REPRINTS OF ECONOMIC CLASSICS

Money and Monetary Policy in Early Times

Money
and Monetary Policy in Early Times

By

A. R. BURNS
B.Sc. (Econ.)

WITH SIXTEEN PLATES, ONE MAP,
AND FOUR FIGURES IN THE TEXT

REPRINTS OF ECONOMIC CLASSICS

Augustus M. Kelley, Bookseller
New York 1965

Original edition 1927. Reprinted 1965 by arrangement with Arthur R. Burns.

Library of Congress Catalogue Card Number 65-19645

Printed in the United States of America
by Sentry Press, New York, N. Y. 10019

PREFACE

THE purpose of this book is to examine from the economic point of view the knowledge which has been accumulating at an ever-increasing rate during the past century concerning money in early times. It aims, in the first place, at an historical account of the emergence of money. In the second place, an attempt has been made to sketch the development of state policy with regard to the control of money from its beginnings, and to correlate policies at different times and places with political and, more especially, economic conditions. The control of monetary policy by governments was thrust into the field of public attention by the war of 1914-18 and the currency inflation of the immediately succeeding years in most European countries. Although in some respects, more particularly in the matter of the use of paper money and credit banking systems, conditions in early times are sharply contrasted with the contemporary situation, it is by no means fruitless to examine the history of the first thousand years of coining and to seek comparison with modern conditions. Indeed, if monetary theory is to be scientific it must be capable of explaining the events of this early period as well as those of the first quarter of the twentieth century. The desire to supply the means of checking our monetary theory and, at the same time, to supply historical background to replace supposititious accounts of primitive conditions has been, therefore, the impelling motive behind the execution of this work.

The evidence upon which a study of this kind must be based is not only sparse, but often also difficult of interpretation. In consequence, dogmatic statement, although perhaps more satisfying to the reader, would be misleading.

The excuse for the presentation of alternative theories, and the not infrequent absence of clear-cut conclusions, is therefore in the nature of evidence. It is as desirable to keep well in mind the things that we do not know, as it is to re-examine from time to time the things we think we know.

The meagreness and the intermittent nature of the evidence available have already produced a mass of speculation by archæologists and, particularly, numismatists. These attempts to yield a satisfying continuity occasionally lack probability, and, more often, consistency, and they have been here subjected to a critical examination which it is hoped will be regarded as a helpful and friendly gesture from economics to archæology and numismatics. It is hoped, too, that the work will make its contribution to the larger synthesis which is now proceeding as a necessary and desirable aftermath of a period of specialization in the pursuit of knowledge.

I take this opportunity of recording my debt to Professor Edwin Cannan, LL.D., to whom I owe my training as an economist, and the anticipation of whose criticism has been a most vigorous and continuously operating influence playing upon this work. Professor Cannan's criticism at various stages, as well as of the final manuscript, has been responsible for the removal of much obscurity and error; for so much as remains I am, of course, solely responsible.

The magnitude of my debt to other writers is revealed in the notes throughout the book, and in the bibliographical note annexed. I am also indebted to the officials of the Reading Room at the British Museum, London, whose resourcefulness and quiet efficiency has made possible the reading necessary for the work.

I am very deeply in debt to Eveline M. Burns, B.Sc. (Econ.), Ph.D. (Lond.), my wife and fellow-economist, for having found time in a very active life to take up the burden of reading through the proofs of the whole work. This service has saved the reader from many errors and obscurities.

Finally, my thanks are due to the officials of the Department of Coins and Medals at the British Museum for providing facilities for procuring the reproductions of Plate VIII., Figs. 2 and 4, Plate IX., Figs. 2 and 5, and Plate X., Figs. 1, 2, 3, and 4. The Trustees of the British Museum have kindly permitted the reproduction of Plate III. from the *Catalogue of Chinese Coins in the British Museum*, of Plate XII., Plate XIII., Fig. 2, Plate XIV., and Plate XV., Figs. 1, 2, 3, and 4, from the *Catalogue of Coins of the Roman Republic in the British Museum*, and Plate XVI., from the *Catalogue of Coins of the Roman Empire in the British Museum*, and Plate I. and Plate IV., Fig. 1, from *Corolla Numismatica; Numismatic Essays in Honour of B. V. Head.* The Cambridge University Press have kindly permitted the reproduction of Plate II. from *Athens: Its History and Coinage before the Persian Invasion* (C. G. Seltman), Plate IV., Fig. 2, Plate V., Fig. 5, Plate VII., Fig. 4, Plate IX., Fig. 1, Plate X., Fig. 5, and Plate XV., Fig. 5, from *The Evolution of Coinage* (G. Macdonald), and Plate IX., Fig. 6, Plate XI., Figs. 2 and 3, from *The Origin of Metallic Currency and Weight Standards* (W. Ridgeway). To the Clarendon Press I am indebted for permission to reproduce Plate IV., Figs. 3 and 4, Plate V., Fig. 3, Plate VI., Figs. 1 and 2, Plate VII., Figs. 1, 2, and 3, Plate VIII., Figs. 1 and 5, Plate IX., Fig. 4, Plate X., Fig. 6, Plate XIII., Figs. 1, 3, and 4, from *Historia Numorum* (B. V. Head), and Plate IV., Fig. 5, Plate V., Fig. 4, and Plate IX., Fig. 3, from *History of Ancient Coinage* (P. Gardner). To Messrs. Jackson, Wylie and Co., of Glasgow, I am indebted for authority to reproduce Plate IV., Fig. 6, Plate V., Figs. 1 and 2, Plate VI., Figs. 3 and 4, Plate VIII., Figs. 3 and 6, and Plate XV., Figs. 6 and 7 from *Coin Types* (G. Macdonald).

To all who have thus made possible the provision of illustrations, I tender my thanks.

A. R. B.

CONTENTS

APPENDICES

LIST OF ILLUSTRATIONS

PLATES

IN THE TEXT

MONEY AND MONETARY POLICY IN EARLY TIMES

CHAPTER I

BEFORE THE INTRODUCTION OF COINS

1. *The First Stages in the Organization of Exchange.*

THE idea of coining is one of the most important, if not the most important, single contribution to the heritage of economic knowledge that underlies the complex co-operation upon which modern life is based. But the idea did not flash suddenly upon the world: it came by such gradual stages that, as we retrace them, very much in the dark, we can never be sure which of them marks the beginning of the story. Coinage evolved, with almost incredible slowness, out of pre-existing conditions: we cannot, therefore, begin a discussion of money with the invention of coining: we are forced to consider the economic conditions in the earliest times of which there is record, that we may know the environment in which the new institution developed and which shaped its early career.

Economists have always suggested that money developed out of the priority in exchange obtained by some commodity in primitive times. Every book on economics introduces the reader to the subject of money, by way of an account of the trials and troubles of life in a community where unorganized barter is the only method of exchange. A community without a medium of exchange or a unit of value has, however, never been found, and the stage is one imagined for simplicity of exposition of the merits of money: it must not be taken seriously. The next supposed stage is where one or a small number of commodities has emerged as a general medium of exchange. The commodity, or one of the commodities so selected, would form one side of every exchange. But in very early times such commodities were often bulky and troublesome to deal with, and it is evident that time and energy would often be wasted in taking over the medium of exchange to pass it on again. Where it was impossible for the goods and services offered and wanted by one party to be fitted to those wanted and offered by the other, some such intermediate commodity might be required. But in early times it must very frequently have occurred that each party to the negotiations could offer a commodity desired by the other, and the real problem was to determine the ratio of exchange. The verb "to sell" corresponds to words in various ancient Teutonic languages meaning to give, to deliver up, to offer, to sacrifice:[1] in its original use it carried no reference to exchange for currency or any common medium of exchange. The first stage in the organization of exchange was the development of a unit of value in terms of which barter could be arranged. The commodity upon which the unit was based was actually transferred in a relatively small number of the exchanges effected, but the preservation of the unit would require that the commodity selected should be one exchanged with some frequency. There is no reason why all the people in a community should use the same unit of value when it is not represented by a medium of exchange. Where a number of sheep are to be exchanged for corn, one man may value corn and sheep in oxen, and the other in bars of bronze, and without any risk of disagreement arising out of the use of different units of value. Specialized persons selling a single commodity would be apt to make all valuations in terms of some easily defined quantity of their produce. In fact, units of value in common use merely developed out of commodities in frequent exchange, and the appearance of a general medium of exchange in the sense of a commodity handed over in settlement of one side of most bargains is a later stage of economic evolution. Such a medium arose only when a commodity was available which was easily portable, divisible, and capable of preservation without difficulty. For this reason the metals provided the first medium of exchange. The introduction of metals may have given rise to a new unit of value, but more probably older units of value were translated into the new material. But

[1] *New English Dictionary: verb*, sell. The derivation of the verb "to buy" is unknown; it is of Teutonic origin (*N.E.D.*, *verb*, buy).

the pursuit of this aspect of the evolution of money will take us too far forward into the subject. It is desirable first to investigate the commodities used in early times as mediums of exchange, and the basis of units of value.

References to these commodities by economists have been supported by casual quotations from classical authors, but their general description of primitive conditions of exchange has been mainly coloured by travellers' stories of the habits of primitive peoples in more recent times. Excavation has proceeded at a very rapid rate during the past half-century, and the progress of archæological research makes possible some, although a very blurred, picture of conditions in early times.

If the commodities which figured largely in primitive exchange furnished the earliest units of value, these latter must have varied from place to place as the staple commodities in exchange varied. Palæolithic man lived mainly by hunting, at least in colder areas, and, so far as exchange occurred, furs and skins must have dominated commerce. In the colder climates they would be valued for clothing and would be less perishable than meat, the other important product of the chase. There is much evidence that furs and skins were so used in later historical times in the ancient world.[1] The cave men of this Old Stone or an early Neolithic Age have left another suggestion of a common medium of exchange. Buried with the most ancient remains of the human race which have been found in Europe are shells. They must have travelled far from their source of production and have possessed considerable value: in consequence, it is not improbable that they were very early a form of money. The use of tortoise and cowry shells as money in China is well authenticated both by mention in early books and by relics of their use which linger in the written and spoken language. The ideogram *pei* (shell) means wealth and riches, and appears in all the words relating to purchase, sale, prices, cheap, and dear,[2] and the expression *kuei hwo* (tortoise-shell money) is still used as an elegant expression for coin. Tortoise-shells of various species and sizes were used for greater values which would have required too many cowries. But this shell

[1] As well as in more recent times in the northern parts of Canada.
[2] Lacouperie, *Catalogue of Chinese Coins*, 193.

money did not come into use in China until 2000 to 1500 B.C. It is well known that in more recent times cowry shells have been very common instruments of barter in widely scattered parts of Asia and Africa, but it is doubtful when they came into use. It has been said that "shells or necklets of shells are found to be used everywhere in the earliest stages"[1] but the *New English Dictionary* offers no encouragement to the quotation of the English phrase "to shell out" in support of the use of shell money in England at any time.[2] For shells to be used as a medium of exchange they must have possessed value. But the demand for shells cannot have been narrowly utilitarian, for they play no direct part in the struggle of man with his environment: they must have appealed to the cave man and woman's passion for adornment. But to ask why their passion should have lighted upon and been satisfied by shells is to strain our archæological resources more than they can at present stand. Professor Elliot Smith[3] holds that primitive people saw in the cowry shell a resemblance to "the portal by which a child enters the world." In consequence, they regarded the shell as a giver of life and used it as a fertility charm. The demand for shells consequent upon the spread of this practice resulted in a great traffic in them in prehistoric times, and they attained a position

[1] Ridgeway, *Origin of Coins and Weights*, 48.

[2] It regards the phrase as a figurative adaptation from the sense of removing seeds from a pod, husk, or shell.

[3] *Evolution of the Dragon*, 145, where he writes that "In delving into the remotely distant history of our species we cannot fail to be impressed with the persistence with which, throughout the whole of his career, man (of the species *sapiens*) has been seeking for an elixir of life to give added vitality to the dead (whose existence was not yet consciously regarded as ended), to prolong the days of active life to the living, to restore youth and to protect his own life from all assaults, not only of time, but of circumstance." The cowry shell was adopted as the chief of these elixirs of life because of its resemblance to the portal by which a child enters the world, which was early regarded as a lifegiver. For this reason shells were worn as amulets and lucky charms, more particularly to confer fertility on women, and to help them in childbirth. They were also buried with the dead to confer upon them fresh vital energy, a fact which, it is suggested, explains their discovery on skeletons of the Upper Palæolithic Age in South Europe (Cp. Ridgeway, 152).

Professor Elliot Smith states that later, when the real reason for burying the shells with the dead had been forgotten, and they were being used as currency, a new explanation was invented, that they were to pay Charon's fare for the journey to the next world. Finally, a coin actually took the place of the shell (*Evolution of the Dragon*, 223).

in commerce that fitted them for use as a medium of exchange and the foundation for a unit of value. Professor Seligman, on the other hand, states that primitive peoples now more often see in cowry shells a resemblance to an eye, and use them to represent eyes in mummies. Because of this resemblance they are used as charms to ward off the evil eye. The reasons which moved primitive men to desire cowry shells are unknown, but it is clear that they were fairly common in exchange in early times. Nevertheless, they seem to have left no impress upon money as it subsequently evolved, for there is no trace of the influence of any shell unit of value. Possibly shells were never more than subsidiary currency.

The Neolithic period is characterized by the cultivation of the soil and the taming of animals. The substitution of settled life for hunting produced the small aggregations of people who first faced the problems of social organization. On the economic side accumulations of agricultural knowledge, the harnessing of the energy of beasts and the development of exchange are the most striking aspects of this new but primitive civilization. It is with the last that we are here concerned. The more durable agricultural products such as grain and oil are known to have been frequently exchanged, but fluctuations in the supply of such products caused by variations in the harvest must have rendered them unsuitable as the basis of a unit of value. Fishing communities have used dried fish in early historical times, and may well have done so soon after the process of preserving by drying and salting was discovered. When some men began to make weapons of superior material, for examples axes of jade instead of stone, these also may have been used as a medium of exchange.[1] Social conditions were doubtless responsible for the use of a great variety of commodities as more or less common mediums of exchange in early as in more recent primitive communities. Some such commodities may have given birth in later times to units of value, and others have left their impress upon the face of the coins: but most of them were swept away when invention or importation presented units that fitted more easily into the needs of the time.

[1] Ridgeway, 48.

2. *The Ox Unit of Value.*

One among the units of this age was the product, not of local conditions, but of features which characterized the civilization as a whole. The taming of animals, their use for food and sometimes for draught, brought them into the market, and made them the subject of frequent exchanges. The ox, in particular, provided the basis of a standard of value[1] more

[1] Laum, in a recently issued volume (*Heiliges Geld*, Tübingen, 1924), disputes the suggestion that the ox unit of value arose because the ox was a common commodity in the market under conditions of barter, and, in consequence, developed into a medium of exchange. Because oxen were of relatively high value, and an inconvenient medium of exchange (Tauschmittel), he thinks that " it is impossible that the ox unit of value (Wertmesser) originated in trade " (14). He " does not see how the ox, because it was a commodity of superior attractiveness, can have become the measure of value " (16), but holds that " the evolution of cattle as a unit of value originated in their religious use " (17). Primitive man made sacrifices, at first to ward off evil spirits, and resorted to magic in manifold forms. Later he sought something more positive and attempted to influence the author of evil, and to reward good and placate malign spirits. Man conceived of the gods as very much like himself, and, as " a simple consequence of this anthropomorphism . . . man in the presence of the divinity, offered the same objects as he used among his fellow men, either to soften their anger or gain their favour. He brought gifts. In this way sacrifices developed " (20). Cattle were selected for religious sacrifices because they were substitutes for human sacrifices. " The redemption of blood vengeance by blood money is the origin of the substitution. The animal stepped into the place of a human being. The substituted animal is next offered to the deceased as a sacrifice. Later it was handed over to the relatives of the dead man. From human sacrifices developed the offering of animals, and from the offering of animals developed the counting of animals as blood money. Blood money is the ransom with which a man buys his life. Ransom is also a reparation sacrifice. Whoever pays ransom escapes his own life being sacrificed " (81). Sacrifices were then made to the gods to expiate misconduct. " The connection of atonement and expiation with sacrifices is undoubted, and it is obvious that there is some relation between the expiatory and sacrificial offerings (Sühn und Opfertieren) of the Greeks and Romans and our blood money in cattle or corn " (69). These sacrifices had a definitely economic foundation (Verkehrsform), and a commerce in them grew up. Private offerings, either in respect of some specific offence or to secure the general good offices of the gods, were left to individuals, relations with the divinity being then clearly individual. But later public offerings became the subject of complete regulation as to quantity and quality. The arrangements for the marking of the months gave rise to the practice of making state sacrifices at regular intervals. " The fixing of sacrificial and feast days served as a calendar, which was also, in the first instance, of religious origin. The public religion must necessarily possess a normative character. The quality and quantity of sacrificial articles, as well as kind and time, are then laid down. The well-being of the state demands that the divinity recognized by the state shall be pacified by offering the gifts due to

widely used, particularly among the Aryan races, than any previous unit. Moreover, it persisted long after man had

---

him" (28). These sacrifices are, therefore, exchanges which have been taken over from secular into religious practice. But "it does not follow that the development of profane and religious commerce in gifts ran parallel. The elementary idea of sacrifice originated in human trade (menschlicher Verkehr), so that, at the outset, both correspond. But religion soon departs its own way, and, indeed, sooner reaches the stage of regulation, of fixed forms between god and man. . . . Sacrifice is merely a higher form of commerce in presents (Gabenverkehr)" (20). The commodity which, selected from the many available, is prescribed in quality and quantity for sacrificial purposes "serves as a unit of account if the relations between god and man are conceived as a debt relation (Schuldverhältnisse). It serves as a medium of exchange if the sacrifice is an act of exchange. Cattle were the accepted sacrificial medium among the Greeks, Romans, and Indians, and Germans. In consequence, cattle have the qualities of money, but so far only for relations between the gods and men" (40). Money originated, therefore, in the religious laws of the state, and first as a unit of value and account.

The translation of the ox unit of value and of account from religious ritual to secular affairs developed out of the custom of paying the fees of the priests in portions of the cattle sacrificed to the gods. "Cattle were used to pay sacrificial fees to the priests because they were the form in which sacrifices (Opfergabe) were made to the gods" (43). "In this way, the norm evolved in religious affairs was translated into private trade. The medium that served as a medium for payment in respect of services in religious matters was also known and used as such in private trade"(43). Although cattle were the principal medium for the payment of sacrificial fees, "they were not the only one offered to the priests. They were also paid in sheep, horses, elephants, slaves, clothes, and many other things. But this variety does not appear always to have existed. In Vedic times the priests were forbidden to accept horses, slaves, and sheep. Cattle were then the sole medium for the payment of fees: as later a part of a fee prescribed in a quantity of cattle was given and received in other goods, it was necessary to fix the equivalents of the cattle. Quite naturally, therefore, the ox became a measure of value in India" (61). Likewise elsewhere the commodities offered in payment of fees increased in variety, and also those offered as sacrifices, and it became necessary to produce a price list in terms of oxen of a defined quality, in order that the equivalents in other commodities of sacrifices and fees prescribed in cattle could be ascertained. Thus arose the custom of valuing commodities in the ox unit of value.

It seems to be agreed that the ox was used in the beginning as a sacrificial medium for economic reasons. The gods were conceived as beings with human qualities. When their anger was aroused by some specific offence, or when events revealed the divine temper without disclosing the moving cause, the gods were appeased by the kind of offering which softened a human heart. For the same reason the aggrieved relatives of a murdered man were mollified, and the good offices of priests were secured by the offer of cattle, because of their generally recognized economic value. If this value was recognized at the very beginning of these practices, they can have done no more than strengthen the position already occupied by the ox in economic life and, if it was wastefully sacrificed, increase the value of the ox. The

become acquainted with the metals, and into the periods of which records are available.

Representations of the heads of oxen on an inscribed clay tablet, from Knossos, part of a palace inventory, probably indicate the use of an ox unit in Crete in Minoan times. In the Homeric poems values are constantly expressed in oxen. The arms of Diomed are stated to have been worth nine oxen, while those of Glaucos were valued at one hundred.[1] A woman slave skilled in industry was worth four oxen, and the three-legged pot, the first prize for wrestlers in the 23rd *Iliad*, was valued at twelve. A cargo of Lemnian wine, which reached the Greek camp before Troy, the chiefs purchased for cattle and hides.[2] Towards the end of the 7th century, the fines fixed in the laws of Draco at Athens were stated in cattle. In the time of Æschylus (the 5th century B.C.), it was said of a man whose silence had been bought, that he "had an ox on his tongue." The Aryans of the *Rig-Veda*, who dwelt in the North-West Punjab, in about the 6th or 7th centuries B.C., also measured values in sheep and cattle. In ancient Persia payment in cows and sheep was common, and in the Zoroastrian *Zend-Avesta*, which was revised and partly re-written at the beginning of

---

main contention is, however, that this traffic with the gods and their servitors first called for the definition of the abstract ox unit of value and the drawing up of price lists in the ox unit. A unit of value arises in the first instance when people begin to appraise values in terms of a commodity. Soon the process of bargaining results in explicit reference to their line of thought: if the commodity selected appeals to a number of buyers and sellers it obtains an established position. In the absence of positive evidence, it is not reasonable to suppose that precision was first given to the unit because of relations with the gods. Although primitive men are often regarded as simple and highly superstitious souls, the existence of exchange on any important scale calls for a unit of value more or less explicit. Transactions with other men came as soon as, if not a good deal before, transactions with the gods, and these secular transactions are most likely to have given rise to the unit in its more abstract form. Religious and profane affairs were closely interwoven, and, where communal organization developed out of religious and magical practices, the first publicly controlled obligations in terms of oxen may have been concerned with these affairs, and the later custom of expressing fines in terms of oxen may be a survival. But when obligations in the ox unit came to be satisfied in other commodities, even the Temple authorities must have looked to market prices for a basis of commutation. The conservatism of the priesthood may have given rigidity to the unit, but its origins are in the more primitive economic struggle.

[1] *Iliad*, VI, 236.

[2] *Iliad*, VII, 274.

the 3rd century A.D., cattle units were still in use concurrently with metallic money.[1] According to the *Vendidad*[2] during the transition from one measure to the other cattle and sheep were still acceptable in all payments, but coins were also accepted at specified rates.[3] Among the first inhabitants of Italy everything was valued and paid for in cattle and sheep, the full grown cow being the principal unit of value, in which accounts were kept both there and in Sicily. The Tarpeian Law of about 452 B.C. provided, for the first time, for penalties fixed in cattle and sheep to be paid in pieces of marked copper.[4] Some twenty years later a tax was substituted by law for the fines expressed in cattle,[5]

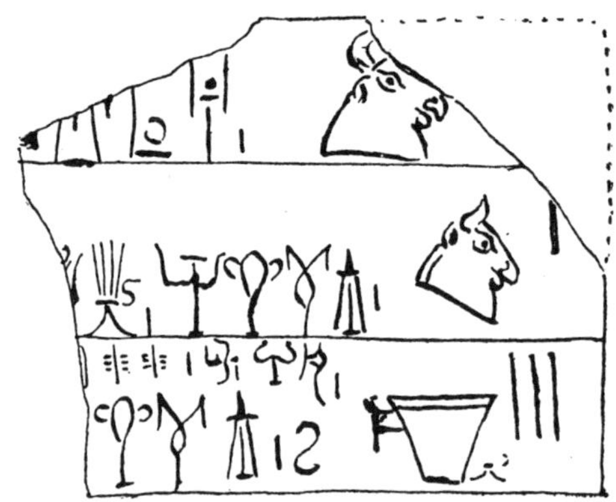

FIG. 1.—AN INSCRIBED CLAY TABLET FROM KNOSSOS.
Part of a palace inventory where representations of heads probably indicate a Minoan unit.
(From Head's *Corolla Numismatica, by permission of the Clarendon Press.*)

which probably means that the fines were expressed directly in copper. At Syracuse the cow was the rateable unit until the end of the 4th century B.C. Written record is supplemented by indirect evidence. Representations of a whole or part of an ox or cow appear on many coins issued on both the

[1] Doctors' fees, for instance (which were payable only on the event of the recovery of the patient), were fixed according to status of the person treated, and varied from an ox, a milch ass, a milch cow, down to a simple piece of meat in the case of the humblest (animal) patients.

[2] One of the books of the *Zend-Avesta*.

[3] Sheep at one *stater*, and ox of medium quality at twenty-two *staters*.

[4] Babelon, V, 31; Ridgeway, 31.

[5] Cicero, *De Rep.*, II, 35.

west and east coasts of Greece,[1] on the coast of Asia Minor,[2] and also in Central Italy, and have been claimed as evidence that these coins superseded an ox unit; but the evidence is weak.[3] More assistance is obtained by tracing the derivation of words relating to money and monetary transactions. It is well known that the Latin *pecunia* is derived from *pecus* (cattle), and "peculation," says Festus,[4] "as a name for public theft, was derived from *pecus* because that was the earliest kind of fraud." The English *fee* is traced through Anglo-Saxon to the Gothic *faihu*, meaning cattle. Another Gothic word for cattle, *skatts*, comes in its Anglo-Saxon form of *skeat*, to mean treasure or money. The Indian *rupee* can be traced to a Sanskrit word *rûpya*, which again is derived from a word meaning cattle. These words all became so generally related to cattle, used as a medium of exchange, that they were applied to anything else which was so used when, in its turn, the cattle medium was superseded.

The wide use of the ox unit shows that it met the needs of the age. As a means of payment, and a form in which purchasing power could be accumulated, cattle were troublesome, requiring care and some degree of skill in their preservation. For overseas trade they were particularly unsuited, but they were not so radically disqualified for use in local and continental trade. They were not quickly perishable, and their capacity for multiplication, for work, and the supply of milk, all counterbalanced the disadvantage that they were costly to maintain. Their bulk was no great disadvantage, as they provided their own transport. But, in spite of their capacity to become current in the most literal sense, they were probably much more used as a unit of value than a medium of exchange—a probability which is supported by such evidence as is available. The size of the ox unit must have limited its usefulness in either capacity. In Homeric times oxen were owned mainly by kings, nobles, and the wealthier classes, the simple man having only goats and sheep and, as a currency, oxen were limited to the settlement of larger bargains. But in more primitive economic conditions, small transactions are much less frequent and important

[1] The isle of Corcyra, and towns in Eubœa, and possibly Athens (*vide infra*).

[2] Phocæa.

[3] *Vide infra*, Chapter V.

[4] P. 237, Ed. Müller.

than in modern times, and there is little doubt that they were effected by some other form of currency. These latter forms of currency doubtless supplied small value units as well. As the basis of a standard of value, the ox was not all that could be desired. But its disadvantages are different in kind from those attaching to its use as a currency. As a value unit it would be as useful as any other in foreign trade, which was not of great importance to most early communities, and must always have been effected by barter. But it is essential in a standard that it shall possess stability, and that it shall be capable of easy and precise definition. Cattle were probably more stable in value than agricultural products and many of the other primitive standards, since the stock of cattle was greater in proportion to the annual accessions to that stock than can be said of agricultural produce. But the stock was liable to sudden reduction owing to epidemic diseases and shortage of fodder, which tended to cause temporary and local enhancement of the value of the unit. Stability of the unit of value must, however, have been of much less importance in primitive communities, where the number of bargains for future fulfilment, made in the terms of the unit, was probably very small, and their duration usually short. It is the increase in the number of such bargains, and in the length of the period between the time of agreement and the time of execution, that renders stability of the unit of value of such primary importance at the present time. Oxen are not uniform in value, and an ox unit of value must be an abstract unit. The abstract unit necessitated precise definition of both quality and quantity. If the word "ox" was applied only to the full-grown beast, a rough natural definition of quantity was obtained. The definition of quality was very much more difficult. The long and searching discussion involved in the negotiation of the sale of an ox in a modern country market shows that the fixing of the values of cattle, which appear to the untrained eye to be of similar quality, is no simple business. Oxen cannot have changed much in this respect, even in three or four thousand years, and the definition of the typical or "money-ox," which was to be the one carried in the mind when values were being quoted, presented great difficulties. Although men probably did not then attempt the exact measurement of values to which the long use of the metals has accustomed us, they did make some attempts to render their unit less vague. Generally the "standard ox" was one of a stated age.[1] But the difficulty of making out of the ox any sharply defined standard of value must have proved insuperable, and probably accounts for the willingness of most progressive communities to turn to the metals and allow the old ox-unit to be superseded.

3. *Metallic Mediums of Exchange.*

The next stage in the evolution of exchange technique accompanied the abandonment of stone tools in favour of bronze. The pursuit of agriculture in the Neolithic Age brought with it the problem of agricultural machinery in its most primitive form. The need for tools was doubtless an incentive in the search for a more tractable material than stone, and the metals provided that material. Gold and bronze are of great age. The latter dates at least from the 4th millennium B.C., and its discovery revolutionized economic life: the Stone Age gave place to the Age of Bronze. The metal which was so useful in providing new implements attained an important position in exchange, and was probably among the first commodities that can properly be described as mediums of exchange. Gold was the other metal to be so used; known, perhaps, even earlier than bronze, it met less urgent economic needs, but became a more universal exchange medium. Silver is rarely found native, and its isolation called for considerable metallurgical skill; in consequence, it was a much later exchange medium than gold. Still greater skill, both in smelting and working, was necessary before iron could replace bronze as a medium for tools and open the Iron Age. Methods of working iron were probably discovered in the

[1] From the *Zend-Avesta* it appears that the Persians not only had a "system of clearly defined relations in value between all their worldly gear, whether the object was a slave, or an ox, or a lamb, or a field," but also "they had evidently strict notions as regards the inter-relations in value of different animals of the same kind; thus the ox of high value, the ox of low value, the cow of three years old or the bull, all stood to each other in a fixed relationship (Ridgeway, *op. cit.*, p. 27). At a very much later date Charlemagne, in his dealings with the Saxons, defined the value of his *solidus* by equating it to the value of an ox of a year old of either sex in the autumn season, just as it is sent to the stall (Ridgeway, *op. cit.*, p. 34).

north of Syria during the 2nd millennium B.C., and among the civilized peoples of the East the Iron Age began with the 1st millennium B.C. Gold, bronze, silver, and iron are the principal metals which were used as mediums of exchange. Other metals[1] have been used, but not over long periods or large areas, and, as they have had no appreciable effect on the subsequent history of money, they can be ignored.

The three most ancient civilizations which have left records—Egypt, Babylon, and China—were all acquainted with bronze, and have left evidence that it was used as a currency. This evidence takes the form either of literary record or the discovery of bronze made up in forms suggestive of currency use. The Egyptians worked the rich copper mines of the peninsula of Sinai from about the beginning of the 4th millennium B.C.[2] Supplies were also obtained from Cyprus and Syria, and the metal was fairly plentiful. Gold, though also fairly plentiful, was too valuable to furnish a convenient unit for the settlement of day-to-day transactions; silver, in very early times, was even more valuable than gold, owing to its greater scarcity, all supplies having to come from a distance. In consequence, when a medium of exchange and unit of value was formally adopted in the middle kingdom about the 12th century B.C. copper was selected. Down to the 6th century B.C. it was a common practice to cast copper in moulds made to contain a unit weight, but, as the resulting bricks of the metal were not uniform in size, they were usually weighed out. The values of goods and cattle are recorded in copper by weight, and wages were expressed in the same terms. In the records of the tomb robberies about the 13th century B.C.[3] values are also reported in terms of copper, and this basis of reckoning continued down to the 3rd century B.C.

Copper was known to the civilizers of China in the 23rd century B.C., and they learnt the use of bronze some five hundred years later. There is more certainty that in China copper supplied an early currency. "Originally any metallic

[1] A code of laws of the 12th and 13th centuries B.C., but probably of much earlier origin, expresses fines in lead (Smith, *Num. Chron.*, 1922, 179). It never obtained any general currency in Babylon on account of its great weight, which made it expensive for the caravans to transport. Nickel is said to have circulated in North-West India soon after 200 B.C. (Hill, 37).

[2] 4th dynasty.

[3] 20th dynasty.

tool or implement of small size, or even a lump of metal, was used in barter. The convenience of this practice led gradually to the practice of casting sham tools or implements for the purpose of exchange only."[1] From at least the 7th century B.C., and most probably very much earlier, small round tongue-like plates of copper, generally regarded as hoes and spades,[2] were in common use as currency. The thinness of the later issues of spades is evidence that they were never intended for use in agriculture. Copper knives were also very commonly used as money. Their issue began in Shantung in the 7th century B.C., and they seem originally to have been graving knives, the point of which was used for writing and the blade for erasing, as they follow the legal regulations as to the length of these knives. The ring shape, which has proved so universally popular a shape for ingots of the monetary metal, is also mentioned in China in the middle of the 10th century B.C., when commutation of punishments and fines was enacted, and the penalties were expressed in terms of rings of copper weighing six ounces. These rings do not appear to have been so widely acceptable as spades and knives, and several unsuccessful attempts were made to popularize them before success was attained in 221 B.C. The *Rig-Veda* testifies to the use of copper among the peoples of North-West Punjab in the 7th century B.C. In Assyria and Babylon pieces of copper of fixed weight circulated together with the precious metals and were in very common use. That copper was held in considerable esteem appears from the prominence given to bricks, plates, and utensils of copper in the accounts of the treasure obtained by Assyrian conquerors as a result of their depredations in Syria and Asia Minor in the 12th and 9th centuries B.C.

In Crete, the half-way house between Egypt and Greece, the Bronze Age began about 2400 to 2100 B.C.,[3] and by the middle of the 2nd millennium B.C. the Mycenæan offshoot of the Cretan civilization appeared on the mainland of Greece.[4] Between 1400 and 1200 the Minoan civilization fell, but in its Mycenæan form survived for a brief period of two or three

[1] Lacouperie, *Catalogue of Chinese Coins*, 1.

[2] But identified by Sir John Lubbock (*Journal of the Institute of Bankers*, vol. i, p. 3) with shirts, and therefore a link with the days when cloth was in circulation as a medium of exchange.

[3] Glotz, 36. [4] Glotz, 46.

hundred years, using bronze for currency as well as tools and weapons. In the district to the west and south of the isthmus of Corinth (Argolis) there has been found beneath the Palace of Mycenæ a copper ingot about $2\frac{1}{2}$ feet long in a shape which is said to represent a hide stretched to dry (with no head or tail). This may even be as old as the 14th century B.C., and

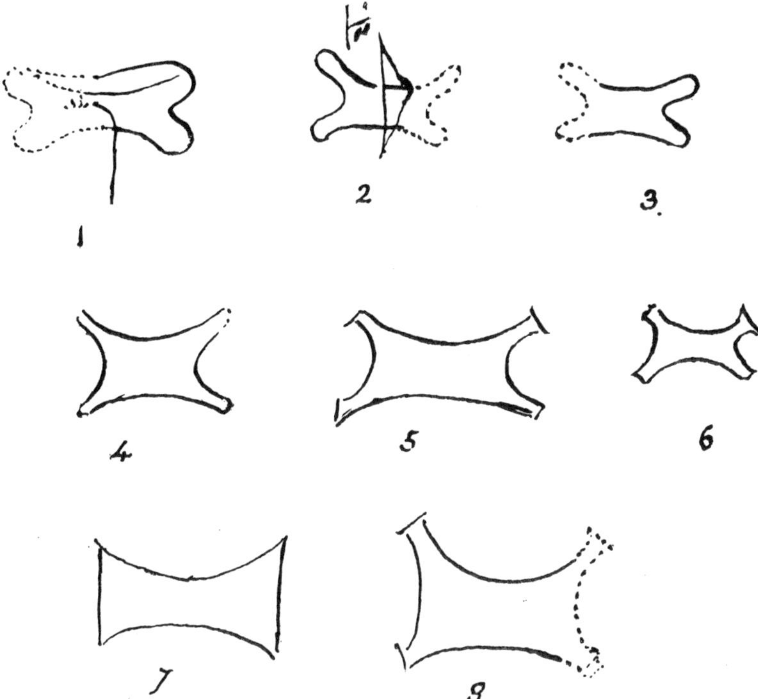

FIG. 2.—IDEOGRAPHIC FIGURES ON INSCRIBED CLAY TABLETS FOUND IN THE PALACE OF KNOSSOS.

The figures probably represent bronze ingots used as currency. (From Head's *Corolla Numismatica. By permission of the Clarendon Press.*)

suggests a transition from the live ox unit to metals by way of a representation of the shape of the hide.[1] Other specimens found off the coast of Eubœa suggest that the circulation of the ingots extended to Attica. A tablet found by Sir Arthur Evans at Knossos,[2] which seems to equate ox-hide

[1] Seltman, 4. An inscription showing part of a picturegram of such an ingot is reproduced in Glotz, 195.

[2] See Fig. 3 (p. 16).

ingots of copper with talents of gold,[1] points to their circulation in Crete. These ingots are of a shape that cannot have rendered them particularly useful;[2] they may have been so shaped to make them convenient to lash.[3] They were of fixed weights which formed a series of multiples, and they often bore a stamp, and it is probable that bronze in this form circulated as a currency in the Eastern Mediterranean[4] for six or seven hundred years into the Homeric Age when copper was certainly used for many payments.

Further west bronze was used by the primitive peoples of Central and North Italy. These peoples, who were making their way to Italy at the beginning of the 2nd millennium B.C., had in circulation from at least 1000 B.C. amorphous lumps of bronze of various sizes, the value of which must have been measured by their bulk. Later it became customary to cast

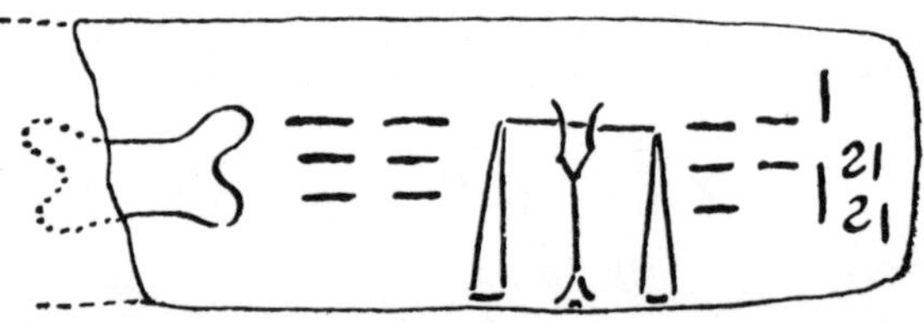

FIG. 3.—TABLET BY OFFICIALS OF THE KING OF KNOSSOS RECORDING THE VALUE OF INGOTS (60 INGOTS WORTH 52 AND A FRACTION GOLD INGOTS), AND RECORDING THE SHAPE OF THE BRONZE INGOT.

(From Head's *Corolla Numismatica. By permission of the Clarendon Press.*)

it in more regular form. Flat pieces, some oblong, and others square, and weighing from one ounce to twelve pounds, have been found, very frequently in votive deposits to the divinities of fountains. Bronze was probably also made up into foot lengths, divided by transverse marks into twelve inches. Still later it began to pass by weight, and was made up into pieces of one pound weight. The advent of weighing made it

[1] Seltman, 112, but Hill (*Camb. Anc. Hist.*, IV, 125) regards the equivalence of these bronze ingots with the gold *talent* as not yet definitely established.

[2] They cannot be regarded as axes, for all the edges are concave (*Camb. Anc. Hist.*, IV, 125).

[3] *Camb. Anc. Hist.*, IV, 125.

[4] Glotz, 194. Nineteen such ingots were brought to light in the excavations at Hagia Triada (Crete). Others have been found in Sardinia and Cyprus (*Camb. Anc. Hist.*, IV, 125).

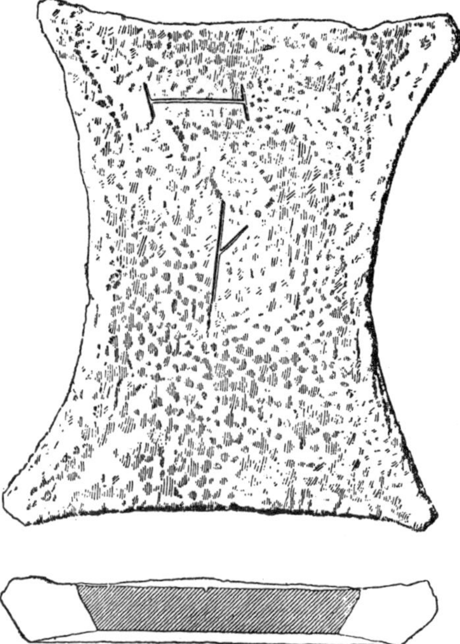

One of the nineteen bronze ingots found in the sealed chambers next the principal chamber in the royal villa at Hagia Triada near Phæstos (Crete).

[*face p.* 16

possible to dispense with definition by measurement, and then the pieces lost their old shape. These lumps or bars, known to ancient writers as *as rude*[1] (raw copper), were, according to Pliny,[2] the common means of payment until the time of Servius Tullius (in the middle of the 6th century B.C.). By 451 B.C. the *as* must have been common as a means of payment, for in that year the Tarpeian Law, while continuing to express fines in terms of sheep and cattle, made provision for their payment in marked *asses*.[3] The three Commissioners sent to Athens in 454 B.C., to study the laws there, doubtless reported that Solon had provided that the fines expressed in the laws of Draco in sheep and cattle might be paid in money,[4] and the Tarpeian Law was copied from Athens. A year or two later, when the twelve tables of laws were drawn up, some penalties were made payable in *asses* and *sesterces* of copper, no mention of payment in cattle being made. But the cattle unit died hard, for twenty years later it was necessary to order by law (the lex Papiria) that payments in copper should replace payments in cattle. Cicero[5] ascribed this law to the fact that "the Censors had, through the vigorous imposition of fines of cattle, converted many private herds to the public use," and in consequence "a light tax in lieu of a fine of cattle was substituted." This may, however, only mean that payment in cattle was inconvenient, owing to the difficulty of disposing profitably of the cattle: it probably marks the end of the practice of assessing fines in cattle and sheep. There is, therefore, no doubt as to the existence of a bronze medium of exchange and standard of value. In fact, the habit of expressing values in terms of copper or *aes* gave rise to the verb *æstimare* and to our words

[1] The word *as* is said to be of ancient Italian origin, and to signify *solidum* in the sense of totality. (The later Roman gold coin was called a *solidus*.) The Sanskrit word *ayas* is analogous to *as*, and bears the same meaning. The *as*, therefore, was a piece complete in itself (Grueber, *op. cit.*, XIX)—complete, presumably, by reference to some accepted standard. Ridgeway (*op. cit.*, p. 354) thinks it is probably connected with *asser*, a rod, bar, or pole. The standard was, therefore, a linear measurement, which, of course, fits in with the suggestion that bronze was originally defined by size.

[2] *Hist. Nat.*, XXXIII, 13.

[3] The ox was to be taken as equal to one hundred *asses*, and the sheep as ten (Festus, *Peculatus*, 237, Ed. Müller).

[4] At the rate of five *drachms* to an ox and one to a sheep.

[5] *De Repub.*, II, 35.

to *esteem* and to *estimate*. A medium similar to the Italian *libra*, or pound, of bronze was used in Sicily,[1] where it was called a *litra*, and circulated in rods similar to those used in Italy.[2] In the Caucasus and Russian Armenia, in certain parts of the Urals, and along the banks of the Volga, bronze rings were in use in prehistoric times. Specimens found there in burial grounds are regular and graduated according to the system of weights. In Scandinavia, and generally in Central European countries, bracelets of copper and bronze were in use during the Bronze Age as a standard of value. Specimens are frequently spiral in form, and the fact that they often appear to have been intentionally broken at one or both ends suggests that the settlement of small transactions was effected by breaking off pieces from the rings. Rings of this kind were also in use among the Saxons, Danes, and other North European peoples until the beginning of the Middle Ages. Bronze probably circulated in other forms too, in double axe heads in Central Europe and in celts in Gaul.[3]

Acquaintance with gold is of such great age that we do not know where or when it was first used. It was often found native, especially in the beds of streams, and the most primitive men in gold-yielding areas must have been familiar with its appearance. The ease with which the metal was shaped must also have been discovered in a remote age. But it was not suited for the making of weapons or tools, and the only explanation of the value which it attained is that it proved attractive for personal adornment. It could be of no use as a currency or to provide a value standard until some demand for it had arisen and it had become valuable and frequently exchanged. Though a pure speculation, it is not unlikely that very early men picked small nuggets out of the streams and used them as trinkets in much the same spirit as they used shells. When they discovered that the new material was easy to work, more complicated trinkets were

[1] The *sikels* appeared in Sicily towards the end of 3rd millennium.

[2] In the latter half of the 5th century B.C. there appeared at Agrigentum a " series of a very strange looking lumps of bronze made in the shape of a tooth, with a flat base, having on one side an eagle or an eagle's head, and, on the other a crab, while on the base are marks of value " (Head, 120), which may represent the " Sicilian *litra* in its mid course from its original full size and shape to that of the ordinary round copper coin of a later age " (Ridgeway, *op. cit.*, p. 350).

[3] Hill, *Camb. Anc. Hist.*, IV, 125.

possible, and they may at first have made imitations of the shells then fashionable. But we must be on our guard when we regard the beautiful lustre of the precious metals as sufficient explanation for their original appeal to man, for social convention and habit make it impossible for us to look with the unsophisticated eyes of primitive man on the many beautiful things produced by nature and to choose impartially. Many attempts have been made to discover the impulses in primitive men to which gold made its successful appeal, thus securing a place in his subsequent economic history out of all proportion to the assistance it has given in his struggle with Nature. He may have seen in the metal a resemblance to the sun which he had already come to see as the author of all life; or its association with the springs of life may have been by its association with the cowry shell; for if, as Professor Elliot Smith suggests,[1] the cowry shell was widely regarded as a giver of life, peoples living at some distance from the sea must have found difficulty in obtaining supplies of the shells. It is supposed that, rather than pay the high prices demanded, they made gold imitations of cowry shells and, finding them to be good, they continued to use them. Later ideas as to the source of the magical properties of the charm became confused, and those properties were associated with the metal and no longer with its shape.[2] Gold was now launched on its long career in the satisfaction of the human desire for personal adornment, and it slipped easily into the position occupied by shells as a medium of exchange. It has often been claimed

[1] *Evolution of the Dragon*, 145, and *supra*.

[2] Professor Elliot Smith suggests that it was somewhere about 4000 B.C. that the inhabitants of the deserts between the Red Sea and the Nile discovered that the abundance of gold which had until then been lying about there unused and unappreciated was soft and durable, and a suitable material for these charms. When they had made these golden imitations of the lucky shells, their lightness and beauty "rendered them more attractive than any of the other surrogates of the shells, or even the shells themselves, and soon the golden amulet acquired a value far transcending that of its prototype, for the æsthetic attraction of the first jewellery devised by men was a very potent factor in enhancing the appeal of these golden trinkets to both sexes, which primarily had been inspired by magic and religion. But in course of time the attribute of life-giving was transferred to the metal itself, and not to the mere form of the objects made from it, and its reputation as an elixir of life seemed to find symbolic confirmation in the fact that it was not subject to corrosion, and not destroyed by fire. Hence the indestructibility of gold became a symbol of immortality" (Professor Elliot Smith in a letter to *The Times* of March 15th, 1924).

for gold that it is the source of life and immortality, and that it preserves the body. These beliefs are found particularly in Chinese and Indian literature; Western peoples have made humbler claims. Pliny says,[1] " Gold boiled in honey with melanthum and applied as a liniment to the navel acts as a gentle purgative upon the bowels. M. Varro assures us that gold is a cure for warts."

It is, however, probable, and even to be expected that, when men discovered gold, their first efforts would be directed to the imitation of shapes with which they were acquainted, and, in particular, shapes already regarded as attractive. Gold imitations of cowry shells have, in fact, been found,[2] and the Egyptians so far associated gold with these shells that " the earliest hieroglyphic sign for gold was a picture of a necklace of amulets " (of shells).[3]

That men began to work gold solely for the purpose of imitating cowry shells, the core of Prof. Elliot Smith's theory from the economic point of view, is entirely unproved. Some modern psychologists contend that metal coins in general, but gold in particular, are valued because, for definite psychological reasons, they are particularly associated with our sense of possession.[4] The popular confusion between money and wealth is not, therefore, to be ascribed alone to inadequate diffusion of economic knowledge. The importance attached to the gold standard, on the other hand, is not the result of pure economic thought; it also is the product of this symbolism. The psychological factors behind the present high value of gold are somewhat different from those of primitive times. The most important modern demand arises out of its monetary use, either directly in coins or indirectly in reserves. This use is founded on the relative stability in the value of gold which results from the absence in recent years (if we may exclude years of war) of rapid variations in either the demand for or the supply of gold. The psychological reasons behind

[1] *Hist. Nat.*, XXXIII, 25.

[2] " The earliest gold ornaments found at Troy were a series of crude reproductions of cowries as pendants to a hair ornament " (Elliot Smith, 222).

[3] Elliot Smith, 222.

[4] They are regarded as " unconscious symbols for excrement, the material from which most of our sense of possession in infantile times was derived " [Jones, *Papers on Psycho-Analysis* (London, 1923), 197, 693].

the general, but now questioned, adherence to gold as a basis for currencies are best sought in treatises on currency theory. The industrial demand for gold is based on the physical qualities of the metal, and these, in particular the fact that it does not corrode, are considerable. Probably a fall in the price of gold would reveal capacity for a very great extension of these uses, and gold would then cease to be regarded as more ornamental than useful. The individual demand for gold is now confined mainly to its use for decoration and jewellery, for the latter of which it is still in great demand—a demand doubtless based in part upon its pleasant colour and lustre. In these, however, it is by no means alone, especially among the metals, although in its freedom from tendency to tarnish it is more uncommon. But the demand probably once based on natural qualities of beauty has caused a rise in value, and gold is now by reason of its value used also as a means of ostentation, a certificate not only of wealth, but of the ability to keep possessions in a form unproductive of economic gain. This motive is indicated by the recent tendency to supersede gold by platinum in jewellery. Platinum, while being harder, is much less attractive in appearance than silver, which possesses a finer lustre, yet silver has already fallen into disuse for jewellery. Gold, if once used as a magical means of securing good luck, is now a certificate of its enjoyment.

The part played by gold has been, and continues to be, of such importance in economic life generally and in currency arrangements in particular, that its origins must be of the greatest interest. It must be confessed, however, that the theories put forward need specialist examination, and, for the economist, the primary facts are that gold was known in very early times, and, for reasons yet not explained, man chose to work gold and make ornaments. In consequence it became a commodity of value, and, in times of recorded history, we find it in use almost everywhere as a medium of exchange. But in these later ages of which there is record, silver was frequently used side by side with gold. It has already been said that silver came into use much later than gold. In common with gold it has rarely been found in directly utilitarian use in ancient times, and the main use of both has been for ornament, and as an exchange medium. Less attempt has been made to account for the appeal of silver.

When it was isolated, gold had long been used, and men were more sophisticated than when they first worked gold. Nevertheless, while gold is said to have made its appeal because of its resemblance to the sun, silver was thought to resemble the moon, and attempts have been made to associate the relation between the periodicity of the sun and moon with the relative values of gold and silver. How any causal connection can be established between the two relations is inconceivable.

The ancient civilizations offer plenty of evidence of the use of gold and silver in exchange. In Egypt gold was playing a part at the very dawn of history,[1] and silver came into use considerably later. Both metals were made up in unit weights, sometimes in the form of bricks, but more commonly in rings carefully graduated in weight down to the smallest units. These rings are frequently mentioned in Egyptian texts. The museum at Leyden contains a number of specimens which were found in Egypt: they are perfectly regular, made of pieces of wire bent round into circles, or into " S " form, but of six different sizes; they are of such small dimensions that they could not have been meant for use as jewellery, but must have been instruments of exchange.[2] They did not, however, bear any guarantee of weight, and it appears from temple paintings that they were verified in the balance. Some of these paintings show great sales of corn being settled by means of gold rings which are being heaped up in the scales to be weighed. These rings were probably used to settle the larger transactions, but copper remained the measure of value, and gold and silver were taken at their current value in copper. In a hieratic papyrus in the Louvre a number of receipts in *sicles* (*shekels*) of silver are mentioned " at the rate of three-quarters of an *outen* of copper to the *sicle*,"[3] the *outen* being the unit of weight for copper. The units of weight upon which the rings are made come from Asia, and it is, therefore, probable that the rings were current there as well; perhaps, as Babelon suggests,[4] they came as tribute from Palestine or Syria. From the 12th to the 7th centuries before our era gold, silver, and copper were all circulating in this form in Egypt, but silver composed the mass of the currency and regulated prices.[5]

[1] Ridgeway, 58-60. [2] Lenormant, I, 103. [3] Lenormant, I, 106.
[4] *Origine de la Monnaie*, 53. [5] Lenormant, I, 111.

The Chinese have been using gold and silver in exchange since about 2100 B.C., and as early as eleven centuries[1] before our era gold in one inch cubes (or *kin*), weighing one pound, is mentioned as a unit,[2] but historical references to its use are very rare. It was probably restricted to the purchase of jewels and to presents from princes and wealthy persons.[3] Both gold and silver also circulated in rings, and attempts to popularize this form, probably introduced from Egypt, were made in 1032 B.C. Ring money is mentioned in connection with commutation of punishments in 947 B.C. Again in 523 B.C. an unsuccessful attempt was made to circulate rings, but in 221 B.C. metal in this form was definitely adopted as currency. Small bean-shaped ingots or metallic cowries, circulated 613–590 B.C.[4] Japan presents a very striking contrast to China, for there a state of pure barter, without the use of metals in any form, is believed to have persisted until the 5th century A.D.[5] The peoples of North-West India of Vedic times (about the 6th or 7th century B.C.) had a gold unit of their own before they knew the use of silver.[6]

In Babylon both gold and silver were known. Gold was scarce and but rarely used in business transactions, although it appears more frequently in temple offerings. Silver provided a generally accepted unit of value at the end of the 3rd millennium B.C. The laws of Hammurabi then set down fixed wages, prices, and fines in considerable detail, and frequently in silver by weight. Both metals at first circulated in irregular ingots, but were later made up into small pieces of exact weight, and must, therefore, have been used as exchange mediums. After the sacking of Babylon by the Hittites, silver served as a unit of value, but much less frequently as a medium of exchange, bargains being settled frequently in corn, and to some extent also in slaves, animals, weapons, and garments.[7]

The Minoan peoples must have used gold, if not silver, from the 3rd millennium B.C., for they were in close communication with Egypt. Recent discoveries reveal how close an approach was attained in Mycenæ and Cyprus, as well as

[1] They were in use from 1091 B.C. to A.D. 200.
[2] Ridgeway, 22.
[3] Lacouperie, *Coins and Medals*, 208.
[4] Lacouperie, XLIX.
[5] Lacouperie, 226.
[6] Ridgeway, pp. 59, 257.
[7] Glotz, 195.

Crete, to the making of coins. The precious metals circulated in lumps, and gold even in discs, the weights of which indicate that they were based upon an organized system of weights. Moreover, when the King of Knossos caused an inventory to be made of his treasure, its value in copper talents was converted into gold.[1]

The Phœnicians, whose culture was probably an early offshoot of the Minoan, rose to power at the decline of the Cretan power in the 12th century B.C., when they were using both gold and silver. So prominent were their possessions of the precious metals that a tradition grew up among the Greeks that the Phœnician ships had anchors of gold.

Among the Jews of the early centuries, the last millennium B.C., all three metals circulated by weight. Gold and silver are mentioned very early in the Hebrew scriptures. Abraham came back from Egypt " very rich in cattle, in silver, and in gold,"[2] and Solomon accepted tribute payments in these metals; he received " vessels of silver and vessels of gold."[3] Probably the metals were frequently in the form of rings,[4] and sometimes bars and bricks. Gold, however, was not used so much for money as for personal ornaments and in connection with the temple. The gift made by the servant of Abraham to Rebekah of a " golden earring of half a *shekel* weight and two bracelets for her hands of ten *shekels* weight of gold "[5] suggests that jewellery was made up of unit weights so that it could be used in lieu of money.[6] A statement of the weight of the ornament would have been the most suitable way of conveying the value of the gifts, but it does not follow that the exact weight is given. Although gold and silver rings were a common form of early currency over a great part of the ancient world, the common medium among the Jews was silver measured by weight. When Abraham purchased from Ephron the cave of Machpelah as a burial-place for Sarah, he " weighed to Ephron the silver which he had named in the audience of the sons of Heth four hundred *shekels* of silver current money with the merchant."[7] Although " money " is referred to, since it had to be weighed

[1] Glotz, 195, and Fig. 3.
[2] *Genesis* xiii, 2, and xxiv, 35.
[3] 1 *Kings* x, 25, and 2 *Chron.* ix, 24.
[4] The Hebrew *kikkar* (talent) also means circle.
[5] *Genesis* xxiv, 22.
[6] Maddon, *Coins of Jews*, 9.
[7] *Genesis* xxiii, 16.

out, it could not have been coined money, of which there is no mention in the Hebrew scriptures. In the law of Moses the prices of slaves and cattle, fines for offences, contributions to the temple, sacrifices of animals, are all regulated by the value of silver.

Numerous other passages in the scriptures bear evidence of the use of gold and silver by weight,[1] although it is probable "that the balance was not called into operation for every small transaction, but that little beads or bullets of silver and of gold of fixed weight, but without any official mark, and, therefore, not coins, were often counted out by tale, larger amounts being always weighed. Such small lumps of gold and silver served the purposes of a currency."[2] In Mycenæan Greece, and also in the dark ages succeeding the Dorian invasion of Greece from the north in about 1200 B.C., both gold and silver were in use, but conditions were very primitive and older units long survived. Later, gold came into more common use as a medium and was dealt in by weight. A special unit (the *talent*) was used for weighing it, and it was probably kept in ingots of *talent* or half-*talent* weight. Two round bullets of gold, which have been found in a late Mycenæan tomb in Cyprus, are believed to be half-*talents*.[3] No single piece of coined money has, however, come down from these times. In Italy, in early times, although copper was the principal medium of exchange, gold and silver were in use in small ingots or bricks, and were probably used to settle larger transactions.[4] There was a considerable supply of gold in England, probably from Ireland, in the middle of the Bronze Age (towards the end of the 2nd millennium B.C.). There is no sign of its use for currency. Thin crescent-shaped sheets are found with bronze celts; a gold plated breastplate intended for a pony indicates the possibility of the use of gold in religious ritual, and the crescents may have been associated with moon worship.[5]

Iron seems to have been first worked in the district to the west of the Taurus Mountains: during the 2nd millennium B.C. knowledge of the process passed eastward with the Vannic

[1] *Joshua* vii, 21; *Judges* viii, 26; 1 *Chron.* xxi, 25; 2 *Sam.* xxiv, 24.
[2] Head, XXXIV.
[3] Ridgeway, *Companion to Greek Studies.*
[4] Cp. Varro, *ap. Non.*, p. 356, *cit.* Ridgeway, 375.
[5] Mr. R. A. Smith of the British Museum.

peoples who lived in what is now Armenia.[1] During the first two or three hundred years of the last millennium B.C., probably at the end of the 8th century owing to the northern campaigns of Sargon,[2] it passed to Assyria, where iron extensively replaced bronze. To the west the Hattic peoples, who lived in Cappadocia to the north of Syria, knew of the use of iron probably from the middle of the 2nd millennium B.C.,[3] and, by the beginning of the 1st millennium B.C., the knowledge had passed southward to the Hittite Carchemish[4] and to Palestine.[5] The general replacement of bronze by iron did not occur in the Eastern Mediterranean until the early part of the 1st millennium B.C., when the civilizations of Egypt and Assyria were beginning to crumble and that of Crete had already fallen. By that time bronze and gold and silver were well established in their use as mediums of exchange. Although the new metal made great changes in economic life, it probably had no marked general effect upon primitive currency. Specimens of iron currency and weapons are much more rare than those of bronze, not only because it was late in coming into use, but also because it so easily oxidizes. In Greece, however, there is definite evidence of the use of iron as an exchange medium. The Dorian peoples from somewhere in the neighbourhood of the wilds of Albania[6] came down into Greece at the beginning of the 12th century B.C., leaving a trail of ruins from Corinth to Sparta. They laid waste Mycenæ, and the native peoples fled. Destructive as they were of the old civilization they brought the seeds of a new, for they possessed a knowledge of the use of iron, and, on their arrival, the Bronze Age in Greece gave way to one of iron. The weapons and implements of Homeric Greece were of iron, which was then held in high regard. It was an important article of commerce, and there is little doubt that it provided the staple currency of the Peloponnese for two or three hundred years down to the beginning of the 7th century B.C. In about 600 B.C. the laws of Lycurgus prohibited the introduction of gold, silver, or even copper in Sparta for commercial circulation. Iron alone was allowed, and that circulated in long bars weighing about $1\frac{3}{4}$ lbs. troy. The broken remains of such bars have been found in excavations at Sparta.[7] The Homeric poems

[1] *Camb. Anc. Hist.*, III, 19. [2] *Ibid.*, III, 186. [3] *Ibid.*, III, 153.
[4] *Ibid.*, III, 162. [5] *Ibid.*, III, 417. [6] Glotz, 53. [7] Seltman, 120.

The bundle of *obols* and iron weight found in the Argive Heræum.

[*face p.* 26

also mention the circulation of iron bars concurrently with precious metals and cattle. Aristotle[1] records that Pheidon dedicated specimens of iron nails or spits in the Heræum, and subsequent excavations on the site of the temple have brought to light a bundle of rounded iron bars about four feet long and pointed at one end.[2] The reason for the dedication is in some doubt. The nails were most probably the form in which iron was used as currency, and their dedication may have been a way of preserving official standards of weight and length for the uncoined metal in circulation. More probably[3] the nails were dedicated as specimens of obsolete currency[4] which had been superseded by the coins which Pheidon is believed to have introduced into Peloponnesus, or perhaps still more likely as obsolete apparatus[5] of the period before the introduction of coins which was no longer required. Such a dedication is in accordance with a prevalent custom of offering up in the temple old and obsolete implements that had ceased to please the owner.[6] The nails, or *obols*, are worth something less than a penny of our money (in gold equivalent), and six of them made a handful, or *drachma*, which has since become an historic currency unit. Small change was probably obtained by breaking pieces off the bars,[7] much as apparently the early farthings were intended to be obtained by breaking coins into four in England. Aristotle referred to iron *obols* in his lost constitution of the Sicyonians,[8] and Rhodopis, the Greek courtesan of Naucratis, is reported to have dedicated a great quantity of iron spits, " such as are fit for roasting oxen,"[9] at Delphi. At the beginning of

[1] Fr. 481, *cit.* Head, 438.
[2] Gardner, 113. Ure, " *The Origin of Tyranny*, 163.
[3] Gardner, 113.
[4] According to Hill (*Camb. Anc. Hist.*, IV, 125) the spits were probably dedicated without any reference to their use as coins.
[5] Seltman (121) identifies a piece of iron found with the *obols* as a standard of weight for 180 *obols*.
[6] Babelon, 210-2. At a later date the Athenians dedicated in the Parthenon the whole of the obsolete apparatus employed to coin gold in 406 B.C. (Woodward, *Num. Chron.*, 1911, 351).
[7] Possibly this explains the relevance of Plutarch's reference (*Lyc.* 9) to the method used by the Spartans for making iron brittle—iron bars being their currency (Seltman, 121).
[8] Seltman, 120.
[9] " Wishing to leave a memorial of herself in Greece she determined to have something made the like of which was not to be found in any temple, and to offer it at the shrine at Delphi. So she set apart a tenth

the 7th century this iron currency was probably superseded,[1] at least in large payments, by the silver coins of Ægina.

4. *The Definition of Metallic Units.*

The metals are obviously superior to oxen as a medium of exchange. They are durable and can be stored without any cost of maintenance, although they do not multiply or supply food. They are more easily hidden than cattle: the precious metals are particularly easy to hide. Gold and silver, though not copper and iron,[2] are also easily portable. The custom of making them into rings and spirals doubtless arose because people desired to carry their most precious possessions with them and, therefore, placed them on their arms and legs. The metals had advantages over cattle in overseas trade. But more important than all of these qualities was the homogeneity and divisibility of the metals. Nature supplies no natural unit of the metals as she does of cattle. Pieces of metal not only vary in size, but can be made of any size that is desired. The quality of metal does not vary so widely as the quality of oxen. But these advantages, this very freedom to determine how large a piece of metal should be the medium of exchange, brought with it the problem of measuring the metals. In the earlier stages of their use as exchange mediums there is a sharp contrast in this respect between gold and silver and bronze and iron. The latter metals have always found their primary use as a material for weapons and implements, and their monetary use seems to have developed out of the exchange of implements rather than out of exchanges of the raw metal. Literary records show that utensils were often used in the ancient Mediterranean as units of value.[3] This development is best illustrated in China. Among agricultural people it would be expected that the implements most likely to develop a monetary use in this way would be agricultural tools. Small implements,

---

of her possessions and purchased with the money a quantity of iron spits, such as are fit for roasting oxen whole, whereof she made a present to the oracle. They are still to be seen there, lying of a heap behind the altar which the Chians dedicated" (Herodotus, II, 135).

[1] Except in Sparta, where iron continued in use.

[2] Or lead, which was used in Assyria. *Vide supra*, p. 13.

[3] *Vide* Hill, *Camb. Anc. Hist.*, IV, 135.

such as adzes, bill-hooks, spades, chisels, and planes, were there used as currency for a long period.[1] Knives began to be used in 7th century B.C. in Shantung, and continued in circulation until 221 B.C., when they ceased to be recognized; they were revived for a brief period in a sharpened and thicker form in A.D. 7.[2] They may have been bill-hooks or possibly graving knives, the point being used for writing and the edge for erasing; the length of these knives was fixed by law.[3] Spades or hoes with hollow handles were in two sizes from about 600–350 B.C.[4] The weighing of metal for currency did not prevent the continued use of these implements, which then passed by weight.[5] But there arose a custom of "casting small implements, which for convenience were used in exchange of a regular shape and approximate weight." But they were no longer useful as implements; some of the spades are too thin ever to have been used as spades.[6] Among the remains of prehistoric peoples in Central Europe have been found bronze double axes pierced with holes too small for a practicable handle, but probably intended to enable them to be strung together, possibly for commerce in exchange. Again in Gaul there have been found hoards of small bronze celts which seem to have been used as currency.[7] Cretan laws express fines, not in cattle, as in Greece and Rome, but in kettles and pots (tripods),[8] a unit of value that would hardly have arisen in any other way than out of a custom of using these commodities for payments or as a basis of valuation.[9] Coins in Crete at a later period bore representations of such tripods, thus supporting the idea that they were once a local currency.[10] The iron *obols*, of which specimens were found at the Heræum, were pointed at one end,[11] and the offering of Rhodopis at the shrine of Delphi was of iron spits "such as are suitable for roasting oxen."[12] They too, therefore, may have been a commodity taken over for

[1] Lacouperie, 201. [2] Lacouperie, XVIII.

[3] The original length was probably the great span of 10·63 inches. (Lacouperie, XLV).

[4] Lacouperie, XLIX. [5] Lacouperie, II.

[6] Money of many shapes was used in China: half-moon money, comb-shaped, fish-scale money, etc (Lacouperie, *Coins and Medals*, 201).

[7] *Camb. Anc. Hist.*, IV, 125. [8] Gardner, 389.

[9] Macdonald (34), *Common Types*, suggests the bowlful of meal was the unit.

[10] Ridgeway, 314-5. [11] Gardner, 23. [12] *Vide supra*, p. 46.

use as currency.[1] Etruria furnishes an interesting parallel to these spits, for between the 8th century and 6th century B.C. first bronze and later iron spits were hung together on ornamental handles in sets of six.[2] It is easy to see why they should have been favoured, for they must have been a convenient form in which to purchase iron for any purpose, even when one had no ox to roast.[3] They were probably the iron billets of the time.[4] Metallic mediums made up in more or less useful forms were directly convertible from currency into commodities. The Cretan could, without difficulty, divert part of the proceeds of the sale of his cow to use in the cooking of food. But there must also have been some means of controlling currency of this kind to prevent its shrinkage. Pots were doubtless conventionally defined by size; where weighing was not in use Chinese knives and Greek *obols* were defined by size, particularly in length: one merit of the *obol* was that its shape lent itself easily to measurement by units of length which were probably based on the human body. The primitive bronze *as* used in Italy was a bar of bronze which shows no sign of any intention to make it directly useful as a commodity. It was a bar probably one foot long and half an inch in diameter. The bar was divided by transverse strokes into twelve parts called *unciæ* (inches), each of which could be again divided into twenty-four parts, each called a *scripulum* (scratch).[5] These subdivisions suggest a monetary use.[6] The Sicilian *litra* was divided in the same way, although possibly at a much later

[1] Plutarch (*Lysander*, 17) thought it probable "that all ancient money was of this sort, some people using iron spits as coins, and some bronze."

[2] *Camb. Anc. Hist.*, IV, 125.

[3] Laum denies that these *obols* were used as currency. He believes that the repeated references to them in temple inventories and the finding of specimens in temple ruins are due to the custom of cooking the meat of the animals sacrificed to the gods. The meat was cooked in the temples, or very near by, and then distributed, and the spits or *obols* were used for roasting (*Heiliges Geld*, 55-56).

[4] According to Pollux (*cit.* Ridgeway, 349), the *obol* was divided into twelve *chalci*, possibly while it was still measured by length, although Gardner (23) considers that, as the *obol* was pointed at one end, division on this basis is unlikely.

[5] In Greek a gramme.

[6] It is possible that they also were the form in which crude bronze was purchased to be worked up and the marks were intended to facilitate marking out.

date.[1] With the application to these metals of measurement by weight the size and shape of the pieces of metal lost all significance, and it was possible to reduce the currency to a more compact form and the Chinese knife became shorter and thicker, first the handle and then the blade disappearing until there was only the ring left as the Chinese cash.[2] The Roman *as* in the same way slowly contracted in length until it assumed the round shape of the ordinary coins.

Gold and silver, on the other hand, were always of high value, and there are no known examples of gold and silver implements used as currency. The nearest approach is the ring of the precious metals which was very common, but which, nevertheless, circulated by weight, and not because of its shape and size. The only example of gold circulating in a form defined by linear units is the *kin*, or inch cube of gold occasionally used in China.[3] The need for accurate measurement of the precious metals must have resulted in their being weighed at a very remote date.

Human ideas of weight arose first as a result of man's efforts to lift and transport commodities, and one of his earliest units must have arisen out of the distinction between what he could and what he could not lift, and this would be expressed in numbers or volume of the commodity. The equalizing of weights probably originated with man converting his body into a balance, and comparing weights by holding them in his hands with his arms full extended. Later the invention of the balance supplied a more accurate means of comparison. Before the end of the old kingdom in Egypt weights of more compact material had been evolved and were probably used to measure out numbers or volumes of commodities. But this latter measure doubtless developed quickly into a new method of measurement by weight, and measurement by capacity fell out of use. One of the first and most important uses of the balance was to measure quantities of the precious metals.[4] The

[1] Pollux (*cit.* Ridgeway, 349) says the *litra* was divided into twelve parts each, an *ungia*, but the term may have been borrowed after the Italian *uncia* had become a unit of weight.

[2] The disappearance of the handle was made up for by increase of thickness of rest.

[3] *Vide supra*, p. 36.

[4] It has been suggested (McLean, *Num. Chron.*, 1912, 333) that at first, however, weight was used in combination with measurement by volume as a means of assessing, by means of its density, the quality of

invention of the balance which supplied the desired method of measurement brought with it the need for standards of weight, the question of the magnitude of the unit of weight, and the preservation of the unit after it had been selected. Of the size of this unit it will be necessary to treat later; it is possible that the habit of making valuations in terms of oxen persisted after gold had come into use, and, therefore, the most convenient unit of weight for gold was that weight the value of which was one ox unit.[1] The preservation of the unit of weight presented serious difficulties; it is suggested that as soon as man gave up dealing in gold by measurement (which was probably very early) he began weighing it against seeds. Seeds were selected which were fairly uniform in weight and of a convenient size[2] and weight, and the unit of gold was defined in terms of these seeds. Nature would then be relied upon to produce seeds of a uniform weight from place to place and from time to time. The grain of wheat is referred to as a unit in the laws of Hammurabi of Babylonia, at the end of the 3rd millennium B.C.[3] The Chaldeans were aware of this

---

the metal, and not as a test of quantity, which was fairly easily measured by volume, wherever standard shapes were used. The standard Egyptian weights would be those which would balance a given volume of metal if it were pure gold. This method of testing may have arisen out of the fact that gold and electrum of varying degrees of quality came into Egypt, partly as tribute.

The frequent appearance on Egyptian wall paintings of the use of the balance for weighing human souls suggests the prevalence of the idea that quality might be tested in the balance. In the early records the measure of gold is given in units of capacity as well as in *deben*, which suggests that the balance was not used solely as a test of quantity. In fact, " there is no word giving an absolute weight in the Egyptian records " (McLean, *Num. Chron.*, 1912, 347).

[1] *Vide infra*, Chap. VIII.

[2] Ridgeway (194) gives a list of the weights of a number of seeds used in ancient times for weighing. The inter-relations between the units are remarkable:

	Troy grains.	
Barley	1	(=1⅓ wheat grains).
Wheat	0·75	
Rice	0·5626	
Carob	3	(=3 barley=4 wheat).
Lupin	6	(=2 carobs).
Maize	2	
Ratti	2	
Rye	0·5	

[3] The *shekel* of silver was subdivided into 180 *se* or grains of wheat. Wages were sometimes also fixed in grain of which 1 *gur*. of about 500 lbs. or 8⅓ bushels was worth a *shekel*. (*Vide* Ridgeway, 254.)

method of fixing weights in terms of grains of corn, and the Assyrians used a unit weighing 0·65 grains, as appears from a weight weighing 14·6 grains, and inscribed "22½," with an ideogram which evidently refers to some kind of corn with a rounded end. If an allowance of a little over 10 per cent. be made for loss of material of the weight by wear and tear the grain referred to can be identified with the present wheat grain.[1] Similar grain units were used in Arabia[2] and among the Semitic peoples.[3] This primitive method of defining standards persisted for a remarkable time, for in England as late as the 13th century A.D. the weight of the penny was defined by equating it to 32 grains of wheat "round and dry and taken from the midst of the ear."[4] The carat weight still used by goldsmiths, and equal to a twenty-fourth part of an ounce, is also based on the weight of the seed of the carob or locust tree.[5] At a very early date, however, the advantage of intervention by the State for the purpose of defining and preserving weight standards was realized. In the ruins ot Nineveh were found in the middle of the last century bronze weights in the form of lions and stone weights in the form of ducks bearing inscriptions, indicating the reign of the King in which they were made, and stating their exact weight according to a defined standard: "there can, therefore, be no manner of doubt that these lions and ducks were officially guaranteed standards of weight deposited from time to time in Royal palaces."[6] The principal specimens found cover the period from about 2000 B.C. to 560 B.C.

It is now possible to sketch the system of exchange in vogue in the ancient empires down to the end of the 8th century B.C. One or more of the four metals, gold, silver, bronze, and iron, provided both a unit of value and a medium of exchange. Made up sometimes in useful forms and sometimes in pieces of standard weight, or multiples or submultiples of the standard they usually passed by weight, and rendered it possible for civilization to reach a high stage of development. The use of scales was not an overwhelming hindrance to trade; even after

[1] Ridgeway, 183. [2] Ridgeway, 182.

[3] The Hebrew gold *shekel* was divided into two *bekahs*, or halves, and each of these into 10 *gerahs*, which Ridgeway (278-79) identifies with Lupin seeds.

[4] Statute *De Ponderibus*, c. 1265.

[5] *New English Dictionary*: *verb*. carat. [6] Head, XXXV.

coinage had been introduced, scales for weighing money were part of the normal equipment of the merchant. It was upon this basis that the commerce of the great empires of Egypt, Crete, Babylon, and Assyria was transacted. The Phœnicians, whose commercial activities, by impelling them to seek the simplification of business records, inspired them to invent the alphabet, have left no coins of a period anterior to the Persian rule; their trade was largely with primitive peoples accustomed to, and probably quite content with, barter, and who would have been likely to show little interest in such an innovation as money. Had the bulk of the Phœnician trade been with civilized peoples, their genius might have evolved coins, although the civilized peoples of the time had turned their energies to the perfection of the exchange, based on metal current by weight. The fact that the Phœnicians were sea-traders doubtless led them to prefer full cargoes in both directions. No coins were issued by the Jews before the Exile, and the Persians and Medes did not coin money until after the conquest of Asia Minor in the 6th century B.C. Carthage and Egypt long resisted the use of coins. In consequence, the integrity of weights and those who used them was vital to the maintenance of trade. In Egypt, Greece, and Rome, and probably among the Jews, there were public weigh-masters to check private weighing. The frequency of the occurrence of the weigh-master and his scales in wall-paintings shows how important a place he had in Egyptian life, especially when tributes and the spoils of war were to be measured. The Book of the Dead makes significant reference to the crimes of tampering with weights and balances.[1] Honesty in weighing was enjoined upon the early Jews, who were commanded that " Thou shalt have a perfect and a just weight,"[2] for " A false balance is an abomination to the Lord."[3] " Italy retained the fiction of weighing copper to legalize a sale long after silver and gold were the currency."[4] Our language also contains interesting relics of the time when the settlement of every bargain necessitated the use of the balance. *Pondus*, from which is derived the

[1] " Je n'ai pas tiré sur le peson de la balance. Je n'ai pas faussé le fléau de la balance " (Babelon, p. 65).

[2] *Deuteronomy* xxv, 15.

[3] *Proverbs* xi, 1.

[4] Petrie, *Social Life in Ancient Egypt*, 5.

"pound," is the oldest Latin word for weight, and *libra*, which meant "balance" as well as "weight," is the source of the French *livre*, and the Italian *lira*. The time when spending meant weighing out is recalled by our word "expend" and the word "spend" itself. In Assyrian and all other Semitic languages, *Saqal* means both weigh and pay.[1]

5. *Summary*.

The commodities that were used as exchange mediums, and the basis for the measurement of values in the ages before the invention of coins, must have varied greatly from place to place. But a small number stand out because of their widespread use and the influence they brought to bear on the subsequent development of the mechanism of exchange. From late Paleolithic and early Neolithic times, shells, useful as trinkets, were an article of frequent trade and possibly used as a means of payment. With the training of animals, and the appearance of settled communities, the ox became a unit of value among Aryan peoples. It is impossible to produce evidence that oxen were generally used for effecting payments, and there is every reason to presume that they were not. The metals were the first commodities widely used for that purpose. Bronze was used in Egypt, Assyria, China, Crete, and probably throughout the Mediterranean. Of the precious metals, gold is older in the service of man than silver, although the ultimate reasons for the use of either metal are at present unknown. Almost all peoples who have left records (except the Indians of Vedic times) used both metals, and their records, together with ancient gold and silver which have been excavated, point to the use of one or both of the metals in varying degrees for effecting payments. Iron is of a later age, and evidence of its use for currency has been mainly confined to continental Greece. The metals brought with them problems of measurement new in kind. There was no natural unit of quantity, and silver and gold required methods of measurement more accurate than would suffice for less valuable commodities. Bronze and iron circulated in the form of commodities of use for non-monetary purposes and probably passed through a period of definition by size.

[1] Babelon, 56.

Gold and silver, on the other hand, were current by weight from a very early period. Weights were fixed in seeds of various kinds, which were convenient in size and regular in weight. The more highly organized empires of Mesopotamia and Egypt probably established official standards of weight, and appointed official weigh-masters. Thus commerce, based upon the currency of monetary metals in uncoined form, was made possible and even easy. It sufficed for all the great civilizations prior to the rise of the Greek culture around the shores of the Ægean. This culture evolved coins, and marks the end of the period with which this chapter is concerned.

CHAPTER II

THE EVOLUTION AND SPREAD OF COINS

1. *Tentative Experiments in Coining.*

WHEN it had become a well-established custom to settle commercial bargains by the transfer of metals by weight, and more particularly to make up the metals in ingots of unit weight, one further step was necessary to produce a piece of metal that could be called a coin. The ingots had to be marked to indicate the weight or purity of the metal, or both. The custom of authorizing transactions by affixing a seal is of very great age. Private seals and signet rings bearing devices for signing contracts were in use in Babylon, Assyria, and Egypt ages before the Lydian and Ionian bankers applied them to the marking of ingots of the currency metals. In Crete a number of seal stones have been found dating from prehistoric times. It is surprising to find, therefore, that the new use for the private seal was not discovered until the early part of the 7th century B.C., for it is to that period that the first coins are ascribed. There is, however, some evidence that sporadic experiments were made in this direction at very much earlier dates.

According to Sir John Marshall,[1] Director of Archæology in India, excavations at Mohenjo Daro (Sind) have brought to light " certain oblong bars of copper which their discoverer assumes to have been coins, since they are similar in shape to the early Indian oblong coins known as " punch-marked," though they do not correspond in weight with any recognized standards used in ancient India. Should this assumption of Mr. Bannerji's prove correct, it would mean that these coins may turn out to be the earliest in existence." Professor A. H. Sayce[2] thought that the seals discovered at the same time as these coins belonged to the 3rd millennium B.C. If the alleged coins can be proved to be such, and to date from

[1] *Illustrated London News*, September 20th, 1924, 528.
[2] *Ibid.*, September 27th, 1924, 566.

the same time as the seals, these issues antedate what have hitherto been thought to be the earliest coins by at least fifteen hundred years.

Texts from Assyria and Cappadocia are said to show that gold, silver, copper, and lead bearing impressed marks were in use there some time between 2250 and 1200 B.C. Lead was the most popular, and was the medium in which fines were expressed. Specimens of "sealed lead," dating from about 1400-1200 B.C., have been found.[1] Cappadocian texts of about 2200 B.C. refer to sums of money "of my seal," "of your seal," "of the seal of——" which may have referred to a known unit of weight.[2] An inscription of Sennacherib, which describes the casting of some colossal bronze bulls in clay casts "as in casting half *shekel* pieces," suggests that the casting of half-*shekel* pieces was known in Nineveh before the commencement of the reign of Sennacherib, in 705 B.C. But it is curious that none of these pieces has been found, even allowing for the fact that the Medes sacked the Assyrian cities.[3] If these texts are correctly deciphered, it would appear that these pieces of lead were a notable step towards the development of coins, and if, as is suggested, these marked pieces passed by tale and at a value above that of the metal they contained[4] they were token coins. But the evidence is obscure.

Again, excavations in Crete have brought to light in the Palace of Knossos blobs of silver which appear to have been dropped, while still hot, on a surface engraved with a special sign.[5] In view of this marking, and the fact that the weights of the pieces correspond with a metric system in vogue in Minoan Crete, we "seem to be justified in supposing that we have here an example of a medium of a small metallic currency closely heralding the appearance of actual coined money."[6] Sir Arthur Evans considers that these Cretan pieces can hardly be later than about the 12th century B.C. Recent excavations in Cyprus have brought to light similar dumps of gold which are also attributed to a date at least as early as the 12th century B.C.[7] and a tomb at Mycenæ

[1] At Kal'ah Sharkat (Smith, *Num. Chron.*, 1922, 179).
[2] *Ibid.*, 177 sqq.
[3] Smith, *Num. Chron.*, 1922, 177. [4] *Ibid.*, 182.
[5] On one piece H and on one about half its weight ⊦ (Glotz, 196).
[6] Evans, *Corolla Numismatica*, 364.
[7] Ure, 128.

contained 700 gold discs stamped with various impressions.[1]

But if, as is quite possible, ingots of the monetary metals were marked in India, Assyria, Crete, and Mycenæan Greece before the beginning of the last millennium B.C., the idea did not develop further. So far as we know, the metals continued to pass by weight; we do not know whether the mark was a guarantee of fineness, but if it was, it is strange that some more recognizable form of coinage was not produced.

2. *The Beginnings of Modern Coinage around the Ægean.*

There is little doubt that modern coinage emerged in the Eastern Mediterranean at the end of the 8th century, or beginning of the 7th century B.C. If the idea of marking ingots was borrowed from Assyria, the Ægean world certainly developed it so far as to claim the lion's share of the credit for the institution of coinage. But the decisive steps in its evolution were possibly taken in more than one of the centres of commercial activity round the Ægean, and it is uncertain whether the first crude coins were made on its eastern or its western shores. Plutarch[2] claimed that Theseus coined silver money in Athens bearing as type the head of an ox, but Theseus is a shadowy figure, and there is no evidence of any issues in Athens before the last decade or two of the 7th century.[3] Credence cannot, therefore, be given to the suggestion that Athens made the first coins, although her later contributions to the technique of currency management are undeniable. Much stronger evidence exists for the claim that the earliest coins in the Ægean were made by Pheidon in Ægina, an island off the Piræus. The period of Pheidon's reign is so uncertain that suggested dates cover a period of over three centuries; the results of recent research, however, suggest the latter half of the 8th century,[4] or more probably the early years of the 7th century.[5] The medieval *Etymolo-*

[1] Glotz, 195.

[2] *Theseus* (Edn. Murray, Sutherland and Co., London, 1876), p. 15.

[3] Seltman, who believes that coins were issued before the time of Solon (*c.* 600 B.C.), does not believe any issues were made before the last two decades or so of the 7th century (p. 5).

[4] Gardner, 112.

[5] Ure, Chap. VI., *Camb. Anc. Hist.*, III, Chronological Note, p. 761. Ridgeway, 266. Head, 395.

gicum Magnum states that, "First of all men Pheidon of Argos struck money in Ægina,"[1] and Strabo[2] records that "Ephorus says that in Ægina silver was first struck by Pheidon, for it has become an emporium, inasmuch as its population, owing to the barrenness of the lands, engaged in maritime trade."

Herodotus[3] says, on the other hand, that "the Lydians were the first people, so far as I know, to adopt a gold and silver coinage." But he does not claim that they were the first to issue coins of any kind, and the fact that the first Lydian coins were of neither gold nor silver makes his evidence inconclusive. Crude bean-shaped ingots bearing a punch mark have been found in considerable quantities within a circuit of some thirty miles round Sardes, the ancient capital of Lydia. These embryo coins are made of a natural mixture of gold and silver, called by the Greeks electrum or "white gold," and probably collected at Sardes from the washings of the little mountain torrent Pactolus, or perhaps from workings in the Tmolus and Sipylus mountains.[4] The appearance of these early Lydian pieces suggests that they are older than any specimens of marked ingots that can be ascribed to Ægina,[5] and as the testimony of the two best and oldest witnesses,[6] Xenophanes in the 6th century[7] and Herodotus in the 5th century, is also in favour of Lydia, the Lydians have a good claim to priority in the production of coins.[8]

But the date of the first Lydian issues is very uncertain. The manner of their execution, a not very certain basis for judgment, suggests that they date from the time of Gyges, who usurped the Lydian throne in the second decade of the 7th century B.C.[9] On the other hand, the excavation of the foundation of the earliest basis in the temple of Artemis at Ephesus brought to light coins that show that the electrum

[1] *Cit.* Ridgeway, 214.

[2] Strabo, VIII, 376: *cit.* Ridgeway, 213. For other references see Head, *Historia Numorum*, 395.

[3] I, 94.

[4] Head, 643.

[5] Hill, however, says (*Camb. Anc. Hist.*, IV, 127) that the coins of Ægina are the most primitive in appearance.

[6] No evidence earlier than Ephorus in the 4th century connects Pheidon with a developed metal coinage.

[7] Xenophanes, *ap. poll*, IX, 83 (*cit.* Ure, 129).

[8] Ure, 129. For a detailed examination of all the evidence relating to the issue of the first coins in Lydia *vide* Ure, Chap. V.

[9] *Camb. Anc. Hist.*, III, 507.

coinage of the Lydian style was already well developed when the foundations were laid. If the date of the foundation is correctly ascribed to a little before 700 B.C., the introduction of the coins is put well back into the 8th century.[1] The discovery of marked ingots issued by the late Minoan peoples in Crete, dating from the 12th century B.C., supports the attribution to the earlier period.[2]

At about this time light dawned upon the dark age that settled on the Ægean world after the Dorian invasion of about 1200 B.C.; brigandage and piracy settled into trade and commerce.[3] Reformed pirates are vigorous people unencumbered by traditional prejudices, and in consequence "the 7th and 6th centuries B.C. constitute, from many points of view, one of the most momentous periods in the whole of the world's history. No doubt the greatest final achievements of the Greek race belong to the two centuries that followed. But practically all that is meant by the Greek spirit and the Greek genius had its birth in the earlier period. Literature and art, philosophy and science, are, at this present day, largely following the lines that were then laid down for them, and this is equally the case with commerce."[4] The foundation laid by the Greeks or their half-hellenized neighbours, the Lydians, for the institution of coinage, was therefore one aspect of an intellectual development that embraced philosophy, art and commerce.

Not only was the period of the 7th and 6th centuries B.C. a time of extraordinary mental alertness. "Thales and the numerous other philosophers of the Ionian school were in close touch with the merchants and manufacturers of their age. They were, in fact, men of science rather than philosophers in the narrow modern sense of the latter word, and most of them were ready to apply their science to practical and commercial ends."[5] Moreover, industry and commerce

[1] *Camb. Anc. Hist.*, IV, 125.

[2] Ure (*Origin of Tyranny*, 128) considers that the discovery of gold and silver dumps in Crete and Cyprus, while it is "no argument against the mass of material which points to a great numismatic development at a date not very far removed from 700 B.C. (does) . . . shift the balance of probability backwards, and make a date in the 8th century as like it as one in the 7th century." Professor Ridgeway (*Companion to Greek Studies*, 446) has suggested that punched pieces were probably in use soon after 800 B.C., and before the time of Gyges.

[3] Ure, 129. [4] Ure, 1. [5] Ure, 1.

were making enormous strides. In Lydia, in particular, the development of commerce was tremendous. Its geographical situation on the trade route from the Euphrates and the Far East to the Ægean put its merchants in a position to become middlemen between the continent of Asia to the east, and the Ionic cities of Asia Minor to the west, and, through them, to continental Greece and western Europe. The Greeks, and particularly those of Ægina and Corinth, were sending forth their wares by sea in all directions from Spain to the Crimea. Egypt had recovered its prosperity, and Greek trade with Egypt grew to considerable magnitude during these centuries. With wits sharpened by such a far-reaching commerce and contact with the Ionian, Greek, and Oriental peoples of Asia Minor, the Lydians entered at the time of the fall of the Assyrian Empire on a period of vigorous independent national life, and Sardes rose to great wealth and luxury. Gyges adopted a policy of maintaining to the full commercial relations with the East, while also extending westward and obtaining a footing on the coast,[1] possibly as a basis for naval power.[2] But at this time also the Lydians began to work their mines of electrum,[3] the metal in which Lydia, above all other countries, was so especially rich. The wealth of its kings down to the time of Crœsus was principally in this form. The device of stamping the ingots of the precious metal sprang not only from the commercial ingenuity of the Lydians, spurred on by their progressive foreign policy, but also from their possession of a supply of the precious metals. This latter factor is of great importance,[4] for subsequent currency

[1] *Camb. Anc. Hist.*, III, 506.

[2] But this is disputed: *vide Camb. Anc. Hist.*, III, 508.

[3] Ure, 129.

[4] The importance of supplies of monetary metals is both over emphasized and placed on a wrong basis by Professor Ridgeway when he says that "where the supply of precious metals is only sufficient to meet the demand for personal adornment, the establishment of a coinage in those metals will naturally be slow, whilst, on the other hand, where there is so abundant a supply of the metals that there is more than sufficient for purposes of personal use, the tendency to produce a coinage will be much greater" (Ridgeway, 372). The demand for gold for ornament will tend to increase when it becomes more plentiful and falls in value. Any increase in the supply cannot therefore be regarded as a surplus available for coinage. It may, however, be argued that ostentation being the underlying reason for the desire for gold, rather than its appearance and peculiar physical properties, a fall in value will tend to restrict the demand for it. But not more than a portion

policy in Lydia suggests that coinage was intended much more as a device for facilitating the export of electrum than to simplify domestic exchange. Different units of weight were in use in the east and in the west, and the first punch-marked ingots were made up on two different weight standards according to the markets for which they were intended. On one standard they were sent forth eastward over the caravan routes to Mesopotamia, and on another westward along the river valleys to the Ionian coast towns of Asia Minor.

3. *The Diffusion of Coining to Asia Minor, Greece, and Central Asia.*

The practice of placing punch marks upon the metallic unit medium, having once been adopted in Lydia, spread quickly during the 7th century B.C. The cities of Asia Minor,[1] which were closely related to Lydia by ties both political and commercial, issued electrum pieces of the Lydian pattern: a number of such very early coins has been found at Ephesus.[2] From Asia Minor the idea passed immediately to continental Greece and the neighbouring islands, where, by the middle

---

of the demand, and probably only a small portion, can be dismissed in this way. If gold were very rare, it would, of course, possess so high a value that it would be inconvenient as a medium for the measurement of other values, and additional supplies would tend, by reducing its value, to make it more suitable for currency. In Lydia, increased supplies of the precious metals, and the desire to market them abroad at better prices than could be obtained at home (where the demand must have been largely for ornament), probably gave rise to coinage, but not a supply of the metals " in excess of the demand for purposes of ornament."

[1] Gardner (69), following Babelon, suggests that it was the Asiatic Greeks who made the first coins, and that the Lydians quickly appreciated and adopted the idea. The point of view rests only upon the assumption that " it would be strange if the Lydian horsemen anticipated the quick-witted and versatile Ionians in so remarkable a discovery as that of striking coins." The types of some of the earliest coins can be called in support of the theory, for they suggest contact with the sea. There is a compromise theory that the coast towns were full of Lydian shop-keepers " who may have privately inaugurated a coinage for their own purposes; or the Lydian Kings may have caused such coins to be struck in the towns under their influence " (Hill, *Camb. Anc. Hist.*, IV, 127). Ure (130) rejects this idea.

[2] Excavations at Ephesus in the temple of Artemis, which was built in the time of Crœsus, revealed the remains of three previous structures, all of considerably earlier date. In these remains were found eighty-seven electrum coins, which may well date from the 8th century B.C. (Ure, 129).

of the 6th century, it was well established. The literary evidence for the origination of the idea in Ægina suggests that it is very probable that, if coining was imported from abroad, it entered Greece by way of Ægina, to which city belongs the credit of having been first to appreciate the importance of the Lydian invention and introduce it into European Greece.

Considerable advance was made in Ægina by way of the addition of a reverse design on the ingots and the application of the idea to silver instead of electrum. In this way Ægina contributed greatly to the spread and popularity of the new invention, and established silver as a coinage metal; so solidly was it established that it remained the monetary metal of Greece for the next 400 years. The Æginetans who had been quick to adopt coining were also well situated to disseminate the idea widely. As pedlars and traders they took coins with them wherever they traded, and coins were soon known throughout continental Greece and the Black Sea, the *pegasi*[1] of Corinth probably being early among the issues following the Æginetan. The establishment of local mints was, however, a slower process, and for some time the issue of money was confined to the maritime cities of Ægina, Corinth, and Corcyra, and to the isle of Eubœa. It is noticeable that Athens does not appear in this list. The coins of Corinth and Ægina were undoubtedly in circulation in Athens, but no Athenian issues seem to have been made until about 600 B.C.,[2] when Solon effected the reforms which, reinforced by the ambition of Peisistratus, prepared the way for the

[1] Possibly issued by the tyrant Periander (*Camb. Anc. Hist.*, IV, 128).

[2] Seltman (5) claims to identify silver coins hitherto ascribed to Eubœa as issued in Athens in pre-Solonian times, probably in the last decade or so of the 7th century B.C., under the influence of the issues of Corinth (*vide* also Ridgeway, 243). The mention of oxen as a unit of account for the measurement of fines in the laws of Draco in 620 B.C. not only suggests that coins were not issued, but that those of Ægina and Corinth then in circulation were not officially recognized, unless it can be contended that reference to oxen is to coins of that name. Professor Gardner (143) rejects the suggestion.

Moreover, the attribution of pre-Solonian issues to Athens is hotly contested on numismatic grounds (Gardner, 143, 148). The weight standards of the Athenian coins of the first half of the 6th century suggest that the city had looked to Eretria in the neighbouring island of Eubœa for inspiration in the organization of her issues rather than to Ægina. But it is quite probable that the Æginetan standard had been in use and was definitely thrown over on political and economic grounds for the Eubœan (*vide* Chap. IX).

greatness of 5th century Athens. The slowness of many cities in Peloponnese to make coins can doubtless be explained by unwillingness to undertake the management of a mint when other and wealthier cities were prepared to do so, and to supply coins for the Ægean world. In the 6th century B.C. some may have been deterred by the policy of Sparta, which prohibited the circulation of coins as well as the precious metals.[1] The Greek emigration of the 7th century to Sicily and Italy and the Corinthian and Corcyran trade of the first half of the 6th century resulted in the introduction of coining in Magna Græcia. In fact, towards the close of the 6th century there was hardly a country[2] in which the Greeks were established where coins were not in use. During the first half of the 5th century B.C. coining had also spread north-west from Asia Minor to Thrace and Macedon. The Cimmerians, from the lands to the north of the Black Sea, who overrran Asia Minor and part of Lydia in the 7th century B.C., seem to have also begun coining, they probably being responsible for the issue of copies of the Lydian pieces.

In 546 B.C. Cyrus the Persian captured Sardes and conquered the Lydian Empire. The Persians had not previously issued coins, but they quickly adopted the idea from the conquered Lydians and their vassal cities along the coast of Asia Minor. After but a short period of delay Cyrus[3] was issuing gold money of the finest quality,[4] probably from the old Lydian mint at Sardes.[5] These issues carried the custom of using coins far afield, although coined money was probably not universally used throughout the whole empire from Asia Minor to Mesopotamia. After the Persian invasion of Egypt, silver coins of the Persian type were issued there, but they are found only on the coast and never far up the Nile. They can never, therefore, have gained any local currency, and were probably intended only for payment of the mercenaries in the army and navy. Until at least the end of the 3rd century B.C., the Egyptians continued to do their business

[1] *Camb. Anc. Hist.*, III, 561.

[2] Very few of the cities of Crete or Cyprus issued coins before the end of the 6th century B.C. (*Camb. Anc. Hist.*, IV, 130).

[3] Gardner, 88. Seltman, 126. Head (*Hist. Num.*, 25) thinks it improbable that any Persian issues were made before the time of Darius.

[4] Herodotus, IV, 166.

[5] Where the processes of minting were understood and skilled die sinkers and moneyers were to be found.

with the scales and uncoined metal. The Persian invasion of Thrace and Macedon stimulated coining there towards the end of the 6th century.[1] The Jews were also brought into closer touch with coins by the Persians, but until the middle of the 2nd century B.C.[2] the former remained content to weigh out their gold and silver or to use the Persian, Phœnician, or Attic coins current in Syria.

The Phœnicians were slow to abandon the old habits of commerce that had served them so well. Whereas the Lydian commerce was based upon transport by caravan, the Phœnician was essentially an overseas trade, and, apart from the fact that the Lydians possessed supplies of the precious metals, such metals were less suited to overseas trade, which requires cargoes in both directions, than to the caravan commerce of Lydia. Not until the middle of the 5th century did the great Phœnician cities of Tyre and Sidon make issues of coins.[3]

In the Ægean, during the 5th century, the number of local issues not only ceased to increase, but was reduced. But there is little doubt that the fine issues and vigorous policy of Athens greatly increased the use of coins. This service of supplying a plentiful currency of good quality and uniform in weight was performed for the East in the later half of the 4th century by Alexander the Great. His conquests carried the custom of using coins to the East, to Southern Asia, and to India. In India, however, there was already in use a primitive kind of coinage, consisting of oblong weights of silver or copper without any type of inscription, but covered with punch-marked symbols. The abundance of his gold issues made them more influential than either the native issues or those of Persia in the Far East. In Egypt, too, Alexander's invasion proved a more effective factor in the popularization of currency. Under the Ptolemies, probably during the 3rd

[1] *Camb. Anc. Hist.*, IV, 130.

[2] In the middle of the 2nd century B.C., by virtue of the right "to coin money for his country with his own stamp" granted by King Antiochus VII. of Syria, Simon the Maccabee issued the first Jewish *shekel* coins (1 Maccab. xv, 6).

[3] The issues of Tyre began in about 450 B.C. (Hill, *Brit. Mus. Cat. Phœnicia*, CXXVI): the types suggest the influence of Athens and Egypt. (Gardner, 345). The issues of Sidon were probably later, and possibly followed the fall of the Athenian Empire, which threw them on their own resources for the supply of coins (Gardner, 340).

century B.C., a mint was set up at Alexandria, but metal by weight continued to be preferred to coin. The circulation of the Macedonian issues, especially of gold, was by no means confined to the empire. The *staters* of Philip and Alexander travelled westward in great quantities. They not only circulated generally throughout the Greek world (and were the first gold coins to do so), but soon obtained even wider recognition. They came into the hands of the Gauls about the time of the death of Philip, towards the end of the 3rd century B.C., through the Greek colony at Massalia (Marseilles), partly along trade routes up the Danube, and partly in the pillage taken by the Gauls in the course of their predatory excursions to Greece. The Gauls, realizing the advantages of the use of coins, began to issue their own pieces, of which the first were copies, though unskilled, of the *staters* of Philip; as time went on, the model was retained, but the copies became more crude and less recognizable. About a century later the Britons of the south took over the idea of coinage from Gaul. They issued gold coins which were rough copies of the Gaulish ones they had seen, and as these were themselves bad copies of the *stater* of Philip, the resemblance between the first British coins and the Macedonian *stater* is often distant. These early coins bore no inscription, but by the time of Cæsar's invasion coins bearing the name of the chief or tribe responsible for their issue had begun to appear.

4. *The Beginnings of Coining in Italy.*

But we have seen that as early as the 7th century the overflow of population from the Ægean had carried the practice of coining westward to Magna Græcia. The native currency of Italy and Sicily consisted of bronze ingots and bars, but the idea of coining introduced by the Greek colonists was not applied to bronze in the south of Italy and Sicily, and no full weight bronze coins appeared. From the end of the 7th century round silver coins were issued, but these were not uninfluenced by the earlier bronze system, for efforts were made to bring the new silver unit of value into simple relation with the native bronze unit. Later, during the 4th century B.C., the Sicilian coins provided a model for the first Carthaginian coins. Carthage was as indifferent to coinage as Egypt and Phœnicia and managed an advanced and prosperous community without the issue of any coins until about 340 B.C. Contact with coinage was made in Sicily in the invasion of 410 B.C., where coins were issued, presumably for the payment of mercenaries more accustomed to the use of money than their employers. The gold and silver of the sacked cities of the very flourishing Hellenic civilization on the island were accordingly coined. The coins, especially the silver, were obvious imitations, unmistakably Greek in style, of the earlier Sicilian coins bearing the head of Persephone.[1]

Greek settlements were confined to Central and South Italy and Sicily, and to the east coast of the peninsula, but their coins were used further north. There, however, native institutions were more vigorous. When coining was adopted it was applied to bronze as the existing monetary metal, and even this step was probably postponed for nearly 200 years after the making of the first silver coins in Magna Græcia. Pliny[2] says that Servius Tullius (who probably lived about the middle of the 6th century) "was the first to make an impress upon copper. Before his time, according to Timæus at Rome, the raw metal only was used." Adam Smith accepted[3] the statement, but no coins of this period have been found, and the suggestion is probably without foundation.[4] Nothing resembling a bronze coin was made in Rome until about the middle of the 5th century. It has been suggested that the Commissioners sent to Athens in 454 B.C. to study the Athenian laws, brought back news of the Athenian currency system, but it is unlikely that the urge to make bronze coins came from this quarter. Coins issued by the Greek cities of Magna Græcia had been circulating in Central Italy for nearly two centuries, and must have taught the native tribes as much of coining as could be learned in Athens. But as in both Magna Græcia and Athens coining had been almost entirely confined to silver, and no full-weight bronze issues had been made, there must have been much of native inspiration in the first attempts to make a bronze coinage.

[1] Head, 877; Gardner, 347. [2] *Hist. Nat.*, XXXIII, 15.

[3] *Wealth of Nations*, I, IV. Babelon thinks that *as signatum* may even have been issued before this.

[4] Two silver coins alleged to have been issued by Servius Tullius do exist; one is in the British Museum and the other at Paris. But both are said to be forgeries, that in London dating from the 18th century.

The first step from the circulation of amorphous bronze ingots (*æs rude*) towards the making of coins consisted of placing types, usually of cattle, on one or both sides of large square blocks of bronze weighing four or five pounds. A block marked in this way was called an *as signatum*. This device was first adopted in Umbria and Central Italy, but the dates of the earliest specimens which have been found are unknown. The practice was copied in Rome about the time of the Twelve Tables, in about 450 B.C.[1] Some broken quadrilaterals of bronze of this kind were found in 1828 at Vulci. These weighed between two and three pounds each, and were stamped with a cow and a trident. There are also in the British Museum some pieces of early bronze, among which are several end-pieces of bars, some bearing stamps or letters. Round bronze coins, however, probably originated in Rome,[2] but, strangely enough, they were not a later development of the *as signatum*. The earliest round Roman coins (*as grave*) are contemporary with the earliest known Roman *as signatum*. Apparently the round coins were regarded merely as subdivisions of the weighty *as signatum*, issues of which seem to have continued, side by side with the *as grave*, at least down to 270 B.C., for if the generally credited explanation of the origin of the types on some of the former be accepted, these types allude to such events as the conquest of the Samnites (295 B.C.) and the victories over Pyrrhus (275 B.C.). Conservatism was doubtless responsible for the maintenance of the old heavy pieces passing by weight for so long a period after the *as grave* had been introduced. Gradually, however, the old *asses* came to be regarded as a relic of an age that had passed and were consecrated in temples,[3] particularly in the sanctuaries of pastoral gods, at the sources of rivers, and in sacred fountains. In such places, as at the source of the Arno, at Spoleto, and at Vulci above-mentioned, existing specimens have been found. They were also handed over at the sale of land or houses to affirm and consecrate the transmission of the property.[4] A sale, according to this form, was said to be

[1] Mommsen, I, 180.

[2] Mommsen, I, 194, thought it could be established "with a certain degree of probability that Rome was the first of all the towns of Central Italy to make coins properly so-called."

[3] As the obsolete *obols* were consecrated in the Heræum by Pheidon.

[4] Babelon, 202.

per æs et libram. It has been suggested that these religious and legal functions were the only ones ever performed by the *as signatum*, but this is not likely.

The first Italian issues of silver resembling those of Magna Græcia and the Eastern Mediterranean belong to Etruria[1] and Campania. Those of the latter were modelled upon the coins of the cities of Asia Minor (more particularly of Phocæa), and became the basis of the first silver coinage issued in Rome towards the middle of the 3rd century B.C. Later, Roman coins were introduced into Spain, Gaul, and Britain, superseding earlier native products. The subsequent issues of Britain were the prototype for still other issues when coinage travelled further north. The early coins found in the western isles of Scotland are rude imitations of Saxon issues, and those of Ireland and Norway were imitations of the issues of Æthelred II.[2]

5. *Early Chinese Money.*

So far the chronicle of the introduction of money has been an account of the spread of the idea from the Ægean. It is often said, however, that the origin of Chinese coins is not to be explained in this way, but that in distant isolation the Chinese came independently upon the idea. Seventh-century B.C. traditions claim that metallic money was cast for the relief of the people in 1985 (?) and 1556 (?) B.C.,[3] Chinese chronology at this early period being too uncertain for the dates to be very definite. But the claim is doubtful, and the coins did not continue in use. Moreover, in recent years there has been a tendency to write up the importance of external influences in China in early times. The introduction of coining has been ascribed to foreign importation. About 670 B.C. some of the sea-traders of the Indian Ocean established a colony in the Gulf of Kiaotchou in the south of Shantung, and introduced the custom of inscribing their large bronze knives (of regular weight) with a distinctive mark or emblem.[4] It is possible that they learned the practice from the western coinages established within the preceding fifty years. During the 4th century B.C. metallic coins of various shapes and sizes

[1] The silver issues of Etruria are thought to date from before 350 B.C. (Sydenham, *Num. Chron.*, 1919, 159).

[2] C. F. Keary, in *Coins and Medals*, edited by S. R. Lane Poole.

[3] Lacouperie, *Cat. Chinese Coins*, I.

[4] *Ibid.*, XI.

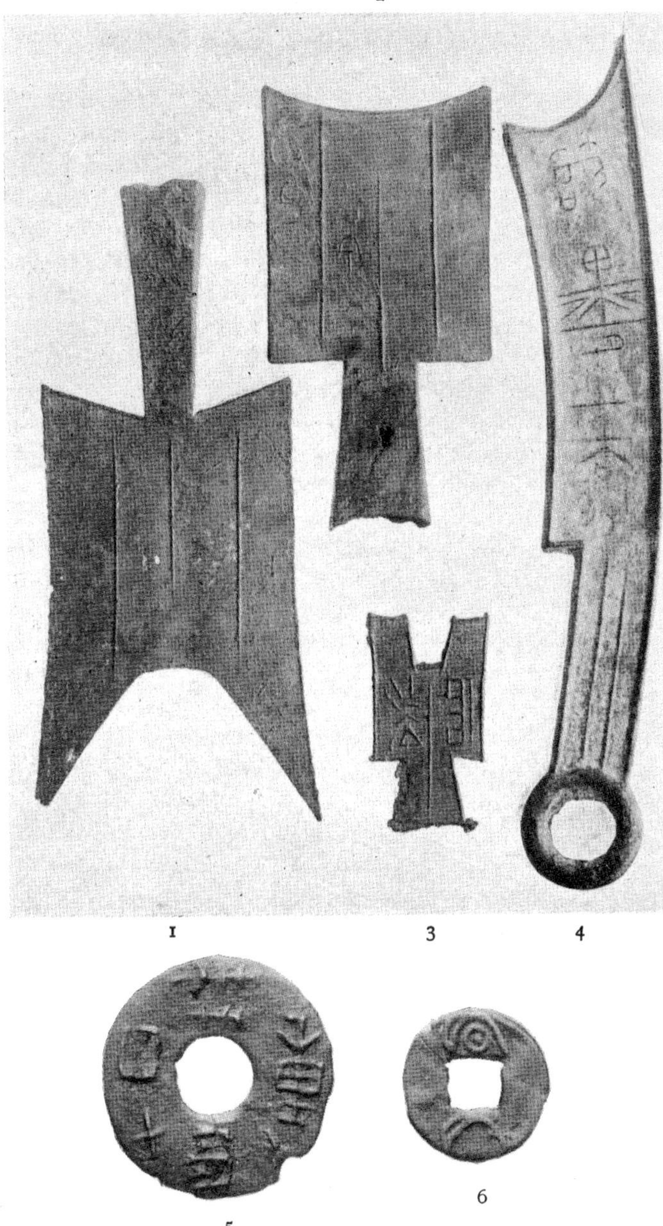

2

1 3 4

5 6

1 Uninscribed Bronze Spade too thin for use in husbandry and intended for use as money. (Twentieth to Seventh Century, B.C.)

2 Inscribed Spade Money of 680 to 350 B.C.

3 Bronze *Pu* Money current from about the Sixth to Third Century B.C. usually inscribed in simplified writing.

4 Bronze Knife Money current from Seventh to Second Century B.C.

5 Round Bronze Money of 481-255 B.C. with round hole.

6 Round Bronze Money with square hole inscribed " Tao of Ming," Ming being the name of a town and Tao originally meaning a knife, but probably by this time a coin.

[*face p.* 50

were issued by private persons in a number of states, and in 335 B.C. the Prince of Ts'in suppressed the then existing shell currency in that province, owing to the difficulty of obtaining an adequate supply of shells. He issued a new round copper currency with a square hole in the centre, which is the direct ancestor of the modern Chinese *cash*. With the foundation of the Empire in 221 B.C. came the first state coinage by the Central Government. The principal money was of copper of the same weight as the earlier issues and round with a square hole—" round as the sky and square as the earth." All other commodities, such as pearls, tortoise-shell, cowries, tin, etc., which had remained in use in many parts of the Empire as mediums of exchange up to this date, ceased to be recognized. In all other countries money once having been introduced, no open reversion by the State to the use of other mediums has occurred, although the war of 1914-18 and post-war inflation in Russia, Germany, Austria, and other European countries had the practical effect of causing such a reversion. But in China the continued use of money has more than once been threatened. During the latter half of the century preceding the Christian era, the counterfeiting of coins had become so great an evil that reversion to the use of grain, silk, shells, etc., as mediums of exchange,, was seriously contemplated. Later, this step was actually taken in the north, but the dishonestly inclined applied their wits to treating fraudulently the new mediums of exchange, and coins had to be reintroduced after a period of forty years. A similar step was taken shortly before the beginning of the Christian era by a usurper desirous of sweeping away all the reforms of the eclipsed dynasty. On this occasion the opposition of traders resulted in the very early withdrawal of the decree. From China the idea of coining spread to Korea and Japan. Japan was content with a currency consisting of imported Chinese *cash* down to the beginning of the 5th century A.D., when the first Japanese coins, consisting of rough silver discs with a small round central hole, were issued.

6. *Summary.*

Thus, although tentative experiments in the sealing of ingots of the currency metals are recorded with varying degrees of credibility in India, Assyria and Cappadocia, and Crete, the effective source of coining in Europe and Asia lies in the Ægean and probably in Lydia. The later 8th century and 7th century B.C. were marked by a great intellectual and commercial renaissance in Greece and Asia Minor. The vigour and independence of mind of the peoples who at this period abandoned their roving life for more settled commercial activities brought forth intellectual movements, increased commerce, and also the first organized coining in the Western World. These products of this time of change interacted—philosophy upon commerce, and commerce upon coining, and, doubtless, coining upon commerce. The last-named reaction has been of immeasurable consequence. The use of coins has revolutionized the commerce of all subsequent time, and it is at the very basis of the organization of large modern co-operative communities. In its own time it enormously facilitated buying and selling for profit and speculation. It was equally momentous in its social and political effects.[1] It vastly increased freedom of movement. By encouraging the growth of commerce it gave rise to a new source of income often of considerable size, which increased leisure[2] and broke up the aristocratic basis of contemporary political organization. The Spartans and Chinese who placed the maintenance of the traditional constitution above all else were, therefore, well advised in their rejection of coining. From Lydia the practice of coining spread to Asia Minor and the Greek mainland, and thence to the Greek colonies in Italy and Sicily, and later to Carthage. At the same time, from Asia Minor it passed to Thrace and Macedonia and to the peoples north of the Black Sea. The Persian invasion of Lydia was followed by the issue of the first Persian coinage, which circulated over a considerable area of the Persian Empire, taking the western product to many a new land. During the 5th century the circulation of coins was greatly increased, although the number of active mints in the Ægean was reduced under the influence of Athens. The next century saw in its first half a revival of local issues, which was overshadowed in its second half by the bounteous output, mainly of gold coins, by Philip and Alexander of

[1] "It changed the nature of wealth, which, more clearly separable now from divine right, was to be as powerful as ever. More than any one thing coinage destroyed the old aristocracies" (*Camb. Anc. Hist.*, III, 542).

[2] Cp. Wells, *Outline of History*, 388.

Macedon. In the east the use of coins was more effectively advanced, and in the west Macedonian gold pieces were the prototype for the first native issues of the Gauls and later the Britons.

Although the Greek emigrants to Magna Græcia in the 7th century B.C. took with them the idea of coinage, and in their new homes began to make silver coins, the peoples of Central and Northern Italy retained their native currency of bronze by weight as the official medium of exchange for nearly two hundred years, although they also used the silver coins of the Greek colonies. In the 5th century large bronze *as signatum* were cast, and at the same time smaller round *as grave* were used as subdivisions of the larger unit. This bronze currency was not superseded in Rome until towards the middle of the 3rd century B.C., when silver coins were made. By the beginning of the Christian era the new Lydian medium of exchange, consisting of a metallic ingot bearing a hall-mark, had spread throughout the greater part of Europe and Asia, driven by the forces of economic and political advantage. The communities that stood out longest against the innovation were Phœnicia, Egypt, Mesopotamia, and Carthage. Their conservatism was due, so far as inland trade was concerned, to the efficient organization of exchange by weight, and in foreign commerce to the fact that commerce was conducted mainly by river and sea, and that bulk in commodities was of less concern than in a caravan trade.

CHAPTER III

THE DEVELOPMENT OF COINAGE AND COINS

1. *Early Improvements in Coins.*

It cannot be too much emphasized that coinage was never invented. Although the appearance of the first punch mark upon blobs of electrum and silver has been taken as the beginning of coinage, the first pieces marked in Lydia and Ægina show very little resemblance to modern coins. A long series of developments separates the ancient from the modern: these developments came at first in rapid succession, and later in more leisurely and less striking fashion. In this chapter it is proposed to examine very briefly the steps by which coins, of the type now used, developed out of the early marked ingots, and the relation between the development of coins and the technique of coining and mint organization.

The electrum ingots found on the plain of Sardes have on one side three incuse depressions made with punches bearing small devices not unlike the hall-marks on British gold and silver. The middle mark was oblong and the two outer ones square. The other side of the ingot was striated. The oldest pieces of electrum of the Greek cities of Asia Minor and of silver in Greece have a similar appearance. The process of manufacture was probably to heat the piece of metal and place it still hot upon an anvil, the surface of which had been striated, to prevent the metal slipping. Punches were then driven into the upper surface of the metal by a blow from a hammer, which reduced the globular mass of hot metal to the shape of a bean. In the latter part of the 6th century the striations gave place to an incuse square, made presumably by an improvement of the head of the anvil. This square was later divided up in various ways. During the 5th century the engraver was called in to decorate the lower die, and a small ornament appeared, often in the middle of the square where the transverse dividing lines crossed. At Athens[1] at the end of

[1] Head, 369.

PLATE IV

THE DEVELOPMENT OF COINS (A)

1 Blob of Silver of about the Twelfth Century B.C. found in the Palace at Knossos with traces of a mark " H " or ⊢ on the under side.

2 Pieces of metal cut from a flat sheet or bar, the original native coinage of India.

3 Lydian Electrum Coin of the time of Gyges (687-652 B.C.) bearing (a) Three incuse punch marks and (b) striated surface.

4 Coin of Crœsus (B.C. 561-546) bearing (a) Foreparts of Lion and Bull and (b) two incuse squares.

5 Silver *drachm* of Clazomenæ of Sixth Century B.C. bearing (a) half a winged boar and (b) incuse square quartered.

6 Silver *tetradrachm* of Syracuse before 500 B.C. bearing (a) Quadriga and (b) incuse square with head of nymph or goddess in centre.

the 6th century B.C., and generally within a short interval, coins with types on both sides were being made. The incuse square continued in common use until the end of the 5th century,[1] but the ornament increased in size. The divisions in the square were abandoned, and the type occupied the whole square, which covered a greater part of the face of the coin. This improvement seems to have occurred in the Ionic cities of Asia Minor, probably Phocæa and Miletus, where the vigour of the Lydians encountered the artistic genius of the Greeks, and possibly also in Ægina.[2] In some places early in the 4th century the incuse square gave place to an incuse circle. But in most the next step was the abandonment of the incuse square in favour of a flat reverse surface.

During the 4th century the Ionic Greeks of Miletus introduced a further notable improvement in the replacement of incuse types by types in relief. The Lydian punch was replaced by an engraved die which produced on the coins an artistic type in relief. Towards the end of the century the coins, which had retained their bean shape, although tending to diminish in thickness, became thin, flat discs of the present kind, and the relief of the types became lower. The more elaborate type, or that which was to stand out in the highest relief, was engraved on the lower die, and that side was regarded as the obverse. This side at first usually bore the crest of the town, and later the head of the divinity. On early coins the types are irregularly placed, and do not cover the whole of the surface of the coin, but in the general improvements in the technique of coining in the latter part of the 4th century attempts were made to place the type in the middle of the coin. By the end of the 4th century the coins of the Greek world had taken on the broad characteristics of modern coins; they were flat discs with types in relief on both sides. The name of the people or the ruler by whom the issue was made had also begun to appear on the coins.[3]

[1] At Ægina until the middle, and at Cyzicus until the closing years of the 4th century.

[2] The incuse square suddenly reappeared in Rhodes in the 2nd century B.C., and in places under Rhodean influence, apparently in a deliberate attempt at archaism.

[3] *Vide* Chap. V.

The coins of the Greek cities of Sicily and Southern Italy did not follow altogether the same line of development as those of the Ægean. The first issues were not as primitive in style as those of Ægina and Asia Minor, the early stages in the evolution of coins being omitted in Magna Græcia. They were already round pieces of silver with types on both sides. In some respects the colonies were ahead of the mother cities. The incuse square found on one side of the Greek coins to the end of the 5th century does not occur in Southern Italy, where the reverse die was round from the beginning. When relief types began to replace the incuse a curious line was taken. Many cities made their coins with the same type on both sides, on one incuse, and on the other in relief.[1] Possibly this was due to a local taste for bronze repoussé work,[2] which was then popularly applied to bronze jewellery, and the decoration of chests, tripods, and other articles; it is also possible that the device was intended to facilitate piling up the coins.[3] But it is more likely to have commended itself for technical reasons; it would have been difficult to strike two relief types on such thin pieces. When the pieces increased in thickness the incuse was abandoned, and often at the same time different types were adopted for the two sides.[4] These early coins suggest that the issues of Corinth were the dominant influence in Magna Græcia, although Corinthian coins display neither the tendency to repoussé nor the incuse circle which were peculiar to Magna Græcia.

The first bronze pieces of the peoples of Central Italy were the large ingots of copper weighing four or five pounds (*as signatum*), and the round bronze pieces of about a pound weight (*as grave*) circulating in the late 5th and 4th centuries. These were cast[5] and not hammered as were the Greek silver issues. But the use of the different process is not to be ascribed to ignorance. The size of the coin alone was a sufficient reason for casting: the equipment then

[1] Gardner, 201.

[2] Gardner, 204. In latter half of 6th century B.C. at Poseidonia, Croton, Sybaris, Metapontum, Tarentum, etc. (*Camb. Anc. Hist.* IV, 117).

[3] This is very doubtful. It would take considerable time to fit the relief types into the incuse, and even where the types were different on the two sides the reverse was usually incuse.

[4] Gardner, 205. [5] Head, 20.

PLATE V

THE DEVELOPMENT OF COINS (B)

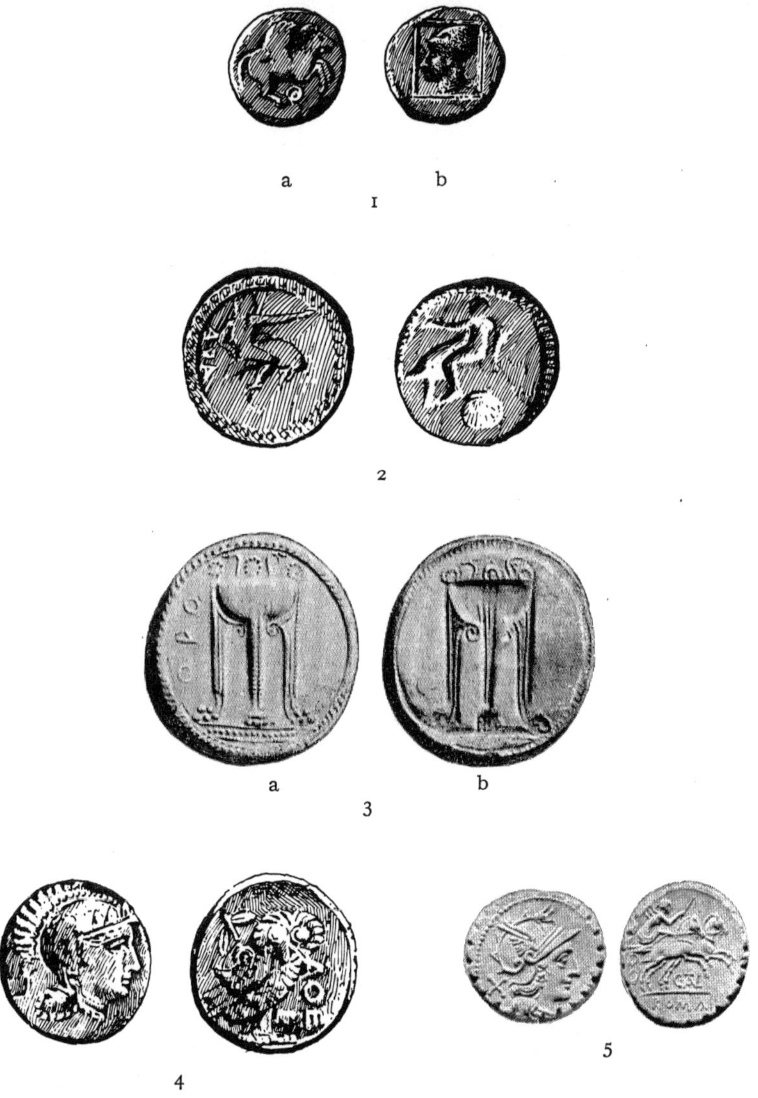

1 Silver *drachm* of Corinth of early Fifth Century B.C. bearing (a) Pegasos and (b) Head of Aphrodite in incuse square.

2 Thin silver Coin of Tarentum issued before 500 B.C. with similar type on both sides, one in relief and the other in intaglio.

3 Silver Coin of Croton bearing Tripod (a) in relief and (b) incuse.

4 Gold *stater* of Athens of early Fourth Century B.C.

5 Serrated Roman Silver, *denarius*, of the Second Century B.C.

available was quite inadequate to the striking of such large pieces,[1] and probably also of the quantities necessary.[2]

The early silver issues of Central Italy and particularly those of Campania, which were the model for later Roman silver, were based largely on Greek patterns. The pieces struck during the 4th century B.C. in the Etruscan towns, however, have no design on the reverse, but towards the end of the century a type appeared, at first in low relief.[3] With the adoption of the Greek principle of coining silver, Greek methods of manufacture were also adopted. When the silver *denarius* was first made in Rome in 268 B.C. it was struck, and from about 260 B.C.[4] all coins of both silver and bronze were hammered.[5] The new method could then be used for bronze merely because the bronze coins had become sufficiently small to be dealt with by the mint equipment then available.[6]

An unusual device was adopted towards the end of the 3rd century, when a *denarius* with a serrated edge was issued, possibly outside Rome.[7] Coins similarly shaped were at about that time issued in Carthage,[8] Syria, and Macedon,[9] and the shape of the *denarius* may have been due to a current fashion. Again, towards the middle of the 2nd century,[10] a

[1] The largest Greek hammered coins were about one-third the size of the one pound *as grave*. The Greeks themselves resorted to casting when they issued a one pound *as* at Agrigentum (Lenormant, I, 276).

[2] Mommsen, I, 275.

[3] Lenormant, I, 264.

[4] Grueber, *Coins and Medals*, 48.

[5] Grueber, I, 30.

[6] The types on certain *denarii* of the Triumvir T. Carisius represent the implements used in the mint (Lenormant, I, 252), and one of the small bronze pieces of the Latin colony of Pæstum illustrates the process of striking: "On the obverse of this piece is a balance containing in one scale a weight and in the other a coin; while on the reverse are two workmen, of whom one is in the act of striking with a hammer a coin die or anvil placed on top of a square block" (Head, 83).

[7] Grueber, I, 102. Mattingly (*Num. Chron.*, 1924, 43) ascribes them to 225 and 220 B.C.

[8] The Carthaginian issue was probably the first (Lenormant, I, 268).

[9] Carthage, 240-200 B.C.; Syria (Bronze), 222-18 B.C.; Macedon, 220-179 B.C. (Grueber, I, 159). *Vide* also Mommsen, I, 266. At Carthage gold as well as silver coins were serrated, but in Syria only copper.

[10] Mattingly (*Num. Chron.*, 1924, 43) suggests that the date of issue was 125-115 B.C., and that it was again an act of the democratic party in opposition to the issue of plated money. Mattingly (*loc. cit.*) ascribes a further issue of serrated pieces to 104-100 B.C. during the period of Marius's ascendancy in Rome. Again, serrated coins are identified with the democrats.

serrated coin is found, and the device was applied to all *denarii* in 92 B.C., and for the next twenty years it was frequently, though intermittently, used. After 70 B.C. serrated coins ceased to be made. Little is known of the method of making the coins,[1] or of the object of the innovation. It is unlikely that it was intended to prevent clipping,[2] because it was ill-designed to that end, or that it was intended to prove the quality of the metal, because it was sometimes applied to bronze and in Rome to plated *denarii*.[3] It is hardly probable that it was intended to make the coins represent "astral bodies,"[4] but it may be that "the exigencies of cutting out the flan from the flat bar of metal" are responsible. "A punch with a plain circular edge would be much more liable to injury than one with a dentated edge, and for that reason the latter was occasionally used."[5] But in general Roman coins after 268 are similar to those of the Greek world, from which, in fact, they were indirectly copied.

In the matter of the development of the coin China took a separate course. In particular, the round coin usually had a hole in the middle, a style peculiar to China in early times. From the beginning of the 7th century B.C.[6] such coins were popular and have, of course, remained in use until the present time.

2. *Currency by Weight and Currency by Tale.*

These developments in the art of coinage have the most direct bearing upon the functions of money in exchange. The crude Lydian punch-marked ingot cannot have passed from hand to hand as easily as a modern coin. In fact, a consideration of some of the more important characteristics of early coins, while still in process of evolution, throws con-

[1] Lenormant (I, 267) says that the serrated edge was fashioned when the blank was cast, and not by filing the coin after it was struck; such a method would have made it too difficult to keep the weight of the coin fixed. The teeth are rounded and not sharp, and the intervening spaces are partially filled with metal.

[2] Lenormant, I, 266.

[3] Grueber, I, 159.

[4] Svoronos (*Bull. de Corr. Hell.*, 1894, 122): *cit.* Grueber, I, 159.

[5] H. G., *Num. Chron.*, 1902, 190.

[6] Coins with a central round hole were popular from 660 to 336 B.C., and were issued with a square hole in 523, 336, and 221 B.C. (Lacouperie, XLIX).

siderable light upon the importance to be attached to currency in the economic life of ancient times.

The type occupied but a very small part of the surface of early Lydian ingots, which also had no reverse type at all. It was, therefore, not difficult to extract much of the metal both by clipping the edges and wearing away the reverse side and yet retain the type undamaged. While extreme maltreatment would be obvious, considerable profit might be made in this way without arousing suspicion. It is fairly clear, therefore, that those who stamped these early pieces had in mind, as Adam Smith[1] suggests, the certification of the quality of the metal, but not its weight. In Lydia and Asia Minor coins were made of electrum, which might easily vary in its composition, and a certificate of quality must have been very useful. In Greece, where coining was immediately adopted, the stamp would guarantee the fineness of the silver. It is probable that for at least 200 years, and, in many areas, much longer, the stamp carried no guarantee of weight and that all early coins were weighed, just as the metals had been weighed before the practice of marking them had been introduced. If this conclusion is correct, it means that no great importance must be attached to the weight of early coins, no more than was probably realised by the peoples who used them. The improvements in manufacture, particularly during the 5th and 4th centuries, render it probable that at about this time the mark on the coin was developing into a guarantee of weight as well as fineness. The types of the coins by this time covered the greater part of both sides of the coin, and clipping and sweating were made more difficult, although it must be admitted that opportunities remained; indeed, they remained until the introduction of the press in the 16th century A.D., and the device of milling the edges of coins in the middle of the succeeding century.[2]

But to secure that coins shall pass freely by tale it is also

[1] *Wealth of Nations*, I, 4, where he said that such stamps "seem in many cases to have been intended to ascertain what it was both most difficult and most important to ascertain, the goodness or fineness of the metal and to have resembled the sterling mark which is at present affixed to plate and bars of silver, or the Spanish mark which is sometimes affixed to ingots of gold, and which being struck only on one side of the piece and not covering the whole surface ascertains the fineness, but not the weight of the metal."

[2] Ruding, 67.

necessary to make them uniform in weight. People abandon the practice of weighing coins when the prospect of profits and losses owing to irregularity in the weight of the coins is reduced to small proportions.[1] This is partly a matter of mint technique. Where coins were cast it was difficult to devise methods that would secure uniformity of weight, and it is probable that before free currency by tale was secured this method was abandoned in favour of the more accurate methods available if coins were struck.[2] Practically all the coins issued round the Ægean were struck, but it is possible that at first moneyers were required to make a prescribed number of coins from a given weight of metal, instead of making each coin of a defined weight. This made variation possible, but in addition many of the early issues were made by cities with no native supplies of the monetary metals, and coining was no more than a spasmodic activity. In consequence, it frequently happened that no public moneyers could be maintained, and a private goldsmith was appointed to make coins, when they were required, under the conditions imposed by the public authority.[3] Other cities borrowed a moneyer from a neighbouring city when coins were wanted.[4] Under such conditions, methods of making coins would be unlikely to make rapid progress. In areas where the precious metals were found, as in Lydia and, later, Persia, Athens, and Macedonia, minting was more nearly continuous. But, for the first two centuries of coining, coins were current by weight, the coin type not being regarded as a guarantee of weight; this currency by weight militated against the type becoming such a guarantee. Probably in the later 6th century the possibility of an expansion of the conception of coinage in this direction was recognized. The developments of mint organi-

[1] Professor Gardner (56) does not agree that we may infer from the variations in the weight of early coins that they passed by weight. It is wrong, he argues, for us so to "project our strict commercial notions into antiquity" and thinks "it is more likely that coins of recognized classes passed as if of standard weight even when they were short of it." He admits, however, that "there is a far greater difficulty of the same kind attaching to the general use of electrum coins which differed in intrinsic value in a remarkable degree."

[2] The fact that the cast coins of China varied as much as 10 per cent. in weight has militated against their success (Lacouperie, XLI).

[3] In consequence, goldsmiths and moneyers are often referred to as of one trade (Lenormant, 250).

[4] Lenormant, III, 251-52.

zation necessary to produce coins of uniform weight probably occurred in the mint at Athens, for the Athenian coins of the 5th century were the first to be of uniform weight and probably the first to circulate by tale. The gold issues of Macedon, that passed throughout the whole of the Mediterranean world, were also of great uniformity.

A further condition precedent to the free circulation of coins is that it shall be easy to distinguish genuine from counterfeit pieces. Crudity of type makes counterfeiting easy work, for it does not exact a high standard of workmanship; but the achievements of the official moneyer must be considered in relation to the state of knowledge at the time. Irregularity of type makes it difficult to distinguish good coins from bad. These matters turn largely upon the processes in the mint. Struck coins are very much more difficult to counterfeit than cast coins. The equipment and personal ability necessary for the successful exploitation of the former process are vastly greater than for the latter. Where the first coins were of electrum or silver, as they were in Asia Minor, Greece, and Magna Græcia, they were small in size. Large coins would have established too large a value unit. In consequence of their smallness it was possible to strike them[1] from the earliest times. Subsequent issues in Persia, Athens, and Macedon were also struck, and the Gauls, when they issued imitations of the gold *staters* of Macedon, adopted the Greek method of hammering.[2] But in Rome the size of the coins made it necessary to cast coins. In India coins were cast from about 250 B.C., and in China they have always been cast.[3] The reason for this adherence to casting is inexplicable, but the principal consequence has been that counterfeiting has always seriously reduced the usefulness of the state coinage.[4] The Romans, on the other hand, did not persist in casting, and by the middle of the 3rd century B.C. all their coins were struck.

Having attempted to make counterfeiting difficult by improving the technical standard of the coin, most states implemented these efforts by punishing with death those

[1] Large coins were issued (*e.g.*, *decadrachms* at Athens and copper pieces up to 1,450 grains by the Ptolemies in Egypt), and were struck, but the number of coins issued was probably small (Lenormant, I, 275).

[2] Lenormant, I, 277.

[3] Lane-Poole, *Coins and Medals*.

[4] Lacouperie, XXIII, and *vide* Chap. XIII.

convicted of issuing bad money. Doubtless many of the less enterprising relied more upon exemplary punishment of counterfeiters than upon exemplary conduct of their mints.

The main requirements of a mint are, therefore, that it should make the hall-mark upon coins, first an acceptable certificate of quality and later also of quantity, that it should maintain coins of uniform weight, and secure general efficiency in the conduct of the mint. If this general efficiency is secured, and the best known methods of manufacture are used, there will be produced types of a degree of excellence difficult to imitate and coins of a uniformity that makes counterfeits stand out even to the less experienced eye. Early mints frequently fell short of these requirements, as we have seen, from lack of knowledge, but in later times the dishonesty of moneyers was a more troublesome cause of shortcoming than their inefficiency. Attempts to remedy this evil left their mark on both the appearance of the coins and the forms of mint organization.

3. *The Control of the Mint to Secure Execution of the Policy Constitutionally adopted.*

The most common method of fixing responsibility for coins was to require the responsible officer to place his mark on all coins made under his surveillance. The method of controlling the mint varied from place to place. In some cities, and particularly those of Asia Minor during the 4th century and after the death of Alexander the Great,[1] the principal magistrate was responsible for the coinage, the production of which he left to officers appointed by him, and working under such measure of control as he thought necessary. The principal magistrate under these conditions placed his name or his official seal upon the coins issued[2] during his term of office. Towards the end of the 5th century the names of magistrates began to appear on the coins, and such names became common in the 4th century.[3] In some cities a high priest or a priestess signed the coins;[4] but as the chief magis-

[1] At Pergamum and Tabæ and at Smyrna during its independence (Lenormant, II, 63).

[2] The names of eponymous annual magistrates on the coins serve also as dates on the coins in the Greek world. Dates in numerals did not appear until after the death of Alexander the Great.

[3] Head, *Coins and Medals*, 39.

[4] *Ibid.*

trate was sometimes invested with the office and dignity of priesthood,[1] it is uncertain whether or not these issues were controlled by the temple authorities. The official seal of the magistrate on the coins sometimes grew in size until it attained the importance of a type.[2] At Lampsacus[3] obverse types change so frequently that it is probable that the coins issued by different magistrates were distinguished by allowing each to select the type for one side of the coins. The Phocæa-Mitylene monetary convention of about 400 B.C. rendered the mint official personally responsible for the quality of the coin. The punishment for dishonest work was death. Here, again, it is probable that one of the types was the signet of the responsible moneyer.[4] This exaggeration of the moneyer's mark is found principally in the cities of Asia Minor, where democratic government was of less sturdy growth than in continental Greece. In other cities money was more carefully controlled. In some, coins were signed by two magistrates. In others, the magistrate and the moneyer signed them, and were jointly responsible.[5]

An alternative and more widespread system placed the powers of controlling the currency in the hands of magistrates appointed for the purpose. Thus the currency control was kept independent of the activities of the chief political officer. The special magistrates were directly responsible to the Senate or frequently to the people. In Athens there were three monetary magistrates who signed the coins, and extreme care was taken to avoid any possibility of collusion between them.[6] There is, however, some doubt how far the appearance of a magistrate's mark can be regarded as rendering him personally responsible for the coins. It may have been more an indication of the time of issue of the coin. It is reasonable to suppose, however, that the monthly magis-

[1] Head, *Hist. Num.*, LVIII.

[2] On reverse at Abdera, Cyzicus, and Phocæa. Head (*Hist. Num.*, LXXXIII) considers that the "types on most electrum coinages . . . were the personal signets of the responsible moneyers and not civic types."

[3] Head, *Hist. Num.*, LVIII.

[4] Head, LXXXIII.

[5] Lenormant (III, 8) says that in Phrygia and Bithynia the name of a priest appears with that of the magistrate.

[6] Lenormant, III, 44, *sqq.* It is believed that one was appointed annually and could not be reappointed, he being in all probability the moneyer proper, and a third seems to have changed every month. All coins have a letter indicating the month of issue, so that the monthly magistrate responsible for bad coins could be identified.

trate in Athens was intended to take his office seriously, and for this reason his term of service was short.[1] It is also possible that the magistrates met the cost of the coining process out of their own pockets, receiving in return the honour of placing their names on the coins.[2] The custom of making donations to the State being well recognized, this is a plausible alternative reason for the appearance of names upon early coins.

Later imperial coinages brought fresh problems. It was impossible for one mint to supply the whole coinage for a large empire. Branch mints were established, and then it was desirable to be able to localize any bad money, at least to the place of issue, if not to the officer responsible at the time of its issue. In consequence Alexander the Great arranged for his issues to be marked with small monograms or combinations of letters indicating the mint from which the issue was made.[3]

Very little more is known of the methods of controlling the mint authorities under the Roman Republic and Empire than in any earlier period. The problem was of much greater complexity in Rome than in the empires of Persia and Macedon or the Greek cities. In the latter the scale of operations was small and more easily compassed. In the Asiatic Empire, although areas were large, political organization was less complex. Under the Roman Republic, on the other hand, particularly during the 3rd and 2nd centuries B.C., efforts were made to secure a formal democratic control of monetary policy, together with security that the policy should be executed by impartial officers independent of the political magistrates. At the same time the high degree of centralization which developed in the later years of the Republic, together with the great area to be controlled, necessitated a more complicated organization. The problem was, therefore, to apply the methods adopted in the Greek cities where the mint was strictly controlled by non-political officers on behalf of the citizens to an area approaching in size that of the empire

[1] Hill, 19.

[2] The Phocæa-Mitylene convention provided that the mint officer, and not the city, should be personally responsible for the quality of the coin.

[3] Much as British pennies made at the Birmingham Mint still bear a distinguishing mark.

of Alexander of Macedon, where ultimate control was monarchical, and where government was much less centralized.

The Senatorial Mint was set up on the Capitoline Hill in the temple of Juno Moneta, probably in 268 B.C., when the issue of the first *denarius* in Rome marked a new era in Roman currency policy, but possibly earlier. The reason for the association of the mint with the temple of Juno Moneta and the origin of the word *moneta* are both doubtful. As to the first, if Juno[1] was regarded as a warlike goddess, it may have been felt appropriate that early issues intended for carrying on wars should be made near her shrine,[2] or if she was generally regarded as a protector of the city and an averter of evil[3] the money may have been placed under her special protection. But more solid and perhaps more Roman reasons may be found in the fact that the site was well fortified, secluded, and near the watch.[4] As to the second it is not even clear whether the goddess gave her name to or obtained it from the money.[5] Nevertheless, the coins were referred to as *moneta*, whence comes the English word money.

[1] Mattingly (*Num. Chron.*, 1924, 186) says Juno ranked at Rome as the patron goddess of Carthage; and Suidas, under the word *moneta*, records that at the beginning of the Pyrrhic wars Juno advised the Romans that " if they fought rightly money would not fail them," which Mattingly interprets as advice to seek the alliance of Carthage and thus overcome her money difficulties.

[2] Hands, *Num. Chron.*, 1910, 4. Mattingly (*Num. Chron.*, 1924, 202) suggests that *moneta* was generally regarded as one aspect of the Carthaginian goddess Astarte, associated with money because silver was first coined by the Romans when in league with Carthage against Pyrrhus, the treasure for the coins having been supplied by Carthage.

[3] Grueber, XL.

[4] Hands, *Num. Chron.*, 1910, 1. The word *moneta* has been traced to μονάς—norm or unit (Giesecke. *Cit.* Mattingly, *Num. Chron.*, 1924, 203, who rejects the theory).

[5] The name of the goddess is first mentioned in connection with the victory over the Aurunci in 345 B.C., when L. Furius Camillus invoked the aid of the goddess and vowed a temple to her. In the following year it was erected on the hill near the Capitol, where the house of M. Manlius Capitolanus had stood (Grueber, XL.). Upon this spot, according to legend, he had been providentially warned by the cackling of geese of the approach of the Gauls to attack the city. The word *moneta* in the name of the goddess was supposed to be derived from *monere* (to warn), but this derivation is etymologically improbable, and the pleasant story of the geese is discredited (Hands, *Num. Chron.*, 1910, 1). Hill (*Historical Roman Coins*, 8), on the other hand, suggested that the goddess received her surname from, rather than gave it to, money.

The control of the mint and the administration, though not the framing, of currency policy, were probably in the hands of the principal magistrates[1] in Rome in early times. They appointed officers to make the necessary coins, and were answerable to the Senate for the manner of their execution.[2] As the consuls issued merely on behalf of the people, they had no right to place their names on the coins. From early times, possibly from 268 B.C., coins were also issued from branch mints[3] in Italy outside Rome, probably to facilitate the operations of the Roman armies stationed at a distance from Rome. Between 240 and 217 B.C. the local issues are distinguishable from the Roman by means of the mint marks placed upon them in accordance with the precedent set by Alexander. Although the coins were issued for military purposes, they were not strictly military issues, for they were controlled, not by the military authorities, but by the Senate. The moneyers were probably appointed by the Senate in much the same way as the Mint Commissioners in Rome[4]; in fact, they sometimes acted in a triumvirate as at Rome. They probably worked under the direct supervision of the quæstors in charge of the military chest at each centre. The cessation of local mint marks suggests that the policy of branch mints had not proved a success, and that by the end of the 3rd century B.C. minting had been concentrated in Rome. For the most part the suggestion is valid: certainly during all the campaigns of the 2nd century in Spain, Africa, and Syria, and against the Kings of Macedon no *denarii* were ever struck abroad.[5] But differences in the fabric of the coins suggest that some of these local mints in Italy continued in operation,

---

Assman, of Berlin, agreed that the surname Moneta given to the goddess was derived from the coinage, but suggests that it came from a Punic word *machanat* meaning camp, which appeared on Carthaginian silver *tetradrachms* circulating in Italy and Sicily before the Punic Wars. Contemporary with Juno, the divine patroness of women, there was a warlike goddess to whom the word *machanat* or camp, might be applied if she was regarded as the goddess of the camp (Hands, *Num. Chron.*, 1910, 1 *sqq.*).

[1] Mommsen, II, 249.

[2] Mommsen, II, 41. Lenormant, III, 146. Babelon, XXXIII.

[3] Lenormant, II, 236.

[4] They were often of the same families as the Roman Mint Commissioners.

[5] Mattingly, *Num. Chron.*, 1919, 224.

although the separate mint marks ceased to appear on the coins until early in the last century B.C.[1]

During the 3rd century the growth of democratic feeling called for some limitation of the power of the consuls, more particularly in matters of currency and finance. In consequence the execution of monetary policy was taken out of their hands and vested in three Mint Commissioners (*Tresviri auro argento aere flando feriundo* or *Tresviri monetalis*),[2] who were appointed especially to administer the mint and issue money, in accordance with decisions arrived at in compliance with the Constitution, and to make the ingots of gold used by the State for making payments by weight.[3] The Commissioners were under the direct control of the Senate[4] as the monetary magistrates had been in many Greek cities. Their responsibility for the coins they issued was, from about 240 B.C.,[5] determined by the practice of placing on the coins issued by each a mark identifying it with the moneyer. Although these marks do not appear until the First Punic War, it is possible that the new method of controlling the mint was instituted in 268 B.C. The initiation of a silver coinage in Rome and the establishment of a new mint probably afforded a suitable opportunity to reorganize the mint administration[6]; perhaps the need for the marking of coins was not realized when the Commissioners were first appointed, and for that reason they did not mark their first issue. On the other hand, because the branch mints set up at about the same time were not placed under special local Commissioners, it can be argued that that system cannot then have been introduced at Rome, and the mint was still under the supervision of the Chief Magistrate. As in early times minting was intermittent, Commissioners were probably not appointed at regular intervals, but only as circumstances demanded. By the beginning of the 2nd

1 Mattingly, *Num. Chron.*, 1919, 222, thinks that a few mints continued to operate until the early years of the last century B.C., but Grueber (*Num. Chron.*, 1911, 118-119) thinks they all came to an end in about 200 B.C., but a few moneyers under the control of the central mint continued to operate at military centres until 89 B.C.

2 Their headquarters were in the temple of Juno Moneta.

3 The State guaranteed the fineness of metal paid out in this way (Lenormant, III, 149).

4 Lenormant, III, 147; II, 249.

5 Grueber, LXI.

6 Grueber, *loc. cit.*

century there is strong evidence of the existence of regular Commissioners, though quite possibly it was not then a regular appointment. Between 92 and 89 B.C. the administration of the mint was considerably dislocated,[1] doubtless by the events of the Social War, and the number of monetary magistrates temporarily increased. By 89 B.C. the coinage commission had become an ordinary annual magistrature, and between 87 and 49 B.C. there was an average of less than two moneyers yearly, judging from the signatures on the coins, although there may have been others who gave only general supervision and did not sign issues.

The moneyers' marks consisted in the late 3rd century mainly of symbols, which were probably the family crests of the moneyers (a fact which accounts for their recurrence). These crests, which consisted of emblems, such as a dog, crescent, dolphin, gryphon, pentagon, knife, hammer, adze, fly, anchor, trident, laurel wreath, etc.,[2] multiplied rapidly, and by 217 B.C. had become extremely numerous. Less frequently initials of moneyers and interlaced letters appeared, and finally, towards the middle of the 2nd century B.C., their full names.[3] The coins of this period bear usually two, and sometimes three, names.[4] During the first century the marks of the Mint Commissioners on the coins acquired a new significance. Honours were added to names, and later the Commissioners captured one side of the coins for advertising the history and exploits of their families. By the early years of the 1st century B.C., in the general decline of the Republic, the Commissioners became entirely out of hand, and their marks on the coins were no longer intended by them to fix their responsibility for coins, but rather to advertise their mastery of the coinage.

From the beginning of the 1st century there appeared special series of coins for which the Senate was responsible, and which were not issued through the regular Mint Commissioners. A superior magistrate was usually appointed to issue the coins, which were marked to show that they were

[1] In 92 B.C. the names of the two censors of the year appear on all coins, and five moneyers seem to have coined. In 91 B.C. there were 6, 90 B.C. 5, and 89 B.C. 3 moneyers. (Grueber, LXVI.).

[2] Grueber, I, LXXXV.

[3] Lenormant, II, 238.

[4] Lenormant, II, 242.

authorized by the Senate.[1] No such mark appeared on the issues of the regular Commissioners, as their authority was well understood. At first such issues were made to meet unusual demands for coin; the first in 100 B.C. was a consequence of a law to provide for State trading in corn, and the second was made in 91 B.C. under similar circumstances. The type of the former issue was adapted to the circumstances as it showed the two quæstors distributing largess[2] and bore a wheat ear. The latter issue bore the names of the quæstors. During the Social War, and the Civil War which followed, the regular issues of money increased, and many special issues were made mostly under the control of quæstors. After the victory of Sulla in 81 B.C. conditions became more normal, but special issues continued in great number. Between 81 and 50 B.C. at least twenty-five special issues were made and, as many bear reference in their types to public games, it is probable that the *curule ædiles* were allowed on such occasions to subsidize the State by making issues of coins at their own expense, as had probably also been the custom in Athens. The coins bore the names of the issuers.[3]

As a result of the Social War and the consequent conferment upon all the free people of Italy of the privileges of Roman citizens in 90 and 89 B.C., local issues of bronze money ceased throughout Italy. Partly in consequence of this the issue of money by generals in command in the provinces was revived. The coins so issued were made either under the direct supervision of the commander or under that of a subordinate appointed by him. At first these issues were probably subject to the control of the Senate as had been those of the 3rd century, but after a short time the Senatorial control relaxed and disappeared.[4] Julius Cæsar took over the coinage of both gold and silver. Soon, however, the coining of silver was handed back to the Mint Commissioners.[5] In 45 B.C. Cæsar increased the number of Mint Commissioners from three to four,[6] and, as he gave the posts to his own slaves, the object

[1] The usual marks on coins of these extraordinary issues are D.S.S. (De Senatus Sententia), P.S.C. (Publice Senatus Consulto), D.S.C. (De Senatus Consulto), Ex S.C. (Ex Senatus Consulto), S.C. (Senatus Consulto), P.E.S.C. (Publice Ex Senatus Consulto).

[2] Grueber, LXXI.

[3] Grueber, I, LXXII.

[4] Grueber, LXXIV.

[5] Mattingly, *Num. Chron.*, 1919, 227.

[6] Grueber, *Coins and Medals*, 56.

of the increase may have been merely to make room for his friends.[1] His own officers continued to issue gold. In 43 B.C., after the death of Julius Cæsar, the dignity of the office of the moneyers was increased: the Senate conferred on them the right of striking and placing their names on gold as well as on silver money.[2] But from 36 B.C.,[3] if not some years earlier, money ceased to be signed by the regular Mint Commissioners. They may have ceased to mark their issues without ceasing to control the mint, but, as there is no obvious reason for a change in that direction, it is probable that control by the Commissioners ceased, and perhaps Senatorial issues of gold and silver were altogether suspended, in consequence of the declining power of the Senate over the currency.[4] Between 17 and 13[5] B.C. the names of Commissioners again appeared on the coins.[6] Probably Augustus reconstituted the commission before, and perhaps in view of, his departure for Gaul. Following Cæsar's example, he made coining one of the services of his household.[7] After 13 B.C. the names of the Mint Commissioners disappeared first from silver and gold, and later from copper as well.[8]

During the first half-century of the empire practically the only coins issued in Rome were of brass and copper from the Senatorial Mint. During this period gold and silver was issued only in the provinces. But by the time of Nero most of the provincial and local issues of silver had ceased. The mint at Lugdunum (Lyons), which had been responsible for the greatest proportion of imperial issues for the preceding half-century, closed in A.D. 38,[9] and the provincial issues in Spain and Africa were withdrawn or lapsed at about the same time. The coining of silver and gold was concentrated in Rome, money of both metals being made in a separate imperial mint. Situated behind the Colosseum near the Cælian Hill, this mint was controlled by the Emperor's Finance Minister, and employed up to 200 men in die-sinking, striking coins,

[1] Only in the first year did all four Commissioners sign the coins. Thereafter three signatures appear.

[2] Grueber, LXVIII.

[3] Grueber, XXXIII.

[4] Grueber, *Coins and Medals*, 56. Lenormant, III, 176.

[5] Mattingly, *Num. Chron.*, 1919, 227.

[6] Lenormant (III, 177) thought that, although no marks appeared on coins until 22 B.C., the Commissioners were reappointed in 27 B.C.

[7] Lenormant, III, 202.

[8] Lenormant, III, 180.

[9] Owing to fear of a nationalist movement.

and keeping accounts. In addition there were *nummularii*, who were probably bankers charged with the duty of placing new coins in circulation and exchanging old coins for new.[1] Mints for issuing gold and silver of imperial issues were also set up by military or civil governors of provinces in Antioch, Ephesus, Spain, Gaul, and Africa. The issues of copper and brass were made from a separate mint near the Capitol controlled by the Senate. As their names never occur on the coins, it is doubtful whether the Commissioners of the mint were ever appointed under the empire : if they were they can only have controlled the Senatorial issues.[2]

At the beginning of the 2nd century A.D. Trajan centralized the control of the central and provincial mints in the hands of a new official called the "Procurator Monetæ,"[3] who took the place of the separate officers previously exercising powers over the issue of money. At the same time to facilitate the technical operation of the mint, and probably also for reasons of economy, he brought together in one building the Imperial Mint (coining gold and silver) and the Senatorial Mint (coining copper and brass), although they were still under separate administration.[4]

During the 3rd century a number of local mints were set up, particularly under Gallienus (A.D. 260-268). By this time the silver issues of Rome had become so debased as to make the issues of bronze by local mints unremunerative, and local mints had to be set up to assist the mint in Rome to supply the volume of currency required. The coins of these provincial mints bear no mark indicative of their origin, but towards the end of the century an attempt was again made to fix responsibility for local issues. Under Diocletian, when the number of branch mints was increased to 14,[5] monograms or initials were again placed on the coins to indicate their place of issue,[6] and Procurators were appointed to control each mint in Rome and the provinces. It had probably become

[1] Mattingly, *Roman Coins in Brit. Mus.*, LVIII.

[2] Grueber (*Coins, Rom. Rep.*, XXXIII) says they were abolished in 3 B.C., but Lenormant (III, 185-98) says that although all numismatic records cease, other records show that they were appointed up to the middle of the 3rd century A.D.

[3] Lenormant, III, 204.

[4] Lenormant, III, 199.

[5] Including one in London (Macdonald, *Evolution of Coins*, 27-28).

[6] Grueber, *Coins and Medals*, 68. Lenormant, II, 421. Webb, *Num. Chron.*, 1920, 229.

evident that a Procurator might take nominal, but could not take real, responsibility for the issues of all the mints. Constantine, not very much later, raised the number of mints to 18,[1] and attempted to co-ordinate the activities of the mints by appointing *Comes sacrarum largitionem*[2] (Overseers of the sacred funds) to control the Procurators of the mints. These branch mints lasted until the fall of the empire in the West and longer in the East.[3]

The Senatorial copper circulated widely in the western empire. Although the first issues were large, they were inadequate to the small change needs of so great an area, and local issues had to be relied upon. Later, as the issues of the Senatorial Mint expanded, local issues diminished. By the end of the 1st century of the present era they were very much reduced. A branch of the Senatorial Mint was established for the eastern empire at Antioch, but no attempt was made to concentrate issues there. The greater volume of the small change was supplied by local issues until the end of the 2nd century A.D. When those issues ceased as a result of the inflation of the 3rd century, arrangements had to be made to replace the bronze coins, many of which had disappeared into the melting-pot. Towards the end of the century Aurelian centralized the issue of copper and turned the old provincial mints[4] into Senatorial ones, issuing copper.

4. *Summary.*

The coin developed by slow degrees from the hall-marked ingots of the early 7th century B.C. by the addition of reverse types, the increase in the size of types, the adoption of relief types in place of incuse, the making of thin coins, and, finally, by greater regularity in the placing of types, the most active years of improvement being the two or three centuries immediately succeeding the first marking of coins at the beginning of the 7th century B.C. The development of the technique of coining is closely bound up with the function performed by the coins. The early crude pieces cannot have been current by tale: the type must have been regarded merely as a certificate of fineness. This was partly because the types were so

[1] Macdonald, *Evolution of Coinage*, 27-28.
[2] *Encyclopedia Britannica :* Article "Numismatics."
[3] Lenormant, III, 210.
[4] Except that at Alexandria.

small as to offer no protection against maltreatment of the coin, partly because coins were rarely uniform in weight when issued, and partly because counterfeiting was common. These imperfections were remedied by the improvements in the technique of coining and mint organization, and by the 5th century B.C. coins were probably beginning to pass by tale.

The control of the mint in order to secure both competence and honesty of work and strict compliance with the decisions of the controlling authority gave rise to serious problems. In the Greek world the mint was sometimes controlled by the Chief Magistrate, but more often by magistrates specially appointed by and answerable to the Senate or the people. Responsibility for the issue of a coin was fixed by requiring those who issued it to place their mark upon it. The later empires needed to maintain a number of mints, and it became necessary to localize responsibility for coins to each mint, if not to the period of office of each moneyer there. Alexander the Great secured this by making each mint place a distinctive mark upon every coin it issued. The Roman Republic combined the demand for independent control of the mint hitherto confined to small city states, with the necessity for maintaining a number of mints as in Macedonia. From the closing years of the 3rd century the Romans adopted the Greek method of appointing independent Mint Commissioners answerable to the Senate. When branch mints were opened their issues bore special marks similar to those introduced by Alexander of Macedon. From the end of the 3rd century to the end of the Republic the issue of money was almost entirely centralized in Rome, and all ordinary issues were controlled by the Mint Commissioners, who placed their marks on the coins. This device of the independent Mint Commissioners, which had been markedly successful in Athens and in Rome, was adopted also in China[1] towards the end of the 2nd century B.C. During the last century B.C., in the breakdown of republican constitution, the Mint Commissioners developed powers far beyond those incidental to the control of the currency. From the time of Julius Cæsar Senatorial control of currency became hazardous as imperial methods of control appeared. Under the Empire all semblance of democratic control of money dis-

[1] In 116 B.C. the mint was placed under control of three Commissioners (Lacouperie, *Cat. Chin. Coins*, XXIX).

appeared, and the mint was controlled by the emperor through officers appointed by him. The titles of these officials changed from time to time, but the essential principles of imperial control remained untouched. The increase in the number of branch mints during the 3rd century revived the problem of tracing coins to their place of issue, and the local mint mark was revived; at the same time attempts were made to correlate the activities of the various mints. In the matter of mint control Rome learned much from her predecessors as in many other aspects of currency policy. Under the Republic methods of mint control resemble closely those in the more democratic Greek states. Under the Empire there is closer resemblance to the imperial methods already evolved in Macedonia.

CHAPTER IV

THE PREROGATIVE OF ISSUE

1. *Private Coining.*

ALTHOUGH there may be wide difference of opinion as to the desirability of state socialism as a method of organizing production, there are now few who take so narrow a view of the functions of the state as Herbert Spencer, and call for coining to be left to private enterprise.[1] Nevertheless, there is little doubt that there have been places and periods in which coining has not been a state monopoly. There is good reason to believe that the punch marks upon the earliest stamped ingots that have been found are neither regal nor civic in origin. In the first place, a comparison of the earliest stamped pieces from each area often reveals a remarkable lack of uniformity.[2] The symbols on the punch marks are of such great variety as to suggest that they are private seals, and many of them cannot be identified with any civic authority.[3] The pieces also vary greatly in appearance and, where coins are of elec-

[1] *Social Statics*, London, 1892, p. 221. He also condemned the hall-marking of silver as superfluous and harmful to trade (*The Man Versus the State*, 1884, 57).

[2] *Vide* Babelon, 183, *sqq*.

[3] The coins found in the temple of Artemis at Ephesus in 1905 exhibit a great variety of types: a lion, a goat, a cock, a stag, head of a bull, a horse, a gryphon, and a human head, a seal, and a beetle. Only two of these types can be even tentatively ascribed to any city (Gardner, 71). Probably some of the very early issues which have, after great difficulty, and with great ingenuity, been assigned to cities, on the assumption that they are civic issues, are private issues, their types being those on private seals.

The oldest known coin bearing an inscription, found at Halicarnassus and now in the British Museum, is an oblong piece of electrum, bearing on the obverse a stag feeding, over the top of which runs a legend in archaic characters, "I am the mark of Phanes." The stag was the symbol of Artemis of Ephesus, but, at the time the piece was probably struck, there was no member of the reigning house of Ephesus bearing the name of Phanes. Adhering to the assumption that the piece was publicly issued, various writers have been forced to invent some tyrant unknown to history to whom its authorship could be credited. But it is more probable that Phanes was an early banker who issued his own coin.

trum, in composition as well. The percentage of gold in the earliest ingots varies from 5 to 95. Taken alone, this variation might suggest depreciation of the coinage by the public authority, but, in view of the variation in types or symbols on the coins, it is more easily explained as a consequence of the system of private issue. A second reason for believing the oldest coins to have been privately issued is to be found in the appearance of the ingots of gold and silver which were the principal medium of exchange in India before the 4th century B.C. The surfaces of these ingots, which were adjusted to a fixed weight, were almost covered with a great variety of punch marks. The variety of the symbols on a single ingot, and the fact that they seem to have been impressed at different times, lends colour to the suggestion that they were simply the private marks of bankers and money changers punched as the metal passed in circulation, more particularly from one district to another.[1] The similar marks upon the early issues of Asia Minor and Greece may probably be explained in the same way.

The object of this private marking of the metals was doubtless to prevent repeated testing of the fineness of the ingots in circulation. Persons through whose hands there passed any large quantity of the precious metals—bankers, merchants, money changers, those working mines of the precious metals, and, above all, the officials of the public treasury, and the temple—tested the metal and punched thereon an impression of their private seals: if the piece came back later in the course of circulation, it could be recognized and accepted without a fresh test. It is possible that in the course of time bankers would omit to test not only pieces bearing their own stamp, but also those bearing stamps of other reputable merchants and bankers. Thus metal marked by a banker or merchant of repute came to be accepted more freely than crude unstamped bullion,and this fact encouraged still more the practice of marking the ingots. At this stage the King or the officials of the public treasury had equal but no greater rights than any private individual to use a private mark on ingots of metal.

The earliest issues in Lydia were probably not a royal monopoly; they were made by merchants and bankers to

[1] Lane-Poole, *Coins and Medals*, 176.

facilitate business at the markets and fairs held in connection with religious festivals in the 7th century B.C.[1] The primitive coins of many cities along the coast of Asia Minor were probably of similar origin. But on the west of the Ægean there is not that irregularity in fabric, style, and quality of metal which in Asia Minor and Lydia suggests free private coining. Moreover, there is much less difficulty in attributing early coins to definite places.[2] In consequence, the private coining is less certain. Again, although the formless *as rude* were probably privately made in Central Italy, the earliest marked ingots were all state issues, in spite of the great variety of symbols upon them.[3] In Russia, however, merchants and goldsmiths apparently made the first roubles without any interference by the state: the coins bore the emblem of the issuer and that of the town in which the pieces were to circulate. In China this practice of stamping ingots in circulation has persisted among money changers down to recent times. Moreover, the earliest issues of knives, spade, and shell money were of private origin. Later, a system of parallel private and public issues was adopted, state-issued money circulating side by side with that issued in the name of, and under the guarantee of, merchants and guilds. The private issues of individuals and local guilds and communities had, however, always to comply with certain state regulations as to the weight and pattern of coins. Subject to these regulations, private issues bearing the name or symbol of the issuer were permitted. In fact, the exchange of private pieces being usually confined to the area of the issuer, either the name of the place of issue or the name or mark of the issuer was essential. On two occasions in 600 B.C. and 523 B.C. attempts were made by the head of the Government to stop private coining and place the currency on a more satisfactory footing, but both attempts failed. Not until 135 B.C. was all private coining forbidden.[4]

[1] The first Lydian "pieces may have been struck as occasion required, and independently of the reigning monarch. . . . I infer (therefore) that during the reigns of the predecessors of Alyattes, Gyges (687-652 B.C.), Ardes (652-615 B.C.), and Sadyattes (615-610 B.C.), the electrum coins struck in Lydia were issued by wealthy traders or bankers to meet the requirements of markets or fairs held in connection with religious festivals, such as those which were celebrated at Sardes in the reign of Gyges" (Head, *Historia Numorum*, 644).

[2] *Camb. Anc. Hist.*, IV, 127.

[3] Babelon, 179; Mommsen, I, 177.

[4] Lacouperie, 213.

2. *The Nationalization of Coining.*

The period of dependence upon private coining seems, in view of the scarcity of specimens of coins of private issues, to have been short, but the circumstances under which a state monopoly was established were not everywhere the same: in some areas economic, and in others political, considerations gave rise to the change. The most important economic reasons for the innovation were that private coining was open to abuses that greatly curtailed the usefulness of the coins, and that nationalization offered a prospect of diverting into the public treasury some of the profits previously made by dishonest private coiners. When stamped pieces of the metal came to be taken in exchange without any test of their purity, a new element entered into the transaction—that of dependence on the good faith of the person to whom the seal belonged. The ingot was taken at a certain value, because it was assumed that the metal was of a certain known degree of purity; but it was possible that the seal might lie. When ingots of electrum were stamped there were obvious opportunities to alter the composition of the metal to the detriment of the public, and in a manner difficult for the ordinary person to detect. The wide variation in the proportion of gold in the early electrum pieces suggests that the opportunity was seen and exploited by many private coiners, although it is perhaps too sweeping a condemnation to say that "the system of free private coining became everywhere a system of false coining."[1] But in consequence of this weakness, pieces bearing some marks gained more general acceptance than others. Marks which experience proved to be reliable would tend to gain this priority, but it was equally important that a considerable number of ingots should bear the mark. Unless the mark was frequently met, it would be unlikely to become familiar, and pieces bearing it could not become common currency for lack of an adequate supply. There is no evidence that, as a general rule, the officers of the royal or public treasury, by their greater honesty, made the royal or civic seal a mark more reliable than the seals of the bankers. In some places, however, this probably happened. The call of the growing commerce of the 7th century B.C. was for a

[1] Babelon, 165.

simplification of exchange and, where the civic seal became generally acceptable, this simplification would most easily be secured by the suppression of the unreliable and self-seeking private coiners, and the attachment of the sole prerogative of coining to the state. But where the public seal did not gain priority because it was notably superior in reliability to any other local mark, the considerable revenue of the treasury must often have resulted in the presence in circulation of a large number of pieces bearing the public mark. Where, as was not uncommon, the state exploited deposits of gold and silver, familiarity with the public seal was better assured. Under such circumstances the state monopoly evolved naturally from the system of private issue—"it sanctioned an existing state of affairs and regularized it, putting a limit to abuses, but it invented nothing."[1]

In the Greek world the temple authorities often exerted a considerable influence on economic affairs, and they must often have played an important part in shaping the development of currency before state mints were set up, and in the circumstances under which the control of the mint was made a civic affair. In some districts the temple occupied a position of economic pre-eminence. The religious authorities controlled great revenues, arising both from offerings to the god and from judicious investments made by the priestly colleges in land, houses, mines, and similar undertakings; in consequence, large quantities of precious metals passed through their hands. In the days of private stamping of ingots these metals were probably put into circulation after being stamped by the temple authorities with the sacred symbol of the deity.[2] If the quantity of ingots bearing the sacred symbol was large, and their quality gave them high repute, they may have performed all the functions secured elsewhere by civic issues, and have rendered the latter unnecessary. The striking of coins in the temple precincts under the auspices of the priests had, moreover, the advantage

[1] Babelon, 141.

[2] "We know that the great shrines of the ancient world served as banks and treasuries, as, for example, the temple of Athena at Athens, that of Apollo at Delphi, and that of Juno Moneta at Rome. The temple priests of Delphi and other rich shrines had at their command large stores of the precious metals, which, in the earliest times, doubtless were in the shape of small ingots or bullets, such as the gold *talents* mentioned in the Homeric Poems" (Ridgeway, 216).

of a greater safety for the mint: in all the insecurity of contemporary life the temples were usually inviolate.[1] Some of the temple issues may even owe their origin to the market for souvenirs of the pilgrimage.[2] But much more important was the fact that the temples were a centre of assembly, at the times of the great festivals. Then, as in the Middle Ages, opportunities for trading must very soon have led to some dilution of devotion by commerce. Something closely resembling the mediæval fair developed[3] and, in consequence of the concentration of trading at such places, special supplies of currency must have been called for in much the same way as concentration of spending at Christmas in England gives rise to the need for greater quantities of currency notes than are normally required. Silver from the temple hoards was put into circulation to facilitate trade as notes are now withdrawn from the banks. Thus it may have been in these assemblies that the need for coins first made itself felt in Greece, and that this need, in the presence of the ability of the temples to satisfy it, produced some of the first coins and resulted in the religious types characteristic of Greek coins. In later years, when the issue of money had passed almost everywhere into political control, coins still issued intermittently from temples. The coins of Olympia, the greatest religious centre in Greece, were probably made in the precincts

[1] Head, *Coins and Medals*, 13.

[2] As medals were struck at the British Empire Exhibition at Wembley in 1924 and 1925, and sold to the faithful.

[3] "The temple shrines of Delphi and Olympia, Delos and Dodona were centres, not merely of religious cult, but likewise of trade and commerce, just as the great fairs of the Middle Ages grew primarily out of the feast-day of the local saint, merchants and traders taking advantage of the assembly together of large bodies of worshippers from various quarters to ply their calling, and to tempt them with their wares. The temple authorities encouraged trade in every way; they constructed sacred roads, which gave facility for travelling at a time when roads as a general rule were almost unknown, and, what was just as important, they placed these roads, and consequently the people who travelled on them, under the protection of the god to whose temple they led in each case, thus affording a safe conduct to the trader as well as the pilgrims; again, at the time of the sacred festivals all strife had to cease, the voice of war was hushed, and thus even amidst the noise of intestine struggles and international strife, peace offered a breathing space for trade and commerce. Hence the probability is considerable that the art of minting money—that is, of stamping with a symbol the ingots or *talents* of gold or silver which had circulated in this simple form for centuries—first had its birth in the sanctuary of some god" (Ridgeway, 216).

of the temple. The great festival was held every four years, but there was a continuous stream of pilgrims needing money, if for nothing else, for paying fees to priests. The nearest town was at Elis, twenty-two miles away, but it is probable that all the Elean coins were minted at Olympia.[1] The gold issued in Athens in 406-5 B.C. was possibly struck in the Parthenon.[2] During the 4th century temple issues were made in Arcadia[3] at Delphi,[4] and in the temple of the Didymean Apollo near Miletus.[5] The latter issue bore the inscription, "Sacred money of Didyma,"[6] but the use of the usual Milesian coin type suggests that they were issued under the authority of the city. Although it might at first appear that the spiritual and temporal powers sometimes shared the prerogative of coining, in fact the Greek world never knew this distinction. The state and temple authorities were generally inter-related in the closest and most ancient bonds, and it is most likely that all these later temple issues were made under civic authority, and possibly civic control, although the mint was in the vicinity of the temple.

But it must be admitted that coining did not always fall thus into the hands of the state in either its secular or its religious aspect. The relative magnitude of the volume of transactions of the public authority and the private bankers was subject to great local variation. In some places bankers were allowed to exploit gold and silver mines, and their private seals may well, on these grounds, have become more familiar than public. But when a banker obtained something approaching an actual, though not legal, monopoly of coining, the situation was charged with political significance. It has been pointed out that the 7th and 6th centuries B.C., which saw the most rapid currency developments, were also, in the Greek world, the age of tyrants, and it is not unlikely that these tyrants "were the first men in their various cities to

[1] Seltman (*Temple Coins of Olympia*, 110) suggests that there were two mints at Olympia in the 5th century—one in the precincts of the temple of Zeus, and the other, opened in about 420 B.C., in the precincts of the temple of Hera.

[2] Seltman, 68.

[3] Hill, *Handbook of Greek and Roman Coins*, 79.

[4] Probably on the occasion of the Pythean festival in 346 B.C. (Gardner, 38).

[5] Gardner, 37. Probably at the rebuilding of the temple in 334 B.C.

[6] Head, *Coins and Medals*, 15.

realize the political possibilities of the new conditions created by the introduction of the new coinage, and . . . to a large extent they owed their positions as tyrants to a financial or commercial supremacy which they had already established before they had attained to supreme political power in their several states."[1] The adoption of coinage was accompanied by, and was almost part of, a great increase in commerce and trade. The economic and social structure of the ancient world was shaken almost as much as the industrial revolution is shaking the world to-day. But there has been a tendency to overrate the part played in the revolution of the 7th century B.C. by coining. If we are correct in believing that in its early days it was nothing more than a means of guaranteeing the fineness of the metals used as mediums of exchange, it was but a small contribution to the large movements of the time. The wider use of gold and silver outside Asia and Egypt is probably of greater significance than coining, although the latter probably facilitated the former. Developments of knowledge and dispersion of population throughout the Mediterranean must have been as great in their effect upon commerce, and this commerce threw up a new class of commercial and financial magnates. Their wealth gave them great power: their business, conducted under the new conditions, made dealings in gold and silver familiar and necessary to them. The volume and popularity of their issues of coins are much more, therefore, an indication of the wealth they had attained, and of the new economic conditions, than a source of power. Kings did not make the first coins, nor did coins make the first Kings. But coinage and tyranny are probably both rooted in the revolution in conditions of life in the Mediterranean. These merchants by their financial prestige probably wielded power comparable to that of the Italian merchant bankers of the 14th and 15th century A.D., and to that of the commercial magnates of the 20th century. But in the ancient East they openly assumed power: an age of tyranny followed in the Greek world during the 6th century B.C. Having risen to power, the tyrant assumed the monopoly of coining. This step was probably part of a policy aimed at the enhancement of his own power and commercial success and the hindrance of rivals. He kicked away the ladder by

[1] Ure, 2.

THE INTERNATIONAL COINS OF THE ANCIENT WORLD (A)

1 Silver Coin of Ægina of B.C. 650-600 bearing (a) Sea Turtle and (b) Incuse Square divided.

2 Silver *stater* of Corinth of Sixth Century B.C. bearing (a) Pegasos and (b) Swastika.

3 Silver *Tetradrachm* of Athens before 500 B.C. bearing (a) Head of Athene and (b) Owl.

4 Silver *Tetradrachm* of Athens of 450 B.C. or later.

[*face p.* 82

which he had risen lest others might attempt to use it. Thus, where economic factors failed to produce a state monopoly of coining, political influences succeeded. Lydia probably affords the best example of the establishment of state coining in this way. Tyranny as well as coinage are said to have originated there,[1] and the tyrant Gyges (687-652 B.C.) was probably responsible for making the right to coin the precious metals a state monopoly.[2] It is notable that "Sparta, the most anti-tyrannical state in Greece, was without a real coinage."[3] But, whether by one path or another, coining had become a public service in Lydia and throughout the Greek world by the 6th century.[4]

3. *The Coinage Prerogative in Lydia and Persia.*

The principal evidence for the state monopoly of minting early in the 6th century B.C. is the greater uniformity that appeared at that time in the appearance, content, and particularly in the types of coins. There are signs, however, that the transition to the new system was gradual: after state issues were instituted merchants and bankers continued to use their punches and marked the new coins, possibly because some of their clients, faithful to tradition, trusted only their banker's mark. Persian *shekels* are often found with their surface almost covered with these small punch marks.

When coining was established as a state monopoly the exercise of the function became an attribute of sovereignty. In general, therefore, an investigation into the allocation of

[1] Ure, 127.

[2] The circumstances of the nationalization of the coinage in Lydia are unknown, "but this is not very surprising if, as the stories of Damonno and Ardys suggest, it was in a series of financial struggles for the throne that the control of the mint became gradually to be synonymous with kingship. When the two were finally equated is a matter of conjecture. The chief part in the process may perhaps have been played by the tradesman king Ardys, but, on the whole, it seems likely that it was Gyges who completed the evolution of metal coinage by making it the prerogative of the state after he had first used it to obtain supreme power. His career falls early enough to make this possible, and the gold of Gyges attained proverbial fame" (Ure, 143). Head (644) suggests that either Gyges or Alyattes may have made the change. Gardner (83) says the issues of Crœsus in the middle of the 6th century were the first state-monopolized issue.

[3] Ure, 14.

[4] Cp. Gardner, 37.

the power to control currency policy identifies itself with the search for ultimate sovereignty in the state. In consequence, we find a sharp contrast in the location of the prerogative between the empires of Asia on the one hand, and the small communities of Greece and Asia Minor on the other. We have seen that in Lydia coining was probably in the hands of the state during the first half of the 6th century B.C. Doubtless it was administered by the King. The Persian conquerors of Lydia brought with them no traditions in the management of money, but, with a quick and very real capacity for administration, they cultivated the developing currency policy of the conquered people. No doubt the economic advantages of coining were recognized both in the market-place and in the imperial treasury. The collection of the tribute payments from each province by the treasury would certainly be simplified by a uniform imperial currency. Political motives were probably also present; the Persians realized the psychological value of an imperial currency and the desirability of superseding the Crœsan issues which were circulating freely in the western provinces of the empire. Perhaps the personal pride of Darius played its part too, for Herodotus, writing in the succeeding century, says of him that being "anxious to leave such a memorial of himself as had been left by no other King, having refined gold to the utmost perfection, he struck money."[1] Moreover, he preserved a very strict monopoly of the issue of gold and enforced its use as far as possible. There is no direct record of decrees or political control, but local issues of gold never appear in the empire where there is no other evidence of relaxation of central control.[2] In fact, the Persian *darics* became famous and superseded earlier issues of both electrum and gold, and were for 200 years the principal gold currency of the ancient world, not only within but also without the Persian frontiers. They circulated in vast quantities throughout the cities of Asia Minor and the islands, and to a considerable extent on the mainland of Greece. In the Athens of Aristotle and Demosthenes, the gold coin in common use was the *daric*, a stock of which was held by most wealthy Athenians. These *darics* wrought as much harm in disuniting various states of Greece as did the gold *staters* of Philip a little later.[3] More-

[1] Herodotus, IV, 66. [2] Hill, 83; Gardner, 39. [3] Ridgeway, 301.

over, wherever the great King exercised direct control, he monopolized also the coining of silver, but where his rule was administered by satraps and tributary dynasts the latter issued silver coins. In the western provinces of Asia the satraps and dynasts were allowed to place their names on the coins they issued, and the army commanders to whom power was delegated to make temporary issues were allowed the same privilege. Probably the names were placed upon the coins in order that responsibility for each issue could be easily fixed. This Persian imperial currency system is typical of the early empires. In their essentials the later systems of Macedon and imperial Rome are the same as that of Persia. In the latter, however, the conquered Greek cities were treated with notable liberality and freely permitted to continue issuing their own coins of silver and copper, and at Phocæa and Cyzicus even of electrum.

4. *The Coinage Prerogative in the Ægean World.*

In the Ægean world, on the other hand, with its small political units, the right of coining was vested in the civic authorities. Where democratic feeling was strong the determination of currency policy was in the hands of either the Senate or the people. In other cities money was controlled by tyrants and chief magistrates. Each city had the power to establish its own mint and issue coins of the size and style which seemed to it best. Some issued no money at all. Even then it is estimated that there were between 1,500 and 2,000 mints. But of these many operated but fitfully, and still more limited themselves to making small change coins for local use.

The commercial sense of the Greeks prevented the establishment of as many unrelated issues as there were mints, but there was in early times considerable variety of material and quality, and more notably of the weights of the coins issued in the cities of Asia Minor, Greece, and Magna Græcia. Units did not always stand in a simple relation to each other and, so far as metal bearing a local stamp was the only generally accepted medium of exchange, travel and foreign trade involved resort to the money-changer, to whom such a state of affairs brought extensive and, no doubt, profitable business.

The need for a money current over an area wider than the territory of one state must have been greater in the first few centuries after the appearance of coins than at any subsequent period. Gold bars were freely used in international settlements in the 7th and 6th centuries B.C., but the reasons which led to the use of coins in internal trade applied equally to foreign trade. Just as in the period of private minting the coins of some individuals emerged as a widely accepted medium of exchange, so the coins of some cities emerged in the succeeding centuries as international coins. Again, priority was gained sometimes for economic and sometimes for political reasons. Reliability of the seal upon the coins and familiarity with it, because of ample supplies, made for success where economic considerations operated freely. Probably the "tortoises"[1] of Ægina were the first to gain wide currency in this way. They were of good quality, and they were widely known because of the great foreign trade of the city to the east and the Black Sea. In consequence, they were the most generally used coins in the Ægean during the 6th century B.C.

Political influences worked also in a manner reminiscent of the period of private coining. Military necessity impelled cities to unite for their common defence. Where these alliances consisted of the grouping of a number of cities under one predominant power, that power often took advantage of its position to secure that its money should become the common currency of the allies. The history of the supersession of the coins of Ægina by those of Athens during the 5th century B.C. illustrates the joint operation of the economic and political influences. From the beginning of the 5th century the "owls"[1] of Athens were excellent in quality and manufacture. They were also plentiful, for Athens possessed the silver mines of Laurium. But the coins were not left to make their way on their own merits. The political influence of Athens grew apace after the temporary set-back to the power of Persia in the Persian Wars of 490-480 B.C. and the fall of Miletus. After the Greek victory at Mycale, Athens was chosen in 478 B.C. to lead the Greek states federated in defence against Persia. But this federation, in which, at first, Athens was a leader of free cities defending their freedom,

[1] So-called because of the type they bore.

THE INTERNATIONAL COINS OF THE ANCIENT WORLD (B)

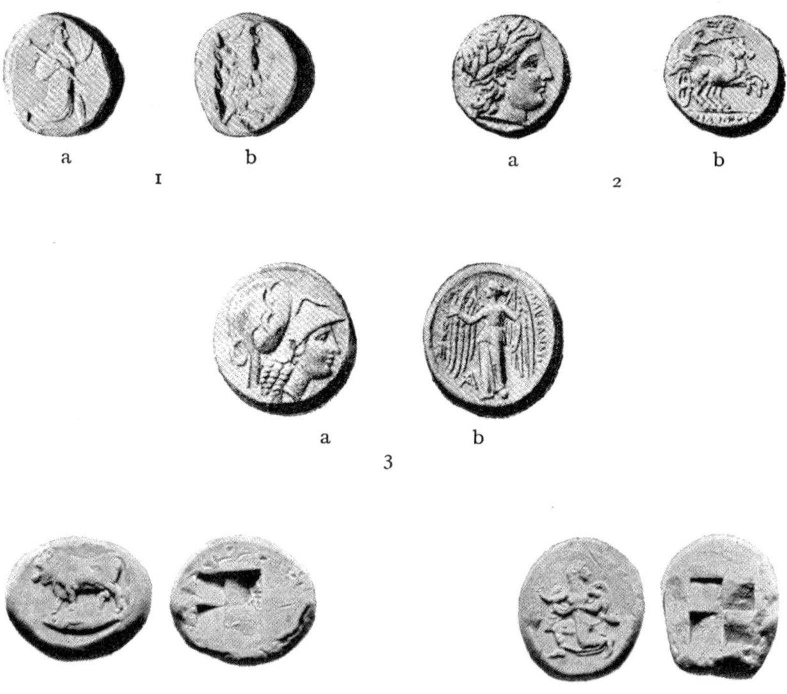

1 Persian Gold *daric* bearing (a) King kneeling and (b) Oblong incuse.
2 Gold *stater* of Philip of Macedon (B.C. 359-336) bearing (a) Head of Apollo and (b) Biga.
3 Gold *stater* of Alexander the Great bearing (a) Head of Athena and (b) Winged Victory.
4 The famous electrum *staters* of Cyzicus of 500-450 B.C.

[*face p.* 86

developed in less than half a century into an Athenian Empire, governed especially in its later years with a harshness not excelled by that of the Persian power, fear of which was the *raison d'être* of the federation.[1] Moreover, if the confederate towns sought to escape the domination of Persian gold, they fled only to Athenian silver.[2] At some date after 480 B.C. a deliberate policy was adopted in Athens of prohibiting the issue of silver currency by cities fully under her power.[3] The evidence for the adoption of this policy is twofold. Inscriptions have been found[4] which refer to a proposal to issue a decree forbidding the use in these cities of any silver money other than that of Athens.[5] A second decree, prompted presumably by the partial failure of the first, provided for the bringing in of coins locally issued, and for the infliction of a fine of 10,000 *drachms* on persons found guilty of non-compliance. This decree was to be exhibited in the market-place and before the mint of each city.

Confirmatory evidence is offered by the coins of most of the confederate cities or, to be more correct, the absence of coins at this period. In Attica and the neighbouring islands, in the islands of the Ægean,[6] the Greek cities of the west coast of Asia Minor, and Ionia,[7] where silver issues had been abundant in the preceding century, they cease in the period succeeding the Persian Wars under the tightening hold of Athens (and sometimes a decline in their prosperity). The areas in which Persia and Athens respectively held sway in Asia Minor in the 5th and 4th centuries can be traced by the predominance of the *daric* and Athenian "owl." Where silver continued to be issued it was often limited to small change, Athenian

[1] Cp. Zimmern, *The Greek Commonwealth.*

[2] It was only Athenian *tetradrachms* that were forced into general circulation; the smaller denominations issued in Athens were intended only for Attica.

[3] Gardner, 226.

[4] Gardner, 226.

[5] The same decree was to enforce the use of Athenian weights and measures. Aristophanes, writing in 414 B.C., alludes to the decree. (*Birds*, 1040-1).

[6] Gardner, 242. Ægina became tributary in 456 B.C., and forthwith limited its issues to small change, which also soon ceased. Coinage recommenced with the conquest of Athens by Lysander, and the re-population of the island (Gardner, 246).

[7] Where the cessation was almost complete in the 5th century B.C. (Gardner, 257). It is doubtful whether any coins were issued at Ephesus during Athenian control (469-415 B.C.), or at Clazomenæ from the end of the Persian Wars until the early 4th century.

"owls" being the basis of the currency.[1] That this was not merely a peaceful acquiescence in the performance by Athens of a function which she admittedly managed with more efficiency than the smaller states, is shown by the alacrity with which local issues were recommenced when the power of Athens was itself eclipsed. Some towns were able to maintain their coinage rights, and we find that they are also towns which do not appear on the Athenian tribute lists. When, at a later date, they were reduced to tributary status, their issues of coins are found to cease as well.[2] The cities of Thrace do not seem to have surrendered their prerogative of coining under the Athenian hegemony, but they and the Kings of Macedon made little use of their right. Their abstinence may be responsible for the complacency of Athens, or the successful invasion of Athenian "owls" may have rendered limitation of local privilege unnecessary. But the burst of coining, which occurred in 421 B.C., suggests that the increasing vigour of Athenian rule gave rise to a determination to use local privilege to the full. In Chalcedon coinage either ceased or was confined to small change for about twenty-five years from the middle of the 5th century.[3] Athenian dominion never extended to Italy or Sicily, all hope of imperial aggrandisement in that direction being dashed by the disaster at Syracuse. The influence of Athens was there confined to the art of the coins, and possibly to the use of the *tetradrachm* instead of the *didrachm* in Sicily. Nevertheless, from Byzantium to Abydos, no currency of any importance was issued while the empire of Athens endured.[4] And over a far greater area from Crimea to Arabia and India to Spain, the Athenian "owls" were famous.

The reasons for this policy of suppressing local issues are, beyond doubt, complex. Exchange difficulties in the payment of her seamen in foreign parts,[5] and in the collection of tribute,[6] would suggest the desirability of an international

[1] Gardner, 53.

[2] *E.g.*, Melos continued to make its own issues, and was not reduced by Athenian forces until 425 B.C.

[3] Gardner, 280.

[4] If the dates given to the coins by Professor Gardner are correct.

[5] Cavaignac, 184.

[6] In the treasure lists at Athens of 434 B.C., coins of Bœotia, Chalcis, and Phocis are separately mentioned. But after 418 B.C. foreign silver was reckoned only by weight (Gardner, 227).

currency in an area then dazed by an intolerable variety of issues. But at the outset it is uncertain whether coins yet passed frequently by tale. If they did not, varieties of issue would matter little. Moreover, the fact that the decrees forced upon the tributory cities not only Athenian coins but also Athenian weights and measures, suggests that the interests of commerce called for edicts so likely to facilitate trade within the empire. Athenian policy at this period was certainly influenced by economic considerations.[1] The extension of the currency of Athenian coin probably facilitated marketing the Athenian silver; a most desirable end, for the silver mines were the backbone of Athenian public finance, and figured prominently in the exports of the city. Civic pride was also a contributory factor.[2] But if the suppression of local issues in favour of Athenian "owls" soon after 480 B.C. was no more than a show of local pride, with the passing of the remaining years of the century it changed from pride to arrogance, and on occasion from arrogance to tyranny. Perhaps the fear of Persia, which had turned the eyes of the Greek world to the East, resulted in contemplation of Persian coins and currency policy by the Athenians: this attempt to make of their silver coins what the Persians had made of the gold *daric* was the result.

This policy of Athens was probably copied by a number of cities in their relations with their colonies. Corinth was prepared to borrow from her great rival, and probably suppressed the issue of imitation Corinthian *staters* which had been made in allied and independent cities in Magna Græcia since the latter part of the 6th century. From about 480 to 450 B.C. Corinthian coins were the main currency of the areas to the north and south of the Gulf of Corinth, on the west coast of Greece, and on the east coast of Italy. It is possible that this spread of the use of Corinthian coins was not the result only of their good quality, but of political pressure, reinforced by economic influences. Early in the 4th century the Corinthian policy broke down like that of Athens, and imitative issues again appeared in Italy, and, particularly

[1] At the time of the second league, Athens prohibited the export of raw material for pottery from Ceos to any place other than Athens, pottery being one of the chief exports of Athens (Cavaignac, 184).

[2] Gardner, 230.

in Sicily.[1] Corcyra seems also to have suppressed coining in her colonies, which commenced to issue only when the misfortunes of the mother city in 375 B.C. threw them on their own resources.[2]

5. *Monetary Unions in the Greek World.*

In areas where the coins of no city took the lead, formal monetary unions were constituted. Such a union provided for uniformity in the exercise of the currency prerogative, and supplied a currency in which trade between the member states could be settled. States with common economic interests could thus encourage mutual trade. Frequently the members took care not to surrender their right to coin. They sometimes issued coins of their own which circulated side by side with the union coins—the former having only local currency and the latter being legal tender without premium or discount—in the markets of all the members without regard to the place of issue. Where all parties to the monetary union were to continue the issue of league coins, the amounts to be issued by each were fixed in order that the profits of issue should be equitably shared. Economy in the cost of maintaining the currency was frequently an important motive behind these alliances, doubtless owing to the fact that most of the autonomous Greek cities were too small to support mints of their own without undue expense. Except where cities worked mines of the precious metals and exported the produce in the form of their own coin, issues were made in most cities only at long intervals, and must on this account have been expensive. Agreements, therefore, sometimes provided for the concentration of the federal issues in one mint and fixed the basis on which the profits and losses of this establishment were to be shared between the members. A number of such early unions are known, their existence being confirmed in some cases by the appearance on their issues of the initials of the league. In others uniformity in weight, and the use of at least one common type on the coins of a number of cities, suggests a union, although the circumstances might be explained by the employment of die engravers trained in the same schools

[1] At Syracuse, 380-330. Locri and Rhegium in Italy about 325, and in Illyria and Acarnania about 425 B.C (Gardner, 370, *sqq.*).

[2] Gardner, 375.

and a practice of borrowing each other's designs.[1] The most important union was that formed in Asia Minor in about 500 B.C.,[2] to issue a uniform electrum coinage. The fabric art and reverse types are uniform, but the quality of the electrum varied in proportion of gold from 20 to 40 per cent.[3] In their effort to free themselves from the domination of Persia, the Ionian cities[4] revived the issue of electrum which they may have regarded as their traditional currency medium.[5] Their weight unit was probably borrowed from Miletus, and the uniform coinage must have been found to assist commerce as well as facilitate payment of the federal forces. Although the suppression of the revolt brought most of these issues to an end, at some date not long after 480 B.C. Cyzicus, Phocæa and Mitylene resumed the issue of electrum on a different standard from that of the cities of the Ionian revolt. They were probably issued after the Athenian victory over the Persians at Mycale, and after the formation of the Delian confederacy.[6] The uniformity of the issues suggests a league, but in any event it is probable that the issues were made under an agreement with Athens.[7] The latter city realized that the currency traditions of Asia Minor would make it difficult to establish the Athenian "owls" there, and the policy of enforcing their currency was not applied; instead, a currency suitable to local tradition was established.[8] Moreover, the Athenian merchants found the electrum coins useful in their trade with the Black Sea. These issues denote a breach in Persian as well as Athenian policy. Electrum was looked upon as a kind of gold, and was therefore a clear infringement of the Persian royal prerogative. The fact that the issue was probably instituted after the victory of the Greeks over the Persians at Mycale probably explains the absence of any attempt to enforce Persian rights. But when the Persian power was reasserted on the shores of the Ægean at the begin-

[1] Head, XLII. [2] Gardner, 93. [3] Gardner, 94.

[4] Chios, Samos, Clazomenæ, Cyme, Priene (*Camb. Anc. Hist.*, IV, 219).

[5] The pieces are a continuation of *staters* issued in Chios in the 7th century, and, as Chios took a leading part in the revolt, it is possible that the issue originated there (Gardner, 94).

[6] Lampsacus and Chios joined in the middle of the 5th century (Gardner, 239).

[7] Gardner, 265.

[8] When silver was issued, competition was carefully avoided by the limitation of issues to small denominations.

ning of the 4th century as a result of the quarrels between Athens and Sparta, the electrum issues continued, possibly because they were now so well established.[1]

The use of electrum rendered a convention more than usually desirable to prescribe a uniform composition of the coins, but no such end was achieved.[2] In weight there was closer agreement. The general agreement upon which this Ionian currency was issued seems in the closing years of the 5th century to have given rise to a desire for more precise and perhaps also more effective arrangements. An inscription of about 400 B.C.,[3] sets out the terms of a monetary convention between Phocæa and Mitylene, which was probably intended to implement the now long-standing general agreement of the league. This convention is one of the very few of which exact details of the terms of the agreement have come down to us. The parties to the convention were to issue electrum coins identical in weight and fineness, and each city was to close its mint in every alternate year while the other supplied all the coins required in that year; in this way a roughly equal division of the profits of issue was secured. No common emblem appeared on the coins, each city continuing to manufacture pieces bearing its own types (as in the Latin Monetary Union in the 19th century). The coins issued by each city were to be legal tender in both. In fact, the electrum issues of Cyzicus, Phocæa, Mitylene, and Lampsacus assumed great proportions, and developed into the international currency of the western part of Asia Minor, during the latter part of the 5th and throughout the 4th century B.C., until electrum fell into disuse.

When the repressive policy of Athens was abandoned, in the closing years of the 5th century, there was a distinct revival of local issues, and when the second confederacy was formed in 378 B.C. the member cities saw to it that the leadership of Athens should not mean also the loss of the coinage prerogative of the members. But the benefits of uniformity of currency had been learned, and the new era of local coining was different

[1] Gardner, 233-36.

[2] The *staters* of Cyzicus varied in composition round about 46 per cent. of gold. The "sixths" of Phocæa and Mitylene were a constant and contain about 40 per cent. gold, 52 per cent. silver, and 8 per cent. copper.

[3] Sir C. Newton, *Roy. Soc. Lit.*, VIII, 548.

from the old. It was marked by a number of local monetary unions, many of which persisted until the Roman conquest supplied a uniform centralized currency such as had existed since the middle of the 6th century B.C. in Asia, where resort to monetary unions had been rendered unnecessary.

Before the end of the 5th century the towns and tribes of Acarnania on the west coast of Greece formed a league of which little is known except from coins. Headed by Stratus, they combined to issue coins based on the silver *stater* of Corinth, and intended for use in the trade with Italy and Sicily. Uniformity extended to the types on the coins, which bore on the obverse a head of Athena and on the reverse a Pegasos. Towards the end of the 3rd century the union was increasing in strength, and its issues continued until about 167 B.C., when, as a result of the Roman invasion, they were first interrupted and then altogether stopped. The cities of Bœotia to the north of Attica had a federal coinage from early times, the legends on the coins identifying the issues of each city. But in 378 B.C. the league was reconstituted, the names of the magistrates, and not the names of the cities, being placed on the coins. In 338 B.C., after the victory of Philip of Macedon over Thebes, the name of the Bœotians only appeared. The league coinage had hitherto been confined to silver, but from this time the bronze coinage was also made uniform. The silver coins were not all struck at one mint, but were uniform in weight and always bore on the obverse a buckler, the type of the league, while the type of the city of issue was placed on the reverse. The union continued until it was dissolved by the Romans in 146 B.C.[1] A league was formed in Chalcidice in 392 B.C., having its headquarters, and probably a central mint at Olynthus, from whence were issued coins of gold, silver and copper. It is to the beautiful silver pieces it issued that the Chalcidean League owes its fame; the gold coins were in all probability only an emergency issue, made as a war measure when Philip of Macedon invaded the province before 358 B.C., which invasion put an end to all local issues. The silver coinage of Arcadia in the 5th century B.C. suggests either a centralization of issue in the religious headquarters of the cities, or a federal arrangement controlling their issues; probably an Arcadian League was formed in the

[1] Gardner, 358.

early years of the 4th century. A later and more ambitious attempt at a monetary union was made in Achaia on the south coast of the Gulf of Corinth. Formed after the battle of Leuctra in 271 B.C.,[1] this union issued both silver and copper during the first ten years of its existence. Each member city made its own issues, but was required to adopt the provisions of the league with regard to weights, measures, and coinage. Early in the 2nd century B.C. it was reorganized and became much more active: its silver issues became the staple currency throughout the Peloponnese for the 134 years from 280 to 2146 B.C., when federal coinage ceased with the constitution of a Roman province. The number of member cities steadily increased throughout this period, and finally reached forty-three, including Corinth (which joined in 243 B.C.), Argos (228 B.C.), and Lacedæmon (192 B.C.).[2] Similar conventions existed in Ætolia on the north coast of the Gulf of Corinth,[3] the island of Eubœa,[4] and Thessaly.[5] Military alliances often resulted in currency agreements of the same kind.[6] Coins issued in temples, or for the sacred games and festivals, developed into federal issues, where the games were held under the joint patronage of more than one city. The policy of the Peloponnese during the 4th century B.C. is in striking contrast with that of the rest of Greece. It was dominated by Sparta,

[1] Professor Gardner (388) thinks league issues began in 373 B.C.

[2] Head, 416-18.

[3] From the 3rd century B.C.

[4] A federal issue probably began when the island was freed from Athenian domination in 411 B.C., and continued until the Macedonian conquest reviving for a short period on the liberation of the island in 197 B.C.

[5] From 196 to 146 B.C.

[6] The cities belonging to the league of Lycia maintained a practical independence, and, while they used the gold *darics* of their Persian sovereign, they received his silver coins only at a rate of exchange fixed by themselves and after the coins had been counterstamped. During the fifth and fourth centuries B.C. a federal currency of silver was issued. Each city continued to issue for itself, but on one side of all league coins there appeared the symbol of the league (Lenormant, I, 74). Some cities continued to issue, in addition, their own coins, not bearing the symbol of the alliance. After the battle of Cnidos (394 B.C.), which freed many cities of Asia Minor from Spartan rule, Samos, Ephesus, Rhodes, and Cnidos formed a military alliance and issued a common silver money bearing the league symbol. More distant cities belonged to the military alliance, but did not join the monetary union.

At the beginning of the 4th century B.C., an anti-Spartan league, formed for military purposes, issued a common coinage of *staters*, and about fifty years later in Sicily a military alliance formed in support of Timoleon, the liberator of the island from the Carthaginians, issued a common bronze currency (Head, *Historia Numorum*, LXXXIV).

which had no commercial or currency policy, its own currency being confined, until the last decade of the century, to clumsy iron pieces. In consequence, no attempt was made to secure uniformity. Rhodes, in the 4th and 3rd centuries B.C., not only permitted but favoured the issue of silver by dependent cities, and allowed the name of the place of issue to appear on the coins in place of that of Rhodes. Although nothing approaching a complete list of the monetary conventions in the Ægean world has been given, the above list amply suffices to indicate the antiquity of the monetary convention, and to suggest the circumstances which were responsible for its popularity round the Ægean, and not on the continent of Asia.

In China monetary unions are known to have existed during the 6th century B.C., when the issue of money was still in private hands. During the two centuries from 580 to 380 B.C. about twenty such have been traced, many being in the form of agreements between guild-merchants to issue knife money.[1] Again, in Etruria during the 5th century B.C., a monetary league was probably in existence and responsible for the issue of *as grave* of uniform types by a number of towns,[2] and as late as the first two decades of the 3rd century Tarentum and Neapolis allied to issue a federal coinage.[3]

6. *The Coinage Prerogative in Macedon.*

When we turn to Macedon we see at work the same imperial forces as in Persia. Philip of Macedon did not, however, proceed immediately to establish a royal Macedonian currency. When the gold mines were taken over, and Philippi was founded, it was given the right to issue its own money of all three metals. It was some thirteen years later, in about 344 B.C., that conquest having aroused his ambition, he began to follow a policy of eliminating autonomous allies and of erecting a great imperial power. The issues of Philippi were then taken over with those of other mints, and imperial issues commenced in Macedon. When Thessaly was joined to Macedon, local issues were suppressed there as well. Philip called a conference of Greek cities at Corinth, which proclaimed him leader of a confederacy against Persia—a position which had been occupied by Athens since the early

[1] Lacouperie, *Catalogue of Chinese Coins*, XLVIII.
[2] Mommsen, I, 226. [3] Head, 61.

part of the 5th century. The assassination of Philip necessitated a second conference, which elected Alexander in the place of his father. Again, it was prescribed that each city was to be free and autonomous, as in the earlier Athenian League. How far the coining privilege of each city was left intact is unknown. In fact, the policy of Alexander in relation to the vast areas over which he secured dominion is not altogether clear. His gold issues and those of his father did in fact supersede the Persian *darics* as the international gold coin. Possibly, in view of the very clear policies of both Persia and Athens, with which he must have been very well acquainted, he preserved to himself the prerogative of coining gold.[1] But the great quantities of gold that he was able to issue in consequence of the spoils of war, and the abundant supplies from Philippi, together with the rapid increase in the use of gold at the time, equally well account for the success of his issues, without any effort by legislation to enforce their currency: they were quite capable of making their own way. His preoccupation with military matters lends plausibility to the suggestion that he continued his father's policy, and left the states under his suzerainty to manage their currency systems for themselves.[2] Whatever his policy in relation to gold, there is no reason to suppose that he forced his silver issues on all his subjects except in Macedon itself, where civic issues were certainly much rarer in his time.[3] Perhaps if he had lived a few years longer he would have set up a coinage for the whole of the ancient world,[4] and enforced its circulation by the same methods as the Persians before and the Romans after him. As it was, the 3rd century B.C. saw the gradual cessation of earlier issues unable to compete with, and no longer required in the presence of, the abundant golden *staters* of Macedon.

7. *The Coinage Prerogative in the Roman Republic.*

The state issues of Roman coin, which commenced about the end of the 4th century B.C., raise two series of problems relating to the coinage prerogative. There are, firstly, questions

[1] Gardner, 428. Little coinage, even of silver, was issued in Athens under Macedonian supremacy (Head, 378).

[2] *Hill*, 83. No local issues seem to have been discontinued on account of Alexander's issues (Gardner, 434). Few tributory states issued gold, however.

[3] Gardner, 428.

[4] Gardner, 432.

concerning the allocation of the exercise of the currency prerogative within the Roman state. Secondly, we must ask who exercised the right of coining within the empire outside Italy, and in the territory of allied and tributory potentates.

Taking first the location of the control of monetary policy within the state, we can say that during the 3rd and 2nd centuries B.C. and the early years of the 1st century B.C. all questions relating to the issue, weight, divisions, types, and metal of money, and the ratio between the metals were decided by the people, the Senate, and the Magistrates assembled together in *comitia* by tribes.[1] In the early years of the 3rd century the supreme magistrate was probably left to carry into effect the popular decision and, within the latitude permitted by it, to decide upon the time and method of making issues. But it has already been seen[2] that a policy of curtailing the power of the chief magistrate led, during the second half of the 3rd century B.C., to the appointment of independent Mint Commissioners answerable to the Senate for their administration of the mint. Their instructions on all the more important matters relating to the currency still came, however, from the people. Indeed, in law, the coinage prerogative was vested in the popular assembly until the end of the Republic. All the more important changes in policy were the result of popular decision.[3] But in practice the break-up of republican and slow introduction of imperial forms which occurred during the last century of the Republic reacted upon the location of power to frame the currency policy. There was, on the one hand, an infringement of the power of the assembly by the Senate. From about 114 B.C. occasional issues were made without reference to the people. A committee of the Senate recommended the issue, and when it was authorized by the Senate a magistrate was also appointed to manage the issue, the coins being always marked to show that they were made on the authority of the Senate.[4] At first these Senatorial issues were made during time of war or other emergency, but from 89 B.C. they

[1] Lenormant, II, 248. Mommsen, II, 41. [2] Chap. III.

[3] Including the Lex Flaminia in 217 B.C., the Lex Papiria in 89 B.C., Lex Livia 91 B.C., with regard to base money, and Lex Clodia, about 104 B.C., with regard to suppression of pieces of 3 *sestertii* (Babelon, *Monnaie Rom. Rep.*, XXXVIII).

[4] Lenormant, II, 251; III, 149-50.

became more frequent and plentiful.[1] On the other hand, the popular prerogative was invaded by the Mint Commissioners. Possibly the appearance of the moneyers' marks upon the coins, towards the end of the 3rd century B.C., can be taken as a symptom of a developing oligarchy.[2] However this may be, it is in the types on the coins that the principal evidence of the declining power of the Senate to control the moneyers is to be found. Although the choice of types was part of the popular prerogative, the Mint Commissioners gave increasing prominence during the 2nd century B.C. to their names and, later, to their family history. Finally, during the first half of the last century B.C., they seized control of the types and used them for the enlargement of their personal reputations; the image of the protective deity of the city of Rome, and even her name was removed from the coin to make way for their personal publicity campaign.[3] During this period also *curule œdiles* were allowed to issue, at their own expense, coins bearing their names. It is notable that the disappearance of republican types did not carry with it any interference with the weight or quality of the coins.

The origins of the system which, by the end of the Republic, swept away what still remained of the democratic currency régime can be traced to the right of military coinage. As early as the 3rd century B.C. the suppression of the silver currencies of Italy and the extending dominion of Rome rendered increasingly serious the problem of providing currency, more particularly for the payment of troops in time of war. The mints which were set up in the provinces, and which made considerable issues during the first and second Punic Wars during the second half of the 3rd century B.C., were not, however, under military control. They were rather branches of the Senatorial Mint, and the Senate kept strict control over them, and probably appointed the moneyers, who were in a position similar to the Mint Commissioners in Rome. The branch mints having been abandoned at the end of the 3rd century B.C., and all minting concentrated in Rome for the whole of the 2nd century, the Senate preserved its monopoly of issue until the beginning of the last century B.C. But after the Social War, and the subsequent admission of all

[1] Babelon, *Monnaie Rom. Rep.*, XXXVIII.
[2] Babelon, *op. cit.*, XXXIII. [3] *Vide* Chap. V.

free inhabitants of Italy to the privileges of a citizen of Rome in 90 and 89 B.C., all local Italian mints which were still issuing bronze ceased to operate. In consequence of this, and the further extension of Roman power, the old difficulty of supplying coin, more particularly for the troops in the provinces, reappeared.[1] Military coinages were again permitted to meet the difficulty. Generals in command were permitted to strike money in the provinces[2] in their own names, or to delegate the work to a subordinate.[3] Some advantage was taken of the new power in Spain and Gaul and in the East between 82 and 72 B.C., the coins sometimes bearing the name of the general, sometimes that of his subordinate authorized to make the issue, and sometimes the names of both.[4] But at first the issue was, as the issues of the 3rd century B.C. had been, under the control of the Senate. The coins were marked S.C. to indicate express Senatorial authority for their issue. For twenty years after 72 B.C. the right fell into disuse, to be resuscitated by Julius Cæsar at the successful conclusion of his Gallic War in 50 B.C.; he then struck coins bearing his name, and distributed them to secure the goodwill of the army.[5] As soon as he arrived in Rome in 49 B.C., Cæsar, by reason of the special military command which he exercised in the city, issued both gold and silver bearing his name, doubtless for distribution to the army; the issue was, however, without authority, for the right of coining in Rome did not attach to the military command there. During the civil war between Cæsar and Pompey in 49-48, the chief partisans of Pompey issued military coins in imitation of Cæsar's Gallic issues,[6] and frankly without the authorization of the Senate. Cæsar's first Roman issues of both metals were made through his own officers, and not marked S.C., but he restored the issue of silver to the Senatorial officers[7] after a short period, compromising with tradition by appointing his own slaves to be Commissioners of the Mint. The coining of gold he kept in his own hands. After the assassination of Julius Cæsar in 44 B.C., Antony succeeded to much of

[1] Grueber, *Num. Chron.*, 1911, 118-19.

[2] The right to coin outside Rome became part of the *imperium militare*, but in Rome it was still part of the *imperium civile* (Lenormant, II, 253).

[3] Grueber, LXXIV. [4] Grueber, III, 342. [5] Grueber, II, 342.

[6] Grueber, I, 499. [7] *Num. Chron.*, 1919, 229.

Cæsar's privilege, and placed his own portrait on the coins. But as a result of a quarrel with the Senate a triumvirate was appointed "to set the state in order," from which mandate its members inferred the fullest powers of sovereignty, including the right of mintage. They issued coins, republican in character, but devoted to their own glorification.

8. *The Coinage Prerogative in the Roman Empire.*

But from 37 B.C. it was clear that the coinage was no longer republican.[1] The names of the moneyers disappeared from the coins for the first time for over 200 years, and the types were thenceforward personal to Octavius, to 27 B.C. as Cæsar (styled *imperator*), and thereafter as Augustus. There then followed a period of uncertainty as to the location of the prerogative. Augustus placed the restored *as* coinage under the Republic in 23 B.C.,[2] but retained the right to coin gold and silver. But for a short interval in 17-13 B.C. the Senatorial Mint seems to have been reopened to issue both gold and silver, which were signed by the moneyers. Then Augustus reclosed the mint and issues ceased in Rome. The Senate was unable to reassert its coinage prerogative and, as Augustus made no attempt to take it over, so far as it concerned gold and silver it lapsed, and coinage passed for about half a century to the provinces.[3] On the one hand, the open seizure of all the coining privileges of the Senate might have offended tradition and conservative thought. It was better, therefore, to let the Senatorial rights to issue gold and silver merely sink into obscurity. On the other, the Emperor's ends could be equally well

[1] Grueber's contention that the imperial currency was based on a Senatorial decree of 36 B.C. is denied by Mattingly in *Num. Chron.*, 1919, 1922.

[2] See Mommsen, III, 12. Both Babelon and Mommsen believed that the imperial control of the mint dated from 15 B.C., but Grueber (II, 43) says: "If the evidence of the types is any criterion, the practical authority over the gold and silver coinages had been invested by the Senate in Augustus at a much earlier date and possibly so far back as 36 B.C." But Mattingly (*Num. Chron.*, 1919, 222) dismisses Grueber's date on the ground that it is "simply inferred and rests on no historical evidence." He argues that the imperial coinage was based on earlier military coinages, and that during the Civil Wars of 49-31 B.C. the military coinage "encroached more and more on the Senatorial coinage of Rome and in the end ousted it" (233).

[3] Mattingly, *Num. Chron.*, 1919, 227.

attained by provincial military issues which, having now been made for nearly 100 years, would excite no comment. Masking reform with precedent, Augustus established the sole Imperial Mint at Lugdunum (Lyons) in 14 B.C., whence the Roman world was supplied with gold and silver coins for half a century.[1] These issues were still founded on the *imperium* of a general in the provinces. It was only in the time of Caligula that the Emperors commenced the issue of their own money from the Roman Mint. The Imperial Mint for gold and silver at Lugdunum was closed soon after A.D. 37, and an imperial establishment for coining those metals was opened in Rome. There were strong practical arguments for locating the mint in the capital. The termination of the frontier wars in Gaul removed one of the advantages of the Lugdunum Mint, and the slow habituation of the people to imperial control of the coinage prerogative removed another, namely the argument which had shaped the policy of Augustus in making his issues outside Rome. From this time practically all issues of silver were made from the Emperor's Mint in Rome. This imperial currency grew clearly out of the right of military coinage, which, although controlled by the Senate in the 3rd century B.C., gradually escaped Senatorial control when revived in 89 B.C. Julius Cæsar assumed, probably without authority, the right to exercise this right in Rome, and laid the foundation of the imperial system. Under the triumvirate the military coinage finally triumphed over the republican, although there was still rivalry for the supreme authority. But after Octavius's victory over Antony the former emerged in supreme control of the military coinage. When finally these issues made in virtue of the military power of the issuer were made in Rome they were truly imperial in type. They were entirely controlled by the Emperor through his Finance Minister and a separate Imperial Mint was established, the cost of which was regarded as part of the household expenses of the Emperor.[2]

The Senatorial prerogative did not altogether disappear. The old mint continued issuing brass and copper, the privilege of the Senate being indicated by the " S.C.," which appeared on all the coins from the old mint. But the Emperors from Augustus claimed some power of supervising the Senatorial Mint, the measure of their powers being indicated by the grow-

[1] Mattingly, *Num. Chron.*, 1919, 231.

[2] Mommsen, III, 13.

ing practice of placing representations of the Emperor on the coins. In the middle of the first century, under Nero, the Senate increased its powers of issue. The first portion of his reign was a period of conservative and constitutional government, which is indicated on the coins of the period. Even pieces of gold and silver, although still struck in the Imperial Mint, bore the letters "Ex. S.C."[1] Clearly the Senate temporarily recovered its lost privilege of controlling gold and silver issues. But after the death, violent or natural, of his conservative advisers, Nero entered upon a period of absolutism. The acknowledgment of the Senatorial prerogative disappeared from the gold and silver coins, and the Senatorial Mint was placed under prefects nominated by the Emperor in A.D. 56. The Emperor's portrait appeared more frequently upon Senatorial issues, and resembled in style the portrait on the other coins. Most probably the powers of the Senate were now purely nominal. At the end of the century Trajan assumed additional control of the mint.[2]

Towards the end of the 3rd century, when continued debasement of the products of the Imperial Mint had rendered the Senatorial right to issue copper ineffective, Aurelian suppressed it. Although it was subsequently restored for a brief period, Diocletian finally deprived the Senate of all coining powers when he reconstituted the empire, and reformed the currency after its complete collapse during the 3rd century A.D. From the beginning of the 4th century the Emperor was in complete possession of the prerogative of coining.[3]

9. *The Control of Coining in the Roman Colonies and Dependencies.*

In the second aspect of the prerogative of issue, the control of currency issues in the empire beyond the Italian peninsula, and particularly in the territory of allied and tributory chiefs, we again notice a similarity between Roman and earlier Persian and Macedonian imperial policy. Authority to issue

[1] Mattingly, XIX. [2] Lenormant, III, 199.

[3] In fact, it was not until the end of the 4th century A.D. that the imperial prerogative covered all issues: the right to issue bronze money was apparently granted to individuals at some period before this, and only annulled by an Act of A.D. 394 (Mommsen, III, 14).

gold was (with one exception)[1] never permitted to any of the peoples, cities, or princes under Roman dominion. The progress of the conquest of Gaul in the last century B.C. can almost be followed by the disappearance of local gold coins. So great was the jealousy of the right to issue gold, that Kings of quite independent countries in the sphere of Roman action refrained from striking gold coins for fear of provoking the Roman wrath. Evidently, to issue gold was to declare independence, and gold gradually disappeared from the outskirts of Roman territory. The issue of silver in Rome in 269 B.C. was commenced only after the defeat of Pyrrhus, the surrender or capture of Rhegium and Tarentum, the submission of the Lucanians and Bruttians, and the establishment of control in Campania in the seventies had given to Rome supreme power throughout all Italy. The issue was part of the policy of consolidating this power. Most of the silver then circulating in Rome had been issued outside the city, possibly in the area of the campaigns of the Pyrrhic Wars, but after the declaration of peace the coining of silver was transferred to Rome.

Throughout Italy a great variety of issues had been made, but from about 264 B.C., or possibly as late as 212 B.C.,[2] the right to issue was suppressed in all the cities of Central and Southern Italy, except Naples, Tarentum, and Rhegium, and they lost their privilege after but a short period.[3] Later, during the conquests of the later 2nd and 1st centuries B.C., this policy of forcing coins upon conquered peoples, which had been that of conquerors since the Persian victories in Asia Minor, was the guiding principle of the provincial governors. In the confusion of the last century B.C. it is difficult to trace the distribution of powers, but the general rule of law under the Republic on monetary matters was that colonies or cities that had been admitted to full municipal rights were absorbed into the Roman people and lost their local sovereignty and, with it, their right of mintage. Those communities, however, that were admitted only to limited municipal rights, (*civitas sine suffragio*) retained certain narrowly circumscribed rights of issue, and a few towns deemed to be free allies[4] were

[1] The Kings of the Cimmerian, Bosphorus (Crimea), whose gold was soon debased to electrum, and by the end of the 3rd century to bronze coins washed with gold (Hill, *Handbook*, 87).

[2] Mattingly, *Num. Chron.*, 1924, 200.

[3] Grueber, II, 142.

[4] Among which were Alexandria, Troas, and Tyre.

allowed to continue to coin silver, but the privilege was exceptional. In the period of transition from Republic to Empire a few cities[1] broke through the tradition and coined silver, but on the establishment of the empire the policy of the Government on this subject became much clearer. Gold was strictly monopolized by the emperor. The attitude of the Government to local silver issues was adapted to the different conditions in the western and eastern empires. In both west and east local money was allowed to continue. In the former, provinces were compelled to base their issues on the Roman *denarius,* and issues not on this basis were demonetized.[2] Thus throughout the whole of the western provinces the only silver currency unit was the *denarius,* although it might appear under different names and forms. In the eastern empire different tactics were adopted. The populations there had for centuries circulated their own silver, and Rome did not attempt a direct attack upon their so well-established customs by forcing her silver *denarius* on them. The vast quantities of local coins were probably allowed to remain, but new silver issues were strictly limited, and official rates of exchange were established between the imperial *denarius* and the main eastern currencies.[3] In consequence of this official rate, a number of the old locally issued pieces were driven to the melting-pot, and room was made for the imperial or authorized local issues. But it is not clear that the rates of exchange were fixed with the object of superseding local issues. The great variety of local coins which persisted in spite of the number of monetary unions referred to above would have called for an extremely complex tariff if it had been desired to preserve them all. Doubtless there was no such desire and, in the hope of simplifying the system, uniform exchange rates were established for large areas.[4] These were unfavourable to a considerable number of the coins in circulation, and the latter were melted in consequence. But Augustus also made Roman coins,

[1] Corinth and Gades (Hill, *Handbook*, 89).

[2] British issues ceased with the Roman invasion, and no coins were made in the island until the end of the 3rd century A.D., when the Romans set up mints, which operated for the next hundred years.

[3] Mattingly, XXIV.

[4] The attic *drachm* was tariffed at one *denarius*, all ancient Greek *tetradrachms*, irrespective of weight, at 3 *denarii* in Asia Minor, and 4 *denarii* in Syria (Lenormant, 107-109).

weights and measures the only ones in which transactions could be legally enforced. All public accounts and tariffs were based on the *denarius*.[1] Furthermore, he abolished the differentiation between free allies and subject states, with the result that colonies outside Italy ceased to coin silver. Only a very few of the old free and autonomous towns were permitted to continue making their own issues,[2] and some of the richest and most famous Greek cities which had preserved their autonomy until this time lost their right to issue silver. By one means or another the coinage of silver was concentrated in the hands of the Emperor, who delegated it to local authorities only in unusual circumstances. The prerogative of coining gold and silver for the whole empire was steadily concentrated in the Emperor. Imperial gold had a complete monopoly, and the whole empire was supplied from the mint at Lugdunum. Silver for the whole of the west, and to a lesser extent for the eastern empire, was also struck at Lugdunum, but a branch of the Imperial Mint was also set up at Antioch to furnish an auxiliary supply of silver for the east. The silver *denarius* slowly drove out all previous issues and supplied the first uniform silver currency in the Greek world.

The Roman attitude to the coining of copper is sharply contrasted with the policy in relation to gold and silver. The evidence of hoards suggests that during the last decade of the 4th century and the first decade of the 3rd century B.C. Rome entered into an arrangement with her autonomous allies for the free circulation throughout the bronze-using district under Roman control of all coins issued from the Roman and Campanian mints and the *as grave* of the allied mints.[3] In later times when copper was sinking to the status of small change money, this policy developed into one of leaving the supply of copper money to the local authorities and, after the middle of the 3rd century B.C., this was generally the only power of minting that remained to them. In Italy itself, the Republic exercised a closer supervision, reserving to itself, in 264 B.C., the monopoly of coinage for Central Italy, and closing all the colonial mints in that area. The ad-

[1] Hill, *Handbook*, 87.

[2] Laodicea ad Mare, Seleucia in Pieria, and others (*vide* Mattingly, XXV).

[3] *Encyclopædia Britannica*: Article "Numismatics."

mission of all free people of Italy to the rights of Roman citizenship in 90 and 89 B.C. had the incidental effect of closing down all the mints in Italy which still issued bronze money. For the next century or more the token money of the Senatorial Mint in Rome was probably not legal tender outside Italy.[1] Imperial copper was issued by Augustus in Africa, Mauretania, and Gaul, and, possibly, Spain, each series being legal tender only in the province of issue. Local town issues were also made in the western provinces. In the east provincial issues were made at Antioch and Alexandria, but the main source of supply was the abundant output of local town mints. Authority to issue copper was freely given to local bodies almost as a normal right, although formal sanction had to be sought for each issue. Sometimes the grant was made by the Emperor personally, and sometimes it came from the governor of the province; in the latter case the grant would be for a limited period only. The fact that some of these local issues were interrupted reveals periods of suspension of the right to coin. Many cities that previously did not coin at all began at this period to issue their own copper. The autonomous towns above referred to, however, possessed the right to issue copper by virtue of their status and did not require any specific grant, but, in fact, they were little better off than subject cities, their only superiority lying in the fact that they were permitted to introduce proud titles of liberty and autonomy into the legends on their issues. In all cases, however, the sovereignty of the emperor had to be acknowledged on these issues, and the effigy of the emperor or one of his family always appears on onc side of the coin, while the name and type of the city is placed on the other. All such issues of copper were on the same basis as imperial money, but no attempt was made to centralize there the issue of bronze for the eastern empire. The difficulty and expense of transporting coin so heavy in relation to its value may have been a reason against centralization, although it did not prevent such a centralization in the west. More probably communities were flattered by the grant of authority to coin, and, as they received little advantage from it, the imperial authorities were content to make use of the weaknesses of local authorities.

[1] Mattingly, XVII.

The general tendency during the first half of the 1st century A.D. was towards the consolidation of the imperial position. Tiberius, in fear probably of revolt, suppressed provincial token issues in Gaul, and apparently the town issues in Spain and Africa, thus throwing the burden of supplying token money for the west on the Senatorial Mint in Rome. On the other hand, he inaugurated an issue of silver *drachms* of a local character at Cæsarea in Cappadocia.[1] As we have seen, Caligula still further consolidated the imperial position by openly exercising the privilege of coining gold and silver in Rome, a step that Augustus and his successors had thought undesirable. The policy of suppressing local token issues in the west was carried to a conclusion, and all local issues ceased, never to recommence. But the Roman Mint was incapable of meeting the demands put upon it. In consequence, local mints seem to have made copies of the Senatorial tokens which, although not authorized, were tolerated in view of the inadequacy of the official mint.[2] After Nero entered upon the more despotic period of his reign, among his other changes of policy, he attempted to solve the problem of the shortage of token currency in the western provinces. He opened a branch of the Senatorial Mint at Lugdunum. Doubtless the fact that the Senatorial Mint was probably now, in practice, under his control was responsible for this step. It is also clear that by this time Senatorial copper must have been made legal tender in the west outside Italy. During the 2nd century A.D. the volume of local issues in the east and the number of mints increased, but in the succeeding century the issues declined again. The debasement of the imperial silver during the first half of the 3rd century A.D. reduced the legal value of the bronze coins below their cost of production. In consequence, issues almost ceased, and existing coins were exported. The increase in the number of branches of the Imperial Mint in the second half of the century resulted in the limitation of local issues to the occasions of festival and the celebration of the games. By the later years of the 3rd century

[1] Mattingly, XVIII. He also permitted local silver issues in many of the cities of Crete, which issues were, however, superseded a few years later by provincial issues.

[2] Mattingly, XIX.

local powers of issue had lapsed,[1] and imperial coins were in general use.

The prerogative of coining in Egypt was always in the hands of the Emperor; the province was always regarded as being under his direct personal control.

10. *Summary.*

We have now traced, on the one hand, the development of the state prerogative of coining, and on the other the correlation between the course of that development and local economic and political conditions. Stamping ingots of the monetary metals was within the rights of every citizen until the early years of the 6th century. Both economic and political forces were responsible for the concentration of the right in the state, to the exclusion of private bankers and religious authorities. The reliability and familiarity of a seal would render it important as the sign of a useful medium of exchange. For this reason either civic or temple issues provided the local medium in the Greek world, and as religious and secular affairs were there so inextricably interrelated civic issues naturally resulted. But where economic forces placed the practical priority in the hands of a banker or merchant, there was a tendency for him to assume tyrannical power and turn his quasi-practical monopoly into an absolute and subsequently legal monopoly. This may have been the course of events in Lydia and some of the cities of Asia Minor. But this monopoly of coining was in early times somewhat narrow. It applied most definitely to gold and less to silver. The latter metal was sometimes coined by local authorities and Kings instead of the superior power. When small change copper was introduced Kings and Emperors took no interest in it and permitted local, though still public, authorities to coin it. The small Greek states coined their own copper as well as silver, and the Roman Republic, having first based its coinage entirely upon bronze, only later took in silver, and finally, towards the end of the Republic, gold. The first three centuries of the empire saw the gradual elimination of

[1] Alexandria retained local rights of issue longer than any other city, but it had become a branch of the Imperial Mint by the end of the 3rd century A.D.

local issues of coins of both silver and bronze, and the inclusion in the imperial prerogative of all three metals. The growth of the right of coining can often be closely correlated with local conditions. The areas in which private coining existed are those in which there was little central control. In Egypt and Assyria it did not occur, and coining was but reluctantly accepted from abroad, while private coining was common in India, China, Russia, and the Greek world. Consequently it has been argued[1] that its existence is a sign of incomplete social organization. But the principal reason for its distribution is that in these large centralized empires before the sealing had become popular better public facilities were provided for passing the metals by weight. The public weigh-masters gave a guarantee of at least equal value to that given by the public seal on a coin. The arrangements for commerce based on the metals by weight were so far advanced that coinage in its earlier and cruder stages offered very little advantage. Their system was, however, in the last resort less suitable than that of the Greek world, and finally the latter triumphed. Again the coinage prerogative in early empires is in some respects contrasted with that of the smaller city states of the Greek world. In Persia, Macedon,[2] and Rome, to coin gold, except in special circumstances, was to claim imperial power. The early empires also made serious attempts to limit the coining of silver and, so far as possible, to keep it in the hands of the monarch or Emperor. Persia and Macedon agree in regarding copper token money as beneath their consideration. Local bodies were usually left to supply the necessary small change. For historical reasons, however, the Roman attitude to coining bronze was somewhat different. Bronze having been the original medium of exchange in Italy, the coining of bronze was there always a state monopoly. But when the *denarius* became popular in the 2nd century B.C., the coining of bronze was narrowly restricted for a very long period. Moreover, in the empire outside Italy, the Romans followed earlier imperial policy in leaving bronze to be supplied locally. In the Greek world, however, where all coins were supplied locally, there was no

[1] Babelon, 141.

[2] Information with regard to Macedon is more doubtful than in the case of either Rome or Persia (*vide supra*).

such disdain of bronze. Even in England silver and gold were coined much earlier than bronze, and not until the last quarter of the 17th century did the state commence a regular coinage of copper.[1] The Romans during the first 300 years of the empire absorbed the supply and coining of bronze into the imperial prerogative, mainly as a result of the inflation of silver during the 3rd century A.D. The location of the power to control monetary policy within the state depends directly, as we have seen, on the form of the local political organization. In Lydia, Persia, and Macedon it was doubtless in the hands of the King or Emperor. In the Greek world it was in the hands of the people, the Senate, or the magistrates, according to the strength of democratic feeling. Rome presents more interest, because it is possible to watch the shift in the control of the currency as the Republic declines and the Empire rises from its ruins. Under the Republic, ultimate power was with the people, and the organization and control of the mint copies the Greek models closely. The Senate and the Mint Commissioners gathered power while they might, but in the collapse of the Republic the Emperor commenced military issues of gold and silver and suppressed the republican tradition, except so far as it related to copper; in Italy control over copper seems to have been small after the middle of the 1st century A.D. Towards the end of the 3rd century A.D., the prerogative of issuing copper was joined to that of issuing silver and gold in the hands of the Emperor, who by the beginning of the 4th century enjoyed full rights to coin all three metals for the whole of the empire.

Lastly, the occurrence of monetary unions is correlated with the occurrence of numbers of small communities, each with separate political organization. The ancient empires provided uniform currencies at least of the more important metals. But the city republics of Greece had each the power to coin, and many, but not all, exercised their power. The large number of issues resulting in the Greek world from these conditions gave rise to a confusion in transactions between cities. During the earlier period before the end of the 5th century B.C., the problem of simplifying foreign exchange was mainly solved by the rise of some coins to an international importance, because of their reliability or their familiarity, or sometimes because

[1] Ridgeway, I, 4.

they were backed by political power. The silver coins of Ægina made their reputation in the 6th century by merit, but those of Athens in the 5th century were assisted by political pressure. The electrum of Cyzicus of the later 5th and 4th centuries was well favoured on account of its relative reliability. The gold of Persia from the middle of the 6th to the middle of the 4th century, and that of Macedon from the later 4th century, circulated within the territory of the issuing power for political reasons, but outside that territory they were far-famed by reason of their reliability and beauty.

It is noticeable that all these coins, with the exception of the Æginetan "tortoises," were issued by powers in possession of supplies of metal. The quantity of the coins available and the consequent familiarity with them were of the first importance, and the pursuit of a policy likely to arouse trust was necessary to those who had stocks to dispose of. In the second period in the Greek world, from the collapse of the Athenian Empire at the end of the 5th century B.C., uniformity was mainly sought by other means, although the Rhodean coins were well known during the 4th century. Monetary unions were formed to bring about uniformity in the issues of neighbouring cities, with a view to the encouragement of trade, or possibly to reduce the cost of coining in cities too small or inadequately blessed with deposits of the precious metals to keep a mint in constant operation. But these unions, found only in Greece, China, and early Italy, where no central government existed for a large area, disappeared when the Romans established such a government. For many centuries the device of the monetary convention was little used. Economy of coining has now become less important as a motive, many modern states being of sufficient size to maintain a mint. Smaller states place contracts with private firms or foreign mints rather than share a mint with a foreign power, although the effect is much the same. The extraordinary development of international trade during the past 200 years has brought into more prominence the advantages of uniformity of monetary units, although the use of bills of exchange reduces these advantages to a mere increase in the rapidity of conversion of prices from one currency to another. Nevertheless, the Latin Union during the 19th century provided for the use by all the members of a common unit and also of a token currency of universal acceptability. The recarving of continental Europe into political units after the War of 1914-18 has, however, brought about a revival of an intense parochial nationalism, which has expressed itself in a variety of new monetary units. Possibly just as the Greek communities were driven to invent the monetary convention, so these small units will wisely turn for assistance to the Greek device.

CHAPTER V

COIN TYPES

1. *Political, Religious, and Economic Origins.*

In the preceding chapters we have traced the evolution and distribution of coining, and finally we have localized the coinage prerogative in the ancient world so far as the evidence will permit. It is now necessary to trace in detail the policy adopted in the exercise of this prerogative. But before any account can be given of monetary policy we must first assemble the evidence. For this evidence we shall have to rely mainly upon the coins themselves. From them we can ascertain what was the monetary metal, whether coins varied in quality, and, a little less certainly, what was the weight of metal in the standard unit, and what were the subdivisions. These subjects can conveniently be assigned to succeeding chapters. There is one matter of considerable interest which first calls for attention—namely, the reason for the types or ornaments upon early coins. This subject can conveniently be dealt with as the first aspect of early currency policy, because the choice of type lay with the authority in whom the prerogative was vested. It can also be conveniently discussed immediately after the coinage prerogative, because the types upon the coins reflect very clearly the real powers wielding the right of coining.

The types on the coins issued by bankers and merchants were doubtless those on their private seals. Presumably the considerations governing the choice of these emblems were very similar to those which have determined the selection of armorial bearings in more recent times. Sometimes a pun on the family name, but more often a reference to the real or legendary history of the family, supplied a basis for the emblem.

It might be expected that when coins came to be issued by the state under a monarchical form of government the coins would bear the personal seal of the monarch or tyrant. The lion and the bull appeared on the coins of Lydia from the middle of the 7th century B.C., and the former is quite likely to have been the emblem on the royal seal.[1] The Persian gold and silver coins issued at the latest by Darius towards the end of the 6th century B.C. bore a representation of the King, and, as his signet, which has been found at Babylon, also bears his image, it is probable that the type on the coin was an impression of the royal seal. From the time of Darius to the fall of the Persian Empire before Alexander the Great towards the end of the 3rd century B.C., all the gold and silver issued by Persian Kings bore a representation of a King, crowned, wearing a long robe, and with a quiver at his back, a spear in his right hand, and a bow in his left.[2] But slight variations in the pose of the figure, its equipment, and more particularly in the physiognomy of the King,[3] suggest that, while originally the effigy on the coin was a copy of the royal seal, it was later regarded as a portrait of the King. We have no information as to the seals of the successors of Darius, and it is impossible to say whether they changed contemporaneously with the types on the coins. Nevertheless, the right of portraiture on the coins was probably slowly developed and recognized in the Persian Empire in the period from the middle of the 6th century to the middle of the 4th century B.C.

Again, in the Greek cities of Asia Minor the variety of types on the electrum of a number of cities suggests that they were not all derived from the public seal. In fact, as we have seen,[4] they were probably the signets of the responsible moneyers, and not civic types. It is possible that the types on the earliest pre-Solonian coins issued in Athens were merely the heraldic devices of the families in power.[5]

[1] Ridgeway, 321, Babelon, 115. But Professor Gardner (71) thinks that it cannot be maintained that the lion was always the regal type of the Lydians. The lion may have been a religious symbol (*vide infra*, p. 115).

[2] Whence they were called " archers " by the Greeks.

[3] Head, 828.

[4] Chap. III.

[5] These early coins, based on the "Ægenetan" standard, are attributed to Athens by Seltman (p. 40 *sqq.*). He identifies their types with the badges of old Athenian families appearing as shield devices on the vases of the 6th and 5th centuries B.C., and the number of devices is explained by the fact that each family, when it was in power, coined with its own seal from 590 to 566 B.C. But the evidence is frail (*vide* E.S.G.R., *Num. Chron.*, 1924, 331). Head (*Camb. Anc. Hist.*, IV, 128) accepts Seltman's view and remarks of the coins in question that " in spite of their varying

In the Greek world generally, where no tyrant emerged, or none strong enough to force money bearing his personal coat-of-arms upon a people who still cherished democratic ideals, other origins of the coin type must be sought. We have already seen that the temple authorities exerted a very important influence on the development of the earliest coins, and this fact alone might suggest that the priestly colleges selected the type to be placed upon the coin. Where coins were struck in the temple, and possibly under the control of the priestly authorities, the authorities would naturally place on the coin either an effigy of the deity or a sacred symbol. The coins from the temple of Zeus would be marked with a thunderbolt or an eagle, those from the temple of Apollo with a tripod or a lyre, the money of Artemis with a stag or a wild boar, and that of Aphrodite with a dove or a tortoise. The number of such ingots in circulation, and the high repute in which they were held, may have induced the civic authorities when they stepped in to take over the monopoly of currency, to continue to invoke the local deity on their own issues.[1] A great variety of types which are probably religious in origin is known. The coins of Ephesus bear the type of a bee or a stag, the emblem of Artemis; those of Miletus a lion, the symbol of Apollo; those of Athens an owl, the sacred bird of Athene; and those of Lydia a lion, which was sacred to Cybele, the deity specially worshipped there. The type on Æginetan coins was the sea-tortoise, which has been supposed to have been the symbol of Ashtaroth, the Phœnician goddess of trade and the sea, a supposition upon which much doubt has been cast. Effigies of the gods were in very early times uncommon, but during later 5th and 4th centuries B.C. the habit

---

types [they] are so uniform in fabric that they must be the product of a single mint, and the presumption is that they represented the Solonian system."

[1] Laum (*Heiliges Geld*, 141-42), while agreeing that the desire to realize temple bullion in the most profitable manner was responsible for the placing of sacred symbols on early ingots, asserts that "the stamp notified that the piece of metal belonged to the god and was sacred to him." And when temple funds had been invested "in order to secure that the exact quantity and metal was paid back . . . and to make quite certain that it was the property of the god, a picture of the god was placed on the metal." "Originally the stamp on the metal signified no guarantee of either quantity or quality; the type was the sacred symbol, and thereon was based the credit which the money enjoyed" (p. 144).

of placing a representation of the deity upon the coins became increasingly common. Where the local seal had been the obverse type it made way during this period for the head of the divinity. The civic seal was either transferred to the reverse or became merely a symbol auxiliary to the head of the divinity on the obverse.[1] By the time of Alexander the Great it was a general custom to place the head of the divinity on the obverse. These types were often accompanied by inscriptions identifying the deity.[2] The religious element in the coin types became more obvious, however, at the time when the powers of representation of the engravers were developing most rapidly, which development reached its zenith during the 5th and 4th centuries.[3] The close contact of the temple authorities with early coining, and the later very definite emergence of religious motives in coin types, has prompted the inference that the sacred motive was present, although veiled, in the simpler badges of earlier times.[4] Burgon, in an " inquiry into the motives which influenced the ancients in their choice of the various representations which we find stamped on their money,"[5] concluded that " from the first striking of money down to the extinction of the Byzantine Empire *religion was the sole motive of the types of coins*, and that this is the invariable principle which is to guide our search in endeavouring to explain them "[6] a good, plain rule. But he ascribed an ultimately utilitarian reason for the selection of religious motives. " No device that could be imagined was so well adapted to the peculiar necessity of the case, or so likely to satisfy the public mind, as the impress by public authorities of the symbol of the tutelar divinity of their city, or some equally sacred and well-known emblem,

[1] Macdonald, *Evolution of Coinage*, 81.

[2] Sometimes in the nominative case, rarely in the accusative, sometimes in the dative (implying possibly dedication to the deity), and sometimes in the genitive (implying possibly that the coin is sacred to the deity). But in the latter case, possibly the words " the badge " were understood—thus notifying that the type was the badge of the deity and city.

[3] The zenith of medallic art as revealed on the coins was reached during the 4th century B.C. before the accession of Alexander in 336 B.C. The best artists were selected and some were allowed to sign their work (a privilege rarely granted in Greece proper).

[4] Head, LVIII. Hill, *Handbook of Greek and Roman Coins*, pp. 166-69.

[5] London, 1836 (Reprinted from *Numismatic Journal*).

[6] Burgon, 21.

COIN TYPES (A)

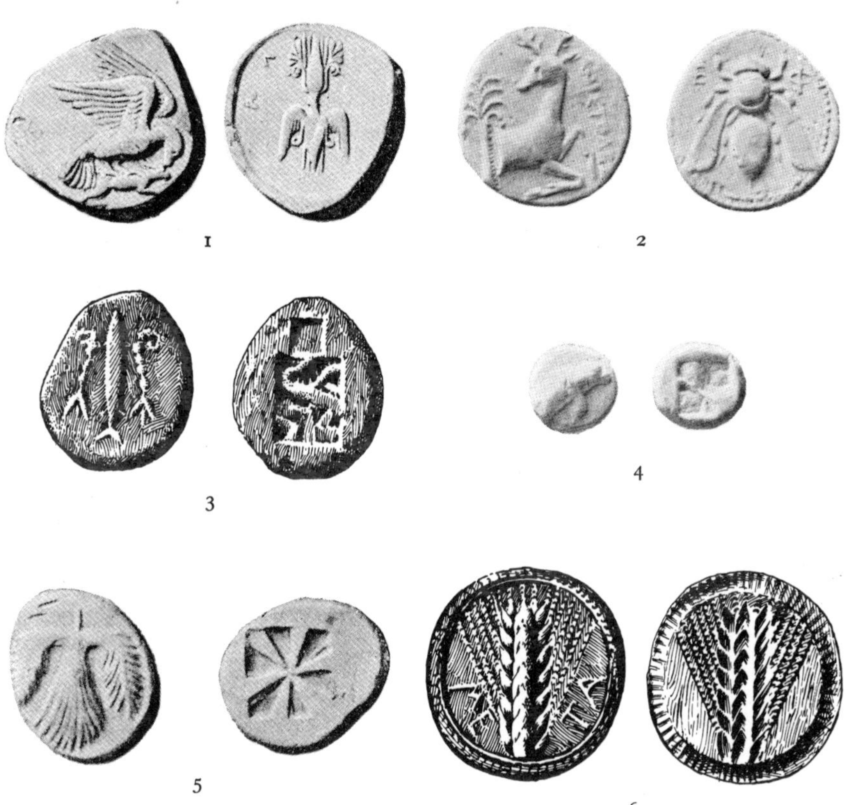

1 Coin of Elis, which was sacred to the Olympian Zeus bearing the thunderbolt sacred to Zeus.

2 Coin of Ephesus bearing a Stag, the symbol sacred to Artemis.

3 Electrum *stater* of Cyzicus of Sixth Century B.C. bearing a tunny fish.

4 Coin of Phocæa bearing a seal (Phoka).

5 Silver *stater* of Selinus (Sicily) of the middle of the Fifth Century B.C. bearing a Selinon (Wild Celery) leaf.

6 Silver *stater* of Metapontum (Lucania) of the Sixth Century B.C. bearing a head of corn.

and even with respect to distant cities, to which the coin might be carried for purposes of commerce, the common reverence for the gods, which was universally entertained, as well as for the sacred games and festivals instituted in their honour, would render sacred symbols, not only grateful to their feelings, but would have the great advantage of speaking a language universally intelligible.[1] At home the association of the currency with the gods was to secure it a free and perhaps respected currency, even where no temple issues had previously been known: it was rather to suggest an origin for the coin more sacred than in fact it had. It was hoped to gain free circulation abroad by the same means, although the foreign origin of the piece was indicated by the type. To this latter hope we shall return later;[2] but it is doubtful whether early issuing authorities concerned themselves greatly with the foreign circulation of their coins unless they had stocks of the monetary metal to export. The interpenetration of religious and secular organization had gone so far in the Greek states that it is not surprising to find religious influences reflected in the coins. But where coins survived for any long period, economic causes, rather than the awe inspired by a religious type, furnish the most probable reasons for their success. On the other hand, it is not reasonable to suggest[3] that religious origins are unlikely, because none of the learned Greek writers of the 4th century B.C. referred to them. Aristotle[4] mentions the function of the type, but does not refer to its origin, but the absence of references to such matters 200 years after the first issue of coins is not surprising. Divine emblems had become heraldic devices and were accepted as a matter of course, particularly as the close relation between religious and secular affairs still existed, and religious references would not be likely to cause surprise. Nevertheless, the inference from later types that earlier ones were all, or even predominantly, religious in origin, is probably incorrect. The concentration upon religious types in the 5th and 4th centuries has probably

[1] Burgon, 22. Head subscribes to this view: " In an age of universal religious belief, when the gods lived as it were among men, and whenever every transaction was ratified by solemn oath . . . what more binding guarantee could be found than the invocation of one or other of those divinities most honoured and most dreaded in the district in which the coin was intended to circulate " (*Coins and Medals*, p. 13).

[2] P. 120. [3] Ridgeway, 336. [4] *Politics*, II, 1257.

a twofold explanation. On the one hand, a fashion was set by Athens. When the tyrant Peisistratus[1] seized power in Athens in 561 B.C., mainly by means of his money, he recognized that the Athenians would be unlikely to tolerate an open display of power on the coinage, and, guided presumably by a delicate political sense, he introduced a coinage bearing, on the reverse, the owl, to which they were already accustomed, and, on the obverse, a head of Athena, a type that would appeal to the pride and religious feeling of every Athenian.[2] Perhaps he wished gently to suggest by the innovation that he was a tyrant by the grace of the goddess. The rise of Athens during the 5th century gave the new style of type a considerable vogue. On the other hand, æsthetic considerations were important. Power of artistic expression was developing with extraordinary rapidity, and artists wished to work upon human subjects, but there was an overwhelming contemporary prejudice against the representation of living persons upon the coins.[3] In consequence, they turned to the gods. Like the Italian and Flemish painters of the later Middle Ages, they probably did not allow themselves to be too much restricted by the fact that their work was required to be religious in form and subject, and, in fact, exercised their powers of portraiture under a thin disguise.

But if all early Greek coin types were not of religious origin, it remains for us to explain those not bearing obviously sacred symbols or the effigies of gods. In the last decade of the 19th century reaction from the rigid and universal religious explanation produced Professor Ridgeway's theory that coin types were purely economic in origin, and probably referred to the staple commodities of the community which, before

[1] Head (369) ascribes the issue to the occasion of the festival of the great Panathenaic games in the summer of 566 B.C., and Hill (*Camb. Anc. Hist.*, IV ,128) ascribes it to Peisistratus.

[2] This was probably the first coin with a clear type on both sides and almost the first to have as type a human head. It is possible that the old pieces bearing heraldic types circulated side by side with these new coins (*vide* Seltman, 40 *sqq.*) down to 546 B.C. The old heraldic types are said to have reappeared for a time when Megacles drove Peisistratus and his party from Athens. But during his exile Peisistratus retained control of the silver mines of Pangaeum in Macedon and continued his old issues. On his return he maintained his issues, the resources of Laurium being added to those of Pangaeum (Seltman, 47).

[3] A few early 6th century electrum coins of Asia Minor had borne portraits of human heads (Head, 369).

PLATE IX

COIN TYPES (B)

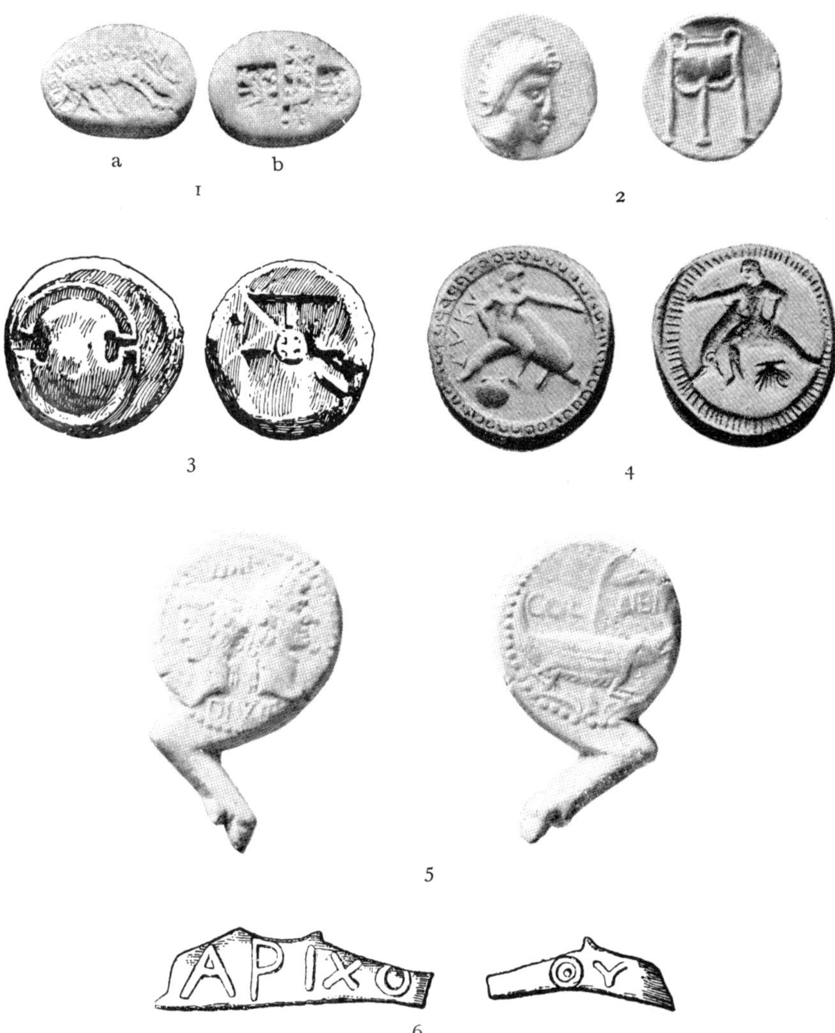

I The oldest inscribed Coin—a piece of Electrum picked up at Halicarnassus bearing (a) a grazing Stag with the words " I am the badge of Phanes " and (b) three incuse stamps.

2 Silver Coin of Axus (Crete) of the Fourth Century B.C. bearing a three legged pot.

3 Silver *stater* of Thebes of the latter half of the Sixth Century B.C. bearing Boeotian shield.

4 Silver *stater* of Tarentum bearing Taras on a dolphin (referring to the legend that Taras was saved from drowning by a dolphin).

5 " Ham-shaped " coins of Roman colony of Nemausus (Nimes) of the last Century B.C.

6 Coins of Olbia (on the Black Sea) said to be in the form of a tunny fish.

the introduction of money, were used as a medium of exchange. The cow, for example, appears on issues from Lydia, Samos, Chalcedon, Byzantium, Thessaly, and other places. The tunny fish appears on the money of Cyzicus and Gades, "where that fish was the chief staple, and where accounts were probably kept in fish as in modern Iceland."[1] The oyster appears at Grygnum, and the wheat ear at Metapontum; the mussel at Cumæ; the wine cup at Naxos, Mende, and Maroneia; the wild celery at Selenus; the sepia at Coresia; the silphium plant at Cyrene.

A few coins suggest that coiners at one time aimed at making the coin a facsimile of the commodity, which was, according to the theory selected, the sacred symbol or the commodity locally used as a medium of exchange in early times. The coins of Bœotia bear a shield on the obverse, while the reverse suggests an effort on the part of the moneyer to imitate the back of the shield. Similarly, the triangular marks on the reverse of coins of Ægina, bearing a tortoise type on the obverse, may be an attempt to copy the marks on the underside of the tortoise.[2] At Nemausus (Nîmes) ham-shaped pieces were made,[3] but perhaps the best example of this tendency is to be found at Olbia, where coins in the shape of a tunny fish[4] were used. In some places the coin type may not only represent the medium of exchange in use before coins were invented, but also the amount of that medium which represented the unit of value. The evidence of such an origin for the types can most conveniently be examined in the course of the discussion of the origin of early coin standards.[5]

It is clear, however, that coin types cannot all be ascribed either to a religious or economic origin.[6] Even where the type can be identified with local religious symbolism, the reason

[1] Ridgeway, 454. [2] Ridgeway, 333.

[3] Hill (3) suggests they were for religious use. The offering of the coin suggested the offering in kind for which it acted as a substitute.

[4] Head (272) says a dolphin.

[5] *Vide* Chap IX.

[6] Hill (166) points out that Professor Ridgeway does not apply his own theory to the explanation of the coin found at Halicarnassus bearing as type a stag feeding and the inscription "I am the mark of Phanes." Professor Ridgeway (p. 320) does not ascribe the type to an earlier venison unit, but regards it as "the particular badge adopted by the potentate Phanes as a guarantee of the weight of the coin and perhaps of the purity of the metal."

for the selection of the symbol must still be sought. There is no doubt that the choice of these sacred emblems was deeply influenced by local economic conditions. For example, the ear of corn may have appeared on the coins because it was the symbol of Ceres; but it may have become the local religious symbol because of the fruitfulness of the soil before the worship of Ceres was introduced, or because the local staple industry was placed under the protection of the divinity, and supplied the sacred symbol of the latter. The local cult may have first evolved and have lent its symbol to the currency, or the local religious symbol and the seal placed on the coin may have evolved separately, their identity being due to the common environment out of which they developed. In any event, economic conditions played a great and probably predominant part in the development of the type.

The claim that the placing of the emblems, symbols, or representations of deities on coins was equivalent to marking them in a language universally understood is not substantiated by subsequent developments. As coins wandered further from their place of issue, it became necessary that they should bear some trace of the place from which they were issued.[1] At first the initial of the name of the town of issue occurs, but in the course of time this develops into longer and more complete inscriptions,[2] stating the place of origin and the name of the people or ruler[3] responsible for the issue.[4] The most important effect of this innovation was that the local emblem or seal lost its real function on the coin, that of identifying its issuer and place of emission. A greater variety of types became possible, and the local emblem disappeared from some coins in order that different denominations might have distinguishing types. In some cases the local seal disappeared altogether, or was retained as a reverse type only. In consequence, partly of this need for a variety of emblems, the coin types became dissociated in later times from the symbol on

[1] Usually on the same side as the local seal (in later times the reverse), while the moneyers' marks appeared on the other side.

[2] The first inscribed coin is that found at Halicarnassus and inscribed "I am the badge of Phanes."

[3] And. in Sicily and South Italy, the name of the artist responsible for the type.

[4] The place name in the nominative case was rare in the Greek world (where it was used only as a description of the type), but in Sicily and Magna Græcia it was common and was later adopted by Rome.

COIN TYPES (C)

1 Coin of Cnidus bearing type of the statue of Aphrodite by Praxitiles.
2 Coin of Athens showing the Acropolis.
3 Coin of Smyrna with portrait of Homer.
4 Coin of Alexandria with allegorical figure of Hope.
5 The first coins minted in Britain being crude imitations in gold of the Macedonian gold *staters* issued in the First Century B.C.
6 Coin of Lysimachus King of Thrace (B.C. 323-281) bearing (a) the head of the deified Alexander with the horn of Ammon and (b) Athena Nikephoros.

[*face p.* 120

the civic seal. Some of the later types clearly refer to events in the real or legendary history of the town,[1] and others to famous temples,[2] statues,[3] bridges,[4] or other monuments.[5] A pun upon the name of the city not infrequently furnished a type, the most famous being the seal (Phoca) on the ancient coins of Phocæa.[6] Occasionally legendary or historical heroes and heroines are depicted and sometimes identified by an inscription.[7] Homer is depicted upon the coins of at least six towns.[8] The types on local bronze issues, made after the Roman conquest of the several Greek states, reveal no sign of the earlier religious motive. The favourite types were the heads of eminent persons[9] and allegorical figures.[10]

More remarkable was the issue by some minting authorities of copies of the coins of other cities. This policy was a by-product of the emergence in the Greek world of certain coins with a wide currency outside the frontiers of the cities that issued them. The types of these coins constituted a valuable trade-mark under which the precious metals could be easily marketed.[11] But frequently imitative issues were made merely to facilitate commerce. The imitated coin became the general medium of exchange in international trade, and any shortage caused a serious hindrance to business, which local issues sought to remove. In other places the ultra-conservatism of backward and relatively isolated peoples made such issues necessary. Where the population had become accustomed to the foreign coin the failure of supplies of genuine pieces necessitated the local manufacture of copies to avoid a dislocation of commerce. When the coins of

[1] Taras on coins of Tarantum, the hare on those of Rhegium and Messana, the mule car on those of the same cities (*vide* Hill, 175.)

[2] The temples of Artemis occur on the coins of Ephesus, and of Aphrodite on those of Paphos and the Acropolis at Athens (Hill, 173).

[3] The Zeus of Phidias at Elis and the Aphrodite of Praxitiles at Cnidus (*loc. cit.*).

[4] At Antiocha (*loc. cit.*).

[5] The harbour at Zancle and at Side (*loc. cit.*). Sometimes where local monuments are depicted, an inscription identifies them.

[6] Also a Rose (at Rhodes), a lion's head (at Leontini), an apple (at Melos), and a table (at Trapezus) (Hill, 177).

[7] At Mitylene persons appeared with identifying inscriptions (Hill, *Handbook*, 185).

[8] Hill, *loc. cit.*

[9] Homer at Smyrna and Herodotus at Halicarnassus.

[10] Hope on coins of Alexandria.

[11] Probably in the 6th century as a guarantee of fineness and from the 5th century of weight as well.

Ægina were widely used during the 6th century B.C. imitations were issued in some cities, and Corinthian coins were imitated more particularly in South Italy. But the fame of the Athenian "owls" attracted more imitations[1] than any previous coin. A great number were issued after 406 B.C. when supplies from Athens were deficient.

2. *The Campaigns of Alexander and the Consequent Injection of Asiatic Traditions into Europe.*

It was mentioned above that there was an unbroken rule in the Greek world that neither the name nor the portrait of any ruler or any living person should ever appear upon the coins.[2] This rule, doubtless an expression of Greek democratic feeling,[3] provides one of the distinctive features of Greek coinage and one in which it is contrasted with modern coins and also with Asiatic practice. In Macedonia, Thrace, and other semi-barbarous countries with monarchical constitutions, the names of Kings not infrequently appeared upon the coins, but never a portrait. For some two centuries down to the death of Alexander the Great the gods had occupied the coins and their types had been looked upon as sacred. Only upon the assumption that the replacement of the divine effigy by the portraits of Emperors would have been regarded as sacrilege, can we explain why neither Philip nor Alexander of Macedon dared to break with tradition. The conquests of Alexander were the cause of the abandonment of the old traditional coin types which followed close upon his death. "In the course of a single decade a new world had been opened up. A great wave of Hellenic

[1] In Syria, Egypt, India, Persia, and Arabia (Head, 377).

[2] "No Greek tyrant, however despotic, no Greek general, however splendid his achievements by land or sea, no Greek demagogue, however inflated his vanity, ever ventured to perpetuate his features on the current coin" (Head, *Historia Numorum*, LVIII).

[3] The dislike of the portrayal of living persons may have been partly superstitious. In some parts of the world there has been such a dread of portraiture of any kind, because it has been thought that a portion of the life of the subject passes to the picture. In more recent times this belief has been strong enough to prevent the portraiture of Kings upon coins. Until the reign of the late King of Siam no Siamesecoins were ever stamped with the image of the King, "for at that time there was a strong prejudice against the making of portraits in any medium" (*vide* Fraser, *Golden Bough :* abridged edn., 193).

influence had swept over the ancient kingdoms of the East, and its reflux had borne back to the West the purely Oriental conception of the divinity of Kings. Petty local interests, local cults, local trade were now merged in larger circles of activity; commerce was now carried on over a wider field and on a grander scale, and Alexander, the one man by whose impetuous energy and insatiable ambition this mighty change had been brought about over the whole face of the ancient world, came to be regarded as a demi-god. The altered political aspect of the world and the inward change in men's minds were at once reflected as in a mirror on the current coin."[1] Alexander did not discourage the worship of the sovereign; whether or not it was derived directly from the Orient and was applied to him in the glory of conquest, it provided a convenient device for imposing an Asiatic imperialism upon the Greek world, without disturbing too much its ancient traditions, which accustomed it to the domination of the gods, but not to any earthly monarchy. But not until after the death of Alexander was the change reflected in the coins. Only then did the features of the god Heracles on the coin "gradually lose their noble ideality and assume an expression in which there is an evident striving on the part of the engraver towards an assimilation of the god to Alexander, now himself regarded as one of the immortals."[2] The next step was taken by one of Alexander's generals who, becoming King of Thrace, placed on his money a portrait of Alexander as a god, "as the son of the Lydian Ammon with the ram's horn over the ear." The slow progress of the innovation is sufficient indication of the unpreparedness of public opinion for the change. But the days of the semi-Oriental monarchies which arose out of the ruins of the Persian Empire afforded ample opportunities for Kings to oust the gods from the coins. They were less shy than Alexander of consecration as gods, and, after no long period, the worship of the reigning monarch became the state religion under the Ptolemaic Kings in Egypt and the Seleucids[3] in Syria. In this way the head of the god on the

[1] Head, *Historia Numorum*, p. lix.

[2] Head, *Coins and Medals*, p. 29.

[3] It is possible to identify one of the types (the anchor) on the coins of Seleucis himself with the device on his seal.

obverse was displaced by the head of the King.[1] The placing of the dates of issue upon the coins was a secondary consequence of this imperial policy.[2]

The coins of Philip and Alexander are of great interest because of the widespread imitation of their types very frequently in areas over which neither had ever ruled. Large numbers of copies of the gold *staters* of Philip were issued from the cities along the western coast of Asia Minor, and their manufacture probably continued until Asia Minor became a Roman province. The earliest gold coins of Gaul and Britain were also imitations of the Macedonian *stater*. Imitation silver *tetradrachms* of Alexander were struck in various cities of Ionia and along the European coast of the Black Sea (where the authority of Alexander had never extended). Some of these imitations made in Asia Minor bear the names of the local magistrates in full. As the only coins for which the apparent country of issue would be responsible were those showing by their mint marks that they were genuine, the addition of the name of the magistrate responsible for the imitation was a more honest course, although it might have been expected that it would have limited the currency of the pieces.[3] Moreover, the types on these coins proved such valuable trade-marks that they could not be permitted to die with Kings. In consequence, the gold *staters* of Philip of Macedon and the silver *tetradrachms* of his son Alexander continued to be issued after the death of the monarchs originally responsible for them, just as the Maria Theresa *thaler* continued to be minted in Vienna (still bearing the date 1780, the year in which the Empress died) down to 1914 because it was preferred in Abyssinia and Arabia to any of

[1] A great impetus was given to medallic portraiture. It was, however, but temporary, for a growing commerce demanded a uniformity of types, which struck a fatal blow at artistic vitality in coin types.

[2] It was not until after the death of Alexander the Great that dates in numerals appeared. Then the date was expressed sometimes in regnal years of the King. The Ptolemies in Egypt usually, though not always, adopted this course. The foundation of the Seleucid Empire was followed by the practice of dating according to the era (in that case from 312 B.C.). This practice became common in Asia Minor and Syria in 2nd and 1st centuries B.C., and was continued under the Roman Empire. (In England dates did not appear on coins until 1547, when Edward VI dated shillings).

[3] This habit of imitating pieces, held in good repute, was also important in the Middle Ages, when copies of the *ducats* of Venice and the *florins* of Florence were issued in great quantities.

the modern issues, the introduction of which had been attempted.

This striking reversal of policy that came with the Macedonian imperialism, and remained with subsequent empires, is not difficult to explain. On the one hand, royal portraiture was traditional on coins in the East, whence came imperial power. The custom had grown up in the Persian Empire of placing the royal effigy upon all coins, probably in the first instance because of the application of the royal signet to the monetary metals. Later conquerors had more practical reasons. A superstitious reverence was paid to the emblems on the coin and, therefore, at least for a time, some similar attitude might be expected on the part of the general mass of the population to any personal emblem which displaced it. But more than this, printing was unknown, and communication with the populace by printed decree was not possible. A coin was something very closely akin to a printed document, and although it demanded brevity to an inconvenient degree, it was much the most convenient and impressive medium for bringing home to almost every class in the community, either the assumption or the continued exercise of sovereign power. Thus the advertising value of the currency was probably mainly responsible for the anxiety of rulers to place on their money their own portraits, and to regard the privilege as one of the most valuable prerogatives of sovereignty, to be preserved at all costs. In this way, the coin changed into a piece of metal, bearing on the reverse a legend signifying a guarantee of weight and fineness which was no longer attested by seal, and on the obverse an advertisement, and thus it still remains in most countries. Certainly the statement frequently made that a coin is a piece of metal the weight and quality of which are guaranteed by the royal or public seal has not been strictly true of the majority of issues for many hundreds of years, and of many it was never true. A less forceful reason for the portraiture of Kings upon coins may be found in the personal pride of those who realized the permanence of the personal record they could bequeath to the world by placing a representation of their features on the currency. Like most changes, the placing of the royal effigy on coins was effected gradually, so as to avoid offending the prejudices of the people.

3. *Greek Traditions in the Roman Republic.*

The early coinage of Rome was deeply influenced by that of the Greek world through the Greek colonies in South Italy and Sicily. In the matter of types, that influence is very obvious, but it is to be explained only partly by the circulation in Rome of the coins of Magna Græcia. Equally important was the similarity of political organization. The Romans of the Republic opposed, as unswervingly as the Greeks, the appearance of the effigy of any living person upon their coins. It savoured too much of monarchy. The types of the earliest bronze issues of *as signatum* were representations of a cow, sheep, pig, elephant, birds, Pegasus, or such implements as an anchor, shield, or trident. According to Pliny,[1] " The form of a sheep was the first figure impressed on money, and to this fact it owes its name *pecunia*." There is no explanation of these types. The *as grave* and its subdivisions issued at about the same time clearly reveal Greek influence, both in their artistic style[2] and their types. They were cast pieces without inscription, bearing on the reverse, in all denominations, the prow of a ship[3] and on the obverse, in accordance with the prevailing Greek tradition, the head of one of the gods and a mark indicating the value of the piece.[4] So long as bronze *asses* were issued under the Republic (to about the middle of the 2nd century B.C.), there was no important change in these types. Possibly this uniformity in the types of bronze money, which is not found on the silver coins, was partly due to the necessity for keeping it distinct from other Italian bronze

[1] *Hist. Nat.*, XXXIII, 13.

[2] " As a matter of fact, the art work of the *as grave* is everywhere borrowed from that of the Greeks, and the degree of excellence attained in any particular district depended on the closeness of its relations, direct or indirect, with some Greek city, or at least with a population imbued with the spirit of Greek art " (Head, 20).

[3] Macrobius, writing in early A.D. 5th century, says (*Sat.*, I, 7) that even then, 500 years after the last " prow " coin was struck, boys tossing coins used to say " Heads or ships " (Macdonald, 81).

[4] The obverse types were:

As	Head of	Janus	and	I
$\frac{1}{2}$	,,	Jupiter	,,	S
$\frac{1}{3}$	,,	Minerva	,,	. . . .
$\frac{1}{4}$	,,	Hercules	,,	. . .
$\frac{1}{6}$	,,	Mercury	,,	. .
$\frac{1}{12}$ (*Uncia*)	,,	Roma	,,	.

(Grueber, 5).

issues.[1] Roman silver enjoyed a monopoly from 268 B.C.,[2] and there was not the same reason for uniform types on silver. Again, in the types on their silver coins first issued in 268 B.C., the Romans reveal their indebtedness to the Greeks. The whole series of the new silver coins[3] bore on the obverse the head of Roma the goddess, who presided over the welfare of the city, and on the reverse the *Dioscuri* (sons of Jupiter). The Romans owed, in respect of these coins, a specific as well as a general debt to the Greek world, for each of the types was a composite design made up by uniting a number of features copied from the coins of various cities of Greece and Magna Græcia. The types on the gold pieces struck during the first Punic War were in the same tradition,[4] as were also those on the silver *victoriatus* struck in about 229 B.C.[5] Until the last few decades of the 3rd century B.C., the Roman coinage is, in its types, much what might have been expected from any Greek city.

The first departure from this tradition was innocent enough in its beginning. The Commissioners of the Mint, who had been appointed somewhere about the middle of the 3rd century B.C. to see that the will of the people was obeyed, were authorized, if not required, to place their marks upon the coins they issued. We have already seen that these marks occurred early in the second half of the 3rd century as symbols, and almost immediately after their names appeared in an abbreviated form in an initial or a monogram. These expanded later into names to which titles were added. But the Commissioners gradually undermined the permanence of the traditional types. The first attack occurred in about 190 B.C., when the *Dioscuri*, which had appeared on the reverse of all silver issues since 268 B.C., were occasionally displaced by Diana or Luna standing in a chariot drawn by two galloping horses.[6] About twenty years later a figure of victory[7] in a

[1] Lenormant, II, 247.

[2] Possibly only from the second Punic War (Mattingly, *Num. Chron.*, 1924, 200).

[3] *Denarius*, *quinarius* ($\frac{1}{2}$), and *sestertius* ($\frac{1}{4}$).

[4] With a bust of Mars and marks of value on the obverse and an eagle on a thunderbolt on the reverse in all denominations (Grueber, I, 27).

[5] Head of Jupiter on the obverse and victory on the reverse. (Grueber, I, 36).

[6] Grueber, I, 66.

[7] Grueber, I, 87.

similar chariot appeared on some coins. It is possible that these innovations were due merely to restlessness at the sterile repetition of types, and to a desire to endow coins with a more vivid interest.[1] But whatever the reason for the first departure from the ancient types, it came at a time when republican forms were showing signs of collapse. This was reflected in the coins. The Commissioners of the Mint seized the opportunity offered by the diminishing control of the Senate, and the fact that the people had become accustomed to a change in monetary types. From 150 B.C., the reverse types change constantly with each moneyer, although the Dioscuri, Diana, and Luna types survived[2] until the beginning of the last quarter of the century, after which each moneyer chose the type that appealed to his fancy.[3] Most of the types selected by them in the last half of the 2nd century B.C. were of a general character. But very soon some can be detected which refer to events more or less intimately connected with the history of the moneyers' families.[4] Types of this kind became increasingly common, some moneyers using more than one type for a denomination. Down to the end of the Social War in 88 B.C., these types were mainly mythological, and when they referred to the history of the family of the moneyer the reference was to some remote period. But between 88 B.C. and the outbreak of the Civil War between Pompey and Cæsar in 49 B.C., the events portrayed on the coins become less remote, and on one occasion contemporary occurrences were recorded.[5]

But before we discuss the changes introduced by Julius Cæsar, there are two other signs upon the coins of the break-up of the Republic. On the one hand, the goddess Roma, whose effigy had appeared on the coins constantly from 268 B.C., remained the obverse type, with minor changes, until about 100 B.C. On two occasions during the first decade of the last century B.C. the goddess was replaced:[6] within the

[1] Victory may have referred to the victorious progress of the Roman armies at that time, particularly in the east. Diana was much revered at Rome. Luna may be associated with the reform of the calendar in 191 B.C. (*vide* Grueber, LXXXVI).

[2] Grueber, I, 117.

[3] Grueber, I, 138.

[4] Examples are quoted by Grueber, LXXXVII.

[5] Grueber, I, 411.

[6] By heads of Saturn (Grueber, I, 170) and Apollo (Grueber, I, 175-80).

next few years this ancient type became rapidly less common,[1] and finally disappeared in 82 B.C.[2] The moneyers had now captured both the types on the coins. The legend " ROMA " had also appeared upon all struck coins of gold, silver, and copper since 268 B.C. Between 150 and 125 B.C. it was on one occasion omitted from the coin, and on another moved to the obverse.[3] From then it was threatened, and by the time of the Social War it was rarely placed on the coins.[4] The moneyers were in complete command of the coinage.[5]

We have seen in the preceding chapter that the coinage of the Roman Empire sprang from the right conferred in the early years of the last century B.C. upon provincial governors and military leaders to issue coins for the area under their control. This right was exercised in the provinces, particularly at the time of the Social Wars; but not even the most ambitious general (*e.g.*, Sulla) attempted to depose the gods from the place they had so long occupied on the coins, or to defy the traditional opposition of the representation of living persons on the coins. These issuers followed closely the policy of the Mint Commissioners in Rome during the first half of the last century B.C. They selected for both sides of the coins such types as pleased them, and frequently elected to record their victories or other notable events in which they had taken part.[6] But never is a portrait of the issuer to be found on his coins.

When Julius Cæsar exercised the prerogative of coining in Rome, he made but a short break with the pre-existing practice of the Mint Commissioners. But his action marks the end of republican and the beginning of imperial money, and again the coin types reflect the change. The almost imperial prerogative which the moneyers had arrogated to themselves had resulted in the rapid change in types already noted. After 50 B.C. much more recent events were recorded on the coins until the record of contemporary affairs became not uncommon. Julius Cæsar recorded his campaigns in Gaul, Africa, and Spain, and the coinage, more particularly that of

[1] Grueber, I, 189, 241. [2] Grueber, I, 316.
[3] Grueber, I, 117. [4] Grueber, I, 189.
[5] An unusual use of the inscription was made on a coin of 100 B.C., upon which it is stated that the issue was made " out of a special grant made by the Senate for the purchase of corn " (Hill, *Handbook*, 191).
[6] Grueber, II, 135.

the provinces, became a medallic history of the time.[1] To some extent this change was a preparation for the striking and unmistakable sign of transition to imperial money which was to come in 45 B.C. In that year the Senate conferred on Cæsar the privilege of representation on the silver[2] coins.[3] This act was a definite breach with the Græco-Roman tradition that no living person should be portrayed upon the money, and an acceptance of the imperial tradition we have seen in Persia and Macedon. It is a sign of sovereignty, although probably not of divinity. During the Civil War which followed Cæsar's assassination, the right to place a portrait on coins was regarded as a privilege of military command, and even the chiefs of the republican party (with the exception of Cassius) claimed and exercised the privilege without regarding such conduct as inconsistent with their republican programme. The triumvirate also adorned their issues, both imperial and senatorial, with their own effigies together and separately. On the one hand, all parties claimed the privilege accorded to Cæsar,[4] and, on the other, they recognized the propaganda value of the coins to which we have already referred. Nevertheless, coins seem to have been allowed to remain in circulation, although they bore the effigy of a rival.[5]

4. *Asiatic Imperial Tradition in the Roman Empire.*

Among the honours accorded to Octavius by the Senate in 36 B.C. it would seem that it was decreed that his portrait should be placed on the coins, that the reverse types should commemorate events in his life, and also that his name should be the sole inscription on the coins.[6] Certainly from 36 B.C. the moneyers' names (which had appeared on Cæsar's issues) ceased to appear on the money, and the coin types were personal to Octavius, as Cæsar until 27 B.C., and thenceforward

[1] Grueber, LXXXV, and I, 500.

[2] There exists a gold coin bearing his portrait, but its authenticity is not beyond doubt. Moreover, Cæsar probably did not permit the Senate to coin gold, and its permission could not, therefore, have applied to gold.

[3] The names of the moneyers continued to appear on the reverse.

[4] But it was mainly exercised in the provinces (Grueber, I, 554).

[5] Mattingly, XXI.

[6] Grueber, II, 3-4. Mattingly (*Num. Chron.*, 1919, 222) points out that there is no evidence of a Senatorial decree in 36 B.C. introducing an imperial coinage.

as Augustus. His portrait occupies the obverse of all his issues,[1] and the reverse bears reference to events in his reign,[2] mainly before 16 B.C. When the new coinage of brass and copper was established it was imperial in style, and after a few years[3] all the token coins bore the head of Augustus on the obverse and the names and titles of the moneyers on the reverse. Towards the end of his reign the proconsuls in Asia and Africa ceased to make coins with their own effigy, and the right to make such issues attached exclusively to and was inseparably bound up with the sovereign power of the Emperor. The generals of the army were regarded as the lieutenants of the Emperor, with no power of issue in normal times: if they made emergency issues they had to be in the name of the Emperor and bear his effigy. Where the right of issue was granted to vassal Kings, they were allowed to place their own effigies on their money,[4] but usually the portrait of the Emperor had to appear as well. Grants of permission to issue local copper also invariably required that the portrait of the Emperor or one of his family should grace the issue, the name and type of the city usually being placed on the other side.

The types of the imperial coinage have not the same interest as those of the Republic. From the time of Augustus to the fall of the Empire the head or bust of the reigning Emperor was the customary obverse type on the gold and silver coins. Occasionally a member of the imperial house was represented,[5] and sometimes a deceased prince or princess. But the opposition of the Romans to the appearance on the coins of the portraits of contemporary women persisted about a century and a quarter longer than their opposition to male

[1] Grueber (II, 46) says from 5 B.C., but Sydenham (*Num. Chron.*, 1919, 116) says that there was an unwritten rule that the Emperor's portrait should appear on no Senatorial money except the *as*, and that the rule was adhered to until A.D. 22.

[2] The improvement of public roads and streets, the erection of statues and arches, conquests in the east, games, and the like (Grueber, II, 44).

[3] During the brief revival of Senatorial issues of gold and silver between 17 and 13 B.C. a few types refer again to events in moneyers' families (Grueber, II, 44).

[4] Mattingly, LXIV.

[5] "The young prince Nero was the first to receive this honour; his mother Agrippina had to rest content with the reverse" (Mattingly, LXV).

portraits. Augustus never permitted Livia's portrait to appear, but, subsequently, by easy stages this change also was effected. At first the features of the woman to be honoured were given to one of the goddesses until, in the time of Domitian, towards the end of the 1st century A.D., women appear not only on gold and silver, but also on Senatorial issues of copper. Domitian himself struck coins in honour of Julia, his niece and mistress, and from this time the practice was not uncommon. The reverse provided an opportunity to commemorate the achievements and history of the reigning Emperor.[1] Inscriptions sometimes make more plain the object of the type[2] or frequently record the circumstances of the issue, especially when it was made on the occasion of periodic festivals,[3] such as those for the safety of the Emperor. The obverse types of the bronze coins were less stable, and there was less insistence upon the imperial monopoly of representation. Nevertheless, during the 1st century A.D., the portrait of the Emperor tended to become the commonest obverse type.

The effigy of the Emperor on the coins seems to have been regarded with some awe. Care was taken, for instance, to avoid placing countermarks on the portrait, and often they were limited to the reverse. The law relating to counterfeiting embodied the idea that falsifying Cæsar's image was a kind of sacrilege.[4] The idea of *majestas* included a religious element, no doubt because of the worship of the Emperors, but the reverence for the coin types may be also partly explained by the fact that on the money the Emperor had succeeded the gods.[5]

The types on Chinese coins follow an altogether different line from any western issues. They consisted only of inscriptions.[6] Many of these relate to the place of issue,[7] and many

[1] *Vide* Mattingly, LXXIII.

[2] Inscriptions on the coins of Vespasian and Titus commemorate the fall of Jerusalem in A.D. 70 (Hill, 189).

[3] These issues sometimes offered an opportunity for a civic puff. A coin of Anazarbus of Cilicia announced that the local games in honour of Elagabalus were " the biggest show on earth."

[4] Pollock and Maitland, *History of English Law*, p. 505, n.

[5] Although the interval of 100 years during which the coin types were captured by the moneyers must have done much to weaken this influence.

[6] Lacouperie, XXXII.

[7] Three-quarters of those listed by Lacouperie (XLVI).

are a proper name often written in an abbreviated form, in later times occasionally by the imperial pencil.[1] Towards the middle of the 7th century B.C., however, coins were inscribed with "their object and weight value" as well as their place of issue.[2] Nevertheless, there is some difficulty in identifying marks of value in early times,[3] and they did not become common until the end of the 3rd century B.C.[4]

5. *Summary.*

It is clear from this brief survey that the types on early coins are intimately bound up with the conditions of political and religious feeling on the one hand, and the economic necessity of perfecting the money as part of the communal equipment for the assistance of specialization and exchange on the other. Nothing could be clearer than the reflection in the coin types of the political conditions under which they were issued. In the Greek world and the Italian to the end of the Roman Republic, democratic opinion ran counter to the practice of placing the portraits of living persons upon the coins. The earliest coins doubtless bore the seals of the private issuers. When State minting commenced civic seals were used. The types upon these seals can be ascribed to no single origin in all places. Religious influences played a very important part, but must have operated within limits prescribed by economic conditions. Economic conditions in some cities probably furnished the local emblem. Directly or indirectly, therefore, many of the types on the coins of the first two centuries of coining are related to local economic conditions. But from the later 6th century the engravers probably seized upon the sacred motive in the coins as an excuse for the portrayal of the human form to which they were attracted by soaring artistic aspirations. Again, economic conditions may have assisted. If divine types were regarded with some degree of awe, and spoke in a language universally understood, circulation was perhaps facilitated and widened. These Græco-Roman republican types are not in quite the same tradition as modern republican types. The earlier

[1] Lacouperie, XXXIII.

[2] Lacouperie, XII.

[3] Numerals were used to denote successive issues of the same kind of coin from the same mint as well as the current value of coins (Lacouperie, XXXIX).

[4] Lacouperie, XXXVIII.

Republics chose a deistic representation of some protective principle, while more recent republican communities do not resort to religious representation. Nevertheless, insofar as it may be broadly and vaguely said that both chose to place on their coins symbols of some quintessential quality of the communal life, some emblem the psychological effect of the contemplation of which would be to raise up in the mind of the individual a realization of his American or French nationality or his Athenian or Corinthian citizenship, the source of the inspiration of the type is the same in the two eras.

In the ancient empires of Persia, Macedon, and Rome, on the other hand, we can watch the development of currency tradition of modern empires and monarchies. Persia probably introduced the practice of placing the effigy of the ruler on the coins, possibly at first because that effigy appeared on the royal seal. In this way the custom of royal portraiture was linked up with the earlier custom of sealing the coins. Towards the end of the 4th century the conquests of Alexander introduced into Europe much of Asiatic influence and institutions. After his death the portrait of the Emperor replaced the traditional religious subjects. When Rome became an empire the same policy was followed, and from that time monarchs have usually regarded the right to place their effigy upon the coins as inherent in their sovereign power.

But coin types were designed not alone as a means of political propaganda, or for the satisfaction of the pride of monarchs. They served two main ends incidental to the exchange function of the coins. First and foremost they signified the origin of the coin, and secondly, in the words of Aristotle, "the stamp was put on the coin as an indication of value."[1] The city responsible for issue was, as we have seen, indicated frequently by religious symbols or divine effigies. The monarch placed his own effigy upon his coins. An inscription was later added in some places to make quite certain that at least those who could read should know the intention of the designer of the type. Perhaps some inscriptions signify that the coin was dedicated to the deity. The value of the coin might be pictorially suggested on the coin by representing an earlier unit of value. Again, an inscription might be added to make more specific the legal valuation. It is notable, however,

[1] *Politics*, II, 1257.

that such marks are very uncommon in Greece.[1] In fact, they were probably introduced by the Greek colonies in Italy, and thence borrowed by Rome, where there was a persistent policy of stating the value of coins upon their face. In Greece, reliance must, in earlier times, have been placed on the size of the coin to distinguish one denomination from another. But in later years the types of the different denominations were varied to make it still easier to distinguish one denomination from another, either in addition to, or in place of, inscriptions stating their value.

The form of the mint organization exercised a third and not unimportant influence on the appearance of the coins. Under less democratic conditions the coin types were selected by the magistrates controlling the mint. But under more democratic conditions the type was civic in style, but the name of the moneyer was often placed on the coins. In later Roman times inscriptions were added to signify the exact political origin of the issue. During the last century and a half of the Republic, when the Senate occasionally made issues without consulting the *comitia*, the coins were marked " S C," or some variant thereof, to make it clear that the Senate was responsible for the issue. During the same period, however, the moneyers became less the efficient servants of the people and more the usurpers of popular, and even also of Senatorial, power, and they assumed control of the types. While on the one hand it is now very long since the royal or civic seal appeared on the coins of most areas, although those seals probably provided the earliest types, on the other the most obvious modern function of the type, to notify the denomination and value of the coin, was not recognized when coins were first issued: it was one of the contributions of the Italian Greeks to the institution of coinage.

Lastly, the types of some coins are mere imitations of the types selected by well-known cities or empires. The most interesting examples of these issues are the early British coins. The Britons of the 3rd century B.C. copied in their first gold issues the gold *staters* of Macedon. Later, after Gaul had been conquered, and shortly before Cæsar's invasion of Britain, the coins used in Gaul were again copied, and the Britons issued copies of the Roman money circulating there.

[1] They occur in Chios, Ephesus, Rhodes, and a few other cities (Hill, 193).

CHAPTER VI

THE MATERIAL OF THE CURRENCY STANDARD

1. *The Selection of the First Coin Materials.*

THE use of coins is no more than an improvement upon exchange based upon the transfer of metals by weight, the system common in the East for some thousands of years before the peoples of the Ægean began to make coins. When they began to strike money they naturally used the metal already circulating as a means of payment. When states took over the business of minting they adopted the same course, confirming the choice of a medium of exchange already made by the community at large, and crystallized in contemporary commercial customs. Such decisions gave the seal of state approbation to the system, and probably had the effect of making it more universally applicable and enforceable than it had previously been.[1]

2. *Electrum.*

The earliest stamped pieces are those found in the Plain of Sardes and, as we have seen, they were of electrum. Until the middle of the 6th century B.C. this mixture of gold and silver was the sole basis of the money of Lydia and Asia Minor.[2] The primary reason for this selection was that Lydia possessed large natural supplies. But there were also secondary, yet important, reasons for the continued use of a medium which soon proved far from ideal as a monetary standard. It was easy to work in times when metallurgical skill was but little

[1] Babelon (366) says iron and lead were punch marked as well as the precious metals.

[2] Professor Ure suggests (132) that the Lydians may have struck silver from the earliest times as well as electrum. One of the earliest striated pieces appears from its specific gravity to contain 98 per cent. silver. But he admits that it has a yellow tint and that its lightness may be due to the presence of copper, which would permit the presence of more than 2 per cent. of gold.

developed, and was hard enough to confine within reasonable limits the loss from wear and tear of the coins.[1] Gold lacked this quality, and it was not then known that the addition of a small quantity of copper would give it the necessary hardness. Further, it so happened that electrum was ten times as valuable as silver; this simple relation made it possible to use the same scale of weights for both electrum and silver, and produce value units simply related to each other. The overwhelming disadvantage of electrum lay in its lack of homogeneity. The first coins were made of a natural mixture at the time thought to be a separate metal. Later electrum was artificially made, but there was never any definition of the proportion in which the two metals were to be combined to secure that the metal should be called electrum and pass as money. Pliny[2] says that " whenever the proportion of silver is one-fifth the ore is known by the name electrum," but he mentions no lower limit on the proportion of gold. Moreover, the earliest stamped pieces found in Lydia vary in the percentage of gold they contain from five to ninety-five. Subsequent (and probably public) issues show a greater uniformity of colour, indicative of a more constant standard in the composition of the alloy, but very considerable variation always persisted. The most usual composition in Lydia consisted of 75 per cent. of gold and the remainder silver,[3] although some of the Lydian ores contained as much as 44 per cent. of silver, and copper had to be added to the mixture in order that it might still be easily distinguishable by its colour from silver. The relative value of gold and silver being about $13\frac{1}{3}:1$, the mixture of three parts gold and one silver gave a relative value of electrum to silver of 10:1.

The manufacture of coins from a mixture of metals that varied from time to time as well as from coin to coin must have favoured fraud and given rise to endless difficulties. If it is true that " there can be no doubt that the Lydian . . . electrum, however variable in purity it may have been, was conventionally accepted at more or less fixed rates of exchange

[1] Ridgeway may be right in thinking that the durability of electrum had little to do with its early use.

[2] *Hist. Nat.*, XXXIII, 23.

[3] Modern analysis of the electrum from Tmolus shows that it consists of 27 per cent. silver and 73 per cent. gold (Hultsch, *Metrologie*, 579).

by weight against both pure gold and silver,"[1] these temptations to fraud must have been intensified: the weight of convention was on the side of the dishonest, for it would tend to force the acceptance of diluted electrum at the value attached by custom to good electrum. This quality of variability was particularly insidious.[2] Variations in the composition of the mixture were difficult for the ordinary person to detect, unless the proportion of gold fell sufficiently to change the colour of the coins.[3] But when differences in the values of coins of equal weight were realized, faith in the royal lion's head which had appeared on the Lydian coins since the time of Gyges was shaken, and merchants and bankers displayed increasing unwillingness to accept it as a guarantee of quality. The spread of the use of electrum from Lydia to the Ionic coast towns of Asia Minor served only to increase the difficulty of monetary transactions by complicating foreign as well as domestic exchanges. Each city adopted its own standard composition for electrum, with the result that the pieces of some cities[4] were of ill-repute, while those of others[5] were well thought of and freely accepted over large areas. In consequence, it became necessary, when fixing prices, fines, or other payments in terms of electrum pieces, to specify the cities whose coins would be accepted in payment. Official rates of exchange were established in some cities for the electrum coins of certain foreign places: an inscription of the beginning of the 4th century B.C. at Olbia prescribes the legal rate at which the *staters* of Cyzicus were to be accepted.[6] But in spite of state control of exchange rates, these intricate monetary arrangements must have brought remunerative business to the tables of the money-changers.

[1] Head, *B. M. Excavations at Ephesus*, 76.

[2] This quality was not, however, peculiar to electrum: gold and silver were not coined in the pure state, and gold and silver coins could also have been changed in composition. In fact, however, electrum was never defined, and it must have obtained a reputation for variability which both gold and silver escaped.

[3] Professor Gardner (34) states that the Greeks, if not the Lydians, used touchstones in very early times, and were able, with their aid, to estimate the quantity of alloy with great accuracy.

[4] Those of Lesbos and Phocæa.

[5] Those of Cyzicus, which usually contain 60 to 70 per cent. of gold.

[6] Babelon, 329.

3. *Gold and Silver Coinage in Asia.*

The last stage of degradation of early electrum money is revealed by the numerous countermarks to be seen on many of the electrum coins which have come down to us. The mark of the state was so little respected that the pieces were tested by bankers and money-changers and marked[1] by them to show the quality of the metal, and the fact that it had passed through the hands of the banker and need not be retested on any subsequent occasion. The disadvantages of electrum threatened to bring down the whole system of State coining, and cause a return to the earlier system of free coinage.[2] But the commercial genius of the Lydians which had been responsible for the introduction of coining proved equal to the task of devising a simple solution to this new monetary problem. They replaced electrum by gold and silver in the middle of the 6th century B.C. The new system was not, however, altogether of their own devising. The earliest coins of Ægina, which had been famous for more than half a century, were made of silver. Since the early years of the 6th century B.C., some of the wealthier cities of Asia Minor had been coining gold. There was, therefore, a precedent for coining both gold and silver. But although with the Lydian currency reform of this period electrum fell into disuse, it did not altogether disappear from currency history. It reappeared in Asia Minor during the 5th century and early in the 4th century B.C.[3] in Carthage[4] and Syracuse. Again, during the bimetallist controversy of the 19th century, it was suggested that escape from the consequences of the shortcomings of gold and silver as monetary standards might be sought in a return to the electrum standard. It was proposed to adopt as a basis for the currency a composite standard consisting of a mixture of gold and silver, a course which Professor Marshall recommended to the Gold and Silver Commission in the United Kingdom in 1888.[5]

[1] "These little punch-marks appear to have been stamped on the coins by money-changers as private indications of weight or value, or marks of acceptance, sometimes, perhaps, at greatly reduced rates of exchange" (Head, *Catalogue of Greek Coins*, XXI).

[2] It is possible that the use of electrum in Lydia may partly explain the introduction of coining there in the first place, a guarantee of the quality of such a mixture being necessary (*vide* Chap. II).

[3] *Vide infra*, p. 144. [4] *Infra*, p. 146.

[5] *Vide* Marshall, *Money Credit and Commerce*, 64.

The more immediate circumstances of the Lydian reform are to be sought in the necessity for disposing of the produce of the Lydian mines and possibly in contemporary developments in metallurgy. It is possible that in early times the Lydians did not know how to separate the gold and silver, but it is doubtful[1] whether they were so ignorant, and, even if they were, they need not have continued to manufacture electrum from silver and gold. The manufacture of gold coins along the coast of Asia Minor was a more forceful influence. With the growing influence of Phocæa, its gold coins became increasingly important and competed severely with the electrum of the time. Crœsus, having been sent by his father to maintain order in the coastal area opposite the isle of Lesbos, in the parts where Phocæan gold was most popular, doubtless realized how serious an innovation the coining of gold was likely to prove for Lydia. The coins of the latter had been one of her important exports, and care had always been taken to make them attractive in foreign markets, as is shown by the weight standards selected as their basis.[2] Towards the middle of the 6th century B.C., the Lydian King, Alyattes, took the first steps to reform, when he issued gold coins. These new pieces competed with those of the Ionic coast towns and provided a channel for at least part of the Lydian ores, which were now rapidly losing ground in the form of electrum. In 561 B.C. Crœsus succeeded his father as King and, perhaps as a result of his experience in the coastal area, carried his father's reforms much farther. Continuing the issue of gold coins, he added to them silver coins, and discontinued the use of electrum. The Crœsan coinage system was the first to include coins of both gold and silver and, when Herodotus writes that "the Lydians are the first people so far as I know to adopt a gold and silver coinage,"[3] it is possible that he is referring to this system rather than to the first coins of any kind. Coins of both gold and silver were of full weight, and it is, therefore, to the Lydians that we owe thanks also for bringing bimetallism into the world with all its attendant problems. But we have no information whether coins of one metal were legally rated in coins of the other and, therefore, whether the Crœsan system was rigidly bimetallic. But, however great the conse-

[1] Cp. Gardner, 34. [2] *Vide infra*, Chap. IX. [3] I, 94.

quences of the Crœsan reform might have been, their emergence was prevented by the Persian invasion and the fall of Crœsus after a reign of only about fourteen years.

We have seen that there is some doubt whether Cyrus, the Persian King who overthrew Crœsus, issued any coins, or whether Darius was responsible for the first Persian issues, towards the end of the 6th century B.C., when he was able to turn from the task of organizing the new empire and suppressing opposition to the new rule. In the matter of the monetary material, though not in other matters, he followed the precedent set by Crœsus, and made full weight coins of both gold and silver. There is no certain evidence[1] that the system was legally bimetallic, but there is a strong probability that the silver *shekel* was rated at $\frac{1}{20}$ of the gold *daric*. It may be that the *shekel* was the only silver coin accepted at the imperial treasury at its face value, all others being accepted only by weight.[2] Some form of bimetallism imposed by the state is rendered probable by the consequences of the fall in the ratio between the values of gold and silver from $13\frac{1}{3}:1$ to about $11:1$ in the declining years of the empire. Then silver was exported on such a scale that silver *shekels* disappeared almost completely from the interior provinces of the empire, leaving a *de facto* gold currency.[3] The stability of the supposed bimetallic systems of Lydia and of Persia until the latter half of the 4th century was due merely to the unvarying ratio between the values of gold and silver until the time of Alexander the Great.

4. *Silver Monometallism in Greece.*

When we turn from Asia to Europe, and more particularly to Greece, we find a different tradition in the material used for money. The original metallic medium of exchange was probably bronze and, later, iron in spits or *obols*. But no coinage developed out of the earlier use of either of these metals. The earliest Greek coins were probably the silver pieces issued in Ægina towards the middle of the 8th century: *obols* of iron or bronze were obviously unsuited to the expanding commerce of a busy entrepôt, and not improbably the

[1] Hill, however, states that "we know that the *daric* was tariffed at 20 *sigloi*" (*Camb. Anc. Hist.*, IV, 135).

[2] Head, *Coins of Lydia*, 30.

[3] Lenormant, I, 177.

electrum coins of Lydia and Asia Minor suggested an improvement. But supplies of natural electrum were not to be found in Greece. Silver, on the other hand, was available in Thrace and Spain.[1] In consequence, when iron *obols* were superseded in Ægina, their place was taken by coins of silver. This decision to make the first European coins of silver was the beginning of a European tradition. As coining spread throughout Greece during the next two or three hundred years, silver monometallism was everywhere adopted as the basis of the currency system. The Athenian coinage was of silver from its beginning at the close of the 7th century B.C., and there is little doubt that the possession of supplies of silver was an important factor reinforcing local tradition, and determining the choice of standard.[2] Control of the Pangæan gold mines was not secured until 463 B.C., by which time monetary policy had become settled and Athenian power had been used to enforce silver standards throughout the Greek world. It was, therefore, an inopportune time for a change of policy. Sparta stands out as a curious exception to the general attitude in Greece. It denied itself any currency but the traditional iron bars (of which no specimens have been found), until about 300 B.C.,[3] when silver pieces were issued in imitation of those of Alexander the Great. Silver was also largely used in the Ægean islands and in a number of the cities of Asia Minor, and by the middle of the 5th century B.C. in practically all of the Greek cities of South Italy and Sicily. In continental Greece silver monometallism lasted as long as autonomous currencies: both passed only when the expansion of the Roman Empire brought Greek liberty to an end.

During this period, however, gold, although not coined, was commonly used in commerce and civic administration. It was often used in bars and in foreign (and particularly Persian) coins to settle considerable foreign trade transactions, and to provide reserves in the temples. On rare occasions, in time of stress, it was coined. Gold bars from the treasury, or the golden statues or ornaments from the temple, were marketed by making them into coins. This emergency

[1] Gardner, 143.

[2] The Athenians had begun to work the silver mines at Laurium by the beginning of the 6th century, but the rich vein at Maroneia was not reached until the end of the century (Hill, *Camb. Anc. Hist.*, IV, 40).

[3] Gardner, 433; Head, 434.

currency policy was probably invented in Sicily, during the Athenian invasion of 415-413 B.C., when Syracuse, besieged by the Athenian forces, melted down the temple plate and *donaria,* and issued gold coins. Ten years or so later, other cities in Magna Græcia[1] followed the Syracusan precedent under comparable circumstances during the Carthaginian invasion. But most important was the adoption of the same policy by Athens in 407-406 B.C. The depression following upon the disastrous failure of the expedition to Sicily was intensified by the interruption of the output of silver from the mines at Laurium owing to the Spartan occupation of Decelia, and the consequent escape of the slaves from the mines. The sacred gold ornaments and statues[2] were melted down and coined to provide the means of meeting the expenses of war. But the issue did not give rise even temporarily to a bimetallic currency. The gold pieces were issued according to a public tariff based on the current piece of gold, but after their issue no attempt was made to fix their value in silver money. They circulated as ingots of guaranteed weight and fineness at their commercial value. Nor was there any effort to make the gold coins of such a weight that their value would be simply related to that of the silver unit. The weight used for silver coin was used for gold without adjustment. Moreover, the coins were of such high value[3] that they were probably very little used in daily transactions. This issue of gold was probably not regarded as a departure from the traditional Greek policy, and there was certainly no intention of superseding the Athenian silver " owls "; nevertheless, it was an important first step away from silver monometallism. A second issue of gold was made at a date which is somewhat doubtful, but not before 394 B.C.,[4] after the great victory at Cnidus. The second issue was more plentiful and varied, *didrachms* appearing for the first time, and there is more evidence of the intention that it should circulate freely as currency. The monopolistic position of the Greek

[1] Agrigentum in 406 B.C., and Camarina and Gela in 405 (Gardner, 291).

[2] The two statues of victory had cost the gold equivalent of about a quarter of a million pounds [200 *talents*] (Zimmern, 412).

[3] They were *drachms,* halves, thirds, and sixths (Gardner, 292).

[4] Köhler has suggested that the issue occurred in 339 B.C., in time of stress, when Philip was marching on Athens (*cit.* Gardner, 292).

silver issues in the Ægean had been lost to the Persian *darics* and the Cyzicene *staters* and, to some extent, to silver of Chian standard, and the gold issue may have been a bid for fresh power, the Athenians having realized that gold was more likely to command general use.

5. *The Conflict of Traditions in Asia Minor.*

Between the area in Asia in which bimetallism was dominant, and that in Greece and Magna Græcia where silver monometallism prevailed, there was one in which the two traditions met, and where policy hesitated between them. This latter area consisted very roughly of Asia Minor and the neighbouring islands, the Black Sea cities and Macedonia. In Asia Minor electrum had been coined in early times, but largely superseded by gold, which had been coined early in the 6th century at Phocæa, Lampsacus, and Cyzicus. By reason of the minting of silver in Lydia and Persia in the East, and in Greece in the West, silver circulated widely in Asia Minor, and was often coined there. It was always less important than electrum, and until the 5th century was limited to smaller denominations consisting of the *drachm* and smaller pieces But when the Ionian cities united to revolt against Persia at the beginning of the 5th century B.C., they carried their revolt into the realms of currency policy. Rebelling against the domination of Persian gold, they returned to what they probably regarded as their native tradition and coined electrum. Their currency was probably suppressed when the revolt was ended, but, after the Athenian victory at Mycale in 480 B.C., a few Ionian cities and some of the neighbouring islands[1] consolidated their position and settled down to an issue of electrum, which lasted well into the 4th century B.C. The electrum staters of Cyzicus and Lampsacus and the *hectæ* ($\frac{1}{6}$ *stater*) of Phocæa and Mitylene[2] were both plentiful and famous during the second half of the 5th century B.C. and the first half of the succeeding century. The issues of Cyzicus were of outstanding importance and abundance; in fact, Cyzicene *staters* and Persian *darics* constituted the main coinage other than silver in the Greek world. At the

[1] Chios coined electrum in the middle of the 5th century B.C.

[2] Phocæa and Mitylene seem to have made no regular issue of *staters*. One *stater* of Mitylene is known (Gardner, 238).

time of the Peloponnesian War Cyzicene *staters* were used for official payments as a special kind of gold. The pay of the troops was sometimes quoted at a Cyzicene *stater* and sometimes a *daric* a month, from which it appears that the two coins were equal in value.[1] If the two coins were thus interchangeable, the popularity of the Cyzicene electrum is partly explained as well as its toleration by Persia. But the fact that Cyzicus, of all the revolting cities, returned to Persian rule without resistance and without punishment also accounts for Persian favour. On the west this electrum coinage seems to have received the patronage of Athens during her period of power in the 4th century. Gold was probably sent from Athens to Cyzicus to be coined.[2] Athens encouraged this rival tradition in coining because trade with the ports of the Black Sea was based on electrum: she found it useful, therefore, to allow the coining of electrum to continue. Thus for various economic and political reasons Cyzicus, a town neither great nor wealthy, was able to maintain its issues under the shadow of the power of both Athens and Persia. This archaic tradition of the electrum standard persisted until the ancient world was flooded with gold coins by Philip and Alexander of Macedon.[3]

But before the time of Alexander the Great a fresh influence came to bear upon currency traditions in Asia Minor and the islands. In the closing years of the 5th century Athenian "owls" lost prestige owing to the military difficulties of Athens and the withdrawal of the pressure she had used to make her coins the general medium of exchange in the Ægean. At the same time she coined gold. In consequence there was a vogue for issuing gold. When the issues were of the smaller denominations they can be traced to the first Athenian issue, and where of *didrachms* to the second. All were based on the weight unit used in Athens, even where other units were used for silver. The supplies of gold from the Crimea, added to the revived commercial influence of Athens, gave rise to a period of rivalry in the coining of gold such as occurred in the Middle Ages. Gold was issued in Abydos,[4] Rhodes, Thasos, and

[1] Gardner, 241. [2] Gardner, 231.

[3] Lampsacus ceased to issue electrum in the first half of the 4th century, and issued gold probably under the influence of Athens.

[4] Abydos had coined gold in the 6th century B.C.

Lampsacus. Issues at Tarentum in Sicily date from 375 B.C., and at Cyrene probably from early years of the 4th century.[1]

The Black Sea ports in the main used electrum during the 5th century, as we have seen, but in the early years of the century bronze was coined at Olbia,[2] the types on the coins suggesting the influence of Athens. These coins were probably not token, but were full weight pieces equal in value to the Athenian half-*drachm*.[3]

6. *Carthage, Macedon, and Egypt.*

Again, in Carthage currency policy cannot be fitted in with the Asiatic or traditional Greek practice. Coining did not commence at all in Carthage until the middle of the 4th century. The idea of coining was obtained from Sicily, as is evidenced by the Carthaginian issues made in Sicily during the invasion of 410 B.C., and the obviously Greek style of early Carthaginian coins.[4] The Sicilian issues were of both gold and silver, and owed much in type to previous issues there. Nevertheless, the Carthaginians did not adopt the Greek tradition of the silver standard; indeed, silver was the last metal to be coined in Carthage: only after the acquisition of the Spanish silver mines between 241 and 218 B.C. did silver coins appear.[5] Down to this time all coins were made of gold, electrum, or bronze. The resort to gold issues in Sicily during the Carthaginian invasion may partly explain the earliest gold coins of Carthage. The electrum was possibly in imitation of the electrum issues in Asia Minor with which Carthage had some ties. But as the gold is rarely pure it is possible that the supposed electrum was merely more than usually debased gold.[6]

In Macedonia there was also some conflict of practice, but silver was the sole basis of the currency in those parts where coins were issued in the 6th century B.C. A few unimportant

[1] The date of the issue has been much disputed, and placed as early as 415 B.C. (Evans, *Syracusan Medallions*, 63), and as late as 218 B.C. (*Num. Chron.*, 1897, 223).

[2] Head, 272.

[3] Lenormant, I, 158. They weighed 3,511 grains which, at a ratio of 105:1 between the values of silver and copper, was worth 33·5 grains of silver, or half an Athenian *drachm*.

[4] Head, 877.

[5] Ridgeway, 289; Head, 879.

[6] Issues of electrum continue as late as the early 2nd century B.C.

bronze pieces were issued a century later, but no radical change was made until the time of Philip. In 356 B.C., soon after his accession, Philip began to exploit the newly discovered gold mines of Pangæum, and some thirteen years later he established a new currency based on both gold and silver. Although positive evidence is lacking, it is not improbable that the silver coins were legally rated to the gold, and that Philip's system was therefore bimetallic. One reason in support of this probability is that when the mines continued ever more abundantly to pour forth gold, Philip's system began to totter. Soon after his accession Alexander was forced to reform the system, and he elected to continue the coinage of silver, but, apparently, not upon a bimetallic basis. The fact that the coins of Alexander persisted so long in times of changing ratio between the values of gold and silver is evidence of the absence of any rigid arrangement rating gold and silver to each other. The two parallel monometallic systems long survived the fall of Macedonian power; the gold coins in particular became famous throughout Europe, from Gaul to India.

Egyptian traditions stood apart from those of the rest of the East. Egypt never willingly adopted coining. The Persians, after their invasion, struck silver coins there, but their issues were probably used only by the invading army and officials. The first purely Egyptian monetary system was set up by Ptolemy I in the last quarter of the 4th century B.C., at first under Macedonian authority. In this currency copper played a larger part than was customary elsewhere at the time, although gold, silver, and copper were all coined. Gold continued intermittently in use until 146 B.C. Silver was the basis of all accounts until the end of the 3rd century, after which they were kept in copper units.[1] Silver coins were issued continuously, but from about 80 B.C. a policy of debasement was adopted which caused the collapse of the whole system on the death of Cleopatra in 30 B.C. The copper of the Ptolemaic issues was probably not token,[2] but little is known of it, or in fact of most of the early Egyptian issues. Under the Roman Empire, in A.D. 19, a new currency was established, the coins being made of a mixture of silver and

[1] Head, 854.

[2] Babelon, 402.

bronze, but two and a half centuries brought it to the same fate as its predecessor, and also that of the Roman silver, with which it was closely bound up.

7. *The Passage from Bronze to Gold in Rome.*

The native peoples of Italy had from early times used a bronze medium of exchange. When the Greek immigrants settled in Sicily and the coast of Southern Italy they brought with them the idea of coining. They did not, however, apply it to bronze; they adhered to the tradition of their mother cities, and introduced a silver coinage in an advanced stage of development. But although silver coins were issued by the colonists soon after their arrival, the native bronze unit of value was not superseded. The new system was grafted on to the old by arranging that the new coins should be equal in value to native bronze units, or by placing on the coins a statement of their value in these latter units. In Central Italy, however, the pound of bronze remained the medium of exchange as well as the unit of value. The practice of marking bronze ingots was probably introduced in Rome, and spread from there, and during the latter part of the 4th[1] and the 3rd centuries B.C. heavy bronze coins, *as signatum* and *as grave*, were in general use throughout Northern and Central Italy. Although bronze must have been cumbrous and inconvenient in all but small transactions, it was the only official money in which fines and official debts could be paid. Doubtless, while trade was of no great magnitude, such a currency met the needs of the great mass of the people. The minority who required a larger unit of value were well able to look after themselves. They used both gold and silver, which were current in bars and in foreign coins, the latter being accepted only by weight and at their commercial value in copper. The silver coins of the Greek colonies,[2] and also of some of the Greek cities themselves, were available from early times, and circulated, particularly in Etruria, where by reason of its

[1] Hæberlin (*Systematik des ältesten römischen Munzwesens*, Berlin, 1905) suggested 335 B.C. as the date of the first bronze issues, but Mattingly (*Num. Chron.*, 1924, 196) suggests that the issue commenced in 300-290 B.C., and was the coinage of the Samnite Wars.

[2] Of Cumæ, on the western coast, from the early years of the 6th century (Head, 42), and of the Greek settlements in Sicily from the later 7th century (Head, 115).

maritime trade native bronze and foreign silver met. A great variety of coins has, in consequence, been found there. Heavy bronze coins are discovered together with silver on various Greek standards, and even a few gold pieces.[1] A variety of silver coins circulated also in Rome, the most common being the coins of Campania, and some of the cities of Sicily, the latter being favoured by reason of the simple relation in value between them and the Roman bronze *as*, weighing one pound. In spite of the competition of these foreign issues, obviously more convenient than full-weight bronze, the latter remained the official unit; but silver issues became popular. At Cumæ, in Campania, silver had been issued from the early years of the 5th century B.C., and in the 4th century the popularity of silver was on the increase, and silver coins were issued from a number of cities.[2] The first issues of silver by the Romans were not made from the Roman mint. Coins marked " Roma " and " Romano " have been assigned to a Roman mint at Capua,[3] at a date as early as 335 B.C. But it is remarkable that the Romans should have issued silver outside Rome, and more than ever remarkable that they should have waited as long as seventy years after initiating the Capuan issue before making any similar issue from Rome. On this account these early silver coins may be ascribed to the period of the wars against Pyrrhus (282-272 B.C.). The types of some of the coins reveal Carthaginian influence, and it is probable that the coins were practically a joint issue, more Roman than Carthaginian because of the place of issue, but made of treasure supplied by Carthage.[4] In fact, it is probable that the form of the Carthaginian treasure determined the material of the coins. These new coins circulated in Rome,[5] and when the war was over the idea borrowed from Carthage (although the cities of Magna Græcia had been coining silver for over 300 years, and the Romans had used them) was not abandoned. In 268 B.C. silver coins were issued from the city mint. The series of reductions in the bronze *as* since the beginning of the century must have reduced

[1] Gold was issued in Etruria probably in the 5th century B.C. (Head, 12).

[2] *E.g.*, Fenseris (Head, 37), Hyria (37), Neapolis (38), Phistelia (41).

[3] Head, 32.

[4] Mattingly, *Num. Chron.*, 1924, 185 *sqq.*

[5] It was probably in the course of the war that they were reduced, so that the silver pieces should be worth exactly three *asses*.

confidence in the bronze coinage, if it was not merely a reflection of the disfavour into which it had fallen because of its obvious inferiority to silver.[1] The conquest of Campania and the capture of Tarentum in 272 B.C. brought considerable supplies of gold and silver coin and bullion to Rome. Public opinion was ready for silver coins and, like Alexander, over half a century earlier, the Romans disposed of their silver booty by coining it.[2]

The new silver issue[3] was made in 269 or 268 B.C.[4] and was based upon the *denarius*, which, as its name implies, was worth 10 *asses*. It was marked with an "X" to define its value in bronze units, and its subdivisions were marked with their respective equivalents in *asses*. The *as* was not the original full pound of bronze, but was probably a reduced coin valued at about its current market value as metal.[5] As the value of silver coins in bronze was marked upon the silver coins themselves, it is probable that the currency was bimetallic, and based on both bronze and silver. The mark upon the silver coins may at first have been intended to facilitate their introduction to people whose only official currency had hitherto been of bronze. But the mark continued to be used, and there is little doubt that the system was legally bimetallic. Until the end of the century, issues of silver were small. The composition of hoards that have been discovered shows that the currency of a great part of Italy consisted of Roman copper coins,[6] and down to 189 B.C. the largess scattered after military triumphs was invariably of copper.[7] But early in the 2nd century B.C., the issues of bronze, previously abundant, were suddenly restricted, and

[1] *Vide* Chap. XV.

[2] Ridgeway (373) suggests that inadequacy of supplies of silver in Rome was responsible for the long postponement of the issue of silver coins. But there is fair evidence of the use of silver coins in Rome for some time previously. If the city could afford to import silver in the form of foreign coin in sufficient quantities to meet its needs, it could with equal ease have imported bullion or foreign coins and have made its own issues. In the latter event it would have had to meet the cost of coining which might be escaped in the former.

[3] Full-weight copper coins remained in circulation for many years in Central Italy, and across the Apennines.

[4] Livy (IV, 60) says 268 B.C., and Pliny (*Hist. Nat.*, XXXIII, 3-13) 269 B.C. Possibly the issue was authorized in the former and made in the latter year (Grueber, XXXIV).

[5] *Vide* Chap. XII.

[6] Mommsen, II, 70.

[7] Mommsen, II, 71.

silver pieces were issued on a larger scale than before.[1] From the middle of the century bronze ceased to be kept in the *ærarium* of the Roman people, silver and gold alone forming the reserve. Moreover, about the same time, the issue of bronze *asses* was suspended for a period of about sixty years.[2] The Romans were moving towards silver monometallism, but there was no clear-cut change from silver and bronze to silver alone. When in 91 B.C., under the pressure of the Social War, copper was reduced to a token money, and monometallism accepted, the Romans were merely accepting in law the situation that had slowly evolved. The manner of the acceptance of silver monometallism in Rome is very similar to that of the adoption of gold in England. Bimetallism persisted in law down to 1816 in England, but, in fact, during the whole of the previous century, gold was the most important part of the currency. And just as in 1816 silver was restricted to token coins in England, so in Rome, in 91 B.C., copper coins became tokens.

But at the time when silver was becoming the sole basis of the standard, the way was being made straight for its future rival—gold. Since early times, gold had circulated widely, but had rarely been coined.[3] It was in much the same position as silver had been before the issue of the first silver coins. The amount of gold in circulation, in the form of ingots and foreign coins, was sufficient during the 4th century B.C. for it to be possible to prescribe that a tax should be paid in gold. But the Roman attitude to the coining of gold seems to have been exactly similar to that of Athens—viz., that it should be coined only in time of dire necessity. The only Roman gold issues before the 1st century B.C. were made during the Punic Wars.[4] There seems to have been an intention to explain the departure from tradition involved in their

[1] Mommsen, II, 72.

[2] Grueber, XXX. The largest bronze coin was the half-*as*.

[3] Cumæ seems to have coined it early in 5th century B.C (Head, 36).

[4] Pliny thought that " The first golden coin was struck fifty-one years after that of silver " (*Hist. Nat.*, XXXIII, 13)—*i.e.*, in B.C. 217, during the second Punic War. But " the evidence of the coins themselves . . . favours the earlier date (*i.e.*, before 217 B.C.), and it is not improbable that the first issue of gold was simultaneous with the introduction of the bronze sextantal standard (*i.e.*, about 240 B.C.), when Rome, hard pressed by the strain of the first Punic War, needed money to meet her necessities and for the payment of her troops, and for that purpose used the gold bullion which was in her treasury " (Grueber, I, 13).

issue by means of the types, for the pieces bore on the obverse Mars and on the reverse an Eagle on a thunderbolt. But, unlike the Athenians, the Romans attempted to regulate the current value of gold pieces in terms of silver, each piece being marked with its value in *sestertii* at a rate of 20 *sestertii* to the scruple of gold.[1] It is unlikely that this marking indicates the existence, even temporarily, of a trimetallic system in Rome; the gold coins seem to have been rated so high that they were tokens.[2] This issue was of short duration, and no further gold coins were made for about 170 years. When it was found necessary, early in the 1st century, to grant to generals in the field the power to issue coins, the way was unintentionally opened to the coining of gold. No limit was placed upon the metals to be coined, and Sulla began a series of gold issues by military commanders. His issues in Greece were for distribution among his victorious troops. Their large size suggests that they may have been issued more as commemorative medallions than coins. For a period of about twenty years, the right of coining fell into abeyance, but it was revived by Cæsar at the close of the Gallic Wars, although he issued only silver in Gaul. But on his arrival in Rome he issued both gold[3] and silver. He brought with him the gold looted from the temples of the Gauls.[4] His troops expected some reward for their support in the Gaulish campaign, and his gold issues were the result of the application of the gold booty to the satisfaction of the expectations of the troops.[5] There is, therefore, a close parallel between the circumstances of the introduction of silver and gold to coinage. The legal position of the currency at this time is uncertain: the *aureus* passed for 25 *denarii*, and it is very probable that this ratio was reinforced by some legal sanction. Soon after Cæsar's death the position of the gold was regularized, and it was used as a recognized currency

[1] If the *sestertius* was still one scruple of silver, the ratio between gold and silver was 20:1, but if the gold was issued during the second Punic War, after the *denarius* had been reduced to $\frac{1}{84}$ of a pound, the ratio was 1:17·43.

[2] *Vide* Chap. XII.

[3] Specimens of Cæsar's gold issues are rare, but it must not be inferred that the issue was small. The later reduction in the weight of the *aureus* probably caused Cæsar's heavy coins to be melted down.

[4] He seized the public treasure in the temple of Saturn.

[5] Grueber, I, 505 n.

metal. The Senate took up the manufacture of gold coins concurrently with the military authorities; apparently they were unwilling that the issue should lapse, and were forced to take active steps to secure its continuance.[1] Gold issues continued throughout the remaining tumultuous years of the Republic, and were finally taken over by the Emperor.

The Empire commenced, therefore, with a gold and silver bimetallism, 25 *denarii* being worth 1 *aureus*,[2] which system continued until the time of Nero in the middle of the 1st century A.D. But after about a century of bimetallism, during which the coinage ratio had been repeatedly altered in favour of gold,[3] the latter became increasingly important. This change was mainly due to a rapid series of alterations in the weight and fineness of the silver currency, and the introduction of the practice of issuing base coins washed with silver among those which were genuine, though poor in quality. At the beginning of the 3rd century, the debasement of silver, and attempts, or anticipated attempts, to reduce the weight of the gold currency, gave rise to the custom of passing gold coins by weight. Repeated efforts were made to secure the acceptance of coins at their nominal value, but without success, and throughout the greater part of the century, although the gold pieces were the only ones of the fineness which had not been seriously tampered with, they were struck without any fixed standard weight, as is evidenced by the wide variations in the weight of the *aurei* that have come down to us from this period. The gold pieces in circulation, like the stamped ingots of earlier times, passed as pieces bearing a guarantee of fineness only. Thus gold was demonetized, and the principal standard of value was a unit weight of uncoined gold, there being no coins representing the unit or simple fractions of it. Towards the end of the 3rd century attempts were made to bring some order out of the chaos. Although in about A.D. 271 plated coins were again issued as tokens, nothing was done to re-establish the gold currency. During the reign of Diocletian there was a series of experiments with gold and silver bimetallism, but reform was finally effected in A.D. 312 by Constantine, who aimed also at a return to gold and silver bimetallism. He issued pieces of both metals, but the gold *solidi* were of such

[1] Mommsen, III, 45. [2] Mattingly, XLIV.
[3] By reducing the weight of the gold coin (*vide* Chap. X).

irregular weight that he must have accepted the custom which had grown up in the period of inflation of passing coins by weight. Not only was there no attempt to force the circulation of the coins at their legal value, but steps were taken to facilitate their circulation by weight. Special standard weights were supplied to the principal cities, and public officials were appointed to verify the weight of gold whenever requested to do so. The silver coins were also irregular in weight, but must often have passed by tale, probably as subdivisions of the pound of gold. Posssibly silver was not freely coined, although silver coins were full weight pieces, and there are signs that gold was preferred. In about A.D. 380 this preference became quite obvious when the silver coins were relegated to the status of small change money, but it was not until the 7th century A.D. that the silver pieces certainly became tokens as well, and Rome emerged with a gold standard currency, supported by silver and copper tokens, similar to that in Great Britain from 1816 to 1914.

Chinese currency before the end of the 3rd century B.C. consisted of bronze circulating with shells, silk, and other commodities. When the first state currency was issued during the last two decades of the 3rd century B.C., bronze was adopted for the standard, and it has remained the sole monetary metal in China until quite recent years.

8. *Summary.*

Looking back over the metallic bases of early currency systems, we find them in close agreement with those of recent times. Electrum, it is true, has not been used for many centuries, but it is notable that its use has been recommended within the last fifty years. For the rest, gold and silver, either jointly or separately, were the basis of most early systems, with the exception of the Roman. The distribution of standards is of interest. Electrum was used in Lydia and Asia Minor, but never in Greece, South of Macedon,[1] and hardly ever in Europe.[2] Gold was probably first coined in the coastal cities of Asia Minor to supplant electrum. In Lydia, when electrum was replaced, both gold and silver were coined, and

[1] Hill, *Camb. Anc. Hist.*, IV, 128.
[2] It was issued at Syracuse (Head, *Hist. Num.*, 178).

the Asiatic imperial tradition in the matter of money remained one of gold and silver bimetallism throughout the supremacy of Persia and the years of the rise of Macedon under Philip. Then rapid changes in the relative values of gold and silver rendered the system unsteady. The first silver coins ever struck were probably made in Ægina, and upon them is based the Greek tradition of silver monometallism, which was generally accepted also in Magna Græcia. But the close of the 5th century B.C. brought the first signs of a rapprochement between Asiatic electrum and bimetallism and European monometallism. Emergency issues of gold in Sicily were followed by similar issues in Athens. Having dominated the Ægean with her silver during the 5th century B.C., Athens led a considerable movement in the coining of gold in the 4th century. The parallel coinage of both gold and silver introduced by Alexander of Macedon towards the end of the century was, therefore, but the more grandiose successor of the system introduced by Athens, while also it went more than half-way to meet the imperial tradition in Asia. Still more important for the future of this system was the fact that it was capable of surviving rapid changes in the values of gold or silver. The reasons for these differences of practice lie mainly in the distribution of supplies of the metals. The Lydians were deeply interested in the disposal of their supplies of electrum, and their monetary policy is doubtless a reflection of that interest. The Persians were influenced, partly by the previous Lydian policy, and partly by the sources of supply of which they had taken possession. The Greek cities did not possess supplies of gold, but at least some (*e.g.*, Athens) commanded silver supplies. But Ægina and Corinth, the earliest cities to coin, do not appear to have possessed silver mines, and the beginning of the tradition of silver monometallism is not easy to trace. The effect of the possession of supplies of gold is again evident in the monetary policy in Macedon. Philip abandoned silver monometallism for bimetallism, and his son entrenched the use of b6th metals by abandoning rigid bimetallism.

In Rome the influences which separately affected the Eastern Mediterranean and Asia were successively brought to bear upon the primitive Italian peoples. Native tradition in favour of a full-weight bronze currency gave way but slowly to foreign innovation. For three centuries foreign silver coins circulated in Rome without arousing sufficient interest or pride to stimulate a Roman issue. In the middle of the 3rd century a mixture of Greek and native tradition produced a bronze and silver bimetallic system which must be unique in currency history. Growing power, widening territory, and increasing public business and wealth, led to the gradual disappearance of the copper element in the currency during the 2nd century, and its elimination by law early in the 1st century B.C. Until this time the Greek attitude dominated Roman policy, the sole issue of gold made during the Punic Wars having been token and looked upon as a purely emergency issue. But the last century B.C. saw an expansion of dominion that inevitably opened the way to Asiatic imperial influence. It brought physical contact with the East and its bimetallic tradition; it brought Rome face to face with imperial problems similar to those already dealt with in the east; and it brought a decay of democratic institutions and a growth of tyranny which had long flourished in Asia. The immediate reason for the coining of gold lay even then in the Gaulish loot in Cæsar's hands and the troops expecting reward. We find, therefore, from the middle of the last century B.C. to the middle of the 1st century A.D., a gold and silver bimetallism in Rome explainable ultimately by contact with the East and the similarity of currency problems in the two areas. But from Nero to Diocletian the question of the material of the monetary standard is overlaid by a debasement of currency so serious that it caused a reversion to the Lydian system of passing the precious metals by weight. Towards the end of the 3rd century Diocletian attempted to re-establish the monetary system, and seems to have aimed at a bimetallic currency of gold and silver for the whole empire,[1] to which end he made a series of experiments which involved repeated alteration of the weight of both the gold and the silver coins to secure a fresh currency ratio between the metals.[2] But none seems to have been a success, and Constantine probably gave up the attempt and coined gold and silver on the same weight basis, probably without making any attempt to establish a legal valuation of silver coins in terms of gold *solidi*. They were more likely regarded as full-weight coins

[1] Sydenham, *Num. Chron.*, 1919, 152.

[2] *Vide* Chap. X.

representing a fraction of the pound weight of gold. In the course of the 4th century gold grew in importance and silver declined. The result was the first gold standard in the ancient world.

In ancient times the earliest metallic monetary medium, at any rate in Europe, was usually copper or bronze. The copper pieces of ancient Egypt, the *obol* of Greece, the *libra* of Italy, and the *litra* of Sicily, and the full-weight bronze pieces of Sparta and Carthage, stand forth as witnesses. With the history of the Roman system fresh in mind, it appears almost natural for development to lie through silver to gold, and there is much evidence that this happened. We find gold and silver both in use in Asia at the beginning of history. But in Europe, perhaps by reason of the distribution of supplies of the precious metals, the path from copper to gold was long. In the Greek world bronze gave way to silver at or before the introduction of coining, and the first coins were of silver. The events of the 4th century B.C. reveal a movement towards the issue of gold, but it was slow and uncertain in the face of the aged silver tradition, and was overtaken by the Macedonian gold; Greek influence petered out without establishing a stable gold currency or even a gold and silver bimetallic system. In Asia gold had probably always circulated as part of a bimetallic system, and it was left to Alexander the Great, impelled by the output of his Pangæan mines, to approach nearest to a gold standard in his parallel currency of gold and silver, with gold as the more important metal. The Romans, in the course of about 800 years from the middle of the 5th century B.C., passed slowly from their heavy bronze coins to silver, and finally to gold. They established a gold standard that was to be the basis of mediæval European issues.

CHAPTER VII

THE FINENESS OF THE COINS

THE definition of the monetary standard requires a definition, on the one hand, of the metal used as the basis of the monetary system and, on the other, of the amount of that metal which constitutes the monetary unit. But the coins in circulation representing the monetary unit do not consist only of the prescribed amount of the pure metal. They always contain at least a small proportion of alloy. In order to discover the monetary standards of the ancient East from a consideration of their coins, it is now desirable to consider what proportion of the weight of ancient coins was alloy and how much was the monetary metal. This consideration may be of great importance when, for any reason, attempt is made to reduce the standard. The change may be effected without any reduction in the weight of the coins, by merely increasing the proportion of alloy which they contain and reducing the proportion of the metal of the standard. If the coins are freely issued they will fall in value until they reach the value of the new mixture in the coins. The mere fact that this debasement enables the issuing authority to keep up appearances while it makes the change renders this method of depreciation attractive. It is necessary, therefore, to examine ancient coins with a view to discovering firstly the proportion of alloy which it was customary to use, and, secondly, the frequency with which the proportion was changed. The result of the second discovery will reveal whether debasement of money was a common means of inflation in early times.

1. *The Composition of Early Electrum.*

We have seen that the earliest royal coins of Lydia and of the cities of Ionia were made of electrum, the currency medium upon which the first experiments in debasement were tried. The early punch-marked ingots of Lydia contained most frequently about 75 per cent. of gold, but pieces have been found containing anything from 5 to 95 per cent. As the earliest issues were probably made from a natural mixture of the metals, variations in their composition may not have been intentional; indeed, so long as electrum was regarded as a separate metal, they may not have affected the value of the coin, unless they were so wide as to affect the colour of the metal coins. But we have seen[1] that variations in the quality of electrum were soon noticed, and it became a common practice to test coins, and in consequence of this disadvantage the coining of electrum almost ceased. When, after a long interruption, the cities of the Ionian revolt recommenced the issue of electrum, and it was continued in a few cities of Asia Minor, led by Cyzicus, its composition was known: it was artificially mixed to make the coins. Moneyers soon found how little the appearance of the coin was altered if they used slightly less than the usual proportion of gold, and they were tempted. The *staters* of some cities certainly contained less gold than those of others, but whether as the result of a decision constitutionally arrived at, or merely of the dishonesty of moneyers, we do not know. Cyzicus was most famous during the latter half of the 5th and first half of the 4th century B.C. for its electrum coins, yet some of them contain as much as 40 per cent. of silver instead of 25 per cent.[2] Those of Lesbos and Phocæa contained up to 60 per cent. of silver, and became known for their poor quality, and passed at a discount in Cyzicene coins.

Electrum, in Asia Minor, and probably also in Lydia, first turned men's minds to the temptations of debasement. It was so very easy, particularly in early times, to tamper with the composition of a currency medium which had never, so far as we know, been precisely defined. The specimens of coins that we have bear out this suggestion.

2. *The Quality of the Gold and Silver of the Asiatic Empires.*

When Crœsus introduced the first imperial coinage of gold and silver, in the middle of the 6th century B.C., the coins commenced with and maintained a very high standard of purity. Although the Lydian currency was swept away a few years after the Persian invasion, its tradition of a high and

[1] Chap. VI.

[2] Lenormant, III, 7.

unchanging degree of purity in the coins of both gold and silver remained. The famous gold *darics* were very pure, containing never more than 3 per cent. of alloy, which was intentionally introduced[1] to harden the metal. The *daric* was never debased, and its reliability in quality explains the fact that it was practically the only gold coin for about 200 years, as well in Asia Minor and the mainland of Greece as in the Persian Empire. The Persian silver coins were a little less pure than contemporary Greek issues; no serious debasement took place until the decadence of the empire, when the royal silver specially struck for circulation in Syria and Phœnicia was reduced. The fineness of the small silver of Pamphilia fell to 0·709, but the larger pieces remained more pure.[2] But this debasement is not to be ascribed to any lack of integrity in the management of the currency. It is more likely that an increase in the supplies of gold during the last century of the empire caused a fall in the silver value of gold from $13\frac{1}{3} : 1$, the ratio upon which the currency was based, to about 11 : 1. In consequence, the silver coins disappeared from circulation. By reducing their fineness it was hoped to prevent their export by increasing the currency value of silver.[3] Darius attached great importance to the fineness of coinage for, if Herodotus[4] is to be believed, Aryandes, governor of Egypt, having become "aware by report, and also by his own eyesight, that Darius wished to leave a memorial of himself such as no King had ever left before . . . resolved to follow his example, and did so till he got his reward. Darius had refined gold till the past perfection of purity, in order to have coins struck of it. Aryandes, in his Egyptian government, did the very same with silver, so that to this day there is no such pure silver anywhere as the Aryandic. Darius, when this came to his ears, brought another charge of rebellion against Aryandes, and put him to death." No specimens of these fatal coins are known, but if the story is true they were probably Persian *shekels*.

[1] Lenormant, I, 187.

[2] A few towns possessing the right to issue silver followed this example (Lenormant, I, 190).

[3] The alteration in the fineness of the coins was so great that some of the semi-independent provinces in Asia Minor refused to take them except at their bullion value (Lenormant, III, 16).

[4] IV, 166.

3. *The Quality of Greek Coins.*

The silver coins of the Greek world varied generally in millesimal fineness from 910 to 980,[1] which compares very favourably with a fineness of 0·925 in the British silver coinage for the period of over seven and a half centuries from the time of Henry II (at the latest) until 1920.[2] The Athenian *tetradrachms* of the finest period during the later part of the 5th century B.C. were about 0·986 to 0·983 fine. During the second half of the 4th century they were reduced to about 0·966, but the alloy consisted of 0·032 copper and 0·002 gold, a not uncommon mixture at that time. The quality of the Attic coins was never reduced by the addition of any considerable amount of alloy.[3] In fact, alterations of the fineness of silver coins among Greek cities generally are rare.[4] When gold was coined in the Greek world, it was nearly always pure. Bronze consisted of not less than 88 per cent. copper, and the rest tin, until about 400 B.C., after which date it became an increasingly common practice to mix lead with the copper.[5]

The Greeks were responsible for introducing a new form of debasement, which wrought great havoc in later currency systems. Debasement by the straightforward mixture of more alloy with the metal was a device of limited utility. When the amount of alloy reached very large proportions, the appearance of the coin was sometimes altogether changed, and it ran a risk of not being accepted. Accordingly, the Greeks invented the device of placing on the outside of the coin what little of the monetary metal it contained: they invented plated

[1] The silver of Chios in the 6th century was 0·975 fine, that of Teos and Ægina 0·960, and of Corinth 0·961 to 0·936. At Miletus, at the end of the 5th century, fineness was about 0·950, and in Chalcedon 0·960, while later at Rhodes it was 0·965, with 0·003 of gold (Lenormant I, 190). In Magna Græcia much the same quality is found. In the 6th century at Tarentum it was 0·948 to 0·970. Early in the 5th century in Messina it was 0·948, and in the 4th century 0·910 to 0·980. It was in Campania 0·980, Syracuse 0·960, Velia 0·966, and Tarentum 0·910-0·930, falling later to about 0·880, the smaller denominations being generally of less fineness than the larger pieces (Lenormant, I, 188).

[2] With the exception of about twenty years from the end of the reign of Henry VIII to that of Elizabeth.

[3] Lenormant, I, 190.

[4] Zimmern (*Greek Commonwealth*, 304) quotes Demosthenes' charge that "the majority of states are quite open in using silver coin diluted with copper and lead" (XXIV, 214), and accuses the Greeks of having habitually and shamelessly debased their coinage, but the accusation is unfounded.

[5] *Encyclopædia Britannica*: Article, "Bronze."

coins. These coins consist of a disc of some metal of low value, of copper, iron, or lead, bearing a thin coating of silver or, more rarely, gold. They were then stamped and issued as genuine silver or gold coins. Plated coins are found among Greek issues of the earliest times, the core usually being of copper or lead. In all probability some private counterfeiter hit upon the idea, and later the State, stimulated by needs similar to those of the counterfeiter, took over his enterprise. Some of the plated coins which have been found are undoubted counterfeits, particularly those bearing obverse and reverse types of different periods, or those with gross errors in the legend: these specimens are also poorest in workmanship. But there are many, perfectly regular in type and legend, and executed with a delicacy which is incontestable evidence of their official origin.[1] To produce such coins with a lead or iron core would need all the equipment and facilities of the State Mint, and they are almost certainly Government issues. Lead coins plated with gold are said to have been issued by Polycrates in Samos some time after 545 B.C., in a desperate but successful attempt to rid the island of the Lacedæmonian invaders.[2] But Herodotus[3] regards it as nothing more than "a silly tale." Perdicaas II of Macedonia issued iron coins plated with silver to meet the cost of the army during the Chalcidian War[4] in the middle of the 5th century B.C. At the beginning of the next century similar pieces were again issued in considerable quantities.[5] Plated coins were also issued in Athens towards the end of the Peloponnesian War. The Athenians had seen the gold statues of victory taken from the Parthenon and melted down for coinage in an effort to replace their lost fleet. By 406 B.C. the coins had all been spent, and silver currency was also scarce. Aristophanes[6] wrote truly of Athens that:

> She has good and ancient silver, she has good and recent gold,
> These are coins untouched with alloys, everywhere their fame is told.
> Not all Hellas holds their equal, not all Barbary far and near,
> Gold and silver each well minted, tested each and ringing clear—
> Yet we never use them ! Others always pass from hand to hand:
> Sorry brass just struck last week, and branded with a wretched brand.

The new brass pieces were probably plated, for the inventories of offerings in the Parthenon refer to *staters* which

[1] Lenormant, I, 222. [2] Ure, 74. [3] LII, 56.
[4] Lenormant, I, 226. [5] Lenormant, I, 226.
[6] *Frogs*, 730, *sqq.* (trans. Prof. Gilbert Murray).

were only gilded.[1] Few specimens of these *staters* exist, but there is in the British Museum a bronze *tetradrachm* which was originally plated.[2] These coins remained in circulation for only thirteen years, after which they were cried down, and silver was again made legal tender. In the 3rd century B.C. so many plated coins are found among the issues of some years as to suggest that the Government must have decided to issue plated coins in a fixed proportion to and mixed with the genuine issues from the mint.[3] There is one specimen of a plated coin of Miletus[4] with a core of lead and a plating of electrum, and a passage in the pseudo-Aristotelian *Œconomica*[5] has been interpreted[6] to mean that the people of Clazomene also struck iron money as silver money under the stress of famine and a large public debt, but it is doubtful whether the reading is correct.[7] A milder experiment in the issue of plated money seems to have been tried in Carthage during the 4th century. Electrum coins were issued in imitation of the revived issues of the cities of Asia Minor, but all the specimens of these coins which have survived have been subjected before issue to a process for the removal of the silver from the surface. Lenormant suggests[8] that these electrum coins were low-quality gold rather than electrum, and were never issued as electrum, but were fraudulently issued as gold in time of necessity. Where there were so many issuing authorities it would be remarkable if no debasement occurred, but in general the Greek cities did not frequently debase their money or issue plated coins although they possessed the necessary knowledge.

4. *The Quality of Macedonian Coins.*

As in many other respects, so also in its attitude to the fineness of coins, the Macedonian Empire followed the Persian tradition. The gold *staters* of Philip and Alexander the Great which superseded the Persian *darics* contained only three per-

[1] Lenormant, I, 226. [2] Head, 373.

[3] Lenormant, I, 227. Possibly this was the precedent for the later Roman practice along the same lines.

[4] Lenormant, I, 225. [5] II, 17. [6] Lenormant I, 221.

[7] The passage states that they "struck iron coinage to represent a sum of twenty *talents* of silver," and it appears from the context that this passage was merely intended to define the total face value of the issue, and not to mean that the coins resembled silver pieces.

[8] I, 199.

mille of silver mixed with the gold.[1] This surprising degree of fineness was probably the highest possible with the methods then in use. The fineness of both gold and silver remained unchanged to the end of the empire. The bronze of Alexander contained up to 12 per cent. of tin. At the death of Alexander his empire fell into a number of separate kingdoms each of which issued coins of its own. In what had once been the old Persian Empire the first silver coins were about 0·990 fine. This standard of purity was maintained for a considerable period, but towards the end of the empire, some three centuries later, the coins had fallen to only 0·678 fine. Silver was rehabilitated under the succeeding Parthian rule, and in the 1st century B.C. coins of a fineness of 0·946 were issued, which standard continued with little alteration to the end of the Parthian Empire in A.D. 227. But the coins struck for circulation in Mesopotamia followed, from about the beginning of the Christian era, the alterations in the issues from the mint at Antioch, and by the end of the empire were about 0·625 fine.[2]

5. *Coinage Debasement in Rome.*

The Roman Empire took over from the people of the Greek world their heritage of knowledge of currency manipulation, and made much greater use of it than ever they had done. The Roman bronze money throughout the period of about four centuries from the issue of the first *as signatum* to the time of Julius Cæsar was always of about the same composition. A fresh alloy was specially introduced when the *as* was struck.[3] It is supposed that the object of the new alloy was to differentiate currency bronze from that used for domestic utensils in order to discourage melting of the coin. The silver money of the Roman Republic varied in millesimal fineness between 0·902 and 0·998. Its fineness was never reduced in any serious measure even during the Punic Wars, when devaluation and the issue of base coin were resorted to.

[1] Lenormant, I, 187.

[2] *Tetradrachms* of this metal were worth only 2½ of the silver *drachms* circulating elsewhere in the empire.

[3] Mommsen, I, 198. It contained from 5 to 8 per cent. tin, from 16 to 28 per cent. lead, and the rest copper. The mixture of lead with copper is unknown among the Greeks until the third century B.C., after which it occurs mainly under the influence of the Romans.

Sulla forbade, under pain of severe penalties, the damaging of the standard of silver coin.[1] The rare occasions on which silver was debased were during intervals of Civil War in the last century of the Republic. Mark Antony, for instance, issued to his legions *denarii* containing 20 per cent. of copper.[2]

The debasements of the Republic usually took the form of issues of plated money mixed with genuine coins. The first was made after the military disasters of the second Punic War. The Lex Flaminia authorized, as well as reductions in the weight of both copper and silver, the inclusion of a certain number of copper pieces washed with silver in each issue of genuine silver coins.[3] The extent to which the Government exercised this power is not known: no very great number of these pieces has come down to us. The base coins were legal tender, and acceptance was enforced when it was known that they were only plated. It has been suggested that "once the issue of base coins mixed with good ones had commenced at Rome, it was never completely given up,"[4] but the only other serious debasement of this kind took place at the beginning of the first century B.C. During the disturbances of the opening years of the century, unprecedented quantities of plated coins were issued, and produced a financial crisis. The Social War of 91-89 B.C. provided an excuse for even further issues, and a law was passed in 91 B.C. authorizing the issue of one base coin with every seven silver coins. Advantage was taken of this authority to issue pieces with cores of iron or lead, and within a few years "the value of money was so fluctuating that no one could tell how much he was worth."[5] Some ten years later the prætor Gratidianus established offices to verify coins and to withdraw the base money by redeeming it in good *denarii*. At the same time he withdrew the forced currency of the base coins, and they ceased to be legal tender. So strong was the public feeling which had been roused by the dislocation and iniquity which had followed on the issue of the base money, that these reforms met with immense public enthusiasm. Gratidianus received almost divine honours and full-length statues were erected to him in every

[1] Lenormant, I, 201.
[2] Mommsen, III, 28.
[3] Lenormant, I, 228.
[4] Lenormant, I, 228.
[5] Cicero, *De Officiis*, III, 20.

quarter of the city,[1] and incense was burned before them. But such popularity was fatal in times of fierce political intrigue. Sulla succeeded Gratidianus, and put him to death after barbarous torture. The statues erected to him were thrown down, and the mixture of plated coins with the genuine pieces was recommenced, the base coin being again made legal tender. After the death of Sulla the silver money improved in fineness and fabric, but there is some doubt how long the plated coins continued to circulate. It is possible that they persisted down to the time of Julius Cæsar,[2] but probable that they were soon discontinued, and no debased coins were issued by Julius Cæsar.[3] The gold coins issued under the Republic were always pure. A law of Sulla forbade the mixing of any alloy with gold, even if it was to circulate as bullion.[4]

At the foundation of the empire in 15 B.C. all old base coins were withdrawn and replaced by the gold and silver coins of Augustus. These were of high quality; the millesimal fineness of gold being 0·998 and of silver 0·980 to 0·990. Base silver was, however, struck for export. Augustus, realizing that the Roman *denarius* was preferred in some parts of India to local money, and believing that the Indian population would not distinguish genuine from base coins, sent it base *denarii*.[5] With the copper of the empire we are not here concerned, as it was admittedly token, but we may note in passing that the old bronze alloy for coins was done away with, and in its place two metals were used. Some coins were of pure copper, the inclusion of an alloy being prohibited by law, and others were of brass, made of four-fifths copper and one-fifth zinc.

During the first three centuries of the empire, the capacity of currency debasement to support corrupt or incompetent Governments was fully tested. But even in the worst periods of chaos, gold was treated with considerable respect. Towards the end of the 1st century after Vespasian, the fine-

[1] According to Cicero (*De Offic.*, III, 20), this fame was gained by an unworthy deceit, for the whole College of Prætors drew up the ordinance, and it was agreed that all should appear together on the rostra to publish it. Gratidianus then forestalled his colleagues, and published it himself before the appointed time.

[2] Lenormant, I, 233.

[3] Grueber, XLII.

[4] Lenormant, I, 201.

[5] Lenormant, I, 235.

ness of gold fell to 0·991, and later to 0·938 per mille. At the beginning of the 3rd century, it was further reduced, but remained remarkably good compared with the silver currency.[1]

Base silver coins appear among the coins of the early successors of Augustus. Four-fifths of the issues of Claudius (A.D. 41-54) are said to have been base,[2] as well as many of the *denarii* of Nero, and of the period of confusion following his death. But the official origin of the base pieces of the period before Nero is open to doubt,[3] and they form but a small proportion of the total circulation. Such of the *denarii* as were not plated pieces were reduced in quality in the time of Nero from 950-990 per mille fineness to 900. But the issues of plated coins decreased during the latter half of the 1st century A.D., were rare in the 2nd, and ceased altogether at the beginning of the 3rd century A.D., under Caracalla. These issues became less important because of the reduction in the fineness of the genuine silver coins, and when the base issues finally ceased, great reductions were made in the fineness of *denarii*. By A.D. 211 they were not more than 500 per mille silver,[4] and still falling rapidly in fineness. In A.D. 215 the device of issuing a new silver coin was tried. This piece, the *argenteus Antoninianus*, at first contained about 500 per mille

[1] The only vassals of Rome allowed to coin gold were the Kings of the Cimmerian Bosphorus. Their issues, at the beginning pure gold, were, by the end of the 2nd century B.C., electrum containing a fair proportion of silver. A quarter of a century later they were not worth their weight in silver, and after another thirty years or so all the silver had disappeared from the pieces, and practically all the gold. By A.D. 268 they were merely gilded copper (Lenormant, I, 203).

[2] Lenormant, I, 235.

[3] Mattingly, XLIV.

[4] Babelon, 411. The approximate percentage of silver in the *denarius* under the various Emperors was:

Augustus	99·1–92·78
Nero	94 3–91·0
Vespasian	88·6–80·0
Trajan	92·8–78·5
Antoninus Pius	93·2–70·0
Commodus	72·0–67·1
Septimus Severus	75·5–43·1
Caracalla	54·0
Alexander Severus	50·0–33·4
Gordian III	58·9–36·1

(Hammer, *cit.* Sydenham, *Num. Chron.*, 1919, 170).

of silver,[1] but steadily declined in fineness, until by about A.D. 270 the *denarius* had ceased to be issued at all, and the *argenteus* contained only about 20 per mille silver.[2] It had driven most of the professed copper currency out of circulation, and was little different in value from plated coin.

A number of copper coins plated with gold in imitation of the *aureus* are also known. Some of the time of Hadrian (A.D. 117-138) and Commodus (A.D. 180-192) are thought by Lenormant[3] to be so well and carefully fashioned that they cannot be counterfeits. Many specimens date from the period of the complete currency collapse from about A.D. 211-270, and only these are certain not to have been the work of false coiners.

Silver coins of good quality were not again issued until the last decade of the 3rd century, when Diocletian made silver pieces of great fineness. He also gave up the practice of issuing plated coins in imitation of either silver or gold pieces. A short time after the death of Constantine plated pieces reappeared. A number of *solidi* which are, in fact, silver pieces plated with gold are known, but are held to be the work of counterfeiters.[4]

We have already noted that no autonomous currency system was established in Egypt until the end of the 4th century B.C., under the Ptolemies. Until then merchants had settled their transactions by paying in the metals by weight. The first coins issued from the new mint at Alexandria, doubtless influenced by this tradition, were finer and heavier than in any other Greek or Hellenized country.[5] But the coins soon commenced to decline in purity, and a few years before the beginning of the Christian era, under Cleopatra, the issue ceased altogether. The mint continued to issue local

[1] Hammer (*cit.* Sydenham, *Num. Chron.*, 1919, 170) gives the percentage of silver in the *Antoninianus* as follows:

Caracalla	62·3–52·0
Elagabalus	42·8
Philip I	50·0–32·0
Decius	75·0–39·64
Gallienus	72·0–34·6

[2] And 820 per mille copper and 16 per mille lead.

[3] Lenormant, I, 237.

[4] Lenormant, I, 238.

[5] Babelon, 384. The silver coins were 0·9674 silver, 0·029 alloy, and 0·0036 gold (Lenormant, I, 188). The bronze contained about 84 per cent. copper and 16 per cent. tin (Lenormant, I, 200).

bronze coins under the Roman Empire, and during the later period they followed in point of fineness the progressive alterations in the copper money at Rome made under the authority of the Senate. In A.D. 19, coins of a mixture of silver and copper were issued from Alexandria. They circulated as silver, although they contained only 25 per cent. silver. But, like electrum, they lent themselves to debasement, which soon appeared. It gained speed towards the end of the 2nd century A.D., but proceeded still faster during the 3rd century, with the decline of the silver of Rome. The coins lost half their weight, and of what remained not 2 per cent. was silver.[1]

6. *Summary.*

Imperial currencies from Lydia to Macedon were of gold and silver of great purity. The only suggestion of debasement occurs in the declining years of the Persian system, and then it appears to be an attempt to maintain bimetallism in the face of alterations in the relative values of the currency metals. The cities of Asia Minor, which resurrected electrum as a monetary medium in the 5th century B.C., debased their issues by reducing their gold content. Very few Greek cities reduced the fineness of silver issues, but some issued plated coins almost always in time of war. While knowledge of the methods of debasement was not wanting, currency remained well preserved in quality. It was left to the Romans to make of these devices the destructive agents that they have since become. Throughout the Republic, neither bronze nor silver was seriously altered in fineness, but plated coins were issued during the second Punic War and the Social War. After all the conflict and disturbance of the last century of the Republic, the empire commenced with a coinage of gold and silver of good quality. But plated coins were almost immediately re-issued, and Nero in the middle of the 1st century commenced the debasement of the silver currency which continued during the 2nd and 3rd century until the natural limit had been reached. The progressive debasement of the so-called good coins made the issues of plated coins less profitable, and they were reduced, and then ceased altogether.

[1] They were 0·018 silver, 0·9138 copper, and 0·0289 zinc, with traces of lead (Lenormant, I, 204.)

Even gold suffered some decline in fineness. Diocletian's reforms again put the currency system on a sound basis of gold and silver of good quality. With the Roman Emperors of the first three centuries of the Christian era lies the discredit for the first full and complete investigation of the possibilities of the devices of debasement known to, but for the most part scorned by, earlier empires and city states.

CHAPTER VIII

WEIGHT STANDARDS BEFORE THE INTRODUCTION OF COINS

THE definition of the unit of value requires not only the selection of a commodity, but also the determination of the quantity of the commodity the value of which is the general unit of value. When the state began to issue money, the duty of defining this unit fell upon the state. In theory the state was at liberty to make its choice without restriction, and to alter the definition of the unit as frequently as it chose. But as soon as the unit of value was used also as a measure of indebtedness, which happened as soon as the practice of incurring debts appeared, changes in the unit of value meant changes in the burden of debts. It was highly undesirable that the state should take action likely to result in such a disturbance of economic relations. Even in a community where no such debts were outstanding, alterations in the unit would give rise to unnecessary confusion. For both these reasons, but principally the former, continuity in the unit of value was desirable. The unit could, in fact, be regarded as an abstraction, which was translated by the state into terms of the commodity in use for monetary purposes at any time. If the commodity was changed, the unit would then be stated in terms of the new material, the state aiming in normal times at a definition which would cause the minimum of alteration in the burden of the debts outstanding at the time of the change. But apart from occasions upon which the material of the standard has been changed, states have not often taken the trouble to prevent alterations in the burden of debts; they have even on occasion deliberately caused such alterations in their own favour. The large amount of continuity in the unit supplies a thread by which modern units of value can be traced back to the very beginning of money. But even this is not far enough, for, as we have seen, the first coins took the place of the pieces of metal of unit weight which were already in circulation. We must, therefore, go back still further and examine the units of weight which were in use in the pre-money era. Deliberate alterations of the unit of value break the thread, and the consequent gaps can be bridged only by considering the monetary policy which gave rise to the change, an aspect of the history of early monetary administration which will be dealt with later.[1]

The introduction of measurement by weight in all probability followed closely on the commencement of frequent exchanges of the precious metals. Rough estimates of weight, sufficient for commodities whose value was small in relation to their bulk, would be clearly inadequate to the measurement of the precious metals. More accurate measurement was obtainable by the balance and the use of generally recognized weights. General recognition of units of weight depended on their convenience in effecting exchanges. This was not a simple matter. Convenience was partly a matter of easy relation to the unit of value to which people had become accustomed prior to the use of the balance, partly in those countries which were interested in foreign trade, of easy relation to the unit used by those with whom they were in close commercial relations, and partly of the convenience of the value unit obtained by applying the weight unit to the metal in use. The problem of accounting for the units of weight used in early times for the monetary metals is further complicated by the use of both gold and silver as a medium of exchange, and the fact, already noted, that there was no uniformity, either as to time or place, in the relative values of the two metals.

No single explanation can account for all the units of weight to be found in the ancient world. Reference has already been made to the considerable evidence of the use in early times of the ox as a barter unit, and a widespread practice of this kind would provide a common foundation on which to base the weight of the precious metal which was to form the unit. On the other hand, some peoples more than others showed aptitude for scientific enquiry and invention. The Chaldeans were pre-eminently of this type, and probably, in the measure that their metrological system proved adequate to the conditions of the time and place, it found general acceptance. When in about 1300 B.C. the empire of Assyria surpassed that

[1] Chap XIII *sqq*.

of Babylon, the learning and science of the older civilization was transmitted to the new, mainly by way of Nineveh. Assyrian conquests and commerce carried them further northward and westward until they reached the Mediterranean. Knowledge of this kind flowed along the channels of trade, so that nations mainly independent would be slow both to spread their own inventions and to receive those of others. The overflow of population from Greece during the 9th and succeeding centuries B.C. took the form of the establishment of a number of Greek colonies throughout the Mediterranean. Greek trade grew quickly, and ousted the Phœnicians from some of their posts, and the consequent lessening of isolation tended more and more to the spread of ideas and the development of uniformity throughout the Eastern Mediterranean. Carrying and trading peoples, depending for their livelihood on the development of trade, became also the carriers of economic ideas, and the Phœnician, and later the Greek, trading ships played no inconsiderable part in the transmission of units of weight.

But improved communication frequently brought about conflict between old units hallowed by long usage, often rooted in local antiquity and desirable for their familiarity, and new units attractive for their simplification of foreign exchange. The conflict could not be resolved, as has sometimes been suggested, by a process of "splitting the difference," for a system so established would possess the benefits of neither of the conflicting units. The difficulty of assessing the relative vigour of the native and the invading foreign institutions is the greatest hindrance to a satisfactory explanation of the origin of early units. The desire for agreement with foreign standards, especially in the period after coins had been issued, has, however, been much over-emphasized.

1. *Babylonian Weight Standards.*

The peoples of Mesopotamia having been the great calculators of the 2nd millennium B.C., we may well commence by asking what units were in use in Babylon and Chaldea. Our knowledge of these units is based upon a number of bronze and stone weights which have been discovered, for the most part in the ruins of Nineveh. They date from the

2nd millennium B.C., and some even earlier. The inscriptions on these weights indicate that they were officially guaranteed standards deposited in the royal palace, and certify the number of units represented by each weight. The unit in which they are all measured is the *mina*, which is the only unit of this period of which there is direct and undeniable evidence, and, strangely enough, it agrees remarkably closely with the kilogramme of the metric system.[1] But, from the evidence of coins struck later, and also of the names and size of the units of weight and coins in places to which the Babylonian system is thought to have spread, a hypothetical Babylonian table of weights has been constructed. For commodities other than gold and silver the system so constructed is:

1 *talent*=60 *minas*. 1 *mina*=60 *shekels*.[2]

These weights were not used for gold and silver, the system for which is thought to have been:

1 *talent*=60 *minas*. 1 *mina*=50 *shekels*.

The *shekel*, in the series of weights used for gold, was identical with that used for goods, and weighed about 126 grains: the *mina* was $\frac{50}{60}$ of that used for goods, and weighed 6,300 grains. The units of weight for silver bore the same names as those for gold, and stood in the same relation to each other, but were not of the same size respectively as the gold units. It is supposed that this differentiation was introduced in order to secure that a convenient number of *shekels* of silver should be equal in value to a *shekel* of gold. If the relation between the values of gold and silver was about $13\frac{1}{3}$: 1 at this time, and the same weights had been used for both metals, $13\frac{1}{3}$ silver *shekels* would have been worth one gold *shekel*, a very inconvenient relation.[3] It is supposed that in Babylonia each silver unit was made equal to four-fifths of the corre-

[1] The *mina*, in the " heavy " form, weighed 1,010 grammes, and in the " light " form 505 grammes, thus presenting, in the " heavy form," a very close approximation to the modern kilogramme.

[2] *Shekel* means to count or weigh. *Shekels* of perfumes (*Exodus* xxxviii, 28) and food (*Ezekiel* iv, 10) are mentioned in the Hebrew Scriptures.

[3] As Professor Cannan points out, it is the relation between the rupee and pound sterling, where the rupee is worth 1s. 6d., but the rupee and pound are not units in the same system. One and a half gold units would have been worth twenty silver units.

PLATE XI

STANDARD WEIGHTS FROM ASSYRIA AND CRETE

1

2

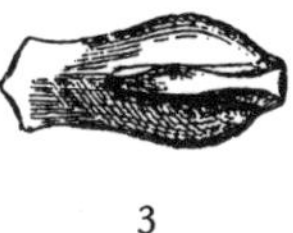

3

1 Standard weight of Porphyry from Knossos (Crete).
2 Lion shaped Assyrian weight discovered by Sir A. H. Layard at Ninevah.
3 Duck shaped weight discovered by Sir A. H. Layard at Ninevah.

[*face p.* 174

sponding gold unit. This would make the gold *shekel* worth 10 silver *shekels* of 168 grains. This unit is known as the " Babylonian " silver standard. In Phœnicia and Syria, however, it is thought that an attempt was made to establish a silver *shekel* worth one-fifteenth of the gold unit. In consequence, a unit, equal to eight-ninths of the gold unit, and weighing 112 grains, was established. This unit is known as the "Phœnician" standard. But a relation of 15 : 1 between the Phœnician silver unit and the gold unit cannot have been very convenient, and was certainly an unusual choice when either a decimal or a duodecimal relation would have been equally easy to arrange, and it is possible that the ratio between values of gold and silver was about 17: 1, and that the unit of 112 grains was the result of an effort to establish a unit worth one-twentieth of the gold unit.[1]

Side by side with these three series of weights for precious metals, there were three series of " heavy " units in which the weight of each unit was double that of the respective " light " units. According to Ridgeway[2] there is complete evidence that the " light " *shekel* system is older than the " heavy " system. There is no very satisfactory explanation of this curious duplication of standards. If the " heavy " *talent* was originally based on the weight that could be lifted by a man in both hands, the " light " unit may be traced to the weight a man can lift in one hand. Or if these early units can be traced to translations of the old ox unit of value into gold, the " heavy " gold *shekel* " may be due to the fact that among certain people, especially those who dwelt, after the fashion of the Sidonians, quiet and full of riches, and who had passed from the pastoral life into the settled agricultural stage, the yoke or pair of oxen would readily be regarded as the unit, instead of the single ox of primitive days. The fact that a ' zeugos ' or yoke of oxen was taken as the unit of assessment by Solon for the third of the Athenian classes lends some support to this view."[3] Or it is possible that the " light " series was peculiar to the Babylonian, and the " heavy " to the Assyrian Empire; or that when the Aramaic peoples began to

[1] $\frac{130 \times 17}{20} = 110{\cdot}5$. Ridgeway (286) suggests large imports of silver from Cilicia and Spain as the probable cause of the low value of silver.

[2] *Op. cit.*, 255.

[3] Ridgeway, 249.

weigh commodities of less value than gold, such as silver, gums, and spices, they felt the need for a larger unit, and were then led to adopt the double series.[1]

The origin of the various Babylonian weights is almost entirely unknown. It has been suggested that the basic unit was scientifically arrived at by the Chaldean scientists in the 3rd millennium B.C., by calculating the weight of a volume of water, based on a unit of length equal to the apparent diameter of the sun.[2] But this and the above explanations of the relation between the various units are pure speculation. Nevertheless, it will be convenient to refer to the "Babylonian" and the "Phœnician" *shekels* without implying that these names carry any reference to the origin of the respective units.

[1] Among the weights found, there was also a series parallel to each of those for gold and silver, but raised above the normal, usually by $\frac{1}{36}$, but sometimes by as much as a twenty-fourth, a twentieth, or a twelfth. It has been supposed that this raising of weights was a means of taxation, metal received by the King being weighed by the raised units, and the excess metal received representing the tax. On this assumption, these series of weights have been called "royal" units. It is notable that such an arrangement obtained in this country from very early times until 1526. Gold and silver were taken in at the mint in troy pounds of 5,760 troy ounces. When, however, coins were issued to the person bringing the metal, these were weighed against a tower pound of only 5,400 troy ounces, or 93·75 per cent. of the troy pound. In this way the King gained, in addition to the prescribed seigniorage charge, 6·25 per cent. of every deposit of gold or silver. The Tower pound was divided into ounces, pennyweights, and grains in the same way as the troy pound.

Professor Gardner (124) suggests that if the *talent* was originally the amount a man could lift, the royal *talent* was the weight the King could lift. It may have been the weight he was reputed to be able to lift, but it would then have a most precarious basis for a standard.

The raising of the "Babylonian" units in this way sometimes brings them into line with units subsequently used in other parts of the ancient world—for example, the heavy gold *mina* raised by $\frac{1}{36}$ gives a *mina* of 6,500 grains ($\frac{1}{50}$ of which gives the "Eubœan" unit). The "Babylonian" silver unit raised by $\frac{1}{36}$ gives a unit of 173 grains (Persian silver *stater*). The "Babylonian" silver unit raised by $\frac{1}{24}$ gives a unit of 175 grains (10 Roman *scripulæ* of 17·5 grains) (Head, XXXVIII). But there is nothing to explain why the royal rather than the normal units should have been borrowed: it is very easy to build too much on the coincidence of weight units. Moreover, the rate by which the units were varied is quite arbitrary. It would be possible to explain any unit in this way.

[2] Hultsch, *Metrologie*, p. 393.

2. *Egyptian Weight Standards.*

The peoples of Egypt, the other great empire of the 2nd millennium B.C., show a striking similarity to the Babylonians in the attention which they gave to astronomy and to associated problems of measurement. A great number of weights, both inscribed and uninscribed, have also been brought to light in Egypt, and from these a good deal is known of the early weight systems of the country. The commonest system used for gold, silver, and copper was:

1 *deben* (*uten*)=10 *kedets* (*kats*).
(1 *kedet* weighed about 136-156 grains.)

The wideness of the range of the size of the *kedet*[1] suggested to Professor Flinders Petrie[2] that there were two standards. One may have been adjusted for use for weighing some particular commodity in the same way as the *shekel* is supposed to have been adjusted in Babylon for weighing silver.[3] The *kedet* unit cannot be identified with the " Babylonian " gold *shekel* of 130 grains, although it shows some approach to it. But the *kedet* is not the oldest Egyptian unit: it is not known to be older than the 2nd millennium B.C. A very much older standard is represented by a weight which was found in the tomb of a king of the first dynasty (about the 5th millennium B.C.). This unit was in common use in the middle of the 3rd millennium B.C. for gold, and ranged from 188 to 215 grains. At about the same time there were also in use weights based on the " Babylonian " *mina*, some of them being marked to denote the number of the gold units above referred to, which are contained in the " Babylonian " unit, showing that both standards were in use. These " Babylonian " weights indicate a *shekel* of 117 to 130 grains. In addition to this variety of units the " Phœnician " standard seems also to have been

[1] Two weights found at Heliopolis of about the 17th century B.C., one inscribed 5 *kedets* and one inscribed ½ (*deben*), 5 (*kedets*) give a *kedet* of about 140 grains (Seltman, 120). Horapollo (*cit.* Ridgeway, 129) says that the *monad*, which the Egyptians held to be the basis of all numeration, was equal to 2 *drachms* (or 135 grains).

[2] *Naukratis*, 75; *cit.* Ridgeway, 241.

[3] McLean (*Num. Chron.*, 1912, 337) considers that the *deben* was a unit of value, and not an absolute weight, and that its weight differed with the precious material of which it was manufactured. In the Harris Papyrus *deben* of gold, silver and electrum are added together.

used. An inscribed basalt weight on this basis has been found, which appears to date from the end of the 4th millennium B.C. This and other specimens reveal the existence of a *shekel* of 208 to 231 grains.

The origin of the units in Egypt itself has naturally attracted speculation, and it has been suggested that weight units were there physically determined by some relation to the standard of length calculated from the dimensions of the pyramids, possibly by weighing a volume of Nile water determined in this way.[1] If this was so, they must then have been propagated eastward and northward to Asia Minor and Babylon. The weights found in Egypt suggest that at least the Babylonian gold unit and the Phœnician silver unit may have originated there.

3. *Minoan and Greek Weight Standards.*

The Minoan peoples of the Ægean had no peculiar system of weights. As might be expected of island people trading with Egypt, Asia Minor, and continental Greece, they used most of the weight units found in those areas. There are traces of the Babylonian gold standard,[2] the "Phœnician" *shekel*,[3] the Egyptian unit,[4] and a unit later known in continental Greece

[1] *Vide* Ridgeway, p. 241.

[2] A truncated pyramid of red limestone found at Knossos, and believed to have been a standard weight, weighed 440,440 grains. If this was a *talent*, then on the Babylonian basis of 3,000 *shekels* to the *talent*, the *shekel* weighed 122 grains—or 4 grains below the Babylonian *shekel*. But bronze ingots found at Hagia, Triada (Crete) weigh about 454,300 grains, and on the Babylonian basis of 3,600 *shekels* to the *talent* of bronze, the *shekel* was equal to the Babylonian *shekel* (Glotz, 194-95).

[3] Glotz, *Ægean Civilization*, 191. A monetiform silver lump found in the Palace of Knossos weighed 56·4 grains, or half a "Phœnician" *shekel* (Evans, *Corolla Numismatica*, 366).

[4] Ten hæmatite "olive" weights from Enkomi (Cyprus) suggest weights of two, three, five, and ten times a unit of 142·6 grains (Glotz, 193)—or the Egyptian *kedet*. In Cyprus "dumps" of gold dating from the 12th century B.C. have been found at Old Salamis. They probably bore no marks, and weigh respectively 132·9, 72·9, and 72·2 grains. The first suggests the Babylonian gold *shekel*, but the two smaller pieces are regarded by Evans (*Corolla Numismatica*, 366) as half-*kedet* pieces, and, therefore, based on the Egyptian standard of the time. Again, at Enkomi in Cyprus, a gold bar has been found weighing 1,113 grains, or 8 *kedets* of 139·125 grains, and twenty-two pieces of gold found in a "sub-Mycenæan" tomb at Amthaus, also in Cyprus, have an average weight of 72 grains, or half a *kedet* (Evans, 360). The pieces found indicate a unit varying from 139·125 to 144 grains (p. 362).

as the " Æginetan " unit.[1] Information as to the smaller units is based, for the most part, upon discoveries of pieces of gold and silver, while the larger units are evidenced either by pieces of stone believed to have been weights or by ingots of bronze. Bronze was apparently weighed in large units related to the Babylonian *shekel*, the Egyptian *kedet* unit, and the unit later famous as the " Æginetan."[2]

During the 2nd millennium B.C. trading relations between Greece and Egypt were close, communication being at this period always by way of Crete. In consequence, it would not be surprising if finds at Mycenæ revealed units similar to those of the Minoans.[3] Although the rings and pieces of gold found in Greece reveal so considerable a variety of weights that it is difficult to trace Egyptian units with certainty, a unit approaching the *kedet* is suggested by the results of excavation at Mycenæ.[4] Again, at Ægina, a unit approaching 135 grains was used for gold in Mycenæan times.[5] The very rough correspondence between Mycenæan and Egyptian units is not necessarily evidence of borrowing from Crete or Egypt, or even from abroad at all. It is possible that this Greek unit was identical with the *talent* of gold used in Homeric times. The unit may have originated locally in the ox unit of value,[6] or in the *talent* of copper which owed its importance to the

1 The Egyptian gold unit of about 188 to 215 grains probably travelled to Palestine, Cyprus, and Crete in the form of hæmatite " olive " weights. A weight found at Knossos weighs 194 grains, or practically the same as the unit later famous as the " Æginetan " (Glotz, 193). This gold unit was apparently used for bronze, for at Cyme (Eubœa) a number of ingots of copper have been found, apparently based upon a *mina* of 9,700 grains (fiftyfold of the unit of 194 grains). A bronze ingot found at Enkomi (Cyprus) weighs 571,250 grains, or a *talent* of 60 of the above *minas* (Glotz, 193).

2 See p. 253.

3 Evans, 354.

4 A cut piece of electrum or pale gold found there weighs 350 grains, and may be a quarter of a *deben* of 1,400 grains. Rings and bars of gold were in circulation there, and the gold rings and spirals which have been found in a shaft grave of about the 17th century B.C. agree fairly well with a weight unit of about 135 grains (Seltman, 112).

5 " It is certain that gold was being weighed in the ancient ox unit in Ægina before the introduction of coinage, for the gold ornaments from a prehistoric grave in Ægina are made upon that unit " (Ridgeway, in *Companion to Greek Studies*, 451).

6 " Before the Greeks came into contact with either the Phœnicians or Lydians, they had a weight standard of their own, the Talanton of the Homeric poems, based on the cow, which was as yet only employed for the weighing of gold "(Ridgeway, 228).

copper mines of Eubœa.[1] But whatever may be their origin, it is clear that in Babylonia, Egypt, Crete, and in Argolis to the west of Attica, the units used for gold in the 2nd millennium B.C. were all within the limits of 125 to 150 grains.[2] In later times the unit of about 130 grains is found in use for measuring gold in Italy[3] and among the Gauls[4] and the Teutonic tribes,[5] but it is impossible to discover whether it was of native origin or borrowed after coinage had been introduced.

In China a *Hwan* unit of 7,800 grains was used, and is claimed to have been derived from the Babylonian *mina*,[6] largely on the ground that the Chinese civilization was a distant off-shoot from a common focus of culture in South-West Asia. But it should be noted that the *Hwan* is 25 per cent. heavier than the unit from which it is said to have been derived.

[1] See p. 206 with regard to the " Eubœan " unit.

[2] Gardner, 114.

[3] The earliest non-Hellenic peoples in Italy to issue coins were the Etruscans. In the 5th century B.C., or later, they struck gold pieces of 44, 22, and 11 grains, which look like one-third, one-sixth, and one-twelfth respectively of the unit of 130-135 grains. Professor Ridgeway suggests that these units cannot have been borrowed from the Hellenic settlements, because " the subdivisions of the unit (are) unknown to the Attic or Syracusan gold " (*op. cit.*, p. 130). But among the gold issues of Athens at the end of the 5th century B.C. are pieces of 22·5 and 11 grains (Head, 373), and at about the same time in Syracuse were issued pieces of 11 grains (Head, 175). The Etruscan issues may have been of purely local origin, but they may also have been borrowed. In Sicily and Magna Græcia, the unit for gold was fairly certainly 130 grains, but whether this was native or brought in by the Greek colonists it is impossible to prove.

[4] The Gauls commenced their issues of gold with an imitation of Philip's *stater* of 135 grains, but they did not reproduce its full weight, scarcely any of their pieces exceeding 120 grains troy. " It would appear, then, that the Gauls had already at that time a gold unit in use, somewhat lighter than the usual weight of one " ox unit," although we cannot, of course, ignore the possibility of its being the form of the Phœnician gold standard which we found above was employed by the Carthaginians both in Sicily and Africa; in other words, it may be maintained that the Gauls followed the standard on which the Phocæans of Massalia struck their *silver* coinage. As, however, the coins of Massalia were *drachms* of about 55 grains, the probability is not very high that the Gauls had no gold standard of their own for gold until they got one from the silver of Marseilles " (Ridgeway, *op. cit.*, 132).

[5] The Teutonic tribes followed the same course as the Gauls, imitating the *staters* of Philip but reducing them to 120 grains.

[6] Lacouperie, XLVI.

4. *The Origin of Ancient Weight Units.*

Before passing on to discuss the units used for the earliest coins, the origins of these early weight units call for enquiry. The idea that the mathematicians and physicists of the second or some earlier millennium, either in Babylon or Egypt, constructed a system of units of weight on the basis of certain measurements, astronomical or mundane, doubtless owes its popularity in the later part of the 19th century, to the adoption by France of the metric system, which directed attention to the possibility of a physical basis for standards. But it is unlikely that the Chaldæan and Egyptian scientists were allowed complete liberty to establish abstract units. The appearance of gold in exchanges led to the use of the balance and to the need of a series of standards of a kind until then unknown. Among peoples with a taste for scientific enquiry, the scientists of the time would naturally play a leading part in the establishment of the new units. But if they were altogether persuaded by a desire for a systematic metrology or for a physical basis for their units, they lacked all appreciation of the need of the moment. The standard weight of gold was to be the unit of value, and if the new standard was unrelated to the unit of value hitherto in use commerce must inevitably have passed through a period of confusion. It is not likely, therefore, from the economic point of view, that the current unit of value was so suddenly and absolutely "scrapped." The archæologist also finds "the theories which derive all weight standards from the scientific investigations of the Chaldæans or Egyptians . . . directly in contradiction to the facts of both ancient history and modern researches into the systems of primitive peoples."[1]

If the units of weight for precious metals had a scientific origin, the considerable uniformity in the magnitude of the units used throughout the ancient world is difficult to explain. Units scientifically calculated in a number of places would be unlikely to agree between themselves owing to the great variety of bases available to the physicist. Considerations of convenience would doubtless dictate limits to the size of the unit. It must not be so small that weights are easily lost, or so large that the unit could be used only when unusually large trans-

[1] Ridgeway, 387-88.

actions were settled. But within these limits would be scope for great variety. In fact, it has never been seriously suggested that more than one or two peoples set up standards in this way; the frequency with which certain units occur in the ancient world is explained as being due to their diffusion from one centre in either Egypt or Chaldæa, whence emigrants and travelling merchants went forth with their weights and balances, introducing their own standards in distant lands. The units in use in many localities can be related to their supposed parent only by admitting that the latter was raised or lowered. But why should peoples borrowing a unit alter it at all? And why in the direction and by the amount which was chosen? Clearly some of the borrowing peoples must have had some unit of value of their own to which the unit was to be adjusted. But when a foreign unit is adjusted it loses its identity, and when it is adjusted to a local unit it is reasonable to say that the local unit was the dominating factor and to throw over the pretence of tracing the unit to a borrowing from abroad. Many assumptions of foreign borrowing have no more substantial foundation than a desire to present a clear-cut explanation of the weights found in ancient times. Even where different areas are found using an exactly similar unit, that fact is in itself no reason for saying that one country must have borrowed from the other or that both borrowed from some common origin. It would, however, be ridiculous to deny that borrowing of units has ever taken place.

If prominence be allowed to local units it remains to explain such uniformity as exists from place to place.[1] The alternative

[1] The standards for gold in the time of the earliest records are brought together in the following table compiled by Professor Ridgeway (*op. cit.*, 132):

	Grains
Egyptian gold ring	127
Mycenæan	130–35
Homeric *talent* (or " ox unit ")	130–35
Attic gold *stater*	135
Thasos	135
Rhodes	135
Cyzicus	130
Hebrew standard	130
Persian *daric*	130
Macedonian *stater*	135
Bactrian *stater*	130–32
Indian standard 7th century A.D.	140

to a single local origin is the possibility of common elements in the economic life of the widely scattered lands, which gave rise independently in each to similar standards. The unit of value in the period before metals were in common use must have influenced the choice of the weight standard, and if it is found that throughout the areas concerned a common unit of value was already in use in premonetary times, this would explain why similar units were evolved independently in different countries.

5. *The Ox Unit of Value as the Basis of Early Weight Units.*

Professor Ridgeway[1] has attempted to prove that the ox was the common unit in premonetary times, and that this provides the foundation for all subsequent units of value. He summarizes his theory in these words:

> "In the regions of Asia, Europe, and Africa, where the system of weight standards which has given birth to all the systems of modern Europe had its origin, the cow was universally the chief unit of barter. Furthermore, gold was distributed with great impartiality over the same area, and known and employed for purposes of decoration from an early period by the various races which inhabited it. . . . Practically all over that area there was but one unit for gold, and that unit was the same weight as the Homeric *talanton*. . . . Gold was the first object for which mankind employed the art of weighing . . . and over the area in question there was strong evidence to show that from India to the shores of the Atlantic the cow originally had the same value as the universally distributed gold unit. From this we drew the conclusion that the gold unit, which was certainly later in date than the employment of the cow as a unit of value, was based on the latter."[2]

On theoretical grounds this hypothesis that the earliest monetary standards were the result in each locality of the valuation of the ox in gold is attractive; it endorses the theories usually put forward by economists that money arose out of the attainment by some commodity of a position of pre-eminence in the premonetary era. The ox would be one of

---

	Grains
Phœnician gold unit (double)	260
Carthaginian	120
Sicily and Lower Italy	130–35
Etruscan	130–35
Gaulish unit	120
German	120

[1] *The Origin of Coin and Weight Standards* (Cambridge, 1892).
[2] Ridgeway, p. 387.

the most valued and also the most easily transported goods of early nomadic as well as later agricultural peoples, and would naturally become suitable as a unit of value, at least for larger and more important transactions. When the precious metals were adopted, the unit of value continued unchanged, but was translated into gold, just as when countries abandon silver and adopt gold as a monetary standard they translate the unit of value from silver into gold.

The evidence for the widespread use of the ox unit of value has already been presented.[1] If gold came into use before the ox, units of weight for measuring it must have been invented at a time when there was no inducement to invent a unit equal in value to the ox. But although it is not possible to prove that the ox unit everywhere preceded the gold unit,[2] there is a strong probability that man was acquainted with the ox long before he ever collected gold from the bed of any stream.[3] Presuming this to have been the order of events, Professor Ridgeway endeavoured to show that gold was the first of the metals to be used in exchange and the first to be weighed. We have already seen that, of the metals, man first became acquainted with gold and copper. Silver, not being found pure, and being more difficult to work, became important much later. As between gold and copper gold is most universally found native, and is most likely to attract the eye and to become important in exchange throughout the area covered by the ox unit from the earliest times.

[1] P. 6 *sqq.*

[2] Ridgeway thinks that of the ox unit and the *talent* referred to in the Homeric poems, the ox unit is the older, because " it represents the most primitive form of exchange, the barter of one article for another before the use of precious metals as a medium of currency " (p. 2). Further, while all values are mentioned in oxen, the *talent* is only mentioned in relation to gold " (for we never find any mention of a *talent* of silver) and we never find the value of any other article expressed in *talents* " (p. 3). The first of these arguments is weak. If we have to prove that gold came into use after cattle it cannot be done by simply stating what it is required to prove—viz., that the latter is the most primitive form of exchange. The second argument is more satisfying. In Italy fines were expressed in oxen and sheep as late as the middle of the 5th century B.C., and were probably commuted into money a quarter of a century later.

[3] " When primeval man first stood on the plains of Europe and Asia vast herds of cattle met his eye on every side. The process of domestication was long and slow, but yet in all the ancient refuse heaps of Scandinavia and Germany, whilst the remains of the ox are found in plenty, there is yet no trace of gold " (p. 52).

There is plenty of evidence of the widespread use of gold over almost the whole of the world in ancient times.[1] But it is not so certain that gold was everywhere the first metal to be

[1] In the Far East the literary evidence of the *Rig Veda* and the legends handed down by historians " show that well back in the 2nd millennium B.C. the gold deposits of Thibet were known and worked. Silver is as yet unknown to the people of the *Rig Veda*. Again, in the region of the Altai and Oural Mountains, the tale of the 'Arimaspian pursued by a griffin' pointed to a great antiquity for gold-mining in this district; the barbarous Massagetæ, who occupied the modern Mongolia and Sangaria, were rich in gold, and to the west the Scythians, who used neither silver nor copper, had abundant store of gold. These tribes stretched right across Russia, until they touched on the west the Getæ and the other tribes of the great Thracian stock. Gold must early have been known throughout all Thrace. Greek tradition and history unite in demonstrating the great antiquity of the first Phœnician gold-seeking in Thasos and on the mainland. The evidence in Greece itself puts it beyond doubt that gold was in use 1500 years B.C. The Balkan Peninsula was occupied on the north-west by Illyrian tribes, some of whom, like the Dardani, dwelt interspersed among the Thracian clans. The Illyrians inhabited all the northern end of the Adriatic, and originally much of the east side of all Italy, although, under the pressure of the Umbrians and Kelts, they had been almost completely crushed out of the Italian Peninsula, only maintaining themselves in the extreme south-east, where the Messapians remained independent of both Italian and Greek alike. The Keltic tribes were their neighbours in Noricum, where they had succeeded the ancient Rhætian stock, the survivors of which, like the Salassi, had managed to maintain themselves in the fastnesses of the Alps. . . . These Rhætians must long have known the art of working gold, for they had devised elaborate pieces of engineering work for the purpose of developing their gold-fields. . . . Added to this . . . gold, as an ornament, seems to have been used by the inhabitants of the Swiss lake dwellings in the Neolithic Age. The Kelts must have been in contact with this people before they ever invaded Italy: again, in Spain, we found every token of great antiquity in the working of gold and silver. Again, before they invaded Italy, the Kelts, must have been long in contact with the Iberians of what in later days was Aquitania, for the Keltic conquest of Northern Spain can hardly be placed later than the 5th century B.C., and it is most probable that the conquest only took place after long and stubborn struggles. The Kelts too, in Southern Gaul must have come in contact with the Ligyes (or Ligurians), whose territory at one time extended from the Iberus (Ebro) along the coast of the Mediterranean to the frontiers of Etruria. The Ligurians had been in touch with the Iberians on their western border; in fact, the two races had blended to a considerable degree, and since they had also had communication with the Etruscans, Phœnicians, and Greeks (with the last from at least 600 B.C., when Massilia was founded in their country), it is impossible to suppose that this people could have remained ignorant of the use of gold. The Kelts thus, at every point along their southern front as they advanced, must have been for centuries in full knowledge of gold before they ever entered Rome. Add to this the fact that when they entered Italy they appear to have brought nothing but their gold ornaments and their cattle, and that in Gaul it had been the habit to dedicate great piles of the precious metal in the sacred precincts of their divinities " (Ridgeway, *op. cit.*, 102).

weighed.[1] The literary remains of the Greeks[2] and Latins[3] suggest that in the early stages of society wool was weighed as well as the metals.[4] The earliest Egyptian weights are so small that they must have been used for some precious commodity, and they were probably used only for the metals. The *Rig Veda* goes back to a much earlier date than any of the above records, and the only reference to weighing associates it with gold. If this is to be explained by the fact that these people were yet unacquainted with silver or bronze, it suggests that gold was there the first commodity put in the balance.

On general grounds Professor Ridgeway argued that weighing would everywhere be first adopted for the most valuable commodities, and would gradually be extended to the more bulky and less valuable, but it does not follow from this that gold would first be weighed. In the first place it is not certain that weighing commenced with the one most valuable commodity, and not two or three. In the second, gold was not always the most valuable commodity. In Egypt and other parts of the ancient world, silver is known to have been more valuable than gold.[5] In fact, Professor Ridgeway says[6] that " it is almost certain that in all countries at one stage silver must have been of higher value than gold." If weighing was adopted during that period, and applied to the most valuable metal, silver units would be the oldest, and we should

[1] If it is suggested that the art of weighing is not likely to have evolved except in one of the centres where civilization had reached a high stage of development, Ridgeway replies with vigour that the Incas had discovered that art, and it is, therefore, " possible for the human race to invent a system of weighing before it has made any advance in letters or science. Hence it is logical that the civilized races in Asia and Europe could have discovered a means of weighing gold long before the Chaldæan sages made a single step in their astronomical discoveries, or a single symbol of the cuneiform syllabary had as yet been impressed on brick or tablet " (Ridgeway, 194).

[2] In the Homeric poems measurement by weight is used only for gold and wool. Thus " the Greeks were using gold by weight when as yet neither silver, copper, nor iron was sold or appraised by that process " (Ridgeway, 121).

[3] There is little direct information with regard to Rome: wool was weighed out to slaves, but apart from this probably " the scales were used for none but precious articles, such as copper, silver, and gold " (Ridgeway, 121).

[4] The evidence of the Old Testament suggests that weighing was confined by the Hebrews to silver, gold, and spices. It is possible, however, that Absalom weighed his hair in *shekels* (2 *Samuel* xiv, 26), because wool was so weighed (See Ridgeway, 120).

[5] Cp. Ridgeway, p. 146.

[6] *Op. cit.*, 146.

seek the origin of weight standards in the basis upon which they were established. But copper or bronze was more useful in meeting the more fundamental needs of life; it was known in very early times, and must have taken a very important place in exchange. Professor Ridgeway himself remarks that "copper is found native in various countries—Hungary, Saxony, Sweden, Norway, Spain, and Cornwall—" and "it is, of course, quite possible that in a region where gold is not native and copper is, the latter may have been the first metal known to the aboriginal inhabitants."[1] In such areas copper was probably the first metal used in exchange, either by measurement of size or by weight. Bronze is known also to have been a very ancient medium of exchange in Greece, where it may be older than any gold unit. It is possible[2] that the earliest bronze unit was the result of the translation of the ox unit into bronze. The large pieces of bronze, in the shape of a stretched hide already referred to, suggest direct translation of an ox or hide unit of value, and their size, some 2½ feet in length, renders this not improbable. Again, in the Peloponnese at a later date, iron bars defined by size were used as a unit of value. They were probably not based on any ox unit of value. The bronze bars of Italy, Sicily, and Greece represent also a metallic medium of great age and long-standing influence on early exchange. It is possible, therefore, that in a number of communities the earliest metallic units of value were based not upon gold, but upon bronze or iron. Moreover, standards in these metals may have been set up before any metal was weighed: bronze standards could be defined by size. The standards used for these metals may or may not have been based upon the value of the ox, and when gold came to be weighed the gold unit may have been established to equal the existing metal unit on either a weight or a value basis. The assumption that when gold was first weighed it would be equated to earlier cattle units is, therefore, invalid, as there may have intervened a stage in which

[1] *Op. cit.*, 58.

[2] It is equally possible that the first bronze unit was arrived at on some other basis. Seltman, for example, suggests (*op. cit.*, 122) that the Ionian Greeks evolved a *talent* unit for weighing copper. During the 8th century B.C., as a result of Asiatic influences, this was divided into *minas* and *shekels* producing the unit of 130 grains. This weight unit for copper was then used for silver and (gold), and fresh units of value were thus established.

the baser metals supplied a unit defined by size. And, secondly, when a gold unit supervened, it cannot be said to have been necessarily based on the cattle unit even at second hand through the bronze unit. The first bronze unit was not everywhere based upon the ox, and the gold unit was not necessarily made equal in value to the bronze unit. It may have been related to it in size.

But if we assume that the ox unit of value was in general use before the metals and that, directly or indirectly, the gold unit subsequently set up was based upon the ox in order to maintain continuity in the unit of value, we should expect to find that local weight standards for gold would vary only so much as could be accounted for by local variations in the values of both the ox and gold. Further, we should hope to find some indication in each district that the ox was worth one of the weight units of gold.

As to the uniformity of weight standards used in widely different areas, Ridgeway infers from the general distribution of both cattle and gold over the area concerned the conclusion: " That the ox, which we have evidence to show was the chief unit of value in all these countries, had the same value throughout, and in like manner that gold would have the same value over almost all the area in which we have shown it was so impartially apportioned out by nature."[1] Only proof of free commercial intercourse would justify the assumption of such uniformity, and he gives considerable evidence[2] of a number of well-worn trade routes in remote times from the extreme west of Europe to Northern India, China, and the Pacific shore. Since this evidence was published, belief in far-flung commercial relations and communication in ancient times has increased, and the probability of uniformity of value has thus been enhanced. But it must be remembered that evidence of this kind can equally be claimed in support of the theory that the units of weight were themselves disseminated.

Direct evidence that the ox was worth about 130 grains of gold is naturally very difficult to find.[3] In Greece, in Homeric times, the *talent* of gold and the ox unit were contemporary units, and there must have been a value relation between them. Professor Ridgeway endeavours to prove

[1] *Op. cit.*, 114. [2] *Op. cit.*, Chap. IV.

[3] In 1914 gold was worth about $\frac{1}{13}$, and in 1926 about $\frac{1}{22}$, as much as it was (according to this theory) in ancient times.

that they were in fact equivalent units, and that the *talent* weighed 130 grains. His evidence rests upon references to customs at the temple at Delos, and to supposed early coins bearing an ox type. But the references to temple customs are ambiguous, and the ox type coins which have been found are of silver and not gold, and while they may support the idea that the ox was an early unit of value, do not assist in the identification of the ox unit and the gold unit.[1] All that

[1] Ridgeway quotes (p. 5) Julius Pollux (*Onomasticon*, IX, 60), who says, in reference to a date about 490 B.C., that at Delos " when the Deleans have their sacred festival, they say that the herald makes a proclamation, whenever a gift is given by anyone, that so many oxen will be given by him, and that for each ox two Attic *drachms* are offered." Thus the ancient ox unit probably lingered on in the conservative regulations of the temple. This passage expresses the relation between old and new units, but does not state whether the new *drachms* were of silver or gold. In view of the rate at which fines expressed in cattle were commuted into coin, it is unlikely that the value of an ox ever sank so low as but two *drachms* of silver. Professor Ridgeway quotes records of an offering of a number of *talents* of frankincense at Delos in support of the suggestion that the *talents* used were gold units of 130-35 grains, and finds more direct evidence in the remark of an anonymous Alexandrian writer on metrology who says " the *talent* in Homer was equal in amount to the later *daric*. Accordingly, the gold *talent* weighs two Attic *drachms* " (*op. cit.*, p. 7). It is probable that at Delos the ox was worth 2 *drachms* (150 grains troy), and " who can doubt that at Delos was preserved an unbroken tradition from the earliest days of Hellenic settlements in the Aegean " (*op. cit.*, p. 7), and that the ox was their unit, and that it was worth about 130 grains of gold? There is also the evidence of tradition. In ancient times in Athens the two-*drachm* piece was called an ox, because it was said that it bore the representation of an ox. Although there is no evidence that any such coins were struck in Athens, " a probable solution may be found in the fact that certain coins bearing the type of an ox head, which in recent years have been assigned to Eubœa, are for the most part found in Attica." Such coins probably constituted the currency of Athens in the days before Solon. " Why the name ox was specially recollected in after years as that of the earliest currency we can well understand: the name derived from the old unit of barter would at once attach itself to the coin which bore the image of the ox, and in the course of time two traditions—one that the ancient unit was the ox, the other that the first coins current at Athens bore the symbol of an ox—would merge into one " (p. 6). But while it is true that the ox is unlikely to have been worth as little as two *drachms* of silver, the positive evidence is unsatisfactory. The coins bearing the ox type which may have been used in Athens before the time of Solon were certainly of silver. No Attic gold *diadrachm* coin was issued in Athens until the closing years of the 5th century B.C., when it cannot have been issued to represent the ox unit. Its weight was probably determined by the application to gold of the weight standards used for silver. The two Attic *drachms*, if coins, must have been silver, and if the *drachm* was merely a unit of weight the metal weighed is open to question, but it is unlikely that if units of weight were intended it would have been omitted to state what metal was weighed (*vide* Gardner, 23).

can be said, therefore, is that the Homeric Greeks, who probably used the ox unit in early times, may have translated it into a gold unit, but it is also possible that they accepted the Babylonian unit, and allowed it to replace the ox unit because of a rough approximation between the two.[1]

From Egypt comes the evidence of wall paintings, which repeatedly represent the payment of tribute by the weighing out of rings of gold and silver. Doubtless the weights employed were those in common use in Egypt for measuring gold and silver. The weights shown in the balance appear again

FIG. 4.—EGYPTIAN WALL PAINTING, SHOWING WEIGHING OF METAL RINGS AGAINST WEIGHTS OF SHAPE OF AN OX'S HEAD.
From Ridgeway's *Origin of Coins and Weights.* (*By permission of the Cambridge Press.*)

and again as " solid images of animals in stone or brass in the shape of recumbent oxen."[2] Now the shape of these early weights " indicates that in the mind of the first manufacturer of such weights there was a distant connection between the shape given to the weight and the object whose value in gold (or silver) it expressed."[3] Later the cow shape was abandoned and other animals are represented, but it may be that the origin of the shape came to be forgotten and the necessity for distinguishing different standards led to variations in the shape

[1] Cp. Gardner, 27.
[2] Brugsch, I, 386; Ridgeway, 128.
[3] Ridgeway, 243.

adopted. Examples of the rings which were weighed have been found, and are based on the unit of 130 grains in one form or the other. There is also some evidence that the ox was worth about 140 grains of silver, but Ridgeway suggests[1] that, as this is difficult to agree with other statements of the value of horses, the quotation must relate to a period towards the middle of the 2nd millennium, when gold and silver were of equal value. Later this unit was confined to gold, as a result probably of the decline in the relative value of silver. But the evidence is clearly very speculative. The identity between the value of the original which furnished the shape of the weight and the value of an equal weight of some metal is weak. There is no evidence that the rings found were those weighed against the weights found, although it is not unlikely. The auxiliary evidence as to the value of the ox is practically useless.

In Macedonia and Thrace the ox unit may have been known, for it is said that " three gold *staters* formed the Macedonian *talent*."[2] This suggests the slave unit which is thought to have been used in some places, but is no proof of the use of the ox unit.

The Hebrew scriptures provide little information as to the value of the monetary unit. Nowhere is the price of cattle given, but the price of a slave is mentioned in terms of silver and, assuming that a slave was worth three times as much as an ox (a ratio which existed in some other parts), and that gold was ten times as valuable as silver, a unit of 130 grains is obtained. But it must be admitted that there is but the most slender basis for these assumptions, although they are not unreasonable. Thc Zend-Avesta offers some evidence, not very direct,[3] that the ox was worth 12 silver *staters* of 130 grains in ancient Persia, or, assuming a ratio between the values of gold and silver of 12:1 (a ratio quite common in the ancient world), 130 grains of gold.

The most direct evidence of the value of the ox in Italy is to be obtained from the law of 429 B.C., when fines previously expressed in oxen were commuted into money. The basis of this commutation was that one ox was worth one hundred *asses* of bronze. But there are great difficulties in the way

[1] P. 147. [2] Eustathius, *cit.* Ridgeway, 125.
[3] Ridgeway, 150.

of any attempt to ascertain the gold value of one hundred *asses* of bronze. One series of assumptions as to the relative values of the metals has produced a value of the ox equal to the unit of 130 grains, but another has produced a result threefold of this. Comparison with records in Sicily seems to indicate, however, that the former is the more probable result.[1] Evidence from the peoples living further north is equally speculative.[2] It has to be admitted, therefore, that the search for solid proof of the identity of the value of the gold unit and of the ox is unsuccessful.

6. *Summary.*

A survey of the explanations of the origins of the weight units applied to gold and silver in the period before coining was introduced leads in the first place to the inevitable conclusion that the units were not based on physical measurements made in one of the two great ancient empires without reference to economic conditions. At least, the size of the resulting value unit must have been considered in order to avoid a unit inconveniently large or small. It is fairly certain, too, that consideration of existing economic conditions would

[1] (*Vide* Ridgeway, p. 136.) Ridgeway rejects (360) the idea that the Roman system was based on the Babylonian *talent* known in Italy as a *centupondium*. He asserts that this latter " must be regarded as a true born Italian unit, not one borrowed from Greece or Asia." He insists, however, that even if this were true, the ox unit would still play an important part in the Italian system. In fact, " On every hypothesis . . . the cow must be retained as the chief factor in the Roman weight system." But the relation would be very indirect, for if the ox unit was about 126 grains of gold, the Babylonic silver *stater* was intended to be worth $\frac{1}{10}$ of this unit when gold was worth 13⅓ times its weight in silver. The unit had then to be multiplied by fifty to obtain the *mina*, or by 3,000 to get the *talent* to obtain the unit which was then used for bronze. The conversion from gold to silver was on a value basis, and from silver to copper on an arithmetical basis.

[2] The laws of the Alamanni, who dwelt in Rhenish Bavaria and Bohemia in later times, assessed the value of the best ox at 5 *tremisses*, or 120 grains of gold, which is exactly the unit on which are coined the gold pieces found in that area, and which are imitations of those of Philip II. Here there is direct evidence of an issue of gold coins on the ox standard (Ridgeway, p. 140). " The Keltic and Teutonic tribes were so intermixed that we may plausibly infer that the Gauls had reduced the weight of the *Philippus* to 120 grains because, owing to gold being less plentiful and cattle more abundant to the north of the Alps, from a remote time the ox unit throughout Gaul and Germany was slightly lower than along the Mediterranean " (p. 141).

proceed much further. Contemporary customs in exchange would be considered, and, in particular, the unit of value in use. Wherever the unit for gold evolved it was, therefore, based on some pre-existing unit. The suggestion that the unit evolved in one place, and was thence disseminated throughout the ancient world, raises much more difficult problems. The uniformity of the gold unit is striking, and there is no doubt that, at least in later times, units were adopted by communities from outside. On the other hand, the mere discovery of equal or approximately equal units in different places must not be taken as evidence of borrowing. In fact, the evidence for the almost universal use of the ox unit in early times is incontrovertible, and it is reasonable to look in later times for consequences of the early use of this unit. While the evolution of economic institutions did not proceed everywhere at the same rate, it is almost certain that some peoples, when gold became available, would seek to value the new metal also in oxen, and that the measure so established would be likely to gain currency. With an easily divisible medium such as gold, it is possible to establish a unit of any size, but there is no particular size which would be more useful than any other. Peoples whose exchange had settled around a value unit of the size of the ox would doubtless find it most convenient to continue using a unit of the same size. If the gold units of the ancient empires of the Nile and the Euphrates were built upon this foundation, their way throughout the world, which had also used the ox unit, would be easy, and, so far as the unit spread from these centres, its success may be thus easily explained. Preparations for its easy and rapid acceptance were already made. But it is equally likely that the translation of the old unit into the new medium was effected in a number of places, and that diffusion from one centre is an over-simplification of the course of events, obtained often by hiding difficulties in adjustments of the unit.

Although recent archæological research all points to much more frequent and widespread communication than had once been thought possible, it must be admitted that the difficulties of transport and travel were so great that journeys were few, and communication between many places was not adequate to support any large trade. But it was probably adequate to the transportation of gold, which proved attractive in very early times, and doubtless served the early travellers as a compact medium for the command of the means of life in new lands. Gold probably became widely known and used, and therefore its value tended to a very rough uniformity. Probably over land areas the ox was also fairly uniform in value. If gold was made up into pieces of standard weight the small ingots would carry with them the suggestion of the new unit. Disparity between the gold unit and the ox unit must have occurred in many areas where communication was poor and infrequent; but where the disparity was small, the change in the unit of value from the ox unit to the gold unit being correspondingly small, it is quite possible that the imported gold unit gained acceptance. When the difference was large, it is equally likely that a new gold unit was established equal in value to the local ox unit. It is at the present time impossible to produce positive proof of the assimilation of gold and ox units of value, but there is no important evidence against the suggestion, and the most reasonable explanation of these early units is that they were based upon this primitive barter unit. Further support for this suggestion is to be found in the origin of subdivisional units in many early communities, many of which are related to early units of value used concurrently with the ox.[1]

But it is quite probable that in Greece and other parts of the Mediterranean the ox unit was translated into bronze before any gold unit was established. The ox unit may have persisted side by side with the bronze unit, and have been later translated into gold, but more probably the gold unit was in some places obtained by the translation of the bronze unit into gold, a fact which may account for differences in the gold units obtained. For, if the relative values of gold, bronze and oxen changed between the time the ox unit was translated into bronze unit, and the latter into gold, the resulting unit would be different from that obtained by direct translation from ox units into gold. But early bronze units were not everywhere based on the ox unit, nor were gold units necessarily established to be of equal value to bronze units.

Early units of weight, which are the foundations upon

[1] See Chap. XI.

which the earliest currencies are built, are the end product of a series of development stretching back into prehistoric time. The standards adopted when gold ceased to be a rare metal are probably continuous as value units with those which grew up in Neolithic ages when man first began the domestication of animals.

CHAPTER IX

THE WEIGHT STANDARDS OF GREEK AND ASIATIC COINS

The monetary standards underlying the earliest issues of coins were based upon the weight units of the premonetary era. The names of early coins, such as the *shekel*, *stater*, *drachm*, *obol*, *libra*, and *litra*, are all the names of early weight units, or refer to an early custom of weighing. The most important of these units, which were discussed in the preceding chapter, were the " Babylonian " gold *shekel* of about 126 grains, the " Phœnician " silver unit of 112 grains, and the " Babylonian " silver unit of about 168 grains, all these units being known in a " heavy " or double form.

1. *Lydian Electrum Standards.*

The earliest pieces of Lydian electrum found near Sardes are based on two weight standards, some weighing 168 grains ("Babylonian" "light" silver standard), and others 215 to 220 grains (" Phœnician " " heavy " silver standard). In addition there are pieces of dark electrum, almost the colour of gold, based on a unit of 246 to 256 grains, which were probably regarded as gold, and are " heavy " " Babylonian " gold *shekels*. The Lydian pieces are based, therefore, on each of the three early Babylonian units. It has already been suggested that the reason for the adoption of these units lay in the desire to make up exports of electrum in a form which would be attractive to the markets of both East and West. But it is not fully explained why the Lydians should have chosen to make up electrum on the same weight basis as silver, although the reason probably lies in the fact that, as electrum was about ten times as valuable as silver, a convenient decimal relation was obtained by making electrum pieces equal in weight to the silver unit. So far as relations with the gold unit were concerned these two units were not inconvenient. Gold was about one-third more valuable than electrum, so the electrum piece of 168 grains was equal in value to the gold unit of just under 130 grains. The piece of 220 grains was worth one and one-third such gold units, a relation less inconvenient than would at first sight appear, as subdivision of coins into thirds and sixths was then quite usual in Asia.

2. *Gold and Silver Standards in Lydia and Persia.*

Under Crœsus, in the middle of the 6th century B.C., these electrum pieces were replaced by a currency of gold and silver, coinage on two standards of weight being retained. The reform rested on the principle that the unit of value was to be left undisturbed, for the electrum pieces were replaced by gold pieces weighing three-quarters as much as the respective electrum pieces they were to supersede and, therefore, equal in value to them. These two new gold pieces weighed respectively 126 and 168 grains, the former being the old "Babylonian" gold unit, but the latter a new unit.[1] Possibly the fact that this new gold coin weighed the same as the "Babylonian" light silver *shekel* proved an attraction by raising the hope of a single standard for gold electrum and silver. But it was a short-lived hope.[2] The weights of the silver coins issued by Crœsus were fixed with a view to establishing a decimal value relation between gold and silver pieces. The principal coins were therefore:

On the "Babylonian" Standard.

A silver piece of about 168 grains.

A gold piece of about 126 grains (worth 10 of the above silver pieces).

On the "Phœnician" Standard.

A silver piece of about 244 grains.

A gold piece of about 168 grains (worth 10 of the above silver pieces).

[1] Born of the use for electrum of a unit originally intended for silver.

[2] According to Professor Ridgeway (p. 299), "the eastern mind was still too much impressed with the necessity for cleaving fast to the original weight unit obtained from the ancient unit of barter" (*i.e.*, the *shekel* of 130 grains of gold derived from the cow unit). But the departure from the old unit of value took place much earlier when the unit of about 220 grains intended for silver was applied to electrum.

Each silver unit being one-third heavier than the corresponding gold unit, the verification of the units was simplified. The system also secured that the coins of both gold and silver should pass easily in the Ionian cities in commercial contact with Sardes, because one or other of its principal coins bore a simple value relation to the more important units in use on the Ionian coast.[1]

The overthrow of the Lydian Empire under Crœsus in the middle of the 6th century B.C. brought the Persians for the first time into contact with the problem of the issue and management of currency. Nevertheless, soon after his successful invasion, Cyrus[2] began the issue of an essentially Persian currency. The policy of the Lydian monetary administration of issuing money according to two different weight standards was abandoned. That policy, dictated by the peculiar interests of a country which was an exporter of the precious metals, had much less to recommend it in an empire so vast in extent as the Persian. Simplicity was the first essential in the currency of the empire. Of the two gold *staters* issued from the mint at Sardes, the smaller unit which travelled eastward circulated over a larger area than the heavier unit. It was, moreover, based on the weight unit which was almost universally used for measuring gold, even where gold in coined form was unknown. This smaller unit was, therefore, chosen as the basis of the new system, and the gold coin representing it became famous in antiquity as the *daric*. The unit appears, however, to have been increased about 3 per cent. The object of the increase may have been to hasten the disappearance of the Lydian issues. If so, we have here at almost the beginning of currency history the use of a device tried many times in the succeeding centuries, and doubtless no more successful at its first trial than it has been since. Or it may even have been that some currency theorist of the time was already impressed with the importance of maintaining intact the metallic content of the coin. If the unit

[1] Three gold pieces of 126 grains were worth two of the electrum *staters* of 252 grains used in Cyzicus and Phocæa, and the new gold piece of 168 grains was identical in value with the *stater* of 224 grains of electrum (the "heavy" "Phœnician" silver *shekel*) used in Miletus and Ephesus.

[2] Gardner, 88. Seltman, 126, bases the attribution of these issues to Cyrus rather than Darius half a century later, as has often been suggested, on a study of Athenian and Corinthian issues.

had been slowly losing weight, he may have urged this deflationary measure for the sake of returning to what he thought the original unit of value:[1] or, possibly, a unit based on the ox had already been evolved in the east, and the currency was now based on it. The silver coin was called a *siglos* (*shekel*), and weighed 86 grains, or two-thirds as much as the gold *daric*.[2] The relative values of gold and silver being $13\frac{1}{3}$: 1, the gold *daric* was worth twenty silver *siglos*. The principal coins of the Persian system were, therefore, the gold *daric* of 130 grains, and the silver *siglos* of 86 grains. The extreme simplicity of this system, together with the constancy of the weight and fineness of the coins, explains the then unprecedented popularity of the issue. Moreover, their ability in dealing with such marked success with problems then quite new to the world reveals the Persians as a people of financial genius.

3. *The Conflict of Standards in Asia Minor.*

These Asiatic currencies influenced the issues of the coast towns of Asia Minor. The 6th century saw the rise of tyrants in most of the Ionian cities; whether or not they had been raised or assisted by the Lydian Kings, the Persians used them as a means of control and found it convenient to insist upon their continuance.[3] This political connection of the coast towns with Asiatic tradition was often reinforced by economic influences. But trade influences were divided between the continental trade from the east, and the overseas trade from the west. The coasts of Asia Minor were, in consequence, the meeting-ground of Greek and Asiatic weight standards. The Persian silver *shekel* of about 86 grains circulated much more freely in the southern areas of Asia Minor; the Greek cities of the southern coast[4] and of Cyprus generally adopted the unit. The Persian admirals generally used the harbours of Cilicia as a base for their naval expedi-

[1] Hill thinks that the weight of both gold and silver coins was arrived at after making a deduction for the cost of minting (p. 26), but there is no evidence to support the suggestion.

[2] The *stater* of two *siglos* was the " light " " Babylonian " silver *shekel*. Hill (*Camb. Anc. Hist.*, IV, 135) says silver and gold were both raised by the same amount over the Crœsan units.

[3] *Camb. Anc. Hist.*, III, 515.

[4] Pamphilia and Cilicia (" heavy " form), Lycia (" light ").

tions,[1] and the use of the Persian *shekel* unit there is not surprising. Again in the north, on the Asiatic shores of the entrance to the Black Sea,[2] Persian domination brought with it the silver *shekel* towards the end of the 6th century B.C.[3] During the 5th century the clash between Athenian and Persian power occurred mainly in this area, but the Persian satraps were always of sufficient power on the south coast to maintain the Persian *shekel*, although in some cities it tended to shrink towards the middle of the century.[4] The Babylonian " light " silver *shekel* of 168 grains had no great vogue: it can be traced in Thasos, and thence to some of the Thracian mining tribes[5] in the second half of the 6th century B.C., if reduction of 10 to 16 per cent. be overlooked as an " adjustment " or a natural shrinkage—a very unsatisfactory line of argument.

The " heavy " " Phœnician " *shekel* is found in the Jewish silver issues of the Maccabees.[6] But in its " light " form it was more popular. The issues of the cities on the west coast of Asia Minor group themselves round the ancient Phœnician " light " *shekel* standard. The coast is divided into two almost equal parts; the cities north of Smyrna used the *stater* of 120 grains, which is generally known as the " Phocæan " standard, and is often regarded as a raised " Phœnician " *shekel*. The southern half of the coast used a *stater* of about 102 grains known as the " Milesian " standard, and regarded as a reduced form of the same " Phœnician " *shekel*. The " Phocæan " standard was used for the gold and dark electrum issues of North Asia Minor in the late 7th and early 6th century B.C., and for subsequent silver issued there.[7] The famous electrum *staters* of Cyzicus and Lampsacus of the 5th century were based on the same unit as well as the base silver issues of Phocæa, Mitylene, and Cyzicus, and the electrum *hectæ* issued under the Phocæa-Mitylene Convention. The unit was taken by colonists from Phocæa to Velia, whence it may have become the basis of the Campanian standard[8] in Italy. Examples of the raising of currency units in the ancient world are very rare, and it is unlikely that this unit

[1] Gardner, 260.
[2] *E.g.*, Abydos, Lampsacus.
[3] Gardner, 179.
[4] Gardner, 265.
[5] Gardner, 269; Hill in *Camb. Anc. Hist.*, IV, 135.
[6] Ridgeway, 284.
[7] Gardner, 176.
[8] Hill, 31; Gardner, 210-11.

is a raised " Phœnician " *shekel.* It was used in early times for dark electrum and gold issues, and only later for silver, and it is, therefore, more probably a gold unit transferred for weighing silver.[1] Why along the north coast of Asia Minor the gold unit should have been 120 grains instead of the 130 grains used elsewhere is not explainable, although reduction of units is always more probable than increase.

The " Milesian " unit was the basis of all early electrum and silver[2] issues along the southern half of the west coast,[3] and in Rhodes and Samos off the coast. The great wealth of Miletus, derived from an entrepôt trade based largely on Anatolian wool, carried the unit far. In particular, it was the prevailing unit at the Milesian settlement at Naucratis in the Nile delta in the 8th century B.C.[4] During the 6th century it spread to Abdera,[5] and thence westward into Macedonia,[6] where it was the basis of the silver issues of Alexander I.

The silver issues of the Phœnician cities of Tyre and Sidon in the 5th century B.C. reveal the light " Phœnician " unit of about 112 grains, shrinking in the middle of the 4th century towards 100 grains. The electrum issued in Carthage suggests a standard,[7] showing more approach to the " Phœnician " or " Phocæan " unit than to the Attic unit upon which issues of silver were made for Sicily.

These Asiatic silver units were almost entirely confined to Asia Minor, and found no favour in Greece. In the Mycenæan Age the people of continental Greece probably used as one, if not the only, unit of value the gold unit of about 130 grains, but there is no trace of this standard in the early currencies of the Greek world. The Hellenes, coming down from the north, seem to have made a complete end of the Mycenæan civilization.[8] " The break between Mycenæan and

[1] As in the case of the " Eubœan " unit below.

[2] Usually only for *drachms* and smaller denominations (Hill, *Camb. Anc. Hist.*, IV, 135).

[3] Gardner, 174, especially Miletus, Ephesus, and as far off as the Isle of Melos.

[4] The " Æginetan " unit fitted more easily into the local Egyptian system, but this can have mattered little, as the Egyptians used the balance. Most of the trade was in the hands of wealthy Ionian merchants (Seltman, 123).

[5] Gardner, 345.

[6] Gardner, 269, and Hill, *Camb. Anc. Hist.*, IV, 135.

[7] Pieces weighed 118, 58, and 27 grains (Gardner, 349).

[8] Gardner, 27.

historic Greece is so complete, it is so clear that a period of barbarism and poverty separates one from the other, that we may well doubt whether so civilized an institution as a weight standard would survive."[1]

4. *Greek Standards—the "Æginetan."*

When, in the 7th century B.C., the Greek cities began to issue silver coins, their standard, so far as can be judged from surviving specimens, was about 200 grains in early times, falling later to about 194 grains. This unit is commonly known as the "Æginetan," a name that can usefully be adopted without any implication as to the origin of the unit. The unit was never used for gold, which was always weighed in Greece by the Babylonian gold *shekel* of about 130 grains: it differs considerably from any of the units yet mentioned. Whence did these Northern invaders obtain their standard? Did they turn to the mature civilizations of Asia or Egypt for weight, and, therefore, coin standards, or did they build upon the crude native institutions which they found? To these questions there are no clear answers. The weight unit probably originated during the 8th century B.C., for there is a strong literary tradition that Pheidon[2] introduced the first organized system of weight standards into Peloponnese. Many attempts have been made to trace the Greek unit to a foreign source. But the evidence for its identity with the "heavy" "Phœnician,"[3] the "heavy" "Babylonian"

[1] Professor Gardner remarks, however (on p. 29), that it might not be unreasonable to suppose that the tradition of Mycenæ had some influence on the "Æginetan" system of weights.

[2] For references see Head, *Historia Numorum*, 395. This evidence has, however, been described as a "somewhat crazy foundation" on which to base "an elaborate system of weights and measures intimately related to each other" (Ridgeway, 214).

[3] The "heavy" "Phœnician" unit weighed 224 grains, and it is supposed to have come to Greece in a reduced form by way of Phœnician trading ships. But a difference of 10 per cent. requires much more adequate explanation than has yet been given. Head suggested that "it is natural to suppose that these weights, as is always the case when there is no definite standard regulated by state authority, suffered a slow and sure degradation until Pheidon's time" (*Journal of Institute of Bankers*, I, 180). But the interests of Ægina were all against a reduction of the standard. It was a small island state relying for its prosperity on overseas trade and an entrepôt traffiç. If the standard declined gradually after it had been borrowed from the Phœnicians owing merely to primitive coining technique, it could not proceed far without

silver *shekel*,[1] or the " light " " Babylonian " gold *shekel*,[2] is unsatisfactory. The close contact between Egypt and Greece by way of Crete and Cyprus during the Minoan period suggests the possibility of an Egyptian origin for the unit.[3] The improbability of its introduction during the Mycenæan Age has already been emphasized. It is possible, however, that it arrived during the 8th century B.C. through the Greek emporium at Naucratis in the Nile delta,[4] or even earlier with pirates visiting Egypt from Greece; but in view of all the evidence, this also is unlikely.[5] Moreover, after all due allowance is made for the recently emphasized importance of trade between Greece and Egypt, the principal carriers were the Phœnician ships which played a great part in seaborne trade: the idea of coining itself reached Greece, not from Egypt (which was almost the last part of the civilized ancient world to adopt it), but by way of Phœnician ships from Asia Minor, and their influence was on the side of the Asiatic units.

The alternative to a foreign origin is that a fresh standard

---

the shrinkage being noticed. Silver weighed out in Ægina must soon have been taken only at a discount by Phœnician traders. It is doubtful whether any individual had the power to force a predetermined reduction on the rest or whether the amount of currency in use was large enough to offer sufficient profit to tempt any currency manipulator. If the coins passed by weight, their prestige was probably not improved by reduction.

[1] Brandis's (*Munz-Mass-und Gewichtswesen in Vorder-Asien*, 153, *cit.* Ridgeway, 217) suggestion that it was obtained by raising by some 12 per cent. the "light" "Babylonian" silver *shekel* of 168 grains has now been generally abandoned.

[2] Dr. Hultsch suggested that the unit was based on the value of six "light" Babylonian gold *shekels*. But no reason is given for the selection of six gold *shekels* as a unit, and the ratio between the values of gold and silver of 13:1 upon which the theory is based is probably inaccurate.

[3] Gardner, 118. A hæmatite " olive " weight found at Knossos weighed about 194 grains (Glotz, 193).

[4] *Camb. Anc. Hist.*, III, 276.

[5] The Egyptians used a unit approaching the " Æginetan " in size (188-215 grains), but in Egypt it was used only for gold (Ridgeway, 218), and in Greece the " Æginetan " only for silver. The custom then was to keep units for the two metals separate, and such agreement as appears in the weight of the units must be purely accidental. Agreement can also be found between the Æginetan *mina* and the Egyptian *deben*, the latter being equal to four of the former. It has never been argued that the *mina* was constructed on this basis, although it is said that in later times this correspondence was an advantage on the side of the " Æginetan " unit at Naucratis. Greek silver was almost always taken by weight, and advantages of the kind can have been of little importance.

was established by Pheidon in Ægina. There are two possible courses in the selection of the unit. On the one hand, the Æginetans, the pedlars of the ancient world, impressed by the universality of the gold unit of 130 grains, may have attempted merely to establish a silver unit of which a round number would be worth the gold unit.[1] By this simplification of foreign exchanges, trade might be assisted. But the decision to coin silver when gold was regarded as the important trade unit, the grave doubt whether coins were at this time at all commonly taken by tale, our uncertainty as to the relative values of gold and silver in the 8th and 7th centuries B.C., and the probability that the gold value of silver was very unstable,[2] all render this hypothesis doubtful. Moreover, there is little evidence that would justify the belief that the Greek peoples regarded correspondence with the gold unit as of first-rate importance.[3] Furthermore, if the unit was borrowed directly from abroad, or based on the gold unit of value, it remains to explain how the new standard was grafted on to the native system of iron or bronze *obols*, the use of which in Peloponnese is generally accepted. If Pheidon left the number of iron bars which would exchange for a silver unit to settle itself,[4] a simple relationship could not be anticipated. But, in fact, the two systems fitted together with unexpected simplicity, giving the series:

1 *talent*	=	60 *minas*
1 *mina*	=	50 *staters* (*shekels*)
1 *stater* (192 grains)	=	2 *drachms*
1 *drachm*	=	6 *obols*

There are three possible explanations of the simplicity of the series. The Pheidonian reformer may have made no attempt to facilitate the transition from the old unit of value to the new.[5] Secondly, the two systems now joined together

[1] *Vide* Ridgeway, 221. Assuming a ratio between the values of gold and silver of 15:1, ten pieces of silver of 195 grains would be worth 130 grains of gold $\left(\frac{195 \times 10}{15} = 130\right)$. Gardner (25) regards this theory as "quite baseless."

[2] Seltman, *Athens*, 116. [3] Seltman, *loc.cit.* [4] Gardner, 119.

[5] Possibly the spits had already begun to shrink in weight, and ceased to be worth as metal the value which they represented in circulation. But it is very doubtful whether a token currency had developed so early; the control of issue necessary to prevent the depreciation of its value to that of its metallic content is unlikely to have been present.

may have sprung from a common origin.[1] And lastly, the Pheidonian system may have been a simple transformation and development of the native system. When Pheidon swept away the earlier currency of spits[2] defined by size,[3] and replaced them by metal measured by weight, the standard selected for silver may have been based on the contemporary relation between the values of silver and iron: the silver *drachm* was, in this event, a translation into a new medium of the value unit represented by a handful of the iron skewers previously current. The knowledge of the relation between the values of iron and silver necessary to confirm this origin is altogether lacking,[4] but this native origin of the standard is the only suggestion against which no heavy objections can be laid. Thus the "Æginetan" is probably a native Greek unit, and the only such unit.

This "Æginetan" unit of about 194 grains (the gold value of which was from $\frac{1}{10}$ to $\frac{1}{8}$ of the British sovereign) was adopted far and wide throughout almost the whole of the ancient world which used silver down to the early years of the 5th century B.C. It was to be found from as far north as Thessaly throughout Greece, and most of the Ægean islands[5] to Crete. Eastward it travelled to Rhodes and the coastal cities of Southern Asia Minor[6] (Caria). The latter, being cut off by high lands from the interior, felt the influence of the west more than that of Asia: by reason of their Dorian origin they tended also to turn towards the Peloponnese.[7] After the fall of Miletus the

[1] *Vide* Chap. VIII.

[2] Except in Lacedæmon. They continued as unofficial currency down to the 4th century (Seltman, *Athens*, 122).

[3] It is possible that the earlier regulation had not been very exact, and that the Pheidonian reform introduced greater fixity of standards as well as a new material.

[4] Gardner (119) suggests a ratio of 1:120 between silver and *bronze*. The bronze *obol*, worth a silver obol of 16 grains, must then have weighed 1,920 grains (20 Æginetan *drachms*), or about $\frac{1}{4}$ pound, and the *drachm* about $1\frac{1}{3}$ pounds. Seltman (120) suggests that Pheidon, in translating the iron units into silver, adopted a ratio between the value of iron and silver of 1:400. The six best specimens of *obols* found in the excavations at the Heræum weighed about 37,250 grains, which would give a silver *drachma* of 93 grains. A ratio between iron and bronze as high as 1:603 has been suggested.

[5] The "Æginetan" unit was used in the Ionic city of Teos—probably because of its connection with the Black Sea (Gardner, 170).

[6] In Asia Minor some of the early electrum *staters* approximate to the "Aeginetan" unit (*Hill, Camb. Anc. Hist.*, IV, 131).

[7] Gardner, 169.

trade of the Black Sea fell for a time into the hands of Ægina, and the unit[1] spread to the Greek settlements in the Black Sea.[2] It was used in Cilicia, in the centre of Asia Minor, and, during the 5th century B.C., in the peninsula of Zephyrium (to the west of Alexandria).[3] Such coins as have been ascribed to 7th-century Athens are based on the Æginetan unit,[4] but the issue of any pre-Solonian coins is much disputed.[5] Victorious as it was throughout the Ægean and Black Sea, it is doubtful whether the unit travelled as far west as Cyprus, where the Persian unit was supreme. Silver coins issued in Sicily,[6] weighing nearly 10 per cent. less than the usual "Æginetan" standard, have been regarded as poor relations of the unit of the Ægean. But the historical improbability that the "Æginetan" unit would find its way to Magna Græcia,[7] and traces of the influence of Corinth in the fabric of the coins,[8] suggest that the standard was based on that of Corinth, which stands out as an exception to the general use of the "Æginetan" standard. The "Æginetan" standard was the basis of the first important silver currency in the world. Independent as it probably was of all the Asiatic gold and electrum units, it spread far and wide, doubtless by reason of the great foreign trade of Ægina, whose own issues became so well known that some of the Ægean islands in the 6th century copied in their issues the type as well as the weight of those of Ægina.

5. *The "Eubœan" Standard in Greece.*

At about the same time[9] as Pheidon introduced his new weights and measures, an experiment was being carried on in the island of Eubœa that was to change completely the currency history of the Greek world. A silver unit of 130-5

[1] The fall from the "Milesian" unit of about 222 grains to the "Æginetan" of 192 may have been merely a shrinkage in the unit and not a definite change of standards, but it brought with it the change from electrum to silver and also division of the unit into two instead of three (a typically Asiatic method of division) (Gardner, 171).

[2] Especially Sinope and Panticapæum in the 6th century (Gardner, 171).

[3] Hill, *Camb. Anc. Hist.*, IV, 131.

[4] Seltman, *Athens*, 116.

[5] Gardner, 148.

[6] Zancle, Naxos, and Himera.

[7] "The earliest coins of the Chalcidean colonies are essentially different in fabric from the contemporary money of Ægina, being flat and circular, not globular or bullet shaped" (Head, L).

[8] Gardner, 212.

[9] The end of the 8th century B.C.

grains was adopted. At a time when elsewhere the new "Æginetan" silver standard was gaining ground, the unit hitherto restricted to weighing gold was in Eubœa applied to the measurement of silver. The origin of the unit in Eubœa is uncertain, but there is no lack of speculation. The island possessed rich mines of bronze, and an early native bronze currency has been suggested[1] as the basis of the new unit for silver. A *talent* unit invented for copper may have been divided as a result of contact with Asiatic systems into *minas* and *shekels* to produce the unit of 130 grains,[2] which agreed with the ancient gold unit by a pure accident. But if Asiatic influence is admitted in the division of units, it probably also affected their size, and the evidence for the early copper *talent* in Eubœa is very fragile.[3] The island of Samos,[4] off the Ionian coast, and Cyrene, on the North African coast, both issued coins on the standard of about 133 grains during the 6th century B.C., and it is possible that the Eubœans obtained the unit from Samos. The Samians were among the most important people responsible for the founding of Naucratis, and a very rough approximation between Samian units and those used in the Nile delta has formed a basis for the theory that the "Eubœan" unit was of Egyptian origin.[5] But the difference between the units is considerable, and as a unit corresponding to the Eubœan was already in use at Corinth, the evidence for the Egyptian origin is weak.[6] It is possible that the unit travelled from Asia to Eubœa and Greece by way of Samos. The fact that within the island of Eubœa the unit was adopted sometimes on the "light" and at other

[1] Lehman-Haupt, *cit.* Gardner, 124. [2] Seltman, 122.

[3] Seltman (113) suggests a ratio between bronze and gold of 1 : 3000, and states that gold ingots from Cyme in Eubœa suggest a bronze *talent* of 22,660 to 27,000 grammes.

[4] Ridgeway (223), however, claims that "the recognized Samian coins are of the 'Phœnician' standard (220 grains) in its slightly reduced state as found at Miletus."

[5] Weights, varying from 127·8 to 148·8 grains, have been found at Naucratis, but they are uninscribed and difficult to identify. At Heliopolis, one of the cities of Egypt most accessible to the Greeks, an unscribed weight indicates a *kedet* standard of about 139 grains, but there is a considerable difference between the unit of Heliopolis and those of Cyrene and Samos which are supposed to have been derived from it (Gardner, 79; Seltman, 123).

[6] *Vide* Gardner, 218-21 and 30; *Num. Chron.*, 1924, 341. "There is no evidence for connecting the Euboic-Attic with Samian electrum or Egyptian *ket*" (*kedet*) (Hill, *Camb. Anc. Hist.*, IV, 134).

times on the "heavy" standard[1] suggests an Asiatic origin. But in Asia the unit was confined to gold, and contact with the East would have also brought knowledge of the two Asiatic silver units[2] with which Phœnician traders were well acquainted. It is unlikely that, when in possession of this knowledge, the Eubœans would choose to use the gold unit for silver. But a unit similar to the "Eubœan" was in use in Corinth from the latter half of the 7th century,[3] and it is quite probable that it was obtained by the Eubœans from Corinth, probably as a result of using Corinthian coins.[4] The Eubœans, however, applied to the Corinthian *stater* the Æginetan method of division into 2 *drachms* each of six *obols*, thus Europeanizing the unit, which in Corinth had retained a very positive Asiatic feature in the division of the *stater* of 130 grains into 3 *drachms*.[5] However, all the arguments against the introduction of an Asiatic unit by way of Samos apply to its introduction by way of Corinth.

If the gold unit was locally evolved by the Greeks, and by other ancient peoples by the translation into gold of the ox unit of value,[6] it might be that this gold unit then ceased to be regarded solely as a unit of value, and became a weight unit which was used for silver. If this change occurred before the Eubœans were familiar with the Asiatic silver units, the explanation is plausible, although supporting evidence is meagre.[7] If the ratio between the market values of gold and silver produced an easy ratio between the values of equal

[1] Later, when the first coins of Chalcis and Eretria, the most famous cities of the island, were issued, they were based on this unit, and weighed from 130 to 135 grains. A number of early coins weighing about 260 to 266 grains, and hesitatingly attributed to Eretria, bear two pellets, the usual indication of a 2-*drachm* piece (Head, *Hist. Num.*, 360). The earliest coins of about 260 grains of Chalcis, on the other hand, are usually regarded as 4-*drachm* pieces.

[2] The "Babylonian" unit of 168 grains, probably best known in the interior of Asia Minor, and the "Phœnician" unit of 112 or 224 grains, used in the coast towns.

[3] Gardner, 134. Corinth alone in the Peloponnese did not adopt the "Æginetan" unit in the 6th century B.C.

[4] "The Eubœans were content—until late in the 6th century, when the first coins, certainly attributable to Chalcia and Eretria, were struck —to use the coinage of Corinth with which they were in such close relations" (Hill, *Camb. Anc. Hist.*, IV, 129).

[5] *Vide* Chap. XI.

[6] *Vide* Chap. VIII.

[7] And the Asiatic units were probably known in very early times.

weights of the two metals,[1] the use of the same unit for gold and silver would be likely to commend itself. Simplicity in units of weight would be combined with simple value relations. But the importance of simple relation to the gold standard may be, and probably is, at this distance of time, easily overemphasized. It is quite possible that no great importance was then attached to it, particularly as changes in the relative values of the precious metals made it clear that such an advantage could be but temporary. Moreover, subsequent currency history in Greece brings out, in a most striking manner, that such a simple relation between the values of gold and silver units was never regarded as important. In contrast with the policy of Asia, the two metals were struck on the same weight basis, and their relative values were left to be settled in the market.

At a very early date the new standard spread from Eubœa. The precious metals flowed steadily into the island: electrum from Lydia, silver from Chalcidice,[2] and gold from the east. By its exports of metals it sent forth, from very early times, the standard it had adopted, and which was soon known as the "Eubœan" by the Greeks of the mainland—a fact which indicates that they borrowed and did not themselves invent it. From the powerful cities of Chalcis and Eretria in the island, more colonists sailed for Magna Græcia than from almost any other cities: these colonists took with them the new silver unit. When coining commenced in Eubœa the new silver unit was the basis upon which coins were struck. Whether or not Athens coined on the "Æginetan" unit during

[1] "If the relative values of gold and silver were as 15 : 1 such a convenient and manageable relation between the values of equal weights of gold and silver was obtained. "Hence there was not the same need in Greece to devise a separate silver standard as there was in Asia, where the relation of the precious metals stood as 13:1—a fact which made simple exchange very difficult" (Ridgeway, 228). But as near as Ægina, where the relation was presumed to be the same, a separate unit was established for silver, on the assumption that in establishing the system it was desired to make ten silver units equal to one gold unit. Evidently in Ægina (and later in Central Greece) a decimal relation was preferred. Furthermore, Professor Ridgeway himself, when discussing the origin of the "Phœnician" standard (286), asks, "Why did the Phœnicians adopt so awkward a scale as the quindecimal?" If economic circumstances supplied the quindecimal system in Eubœa, there was more excuse for its maintenance; but the evidence of the "Æginetan" standard, established under circumstances similar to those in Eubœa, weakens the explanation. Quindecimal systems were not popular.

[2] Where many colonies had been settled from Chalcis (Eubœa).

the 7th century, which is doubtful, it certainly used coins based on it. At the end of the century the "Æginetan" and the "Eubœan" units met in Athens, the clash between them being perhaps one aspect of that conflict between Dorian and Ionian culture and institutions of which Athens was the centre.[1] In the reform effected by Solon in about 594 B.C., the "Eubœan" unit was accepted as the basis of the new currency. Thus across the middle of the zone using the "Æginetan" unit was placed a belt of cities using the "Eubœan" unit (Corinth, Athens, and the cities of Eubœa). At the beginning of the 6th century B.C. the standard was confined to the isles of Eubœa and Samos, and the cities of Athens, Corinth, and Cyrene.

In the course of the 6th century the "Eubœan" unit was increased in a number of cities by about 5 grains.[2] Peisistratus probably introduced the change,[3] and the suggested reasons for the step, that he aimed at enhancing the prestige of Athenian coins,[4] or that it was forced upon him owing to a similar raising of the Persian unit, will be examined later.[5] Similar increases occurred at Corinth and Eretria.[6] During the 6th century the "Eubœan" unit spread rapidly, and superseded the "Æginetan" unit in most areas. Its most notable successes were in Magna Græcia, where, owing to the dominant influence of Corinth, it was widely adopted.[7] In consequence of this Corinthian influence, the *stater* was usually divided there into three *drachms*.[8] In Sicily the same unit was probably the basis of most issues,[9] although in some cities *didrachms* of about 90 grains were made[10] instead of *tridrachms* of the "Eubœan" standard.[11] But when the Corinthians raised their unit, the cities of Magna Græcia

[1] Cp. Seltman, 122.

[2] Thus producing the Attic as distinct from the "Eubœan" unit.

[3] Seltman (62) suggests 546 B.C. as the date of the change.

[4] *Camb. Anc. Hist.*, IV, 67.

[5] Chap. XIII.

[6] Gardner, 126.

[7] Before it was raised at Athens: it was usually somewhat light—about 128 grains (Gardner, 206).

[8] *E.g.*, at Croton, Metapontum, etc.

[9] Even the Sicilian issues, thought to be "Æginetan" *staters* (*e.g.*, at Naxos, Zancle, and Himera), may be Corinthian *tetradrachms* (Hill, *Camb. Anc. Hist.*, IV, 132).

[10] *E.g.*, at Zancle, Himera, and Naxos (Gardner, 212).

[11] Towards the end of the 6th century Syracuse and a number of towns on the east coast of Sicily issued *tetradrachms* on the Athenian basis, while those on the east struck pieces equal to Attic *didrachms* or Corinthian *tridrachms* (Gardner, 214).

showed no disposition to follow their example. In fact, in Italy the unit tended to shrink rather than expand.[1] The earliest issues of gold and silver in Etruria in the 5th century B.C., or later, were probably based on the " Eubœan " unit,[2] and those of Cyrene, on the north coast of Africa, had been made on the " Eubœan " standard from at least the middle of the 6th century.[3] Much later, in the 4th century, the Carthaginians issued silver in or for Sicily on the same standard, although at the same time they were issuing gold and electrum on the " Phœnician " standard. In Macedon and Chalcidice the same unit is found. But in Asia Minor, and in fact in Asia[4] generally, it never became popular, and there are very few examples of coins based on it. Most Asiatic cities preserved their own standards, among which there was great variety, although the standards of many cities were well preserved for long periods.

In Greece and the Ægean islands, on the other hand, the Athenian unit prospered.[5] With the growth of Athenian power and commerce the unit spread rapidly. After the formation of the Delian Confederacy, early in the 5th century B.C., the enforced suspension of allied issues by Athens, and the pressure brought by Athens to give her coins wide circulation, made the silver unit of about 130 grains even better known. But towards the end of the century, when the power and influence of Athens were shaken by disaster, her repressive imperial policy was abandoned, and the peoples of the Ægean were left to use Athenian " owls " or not as they pleased.

[1] Gardner, 206.

[2] Seltman, 130; Head, 12 *sqq*. They were based on the "Eubœan" unit and tenths thereof, but it is impossible to say whether the tenths (as translations into silver of the old bronze unit) or the " Eubœan " unit (borrowed from Magna Græcia) was the real basis of the issue.

[3] Hill, *Camb. Anc. Hist.*, IV, 133.

[4] It never took root in India or in Phœnicia.

[5] The standard used in Corcyra off the west coast of Greece was probably based on the " Corinthian " standard. The *stater* weighed 180 grains. This may be simply an " Eginetan " unit in a decline (it is 6 per cent. below the usual "Æginetan" unit). Rather more probably it is a *stater* of 4 Corinthian *drachms*, although such a *tetradrachm* should weigh only 172 grains on the Corinthian basis. Nevertheless, Head (*Hist. Num.*, XLIX) and Hill (*Camb. Anc. Hist.*, IV, 132) hold this view. Professor Gardner (137) suggests that there was a conflict of standards at Corcyra, but does not explain the basis of the standard used. In the 4th century the local standard fell to 160 grains, when also the "Corinthian" unit was falling (Gardner, 376).

In Athens the standard continued unchanged until the end of autonomous issues, probably in 86 B.C., when Sulla captured the city.

6. *The "Chian" or "Rhodean" Standard.*

The isle of Chios, off the coast of Asia Minor, seems to have supplied a new standard for coins struck to replace the Athenian issues. From about 480 B.C. Chios had coined fairly continuously silver *tetradrachms*[1] of 240 grains. This gives a *stater* of 120 grains, about 8 per cent. lighter than the "Eubœan" unit, and identical with the "Phocæan" unit. The latter was originally used for dark electrum and gold on the west coast of Asia Minor, but was applied to silver in the 6th century, and was, therefore, arrived at in the same way as the "Eubœan," of which it might be regarded as a poor relation. But the considerable difference in weight has led to this Chian unit being regarded as a separate standard from the "Eubœan." During the 5th century the "Phocæan" standard of 120 grains maintained its position as a rival to the Athenian unit with great tenacity. In fact, its maintenance at Cyzicus, Phocæa, Lampsacus, and Mitylene may be due to an arrangement with Athens.[2] After the middle of the century its popularity began slowly to increase, and at the end of the century, when the power of Athens was eclipsed, and the Persians made no attempt to secure the place left vacant by the Athenian "owls," the standard of Chios began to spread[3] with great rapidity. About 400 B.C. the unit was adopted in Rhodes, and thence everywhere along the west coast of Asia Minor, and as far as Byzantium. There are also signs of the unit in Chalcidice and Macedon.[4] In the 4th century the old "Phocæan" unit, often called in this period the "Chian" or "Rhodean" unit, became the best-known standard. It is found in all the isles of the Ægean into the

[1] In the first issues these coins represented six units, but later the division into four, common in the Greek world, was introduced (Gardner, 250).

[2] At some cities it fitted fairly well into the Persian system: the "Phocæan" unit equalled two-thirds of the "reduced" Persian *siglos*.

[3] After the Chian revolt of 412 B.C. At first to Ephesus and at the entrance to the Black Sea in about 408 B.C. (Gardner, 287).

[4] Gardner (325) says Philip adopted it in a reduced form for his silver currency, but it then becomes the old "Phœnician" unit.

3rd century,[1] and most frequently around its shores, although the Æginetan[2] and Attic[3] units kept a footing in some districts.

The standards used for gold in the Greek world show much less variety than the silver units. Broadly speaking, the "Babylonian" *shekel* of about 130 grains was supreme.[4] Along the northern half of the west coast of Asia Minor the unit of 120 grains used for silver was applied also to gold: it is possible that it was merely a reduced "Babylonian" unit.

7. *The Relation between Early Greek Silver Standards and Primitive Local Barter Units.*

It is not easy to reduce the number of standards used in the Greek world to a small number. Attempts to do so call for much ingenuity in fitting the very great variety of coin weights into the simple framework of a few recognized units, and it must be admitted that the coins of many cities obdurately refuse to be fitted in. Professor Ridgeway, rebelling against the hard and fast doctrines of those who would account for all similarities in the institutions of different areas by the borrowing by one from the other, has attempted, with the assistance of the types on many early Greek coins, to show[5] that the Greek units were often merely translations into silver of an early barter unit. He contends that the coin types reveal, not only what was the staple commodity in local trade in early times, but also how much of that commodity constituted the unit of value. The types were marks of value. Aristotle had said that "the stamp was put on the coin as an indication of value,"[6] but he is as likely to have meant that the stamp was put on the coin to guarantee that it was of full weight and good quality as that it signified its purchasing power.[7] The appearance of a sprig of olive found on the coins

[1] Gardner, 433. The people of Samos issued an abundant coinage on this basis after their restoration to the isle in 322 B.C. (Gardner, 436).

[2] At the entrance on the shores of the Black Sea (Gardner, 263). The Chian unit fitted easily into the "Æginetan" system, the former unit being $\frac{5}{8}$ of the latter (Gardner, 252). ($60 = \frac{5}{8} \times 96$.)

[3] Clazomenæ. It is almost possible to judge whether cities looked to Sparta or to Athens for leadership according as they used Chian or Attic units (Gardner, 287).

[4] In 411 B.C. Thasos issued gold on the standard of 135 grains, to be followed a few years later by Athens and, at the beginning of the next century, by Rhodes. In Cyzicus the unit of 130 grains was favoured.

[5] *Op. cit.*, Chap. XII.

[6] *Politics*, 1257a, 38.

[7] Cp. Hill, 169.

of Athens from the earliest times, and the religious care bestowed on the sacred olive trees, which belonged to the state, show that the olive must have been one of the most important products of Attica. It is possible, therefore, that a measure of oil was the early barter unit which the later silver coin represented.[1] Plutarch[2] regarded the *drachm* as worth a measure (presumably of oil or corn) as well as a sheep.[3] But as Athens did not issue coins of its own until long after it had become accustomed to those of other cities, the connection between the types on its first pieces and conditions in the barter state cannot be very direct.

At Ægina the sea turtle was the constant type on the coins from the middle of the 7th to the end of the 5th century B.C., when, for a further half-century, the land tortoise was substituted. The coin may therefore have replaced an earlier tortoise-shell currency. These shells had probably been the principal article of export from Ægina in early times on account of their beauty and their usefulness for bowls. Later pottery, made in imitation of the shells, suggests their earlier use for this purpose.[4] The shield on the coins of nearly all the Bœotian towns may indicate that a shield of ox-hide had been one of the early units of value in the island. The double axe, which appears on the earliest coins of Tenedos, may have been an especial product of the island which was locally used as a medium of exchange and a unit of value.[5] The wine cup on the coins of the isle of Naxos suggests that a measure of wine was the unit of value which they replaced. The sheep or sheep's head on Phœnician issues at Salamis in Cyprus and elsewhere may indicate a sheep unit in early use. The earliest coins of Cyzicus invariably bear a representation of the tunny fish: in a town which depended on fisheries and trade rather than agriculture, the tunny may have been a staple commodity, " and singly or in certain defined numbers,

[1] Ridgeway (325) says: " It is hardly possible to doubt that the first Attic coined silver *drachm* was equated to the old barter unit of a measure (either of corn or oil)."

[2] *Solon*, Langhorne trans., p. 70.

[3] This evidence proves too much, for the unit cannot have originated from all three, the sheep, the measure of oil, and the measure of corn. If it originated in one it is unlikely that it could be used indiscriminately for any one of the three, for the values of the three must have changed frequently.

[4] Ridgeway, 328.

[5] Ridgeway, 318.

as by the score, or hundred, and the like, would naturally form a chief monetary unit."[1] Here the definition of quantity of the commodity is not so directly conveyed by the type on the coin. Ridgeway, by implication, admits that the coin probably was not the translation into electrum of the unit of value based on one tunny. But he points out that Olbia, a Milesian colony on the northern coast of the Black Sea, issued bronze coins shaped like a tunny. The small pieces bear an inscription, which has been read as an abbreviation of the word "tunny," while the inscription on the larger ones has been read as a basket, presumably a defined multiple of the smaller unit.[2] The cuttle fish on the coins of Croton in Southern Italy and Eretria may possibly be explained in the same way.[3] The early Cretan coins of the 5th and 4th centuries bear traces of the tripod and the bowl, which are believed to have been used in early times as a unit of value.[4]

Although there is almost complete lack of evidence that the subjects of types were ever used as a local unit of value,[5] that lack of support is not ground for rejection. But in cities where the coins developed in this way out of earlier units we should expect the representative type to occur, at least in the earliest issues, only on the denomination which superseded the earlier commodity standard. The coins of the cities which have been called in evidence hardly ever bear this out. On the first coins of Thebes the famous Bœotian shield appears on pieces of 2, 1, $\frac{1}{2}$, $\frac{1}{6}$, and $\frac{1}{24}$ of the *drachm*, while a half-shield appears on the $\frac{1}{12}$ *drachm* (half *obol*). In fact, throughout Bœotia, from the earliest issue of coins in the first half of the 6th century B.C., there is no city which confined the shield type to one denomination. At Ægina[6] the sea-tortoise appears from the earliest times on pieces of different denomination, and the same is true of the double axe at Tenedos,[7] the wine cup in the isle of Naxos,[8] and the ram at Salamis.[9] At Lycia[10] the boar, or the fore-part of a boar, is the earliest type, but the same types appear on coins of different denomina-

1 Ridgeway, 317. 2 *Ibid.* 3 Ridgeway, 327.
4 Gardner, 392; Ridgeway, 314.
5 Crete is probably the only exception: there is evidence that in Crete the three-legged pot was used as a unit of value, and it also appeared on the coins.
6 Head, 396. 7 Head, 550. 8 Head, 448.
9 Head, 742. 10 Head, 688.

tion. It is admitted that the Cyzicene electrum *staters* bearing the tunny cannot have been identical with a tunny unit of value, and the evidence of the Athenian types is of no great assistance owing to the lateness of the first issues. There is little doubt, therefore, that these types do not indicate the value of the coins in barter units. Professor Ridgeway himself relaxes the theory when he discusses the origin of the coins of Ægina and Bœotia, for he says that " when silver money came to be struck it was natural that the barter unit which came nearest in value to the silver *didrachm* would be equated to it, and the piece of silver would accordingly be termed *shield* or *tortoise* . . . and in due course the corresponding device would be impressed on the silver coinage."[1] This is very different from the suggestion that the silver unit was a translation into silver of the barter unit. In fact, Professor Ridgeway has already suggested that the " Æginetan " and " Eubœan " units were established as convenient subdivisions of the gold or ox unit of value. The smaller unit cannot have originated from both an older barter unit and a desire to set up an easy submultiple of the gold unit, unless it can be proved that the relation between the value of the ox and the smaller barter unit suggested the number of units into which the gold unit was to be subdivided. But this is not a very credible theory, because it is unlikely that the tortoise shell, the ox-hide shield, the measure of wine, and other local units, when translated into silver, would produce, not only units bearing a simple value relation to the gold unit, but also units of almost equal size in a number of cities. This is admitted by implication when it is suggested that the barter unit " which came nearest in value " gave its name to the new coin. It seems that the old units were not translated into the new medium, but were adjusted to it, which means that they ceased to exist except possibly in name.

8. *The Standards of Macedon, Egypt, and Carthage.*

Thrace and Macedon were the meeting-places of a number of European and Asiatic standards,[2] and, in consequence, there was confusion of units both from time to time and place to place. The earliest silver standard was the unit of about

[1] Ridgeway, 332.

[2] By way of Abdera and Thasos.

220 grains adopted, probably, in the time of Alexander I. The usual alternative explanations can be offered, based, on the one hand, on the borrowing of the unit from abroad,[1] and, on the other, on an attempt to secure simple exchange relations with the gold unit.[2] During the closing years of the fifth and the opening years of the following century the unit in Macedon and Abdera made way for a standard of 168-173 grains,[3] which again fell in the early part of the 4th century to 140-152 grains. When Philip opened the hitherto unworked mines at Philippi, and established a coinage of both gold and silver, the standard for gold was the " Babylonian " *shekel* raised to 133-5 grains, which had been used in Athens half a century earlier. For his silver coins Philip returned to the " Phœnician " unit, although probably in its " light " form based upon a *drachm* of about 56 grains.[4] Twenty-four silver pieces of this weight were equal in value to one gold unit. But the continued outpouring from the new mines caused a fall in the silver value of gold that threatened the existence of the silver pieces, and Alexander abolished them and coined silver as well as gold on the unit of 133-5 grains. The unit adopted in Macedon was carried far and wide throughout the vast empire, from Macedonia to the Punjab.[5]

These issues of Alexander the Great were the first coins which obtained any general circulation in Egypt. But, in the early years of the 3rd century, they gave way there to the " light " " Phœnician " standard, and gold coins were

[1] From Miletus and the Ionian cities by way of Abdera, possibly at first in the form of foreign coins that obtained local popularity.

[2] The Bisaltian silver mines may have produced such plentiful supplies of silver before the Persian invasion that the relative values of silver and gold fell to about 17 : 1. The piece of 220 grains of silver would then be worth one-tenth of the gold unit of 130 grains.

[3] Possibly obtained from the Isle of Thasos, a rich source of the precious metals, and, particularly, gold. The unit at times approaches the "Babylonian" silver unit of 168 grains (Gardner, 186 and 269).

[4] Both his gold and silver units were already in use in Chalcidice, and they may have been borrowed from there (possibly from Olynthus) (Gardner, 422).

[5] After the decline of Macedonian power the Kings of Bactria made their own issues of gold (Ridgeway, 126). Whatever may have been Alexander's reasons for rejecting the standard of the *daric* in favour of the Attic standard, they did not appeal to the peoples of Bactria. As soon as occasion offered, they abandoned the standard of 135 grains, and issued pieces of 130 grains, either because this was the ox unit to which they were accustomed (Ridgeway, 349), or possibly merely to profit by the reduction of the unit.

issued, weighing about 110 grains—a very unusual gold standard. In about 270 B.C. a monetary reorganization resulted in the adoption of a similar standard for silver. The reasons for this change, directly counter to the trend elsewhere, are not at all clear. The "Eubœan" system did not perhaps fit in with the local units either for gold and silver[1] or for copper. We do not possess adequate knowledge of the use and popularity of the respective units in use in this period to resolve the problem.[2] Between 246 and 221 B.C. coins of both gold and silver were again issued on the Athenian standard, possibly called for by the war in Asia Minor.

The standards of the Carthaginian coins were all borrowed. During the occupation of Sicily in the 4th century B.C., coins were made for circulation there on a gold unit of 118 grains, probably that used by Phocæa and the cities of the northern coastal area in Asia Minor. Silver was issued, however, on the basis of the Athenian standard then in use in Sicily. When coins were issued in Carthage itself, during the second half of the 4th century B.C., electrum and gold were again based on the "Phocæan" unit. When silver coins were issued a hundred years later the same unit was used.[3] Discoveries at the end of the last century revealed large bronze coins similar to those used in Egypt, but weighing about 1,850 grains.[4] Although there were active commercial relations between them, Carthage and Egypt appear not to have used the same weight standard for these heavy copper coins.[5]

[1] The most important unit for gold and silver was the *kedet,* which shows some affinity to the "Eubœan" unit; but, on the other hand, the "Phœnician" unit was also of very great antiquity in Egypt.

[2] Head, 846. During the 3rd century large copper coins, of about two inches diameter and weighing 1,400 to 1,500 grains (20 Attic *drachms*), were in circulation. These coins must have been very inconvenient to handle, but people accustomed to dealing with bronze ingots may have been satisfied with them. The largest are made up on the *tabnou* standard, a unit used for copper in Pharaonic times (Babelon, 385), but one which at the then probable silver price of copper may have been nearer in value to one-tenth of the "Phœnician" unit than the tenth of the "Eubœan" unit.

[3] Head, *Hist. Num.*, 877 *sqq.*

[4] Head (*Hist. Num.*, 881) remarks that they are about equal to two of the contemporary Roman *asses* (of about 840 grains). At the ratio between the values of silver and copper of 107:1, this coin would have been worth about one "Æginetan" *obol,* or one-eighth of the "Eubœan" unit.

[5] Babelon, 387.

9. *Summary and Conclusions.*

The earliest metallic units of value of which there is record are gold and silver units of Babylon and Egypt. The gold unit of about 130 grains stands out as the most stable of all the weight units applied to the monetary metals in the ancient world. After coinage commenced it remained the unit of almost all gold currencies, except some of the early issues in the north of Asia Minor. The first great imperial coinage was that of Persia, and its successful management must have given great impetus to this standard by reason of the fame to which the *daric* attained. At the end of the 5th century B.C., and again at the beginning of the 4th century, the unit was used for the Athenian issues, and for the local issues in imitation of them, and finally in the latter half of the 3rd century its position was definitely established by its use for the abundant issues of Macedon. The other early unit was the value of a quantity of bronze measured by weight or size in Italy and Sicily, and also in Greece in very early times. This unit did not survive in either area, although it persisted much longer in Italy and Sicily than in the Greek world—the native institutions of the former being more vigorous than those of Greece. In consequence, it plays an important part in the evolution of the Roman monetary system. In the Greek world it gave rise to the "Æginetan" unit for silver and, possibly, the "Eubœan" unit.

Silver had been used as a standard of value in Babylon and Egypt, but it was in the Ægean that it was used for coining, and took up its position as sole monetary standard. The size of the units used for silver admits of no simple explanation. In the present chapter the number of silver standards has been reduced to five, viz.:

	"*Light*" *Grains.*	"*Heavy*" *Grains.*
"Babylonian" *shekel* (Persian, 2 *siglos*)	168	336
"Phœnician" *shekel*	112	224
"Æginetan" *stater*	200 to 192	
"Eubœan" *stater* (Attic, a little larger)	130	260
	Tetradrachms.	*Didrachms.*
"Phocæan" ("Chian" or "Rhodean")	240	120
"Milesian"	204	102

The origins of these units are altogether uncertain. The "Æginetan" unit is most reasonably traced to the primitive iron units which it succeeded. Nevertheless it, as well as all the remaining four units, has been traced, directly or indirectly, to the gold unit. The relations of the silver unit to the latter are, however, of two different kinds. On the one hand, the "Eubœan" and its shrunken relative, the "Phocæan," seem to have arisen out of the transference to silver of a weight unit originally used for gold. The value unit which resulted from such a transference depended entirely upon the relation between the values of gold and silver. In communities where the gold unit had been coined, a silver unit would be unlikely to be adopted in this way unless a simple relation existed between the values of gold and silver. This condition was satisfied in the Greek world where a 12 : 1 ratio existed.

The "Babylonian" and "Phœnician," with its dependent Milesian and also the "Æginetan" unit (if the bronze basis is not accepted), all bear a value relation to gold. They result from a division of the gold unit of value and a translation of the resulting unit into silver. It is of the essence of the process that the resulting units shall bear a simple value relation to their parent gold unit, although their weights may be unrelated to that of the gold unit. For this purpose the gold unit of value was never divided on the duodecimal basis, common in Greece in later times; where such a relation was desired, it was approximately obtained by using the same weight units for both gold and silver. Accepting the desirability of decimal divisions, units equal $\frac{1}{10}$ to $\frac{1}{20}$, and perhaps $\frac{1}{15}$ of the gold unit might be expected, and if such units were established separately in different places, there would be much agreement between them. Local variations in the relation between the values of the precious metals explain minor disagreement without the assumption of any "adjustments." The theory that all the silver units were based on the universal gold unit is based on the assumption that "from first to last the Greek communities were engaged in an endless quest after bimetallism."[1] But it would be rash to assume that everywhere the weight of silver coins was controlled by the price of gold, or that denominations of silver must always have been exchangeable in round numbers with contemporary

[1] Ridgeway, 338.

units of gold.[1] The desire for a simple gold exchange was, in all probability, can unimportant factor. But if for the moment it be assumed that such a motive played a leading part in the establishment of these units, it cannot be seriously maintained that it was a continuing element in monetary policy, and that the weights of the silver units were changed as frequently as the relative values of gold and silver changed.[2] A gold exchange standard, with a full value silver currency in circulation, is an administrative impossibility. Moreover, to explain all silver standards by this means, it is necessary to prove considerable differences in the local ratio between gold and silver in different areas—a phenomenon unlikely to prove as permanent as the different standards. Assuming the universality of the gold unit, any of these silver units may have been arrived at locally. But there has been a

[1] Head (*Hist. Num.*, XLIII).

[2] This argument has been applied to alterations in the standard at Abdera on the southern coast of Thrace, where it has been suggested that there was an attempt to maintain a gold exchange standard. The city was founded in the 7th century, and refounded in 544 B.C., by inhabitants of Teos unwilling to submit to Persian domination. In 544 B.C. it commenced to issue (not on the "Æginetan" unit used in the mother city) but coins weighing 240 to 224 grains. This may be the "heavy" "Phœnician" standard, but that unit rarely exceeded 220 grains, and a people fleeing from domination of Persia and Phœnician allies at Teos might not be expected to use the "Phœnician" standard. But during the last quarter of the 5th century the unit fell to 198 to 190 grains, thus becoming identical with the "Æginetan" unit. At the fall of Athens in the 5th century, when the power of Persia was increasing, and great issues were being made by the Persian satraps in support of the naval campaigns, the Persian unit was adopted (Gardner, 322), and the local standard fell to between 176 and 160 grains. At the end of the 4th century the city came under the domination of Athens, and in about 350 B.C. was absorbed into the empire of Philip of Macedon, after which autonomous issues ceased. The continued fall may have been rendered necessary by changes in the relative values of silver and gold, but the dominant unit, and that with which easy relations would be sought in the 5th century, was undoubtedly the Attic silver *tetradrachm,* and not the Persian gold *daric.* Moreover, it is unlikely that one city would strike out alone on a novel policy of a gold exchange standard. The coins do not fall steadily, but are thought sometimes to increase in weight, and the dates of the fall in value of gold do not correspond with changes of standard. The evidence for the existence of a gold exchange standard is, therefore, weak: more probably the various changes of unit are explained by the general causes inducing shrinkage of standards together with political influences. The "Æginetan" unit was borrowed for political reasons after the failure of the Athenian expedition to Sicily, and in a revolt against the enforced use of the Attic unit. The presence of the Spartan fleets probably also suggested the use of their "Æginetan" unit (Gardner, 53).

tendency to infer close trading or political relations between places using similar currency units. Where agreement between units is very close, and two cities are known to have traded with each other, or to have been subject to a common political influence, there is a presumption in favour of the borrowing of the unit by one from the other.[1] But it must be remembered that few of the early issues of coins before the "owls" of Athens can have been taken by tale in any large transactions. If coins passed by weight, there is little object in fitting silver denominations so as to be simply related to the gold unit of value. For the same reason one would not expect to find one city adjusting its standard to that of another: and there is, in fact, very little direct evidence of such adoption of foreign standards.

In fact, the study of early monetary standards is in a profoundly unsatisfactory condition. In order to reduce the number of standards to the manageable number referred to above, and to fit all coins into an easily comprehensible scheme, it has been necessary to grasp at an approach to one of the known standards, and to under-emphasize the extent of the disagreement with the standard (sometimes as much as 20 per cent.). Disagreements of this kind are not disposed of by calling them adjustments, for then attention should be directed to the unit to which they were adjusted. The standards set up often rest on nothing more stable than a tendency for units to cluster a little more thickly at some magnitudes than at others, the whole being, of course, confined within the limits set by convenience in the size of units. The attempt to trace each silver unit in the Greek world to a local origin in the earlier unit of value, which was later placed on the coins, has failed. The only certain influences at work seem to have been a tendency to select units of a convenient size, and then a tendency for the unit to shrink. Shrinkage of the unit is what has often been explained as the adoption of a new standard. The "Eubœan" unit of 130 grains shrinks, and it soon becomes the "Phocæan" of 120 grains, and if the reduction continues, the "Phœnician" of 112 grains, the Milesian *didrachm* of 102 grains, and finally the "Æginetan" *drachm* of 96 grains. When it lies between two of these units, it is a raised or reduced form respectively of its lower and

[1] *Num. Chron.*, 1918, 127.

upper neighbours. Various combinations of the influences causing reduction operated at different rates in different places. Sometimes a long period of stability was secured, and at others change was frequent. This kind of process more satisfactorily explains the variety of standards which is found, than neat classification into standards. Borrowing by one place from another must, of course, have occurred: the cities which first issued silver coins may have based their issues on Asiatic silver units, when they did not find to hand a bronze unit of value to translate into silver. In later times, more or less voluntary borrowing often gave place to the imposition of standards by imperial power. In particular, Athens enforced the use of silver " owls " coined on the " Eubœan " unit over a great part of the Greek world, and by the end of the 5th century B.C. it was the best known silver unit. During the 4th century the " Chian " or " Phocæan " unit is supposed to have spread, but as it weighed 120 grains this must often be merely a way of recording a general tendency for the Athenian unit to shrink. But in the latter half of the 3rd century B.C. Alexander based his silver coins on the " Eubœan " unit and, at the time of his death, it was in general use outside Phœnicia and possibly Egypt. It survived as the most important Greek silver unit until the loss of Greek independence, and then it practically disappeared.

These early units bear a strikingly close resemblance to some of our modern units. The ancient gold unit approached closely to the gold equivalent of the pound sterling, 123 grains of standard gold. The *daric* and the gold *stater* of Macedon were worth about £1 2s. (gold), but we know nothing of their purchasing power, and are, therefore, unable to compare it with the sovereign as a unit of value.[1] But not only was the gold basis of these systems similar to that of our own day; in each was a silver unit of $\frac{1}{20}$ of the value of the gold unit. These silver units recall the shilling, but they differed from it in being full-weight coins. The Athenian silver unit, worth $\frac{1}{24}$ of the gold unit, still more closely approached in value $\frac{1}{20}$ of the British gold pound.

[1] Gardner (19) says a family could live on about an Attic *drachm* per day.

CHAPTER X

THE WEIGHT STANDARDS OF ROMAN COINS

1. *Native Bronze Units in Italy.*

BEFORE coins were made in Italy or Sicily the native population must have had some means of measuring the bronze which they used as a medium of exchange. The *as rude* of Central Italy is our earliest link with their primitive system of exchange based on bronze, but it is not very helpful. We do not know when it came into use, although it lingered on some time after the practice of stamping was adopted, for specimens have been found with stamped pieces. The specimens found are sometimes oblong or square, but are frequently quite shapeless. They vary in weight from over 12 pounds to less than 1 ounce, and although at least the amorphous lumps must have passed by weight, we do not know the weight unit employed.[1] When the practice of stamping ingots of bronze was introduced in Umbria and Central Italy in the middle of the 5th century B.C., the metals were made up into pieces of defined weight.[2] During the succeeding century these bulky *as signatum* were supplemented throughout Northern and Central Italy, Etruria and Latium by heavy round coins (*as grave*), which offer the first information worth considering as to the weight units for bronze in Italy. It is now fairly generally agreed that these round pieces were based upon the pound or *libra* of bronze, but it is not easy to determine the size of the *libra* from an examination of the many specimens of *as grave* that we possess.[3] They are all cast, and, in consequence, are irregular in weight. But the fact that the *libra* varied also

[1] Grueber (XV) suggests that there is some uniformity in the weights of the pieces found.

[2] The specimens in the British Museum weigh 27,627 and 21,445 grains respectively; others are known, weighing 26,179, 21,543, and 21,914 grains (Grueber, 4). These weights have been thought to indicate pieces of four or five Roman pounds.

[3] Numbers of these *as grave* have come down to us, one find alone containing 1,575 *asses*, all of which are known to be of early date.

from district to district[1] also explains the variety in the weight of the *asses*.[2] In most parts of Etruria, Umbria, and generally in Central Italy, a *libra* of about 5,045 grains[3] (the "Roman" or "later Roman" pound) was in use from the middle of the 4th century to 268 B.C. Of the other pounds, the most important in its relation to coining was the *libra* of 4,210 grains (the "Oscan" pound) or $\frac{5}{6}$ of the "Roman" unit. A *litra* unit, comparable to the Italian *libra*, is believed to have been used in Sicily, but the only evidence of its size is obtained from later silver coins, which are believed to have been worth a *litra* of bronze. As information as to the relative values of silver and bronze at the time of the introduction of these coins is very speculative, the resulting weights obtained for the *litra* do not command confidence.[4]

The origin of the *libra* standard has been explained, on the one hand, as the result of the importation of parts of the Babylonian series of weights and, on the other, as a purely native growth. The hundredfold of the "Roman" and "Oscan" pounds bear a close resemblance to one of the "Babylonian" silver *talents*. One hundred "Roman" pounds (504,500 grains) are equal in weight to a *talent* of silver, consisting of 60 *minas* of 50 "Babylonian" silver *shekels* of 168 grains. One hundred "Oscan" pounds are equal to fifty of these *minas*, the pound being exactly half a "Babylonian" silver *mina*, but bearing no direct relation to the *talent*.

1 In some parts of Etruria the *libra* weighed only 3,368 grains, or 20 per cent. less than the "Oscan" pound. In Picenium it rose to the unexplained size of over 6,000 grains, or about 20 per cent. more than the "Roman" *libra* (Head, 23).

2 Only one known specimen of an *as* weighs over 4,847 grains, and that weighs 5,900 grains. Of the above find, 591 *asses*, selected at random, were weighed, and of these 206 (about 35 per cent.) weighed over 4,210 grains, the heaviest weighing 4,847 grains and the lightest 2,100 grains. *Asses* at Ariminium (Umbria) weighed 6,000 grains (Head, 21).

3 The English troy pound weighs 5,760 grains, or about 14 per cent. more than the "Roman" pound.

4 On the two assumptions that the subsequent silver coins called by the same name were made equal in value to the bronze unit they superseded (like the *obols* in Greece), and that the relative values of silver and bronze were 125:1, the *litra* of bronze must have weighed about 1687·5 grains, or about one-third of the "Roman" pound (Head, LIV). Ridgeway (348), however, takes a ratio of 300:1 between the two metals, which gives a *litra* of about 4,050 grains. This is less than either of the "Roman" or "Oscan" units, but approximates more satisfactorily to them. Sydenham (*Num. Chron.*, 1918, 157) rejects the possibility of so high a ratio.

This correspondence between "Roman" and "Babylonian" units has suggested[1] that the *centupondium* was the Assyrian *talent* which came to Italy either by way of visiting trading ships or the Greek colonial settlements, the earliest of which date back to the 8th or 7th century B.C. But none of these settlements[2] coined on the basis of the *shekel* of 168 grains; they were probably using the *talent* as a unit of weight for commodities other than gold and silver, but the *talent* for gold and commodities, if the same as that used in Babylon under the same circumstances,[3] was about 10 per cent. less than even the "Oscan" pound. If, therefore, it is argued that the "Roman" pound was obtained by borrowing the "Babylonian" silver *talent*, and dividing it into one hundred parts, it remains to be explained why the new unit, which was largely used for copper, was based on a silver *talent* rather than a *talent* used for gold and commodities (including copper), and why, even then, on the "Babylonian" rather than the "Phœnician" silver unit. Moreover, the *talent* in the Babylonian systems was invariably divided into 60 *minas*, and it is not explained why it should have been divided into a hundred parts in Italy, more especially as the Italians were accustomed to a duodecimal division.[4]

There are two separate theories which give the *libra* a native origin. It may be that the unit was invented for measuring copper before the art of weighing was known, and measurement was made by length units based on the human body.[5] The pound of copper may have been a piece 1 foot long and of prescribed width and thickness. The smallest subdivision of the *as* was called a *scripulum* (scratch), a fact which lends support to this explanation. Variations in the pound from district to district in later times might then be explained by differences in the local foot unit, although these differences would then require explanation. To weigh one "Roman" pound, the piece of copper would have to be about ½ inch in diameter, and would bear some resemblance to the nails or spits in use in Greece, and there known as

[1] Soutzo (*cit.* Ridgeway, 136).

[2] With the possible exception of Rhegium at the end of the 6th century B.C.

[3] 378,000 grains (60 × 50 × 126).

[4] *Vide* Chap. XI.

[5] Ridgeway, 358.

obols.[1] In fact, " we may with some plausibility suggest that the ancient Greek copper '*obol*,' or spike, and the Italian '*as*,' or rod, were identical in dimensions[2] and in origin," and " it is not improbable that the 'Roman' *libra* and 'Sicilian' *litra* were almost equal in weight."[3] When weighing was introduced, the unit of weight would naturally be the weight of the standard bar already the medium of exchange. Ridgeway, on the other hand, suggests[4] that the highest weight unit was that amount of copper which was worth an ox. This unit appears to have been one hundredfold of the bronze *as*, if we may adopt the ratio upon which the Tarpeian Law of 451 B.C. was based. Then " the *as* having been once subjected to weight, its hundredfold, the *centupondium* or 'hundred weight,' became the highest Roman weight unit." But so convenient a relation between the *as* and the ox unit suggests design, and we must choose whether the *as* was obtained by dividing the ox unit in bronze into one hundred parts, or whether it developed from a mass of bronze defined by linear units based on the human body. We cannot accept both origins. Ridgeway, after having suggested that the *as* was a copper rod one Roman foot long and half a Roman inch in diameter, proceeds: " No doubt from time out of mind 100 of the bars of copper, which formed the chief lower unit of barter, made one cow."[5] He seems to think that the *as* and the ox unit were of independent origin, and that the hundredfold relation between them was a pure coincidence.

When in the later years of the 4th century or early years of the 3rd century coins were first issued in Rome, they must have been based upon the units previously in use, but it has already appeared that specimen *as grave* do not point to any exact standard. If, however, we ignore one or perhaps two specimens which are unusually heavy and ascribe their weight to " a blunder of the workman who cast them,"[6] the remaining specimens may all be based on either the "Oscan" (4,210 grains)

[1] According to Pollux ix, 80 (*cit.* Ridgeway, 349), Aristotle, in his *Constitution of the Himærans*, said the Sicilian *litra* was equal to one *obol*, and, in his *Constitution of Agrigentum*, that it was worth an "Æginetan" *obol*, although in later times, when the *litra* had been translated into silver and coined, it weighed 13·4 grains as against an "Æginetan" *obol* of 16 grains.

[2] The iron spits found in the Heræum were, however, four feet long.

[3] Ridgeway, 360.

[4] *Ibid.*

[5] *Op. cit.*, 360.

[6] Grueber, XXI.

or the later "Roman" pound (5,045 grains).[1] If it is the fact that from the beginning the issues in Rome were based on the unit of 4,210 grains,[2] it is clear from hoards[3] that *as grave* weighing considerably more than this circulated in Latium. Either these were issued in other districts, or else the monetary standard in Rome[4] was from the beginning the unit of 5,045 grains.[5]

There is no doubt, however, that the *as* did not long continue to be coined of a full pound in weight. In a little more than a century it was reduced to but $\frac{1}{12}$ of the Roman pound. The earlier stages of the reduction are difficult to trace. Literary evidence is altogether absent, the dates of the various issues are uncertain, the weights of the coins are irregular, and their denominations often in doubt. It is possible that there was no deliberate alteration of the standard in the earlier stages. The *as* may have fallen gradually "by a natural process."[6] Mommsen held that the *as* gradually declined to 10 or 9 ounces, and, after remaining at that weight

[1] Some bronze coins issued from Capua in the second half of the 4th century B.C. suggest that a standard different from either of these two was in use in Campania, the pound weighing 5,260 grains, or about 25 per cent. greater than the "Oscan" pound.

[2] Sydenham, *Num. Chron.*, 1919, 155. Head (17) suggests that the heavier pound was adopted at some date between 290 and 268 B.C.

[3] Thirty-five per cent. of the early cast *as grave* referred to above weighed more than 4,210 grains (Grueber, XXI).

[4] Mommsen (I, 253-54) says "it is an error to suppose that the weight (of the ancient cast *as*) was a pound." His explanation is that at Rome and in Latium silver was taken only by weight, and the quantity of silver equivalent in value to the coined *as* was regarded as the unit for accounts in silver. But we shall see that this weight was the scruple. In fact, when the coinage of silvèr was commenced at Rome, a money was struck which represented the value of the ancient copper *as* and which weighed exactly a scruple. Then, in the course of an attempt to prove that the ratio between the values of silver and copper was 250:1, he suggests that it was in order to give to it the same value as its equivalent in silver that the ancient cast *as* was never made to weigh more than 250 scruples or $10\frac{5}{12}$ ounces. As the pound always contained 288 scruples, the ratio must have been 288:1 when the scruple of silver was worth a pound of bronze. The suggestion is, therefore, that this ratio moved to 250:1 by the time the first cast *asses* were issued, and then a bronze unit identical in value with the scruple of silver was preferred to the pound weight of bronze. If this is true the traditional unit of value had already been abandoned for a silver unit.

[5] Grueber, XXI. This theory is reinforced by the fact that the scruple unit seems to have remained unchanged at 17·5 grains, and that all ancient writers agree that it was $\frac{1}{288}$ of a pound, which must have weighed 5,045 grains.

[6] Grueber, XXIV.

for some time, fell suddenly to 4 ounces in 268 B.C.; Bahrfeldt thought that a gradual fall explained the decline from 12 to 3 ounces by the time of Pyrrhus. The existence of coins supplying a continuous series of weights must not, however, be taken as conclusive evidence of a gradual shrinkage of the *as*. Worn heavy coins and less worn light coins would tend to supply a continuous series, and would be aided by the inaccuracies inevitable in a cast coinage. D'Ailly[1] thought that the *as* was reduced to a weight of 6 ounces, then to one of 3 ounces, and finally, in 268 B.C., to one of 2 ounces. The reduction from 12 to 6 ounces probably occurred in about 286 B.C.,[2] when a strange compromise seems to have been adopted. The *as* was coined of the weight of half the "Oscan" pound and weighed, therefore, about 2,100 grains, but the subdivisions were based upon the standard of half the heavier pound of 5,040 grains used in Campania.[3] The *as* weighed, therefore, ten and not twelve times as much as the *uncia*, the half *as* $\frac{6}{10}$ of the *uncia*, the intervening units being on the same basis. The only explanation of the use of the two series of standards is that the Romans were anxious to harmonize their bronze coins with those of their near neighbours.[4] Mattingly[5] has put forward a fresh theory that the *as* introduced in 300-290 B.C. remained a full pound in law until 268 B.C., and between that date and the close of the first Punic War it fell by a series of reductions more or less defined to a weight of 2 ounces. Some support for the theory that the *as* was still a full pound in 268 B.C. is drawn from the fact that the pound was the standard in Roman colonies set up in 286 and 268 B.C. The weights of the silver coins issued under

[1] *Mon. Rom.*, I, 6.

[2] Head, 18. It may have been contemporaneous with the halving of the Campanian silver units (Sydenham, *Num. Chron.*, 1918, 163).

[3] Hæberlin, *Aes Grave*, 105. Mattingly (*Num. Chron.*, 1924, 192), however, does not accept the theory. He thinks it more probable that as the *as* fell in weight some denominations were more issued at one time and others at another.

[4] Sydenham, *Num. Chron.*, 1918, 164.

[5] Mattingly, *Num. Chron.*, 1924, 198. The main weakness of the theory is that if a *denarius* was worth 10 *asses* (as was stated in its inscription) the coinage ratio between the values of silver and bronze must have been 720:1, an impossibly high ratio. The only way of getting over this difficulty is to assume that, although legally the *as* was still 1 pound in fact it was very much less—*i.e.*, that the Romans expressed the value of the *denarius* in *asses* which were below legal weight by at least 50 per cent.

Roman influence in Campania give no assistance in fixing the weight of the *as* from time to time, because the value of silver coins in *as* coins is not known, and neither is the ratio between values of bronze and silver in the market.[1] The silver coins issued in Rome in 268 B.C. were marked to show that they were worth 10 *asses*,[2] but the relative values of silver and copper are still in doubt, and it is not possible to calculate the weight of the *as*. If a ratio of 250 : 1 existed[3] the *as* must have weighed 4 ounces and if 120 : 1,[4] 2 ounces.[5] The theories of Grueber, Mattingly, and Head all converge in about 240 B.C., when it is agreed that the *as* was reduced to 2 ounces. We can say, therefore, that at least by 240 B.C., and probably in 268 B.C.,[6] the *as* had fallen to 868 grains.

2. *Early Silver Units in Italy.*

Before pursuing further the history of the bronze unit it will be desirable to trace the origins of the silver units. These are to be found immediately in the south and in Sicily, and mediately in the cities of the Ægean. The latter sent forth bands of colonists from the later 8th century B.C., when a body of Eubœans established themselves at Cumæ, on the coast of the Bay of Naples; later, Zancle was established, on the

[1] The reduction in the weight of the silver coins issued by Rome in Campania to about 108 grains in 312 B.C. was probably intended to bring about a simple relation between Romano-Campanian silver and Roman copper. If the values of silver and copper were as 120:1, the basis of the assimilation was probably that a scruple of silver (17·5 grains) was worth half an *as*, and the *as* weighed 4,200 grains or 10 ounces ($2 \times 17{\cdot}5 \times 120$) (Head, 19). If the *as* was reduced between 286 and 268 B.C. to 2,100 grains, the *as* must then have been worth 1 silver scruple (Head, 19). If, however, the ratio was 1:250 the basis of assimilation must have been that a scruple of silver was worth an *as* in 312 B.C. (Grueber, 16).

[2] Pliny (*Hist. Nat.*, XXIII, 13) states that these new pieces passed for "decem libris aeris." If this means that they passed for 10 full pounds of bronze, we get a ratio between the values of silver and bronze of 720:1. But this is so improbable a ratio that we must assume an error.

[3] $\frac{72 \times 250}{10}$ =about 1,728 grains, or 4 ounces (Grueber, XXV).

[4] $\frac{72 \times 120}{10}$ =864 grains, or 2 ounces (Head, 19).

[5] Mattingly, *Num. Chron.*, 1924, who supports a full libral *as*, thinks that, in fact, the coinage was worn, but suggests a ratio of 360:1.

[6] Sydenham, *Num. Chron.*, 1918, 166.

Sicilian, and Rhegium, on the Italian, shore of the Sicilian straits. During the next two centuries the stream flowed steadily and with increasing volume until almost every creek on the Italian and Sicilian coasts that afforded a landing was the seat of a Greek colony. By the 6th century the overseas trade of these colonies had developed rapidly and, with it, their issues of currency became important. Although the local medium of exchange had been the *libra* (or the *litra*) of bronze, the arrival of the Greek colonists with their silver coinage prevented the development of any heavy bronze coinage,[1] as in Etruria and Latium. The Greek population issued silver coins which circulated side by side with the native bars and ingots of bronze which continued in use. In order to encourage the use of the silver coins their value in local units was inscribed upon them, and some were made so as to be equal in value to the old bronze unit of value. In the Sicilian settlements,[2] when coining began, at the end of the 7th or beginning of the 6th century B.C., the silver unit was about 88-90 grains. This unit was adopted at Rhegium in about 530 B.C., and the same unit was adopted thirty or forty years later at Cumæ, where it was 3 or 4 grains short of its weight elsewhere. We have already seen this unit is unlikely to have been the " Æginetan " *drachm*,[3] of which it fell short by some 5 grains.[4] Most probably the unit is a Corinthian 2-*drachm* piece. Perhaps it was obtained by

[1] In Apulia, and possibly in all the provinces east of the Apennines, there was an *as grave* which may have been based on the value of the 2-*obol* silver piece (of 22 grains) of Tarentum (Head, 43). Full-weight copper may have been coined during Timoleon's campaign in Sicily at the middle of the 4th century. It is probable, however, that the *litra* had then shrunk below its original size (Hill, *Handbook*, 43; Hill, 117).

[2] *E.g.*, The Chalcidean settlements at Naxos, Zancle, and Himera.

[3] Imported possibly, together with the worship of Dionysus, from Naxos (Head, 115).

[4] If the unit was the "Æginetan," it is strange that people from Chalcis (where the " Eubœan " unit was used) should have introduced it. Possibly, as Head suggests (L) the colonists came really from the mainland, where the "Æginetan" unit was used, and merely sailed from Chalcis. It is also just possible that they found the native population using a copper unit (the *litra*), which was exactly the same as that used in Greece. When they commenced to coin silver, the desire to establish a standard, which would correspond accurately to the native Sicilian unit, and could also be conveniently related to the gold unit, may have led them to the " Æginetan " standard. But when the *litra* was later translated into silver it weighed 13·4 grains, which does not agree with the Greek *obol*, and does not fit into the unit of 88-90 grains adopted in Sicily.

way of Corcyra,[1] which was the last port of call on the westward route from the Eastern Mediterranean, and could offer plentiful supplies of silver. If the colonists obtained their supplies there, they were probably made up in 2-*drachm* pieces, which provided the standard for the Sicilian cities. But the general appearance of the coins, and the fact that the principal trade route to the eastward crossed the Gulf and Isthmus of Corinth, in order to avoid the open sea voyage, render it more probable that the standard was obtained from Corinth. The unit possessed the advantage that it offered simple exchange relations with Athens and Chalcis and all cities using the " Eubœan " standard; the piece of 90 *drachms* was one-third of the Athenian *tetradrachm*. In the middle of the 6th century, when the " Eubœan " unit was spreading rapidly, the Dorian colonies in Sicily[2] issued coins based on the " Eubœan " standard of 129 grains. This unit was probably adopted because of the ease with which the native *litra* could be grafted on to it; the latter, when translated into silver, was about $\frac{1}{10}$ of the former. *Litra* coins were issued soon after 600 B.C., and remained common in Sicily throughout the century.[3] Thus simple foreign exchange relations with the more important cities of the East were established, while at the same time currency relations with the native population were simplified. But these silver *litra* coins cannot have been based both upon the silver value of the bronze *litra* and also upon $\frac{1}{10}$ of the " Eubœan " unit, unless by a very remarkable coincidence. Ignorance of the relative market values of silver and copper makes any further search for their origin impossible, but it is probable that they were tenths of the " Eubœan " unit, which approached sufficiently closely to the value of the *litra* to be called by the same name. This agreement with the *litra*, and also with the most common unit in the Ægean, caused the unit of 129-135 grains to supersede that of about 88 grains in most of the cities of Southern Italy and Sicily early in the 5th century. But the coinage of Syracuse suggests that the *litra* unit was a very strong influence, if not the

[1] Head, L. Corcyra probably did not obtain its unit from Corinth, but from Miletus, Rhodes, and Cyrene, and ultimately from Asia (Head, 326). But the "Corcyrean" unit was equal to two Corinthian *drachms*.

[2] *E.g.*, Syracuse and Agrigentum.

[3] A bronze *litra* of full weight was issued in Syracuse, but elsewhere the *litra* was coined in silver only.

real basis of the standard. Up to 310 B.C., with the exception of the *litra* coin, all the pieces represented a well-known Attic denomination, and also a whole number of *litras*, but after this date, while continuing to represent a round number of *litras*, coins were often issued which were quite foreign to the Attic system. The standard was also adopted in Etruria, although it was separated by a territory unfamiliar with the unit from the southern cities using it.[1]

A fresh unit made its appearance at Velia, a settlement established on the coast of the Tyrrhenian Sea by a number of Phocæans who emigrated in about 544 B.C. in consequence of the Persian conquests. Their first coins are reminiscent in their fabric of those of Asia Minor, and it has been suggested that they were based upon the " Phocæan " unit of 58-60 grains brought from Phocæa. But they resemble closely the coins based upon the Corinthian standard in the south,[2] and it is possible that the Velians at first used the Corinthian standard. The people of Poseidonia (Lucania), however, used the standard of 120 grains from the middle of the 6th century,[3] and from about 480 B.C. it was certainly in use at Cumæ[4] as well as Velia. From this time the " Phocæan " unit became increasingly popular in Campania, where it is known as the Campanian standard. But it is impossible to say whether the unit was introduced from abroad or emerged locally from the shrinkage of the " Eubœan " unit. Moreover, it is possible that what is seen as a tendency for the " Phocæan " unit to supersede the " Eubœan " is merely a general tendency for the " Eubœan " unit to shrink. Cities may have affected each other in this respect, but it is more likely that the fall in the unit was due to similar causes operating in many places. The most important issues on the Campanian standard are those silver coins marked " Roma " and " Romano," formerly

[1] It was superseded at Naxos soon after 498 B.C., at Zancle 493-480 B.C., Himera 482 B.C., the " Eubœan " becoming universal throughout the island. In Rhegium the " Eubœan " unit appears between 494 and 480 B.C., and in Cumæ in about 490 B.C. (Sydenham, *Num. Chron.*, 1918, 159).

[2] Gardner, 210.

[3] The standard in use in Tarentum (Calabria) was the same. The *stater* of 120-23 grains was divided into 2 *drachms*.

[4] At Cumæ the unit of about 90 grains was given up for the " Eubœan " of 129 grains in about 490 B.C., and only ten years later that was superseded by the Phocæan.

thought to have been issued from Capua in about 335 B.C., but now more convincingly ascribed to the period of the war with Pyrrhus in 282-272 B.C. Considerable quantities of *staters*, of about 117 grains, were issued, probably with the aid of Carthaginian treasure. These coins could not be at all simply related to the bronze *asses* issued in Rome, and after a time[1] they were reduced in weight from 117 to 105 grains, either to establish such a simple relation[2] or as a means of financing the war.

The reduction of the Campanian *stater* was, in fact, the adoption of a new standard, the origin of which is difficult to find. It is possible that it came from Etruria, where, during the 5th and first half of the 4th century B.C., while the " Eubœan " standard was used with its subdivision into ten *litras* in the Syracusan style, there was another series of coins bearing marks of value, which indicate a standard of about 35 grains.[3] The former unit was probably borrowed from Syracuse, although it is possible that both units were " the silver equivalents of two Etruscan pound weights of bronze in use contemporaneously in different parts of the country."[4] If the unit of 35 grains circulated in the ports in contact with the east coast, the pieces of 175 grains would be equal in weight to the Corcyrean *staters* current there, and it is possible that the latter were reduced to fit the local Etruscan unit (based on the value of a local pound of copper), or that the local unit was made equal to the Corcyrean one.[5] At some

[1] If the *staters* are assigned to 335 B.C., the reduction is supposed to have occurred twenty-five years later (Head, 32). It is difficult to understand how the Romans can have permitted the two unrelated systems to co-exist. Grueber (I, 39) suggests that " the difficulty of communication, and the absence of regulations in commercial transactions between the two districts," was responsible, but there is no explanation of the absence of regulations. Mattingly (*Num. Chron.*, 1924, 187) believes that the reduction was made during the Pyrrhic War, and, therefore, within ten years of the institution of the coinage. It may have been merely a piece of inflation (*vide* Chap. XV).

[2] If the ratio between the values of silver and copper was 250:1 the *stater* was probably worth six *asses*, and if it was 120:1 the *stater* was probably worth three *asses*.

[3] Head, 14; Gardner, 401; Sydenham, *Num. Chron.*, 1918, 159.

[4] Head, LIV. Those on the *litra* basis may have circulated on the coast, where contact was made with Corsica, Sardinia, Sicily, and Africa, while the scruple series circulated in the interior and ports in contact with the east coast, which was dominated by Corcyra, whose *staters* of 175 grains and *drachms* of 87 grains represented respectively 10 and 5 reduced Etruscan units (Gardner, 401).

[5] Gardner, 402.

time, in the middle of the 4th century B.C., both series of units were halved,[1] thus making the basis of the second series a unit of 17·5 grains, known as a scruple. When the Romans reduced the Campanian *staters* to 105 grains, they were, therefore, making them equal in value to 6 scruples. But it is usually supposed that the object of the alteration of the Romano-Campanian unit was to bring the silver into a simple value relation to the Roman copper money, by taking advantage of the fact that the scruple of silver was then worth either half an *as* or one *as*, according to the relation between the values of silver and copper that we may accept. It may be, however, that the scruple unit was obtained in Rome as well as in Etruria, Central Italy, and Tarentum, by translating the value of the bronze *as* into silver.[2] In fact, when the Romans placed the Campanian issues on a scruple basis, they were adhering strictly to their old unit of value based on the pound of bronze. The agreement between the Etruscan and Roman scruple units may be due to a deliberate adjustment of the 2-scruple unit[3] to the former,[4] or to the fact that both were translations of equal pounds of bronze into silver at the same value ratio between the metals. In the early part of the 3rd century B.C. the scruple standard spread in Central and Southern Italy.[5] Again, it may be possible to argue that standards were shrinking because of the incompetence or dishonesty of those in control of the coinage, but the extend-

[1] This reduction may have been connected with, although later than, the similar halving of units by Dionysus of Syracuse.

[2] " We are then forced to the conclusion that at Rome and in Latium silver was accepted only by weight, and that the quantity of silver equivalent in value to the coined *as* was regarded as the unit in contracts made in silver. But we shall see that this weight was the scruple " (Mommsen, I, 254).

[3] Or the one scruple unit if the relative values of bronze and silver were as 1 : 240.

[4] Gardner, 402.

[5] In Heraclea (Lucania) the reduction of the old unit was made in about 272 B.C. In Thurium the standard was increased from 120 to 128 grains before being reduced to 105 grains in about 281 B.C. In Rhegium the reduction took place after 270 B.C. Tarentum was one of the last towns to give way to the *scruple* unit. In 302-281 B.C. it was issuing pieces of about 116 grains, which slowly declined in value and, at the time of the Pyrrhic Wars, in 282-274 B.C., were definitely reduced to 105 grains to bring them into accord with the Campanian issues. Mattingly suggests (*Num. Chron.*, 1924, 187) that Tarentum may have first made the reduction and Rome merely copied the enemy's device.

ing power of Rome is a more obvious cause. When the Romans began to issue silver in Rome, their principal coin, the *denarius,* weighed 4 scuples or 70-72 grains.[1] The suppression of all local issues and the enforced circulation of Roman silver made the scruple standard supreme in Italy.

3. *Early Gold Units in Italy.*

Although gold was commonly used in Italy for jewellery and ornaments, and also in bars in exchange, it was usually valued in bronze. It was not coined in Rome until 240 B.C., but occasional issues were made in earlier times in the Greek settlements. An altogether unique gold issue was made in Campania at Cumæ as early as 480 B.C. upon a "Eubœan" standard,[2] which is also found, divided in the Syracusan style into *litras,* in the gold issues of Etruria[3] in the 5th century or later. This unit was probably borrowed from the Greek peoples by way of Syracuse,[4] although it may be that the ox

[1] The closeness of the weight of the new unit to the "Eubœan" *drachm* of about 67 grains has suggested that the previous use of the Greek *drachm* as a unit of weight in Rome accounts for the weight of the coin. According to a quotation given in the *New. Eng. Dict.* (*denarius—cit.* Raper, *Phil. Trans.*, LXI, 492; 1771), "The Romans did not use the *denarius* as a weight . . . till the Greek physicians . . . prescribed by it, as they had been accustomed to do by the *drachm* in their own country." But this is very inconclusive, and may merely refer to a custom of allowing the use of coins as weights in the measuring of drugs. Many ancient writers regarded the *denarius* and the Attic *drachm* as equal in weight, and even referred to the *drachma* of the Greeks as a *denarius* (Stevenson, *Dict. of Roman Coins*, 358). The type and style of the *denarius* indicates that the Romans had copied the *drachm* of Magna Græcia. But this is no more than is to be expected, and does not necessarily indicate a borrowing of the weight standard. The raising of the Greek unit by 5 grains is very unlikely. There is little doubt that the *denarius* was based upon the *scruple.*

[2] Head (36) suggests that at a ratio between gold and silver of 15:1 the gold half-*obol* was worth exactly one "Æginetan" *drachm.* Gardner (208) contends that the silver coins were in fact Corinthian *didrachms,* and if the gold half-*obol* was worth 2 Corinthian *drachms,* the ratio between gold and silver must have been 16:1, which is unexpectedly high.

[3] Head, 12; Ridgeway, 130.

[4] The denominations 44 grains (=50 silver *litras*)
22 ,, (=25 ,, ,,)
11 ,, (=12½ ,, ,,)
9 ,, (=10 ,, ,,)

(Gardner, 399), at a ratio of 15:1 between gold and silver, suggest Sicilian influence, which seems to have affected both the gold and the silver units of Etruria.

unit[1] was a native unit in Italy. The gold issues made in Sicily[2] at the end of the 5th century are difficult to fit into any known standard.[3] Some suggest translations into gold, at the current market rate, of various numbers of silver *litras* and " Eubœan " *drachms*,[4] while others may have been coined on the Athenian system of using the same weight standards for both gold and silver.[5] In Syracuse, where gold was coined almost throughout the 4th century, the issues of the latter half of the century are fairly clearly based upon the Attic standard,[6] then popular throughout the Ægean and in Macedon.[7] But it is probable that the relative market value of the metals was such as to establish a simple relation between coins of the two metals, although the gold unit was not intentionally based upon the silver unit of value.[8] The same Attic unit is found at Tarentum,[9] in Calabria, in the latter part of the century, and at Metapontum, although the only pieces known weigh 44 grains, which may be either one-third of the " Eubœan "

[1] Ridgeway (359) suggests that the ox unit was used in Italy in early times. In Sicily and Southern Italy there was a *talent* equal to three ox units. When the native peoples first weighed their copper rods they used this *talent* of 405 grains, and found that 1 inch of the copper rod closely approximated to it in weight.

[2] In Agrigentum, just before 406, Camarina and Gela before 405, and Syracuse in 413 B.C.

[3] The coins weigh 27, 20, 18, 13, and 9 grains.

[4] The pieces of 18, 11, and 9 grains issued in Syracuse in 413 B.C., at a ratio between silver and gold of 1:15, represent 4 *drachms* (20 *litras*), 2½ *drachms* (12½ *litras*), and 2 *drachms* (10 *litras*) (Head, 175).

[5] The pieces of 20 grains issued at Agrigentum suggest one-sixth of a "Phocæan" *stater*.

[6] A gold coin of 33·7 grains was issued between 357 B.C. and 317 probably worth 30 *litras* (Head, 179). Under Agathocles (317-289 B.C.) gold *didrachms* and divisions thereof were made. In 304 B.C., however, he issued Corinthian *didrachms* of 90 grains and divisions, but after some twenty years the Attic *didrachm* again became the standard, and remained so until the end of the century.

[7] Macedonian influence is evident in the fact that the types of the larger denominations were borrowed from the issues of Philip of Macedon (Head, 181).

[8] As gold was then only twelve times as valuable as silver, the piece of 90 grains was worth 80 silver *litras* instead of 100 (when gold was fifteen times as valuable as silver) (Head, 182). The Attic *drachm* of gold was worth 12 Attic *drachms* of silver and 60 *litras*.

[9] Gold was first issued at Tarentum in about 340 B.C., and continued for about sixty years. The *stater* weighed 133 grains, although gold *litras* of 13·2 grains were also issued. The issue was probably made owing to the drain on the Treasury resulting from the employment of Greek mercenaries to defend the city against its barbarous neighbours (Head, 60).

stater or one Corinthian *drachm.*[1] It is fairly clear that, during the latter part of the century, the unit of the Attic *stater* and the Macedonian *stater*, weighing 133·5 grains, dominated the gold issues of the Greek cities in Magna Græcia.

4. *Early Reductions of the Bronze "As."*

In 268 B.C. the Roman coinage of both metals was based upon the scruple, possibly, as we have seen the old *libra* of bronze translated into silver. The *denarius* weighed 72 grains or 4 scruples. The weight of the *as* is variously suggested as 864 grains (2 ounces) and 1,728 grains (4 ounces), but it is not disputed that the value of the *as* was $\frac{1}{10}$ of that of the *denarius*. Mommsen,[2] accepting 4 ounces as the weight of the *as* in 268 B.C., because of the standards adopted in Latin colonies which accepted the Roman unit,[3] believed that the *as* fell by a series of small unauthorized reductions made by the moneyers to a weight of only 1 ounce in 217 B.C. In that year its weight was fixed legally at 1 ounce, and Mommsen regarded the act as merely accepting and recognizing the existing state of affairs. Grueber,[4] however, while agreeing with Mommsen that the *as* weighed 4 ounces in 268 B.C., states that the coins of the succeeding fifty years indicate that at some stage the *as* was deliberately reduced to a 2-ounce standard. The coins of this weight differ markedly from preceding issues: they were struck and not cast, as hitherto. As a result, some of the higher denominations, such as the 10-, 3-, and 2-*as* pieces, had to be abandoned, because the coiners had neither strong enough dies nor powerful enough presses to make coins so large. The small $\frac{1}{4}$-ounce pieces had to be given up, because on the new scale they were inconveniently small. It is unlikely that such changes were made without consideration or remark: they must have been the result of deliberate decision.[5] As to the date of this decision there is considerable doubt. The literary authorities do not agree. Festus attributes the change to the period of the second Punic War, but his other remarks on the subject cast doubt on the accuracy of his

[1] Head, 78.

[2] II, 14.

[3] He points out that when the Latin colony of Brundusium, which was established in 244 B.C., began to issue money, it made the *as* of 1,728 grains.

[4] I, 16.

[5] Grueber, I, 30.

record.[1] Pliny attributes it to the first Punic War (268-241 B.C.), but he also is not clear as to the circumstances of the change.[2] Nevertheless, his date is more acceptable. The coinage bears some signs of the prevalence of war conditions,[3] and it is possible that the reduction was itself a war measure. The monetary standard established at Brundusium at some date after 244 B.C. suggests that the 2-ounce *as* was introduced in Rome between 244 and 240 B.C. If this reduced *as* was not adopted in Rome in 268 B.C.—a still more probable solution—it is fairly clear that it was in use by 240 B.C. The introduction of gold about 240 B.C. was probably another aspect of the reaction of war upon the currency. The gold coins were based upon the scruple standard, pieces of 3, 2, and 1 scruples being known. They are respectively marked 60, 40, and 20, to indicate the number of *sestertii* for which they passed. But the issue of gold was no more than a passing phenomenon.

5. *The Reduction of Standards during the Second Punic War.*

The only certain and important currency reduction under the Republic was made during the second Punic War (218-201 B.C.). The Lex Flaminia of 217 B.C. contained four important provisions:[4]

[1] According to Festus (*cit.* Ridgeway, *Comp. Latin Studies*), it was "on account of the second Punic War which was waged with Hannibal (that) the Senate decreed that out of the *asses* that were then *libral* (a pound in weight) should be made those of a sextans (one-sixth of a pound) in weight." But all the evidence goes to show, in the first place, that by the beginning of the second Punic War (218-201 B.C.) the *as* certainly did not weigh a full pound. It is equally improbable that the reduction to a 2-ounce *as* was so long delayed, in fact it was probably the 1-ounce *as* which was introduced in 217 B.C.

[2] He says that "the *as* of a pound weight was . . . reduced during the first Punic War . . . and it was decreed that *asses* should be struck of the weight of 2 ounces, so five parts of it were thus gained." He thought that the reduction was made in one stage from 12 to 2 ounces —a proceeding which, in view of the evidence already considered, is improbable.

[3] "Not only was the bronze money placed on a reduced standard, but the silver appears to have been affected also, as it is to this time that we would assign the first variation in the type of the *denarius*, when, not only did it fall in weight, but also its fabric, and somewhat careless execution show that the mint was in a state of disorganization" (Grueber, I, 30). The reduction in the weight of silver was not more than a few grains.

[4] Pliny's record is that "When the state was pressed upon by the war with Hannibal and during the dictatorship of Q. Fabius Maximus *asses* of an ounce weight (*unciales*) were minted, and a *denarius* was

1. The legal weight of the *as* was reduced from 2 ounces to 1.

2. The legal weight of the *denarius* was reduced from $\frac{1}{72}$ to $\frac{1}{84}$ of a pound.

3. The *denarius* was to pass for 16 *asses* instead of 10.

4. In military pay a *denarius* was to be given for every 10 *asses* due.

We are here concerned only with the reductions in weight standard. It is notable that the reduced weight of the *denarius* was about 60 grains or, roughly, equal to the "Phocæan" *drachm* which was so popular in Magna Græcia and the Eastern Mediterranean after the fall of Athens at the end of the 5th century. The occasion of the change and the accompanying issue of plated money suggest that the reform originated in the financial difficulties of the state, but it is probable that at least part of the advantage likely to accrue from the reductions had already been obtained by moneyers who had brought about a reduction of both silver and copper coins below their previous legal weight.

6. *The Reduction of Bronze and Introduction of Gold during the Last Century B.C.*

We have seen[1] that the bronze coin ceased to be of importance in the middle of the 2nd century B.C. When the coining of bronze *asses* recommenced in B.C. 91, after a lapse of sixty years, the Lex Papiria was passed, fixing their minimum weight at half an ounce (210 grains). The *asses* then in circulation were, however, much reduced in weight, and it is probable that the act legalized the reduction already made.[2]

When gold coins were revived by generals in the field at the beginning of the last century B.C., the weight standard seems to have been the 10-scruple unit[3] used in early times in Etruria. The *aureus* was rated at 25 *denarii ;* it may be,

---

made exchangeable for sixteen *asses*, a *quinarius* for eight, and a *sestertius* for four. . . . In military pay, however, a *denarius* was always given for ten *asses*" (*Nat. Hist.*, XXXIII, 13).

[1] Chap. VI.

[2] Head (20) says that the reduction was "merely a legal authorization of a custom which *de facto* had prevailed for some years before that date, if not in Rome itself, at any rate in some of the confederate towns."

[3] About $\frac{1}{30}$ of a pound.

therefore, that its weight was determined with a view to making it equal in value at the market rate to 25 silver *denarii*. If the *aureus* was originally established on a scruple basis, its value in *denarii* is probably responsible for the steady reduction in its weight that continued until the end of the Republic. When 10 scruples of gold were rated at 25 *denarii*, the coinage ratio between the values of gold and silver was 9 : 1. This ratio was less favourable to gold than the market ratio, and the former was slowly raised to about $12\frac{1}{2}:1$ by reductions in the weight of the *aureus*,[1] unaccompanied by any reduction in the number of *denarii* to the *aureus*. Perhaps growing familiarity with gold coins made it possible to bring the coinage ratio into line with that in the market.

7. *The Augustan System and its Collapse.*

The monetary standards at the commencement of the empire were, for the *aureus*, about 120 grains,[2] and for the silver *denarius* a unit of exactly half that of the *aureus*. These standards continued unaltered from 14 B.C. to A.D. 64, when Nero reduced both gold and silver. The *aureus* then fell to about 114 grains,[3] and the *denarius* to about 52·5 grains,[4] while the fineness of the latter was reduced nearly 10 per cent. Although on subsequent occasions the *denarius* was most seriously debased, its weight was never reduced below the 3 scruples of the Neronian standard. The gold standard was more variable, but it mattered less because, in the course of time, it became increasingly common to pass gold by weight. During the second half of the 1st century A.D., after increasing some 3 or 5 grains, the *aureus* fell, by the end of the century, to the $6\frac{1}{2}$ scruples fixed by Nero.[5] Some profit was still to be made out of reducing the *aureus*, for, during the succeeding century, when the debasement of the silver coin was proceeding apace, the *aureus* was reduced, and by the early years of the 3rd century A.D. weighed only just over 100

[1] Sulla's issues weighed about 170 grains ($\frac{1}{30}$ of a pound); those of Pompey the Great, 140·5 grains ($\frac{1}{36}$ of a pound). Cæsar's gold at first weighed 144 grains ($\frac{1}{38}$ of a pound), and later 126·7 ($\frac{1}{40}$ pound), and by the end of the Republic the *aureus* weighed 122·5 grains ($\frac{1}{42}$ pound).

[2] Seven scruples or $\frac{1}{42}$ of a pound. The gold content of the *aureus* was almost identical with that of the British sovereign.

[3] Six and a half scruples, or $\frac{1}{45}$ of pound.

[4] Three scruples, or $\frac{1}{96}$ of a pound.

[5] Mommsen, III, 24.

grains.[1] It is useless to attempt to pursue the silver and gold standards during the greater part of the 3rd century.[2] Silver coins were so irregular in quality that it is impossible to trace any standard. The gold standard was also suspended. Coins were irregular in weight, and passed by weight and not by tale. The principal standard of value was the pound weight of gold.

8. *The Standards of the Reconstructed Systems.*

The first attempts to re-establish money of a fixed standard were made by Aurelian, but he did no more than stem the tide of debasement and issue a plated coinage of stable value. Diocletian made a series of experiments, probably in an attempt to establish an imperial bimetallic coinage. Before A.D. 290 he began to issue *aurei* of about 72·2 grains ($\frac{1}{70}$ of a pound).[3] In about 290 he probably called in old coins and issued new ones of gold, silver, and copper, the most important being those of silver. He seems to have aimed at the restoration of the Neronian *denarius* of about 52·5 grains or $\frac{1}{96}$ of a pound.[4] At the same time he raised the *aureus* to 84 grains ($\frac{1}{60}$ of a pound). The *aureus* was still worth 25 *denarii*, as at the beginning of the empire, and the system proved unstable; six years later the *aureus* was made equal to only 20 *denarii*. A further reform was necessary after only five years, in A.D. 301, when the *aureus* was raised to about 101 grains ($\frac{1}{50}$ of a pound) as it had been in the time of Nero, and apparently the *denarius* was also increased to a standard of 60 grains ($\frac{1}{84}$ of a pound),[5] But the experiment proved a failure, for in the next year both silver and gold returned to their weights before this change was made, silver being on Nero's standard of 52·5 grains, and gold 84 grains.[6] These many changes may have been due to difficulty in hitting the

[1] Under Marcus Aurelius (161-180 A.D.) it weighed 112 grains, and under Caracalla 100 grains, or $\frac{1}{50}$ of a pound.

[2] Alexander Severus seems to have made an unsuccessful attempt to establish the *denarius* on a 3-scruple standard (53 grains), and an *aureus* of about 92 grains.

[3] Equal in weight to the original *denarius* of 4 scruples.

[4] The numeral "XCVI" on some leaves no doubt as to the intended normal standard (Sydenham, *Num. Chron.*, 1919, 155).

[5] The *denarius* was then worth $\frac{1}{1000}$ of a pound of gold—which gave rise to the name *miliarense*.

[6] Sydenham, *Num. Chron.*, 1919, 159.

market ratio between gold and silver,[1] especially as there seems to have been a desire to retain in each system one of the traditional units for either gold or silver. Variations in the relative values of gold and silver in different parts of the empire may also have made it very difficult to establish a bimetallic system. Finally, Constantine laid the foundations of an enduring system in A.D. 312. Alexander, nearly 650 years before, abandoned his predecessor's unsuccessful attempt to establish an imperial money based on both gold and silver, and took refuge in the Athenian principle of coining both gold and silver on the same weight standard. Constantine followed much the same policy. He reverted to the piece of 4 scruples,[2] which had been the standard of the first silver coins ever issued in Rome,[3] and made both gold and silver coins of the same weight. The silver piece of 4 scruples was worth $\frac{1}{1000}$ of a pound of gold,[4] and was, in consequence, called a *miliarense*. But it is improbable that, as in Macedon, gold and silver were parallel and independent currencies. The silver coins were probably valued in terms of pounds of gold.[5] From about the middle of the 4th century A.D. the *siliqua*, the half of the *miliarense*, became increasingly important, at the expense of the small silver coins of Diocletian still in circulation. The new gold coin was the *solidus*, which was the basis of Roman coinage until the end of the Byzantine Empire in 1453 A.D. The *solidus* was never lowered in weight,[6] but was later debased, although only after the unit had spread far and wide. It was this *solidus* that circulated as the *byzant* throughout Western Europe in the Dark Ages, after the fall of Rome. Charlemagne based his currency arrangements on those of the Byzantine Empire, and thus made the *byzant* the basis of most medieval European currencies. The *solidus* was later divided in Rome into three *tremisses*, each of

[1] The ratios tried were:

1:15·6 (25 *denarii* of 52·5 grains each to the *aureus* of 84 grains)
1:12·5 (20 „ 52·5 „ „ „ „ 84 „)
1:12 (20 „ 60 „ „ „ „ 101 „)
1:12·5 (20 „ 52·5 „ „ „ „ 84 „)

[2] 71·5 grains, or $\frac{1}{72}$ of a pound.

[3] Diocletian experimented with gold coins on this basis in 290 A.D. (*vide supra*).

[4] At a ratio of gold to silver of 13·88:1.

[5] *Vide* Chap. XVI.

[6] With the exception of a passing alteration in A.D. 963-9 (Mommsen, III, 65).

24 grains. The first statute on the subject of the monetary standard in England, passed in about 1265, ordained that a silver penny should weigh 32 grains of wheat, round and dry, and taken from the midst of the ear; $1\frac{1}{3}$ wheat grains, being equal in weight to one troy grain, the silver penny weighed 24 troy grains, or the same as the Roman *tremiss*. But the statute introduced no new standard: the unit goes back to the time of the Norman invasion, and, in all probability, to a very much earlier date, it being quite possible that some of the Saxon issues are based on the same standard. The English silver penny is thus also descended from the *tremiss*. The beginning of the modern series of gold currencies is to be found in the first issues of gold florins at Florence in 1252. These coins weighed 72 Florentine and 53 English grains.[1] Five years later Henry III. followed with the first recorded issue of gold in England. These new gold pennies also weighed two sterlings or 48 grains.[2] No more is heard of the issue of gold coins until 1344, when an issue was made, based on a unit said to be "equal in weight to two petit florins of Florence of good weight,"[3] and to weigh 108 grains ($1\frac{1}{2}$ times the weight of the *solidus*). These pieces were unsatisfactory (probably because the gold was rated too high), and they were melted and recoined in the same year. The new piece was the *noble* of 138·5 grains, but the story of the evolution of the British existing currency system from these early English gold and silver units cannot be pursued here.

9. *Summary.*

The oldest metallic unit of value in Italy was clearly the *libra* of copper. Although it is possible to discover in the silver issues of the Greek cities of Magna Græcia and Sicily traces of almost every silver standard used in the Greek world, it is fairly clear that the bronze unit always dominated in the end. The Æginetan coins, identified with the *drachm*, are probably based, in fact, on the Corinthian *didrachm*. But the "Corinthian" unit was largely superseded by the "Eubœan" unit of 130-135 grains. As a silver unit it was successful because it made concessions to the native system. It was

[1] Ridgeway (385) states that the florin weighed 48 grains, or exactly 2 *tremisses*, whereas it seems to have weighed about $2\frac{1}{2}$ in fact.

[2] Ruding, *Annals of the Coinage*, I, 186.

[3] *Ibid.*, I, 217.

divided into tenths, which were called *litras*, which the population was persuaded to accept as equivalent in value to their old bronze unit, although correspondence was probably not exact. As a gold unit the Attic standard requires little explanation, agreement with the gold issues of Athens and Macedon being sufficient to ensure its success. Further north the unit of 120 grains, introduced perhaps from Asia Minor, although attractive enough to gain general acceptance in Campania, and even to be adopted as the basis of the first issues of silver by the Romans, just failed to become the basis of the Roman republican silver coinage because it could not be conveniently grafted on to the Roman *as*. In the conflict between the two units the silver unit was abandoned, and a standard, based on the scruple weight of silver, became the basis of the Roman system. In all probability the silver unit was merely the *libra* of bronze expressed in silver. All these standards, including the scruple (in its tenfold multiple), can be recognized in the Eastern Mediterranean, and may be explained merely as having been brought by colonists and traders. But the fact that, in the procession of standards in Italy, the later standard is almost invariably lower than its predecessor, at least suggests that the influences tending to the reduction of units in the Greek world[1] were also at work in Magna Græcia. Agreement between standards was often accidental and sometimes an excuse for further reduction. The bronze standards have themselves been related to the Babylonian standards, but the relation is at best distant, and a native origin is more probable. Primarily the *libra* may be traced to a piece of bronze defined by size, but the units of length upon which it was based may have been derived from the human body or arranged so that the resulting piece of copper should be the successor of some earlier barter unit of value or a fraction of it. Once established, the bronze *libra* was the basic value unit until the second Punic War, if we regard the scruple standard used for silver in 268 as the silver equivalent of the *litra*. Slight reductions were made in the silver *denarius* in 217 B.C., and again in the middle of the 1st century A.D. by Nero, and in the orgy of inflation during the 2nd and 3rd centuries coin standards were swept away. When they were finally restored by Constantine, we find

[1] *Vide* Chap. IX.

both silver and gold being coined on the scruple standard. Silver becoming less important, it was the *solidus* of 4 scruples of gold that became the principal monetary unit. This *byzant* was not the old pound of copper unit of value translated into gold, or any easy multiple of it. It was a new value unit, born of the transference of a weight unit from silver to gold.

CHAPTER XI

SUBDIVISIONS OF THE MONEY UNIT

1. *The Functions of Divisional Money.*

It is obvious that the introduction of coins could not be limited to the establishment of a single unit of value, and a coin of a single denomination as its representative. The unit of value and the standard coin are merely a basis, and it is now necessary to consider what kind of system has been erected on their foundation in each place.

As soon as the processes of addition and multiplication are understood, large values can be expressed in multiples of the unit of value. But if subdivision of that unit is not provided for, inaccuracy will necessarily exist owing to limitation of the expression of value to whole numbers of the unit. Moreover, goods and services of smaller value than the unit selected cannot be valued at all. Then, either a smaller unit of value is adopted on some basis independent of the main unit, or else a knowledge of division leads to the subdivision of the principal unit on a mathematically convenient basis. By one or other of these methods a series of units of value is obtained. Our first enquiry must, therefore, relate to the series of units used in each area and their origin. But expressions of value are commonly preliminary to an exchange in which money is required to settle the bargain on one side. Then it is necessary for the subdivisions of the unit to be represented by coins, and questions arise as to the material of which these coins should be made. Where the divisions are small, considerations of convenience make it undesirable for the small change money to be of the same material as is used for the standards. If gold and silver are the monetary metals, then the small denominations are represented by coins so small that they rapidly lose weight owing to the wear and tear of circulation, and are difficult to handle and easy to lose. On the other hand, if copper, tin, or iron were used for all coins, although the pieces representing small denominations would be of convenient size the larger units would not. This difficulty can best be surmounted by using different metals for the large and small denominations respectively. But if all the coins are of full weight, and freely coined and melted, the system will be bimetallic and subject to all the disturbing effects of changes in the relative market values of the two metals. This, and the difficulty of the inconvenient coins resulting if all are made of the same metal, can both be avoided by making the smaller coins tokens.[1]

This matter of small change money is by no means unimportant. In early times, larger bargains were probably capable of easy settlement by barter, but the smaller and more personal exchanges must have called first for some common medium of exchange to facilitate them. Now many of the comforts of modern civilization depend upon the effectiveness with which the need for small money is met. When people were little specialized, and supplied most of their own needs, the efficiency of arrangements for exchange was of no great moment. But economic development has been along lines of increasing specialization, so that we have now become accustomed to obtain by exchange the greater part of the goods and services we enjoy. These having increased in both quantity and variety, some of the exchanges are of quite small values. The smooth running and effectiveness of this complicated system demand a suitable series of small units of value and small change money.

2. *The Origin of the Babylonian, Egyptian, and Minoan Divisional Units.*

The weights of the basic currency units were founded upon the weights in use before coining commenced, and it may be asked whether the multiples and submultiples arose in the same way. There was a series of units of weight for gold and silver in Babylon and Assyria long before any coins were issued, and we may first discuss the origin and basis of the series. To take the second problem first, it is difficult to locate the basis from which multiples and submultiples were calculated. Those who have credited the Babylonians

[1] See Chap. XII.

with the invention of all the weight units of the ancient world have often assumed that the basis of the Babylonian system itself was the *talent*. But the *talent* was probably not the earliest unit.[1] In the first place, it contained 60 *minas*, while it is probable that the sexagesimal was not the earliest basis of subdivision in Babylon.[2] More probably division by fifty, derived from the practice of counting upon the fingers, is older: gold and silver were probably the first commodities to be weighed, and we find that the *mina* used for gold contained 50 *shekels*. When later the *mina* for other goods was established, the sexagesimal had become popular, and the new *mina* was sixtyfold of the *shekel*. It was probably at this time that the *talent* was added to the system, and for this reason it was sixtyfold of the *mina*. Of the *mina* and the *shekel* it is probable that the *shekel*[3] is the older, although ancient records of Babylonian and Assyrian weights are confined to the *mina*, which is the only unit of the existence of which in Babylonia there is positive evidence. But the *shekel* is the unit which is common to the table for both commodities and gold. In the Hebrew scriptures, gold and silver are measured in *shekels* and not *minas*.[4] Moreover, if ancient units for gold are to be derived from the previous use of the ox unit of value, the *shekel* would be the unit first established.

Commencing from the *shekel* as a basis, we must account for the *mina* of 50 *shekels*, and the *talent* of 60 *minas*. In the formation of all early metrical systems, two not altogether harmonious influences were at work. On the one hand units tended to emerge independently of each other in primitive times. Units of measurement based on the human body gave rise to measurement by size, which ultimately produced weight units. Weight units also emerged from the translation into gold or silver of value units, based upon commodities that played a large part in primitive exchange. On the other hand, there might be a desire for a system of weights in which the units were simply and uniformly inter-related on a mathematical basis. The Mesopotamian peoples were peculiarly sensible to this latter influence. In consequence

[1] See Chap. VIII. [2] Ridgeway, 268.

[3] Ridgeway, 254. Head (*Hist. Num.*, XXXV) also regards the *shekel* as the "unit on which the entire sexagesimal scale of weights was constructed."

[4] Ridgeway, 246.

of the close attention which they gave to the heavenly bodies they invented methods of measuring time and the movements of the heavenly bodies which have lasted to the present. They laid the foundations of mathematics and of metrology. Therein lay their most lasting legacy to the world. It is possible, therefore, that the *mina* and the *talent* were both established as convenient multiples of the *shekel*, the former in the earlier period when decimal inter-relations were preferred, and the latter when the advantages of the sexagesimal basis had been realized. Apart from the ease of manipulation offered by a sexagesimal system, there is no explanation of its adoption by the Babylonians. But as against the suggestion that the *talent* was a mathematically obtained multiple of the *shekel*, there is the possibility that it is based upon a very old unit equal to the amount a man could carry. The root of the word talent is τλατλάω (I bear), and it is extremely probable that a load unit of this nature would be one of the earliest to be established. The Babylonian gold *talent* (of 3,000 *shekels*) would weigh nearly 70 pounds troy, while that used for commodities and bronze (of 3,600 *shekels*) would weigh over 80 pounds,[1] or just about a reasonable load. But perhaps when the sexagesimal system was introduced, it was found that 60 *minas* approached in magnitude the load unit, which had either been invented locally or borrowed from Greece,[2] and the load was then adjusted to make it exactly equal to 60 *minas* for the sake of an orderly system. No independent origins are suggested for the *mina*. Although it is the one unit certainly contributed by the Babylonian civilization to the Attic, the only explanation of its origin is that it was established as a multiple of the *shekel* when decimal relations were still popular.

There is some evidence that there was in early times a multiple of the gold *shekel* based upon a slave unit of value. One of the earliest gold units in use in Macedon was threefold of the ox unit, and in later times a piece equal to three gold *staters* was referred to in Egypt as the Macedonian *talent*,

[1] It is possible that the gold *shekel* was itself arrived at by translating a copper *talent* unit of value into gold (Gardner, 23).

[2] Seltman (123) claims that it was a unit invented probably in Eubœa for weighing copper, and that it passed in the hands of the Æolian and Ionian Greeks to Lydia, Asia Minor, and the East. When it came again to Greece, it was in fact a native unit returning.

probably because it was introduced by the Macedonian dynasty of Lagidæ, set up in Egypt after the death of Alexander. A similar unit existed in Magna Græcia and Sicily, and is presumed, therefore, to have been in use at one time in Greece proper.[1] As there is evidence that in some parts a slave was equal in value to about three cows, it is possible that this unit is the direct successor of an early slave unit. But no coins were based upon this unit in later times.

We have already seen that in Asia a still smaller unit than the *shekel* was used for weighing gold. The inscription on the Assyrian "duck" weight in the Louvre is probably to be read "22½ grains," the grains possibly being wheat grains.[2] The *shekel* of 130 grains (troy) probably contained 180 of these grains, and Professor Ridgeway has suggested that they were the basis of the whole Assyrian system in its original form.[3] The origin of the unit is doubtless to be found in the weight of some familiar seed, if not the grain of wheat, and the relation between it and the *shekel* is simply the resulting relation between two independently obtained units.

It now remains to attempt to explain the origin of the Babylonian silver units. The only theories that have been advanced regard them as derived from the gold unit to which they are supposed to have been related on a value basis. The weight was designed so that unit weight of silver would be worth $\frac{1}{10}$, $\frac{1}{15}$ or $\frac{1}{20}$ of the gold unit. They were, therefore, subdivisions of the gold unit of value.[4] A decimal or quindecimal relation may have been chosen for ease of calculation in the period before the convenience of duodecimal relations was appreciated, and the system based on the use of the fingers for counting was still in vogue. But there is no evidence for or against the suggestion that the silver units were subdivisions of the gold unit. They may have their own separate roots in the period when domesticated animals provided the principal

[1] Ridgeway, 304. [2] *Vide* Chap. I.

[3] Ridgeway, 183, 191. He considers that as the "duck" weight was inscribed with its weight, not in fractions of a *shekel* or *obol*, but in numbers of lower units, it was regarded as a multiple of the lower unit. It has been suggested that if the *talent* was the basic unit, it may have been obtained by weighing an accepted volume of corn (Ridgeway, 185).

[4] The principal Asiatic coin standards "point clearly to a recognized system of interchangeable values in the different metals, and, moreover, to the fact that a Babylonian gold unit, ranging in weight from 126 to 135 grains in the *root norm* which, at the rate of 13⅓ : 1, accounts for all of them" (Head, XL).

units of value. There is some evidence that the sheep was the basis of an early unit of value in many parts of Greece, Syria, and Palestine. The Hebrew word *qesitah*, translated as "a piece of money" in the Old Testament,[1] is also translatable as "a lamb." Moreover, weights in the form of sheep have been found in Syria, and in Palestine tribute was calculated in sheep.[2] Plutarch[3] states that Solon reckoned a sheep equal to a *drachm* in sacrifices. If the sheep was worth $\frac{1}{10}$ as much as an ox, and when the latter was translated into gold the former was translated into silver, the tenfold relation between gold and silver units would result. Wherever both gold and silver units were coined in early times, the resulting series of values is, in consequence of the duodecimal division of units of each metal, and the decimal relations between the value of the units of different metals, a combination of both factors.

Those who consider that the early use of the ox was due solely to its use in sacred ritual suggest that all subdivisional units had a similar origin. This supreme unit was now divided into smaller denominations (untere Nominale). The head, hide, leg, and tongue were all units (Zahlungseinheiten), which it is claimed originated in the slaughter of sacrificial animals. This was governed by the rules of religious ritual, customary compliance with which gave rise to an established system of subdivisions of the unit in the most literal sense. No value relations grew up between the different small units nor between them and the principal unit, because, while the ordinances on the matter of religious ritual specified the parts of the sacrificial animals to be given to the gods, and also to the priests and ecclesiastical and state officials, the substitution of one part by another was forbidden by the code. In consequence, the value of one in terms of another part was never determined in the earlier period. Such values were first worked out "when the animal was commuted for other goods, which were now taken as a means of payment in its stead. In remote districts (the use of animal units) was maintained down to hellenistic times."[4] Parts of beasts may have been used for barter, and there is nothing improbable

[1] *Genesis* xxxiii, 19; *Joshua* xxiv, 32; *Job* xlii, 11.
[2] Ridgeway, 270-71.
[3] *Solon* (Langhorne trans.), 70.
[4] Laum, *Heiliges Geld*, 78-79.

in the statement that "the hide was a regular submultiple of the cow,"[1] for the two commodities are likely to occur together in commerce. But there is no adequate evidence that tongues and heads were a medium of exchange, or, even if they were, that the need for small units was first felt in connection with the settlement of accounts with the gods. Moreover, no attempt seems to have been made to trace known units to specific parts of the ox.

The Egyptian weight system was, as we have seen, complex. The most commonly used units were the *deben* and the *kedet*, ten of the latter being equal to the former. Of the relation between the two units nothing can be said, except that the Egyptians, having, like the Babylonians, been interested in mathematics and mensuration, are likely to have constructed the *deben* in a mathematical relation to the *kedet*. Apparently they favoured decimal relations between units. But the series throws no light on subsequent coins.

The Minoans had no native units, but used those found also in Asia and Egypt. But they do not always seem to have accepted the whole metric systems used there. Weights that have been found suggest a strong preference for a duodecimal system. They probably had a unit equal to 144 Babylonian gold *shekels*.[2] In Cyprus, however, the Egyptian series of 10 *kedets* to the *deben* was probably adopted.[3] But in the Ægean duodecimal systems were again most favoured during the Minoan period, and there seems to have been a unit equal to 144 *kedets*. The influence of the Babylonian methods of subdivision is also very evident.[4] The Babylonian *talent* was borrowed,[5] and probably the *shekel* as well, the two being related as in Babylon.[6] The *kedet* seems to have been

[1] Ridgeway, 332.

[2] A marble cylinder found at Siteia (Crete), believed to have been a weight unit, weighs 17,566 grains (144 × 122 grains) (Glotz, 191-92).

[3] Ten hæmatite olive weights from Enkomi (Cyprus) suggest weights of two, three, five, and ten times a unit of 142·6 grains (Glotz, 193).

[4] The full series was 12 *kedet* = 1 *deben*, 12 *deben* = 1 "gross" (Glotz, 193).

[5] It may have been re-borrowed, Asia having at an early period borrowed it from Greece.

[6] A number of units of copper found in Sardinia weigh 512,800 grains (3,600 × 143) (Glotz, 193).

accompanied by a unit 3,600 times as large,[1] used for copper, and presumably a *talent* comparable with the *talent* based on the Babylonian *shekel*. A further complete series seems to have been built upon the unit of 194 grains in the Babylonian style, including *minas*[2] and *talents*.[3] Other weights which have been found are not easy to fit into any of these systems.[4] Where the internal relations of these systems are comparable to those of the Babylonian, imitation probably explains them. But for the rest a desire for an orderly system, based usually on a preference for a duodecimal relation, is the only explanation. Of these the series which most affected coining in the Greek world in later times is that based upon the Babylonian *shekel*. In a previous chapter, the origin of the *shekel* in Greece has been discussed; it may or may not have been borrowed from Babylonian sources. The *talent* is as likely to have originated in Greece[5] as in Asia. But the *mina* almost certainly arrived in Greece from Asia. It is usually associated in Greece with the weighing of silver, and was probably adopted as a more convenient unit than the *drachm* for a metal considerably less valuable than gold. The Greeks, however, contributed new divisions of the *mina*. The Asiatic system came into contact with the native iron *obols* and *drachms* at Ægina, where there was a *mina* which was divided into 100 *drachms* each of 6 *obols*. The basis of the Greek system will be considered below, but it may be supposed that the new *mina* was established to equal, at current market rates for iron, 100 iron *drachms*. These *drachm* units passed back to Asia, and certainly in the Greek cities of Asia Minor superseded the *shekel* unit.[6]

[1] See Chap. VIII. One specimen suggests a *talent* of 3,000 *shekels* (as used in Babylon for gold) and one a talent of 3,600 *shekels* (as used in Babylon for other than gold and silver).

[2] Nineteen ingots found at Cyme in Eubœa seem to be based on a unit of 9,700 grains (50 × 194). Twenty-five *minas* seems to have been a common multiple (Glotz, 193).

[3] An ingot of bronze from Enkomi (Cyprus) weighs 571,250 (Glotz, 193). (A *talent* of 60 of the above *minas* would weigh 582,120 grains.)

[4] Geese of hæmatite or cornelian, in a form well known on the Nile and in the east, weigh 2,572 grains (considerably more than 20 Babylonian *shekels*), 40 grains ($\frac{1}{3}$ Babylonian *shekel*), and 25 grains ($\frac{1}{5}$ Babylonian *shekel*) (Glotz, 191-92).

[5] But it is doubtful whether at any time in Greece proper the *talent* of gold was ever considered as a monetary unit " (Ridgeway, 308).

[6] Seltman (115) claims that the *talent* was a unit for copper, the *drachm* for iron, the *stater* for gold, and the *mina* and *shekel* for silver.

3. *Divisional Coins in Lydia and Persia.*

In the period after the introduction of coining, interest centres mainly round the denominations which were represented by coins. The *talent* and *mina* were never coined, although they were frequently used as large units of value. We must turn to the *shekel* and its divisions. In Lydia, from the time of Gyges (687-652 B.C.) to the middle of the 6th century, punch-marked pieces represent $\frac{1}{2}$, $\frac{1}{3}$, $\frac{1}{6}$, $\frac{1}{12}$, $\frac{1}{24}$, $\frac{1}{48}$, $\frac{1}{96}$[1] of the "Phœnician" unit.[2] Excavations on the site of the Crœsan Artemision at Ephesus in 1904-1905 revealed a number of coins of all of these denominations. The half-*staters* were generally about $2\frac{1}{2}$ grains under their proper weight, a deduction which may have been "purposely made in order to cover the cost of mintage, and to bring in a profit as well."[3] The small denominations of $\frac{1}{96}$ of a *stater* (2·1 or 2·2 grains) are hardly coins at all, as they bear no type. They can "have been of very little practical use except as make-weights for money changers, as they are far too small to have commonly passed from hand to hand as current money. But as make-weights extremely small fractions would be indispensable to dealers so long as gold, electrum, and silver, whether in the form of bullion or as coin, continued to be exchanged by weight and not merely by tale."[4] It is clear that, although some profit may have been made out of the issue, the pieces passed by weight and were not tokens. The size of the pieces can, therefore, have been of very little importance, although a variety of sizes with some small pieces would, as is suggested, be necessary if exact weights were to be made up. There is no known reason why the division should have been by 96. The series as a whole suggests that a duodecimal basis of division was desired, and that the smaller pieces were obtained by repeated halving of units. All the subdivisions of the silver unit must, therefore, be explained as mathematically ascertained fractions of the larger unit. It is notable that the

[1] Head, *Hist. Num.*, 644-45; *Brit. Mus. Excavations at Ephesus*, IX, 77. The pieces representing $\frac{1}{96}$ of a *stater* bear no type.

[2] There seems to be no record of a similarly complete series based on the "Babylonian" units.

[3] Head, *Brit. Mus. Excavations at Ephesus*, 78.

[4] *Ibid.*, 78-79.

Lydians in their selection of subdivisions showed that concern for the disposal of electrum which runs through their whole monetary policy; they coined on an adequate but simple series calculated to make their coins attractive. Their currency also marks a stage when all the coins were made of one material, and none were token.

With the Crœsan reform, gold and silver coins superseded electrum. The gold unit of 130 grains was divided into $\frac{1}{3}$, $\frac{1}{6}$, and $\frac{1}{12}$, and the new silver *stater* which was worth $\frac{1}{10}$ of the gold unit, into $\frac{1}{2}$, $\frac{1}{3}$, and $\frac{1}{12}$. The gold and silver coins of this series, taken together, form a series,[1] of which the smallest unit is $\frac{1}{120}$ of the largest. The other series was based on a gold *stater* of 168 grains with subdivisions of $\frac{1}{3}$, $\frac{1}{6}$, and $\frac{1}{12}$ and a silver *stater* of 220 grains worth $\frac{1}{10}$ of the gold unit.[2] The series of subdivisions[3] of this unit of value appears to be less complete than the former, but it is probable that other denominations were made, although we have no specimens of them. The very small subdivisions of electrum were abandoned, partly because some of the subdivisions of the silver unit approached some of the electrum subdivisions in value and confusion might result, and partly because silver pieces were more convenient to handle in the small denominations than those of electrum, which was ten times as valuable as silver. The duodecimal principle of division, characteristic of the earlier Lydian system, is very obvious in the subdivisions of the unit of each metal, while decimal relations between the values of units of gold and silver respectively were taken over from the ancient Asiatic systems. In consequence, the values of the whole series of coins of both metals rest upon both decimal and duodecimal factors. The Crœsan system is notable in that it is the first in which divisions of the principal unit of value were not all represented in the same metal. But the use of tokens for small denominations did not then appear. The use of silver instead of electrum for small denominations made possible a more extensive series, and the smallest unit was $\frac{1}{120}$ of the largest, instead of $\frac{1}{96}$ as in the earlier system.

Our knowledge of the subdivisions of the Persian *daric* and *shekel* is meagre. The only known subdivisions of the

[1] 1, $\frac{1}{3}$, $\frac{1}{6}$, $\frac{1}{10}$, $\frac{1}{12}$, $\frac{1}{20}$, $\frac{1}{30}$, $\frac{1}{120}$.

[2] Head, *Hist. Num.*, 646.

[3] 1, $\frac{1}{3}$, $\frac{1}{6}$, $\frac{1}{10}$, and $\frac{1}{12}$.

gold unit represent $\frac{1}{12}$ and $\frac{1}{54}$ of it,[1] while pieces representing $\frac{1}{3}$ and $\frac{1}{6}$ of the silver *shekel*[2] are known.[3] Again, we find that the Persians were indebted to the people they conquered. It is fairly clear that they accepted the duodecimal basis of division; probably they were familiar with it before they met it in Lydia. The series seems very short, and it is reasonable to suppose that some denominations have been lost. But it is quite possible that there were fewer coins in the Persian than the Lydian system; the Persians placed considerable emphasis on the simplicity of the monetary system. The decimal relation between silver and gold units was adopted for similar historical reasons. Like the Lydians, they used metals for the complete series, and did not resort to tokens for the smaller pieces. As a whole the system[4] was moderately comprehensive, the smallest unit being $\frac{1}{120}$ of the largest, as in the Crœsan system.

The cities of Asia Minor followed in their coinage of electrum a policy of dividing the unit into $\frac{1}{3}$ and $\frac{1}{6}$ (*hecté*) and downwards to the ninety-sixth[5] part, the *hecté* being the most famous unit. The series is similar to that in Lydia at the same period, and doubtless has a similar origin. Where silver was coined it ranged from 2 *staters* to $\frac{1}{96}$ of the *stater*,[6] denominations being roughly parallel with those used locally for electrum and those used in Greece for silver.[7]

4. *Divisional Coins in Greece and Magna Græcia, and their Origin.*

The earliest coins of Greece were those of Ægina, where the Asiatic and native Greek systems of weights for the precious metal met. The *mina*, as we have seen, was assimilated in Ægina to 100 local *drachms*. The *drachm* was again divided into 6 *obols*, which each contained 12 *chalci*[8]

[1] Cyrus on one occasion agreed to pay soldiers a *daric* and a half a month instead of a *daric* (Xenophon, *Anabasis*, I, 3, 21), but although the half-*daric* was used as a unit of account, it was not coined. Double *darics* were issued in the latest period of Persian rule, but possibly Alexander and his generals were responsible for them.

[2] Probably the subdivisions of the *shekel* were not issued at first.

[3] Head, *Hist. Num.*, 827-28.

[4] 1, $\frac{1}{12}$, $\frac{1}{20}$, $\frac{1}{54}$, $\frac{1}{60}$, and $\frac{1}{120}$.

[5] 1, $\frac{1}{2}$, $\frac{1}{3}$, $\frac{1}{6}$, $\frac{1}{12}$, $\frac{1}{24}$, $\frac{1}{48}$, $\frac{1}{96}$ (Head, *Hist. Num.*, 564).

[6] *Ibid.*, 564 *sqq.*

[7] *Ibid.*, 564 *sqq.*

[8] Aristotle is believed to have referred to the division of the *obol* into twelve parts (cp. Pollux, *cit.* Ridgeway, 349).

(each weighing 1·375 grains). Later, when the Eubœan system was adopted in Athens at the end of the 7th century B.C., practically the same *mina* was used, but it was divided into 150 *drachms* (of about 130 grains).[1] These were divided, as in Ægina, into 6 *obols*, but the *obols* were divided into only 8 *chalci*. The Æginetan and Attic systems are, therefore, almost identical in their largest and smallest units, only the intermediate units being different. The Æginetans coined on the basis of this weight system, thus introducing the *obol* as a coin. From the middle of the 7th century the normal series of coins was 1, $\frac{1}{2}$, $\frac{1}{4}$, $\frac{1}{6}$, $\frac{1}{8}$, $\frac{1}{12}$, $\frac{1}{24}$, $\frac{1}{48}$[2] *staters*, or from the full 144 down to 3 *chalci*,[3] pieces of 2, and somctimes 5 *staters* being also issued.

Where the "Eubœan" unit was used, the subdivisional coins again followed the weight system. In Athens, from the early years of the 6th century, there were pieces ranging from 4 *drachms* to $\frac{1}{12}$ of a *drachm*,[4] and down to the end of the 5th century very little change was made.[5] The emergency gold issues of 407-406 B.C. were parallel in their denominations to the silver issues.[6] But if gold was then twelve times as valuable as silver, such a duodecimal division produced coins easily valued in silver coins. These gold issues did not, however, greatly increase the series of denominations. The second gold issue, made some time in the 4th century B.C., differs from the first only in that it included 2-*drachm* pieces. Between 393 B.C., when the plated siege pieces were decried, and 339 B.C. there was a very obvious attempt to increase the range of denominations. There may have been a growing demand for small change. It is also possible that the tokens had so sunk in value as to act as small change, and their with-

[1] *Encyclopædia Britannica:* Article "Weights and Measures."

[2] Head, *Hist. Num.*, 396.

[3] In Phocis, from the middle of the 6th century, fractions of $\frac{1}{2}$, $\frac{1}{4}$, $\frac{1}{6}$, and $\frac{1}{12}$ of the *stater* were issued, and later the *stater* (Head, *Hist. Num.*, 338). In Delphi the divisions at the end of the 6th century were $\frac{1}{4}$, $\frac{1}{6}$, $\frac{1}{8}$, $\frac{1}{12}$, $\frac{1}{24}$, to which were added, in about 480 B.C., the $1\frac{1}{2}$ and 1 *stater*. In Bœotia the pieces coined in the middle of the 6th century were 1, $\frac{1}{2}$, $\frac{1}{12}$, $\frac{1}{24}$ *staters* (Head, *Hist. Num.*, 343).

[4] 4, 1, $\frac{1}{2}$, $\frac{1}{4}$, $\frac{1}{6}$, $\frac{1}{12}$.

[5] During period from 514 to 407 B.C. 2-*drachm* and 10-*drachm* pieces appeared. Seltman suggested that the latter were issued in connection with the distribution of the proceeds of the silver mines referred to by Herodotus, but the suggestion has been severely criticized (*Num. Chron.*, 1924, 338).

[6] 1, $\frac{1}{2}$, $\frac{1}{3}$, $\frac{1}{6}$ *drachms* (Gardner, 292).

drawal brought to a head the demand for a more complete system. Consequently, a very full series was issued from 10 *drachms* to $\frac{1}{48}$ of a *drachm*.[1] Similar systems were found in most of the Greek cities and islands.[2]

The origin of these series of subdivisions is not easy to trace. It is unlikely that the whole series was introduced from abroad. Even if it was, the problem is but moved back a stage. But we have seen that the *drachm* was probably of native origin,[3] and it is probable that such can be said of the whole series. The *mina*, although bearing an Asiatic name, is not identical with any of the Asiatic *minas*.[4] More probably in its Greek form it was built on the "Æginetan" *drachm*, of which it was made a hundredfold. So far the upper unit is mathematically obtained from the *drachm* on a decimal basis. But as the Asiatic name was used, the Asiatic units probably had some influence on the multiple chosen.[5] If the *drachm* was the result of the translation into silver of the earlier "handful" of iron spits, its division into *obols* certainly dates from the same system. The sixfold division is explained by the fact that six of the old iron spits could be grasped in one hand. The 2-*drachm* piece, or *stater*, was from the earliest times the favourite denomination in Greece. Possibly it also represented a unit commonly used before coins were current, because it "is the equivalent of the bars of bronze which a man carries when he has both his hands full of bars, six in each. It stands for a man, while a *drachm* represents only half a man"; perhaps the issue of *didrachms* in Ægina from the beginning of coining is explained in this

[1] 10, 4, 2, 1, $\frac{10}{12}$, $\frac{2}{3}$, $\frac{1}{2}$, $\frac{1}{3}$, $\frac{1}{6}$, $\frac{1}{8}$, $\frac{1}{12}$, $\frac{1}{16}$, $\frac{1}{24}$, $\frac{1}{48}$.

[2] At Chalcis, in Eubœa, in the 6th century, pieces represented 4, 2, 1, $\frac{2}{3}$, $\frac{1}{4}$, $\frac{1}{6}$ *drachms* (Head, *Hist. Num.*, 357). In Eretria, in Eubœa, the range was only 4, 2, $\frac{1}{6}$, so far as is known, 1, $\frac{1}{3}$, $\frac{1}{12}$ being added towards the close of the century (Head, *Hist. Num.*, 360). In Salamis (Cyprus) the usual divisional silver money was $\frac{1}{3}$, $\frac{1}{6}$, and $\frac{1}{12}$ of the unit. When, however, the first gold pieces were struck at the end of the 5th century B.C., they were divided into 3rds, 10ths, and twentieths, but towards the middle of the 4th century the innovation disappeared, and division into twelfths replaced it (Head, *Hist. Num.*, 742-43).

[3] See Chap. IX.

[4] The Greek *mina* weighed 9,750 grains, while the Babylonian gold *mina* weighed 13,000 grains, the "Babylonian" silver *mina* 17,200 grains and "Phœnician" silver *mina* 11,500 grains.

[5] The *talent* was sixty-fold the *mina* by analogy with the system in the East.

way;[1] although, under these circumstances, it might have been expected that the unit would have been called by a name that would give some clue to its origin.[2] Convenience in size of the resulting coin seems a more solid reason for the existence of the *didrachm* coin. Professor Ridgeway claims, of course, that the *stater* was the descendant of the Homeric *talanton*, and the basis of the whole system. The use of the term *stater* is itself claimed as evidence of the fundamental importance of the *stater*.[3]

The division of the *obol* into 12 *chalci*, reminiscent as it is of the division of the Roman *as* into *unciæ*, can only be explained by a desire for duodecimal division, which had been popular in the Ægean for many centuries. The origin of the "Eubœan" *drachm* has already been discussed.[4] Its division into 6 *obols* is copied from the Æginetan, while the division into *chalci* is designed to make the *chalcus* a unit common to both systems.[5]

The coins of Corinth were related to each other in much the same way as those of other Greek cities. Pieces ranged from the *stater* to its $\frac{1}{24}$ part.[6] Moreover, the *stater* was similar to the "Eubœan" unit. But Asiatic influences were stronger in Corinth than elsewhere, and the *stater* was divided into thirds and sixths as in Asia, instead of into halves as elsewhere in Greece. This division had the advantage that the resulting coins could be easily related to both the Æginetan and the Eubœan. The "Corinthian" *stater* (of 3 *drachms*) was equal in value to the "Eubœan" *stater* (of 2 *drachms*), while the "Corinthian" *drachms* were practically equal to the "Æginetan" *drachm*.[7] In consequence,

[1] Gardner, 120.

[2] It was called a *stater*. This word was used by the Greeks for the standard or unit coin in any system, as the word *shekel* was used by the Oriental (Hill, *Camb. Anc. Hist.*, IV, 131).

[3] "As long as no other unit than the ox unit or *talanton* was employed, the *talanton* or "weight" *par excellence* was sufficient to describe it: but when under Asiatic influences the higher unit of the *mina* and *talent* were introduced, a term was substituted which indicates clearly that the gold unit of 130 grains was the weight or basis of the whole system" (Ridgeway, 308).

[4] Chap. IX.

[5] Professor Ridgeway states that the smallest unit in the Greek weight system of weights was the wheat grain. The *drachm* contained 18 *kerata* (or carob seed units), which each contained 4 wheat grains (*op. cit.*, 181).

[6] 1, $\frac{1}{2}$, $\frac{1}{3}$, $\frac{1}{6}$, $\frac{1}{8}$, $\frac{1}{12}$, $\frac{1}{24}$ *staters* (Head, 399).

[7] Head, *Hist. Num.*, 399; Ridgeway, 311.

the Corinthian coins were not limited to the narrow isthmus of Corinth, but travelled far, particularly to the west, to her colonies on the shores of Epirus and Acarnania, and to the Achæan cities of Magna Græcia.

Although most of the South Italian cities adopted the Corinthian division of the *stater* after the "Æginetan" unit disappeared, those of Sicily, and possibly Tarentum and a few others on the mainland, adhered to the Athenian series. Moreover, many of the cities in both areas divide the *stater* by ten.[1] Decimal division of the unit could never have been learned from the Greek cities. It is probably explained by the fact that the unit so obtained was practically identical in value with the bronze *litra*, which was the native unit of value. In this way, the native system, and that of the Ægean, were easily related to each other. The Greek subdivisional units, therefore, are mainly divisions of the various Greek *drachms* arrived at by a duodecimal division, influenced in part by the earlier currency of *obols*, and doubtless also by the tradition of long standing in the Ægean in favour of duodecimal division. In Corinth Asiatic influences, and in Magna Græcia and Sicily native tradition, imposed a second method of subdivision.

The representation of small subdivisions of the local unit in coins was not easy in the Greek world. So long as a policy of rigid silver monometallism was adhered to, the small denominations were inconveniently small. The silver *chalcus* in Athens, for example, weighed 1·4 grains or about $\frac{1}{15}$ as much as the British three-penny piece.[2] The wear and tear on such small coins was high, and their elusiveness was probably responsible for the Athenian habit of carrying small change in the mouth. The comic possibilities of the custom have been exploited by Aristophanes.[3] Euelpides, excited at the appearance of a kite, swallowed his cash balance;[4] and another unfortunate being handed mullet scales instead of small coins by a practical joker in the market thrust them unsuspecting into his mouth.[5] The solution to this problem of small change money was not discovered until more than 300 years after the introduction of coining. The cities of Sicily were the first to use a separate metal for the smaller

[1] *E.g.*, Tarentum (Gardner, 206).
[2] Which weighs 21·8 grains.
[3] *Ecclesiazusai*, 818.
[4] *Birds*, 503.
[5] *Wasps*, 785.

denominations, and one which, being less valuable than silver, made the small change of a convenient size. In fact, bronze, the metal chosen, was so much less valuable than silver that, had the small denominations contained their face value of metal, they would have been too large instead of too small. But this difficulty was easily avoided by making the coins tokens, an aspect of early coinage that will be discussed in the next chapter. The first bronze coins were probably made by the people of some of the Greek cities in Sicily a little before they made the other great innovation for which they were responsible—the coining of gold in the West. Like the latter, the coining of bronze was probably an emergency device, and it was almost immediately copied in Carthage and in Athens. The copper issue in Athens in 407-406 B.C. was not, however, an attempt to solve the small change problem. The pieces were probably issued as substitutes for larger denominations as a means of obtaining revenue. In fact, their experience with these emergency coins seems to have hardened the Athenians in their determination never again to depart from their traditional silver monometallism.[1] As we have seen, they issued at this time a more extensive and numerous series of denominations than ever before, but they were all in silver. This system, with all its inconveniences, remained in use until 339,[2] and probably until the city fell under Macedonian rule in 322 B.C. Then the *chalcus* and many other small denominations were replaced by bronze coins. But, in adopting bronze small-change money, Athens showed greater reluctance than is usually apparent in the Greek world. Most cities adopted it early in the 4th century, and nearly every Greek city was making bronze small-change money by 350 B.C.[3] Cities that relied upon foreign coins for

[1] Halliday (*Growth of the City State*) suggests that these very small denominations were preferred by the Athenians, because the absence of pockets in their garments forced them to carry their money in their mouths. This theory does not explain why the Athenians lagged so far behind other cities in the adoption of copper, nor does it explain why the coppers could not have been carried wherever the Athenians kept the silver pieces too large to be conveniently transported in the mouth.

[2] Head, *Hist. Num.*, 376.

[3] Clazomenæ (Head, *Hist. Num.*, 567) and Mitylene (561) probably coined in the later years of the 5th century. The cities of Bœotia (343), Eubœa (355), Samos (605), Phocæa (589), Miletus (586), followed during the first half of the century, Ægina (398) and Corinth (401) following towards 350 B.C.

their principal money usually made their own small change. In the Greek world generally, therefore, there was usually a fair supply of coins of a good range of denominations. During the 4th century the introduction of bronze pieces, usually based on the *chalcus*,[1] improved the currency arrangements, and in this condition Greek coinage continued until the Roman conquest. In Greece and Asia Minor there was no attempt to indicate on the coins their legal value; they had to be judged by their size and appearance. But in Magna Græcia marks of value were very common, and in the 5th century types were used to signify denomination. At Argos the wolf was the type of the *drachm*, half a wolf of a half-*drachm*, and a wolf's head of an *obol*.[2] At Syracuse, in the time of Gelon, the type for 4 *drachms* was a quadriga, 2 *drachms* a horseman leading a second horse, 1 *drachm* a horseman, and for an *obol* a wheel.[3] But in later times types, although different for each denomination, were unrelated.

5. *Divisional Coins in Macedon and Egypt.*

The bimetallic coinage introduced by Philip II of Macedon included a plentiful series of subdivisions. In gold the *stater* (of 2 *drachms*) was the common coin, but there were also issued pieces of 1, $\frac{1}{2}$, $\frac{1}{4}$, and $\frac{1}{6}$ of a *drachm*. The silver pieces were of 4, 2, $\frac{4}{3}$, 1, $\frac{2}{3}$, $\frac{1}{2}$, $\frac{1}{3}$, and $\frac{1}{6}$ of a *drachm*.[4] Taking both metals, and assuming gold to have been ten times as valuable as silver, a wide series[5] of values was represented, of which the smallest was $\frac{1}{144}$ of the largest. The duodecimal division of both the gold and silver units probably denotes the adoption of the Greek division of the *stater* into 2 *drachms* each of six *obols*. There is no evidence that this method of division emerged out of any native Macedonian system. But the arrangement that the silver unit should represent $\frac{1}{12}$ of the gold unit is altogether new. The fall in the value of gold broke the tradition of a decimal relation. The values of gold and silver had so changed as to establish a duodecimal relation between the two units already used by the Chalcidian League. The gold subdivisional coins followed the accepted practice of duodecimal division, and a twelvefold value relation

1 Babelon, 404.
2 Macdonald, *Evolution of Coinage*, 132.
3 Hill, 66.
4 Head, *Hist. Num.*, 225-26.
5 1, $\frac{1}{2}$, $\frac{1}{4}$, $\frac{1}{6}$, $\frac{1}{8}$, $\frac{1}{12}$ (in both gold and silver), $\frac{1}{16}$, $\frac{1}{24}$, $\frac{1}{32}$, $\frac{1}{48}$, $\frac{1}{64}$, $\frac{1}{144}$.

between the gold and silver unit must have facilitated business. The gold coins could be equated to simple numbers of silver coins. The fulness of the series may be ascribed to the policy of facilitating the disposal of local supplies of the precious metals, and gold in particular. The reformed currency of Alexander, established about twenty years later, consisted of a series of gold coins based on the *stater* of his father and representing 2, 1½, ¼, and ⅛ *staters*,[1] and a series of silver pieces based on the silver *drachm* and representing 4 and 1 *drachms*.[2] The coins of the two metals furnish a series[3] in which the smallest denomination is $\frac{1}{20}$ of the greatest, 10 silver *drachmas* being taken as equal to a gold unit. This is a much smaller variety than Philip had supplied, but the series was probably supplemented by small issues of bronze[4] *chalci*. The adoption of bronze tokens for small change was part of the general movement that had been spreading throughout the Greek world for the preceding half a century. But as the bronze coins were limited to one denomination, they did not greatly extend the series. It is possible that the supplies of the smaller denominations issued by Philip remained in circulation, but the silver pieces cannot have been very convenient, for they were based on a different silver standard from that introduced by Alexander. It is more likely that local issues supplemented these imperial coins of Alexander.

During the last quarter of the 4th century after the death of Alexander, Ptolemy I began to issue coins in Egypt. These coins are yet so imperfectly classified that it is difficult to discuss their subdivisions. The denominations of the copper coins are largely unknown. In gold and silver there was a leaning to large denominations, such as *octodrachms*, *decadrachms*, and sometimes *dodecadrachms*.[5] When divisions of the *drachm* were coined, they usually, but not always, followed the customary Greek methods of division. The basic unit was apparently borrowed from abroad, but multiples

[1] The *stater* is the only denomination which is at all common.
[2] Head, *Hist. Num.*, 228.
[3] 2, 1, ½, ⅖, ¼, ⅛, $\frac{1}{10}$ gold *staters*.
[4] Small bronze issues had been made since the time of Archelaus I, 413-399 B.C. (Head, *Hist. Num.*, 220-21).
[5] Ptolemy III. issued 5 and 2½ *drachms* of gold (Head, *Hist. Num.*, 852).

and submultiples were not so much borrowed, they were frequently selected for convenience of manipulation under circumstances of which little is certainly known.[1]

6. *Divisional Money in China.*

Chinese knives and spades were not all of one denomination. They were regulated by size, the "great span" of about 10·63 inches being the unit. Knives seem to have been made of a length $\frac{2}{3}$, $\frac{1}{2}$, $\frac{1}{5}$ and $\frac{1}{6}$ of the great span. Spades measure $\frac{1}{2}$, $\frac{3}{8}$ and $\frac{1}{4}$ of the span in length, and other forms of money can be related to it.[2] But the values of pieces of money of these eccentric shapes were not proportional to their lengths. Weight provides a more reliable basis. M. Lacouperie has, as a result of a detailed study of ancient Chinese coins of all kinds, produced[3] a scale of weights based upon a unit weighing 378 grains. Coins indicate units of $\frac{1}{6}$ of this unit, and multiples of 2, $3\frac{1}{2}$, 4, 8, 32 (the oldest knife coins), 80 (probably the ancient *kin* or cubic inch of gold), 160, and 320 units. But the scale is itself very speculative, and it embodies units of different periods: its origins are altogether unknown.

7. *Ancient Italian Divisional Units and their Origin.*

The predominant unit in Italy was the *libra* of bronze, but enquiry into its origin[4] has revealed the possibility that it was part of a series of units of value, and little or nothing is known of the age of the different denominations. The highest unit was the *centupondium* of 100 *libras*, which, as we have seen, may have been a unit of weight for silver transferred for the measurement of copper, or the result of the translation of the ox unit of value into copper. While there is little to be said in favour of the former origin, beyond a coincidence of weights, the latter is quite credible. The Tarpeian Law of the middle of the 5th century B.C., in fixing the rate at which fines and payments in oxen were to be paid in bronze *asses*, valued the ox at a 100 libral *asses*. It also revealed an intermediate sheep unit worth $\frac{1}{10}$ of an ox and 10 *asses*. At that time, therefore, there was a simple system:

1 ox=10 sheep. 1 sheep=10 libral *asses*.

1 Head, 847 *sqq*.
2 Lacouperie, XLIV.
3 *Op. cit.*, XLII.
4 *Vide* Chap. X.

The same system was in use in Sicily, the *litra* being roughly equal to the "Roman" *libra*.[1] So neat a series on a decimal basis requires explanation. The chance fact that 10 sheep were worth an ox may account for the units above the *as* being on a decimal basis, while, as will emerge later, those below it were on a duodecimal basis. The same preference for decimal multiples in the upper portion of the series of units was observed in Lydia, Persia, Greece, and Macedon, although there, too, subdivisions were duodecimal. But while in the East the decimal multiple of the silver unit was represented by a gold unit, in Italy all denominations were represented in copper. The further division of the sheep unit into 10 *libras* is more difficult to explain. A desire for a systematic series might suggest a repetition of the division by ten already applied to the *centupondium*. The use of a decimal notation might also account for it. But we have seen that the *libra* may have originated independently in an *as* rod of bronze defined by size: if the rod was a foot long and half an inch in diameter, it could only by a second lucky chance be worth exactly one-tenth as much as a sheep.

But the subdivisions of the *libra* support the idea that the *as* was originally a rod of prescribed size. The *libra* of 5,045 grains was divided into 12 *unciæ*, each of which contained 24 *scripulæ*. The origin of the division into 12 *unciæ* is unknown, but attempts to explain it have given rise to interesting suggestions.[2] If we accept for the moment the theory that the libral *as* was originally a rod, and that the *libra* was obtained, when weighing was introduced, by ascertaining the weight of a rod of a prescribed size, the *uncia* must also have been a unit of length.[3] It is possible that "the division into 12 *unciæ* is simply the result of the fact that a certain natural relation exists between the breadth of the thumb and the length of the foot." If this is so, duodecimal systems in many parts may have arisen in the same way. The word *uncia* is, then, derived from *unguis*, "a nail," common as a measure in Latin. The same method of subdivision was adopted in at least some of the cities of Sicily. Aristotle, in his now lost Constitutions of both Himera and Agrigentum, is believed to have said that one local *ungia* was worth a

[1] Ridgeway, 371.

[2] Ridgeway, 353 *sqq*.

[3] The word "inch" as well as the word "ounce" is derived from *uncia*.

chalcus. If this was so, the " Sicilian " *litra* and " Roman " *libra* were worth an " Æginetan " *obol.*[1]

The origin of the scruple unit is also quite unknown. The division of the *libra*, first by 12 and then by 24, has again all the appearance of design, and would suggest that the *scruple* was merely a subdivision of the *uncia*. But we have seen that by the early years of the 3rd century the scruple of silver was worth exactly half a pound[2] of bronze. It is possible that the conditions of supply of and demand for the metals resulted in a relation between their values of 288 : 1 the ratio necessary to make the predetermined units of the pound of bronze and the scruple of silver of equal value, but it would be a remarkable as well as a useful coincidence. On the whole, it is more probable that the scruple was the silver equivalent of the half-*libra* of bronze, because it was made so.[3] The fact that it was also $\frac{1}{24}$ of an *uncia* must, however, then be explained by a coincidence. Subdivisions of the scruple are occasionally referred to. The *obolus* was sometimes regarded as half a scruple.[4] A unit of one-sixth of a scruple, called a *siliqua*, has led to the suggestion that the scruple was originally the weight of a certain number of seeds.[5] The Greek word for *siliqua* was κεράτιον,[6] which was the seed of the carob,[7] the weight of which was equal to that of the *siliqua* unit. The scruple was, therefore, equal in weight to 6 carob seeds. The carob was equal in weight to 4 wheat grains, and Ridgeway[8] claims that the Roman system took as its unit the grain of corn. The weighing of the metals against seeds is found in Italy just as in the ancient East. It is unlikely that the scruple was a weight unit sixfold of that of the carob seed. The seeds are more likely to have been adopted because they provided the means for a convenient definition of the scruple.

1 Pollux, IX, 80, *cit.* Ridgeway, 349.

2 Or 1 pound if a ratio of 240 : 1 between values of silver and bronze is accepted.

3 Mommsen (I, 253) thinks the scruple was based on the copper unit; but as he believes in a ratio of 240 : 1 between silver and bronze, he thinks the scruple was made equal to a *libra*.

4 An Attic *obol* of 11 grains is the nearest to a half of a scruple of 17·5 grains.

5 Smith, Article "Scrupulum," in *Dict. of Greek and Roman Antiquities.*

6 From which comes the English *carat.*

7 St. John's Bread (*Ceratonia siliqua, L.*).

8 *Op. cit.*, 181.

8. *Coin Denominations in the Roman Republic.*

The denominations of the coins follow the scale of weights. Multiples of the *as* are always in decimal relation with it. The *as signatum* of the second half of the 5th and first half of the 4th century B.C. weighed 4 or 5 "Roman" pounds.[1] But the bricks or bars of bronze, issued in Campania under the Romans between 312 B.C. and 268 B.C., although apparently intended to provide a regular series of coins, do not seem to represent multiples of the *as* in weight.[2] In 268 B.C. bronze 10-*as* pieces were made. It is notable, too, that the silver *denarius* was made equal to 10 *asses*. Although these *asses* were much reduced from the old libral standard, Ridgeway holds that "it is quite clear that this silver *denarius*, which represented a reduced *decussis* of bronze, had its ultimate source in nothing else than the 10-libral *asses*, which represented the value of a sheep."[3]

The variations in the weight of the earliest *as rude* suggest the possibility that the lumps of bronze were made up in pieces of unit weight according to the *libra* and its subdivisions. The problem of obtaining small change was solved with the hammer and chisel.[4] Pieces were broken off the *asses* or the bars then in circulation (which were probably divided by transverse markings into 12 *unciæ* to facilitate division). Small pieces obtained in this way have been found: they must have passed by weight. With the issues of *as grave*, in the last half of the 4th century B.C., a series of subdivisional coins appeared representing 1, 2, 3, 4, 6, and 12 *unciæ*.[5] Each piece was marked with its value: the *as* "I," the half *as* or 6 *unciæ* "S" (Semis), and the remainder with a number of pellets or globules representing the number of *unciæ* in the coin.

The denominations of coins in the new system set up in

[1] Grueber, I, 3. In *Coins and Medals*, 43, the same author says the 2-, 5-, and 10-*as* pieces which are known were not issued in Rome but in neighbouring cities.

[2] Head (26) says that they "can hardly have been intended to represent exact multiples of the *as*. They may not even have been regarded as coins, although, as Hæberlin has pointed out, their types suggest a correspondence with a regular series of coins. They may have been meant for all those purposes for which the obsolete *æs rude* had served—such, for instance, as dedication to the gods."

[3] Ridgeway, 374.

[4] Babelon, 193.

[5] Head, 18.

268 B.C., together with those issued until the end of the Republic, are set out in the following table:[1]

DENOMINATIONS OF ROMAN COINS 268-216 B.C.

Period B.C.	*Bronze.*										*Silver.*				*Gold.*		
	Asses.										*Denarii.*			*Victoriatus.*	*Sestertii.*		
	10	3	2	1	½	⅓	¼	⅙	1/12	1/24	1	½[2]	¼[3]		60	40	20
268–240 ..	1	1	1	1	1	1	1	1	1	1	1	1	1				
240–229 ..				1	1	1	1	1	1	1	1	1	1		1	1	1
229–217 ..				1	1	1	1	1	1	1	1			1			
217–197[4] ..			1	1	1	1	1	1	1		1			1			
197–173 ..				1[5]	1	1	1	1	1		1			1			
172–151 ..				1	1	1	1	1	1		1						
150–125 ..					1	1	1	1	1[6]		1						
124–103 ..					1	1	1	1	1[7]		1						
102–92 ..					1	1	1	1	1		1	1		[8]			
91–89 ..				1	1	1	1	1	1		1	1					
88–86 ..				1	1	1	1	1	1		1	1	1				
85–82 ..				1	1	1	1	1	1		1	1[5]					
81–73 ..											1				*Aurei*		
72–50 ..											1				1	½	
49–44 ..				1[5]							1	1[5]	1[5]		1	1	
43–37 ..											1				1		
36–17 ..											1				1	1	

The reduction of the weight of the *as* in 268 B.C.[9] resulted in the issue of larger bronze denominations than in the previous series, such as the 10-, 3-, and 2-*as* pieces. With the introduction of struck, instead of cast, coin, smaller denominations of the ½ and ¼ *uncia* were issued, but the addition of silver to the coinage metals made very little immediate difference to the series of denominations represented.[10] The silver pieces merely added coins of 5 and 2½ *asses* to the series. But after 240 B.C. denominations over 1 *as* ceased to be coined in bronze, and the silver coins represented 2½, 5, and 10 *asses*. The

[1] Based on information obtained from Grueber, *Coins of the Roman Republic*, Vols. I and II.
[2] *Quinarius.*
[3] *Sestertius.*
[4] From 217 B.C. there were 16 *asses* to the *denarius*.
[5] Rare.
[6] Rare towards the end of the second century.
[7] Attempt was made to introduce the *dodrans* and *bes*, respectively ¾ and ⅔ of the *as*.
[8] *Victoriatus* withdrawn from currency and demonetized.
[9] Mattingly believes that it had been reduced in fact though not in law (*Num. Chron.*, 194, 198).
[10] From 10 *asses* to $\frac{1}{24}$ of an *as*.

emergency gold coins added denominations equal to 150,[1] 100, and 50 *asses*.[2] The silver coin of 2½ *asses*—the *sestertius*—is of some interest. It weighed 1 scruple, and was adopted as the unit of account: if it was equal in value to a full pound of bronze,[3] the unit was thus continuous with the bronze *libra*.[4] The *sestertius* coin bears a resemblance to the smallest coin in the Etruscan series, based upon the "Eubœan" unit. Up to the middle of the 4th century the Attic stater of 135 grains had been divided into 10, presumably in imitation of the Sicilian device of dividing into 10 *litras*. But between 350 B.C. and 268 B.C, coins of that weight were marked XX instead of X. At this time the smallest of the series was marked "ΛII" (2½),)[5] and weighed about 18 grains. As this is almost identical with the weight of the *sestertius*, it has been suggested[6] that the Etruscan unit was the model for the *sestertius*. But we have seen that it is probable that the scruple was the equivalent in value of half a pound (or possibly a pound) of bronze. It is probable that the marks of value on the Etruscan coins denote their value in bronze units. Presumably, bronze units were reduced contemporaneously in Campania and Rome, so that the same weight of silver could bear the same mark of value in each place.[7] But after no more than forty years the *sestertius* and the *quinarius* (of 5 *asses*) ceased to be coined, although the *sestertius* was the coin representing the unit of account. Except for past issues still in circulation there was no coin between 10 *asses* and 1 *as*. But at the time of the suspension of these silver pieces there appeared a fresh silver coin called a *victoriatus*. The introduction of the *victoriatus*,[8] during the last half of the 3rd[9]

[1] Probably false (Mattingly, *Num. Chron*, 1924, 192).

[2] Thus providing a series of which the largest unit was worth 3,600 of the smallest.

[3] Assuming the *as* of 268 B.C. to have weighed 4 ounces, and the ratio between silver and bronze to have been about 250:1. Otherwise if the ratio was 120:1, it must be assumed that the scruple was assimilated to the *as* after it had been halved.

[4] Fines assessed in *asses* in the Twelve Tables could be paid in an equal number of *sestertii* (Mommsen, II, 32-4).

[5] Head, 14.

[6] Ridgeway, 363.

[7] It must have been an incidental advantage of the *sestertius* that in silver it was equivalent to one-eighth of the "Eubœan" unit (and an "Æginetan" *obol*).

[8] So called from a figure of victory on the coins.

[9] The actual date of its introduction is in doubt (*vide* Grueber, XLVIII).

century, was an innovation. Alone among the Roman issues it bore no mark of value, although its half,[1] which was occasionally issued, was marked " S " (Semis). Its weight did not fit conveniently into the Roman series, and it was probably never regarded as a subdivision of the *denarius*, and never legal tender[2] in Rome, or even in circulation[3] there, to any extent. The *victoriatus* weighed originally 3 scruples (about 54 grains), or three-quarters of the weight of the *denarius*. As its weight approaches that of the " Phocæan " or " Campanian " *drachm*, it is possible that it was issued for circulation in some districts where such a *drachm* was still preferred. A certain similarity between the types of the Romano-Campanian issues of copper and those of the *victoriatus* led to a suggestion that it originated in Campania.[4] If this was its origin, it is clear that the *scruple* standard for silver did not easily supersede the " Campanian " unit, and that for at least half a century the Romans compromised and coined on both standards. It is also exactly one-half of the weight of the coins, bearing as a type Jupiter in his *quadriga*, until recently ascribed to about 286-268 B.C. and the Campanian Mint,[5] but now thought to have been made after the victory over Pyrrhus, and probably in 268 B.C., when the first *denarii* were issued from Rome.[6] These *quadrigati* continued to be issued for some thirty or forty years. At some time after 240 B.C. the *victoriatus*, the half of the *quadrigatus*, began to be issued from Rome, and finally superseded the piece of twice its weight. The *victoriatus* may therefore be a continuation of a coinage on the reduced " Campanian " standard. But the unit also agrees with the " Illyrian " silver *drachm*, then the principal coin in the markets of the Adriatic.[7] Moreover, during the last two or three decades of the 3rd century, as a result of appeals from the Greek settlements on the Adriatic coast, the Romans freed the coast of Illyrian pirates, and a great part of the Illyrian and Dalmatian coastland was brought under

[1] Double as well as half *victoriatus* coins occur, but both were issued only on rare occasions and probably in the provinces (Grueber, XLVIII).

[2] Grueber L; Mommsen, II, 87.

[3] *Encyclopædia Britannica :* Article " Numismatics."

[4] Zobel de Zogroniz, *cit.* Mommsen, II, 104–7.

[5] Head, 33.

[6] Mattingly, *Num. Chron.*, 192.

[7] It had probably come originally from the East.

Roman control.[1] It is quite probable, therefore, that the *victoriatus* was made to facilitate trade with these Greek colonies,[2] and its agreement with the " Campanian " *drachm* is due not to a direct imitation, but to the fact that the " Illyrian " and " Campanian " units had a common origin, and that the Romans copied the former. It is clear that it was not part of the Roman system proper, and that it neither circulated nor was issued in Rome in any quantity. But in 217 B.C. the *victoriatus* was reduced in the same proportion as the *denarius*. It fell from 54 to 45 grains, as did also the "Illyrian" unit. At its new weight it was identical with the Corinthian *drachm*, the standard of the Achæan League then current throughout the Peloponnese.[3] But from about 196 B.C. in Rome, and 173 B.C. in the provinces, the issue of the *victoriatus* was suspended, never to be revived. For the last three-quarters of the 2nd century B.C. the *denarius* was the only silver coin issued.[4]

Meanwhile the Lex Flaminia had introduced, in 217 B.C., the first serious disturbance of the imperial system. For reasons later to be discussed, the bronze *as* and the silver *denarius* were reduced, and a fresh relation was established between them. The *as* became $\frac{1}{16}$ of a *denarius*. Little importance is to be attached to the relation: it was merely the resultant of the reductions in the two units, and the measure of that reduction depended partly on the object in view, and partly on the amount of monetary disturbance the people could be expected to tolerate. In the middle of the 2nd century (when the *denarius* was worth 16 *asses*) the gap between the silver and copper denominations was widened by the suspension of the issue of the bronze 1-*as* piece for about sixty years. An attempt was made to bridge the gap in 89 B.C. by the re-issue of the *quinarius* and *sestertius* in accordance

[1] Grueber, XLIX.

[2] Mommsen, II, 96. Pliny says: " The coin that is known at the present day as the *victoriatus* was first struck in accordance with the Clodian Law, before which period a coin of this name was imported from Illyricum, but was only looked upon as an article of merchandise " (*Hist. Nat.*, XXXIII, 14).

[3] It also served as a prototype for the coins of Rhodes and Marseilles which were similarly reduced (Grueber, LI).

[4] From 217 B.C. to 82 B.C. the scale of values did not vary greatly. Throughout the period it covered a range, where the largest unit was 192 times as large as the smallest; but during the second half of the 2nd century B.C., the variety of issues was smaller than during the rest of the period.

with the Lex Papiria,[1] but after four or five years the issues of the *sestertius* again ceased, and also, to all intents and purposes, those of the *quinarius*.[2] Possibly the *sestertius* was unpopular because of its smallness.[3] All copper issues ceased at the same time, and for about thirty years the silver *denarius* was the only coin of any kind issued in Rome. Julius Cæsar attempted to renovate the currency by recommencing the issue of bronze *asses* and silver *quinarii* and *sestertii*. The similarity of the efforts of 89 B.C. and 49 B.C. suggests that the gap between the silver and copper units was inconvenient. But both efforts to fill the void were unsuccessful. In 44 B.C. all Cæsar's new silver and copper denominations ceased to appear, but the gold *aurei* and half-*aurei*, which he had also initiated, remained. To the end of the Republic the principal issues were the silver *denarius* and the gold *aureus*, occasionally accompanied by a half-*aureus*, the latter coins representing respectively 25 and 12½ *denarii*.

9. *Coin Denominations in the Roman Empire.*

The series of denominations at the beginning of the empire was the gold[4] *aureus* and its half,[5] the silver *denarius* and its half,[6] the brass 4-[7] and 2-*as*[8] pieces, and the copper 1-, ½-,[9] and ¼-*as*.[10] At current values this gave a series in which the value of the largest was 1,600 times that of the smallest.[11] The denominations of the coinage from the time of Augustus to

[1] The *sestertius* not having been coined for 150 years was so unfamiliar that it was marked "E.L.P." (Ex lege Papiria) to indicate the authority for its issue (Grueber, I, 250).

[2] Grueber, 316.

[3] The British threepenny-piece weighs nearly 22 grains, while the *sestertius* then weighed only 15.

[4] Augustus also issued a few 4-*aureus* pieces (Mommsen, III, 19).

[5] *Quinarius aureus*—not very common.

[6] *Quinarius argenteus*—rare, but issued by all the Emperors (Mommsen, III, 27).

[7] The *sestertius*. Under the empire the *sestertius*, hitherto a silver piece worth one-quarter of a *denarius* of 16 *asses*, became a brass coin.

[8] *Dupondius*. A copper *dupondius* was added in 5 B.C. (Sydenham, *Num. Chron.*, 1919, 117).

[9] A brass half-*as* was coined at Lugdunum from 3 B.C. to A.D. 21 (Sydenham, *Num. Chron.*, 1919, 117).

[10] Mattingly, LI.; Sydenham, *Num. Chron.*, 1919, 115.

[11] The full series ran 1,600, 800, 64, 32, 16, 8, 4, 2, 1.

the collapse of the system he set up are shown in the following table:

DENOMINATIONS OF ROMAN COINS 15 B.C. TO A.D. 258.[1]

Period.	*Gold.*		*Silver.*		*Brass and Copper.*								*Argenteus Antoniniánus.*
	Aurei.		*Denarii.*		*Asses.*								
	1	½	1	½	4[2]	2[2]	1[2]	1[3]	½[2]	½[3]	¼[2]	¼[3]	
B.C. 15–A.D. 14	1	1	1	1	1	1		1	1			1	
A.D. 14–37	1	1	1	1	1	1		1	1				
37–54	1	1	1	1	1	1		1				1	
54–68	1	1	1	1	1	1	1	1	1	1	1	1	
68–69	1	1	1	1	1	1		1					
69 (Otho)	1		1										
69 (Vitellius) ..	1		1		1	1		1					
70–79	1	1	1	1	1	1		1			1	1	
79–81	1	1	1	1	1	1		1					
81–96	1	1	1	1	1	1		1			1		
98–117	1	1	1	1	1	1		1	1			1	
117–138	1	1	1	1	1	1		1	1		1		
138–180	1	1	1	1	1	1		1	1				
180–192	1	1	1	1	1	1		1					
193–211	1		1		1	1		1					
211–217	1		1		1	1							1
222–238	1		1		1	1							
238 (Pupienus Balbinus)	1		1		1	1							1
238–244	1		1	1	1	1							1
244–249	1		1	1	1	1							1
249–251	1				1	1			1				1

When Nero reformed the currency he added a few denominations, and established the most complete series ever current in the empire.[4] But upon his death the elaborate brass and copper series was replaced by 4-, 2-, and 1-*as* pieces, almost a complete reversion to the Augustan series, which continued in use until the early 3rd century without any great alteration. Supplies of small change were not always adequate, however, and in the West broken halves, thirds, and quarters of larger coins circulated, particularly in Gaul.[5] The whole of the

[1] Based upon Sydenham, *Num. Chron.*, 1919, 168.
[2] Brass. [3] Copper.
[4] *Aureus* and half of gold, *denarius* and half of silver, 4, 2, 1, ½, and ¼-*as* of brass, and 1, ½, and ¼-*as* of copper (Sydenham, *Num. Chron.*, 1919, 125). Mommsen (III, 19) thought that the ¼-*as* was abandoned by Trajan at the end of the 1st century, and the ½-*as* forty years later.
[5] Mattingly, XXIV. Silver coins used to be broken in England to provide smaller change.

monetary arrangements of the 3rd century are overshadowed by the unrestrained inflation that occupied its first seventy-five years. The final period of depreciation began with the addition by Caracalla, in about 215 B.C., of a new coin to the series of silver pieces, which then consisted of only a *denarius* and its half. The legal value of the new coin, since called an *argenteus*,[1] is uncertain. The *argenteus* coins were distinguishable from other silver pieces by the special types placed on them. They were so irregular in weight that their normal weight is extremely uncertain, although it was probably between 75 and 80 grains. Their original legal value is also in doubt. The first issues having weighed about 50 per cent. more than the *denarius*, and having been of metal of about the same quality, they were probably worth more than a *denarius*. If they were worth $1\frac{1}{2}$ *denarii*,[2] and if at the same time as the *argenteus* was introduced the number of *denarii* to the *aureus* was increased to 30 owing to the declining quality of the former, the new *argenteus* was $\frac{1}{20}$ of an *aureus*. This would provide an easy relation between gold and the now debased silver, but it is perhaps more probable that the new coin was introduced to take the place of the *denarius* as $\frac{1}{25}$ of an *aureus*.[3] The *aureus* was then worth $37\frac{1}{2}$ *denarii*, and the inconvenience of this relation may account for the subsequent decline of the *denarius*. The rapid debasement of the *argenteus Antoninianus* during the next few decades destroyed what remained of the series of denominations set up by Augustus. The silver *denarius* and *quinarius* could no longer compete with the *argenteus* unless they also were debased. In consequence,

[1] Also *argenteus Antoninianus*. The name *Antoninianus* occurs in a doubtful rescript of Aurelian (Oman, *Num. Chron.*, 1916, 37). Mommsen (III, 71) identified it with another coin, the *argenteus Aurelianus*.

[2] Mommsen (III, 143) thought that in view of the abundance of the subsequent issues of *argentei*, they must have been more profitable than *denarii*, and as there is evidence that under Valerian in the middle of the 3rd century the *argenteus* was accepted as good for 2 *denarii* in payments to the Treasury, it was probably issued in the first place as 2 *denarii*, but Professor Oman (*Num. Chron.*, 1916, 37 *sqq.*) has largely disproved Mommsen's theory. He argues in particular that the general reduction of the *aureus* to 100 grains did not occur. Heavy and light *aurei* were contemporaneous (p. 40). It is incredible that it should have been a double *denarius*, because if both were full weight coins, the *argenteus* would have driven the *denarius* out of circulation (p. 37).

[3] Oman, *Num. Chron.*, 1916, 44.

although they continued to be issued in very small quantities, they ceased for all practical purposes to form part of the currency from about A.D. 242.[1] During the same period the series of denominations of gold increased, although for most purposes gold circulated by weight. Elagabalus issued a decree in about A.D. 220 commanding the payment of all taxes in gold. The measure was followed by the issue of fresh denominations of gold equal to 2, 3, 4, 10, and even 100 *aurei*, but, on the death of Elagabalus, they were demonetized. In the sixties multiples were again issued, but were limited to pieces of 2 and 3 *aurei*. Soon after the middle of the century new subdivisions of the *aureus* also occur. Pieces of one-third (or *tremisses*) are fairly common, and pieces of two-thirds less so. Twenty years later pieces of four-thirds were added to the series. Although a period of thirty years elapsed after the decree requiring payment of taxes in gold, the decree was doubtless one of the causes of the elaboration of the series of gold coins, from 1 and $\frac{1}{2}$ *aureus* at the beginning of the empire to $\frac{4}{3}$, 1, $\frac{2}{3}$, $\frac{1}{2}$, $\frac{1}{3}$ by the time of Aurelian. Provision was doubtless needed for the payment of small sums and fractions of the larger gold units to the state.[2]

Bronze issues were, on the other hand, adversely affected by the inflation. Although continued in some denomination or other throughout the century, they were unimportant except under Alexander Severus (A.D. 222-35). The half-*as* was issued up to the second decade of the 3rd century, and again in A.D. 249-51, under Trajanus Decius, while the 2- and 1-*as* pieces continued to the latter date, if not beyond. Trajanus Decius also issued a few specimens of a hitherto unknown denomination, which probably represents a 6-*as* piece.[3] It may have been thought that as the *denarius* had been accompanied by a *sestertius* worth one-quarter of a *denarius*, it would be convenient for the *argenteus* to be accompanied by a piece of one-quarter of its value. The radiate crown worn by the Emperor, in the types of both the *argenteus* and the new bronze pieces, suggest that they were of the same series.[4] The *sestertius* (4-*as* piece) survived longer than any of the other pieces, for it is still to be found occasionally in A.D. 276, although its

[1] Mommsen, III, 70; Sydenham, *Num. Chron.*, 1919, 137.
[2] *Vide* Mommsen, III, 59-60.
[3] It has been thought to be a *quinarius*.
[4] Sydenham, *Num. Chron.*, 1919, 138.

weight was less than in the time of Alexander Severus.[1] By the time of Aurelian, however, the system had to all intents and purposes collapsed, leaving the *argenteus Antoninianus* the only denomination regularly and plentifully issued, although is value is unknown.

After 271 Aurelian faced the task of building a fresh system on the ruins of the Augustan currency. He issued plated copper or mixed metal coins marked "XXI" and "VSV." Nothing definite is known either as to the face value of these coins or the meaning of their inscriptions. The coin marked "XXI" is the core of the reform, and it may have been a new *denarius*.[2] The inscription has been variously suggested[3] to mean that the new coin was worth $\frac{1}{21}$ of a *denarius*,[4] 20 *asses*,[5] 20 *denarii*,[6] 2 *denarii*,[7] and $\frac{1}{20}$ of an *aureus*:[8] if the new piece was a *denarius*, it is not improbable that it was intended to pass for two old *denarii*.[9] But there is no mention of any currency reform establishing a new unit equal to two old units. Moreover, the new "XXI" coins were similar in size, colour, and in their type to the original *argentei* of Caracalla, to which they bear much resemblance. In fact, it is possible that Aurelian aimed merely at the

1 Mommsen, III, 93.

2 Sydenham, *Num. Chron.*, 1919, 142.

3 The suggestions are examined by Sydenham (*Num. Chron.*, 1919, 143 *sqq.*).

4 De Salis (*Num. Chron.*, 1867, 325). But there was no current *denarius* that could be adopted as a unit. Either some older *denarius* standard was used or the *denarius* was regarded as $\frac{1}{25}$ of an *aureus*. But the *aureus* was also very irregular in weight. The *denarius* had been diminishing since the beginning of the century, and it is unlikely to have been worth twenty-one of the new coins. To these objections to this theory is added the fact that 21 : 1 is a most inconvenient relation for a reformer to establish.

5 Dattari (*Riv. it.*, 1905, 443-49). If "XXI" means 20.1 or 20 *asses*, its half would have been marked "X.1" or "VV.1."

6 Finlay (*Hist. of Greece*, I, 439) believed that the *denarius* had fallen from $\frac{1}{25}$ to $\frac{1}{500}$ of an *aureus*. A piece worth 20 *denarii* was, therefore, worth $\frac{1}{25}$ of an *aureus*, and was equal to the Augustan *denarius* of account. Sydenham (*Num. Chron.*, 1919, 145) criticizes the theory on the ground that so great a fall in the value of the *denarius* is improbable. It suffers also from the absence of any *aureus* unit of this period. The *denarius* referred to in Diocletian's Price Edict was worth more than $\frac{1}{20}$ of the plated coin (Sydenham, *Num. Chron.*, 1919, 145).

7 "XX" signifies that it is a double *denarius*, and "I" that it is a unit of reckoning (Hill, *Handbook of Greek and Roman Coins*, 51).

8 Webb, *Num. Chron.*, 1918, 241.

9 Sydenham, *Num. Chron.*, 1919, 147.

restoration of the *argenteus*,[1] although it must be admitted that such would be a hopeless and ill-advised policy. The other coin marked "VSV" is equally difficult to identify. If the larger coin was a *denarius*, the smaller piece was probably a half of it, and its inscription must mean that 2 old *quinarii* are equal to this new half-*denarius*. The scales of denominations must then have been 1, 4, 8, and 16 *asses*.[2] But if the larger coin was a restored *argenteus Antoninianus*, the smaller piece was a *denarius*. It bore a close resemblance to the old *denarii*, and its weight is roughly $\frac{2}{3}$ of that of its larger companion, and thus the old weight relation between the *denarius* and the *argenteus* was preserved.[3] The inscription is difficult to reconcile with this system; but it appears only upon a few coins in one reign, and it is very possible that the letters are not intended to be marks of value.[4] From A.D. 290 onward Diocletian was engaged in the series of experiments already referred to, which it was hoped would result in the establishment of a bimetallic coinage of silver and gold. From about A.D. 290 both the *aureus* and the silver *denarius*[5]

[1] Webb, *Num. Chron.*, 1919, 241. Mommsen (III, 98) assigned these coins to A.D. 296-301 in the reign of Diocletian, but regards them as related to the *argenteus:* he points out *inter alia* that the latter was the only coin in earlier times, bearing a mark resembling "XXI." It is possible that the *argenteus* coin was then worth approximately 20 *denarii*. It would be expected that the abundant issues of *argentei* would have reduced rather than increased their value (originally $1\frac{1}{2}$ or 2 *denarii*). The only explanation of the rating of the new unit to the old is that the *denarius* was a unit of account not related to the *denarius* coin. This unit of account had steadily declined (Mommsen, III, 146), although from what causes, and by what stages, is unknown. It is possible that after the issue of *denarii* had ceased depreciation took the form of increasing the legal value of the *argenteus* coins in *denarii* of account as well as debasing their material. This is the method of depreciation which was applied to the *rouble* and *mark* in modern times; when the value of the unit had fallen to the value of the paper on which the 1 *mark* or *rouble* note was printed, it was further depreciated by issuing fresh notes of the same commodity value but higher nominal value. Webb (*Num. Chron.*, 1919, 241) suggests that the "XXI" means that the new coin was $\frac{1}{20}$ of an *argenteus*—probably the same ratio as in the time of Caracalla, whose system he may have been attempting to restore.

[2] Sydenham, *Num. Chron.*, 1919, 150. Sir Arthur Evans suggested that they meant "Vota Saluta Quinquennalia."

[3] Webb, *Num. Chron.*, 1919, 241.

[4] *Ibid.*

[5] Or *argenteus minutulis*. A few silver *quinarii* were issued. Large silver pieces of $\frac{1}{4}$, $\frac{1}{10}$ (or $\frac{10}{96}$), $\frac{1}{24}$, $\frac{1}{48}$, and $\frac{1}{60}$ of a pound were also issued, but these were more in the nature of commemorative medals issued on the occasion of great fêtes (Mommsen, III, 73).

were again in circulation. Up to A.D. 296 the *aureus* was worth 25 *denarii,* but thereafter only 20.[1] Diocletian also issued three copper coins, the *follis,* the *communis,*[2] and *centenionalis.* The *follis*[3] was the most important of these, but its value in silver is uncertain, $\frac{1}{25}$,[4] $\frac{1}{20}$,[5] and $\frac{1}{16}$[6] of a *denarius* having all been suggested, and $\frac{1}{16}$ of a silver *denarius* being the most probable.[7] The *communis* and *centenionalis* were probably a mere continuation of Aurelian's issues of the pieces marked "XXI" and "VSV" respectively. The *follis* was worth $2\frac{1}{2}$[8] of the *communis* coins, or 5 of the *centenionalis* pieces. During the first decade of the 4th century, a fresh copper coin appeared similar in style to the *follis,* but apparently worth only two *denarius communis* coins, and in the course of the next few years the *follis* sank in weight to that of the 2-*communis* piece.[9] The Edict of Maximum Prices, issued by Diocletian in A.D. 301, uses the *denarius* as the smallest unit of value, and mentions that 50,000 were worth a pound of gold. These cannot be based on the value of the early imperial silver *denarius* issued by Diocletian. The prices fixed indicate that the purchasing power of the *denarius* referred to cannot have been less than $\frac{1}{25}$ of the Neronian silver *denarius*[10] (*i.e.* $\frac{1}{26250}$ of a pound of gold). Probably the unit was the *denarius communis* of $\frac{1}{50000}$ of a pound of gold, and of which there were $2\frac{1}{2}$ to the *follis* and 50[11] to the *denarius argenteus* (*miliarense*).[12]

The reform effected by Constantine in A.D. 312 introduced gold coins representing the new *solidus* and its third and half[13]

1 Sydenham, *Num. Chron.*, 1919, 155.

2 Or *denarius aeris.*

3 *Follis* originally meant a bag or purse containing a fixed amount of money. Later it was transferred to the coin (Mommsen, III, 105). The *follis* coin was also called *major* and a *majorina* (Mommsen, III, 98).

4 Seeck, *Zeitsch. für Num.*, XVII, 36.

5 Lapaulle, *Rev. Num.*, 1889, 119.

6 Dattari, *Riv. it.*, 1906, 375-96.

7 Sydenham, *Num. Chron.*, 1919, 156.

8 Sydenham, *Num. Chron.*, 1919, 159. Dattari, Lepaulle, and others (*loc. cit.*) have suggested that the *follis* was equal to 2 *communis* pieces only.

9 Later specimens of the *follis* are marked "XXI"—thus indicating that they were worth 2 *denarii,* as in the case of Aurelian's plated coins.

10 Sydenham, *Num. Chron.*, 1919, 161.

11 Mommsen (III, 164) suggests there were 21 *denarii* to the *follis.*

12 It is possible that there was a bronze coin called a *denarius nummus* or *libella* (Mommsen, III, 106-7; *Encyclopædia Britannica:* Article, "Diocletian, Edict of").

13 Rare.

and, for a time, $1\frac{1}{2}$ *solidi* as well.[1] With the exception of a temporary alteration in A.D. 963-69, this series remained unchanged till the fall of the Byzantine Empire. The new silver *miliarense*, called a *siliqua*,[2] was accompanied by a piece of half its weight. These new issues, at first issued concurrently with the *argenteus* series, gradually replaced them, and in A.D. 360 an end was put to the issue of the latter. From that date the issues of the *miliarense* and *siliqua* were more abundant, and they became the customary small change for the rest of the century. Constantine made no great alteration in the bronze coins, which during the 4th century are very difficult to fit into a series of denominations. Their face values are very inadequately understood; they vary considerably in weight from coin to coin, and during the century gradually fell in weight until their metallic value was very low indeed.

10. *Summary.*

The origin of subdivisional and multiple monetary units is for the most part an unsolved problem. We have seen that many units may have had their own origin separate from that of other units in the series, the mathematical relation between them being the result of the choice of units. Weights originated sometimes out of the translation of a primitive barter unit of value into a monetary metal, out of the transfer of a unit of weight for one commodity to another, or out of the subsequent weighing of units at first defined by length, or by the lifting capacity of the human body. Examples of suggested origins of this kind have emerged from the foregoing discussion. But the simple mathematical basis of nearly all series of weight standards suggests that some units must have been mathematically obtained from one unit that may be regarded as the basis of all. Such explanations are possible in countries where mathematical processes were well understood as in Egypt and Mesopotamia. But many systems require some combination of the two explanations. In the strictest sense no such compromise is possible; units of one origin, adapted to another unit, cease to exist in their original

[1] Mommsen, III, 64-5.

[2] *Siliqua* was the name of an old unit weighing $\frac{1}{6}$ of a scruple (*vide supra*).

form. This must frequently have happened. It is possible that in times when money was little used, barter units were selected with a view to their simple mutual relation. In subsequent times, when both units were translated into monetary metals, they would still be simply related, unless there had been changes in their relative values.

One of the most remarkable facts which has emerged in this chapter is the preference from Babylon to Rome for decimal divisions of the unit of value which may have been based upon the ox. In the East, silver units were probably $\frac{1}{10}$, $\frac{1}{15}$, or $\frac{1}{20}$ of the universal gold unit. In Rome a sheep unit existed, and its size suggests that ten sheep were worth an ox in very ancient times. But it cannot be argued that this convenient relation with the ox unit alone explains the adoption of the sheep unit. Where the environment suited sheep rather than cattle, they would naturally serve as a unit of value. This preference for decimal multiples may merely be the result of the chance fact that ten sheep were worth about one ox over a very wide area. The use of a decimal notation in counting, derived from the use of the fingers as a counting machine, is not sufficient explanation, because, when we turn to the subdivisions of the sheep unit, we find a general preference for duodecimal division.

In Babylonia perhaps the mathematical advantages of the duodecimal methods of counting may explain the adoption of the sexagesimal scales, and these may have served as models for other peoples. In Greece the silver unit was divided by twelve and by twelve again. In Italy, however, the sheep unit was first again divided by ten before division by twelve. The further division by twenty-four must have come at a later period. It is possible that all the subdivisions were evolved at a much later date than the higher units. They were established only when there was need for a greater accuracy in exchange and valuation. It might be argued that by this time the advantages of a duodecimal system had impressed themselves upon the peoples concerned. But it is known that the Ægean peoples preferred a duodecimal scale as early as the 2nd millennium B.C. The general explanation of the systematic nature of these early weight series must be that, where people evolved units of different sizes, and later translated them into the monetary metals, desire for a simple mathematical scale led to old units being squeezed into the scale and losing their identity. Desire for simplicity did not lead to the complete adoption of either the decimal or the duodecimal scale, presumably because tradition was too strong. But it is not for British critics to comment too severely upon failure to produce a completely orderly system, when the value relation between gold and silver units in the British system is on a decimal basis, and between silver and copper on a duodecimal.

When the time came to represent these divisions in coins, the old system of weights nearly everywhere determined the coin denominations to be issued. But wherever coins were limited to one metal, as in Lydia, and later in Rome, the length of the series was likely to be curtailed by the rapid diminution or increase in the size of the coins as the ends of the scale were approached. Bimetallism in Persia, and later in Rome, tended to lengthen the series, and make the denominations at either end of a more convenient size. The invention of the bronze token for small change greatly facilitated the supply of convenient denominations, and was adopted throughout Magna Græcia, Sicily, and the Ægean world during the fourth and subsequent centuries B.C., the denominations represented being still confined, however, to the ancient scale of weights.

In Macedon the old 10 : 1 value relation between coins of gold and silver was swept away by changes in the relative values of gold and silver. In Rome, when bronze and silver bimetallism was inaugurated, the old 10 : 1 value relation is again found with a decimal division of the bronze unit. But towards the end of the 3rd century units were altered, and, as a by-product of these changes, fresh relations between the units were set up. The *as* became $\frac{1}{16}$ instead of $\frac{1}{10}$ of a *denarius*. The relation of 25 : 1 between the *aureus* and the silver *denarius* was probably also accidental. The 10-scruple weight for silver was used for gold, and the 25 : 1 was the nearest convenient value relation: it made the *aureus* just worth 100 *sestertii*.[1] In this case the gold unit fell until the 25 : 1 relation was attained. By the beginning of the empire the scale of currency denominations was based on a series of historical accidents, the old twelve- and tenfold divisions

[1] Which may have been based on the *libra* of bronze, which may have been $\frac{1}{100}$ of the ancient ox unit.

being almost altogether lost. After the inflation and collapse of the currency in the 3rd century A.D. the reformed coinage shows a considerable hankering after the units of better days, and the systems set up by Diocletian and Constantine are merely the result of compromise between the ancient systems and the demands of new economic conditions.

CHAPTER XII

TOKEN COINAGE

THE value of coins is not determined when we know their weight and the material of which they were made. Their value as money can never, for any long period, fall below their value as a commodity, because they can always be converted from coin into metal by melting. But the coin may rise above its metallic value. Whether it does so rise depends upon the supply of coins made available. If there is no restriction upon their issue, or if the state, although reserving to itself the initiative in coining, continues to issue so long as coins can be sold to realize anything over their cost of manufacture, they will never be worth more than the value of the metal which they contain. But if, by accident or intention, restrictions are placed on the quantity of the coins, it is possible that they will circulate at above their bullion value. They are then token coins.[1]

1. *The Origin of Token Money.*

The origin of token money is not at all clear. It is possible that a medium of exchange, the value of which depended on the credit of the issuer, had developed before coins were invented. In Babylonia and Chaldea in the 9th and 8th centuries B.C., instruments very like bills of exchange are known to have existed. They were inscribed on clay bricks, and were drawn by one person on another in a different place for a sum expressed in weights of silver and copper. They were payable after a stated period, interest sometimes being provided for. No endorsement or acceptance appears; but as the bill was drawn on the clay when it was soft and then baked, subsequent inscription would have been difficult.

[1] The term "token" was first used for the counters or tokens issued by tradesmen in Great Britain to supply a deficiency of small change. Now it is used to describe any money which circulates for more than its commodity value.

These early bills were used as a means of reducing the transport of money at a time when trade was carried on by means of caravans which passed over routes infested by robbers. In similar circumstances they were reinvented by the Jews and Italians as the *lettres de change* of the Middle Ages. They were certainly a kind of fiduciary money, for their value was kept up because buyers relied upon bills being limited to the quantity which could be met, and because the sellers and drawees saw that this condition was fulfilled. Again, classical writers record the use of leather money in very early times. Skins may have served as a medium of exchange at their commodity value, and have been a full value medium of exchange. The leather money reported to have been used in Carthage[1] has been explained in this way by an early commentator.[2] Seneca's reference[3] to debts incurred in " leather, coined with the public stamp, such as was current among the Lacedæmonians, that standeth instead of ready money," suggests a token issue made by public authority and used, moreover, as the basis of a unit of account. But the evidence is unsupported and doubtful. It is more probable that leather money, at least in some places, was a promise to pay gold or silver written on parchment and sealed by a well-known firm. Bills of exchange or promissory notes in this form are, in all probability, older than coins.

These early instruments of exchange may have revealed that a medium of exchange need possess no value as a commodity. But how was this discovery applied to coins? We way dismiss the idea that " in order that tokens shall serve as payment, religion is necessary."[4] Religious institutions might influence standards of valuation, but they alone could not cause a coin to pass in profane commerce for a value greater than that of its metallic content. If religious

[1] Lenormant, I, 220. [2] Aristides, *Orat. Platon*, 145.

[3] *De Benef.*, V, 14.

[4] Laum suggests that tokens were invented owing to the substitution of one sacrificial commodity for another in very early religious practices. " The substitution for valuable goods of valueless symbols had its origin and meaning in religion. In magic there was no distinction between object and counterfeit. Real goods and tokens were in practice the same. In order that tokens shall serve as payment, religion is necessary. . . . The transfer of sacred forms to profane commerce first called forth conflict between the substantial and functional elements of money " (*Heiliges Geld*, 159).

influences tended to raise the value of a coin increased supplies would as effectively reduce it. The reasons for the appearance of tokens are to be found in economic circumstances. Broadly, there are three ways in which they might emerge. In the first place, they may have developed out of the clumsy, heavy standards of iron, lead, and copper used in early times. The first stamps placed on ingots of these metals did not prevent their continuing to pass at their full value; but, with the appearance of smaller and more convenient silver and electrum coins, the size of the iron and copper units may have been reduced. But if the evolution of tokens is to be so explained, we must show that the value of the copper money did not fall with the decline in its weight, or did not fall so much as its weight. In the second place, tokens may in some communities have been first issued as a means of raising revenue. If this was so, and restraint was exercised in their issue, their value might be maintained, and profits would be derived from the sale of the metal taken from the coins. But if this metal was minted, the additional supplies of coins would reduce their value, and the coins would tend to lose their token quality. The fall in the metallic content of the coin might precede in time the fall in their value, and during the period when there was a lag between their bullion value and their value in circulation, they were tokens in the technical but not in the generally accepted sense. Lastly, they may evolve owing to the inconvenience referred to in the previous chapter, attendant upon the use of gold or silver for small transactions. In order to obtain coins of a useful size, a material less valuable than silver was sought. Then, in order to avoid, on the one hand, too large bronze coins, and, on the other, the trials and troubles of bimetallism,[1] resort was had to token bronze. But while token coins may have emerged to solve the difficulties of small change, they need not be confined in their use to small denominations. And all small change money need not be token money. These theories can be best examined

[1] Small change silver was reduced (in 1816) to token status by reducing its silver content without reducing its legal value, in order to protect the silver coinage from melting. The intention at the time was, however, to continue the free coinage of silver, and free coinage was abandoned only as a result of the failure to issue the Proclamation provided for in the Act of 1816—a failure that was probably accidental, and not aimed at the abandonment of bimetallism.

in the light of the very tenuous evidence of the existence of token money in ancient communities.

When we enquire what coins did circulate as tokens in ancient times, we find that this is the most difficult enquiry of all. We have specimens of coins from which we can ascertain the monetary metal, the weight standard, and the fineness of coins, but we cannot tell from the coin the value at which it circulated. Literary evidence is extremely sparse. Sometimes the coins are marked to show their value in coins of another metal, and if we have reliable records of the relative values of the two metals at the time we can determine whether one was a token coin, provided that we know definitely that the other was not. It is certainly not correct to assume that early coins of copper, bronze, and iron were always tokens; some of them were not: they were full-weight coins, and circulated under the same conditions as those of gold, silver, and electrum.

2. *Token Coins in the Greek World.*

The first two or three hundred years of coining passed without any tokens. They were unknown in Lydia, in Persia,[1] in Asia Minor, and in Greece. The electrum issues of the Ionian cities during the 5th century B.C. have been claimed[2] as the first example of a currency in which the principal coins were tokens. When these pieces were first issued, they were accepted at the traditional value for electrum of three-quarters of the value of gold. But as the new issues never contained more than 60 per cent. of gold, the quotation was much above their bullion value. Moreover, at Phocæa and Lesbos the proportion of gold in the coins fell to 40 per cent., and they were quoted at a discount in the coins of Cyzicus and other cities issuing money of good quality. In order to avoid this discount, and to provide " a true and conventional currency of electrum *hectæ* (pieces of one-sixth of a *stater*), which were to circulate throughout the whole territory of the union with a nominal value much above their metallic value, without incurring the disfavour which would fall on such a currency

[1] Babelon, 403.

[2] A few bronze coins of uncertain date have been hesitatingly attributed to some of the Persian satraps (Head, *Hist. Num.*, 830).

abroad,"[1] the Ionic cities concerned formed a monetary convention. "Some of the towns in the convention, those of Lesbos in particular, completed the system of conventional money, and applied it to all metals, striking, besides low-quality electrum, 'billon,' in the guise of silver not more than 40 per cent. fine. This had the same value in low-value electrum as had good silver in good electrum."[2] By thus forming a league to issue low-value electrum, the discount on the coins in foreign exchange transactions could be avoided in transactions with other members of the League, but this in no way indicates that the electrum was a token currency. It may have been circulating at its metallic value, the absence of discount in exchange being merely due to the equally low bullion value of all the currencies issued by members of the League. The low-quality silver was probably issued because it was found that the reduction in the quality of electrum caused its value to fall in terms of silver of the old weight and fineness. To avoid this, silver was debased equally with electrum. It is possible that the poor-quality electrum and silver were so restricted in quantity that they passed within the city of issue for more than their bullion value, if not for as much as the coins of Cyzicus. But it is very unlikely. There is no evidence that at this period anything was known of the methods of controlling the value of money by restricting its issue. Moreover, it is probable that the reduction of the fineness of silver was merely a repetition of a trick successfully tried on electrum, and that both constituted a simple debasement of the money.

3. *Emergency Issues of Tokens.*

There is, in fact, no evidence that any of the silver issues of the Greek cities were ever managed with a view to maintaining them above their bullion value. Token issues must be sought, therefore, among the bronze coins, and as the cities of Asia Minor, the islands, continental Greece, and Magna Græcia confined their issues to gold, silver, and electrum, until the last two decades of the 5th century B.C., no tokens are found before then. Tokens first appeared in Sicily, and probably in Syracuse,[3] as an emergency issue at the time of the Athenian

[1] Lenormant, I, 197. [2] *Loc. cit.*

[3] Head (*Hist. Num.*, 175) merely states that the first bronze coins of Syracuse belong to the period 478-413 B.C.

invasion. The idea soon spread to other cities on the island.[1] There is no means of proving that these issues were tokens. They were made in times of financial stress, and were, therefore, probably intended to yield a profit. The market values of silver and copper are not known with any certainty, but such marks of value as occur on the bronze coins suggest that bronze was much over-valued in coins[2]; also the amount of bronze to the *litra* varied considerably from place to place.[3] These facts all point to a very fair probability that in the issue of these bronze coins the Greek colonists departed from the native tradition of full-weight bronze money. This tradition persisted in Central Italy, but it had been dead in Sicily for over 200 years, and the departure is not surprising. The bronze coins of Sicily were therefore tokens. Both the Athenian and the Carthaginian invaders of the island borrowed the device of coining bronze. The first issue was made in Athens in 406 B.C.,[4] there also in a period of extreme financial strain when the ornaments from the temple had already been melted down and sold. The types on the coins resembled exactly those on the contemporary silver coins,[5] and the pieces were probably plated. They were intended to replace the silver issues,[6] and pass at the same value. The former they did, for Aristophanes complained that good money was used to pay debts abroad, while at home only bad copper pieces carrying the crudest imprint had to suffice.[7] This would not

[1] The Carthaginian invasion towards the end of the 5th century probably gave rise to issues at Agrigentum, Camarina, Gela, Himera, and Selenus.

[2] Gardner, 407. The issues of Himera and their marks of valu suggest 72 grains of bronze represented a *litra*, whereas the market rate is thought to have been 218 grains. The highest coinage rate for bronze is found at Lipara in the 4th century, when coins are thought to have contained bronze worth half their face value.

[3] The bronze coins of the Syracusan mint were used as blanks by other cities because of their uniformity. On one occasion, a *hemi-litra* of Syracuse was used as a blank for a *litra* (Gardner, 419).

[4] The first issues of bronze in Athens have been placed (Lenormant, I, 153) as early as the middle of the 5th century B.C., when the coinage ratio between silver and copper is said to have been as high as 1:72. The coins may have been full-weight pieces, and this also the market ratio, for the rich mines of Laurium probably depressed the local value of silver. It is equally probable that the market ratio was higher, and that the coins were tokens. But no specimen of this issue is known, and subsequent writers agree that the first bronze issues were those of 406 B.C.

[5] Babelon, 399; Head, 376.

[6] Fox, *Num. Chron.*, 1905, 1.

[7] *Frogs*, 730 *sqq*.

have greatly mattered if the supply of the new pieces had been sufficiently restricted, but it appears that it was not, for in 394 B.C. the copper was hurriedly declared no longer legal tender. In future, silver alone was to be receivable in commerce and at the Treasury. This step would probably not have been taken had silver and copper tokens both been of approximately equal value. But complaints about this demonetization[1] suggest that the metal was still worth more coined than uncoined and that the plated pieces were still tokens.

A little later in the 4th century Timotheus the Athenian made bronze coins in the course of the war with the Olynthians. According to the writer of the pseudo-Aristotelian *Œconomica*,[2] the issue was made when Timotheus was short of money, and it aroused the protests of the army. These two facts suggest, although they do not prove, that the coins were tokens. The record also suggests that Timotheus realized how the value of the tokens could be maintained. He encouraged shopkeepers freely to accept and pay out the coins, thus securing them a status as coins, and he made them convertible, although, unfortunately, the rate of conversion offered is not recorded. But the Athenians did not take kindly to token money. At home they were so disgusted with their first experience of it that they refused to adopt it for small change.[3]

4. *Token Small Change.*

We have seen in the previous chapter that the movement to use token bronze coins for small denominations spread throughout the Greek world, from Sicily to Asia Minor, during the first half of the 4th century B.C. The Athenians contrived to manipulate their silver *chalci*—hardly larger than the head of a large pin—until the thirties or twenties of the century,

[1] Aristophanes, *Ecclesiazusai*, 816-22.

[2] "Timotheus the Athenian, when he was at war with the Olynthians, and in need of money, struck a bronze coinage and distributed it to the soldiers. When they protested, he told them that the merchants and retailers would all sell their goods on the same terms as before. He then told the merchants if they received bronze money to use it again to buy the commodities sent in for sale from the country and anything brought in as plunder, and said that if they brought him any bronze money they had left over they should receive silver for it" (*Œconomica*, II, 2).

[3] Professor Gardner suggests (*op. cit.*, 226) that the Athenian habit of carrying small change in the mouth was a part cause of the reluctance of the Athenians to use bronze coins.

when bronze tokens were at last issued. It is not certain that these issues were tokens, for there is no means of knowing for certain the value at which they circulated.[1] The most important copper pieces bearing a uniform type varied in weight from 74 to 100 grains, and probably represented the silver *chalcus*.[2] If they all passed at the same value some must clearly have been tokens, and quite possibly it was only the fact that all were tokens that led to such carelessness in manufacture. In fact, there is a strong probability that all the Athenian bronze pieces were tokens.[3] The Spartans, of course, held aloof from the general movement to make bronze tokens. But when, at the beginning of the 3rd century, they set up their first mint, they commenced immediately to issue small denominations of bronze.[4] The Milesian colony at Olbia, on the north-west coast of the Black Sea, issued bronze in the 5th century, but the early pieces were probably all full value coins. The use of bronze for higher denominations than those to which it was limited in the Greek world resulted in pieces of very much like the *as grave* of Rome. In fact, the coining of heavy bronze pieces may have done no more than give a monetary form to bronze ingots already in circulation for smaller units of value.[5] These pieces were issued down to the end of the 4th century B.C., and survived in circulation for three-quarters of a century longer, to the time of Alexander the Great. The lighter bronze coins were issued after the fashion then prevalent in the Greek world, and in all probability the light pieces circulated as tokens.

It appears that Dionysius of Syracuse, under the influence of financial pressure in the early years of the 4th century, experimented with the issue of token coins other than for small change. He is said[6] to have issued tin coins, which he persuaded the people to accept as silver and, presumably, at

[1] Head, *Hist. Num.*, 366 *sqq.* [2] Babelon, *op. cit.*, 402.

[3] The coinage ratio between silver and copper was round about 1:96, but this is of no assistance in the absence of information as to the relative market values of the metals.

[4] Head, *Hist. Num.*, 435. [5] Lenormant, I, 157.

[6] Pseud-Aristotle, *Œconomica* (II, 2), which states that Dionysius of Syracuse, "when he was in need of money, struck a coinage of tin, and, calling an assembly together, he spoke at great length in favour of the money which had been coined; and they, even against their will, decreed that everyone should regard any of it that he accepted as silver, and not as tin" (1 *drachm* of tin is said to have been coined to pass for 4 Attic silver *drachms*).

above their metallic value. But the authenticity of the record is disputed; no specimens of the coins have been found,[1] and no later record refers to the subsequent history of the issue. A tin-plated coin has, however, been found, and it is possible that the money referred to was plated money made to imitate the silver issues.[2] During the second half of the 4th century there was a curious move, first in Syracuse[3] and later in a number of Sikel cities,[4] to issue large heavy bronze coins without any marks of value. It would appear at first sight that there was an intention to abandon token bronze, and substitute for it full-weight coins. But it is probable that, although the commodity value of the coins was raised, it did not reach their currency value, and they remained tokens. The change of policy was probably due to the campaigns of Timoleon aimed at the liberation of the island, in the course of which the previously little disturbed native Sikel districts were brought into closer contact with the Greek settlements, and particularly with Syracuse. In deference to the native tradition, which favoured full-weight bronze money, the change was made.

The people of Byzantium[5] in Thrace, and of Clazomenæ,[6] are said to have made iron coins, but no such pieces have been preserved. They may have been marked pieces of iron circulating at their metallic value,[7] or token small change money with a purely local circulation, or even tokens to replace the larger denominations issued to meet the needs of the Peloponnesian War.[8] Byzantium had ample supplies of silver coin, and an emergency issue of iron is perhaps less likely there.

The excavation at Athens of baked earth moulds of the silver and gold coins of various countries, but mainly of the 5th century, has led to the not very plausible suggestion that such moulds had a fiduciary circulation;[9] more probably they

1 This is not, however, surprising, as tin oxidizes quickly in the earth.

2 Evans, *Num. Chron.*, 1894, 219. Gardner (414) thinks that the plated coins were probably not those referred to.

3 Head, *Hist. Num.*, 179.

4 *Ibid.*, 117.

5 Aristophanes, *Clouds*, 247 *sqq.; Pollux*, VII, 107.

6 Pseud-Aristotle, *Œconomica*, II, 2.

7 Lenormant, I, 217.

8 Babelon, 418.

9 "It may be conjectured that such pseudo baked earth money moulds of existing coins must have had a fiduciary circulation, but quite a private one like that of notes, the issue of which is authorized in some countries by a private institution (Lenormant, I, 216).

were merely the equipment of counterfeiters, but there is no evidence to confirm the suggestion. There are also references[1] to the use of baked clay, and even to wooden money in early times, in periods of difficulty in Southern Italy and Sicily, but the evidence is too unsubstantial to be worth consideration.

5. *Token Issues in Macedon.*

No bronze or any kind of token was issued in Macedon until the towns of Sicily and Attica had led the way. From the beginning of the 4th century small bronze coins appeared in many towns in Chalcidice and Macedon, and were also issued by the Kings of Macedon in small quantities. Philip of Macedon and Alexander the Great maintained the issue, but restricted it to a small volume, and also to the lowest denominations. Thus confined, it continued to the end of the Macedonian Empire. The copper issues of Alexander the Great consist of pieces thought to be *chalci*, which vary in weight from over 131 grains to 86·4 grains.[2] Unless they passed by weight, some at least must have been tokens. The coinage ratio is said to have been 1 : 96,[3] but such great variety in the weight of the coins renders the calculation of a ratio difficult, and the fact that the market ratio is not known renders it useless. After the death of Alexander the Great at the end of the 4th century, the *chalci*, issued in Macedon under Cassander, and in Thrace and Macedon under Lysimachus, rarely weighed more than 92 grains. Those in what had been the Persian Empire varied from 138·6 to 103·4 grains. This laxity in the coining of bronze in the Macedonian Empire, and the kingdoms into which it was parcelled out on the death of Alexander, suggests that the value of bronze coins as metal was never important, and that they were tokens.

6. *Chinese Knife Money.*

The bronze knife money of China commenced as a full value currency, but in later times showed a persistent tendency to shrink. When first the knife was shortened, its thickness was increased in order to maintain its weight.

[1] *Vide* Lenormant, I, 215.
[2] Babelon, 403.
[3] Lenormant, I, 154.

But later, when the blade of the knife was dispensed with, nothing but the ring was left as a symbol of the original knife, nearly a foot long. It is suggested[1] that the ring circulated for the value previously attaching to the whole knife, but the Chinese have always exploited so fully any weakness in the monetary system that it is very unlikely that bronze rings would not be abundantly produced by unauthorized coiners if they circulated for a value greatly in excess of their cost of production. Later, the material of which the pieces were made was debased: at first copper, it changed to iron, then to zinc. This also might have given the coins a token status. But again, the presence of counterfeiters must have made it impossible for any token money to survive.

7. *The Status of Roman Bronze under the Republic.*

The discussion of token coins in Rome is complicated by the difficulty of determining when token coins came into use. We have seen that the native medium of exchange in Italy was the pound of bronze, and that the first round coins were pounds of bronze. But later coins show a chronic tendency to decline in weight. If their value declined contemporaneously with their weight, the coins remained full-weight coins. If, on the other hand, they did not decline in value, or did not decline in proportion to their weight, they must have become tokens. As we may safely assume that early Italian silver coins were not tokens, the most direct method of proving whether copper pieces were tokens would be to ascertain the relative market values of silver and copper, and then to enquire their relative values in the form of coins. A higher relative value for bronze in coins than in the market would prove their token status. But we have seen that there is no information available as to the relative values of silver and bronze in early times. We might then fall back upon the changes in the currency ratio of the two metals at different times. If we can discover an upward tendency in the currency ratio of bronze to silver,[2] the development of tokens might be suspected. But it must be borne in mind that if the value of bronze, in relation to that of silver, rose

[1] Babelon, 157. Sylvestre, *Notes on Money and Medals of Annam*, 44-45.

[2] *E.g.*, if bronze coins, although reduced in weight, continued to be rated at the same value in silver coins.

also in the market, the rise in the currency ratio of bronze might be aimed at preventing it from being under-valued in coins, and not at causing it to be over-valued. But we have no records of the relative market values of the metals, and when we turn to the coins themselves for evidence we find that even the currency ratio between the two metals is doubtful. The appearance of almost identical types over long periods makes it difficult to date the coins, and therefore to determine the times at which, and amounts by which, the coins were reduced in weight.

Mommsen suggested[1] that the earliest *as grave* issued in Rome had an official value, independent of the value of its metallic content. The ancient writers who said that the value of the coins depended on their content are dismissed: "if it had been so, there would have been no difference between their value and that of crude ingots or copper utensils, and the state would have lost the expense of coining, and its trouble in putting on the pieces an indication of their legal value would have been useless."[2] Nevertheless, it is more probable that the ancient writers were correct. In the first place, Mommsen himself suggested that the weight of the *as* was arranged so that its metallic value should be exactly equal to that of a scruple of silver; but if the *as* was not to circulate at its metallic value, there is no object in such policy. Secondly, an arrangement that a piece of 10 ounces should pass for 12 ounces to cover the cost of minting is improbable, because the allowance for brassage (16 per cent.) is far too high. After all, the cost of minting should not have been great, especially if the introduction of lead into the bronze had proved effective in making it unsuitable for copper utensils, and limited the melting of coins. On the other hand, it is suggested that the weight of the *as* was deliberately reduced, to render it a token coin and to yield a profit to the state.[3] The quantity of *asses* must have been limited in order to preserve the *as* as a token, and there must have been a criterion according to which the supply was controlled. British silver token currency

[1] Mommsen, I, 209 *sqq*. [2] I, 209.

[3] Ridgeway (370) says the reduction was made "when the idea of a real copper currency for local purposes gained ground, and it was found that it was not necessary to have the *as* of account of full weight, and at the same time to enable the state to make a profit of this currency, which was solely for home use (just as our mint makes a large profit out of our silver coins)."

is but small change money, the value of which is stabilized by reference to the full value money or convertible notes. But if the *as* was itself the principal money, it could not be so easily stabilized. It is too much to suppose that an attempt was made to preserve constancy of general purchasing power. The only possible solution is that its value was fixed in terms either of Campanian silver pieces or of bronze by weight. The latter explanation has been advanced,[1] and would mean that there was a bronze standard in operation but only bronze tokens in circulation; the general level of prices would depend upon the market value of bronze. An arrangement of this kind would be easily possible if convertibility were maintained. But it is doubtful whether the Roman financial authorities had yet reached the stage of issuing tokens, and still more of maintaining convertibility. In no country had the principal coins yet been tokens; in fact, it is more likely that the reduced *as* passed at its bronze value, and that the general level of prices varied inversely as the market value of bronze, and as the quantity of bronze in the coins.

We have seen that, although it is known that the *denarius* of 268 B.C. was worth 10 *asses*, we do not know whether the *asses* then issued were those weighing 4 ounces or only 2 ounces. If they were the former, the currency ratio between the values of silver and bronze must have been about 240 : 1, and if the latter 120 : 1. The first definite information comes from the Lex Flaminia of 217 B.C., which altered the weights of both bronze and silver, stating both the new weights of the coins and the relative values of the coins. The relative values of bronze and silver in currency were then 112 : 1. Those who hold that silver was 240 or 250 times as valuable as bronze in early times have to explain the change to a ratio of 112 : 1 by the end of the 3rd century. Although Mommsen argued[2] that the *as* fell gradually from 268 B.C. to 217 B.C., we have already presented evidence in support of a sudden reduction about 240 B.C., if the 2-ounce *asses* are assigned to 268 B.C. But there is no evidence of any change in the number of *asses* to the *denarius*, so the reduction of the *as* would mean a change in the currency ratio from 1 : 240 to 1 : 120, and Grueber holds that it was this change that reduced the *as* to the condition of a token; if his hypothesis of a ratio of

[1] Cp. Ridgeway, 382.

[2] *Op. cit.*, II, 14.

1 : 240 prior to this date be accepted, such a result is possible. But the alteration was made in time of war, and one might suspect that desire for profit would have encouraged a liberal issue rather than the restraint necessary to maintain the coins as tokens. In the absence of any right of conversion, a plentiful issue would either reduce the purchasing power of the bronze pieces in relation to that of the silver pieces or drive the latter out of circulation. But there is no evidence that either of these things happened. Either the issue, though made in time of war, was closely controlled, and the *as* continued to be worth $\frac{1}{10}$ of a *denarius*, or the value of the *as* remained unaltered because it was a full-weight coin. In the latter event, the relative values of silver and bronze must always have been 120 : 1, and no change was made in 240 B.C., or thereabouts.

This latter explanation, indeed, is the most satisfactory.[1] The *scruple* of silver was then rated at half a pound of bronze during the later 4th century, and the new Campanian coins weighing 6 scruples were worth 3 *asses*. When, in about 286 B.C., the *as* was halved in weight, the number of *asses* to a given weight of silver was doubled, thus retaining the same ratio. In 268 B.C. the *as* was reduced, on the introduction of the silver *denarius*, by $\frac{3}{5}$ of its weight. But again, the silver value of the *as* fell in exact proportion from 1 scruple of silver to $\frac{2}{5}$ of a scruple.[2] Still, the ratio of 120 : 1 persisted, and there is no sign of any attempt to make tokens of the bronze money, unless the market value of copper was falling, and there is no evidence of such a fall.

There is little doubt that the currency ratio between bronze and silver remained unaltered from the first issue of coins in Rome until at least 240 B.C. If the earliest reductions from the full pound of bronze were gradual, they must have soon resulted in a fall in the value of the coins, and it is highly improbable that in the course of its early reductions the *as* ever remained a token coin for any long period.[3] If the

1 Head, 19; Sydenham, *Num. Chron.*, 1918, 165.

2 In other words, the *denarius* of four scruples was worth 10 *asses*.

3 When Grueber says (XXIV) that " the early reductions in the *as* probably had no effect on the current value of the coins which would pass at their face value," he must mean that the purchasing power of the coins remained unchanged, and that they became tokens. Their face value was " I," or 1 *as*, and of course, they continued to pass for that.

reduction was the work of dishonest moneyers, or of state officials exploiting the currency for profit,[1] it would be expected that as many reduced coins would be issued as could be sold at a profit—*i.e.*, that coins would be issued until their value was sufficiently reduced to prevent them being tokens. If the reduction was a consequence of the inefficient methods of

[1] Ridgeway (376) suggests that the first reductions from 12 to 10 ounces were made " when the idea of a real copper currency for local purposes gained ground," and that the state made a profit out of the issue of *asses* much as the state now makes a profit on the sale of silver currency. In a subsequent passage (382) dealing with later alterations, he enters into more detail, and suggests that " All penalties due to the state would be paid, not in reduced *asses* of only 5 or 4 ounces, but in full libral *asses* as weighed in the balance. On the other hand, although reduced *asses* were used by the state in paying debts to private individuals, they were only received as tokens, and, no doubt, the state was bound, if called upon, to pay a full pound of bronze for every stamped reduced *as* presented to it, but in ordinary times this made no practical difference, for the bronze currency was purely local all over Italy and Sicily. . . . It was far too cumbrous to be used as a medium of international trade." In the first place convertibility is incompatible with the refusal of the state to take the coins except at their bullion value. If reduced *asses* were accepted by the state in payment of penalties by weight only, why should anyone pay fines in reduced *asses*? " The state was bound, if called upon, to pay a full pound of bronze for every stamped reduced *as* presented to it"; why not, then, have them converted into full-weight *asses*, and use those for the payment of the fines ? Indeed, if the state would not accept the tokens at their legal value, it would be difficult to get private citizens to do so, and there would be a strong tendency for *asses* to fall to their bullion value. But if the convertibility was real, and resulted in the automatic adjustment of the supply of *asses*, they would tend to be worth the amount of uncoined bronze into which they were convertible, and would have been tokens. But it is doubtful whether, in fact, *asses* were convertible; there is no evidence of it, and the suggestion is incidental to the idea that *asses* were tokens, which is also unproved. When he comes to explain the introduction of the *denarius*, Professor Ridgeway writes: " Are these pieces real representatives of the *as* of account, or do they rather simply represent the value of the then normal *as* of currency, which was probably not more than a *triens*, or 4 ounces, or perhaps not more than a *quadrans*, or 3 ounces ? The latter is the more likely hypothesis. The Romans had been long accustomed to a bronze token currency, and it is most likely that the new silver currency would be adapted to it. It is then likely that the *denarius* equalled 10 *asses* of at least 3 ounces each, in which case silver was to bronze as 180 : 1 " (383). In other words, when the value of the *as* was fixed in terms of *denarii*, the value of the reduced copper content of the *as* was the basis of the relation. From this it must be clear that the supposed token quality of the coins which enabled them to circulate at above their bullion value had disappeared, if, indeed, it had ever existed. Professor Ridgeway himself passes on in the next sentence to emphasize that " in transactions inside the state the balance would be commonly and, in dealing with strangers, invariably employed in all monetary transactions, ancient states being very jealous of alien mintages." Balances play no part in dealings with token coins.

the mint, although it is unlikely that at this early date the Romans understood that the preservation of a token currency was a matter of limiting its issue, it might be that issues were limited, in fact, by customary arrangements as to the quantity of money made at the mint, or the periods during which it should work. But any token character which the coins possessed must have been very temporary, for in 268 the coinage ratio was probably the same as in 335 B.C.

It is, therefore, fairly certain that from 240 B.C. the coinage ratio between silver and bronze was 120: 1, and it is probable that this was approximately the ratio in the market between the values of the two metals. The first Punic War was probably the moving cause of the first issue of gold in Rome. The marks on the gold pieces show their value in silver *sestertii* at a ratio of 20 : 1 between the values of gold and silver. There is little doubt that the market ratio at this time was no higher than 12 : 1. The gold coins were, therefore, much overvalued and must be regarded as tokens. The fact that they were issued in time of war makes their token status all the more probable. They were money of necessity, and the Senate may have been legally compelled to redeem them on request at any time at their current value.[1] These coins appear soon to have disappeared from circulation, and there is no evidence as to the rate at which they were in fact exchanged for *sestertii*.

The alterations of the currency in 217 B.C., during the second Punic War, took the form of a reduction of the *as* by half, and of the *denarius* by about 14 per cent. But at the same time it was decreed that the *denarius* should be worth sixteen *asses* (instead of ten as before). There has been much confusion in attempts to explain the significance of this law.[2] The net effect of the changes was to reduce the

[1] Grueber, LV.

[2] Mommsen argued that the Lex Flaminia authorized the introduction of bronze tokens for the first time. But this view was inferred from his argument that the 4-ounce *as* introduced in 286 B.C. suffered in the succeeding period from unofficial reductions made by dishonest moneyers. The Lex Flaminia, by reducing the legal coinage ratio from 250 : 1 to 112 : 1, merely accepted a situation well established in fact. He thought that the market ratio was still 250:1, and the *as* was, therefore, a token. Apparently the moneyers did not over-issue it.

Lenormant, writing (III, 24) of the same Act, after making frequent reference to Mommsen, says that it "gave to the money by public decision an arbitrary and conventional value other than that which

coinage ratio between the metals from 120 : 1 to 112 : 1, bronze in coins being given a slightly higher silver value than before. If bronze money was token before, it was now slightly more so, and if it was not token before, it now became so, unless the market value of bronze was rising in relation to that of silver. But the maintenance of a ratio so near to the previous one lends support to the idea that it was probably also the market ratio, and that bronze coins remained full value money. Nevertheless, token money did appear during the second Punic War. Hannibal's invasion drove the Roman administration to resort to the issue of silver-plated coins. No great number of these pieces has been found, and there is no evidence as to the number of such pieces that was issued. In the absence of records of severe inflation, it can only be supposed that they were not issued in sufficient quantities to reduce their value to that of their bullion content. They must, therefore, have remained tokens during the period of their circulation.

---

it would have had as a simple commodity." But he is not at all clear as to its provisions, for immediately before the passage above quoted he refers to the Act as "*suddenly reducing the* '*denarius*,' which became from this moment the real regulator of the value of things, from $\frac{1}{72}$ to $\frac{1}{84}$ of a pound," making no reference at all to copper money. He seems to think there was an attempt to maintain the value of the *denarius* in spite of its reduction in weight, and that it was the silver currency which became token. But had this been attempted, the *denarius* would have been rated at 20 reduced *asses* instead of 16, the number actually fixed by the Senate. Again in an earlier passage (I, 169) he writes of the same Act that "it effected a reduction of all the money. The weight of the *as* was fixed at 1 ounce, that is to say, $\frac{1}{12}$ of a pound, and at the same time it was provided that the *denarius*, *the weight of which remained the same*, should be worth 16 instead of 10 *asses*." From this it might appear that because the reduced *as* was rated at $\frac{1}{16}$ instead of $\frac{1}{20}$ of a *denarius*, the former was becoming token. But he proceeds (*loc. cit.*) to remark that " under the operation of this law, copper money continued as *une monnaie effective ou representative*, as it had been at Rome since the commencement of coining. The nominal value of the *as* continued to conform approximately to its metallic value." In fact, he goes on to say that it was in 89 B.C. when the *as* was again halved that it became a token. His evidence is very confused. Babelon followed this line of argument, except that he also thought the *denarius* remained unchanged. His conclusion was that the Lex Flaminia "had the immediate effect of depriving the bronze money of the character of real and effective money, which it had, in spite of all, preserved up to then; its nominal value ceased to bear any relation to its intrinsic or metallic value; in short, bronze money at Rome ceased to be what we now called *monnaie droit*, and fell to the rank of *monnaie d'appoint*" (I, 376).

For a century and a quarter the standard of the copper currency remained unchanged, although it diminished greatly in importance during the latter half of the 2nd century B.C. When the coining of *asses* was resumed in the troublous opening years of the 1st century B.C., the *as* began to fall in weight, and in 89 B.C. the Lex Papiria authorized a reduction of its legal weight to one-half an ounce. Again, as the alteration was made under stress of war, we might expect that full profits were sought by the state, and that the reduction was followed by a fall in the purchasing power of the *as*. But this does not appear to have happened. Before the reduction, the *denarius* was marked X̶ and probably passed as one-sixteenth of a *denarius*, and after the reduction, although the X̶ disappeared for a time, one moneyer revived the same mark of value in 76 B.C., thus indicating that the last reduction had not caused a fall in the value of the *as* in *denarii*. That such was the case is further borne out by the fact that when Julius Cæsar later raised the pay of the troops, and withdrew their privilege of receiving a *denarius* for every ten *asses*, he arranged that the *denarius* should be worth 16 *asses*. This is the first occasion upon which it is certain that the weight of the *as* was reduced without a corresponding reduction in its value in silver. As the currency ratio of bronze to silver was about 56 : 1 in the face of a market ratio of about 112 : 1,[1] the bronze coins then became tokens as they had been in the Greek world for about 300 years. The value of the pieces may have been maintained at first, because the metal gained by diminishing the coins was not put back into circulation in Italy, but was exported to finance the campaign in the East against Mithridates. But almost immediately the *as* began to lose weight again. By 35 B.C. the *as* was only a quarter of an ounce,[2] although *asses* of so low a weight as one-eighth of an ounce were issued.[3] At the same time, political strife gave rise to a second resort to plated coins. The quantity of such pieces was fixed by the law of 89 B.C. at one-seventh of each issue of good *denarii*. It is impossible to say whether these pieces were tokens. Complaints that it was difficult to know how much money one was worth indicate that the plated pieces were not as valuable

[1] Lenormant, I, 170; Babelon, 408.

[2] Sydenham, *Num. Chron.*, 1918, 181.

[3] Babelon, 408.

as genuine *denarii*, but whether they sank so low as the value of their metallic content is not recorded. In the years of conflict, from the time of Sulla down to the end of the Republic, no copper was issued,[1] but previous issues continued to circulate as tokens. At the close of the Republic, therefore, gold and silver were both full-weight coins, and copper was token. In those Greek cities which had been permitted under the Republic to make local issues of copper the weight of the pieces followed the reductions at Rome, doubtless with similar consequences.

8. *Token Coins in the Augustan Imperial System.*

Augustus reformed the currency, and at some date between 23 and 15 B.C.,[2] recommenced the issue of small change token coins of which no adequate issue had been made for sixty-five years. In two important respects he departed from tradition: the *sestertius* (hitherto a silver coin) became a (brass) token coin, and a new unit, the 2-*as* piece, was also made token,[3] and two metals were used for tokens. Republican bronze had consisted of a mixture of copper, lead, and tin, but it was replaced under the empire by a mixture of copper and zinc,[4] a kind of brass then called orichalcum or golden bronze. This mixture had been used for an experimental issue in 45-44 B.C., and also for issues in Asia since 29 B.C.[5] It was practically indistinguishable in appearance from the republican bronze, and was almost identical in value with it. The new *sestertius* and *dupondius* (2-*as* piece) were made of this brass, and weighed respectively one ounce and half an ounce.

[1] With the exception of a little in 45-44 B.C., when Pompey issued bronze on the basis of an *as* of a full ounce again. It is possible that the issue was made in Spain when copper was very plentiful (Grueber, *Num. Chron.*, 1904, 220-24). The coins circulated widely, and Pompey may have endeavoured to restore copper coinage to its old dignity (Sydenham, *Num. Chron.*, 1918, 174). In 45-44 B.C., one moneyer (Clovius) coined in yellow bronze, and the other struck lighter coins of pure copper. The coinage ratio between brass and copper seems to have been $1\frac{2}{3}:1$. The experiment was unsuccessful, but it may have been the basis of the brass and copper coinage later instituted under the empire (Sydenham, *Num. Chron.*, 1918, 177).

[2] *Vide* Sydenham, *Num. Chron.*, 1918, 184.

[3] Both these coins had already been issued in Gaul, Asia Minor, and the East (Sydenham, *Num. Chron.*, 1918, 182).

[4] About 75-80 per cent. copper and the rest zinc.

[5] Sydenham, *Num. Chron.*, 1918, 181.

The *as* and quarter-*as*[1] were both made of pure copper, and weighed respectively about 168 grains (two-fifths of an ounce), and 52·5 grains (one-eighth of an ounce). Thus brass was coined at the rate of a quarter of an ounce to the *as* and copper in the quarter-*as* at half an ounce to the *as* and in the *as* at two-fifths of an ounce to the *as*. Attempts have been made to explain this series of weights by reference to the relative values of brass and copper.[2] As it is generally admitted that the coins of both metals were tokens, there was no need to attempt to make their metallic value bear the same proportion to their current value in all denominations. It is certainly misleading to assert that the change involves "the introduction of the bimetallic principle into the Roman system."[3] That principle was probably introduced in 268 B.C., and the reform of Augustus introduced merely two metals for small change, but neither was used for full-weight coins. The use of the quarter-ounce standard for brass is not surprising; the bronze coins of the later years of the Republic, although very irregular in weight, approximated to this standard. The quarter-*as* was probably based on a half-ounce standard for copper for reasons of convenience, the quarter *as* on the quarter-ounce standard would have weighed only 26 grains and on the same basis as the *as* 44 grains. But presumably as these coins would have been small, and because the issue of quarter-*asses* was unimportant in volume, the Government never reduced them from the half-ounce standard.[4] But the *as* cannot be thus explained. It has been suggested that the explanation lies in the use of the *as* in military payments. The countermarks on the coins suggest that such was their particular destination. From 217 B.C., for 150 years, military pay was expressed in *asses*

[1] The weight of the smallest copper piece suggests one-third rather than a quarter of the *as*, but there is no record of such a denomination (*vide* Sydenham, *Num. Chron.*, 1918, 186).

[2] Sydenham (*Num. Chron.*, 1918, 183) suggests that brass was $1\frac{2}{3}$ as valuable as copper. The copper equivalent of the *sestertius* of 420 grains was $\frac{420 \times 5}{3} = 700$ grains. The copper *as* on this basis would weigh 175 grains, which may have been its normal weight. The weight of the quarter-*as* cannot be similarly explained. Beanlands (*Num. Chron.*, 1918, 189 *sqq.*) puts forward much the same theory.

[3] Sydenham, *Num. Chron.*, 1918, 183. *Vide* also Beanlands, *Num. Chron.*, 1918, 189.

[4] Mattingly, XLIX.

which were one-tenth of the *denarius*, although *as* coins were one-sixteenth of *denarius*, but Julius Cæsar made the latter unit also the unit for the payment of troops. It is suggested[1] that it was merely with a view to " honouring the old tradition under which the *as* was an important and imposing part of the Roman money system " that the *as* was made equal in weight to one-tenth of a *denarius* of sixteen quarter-ounce *asses*. Although the military unit of one-tenth of the *denarius* had disappeared over thirty years previously, a unit identical with it was probably still in use in retail trade, and may have provided a crazy foundation for the innovation. Little purpose can have been served by maintaining a weight relation between *sestertii* and *asses* corresponding to an obsolete value relation.[2] The weight of the *as* cannot be satisfactorily explained, but it is clear that all these coins were tokens. As the copper quarter-*as* based on a half-ounce standard survived,the *as* which was based on a lighter standard must have been a token. The brass coins were based upon a still lower standard, and although brass was more valuable than copper, it was probably not twice as valuable, $1\frac{2}{3}:1$ being a more probable value relation between the two metals. Brass was then token. But there is little doubt that the quarter-*as* piece was also a token; the coinage ratio between the copper in it and the silver *denarius* was 1: 56, but the market ratio must have been at least 112 : 1 and perhaps twice as much. The introduction of two metals for small change is not adequately explained by the fact that when the *as* had been raised to one-tenth of a *denarius* of sixteen *asses* of a quarter of an ounce each, it approached too close in weight to the 2-*as* piece.[3] It is true that the great irregularity of the weight of Roman coins would soon cause confusion between units of 168 and 210 grains, and the use of brass for the latter would make it easier to distinguish between the two, but the raising of the *as* has to be first explained and no explanation offers. It is much more probable that the reform was a part of the imperial policy of Augustus. In the Greek-speaking parts of the empire, and in

[1] Mattingly, XLVIII; Beanlands, *Num. Chron.*, 1918, 198.

[2] The *sestertius*, while four times as valuable as the *as*, was about two and a half times as heavy.

[3] Mattingly, XLVIII.

Spain, copper was current for small change. The Roman bronze was more valuable in currency than copper, and the two were not interchangeable at a simple rate. If Augustus was to supplant local issues and obtain the resulting profits, the imperial system had to be assimilated to the local copper. The *as* and its quarter of copper would gain rapid acceptance by copper-using peoples, and the *sestertius* and *dupondius* would appeal to the Romans. The simple relations between the two made them part of a coherent system.[1]

The Augustan system remained substantially unaltered for about 250 years. Minor alterations were made. In the second decade of the 1st century A.D. the quarter-*as* piece ceased to appear.[2] From about 22 B.C. the brass coins increased in weight,[3] although pieces of the original weight continued to appear as well. The appearance of the coins leaves no doubt that both heavy and light pieces were intended to pass at the same value. As the coins were all tokens, it is not likely that a fall in the value of brass gave rise to the increase of the coins.[4] It was against the economic interest of all concerned to increase the cost of manufacturing tokens, and the caprice of the coiners is the only, and that a profoundly unsatisfactory, reason for the increase in weight. During the first nine years of Nero's reign the issue of tokens was altogether suspended. When it was resumed in A.D. 60 it was confined to copper one, half, and quarter-*asses* and a few two-*as* pieces, *brass* not being coined at all. But after A.D. 63 brass pieces of four, two, one, one-and-a-half and quarter-*asses* were added, and two years later copper half and quarter-*asses* ceased to be coined. But the brass *asses* were not a success, and on their suspension the token system consisted of:

Copper.

1 *as* weighing 168 grains

---

1 Sydenham, *Num. Chron.*, 1818, 183. 2 *Ibid.*, 1918, 118.

3 The two-*as* piece first, and the *sestertius* A.D. 37. The two-*as* piece weighed sometimes as much as 250 instead of 210 grains, and the *sestertius* 470 instead of 420 grains.

4 Sydenham (*Num. Chron.*, 1919, 120) suggests that the relative values of brass and copper may have fallen from $1\frac{2}{3}$ to $1\frac{1}{3}:1$. The great variety of weights is also unlikely to have been due to changes in the relative value of brass and copper, nor is Nero's abstention from coining brass to be thus accounted for.

Brass.

4 *as* (*Sestertius*)	weighing	420	grains
2 ,, (*Dupondius*)	,,	230	,,
½ ,,	,,	57	,,
¼ ,,	,,	33[1]	,,

The *as* and the *sestertius* remained of the weight established by Augustus, but the subdivisions of the brass *sestertius* are not at all exactly related to the *sestertius*. After the death of Nero, his new coins were almost all suspended and the Augustan system was reinstated. The brass *sestertius* and *dupondius* returned to their respective ounce and half-ounce weights, and the copper *as* remained about 168 grains in weight. Until the second decade of the 3rd century, the system changed little, the brass *sestertius* and *dupondius* and the copper *as* being the most important tokens, although brass half and copper half and quarter-*asses* occasionally appeared and varied much in weight.[2]

The debasement of the silver coinage and the issue of plated coins, which was accelerated during the 3rd century after the introduction of the *argenteus Antoninianus*, did not, so far as is known, result in the debased coins becoming tokens.[3] As their silver content declined, their value must also have declined, for it is to be presumed that desire for profit induced the issue of coins so long as profit was to be had. But as the currency ratio between silver and copper remained unchanged, the face value of copper in *denarii* represented a continually falling purchasing power, until at last copper pieces became full-value coins, and later were actually worth more as metal than as coin. They were, naturally, exported and melted down. The weight and the quality of the coins were both reduced. But denominations below the *as* ceased to be coined after A.D. 180, *asses* after A.D. 217, and *sestertii* and *dupondii* were issued only in small quantities.[4]

Before passing on to consider the token issues set up after the complete collapse of the currency in the middle of the 3rd century A.D., we must first note certain other token

[1] Sydenham, *Num. Chron.*, 1919, 125. [2] *Ibid.*, 1919, 127.

[3] The baked earth moulds believed to have been the casts used by counterfeiters suggest that the *argenteus* was not worth counterfeiting —*i.e.*, that there was no great margin between cost of production and face value.

[4] Sydenham, *Num. Chron.*, 1919, 131.

issues made during the first three hundred years of the Roman Empire. At the end of the 2nd and beginning of the 3rd century A.D., there was an issue of tin coins in Gaul. Some seven hundred specimens have been found at Lyons struck with the dies used for the silver *denarius* under Septimus Severus, Caracalla, and Geta. They are of too fine workmanship to be counterfeits, and the absence of any plating of silver shows that they were not plated coins. They must have been issued as tin coins and, as they are dated subsequently to the great expedition of Severus to Britain, they may be of British tin, taken to Gaul and coined with the dies used for the *denarius*, with a view to evading the Senatorial monopoly of the issue of bronze tokens. Desire for profit may not alone explain the issue, but rather the inadequate supplies of copper sent from the Senatorial Mint in Rome.[1] But the issue was not a success, mainly because it was difficult to distinguish from silver, a difficulty enhanced by the fact that the types on both were identical. The issue may have been token. Nothing is known of the value of the coins. Gaul also saw the issue of lead coins in the 1st and 2nd century A.D., although only for very small denominations and for local use. It is possible that they were not even public issues.[2]

Up to the 2nd century B.C. special issues of token bronze coins are thought to have been issued by the gold, silver, and copper mining concerns in different parts of the empire.[3] These pieces, bearing on the obverse the head of the Emperor (often Trajan and Hadrian), and on the other the name of the mines, do not bear the mark " S.C." of the Senate, and cannot, therefore, have been universal legal tender. They must have been small change coin restricted in circulation to the mining district. The mines were responsible for the only large industrial concentrations of workers, and called for considerable quantities of small change money. Senatorial copper was issued only from Rome and Antioch, and was difficult to transport. In consequence, special arrangements had to be made in mining districts. The proportion of the metallic to the legal value of the pieces issued was less than

[1] Lenormant, I, 214.
[2] Lenormant, I, 210.
[3] Lenormant, I, 239.

in the bronze issued contemporaneously from the Senatorial and provincial mints.[1]

Another form of token issue is said to have arisen under the empire, owing to the withdrawal from generals in the field of the right to issue their own money. Deprived of this convenient device by the jealousy of the Emperor, they gave, when pressed by military necessities, a temporarily enhanced value to money already in circulation by placing thereon a countermark. Lenormant[2] says that "it is evident, in spite of the absence of texts which state it formally," that after the necessity had passed a date was fixed up to which the pieces were redeemed at their enhanced value in current coins. After the appointed day, countermarked coins passed at the value at which they were originally issued, to the loss of those who had neglected to exchange their holdings. The countermarked pieces were then re-issued by the public offices, and the countermarks ignored. "In this way the frequency with which copper pieces bearing several countermarks occur in finds of Roman imperial money can be explained."[3] But these conclusions are not evident. These countermarks were confined to copper pieces which were tokens. If all the pieces called in were raised in value and re-issued, the effect would be to increase the number of copper units and reduce their value. The copper unit could only be kept at its old value by leaving the quantity of units unaltered. If the general took a number of the pieces out of circulation and sold them as metal, the copper unit might remain unchanged and he obtain the needed financial relief. But if, as is more probable, he paid out all the new pieces in settlement of his debts, they would pass at less than their legal value, although they might remain tokens. If pennies were called in and all re-issued marked "twopence," and not reduced in number by conversion or other means, the twopenny pieces would tend to sink below $\frac{1}{120}$ of a pound, and prices in pennies would rise. When the redemption took place, the reverse effects would be encountered. In its effects the device is exactly similar to a reduction in the

[1] Lenormant (I, 248) attributes to this arrangement, which gave rise to pieces of copper of different metallic value passing at the same value in exchange, the development of the idea of *monnaie signe*, which led to the crisis of the 3rd century.

[2] I, 250.

[3] Lenormant, I, 250.

weight of full-weight coins. It is possible that these pieces remained tokens, but we have no knowledge of the value at which they passed, and certainty is impossible. No other explanation of countermarks on copper pieces is available.

9. *The Token Coins in the Reconstructed Roman Imperial System.*

The first reform after the collapse was but a modest effort. It aimed at issuing plated money of a stable value. As we have seen,[1] the legal value of these new plated coins (marked "XXI" and "VSV") is a matter of dispute; it is most probable that they were tokens, as presumably were the copper pieces, probably *sestertii* and *asses*, issued by Aurelian. In fact, the plated pieces appear to have been very much more overvalued as coin than was the bronze in the smaller denominations. The denominations and value of the reformed currency are so disputed that little can be said as to their status. Diocletian issued copper coins, the *follis*, the *denarius communis*, and the *centenionalis*, the legal value of the former being doubtful, while the two latter are probably continuations of Aurelian's coins. But it is clear that from this time copper coins were only used for small change, and were always token coins.

In Egypt all the evidence points, as we have seen,[2] to the entire absence of coins in general circulation throughout the period of Persian domination.[3] After the death of Alexander, a coinage of gold and silver, with bronze pieces for the small denominations, was issued from a new mint at Alexandria. The currency ratio has been calculated as 161 : 1, and it is not impossible that this was about the market ratio, and that neither bronze nor silver was token.[4] But there is no reliable evidence as to the relative commercial value of the metals.[5] This issue continued, with interruptions, throughout the 3rd, 2nd, and 1st centuries B.C. down to the death of Cleopatra. Some of the copper pieces of Cleopatra

[1] Chap. XI. [2] P. 45.

[3] There was, however, one issue of bronze at Naucratis in the 4th century B.C. Little is known of it, and Head says it "must owe its existence to quite exceptional circumstances" (*op. cit.*, 845).

[4] Babelon, 403.

[5] Lenormant (I, 153) gives it as 1:183, thus making the bronze token pieces.

bear marks which appear to indicate the number of copper *drachms* in each piece, and indicate that 4 or 5 grains of bronze represented the *drachm*. Although possible, it is not probable, that the coins were tokens passing for very much more than they were worth as metal. The bronze *drachm* was different in weight from the silver *drachm*, but very little can be ascertained as to the status, token or full value, of the later bronze issues. The Roman imperial billon money, issued in Egypt from about A.D. 19, suffered the same extreme debasement as did the imperial silver in Italy. There is little doubt that, also as in Italy, the issue was not "managed," but the pieces fell rapidly in value. This is indicated by the cessation of the issue of full-weight bronze during the 3rd century A.D., owing to the competition of the debased billon pieces. Throughout the inflation of the 3rd century the daily needs of the ordinary population were met by local issues of lead coins, which one may surmise with fair confidence to have been tokens. Together with these lead, and sometimes iron, counters there existed also monetiform pieces of Egyptian porcelain and baked clay, bearing on their faces Greek letters and various symbols, of which pieces, it has been suggested, a number were fiduciary money of necessity. If they were used as money at all they certainly must have been tokens.[1] Lenormant also states that "we possess undeniable proof of the use of glass money in Egypt from the time of the Roman Empire, a practice which continued there under the Byzantine Empire and under the Arabs." These glass pieces bore an indication of a monetary value.[2]

10. *Summary.*

It is clear from the available evidence that token coins were a relatively late invention. For three hundred years or more, until the last decade or two of the 3rd century B.C., they seem to have been unknown. When the peoples of Sicily coined bronze at the time of the Athenian invasion, they opened a fresh period in the history of money. The circumstances of the resort to tokens are fairly clear. Nowhere were they adopted as a way out of the inconveniences of the use of heavy standards of iron, lead, or copper, although

[1] Babelon, 419.

[2] Lenormant, I, 214.

such an origin has often been suggested. Over a greater part of the ancient world these difficulties were avoided by adopting another monetary medium. In Rome, where the bronze tradition was more vigorous than anywhere else, silver was made a currency metal, in theory co-equal with bronze. In the course of time bronze was restricted to the smaller denominations, until for practical purposes the Roman system was based upon a silver standard. But copper coins remained, in theory at least, full-weight money, and only at the beginning of the last century B.C. did copper money become token.

The predominant reason for the issue of token money was the need for a small change money, less fragile and elusive than the small denominations of silver which had hitherto been used. As coins came into more general use during the 5th and 4th centuries, particularly for the everyday transactions of poor people, convenient small denominations were more than ever necessary. In consequence, the issues of bronze in Sicily were the beginning of a movement that spread during the 4th and 3rd centuries to South Italy, Carthage, Greece, and Asia Minor. These coins were all of bronze or copper. In Rome, during the 2nd century, bronze coins were used for the small denominations, but, as we have seen, they became tokens only in the early years of the 1st century. From that time small change money was always token. Augustus used both brass and copper, but after a life of about two hundred years his system collapsed. When order was again restored, we find that the use of token money for small change was the accepted practice, and was embodied in the new systems then established.

It is clear from the position in Rome until 89 B.C., and from other cities in the ancient world, that copper coins were not always tokens. But in the Greek world and in Macedonia after the 5th century B.C., and in Rome after the beginning of the last century B.C., they nearly always were. It is not possible to prove that this was so, because the market value of bronze in other monetary metals is unknown. In Rome, in particular, there is wide difference of opinion as to this market ratio throughout the whole period of the Republic. Throughout the Greek world and Macedonia, and in both the Roman Republic and Empire, there is a very evident carelessness in the determination of the weight of the coins, even where uniformity of types suggests that coins passed at the same value. The coinage ratios between silver and copper varied considerably from place to place; and the variations cannot always be explained in terms of local differences in the relative values of the metals. The denominations of Roman imperial coins are usually very difficult to determine. But whenever marks of value indicate the face value of the coins, it is believed that their value exceeded their contemporary value as metal.[1] Moreover, no difficulty seems to have been encountered in keeping both silver and copper in circulation together. Unless we can assume there were no changes in the relative values of bronze and silver, the only possible explanation is that coins of one or other metal were not full weight. In the face of all this evidence, we are justified in concluding that bronze coins were tokens.

Although the first issues of tokens in Sicily were probably intended to yield a profit, they were very rarely so used in the ancient world. The issues in Athens after the disaster at Syracuse, and the somewhat doubtful issues of Byzantium and Clazomenæ, exhaust the probable examples of such a use. The Romans, however, made token coins serve this end on more than one occasion. In 240 B.C., during the first Punic War, they made an emergency issue of gold pieces, and fixed their legal value above their metallic value. In 217 B.C., during the second Punic War, and in 89 B.C., during the Social

[1] Lenormant is not very clear on this matter. He writes (*op. cit.*, I, 155) that "If we had to fix approximately a general average for the most common ratio between the values of the two metals (silver and copper) in the Greek world, it would be between 100 and 120:1. These are the most probable as both commercial and monetary ratios in the countries which, during the second half of the 5th and the 4th century, struck copper on the basis of the silver *drachm*." If both commercial and monetary ratios were the same, either both silver and bronze were tokens, or neither. It is inconceivable that both were tokens, and it follows, therefore, that both were full-weight coins. But four pages later he writes (*op. cit.*, I, 160) that "copper money has never been used among the Greeks but as a small change money (*monnaie d'appoint*), the use of which spread but slowly amongst them. In consequence, they attached, so to speak, no importance to the size and weight of the pieces of this metal. . . . Nowhere after Alexander outside Egypt and Carthage, two countries different from those in the Greek world, did copper money contain a weight of metal equivalent to the value given it by law. It was a conventional currency no longer representative, the study of which teaches nothing of the commercial value of copper in relation to silver."

War, plated coins were issued among the good silver coins, and probably continued to circulate at a value above that of their metallic content. Under the Empire, plated issues were again made in the course of the feverish inflation of the 3rd century, but there is no reliable evidence as to the value at which they circulated.

It is not surprising that practically the only token coins in early times were small change money. Tokens tempt the counterfeiter, and the greater the difference between legal value and metallic value the greater the temptation. Counterfeiters have always existed, and when coins were often roughly made with simple equipment, the illicit coiner could compete with the mint on almost equal terms. Coins of high denomination, maintained much above their bullion value, would doubtless have called forth a supply of counterfeits, which would soon have brought down the value of the genuine pieces. Early Governments were well advised, therefore, not to attempt to manage their currencies so as to keep the value of any of the principal coins above their commodity value by restriction of supply. That they succeeded in maintaining the token status of their small change suggests that they realized that there must be some restriction of the supply of such pieces, and that desire for profit had to be repressed if a convenient system of small currency was to be supplied.

CHAPTER XIII

MONETARY POLICY IN THE EARLY ASIATIC EMPIRES, MACEDON AND EGYPT

1. *The Conditions affecting the Value of Money in Early Times and the Consequences of Changes in its Value.*

In the preceding chapters an attempt has been made to deal separately with the main problems of monetary administration in the ancient world. Who was allowed to issue money ? What metal or metals were used for money ? How pure was the currency metal ? What was the weight of the currency unit from time to time ? Did the value of money depend on the value of the material of which it was made, or did the state limit the amount of currency so as to give the coins a value above that of their metallic content ? Taking such answers as we have been able to give to these questions, we must now attempt to weave them together and obtain some general view of the aims of states in relation to currency, of their conception of their duty in this most important province of government. Contemporary pronouncements on monetary administration are almost entirely wanting. The Greek philosophers made passing references to money in their treatises on politics and ethics, to which the Romans added little or nothing. Apart from these, we are limited to the evidence of the coins themselves, and a few references by historians to important currency changes. In the main, we must rely for an understanding of early policy upon monetary changes. By reference partly to the probable consequences of such changes, and partly to other available material, some sketch of the reasons for reform can be attempted. But there is, of course, much room for error. Our estimate of the consequences of a reform may be altogether different from that made by those introducing the reform. The latter may have been more or less correct than we, but to give a true account of monetary policy we should require to know what was the contemporary reading of the facts, and the remedy at which the reformers aimed (whether they attained it or not). But we can only make the best of the material to hand, and out of the conclusions arrived at by this method attempt to see the currency policy of each state changing with changing times. So far as material will permit, differences in policy from place to place and time to time must be correlated with economic and political conditions.

The motive which first inspired monetary policy was a desire to simplify exchanges, to improve upon the ancient method of settling bargains by the transfer of metal which was tested and weighed on each transfer. But, in the course of time, coinage became more familiar, and the ends to which it might be controlled wider and more varied. The desire to facilitate exchange extended to embrace foreign as well as domestic exchanges. Policies were sometimes greatly influenced by attempts to remove hindrances to trade with a neighbour. With the emergence of large empires under single and political control, the monetary system was often influenced also by the desire to simplify public finances, and more especially the collection of taxes and tributes. Different but nevertheless closely related aims also developed. Currency was manipulated with a view to improving the market for precious metals, supplies of which were possessed by the state; to promoting the political aims of the state, and, most important of all, to promoting the economic ends of those controlling the government. The management of currency, with a view to economic gain, is somewhat complex in its working out, and it is worth while to make some theoretical analysis of the causes affecting the value of money and, in particular, of the kind of manipulation of these causes which will yield profit, before proceeding to discuss the policies of the various ancient states.

The value of money depends upon a number of causes, which operate either by influencing the demand for money or the supply of it. Our knowledge of the demand for money in ancient times is woefully inadequate. The amount of currency needed must have varied greatly. Populations did not, so far as we know, fluctuate widely in numbers, so the need for more currency from this quarter is unlikely. But where new empires extended their territory there was an increased demand for the money of the imperial power concerned. More than this, the early empires must often have absorbed peoples who had hitherto used little or no metallic money; as the vanquished became more accustomed to the use of coin, more was wanted. Increased demands for money must, therefore, have been potent causes of changes in prices in ancient times, unless changes in supply kept fairly well in step with the changing demand.

The conditions of supply were equally important with conditions of demand, and we know a little more about them. The principal decisions on matters of currency policy centre round the mechanism set up to control the quantity of money. If the control was kept in the hands of the state, we must seek the principles according to which control was exercised. If the Government adopted any principle other than that of selling as many coins as it could without incurring loss, the value of the metal contained in the coins would impose upon them a minimum value which would generally be exceeded. In the event of the currency being thus managed, attention must be concentrated upon the criteria according to which the supply of currency was fixed. If, however, the supply of money was determined only by the quantity of coins that could be struck and sold without loss, the value of money would be the same as if the state freely coined metal for private persons, charging them no more for the service than the cost of striking the coins. The value of the unit would then depend on the value of the metal contained in the coin, and no coin would long remain a token. Under a system so controlled the value of the unit can be altered by (1) a change in the value of the material chosen for the standard, caused by a change in either the supply of it or the demand for it for other than money; (2) a change in the weight of the standard; and (3) a change from one material to another, the new standard not being adjusted so that the unit weight of the new material is exactly equal in value to the unit of the old. A change in the weight of the standard may itself be made in two ways, either by altering the weight of the standard coin, or by altering the proportion of the monetary metal which it contained. When these latter changes were in the downward direction, the former constituted a devaluation and the latter debasement.

Changes in the weight of the standard were not necessarily

made for profit. They might be prompted by a concern for trade, and particularly foreign trade, and standards might be changed in order to establish easily manageable rates of exchange with communities with which an important commerce was carried on. But reductions in the weight of the standard usually produced profit whether such profit was the sole aim of the reduction or not. This profit came from one or both of two sources. Firstly, profits could be made out of recoinage. If old coins were recalled and exchanged by tale for new ones of less weight, to the extent that people submitted quietly to the change, the state gained a certain amount of metal. So long as this was not used to increase the number of coins, by having it coined and issued, the new light coins might pass at as high a value as the older, heavier ones did. The metal could be sold in the market, and the profits of recoinage thus realized. But this implies " management " of the currency and the maintenance of token coins. The more likely course is that the metal was coined and issued, thus adding to the quantity of coins in existence and reducing the value of each. Their value could continue to fall until it reached that of the (reduced) bullion content of the unit. Beyond that value it could not go, for holders would melt coins or sell them as metal as soon as it began to pay.[1] Furthermore, the purchasing power of the unit would fall but slowly as the additional coins flowed into circulation, not falling to the bullion value of the coin until all or nearly all the surplus metal had been coined. The first additional pieces would, therefore, fetch in goods nearly as much as the old heavy units, but as the issue continued the purchasing power of the pieces would steadily decline towards its lower limit. Even if no profit at all was to be made out of the recoinage of old pieces on a reduced standard, if new pieces were issued of less weight than the old, and people could be made, by any means, fair or foul, to accept them at a price above their cost to the mint, profit would accrue. Thus the first direction in which profit is sought in reductions of the standard is out

[1] If the population or the demand for money was increasing at the same time, the value of the coins must have been above their bullion value, even when all the metal extracted from them had been coined; but the issuer would be tempted to go on coining so long as the profit continued, buying fresh metal for the purpose. In the end the value of the coin must have tended to be that of the metal it contained.

of recoinage, and the slowness of prices to adjust themselves to new conditions. Secondly, in a quite primitive stage of civilization, the monetary unit was more than a basis for a medium of exchange and unit of value; it was also a unit in which debts could be recorded. If the coin which could legally be tendered in discharge of a debt expressed in the local standard was reduced, debtors paid and creditors received less than was expected. Where the state was a debtor on a large scale, this alteration of the standard was a great relief to an over-burdened treasury. Where the unit was changed without any intent to obtain relief in this way, proclamation could be made of the number of the new units that would discharge a debt of one old unit. But whatever the objects of the reduction, the consequences vary little, although other changes might on occasion mask their effect. In the absence of "management," a reduction in the unit would cause a rise in domestic prices, and a decline in the foreign exchange value of the currency. And in the absence of a regulation rating up old debts, debtors would profit at the expense of creditors.

2. *Motives affecting Monetary Policy.*

The first monetary policy arose, as we have seen, out of a desire to facilitate exchange, to improve upon the system of settling bargains by weighing out crude metal after its quality had been tested by the future recipient. The small punch marks upon the earliest, and probably privately issued, coins were guarantees that the metal was not below a standard quality, and that testing could be dispensed with. This policy brought with it the temptation to have affixed to inferior metal a mark which would generally be taken as a certificate of good quality, a temptation grounded in a profit motive in conflict with the primary one of simplifying exchange. The variability of the quality of the coins which probably belong to the era of free coinage suggests that the profit motive is traceable before state coining had appeared, or at least before coining was generally regarded as an industry which could best be administered by the state. The conflict of motives shaping the policy of the private issuer was partly responsible for the nationalization of coinage, but other factors were present. Where the state exploited mines of the precious metals, and made the produce up into small stamped ingots, the public seal became the most common, and, in time, the most popular. But where there were no local mines, or they were under private control, pieces bearing the public seal circulated side by side with others bearing private marks, and those were best favoured which were found most worthy of confidence and sufficient in quantity. Where all individuals were suspect, where ingots were not true in quality and quantity, refuge might be taken in the power of the state to arrange for an adequate supply of ingots bearing its stamp always to be available, and that, in the interests of all, they should be as true as possible. But where a private seal gained pre-eminence, the circumstances that conferred priority in finance made for political priority as well. The owners of such seals became local tyrants, and, as a first essay to maintain their position, made the marking of ingots a royal monopoly. Their action was dictated by their own economic or political interests, or both. Thus at the outset, in the period when national policies were in process of establishment, there was a conflict of motives. From the first issues made by democratic states or tyrants, the simple desire to supply a machinery to economize labour in the market was mingled with the desire for profit.

3. *Lydian Policy.*

We may now usefully turn to the public monetary systems of the ancient world. In Lydia, the birthplace of coining, the period of private coining by bankers and merchants was brought to an end by Gyges during the first half of the 7th century. He took over the monopoly of coining in the course of his open assumption of political power, which followed naturally from the wealth he had amassed in trade and commerce. There was a political motive behind the initiation of state coinage, and, as might be expected in such circumstances, the prerogative of coining was kept in the hands of the King: the lion and the bull that appear on early Lydian issues were possibly the marks on the royal signet. But once established, the state coinage shows little sign of a strong political motive in its control. Lydian policy falls into two periods: the first covering the hundred years from the time of Gyges to the accession of Crœsus, and the second the brief fourteen years before Crœsus was defeated by the Persians.

During the earlier period, all coins were made of electrum, doubtless because the mixture was found naturally in the country—a fact which probably dominated Lydian monetary policy. The desire to make Lydian coins a useful medium of domestic exchange was overshadowed by the necessity for securing their acceptance abroad. The coins were made up on two weight standards, that they might appeal to the peoples of the East as well as those of the West. Merchants from the East met those from the West in Sardes, and both units were doubtless used within the city. Nevertheless, the adoption of two weight standards stands out as a unique policy in early times. The careful series of divisions of the standard down to $\frac{1}{96}$ of the *stater*, a series that fitted easily into the units of weight used, particularly in Asia Minor, reinforces the suggestion that the disposal of electrum was important. The weight standards used for electrum were those used in Asia for silver. For a considerable period electrum was ten times as valuable as silver, and an easy decimal value relation was established between equal weights of the two metals. Tradition in the East favoured a decimal value relation between units of silver and gold, although each metal was divided duodecimally, and decimal relation between units of silver and electrum would be likely to find favour.

The attempt to profit by the control of currency reveals itself at this early period, however. It is very unlikely that any of the Lydian coins ever passed by tale. They were but oval blobs of metal, bearing a small hall-mark on one side and often no type on the other. In consequence, debasement was the only means of depreciating money. As the proportion of gold in ingots found varies from 5 to 95 per cent., it is not unfair to suggest that debasement was resorted to, by those in recognized authority, by the moneyers, or by counterfeiters, although it must have reduced the value of coining as a means of improving the market for electrum. The ease with which the money could be depreciated in this way probably caused electrum to be abandoned as a monetary metal, and brought to an end the first imperial currency of the world. The failure of this early experiment in symmetallism might easily have resulted in the abandonment of coining, which was saved, however, by the practice of private countermarking, and, most of all, by the abandonment of electrum for gold and silver.

The first monetary reform was made by Alyattes, the father of Crœsus, when he determined to issue gold as well as electrum, and a completely new system was established by Crœsus when he suspended the coinage of electrum and introduced silver coins. In the period of its duration the Crœsan system is unimportant. But in spirit it lived on, for it formed the basis of the later famous Persian system. Solicitude for the disposal of the metals was still evident as a dominant force in the new policy. The two weight standards were maintained, the coins of both gold and silver were of a metal of a very high degree of fineness, the subdivisions were again adequate and such as fitted easily into foreign systems. The extension of coining to silver is no matter for surprise: silver had been coined in Ægina and Corinth for at least 150 years. Moreover, if the gold coins of Asia Minor forced the Lydians to separate the metals in the natural electrum and make gold coins, it was reasonable to apply the same methods to the disposal of the remainder of the mixture.

Both gold and silver coins were, so far as we know, full-weight coins, but there is no evidence of any legal ratio between the values of the two metals, which were probably not current by tale. Nevertheless, it is quite possible that the Lydians introduced bimetallism. In their choice of units they seem to have regarded the gold pieces as the successors of the electrum units. Each of the latter was superseded by a piece three-quarters of its weight, and, therefore, of equal value. Apparently, the standard of value was translated from electrum into gold. The silver pieces being equal in weight to the old electrum were worth $\frac{1}{10}$ as much as their corresponding gold units. Thus the tradition of a decimal relation between the values of gold and silver units persisted, although the units of each metal were still divided duodecimally. The use of two metals for coining made it possible, on the one hand, to arrange a somewhat fuller series of subdivisions of the unit of value, and, on the other, to make the coins representing the smaller values of a more convenient size by making them of the less valuable metal. The decay of the electrum currency may have convinced the Lydians of the desirability of a metallic currency managed without any attempt at profit. It is true that the Crœsan system was shortlived, but while it survived there was no sign of debasement of the material of the coins, the quality of which remained consistently high. There can be little question that the coins still passed by weight, and that depreciation other than by tampering with the quality of the metal was yet impossible.

4. *Persian Policy.*

The second imperial currency, that of Persia, was built upon the foundations laid by the Lydians. The system set up by the latter was incidental to, if it had not given rise to, a monarchical form of political organization. As the Persians had already such a political Constitution, the Lydian system fitted easily into the Persian organization, which had never previously controlled a currency. The prerogative of coining was largely, but not entirely, monopolized by the Great King. The frontier of the monopoly is notable. The Great King claimed and upheld an absolute monopoly of the right to coin gold wherever Persian power was recognized. He claimed a monopoly of silver coinage where he himself held sway, but permitted his satraps to make silver money in the provinces. This idea that coining one material was more important than another recurs in later years, more particularly in Rome. It is possible that in Persia the monopoly might be due to the fact that tribute was paid in gold and, therefore, its control by the central power was particularly desirable; but, on the other hand, it was probably good practical psychology to associate the ruler, to the exclusion of all other persons, with the most valuable metal in the minds of the people. It may have been with this same end in view that the principal type on the gold *darics* was developed into a portrait of the Great King. As a somewhat crude figure of the King had probably appeared on the royal signet, the new tradition was easily developed out of the old. At the outset, therefore, the Persians recognized the psychological value of the coins for the promotion of political ends, a recognition which may have been potent in persuading them to adopt coining and to supersede the Crœsan coins. The obverse of this policy of securing docility in the ruled was the opportunity furnished to the ruler to satisfy his own pride, and, as we have seen, Darius has been credited with a desire to leave a permanent monument to himself in his gold coins. It is possible to explain the sustained high quality of the coins and the constancy in their weight as a part of this same policy, although it is probably not the whole explanation.

The desire to secure wide markets for supplies of the precious metals was probably less dominant than in Lydia. A suitable currency would introduce the use of coins throughout the whole empire, which alone would absorb a great quantity of the precious metals. Nevertheless, the policy pursued resulted in a wide market for gold. From the later 6th century for a period of 200 years throughout the finest period of Athens to the rise of Macedon and the appearance of the Macedonian *staters*, the *daric* became the gold coin of the Ægean as well as of the Persian dominions in Asia. The export of gold must, therefore, have been important, although it is impossible to distinguish cause and effect in the wide use of *darics* and the constancy of their purity and weight. The silver *shekels* did not circulate much outside the empire, but they were the first silver coins to have at all a wide circulation in Asia, and were current in areas where hitherto no coin had been used. Leaving the desire to secure markets for gold as an unknown factor, there is still the probability that the facilitation of the work of the royal treasury was a powerful influence in the building up of monetary policy. The Persian dominions were far more vast than those of Lydia had been. The problem of currency administration was far greater in its dimensions in Persia than in Lydia, which was little more than an entrepôt station. The principal departure from Lydian practice, the abandonment of coins of both silver and gold on two standards, was probably due to this difference in conditions. The great empire called for a simple currency, and the Persians furnished it by establishing a gold unit about equal to the supposed " ox unit," and a silver *shekel*, of which twenty were worth the *daric*. Even the series of subdivisions seems to have been shorter and simpler than in Lydia, although there may have been many subdivisions that have left no survivors. This new simple system, together with the very close control over the issues of gold, was well calculated to facilitate public financial transactions. It is said[1] that much of the Persian money was struck in the first place for the fighting services, gold being struck for the army and silver for the navy. This curious division is probably accounted for by the fact that the army operated in Asia where gold was generally current, while the fleet operated in the Mediterranean where silver was the common currency. Gold coin was principally used in Asia Minor for the remuneration of mercenaries and for the payment of tribute, although for this purpose it was probably more used in the West than in the East. In Persia and Mesopotamia[2] bars of the precious metals continued to circulate by weight as they had before the Persians had learned coining from the Lydians. Issues of coin must have been most plentiful, especially during the reigns of Darius and Xerxes, for Pythius, the wealthy Lydian, had amassed 3,993,000 *darics* at the time of the expedition of Xerxes,[3] and Alexander captured great hoards of *darics* as well as uncoined gold and silver at Ecbatana and Susa. In the latter city, the capital of the empire, he found in the royal treasury 40,000 *talents* of bullion and 9,000 *talents* of coined gold. The large proportion of the reserve in uncoined gold suggests that coining had not yet taken firm hold of the people.

Of the two series of units used in Lydia the Persians selected the series intended to circulate east of Sardes. The coins were based upon weight units already well known over the greater part of the empire—a circumstance calculated further to facilitate administration. As the gold unit approximated to that used for gold throughout the ancient world, foreign trade was probably somewhat facilitated. Like the Lydians, the Persians issued both gold and silver of full weight, but evidence that the system was legally bimetallic is wanting. Xenophon[4] says that *sigli* passed at twenty to the *daric*.[5] It is possible that the *siglos* (*shekel*) was accepted at the Persian Treasury at the value of one-twentieth of the *daric*, in which case its purchasing power would be prevented

[1] Lenormant, I, 137.
[2] Gardner, *op. cit.*, 258.
[3] Herodotus, VII, 28.
[4] *Anabasis*, I, 7, 18.
[5] *I.e.*, relation between values of gold and silver must have been 13⅓:1, which is a highly probable ratio.

from falling below that level. If any such arrangement existed, the silver *siglos* probably exercised a strong influence on local silver issues. But the most concrete evidence in favour of the suggestion that the Persians favoured bimetallism lies in the reduction which was made in the fineness of the silver coins in some of the provinces in the declining years of the empire. The silver value of gold having fallen below the ratio of $13\frac{1}{3}:1$, upon which the $20:1$ relation between the *daric* and the *siglos* was based, silver was undervalued in coins and had disappeared from circulation. Until then bimetallism must have been fairly easy to maintain, because the relative values of gold and silver had been stable. When the difficulties of the system were revealed in the 4th century, the reduction in the fineness of the silver coins may have been the contribution of some early Lord Liverpool to the solution of the difficulty. Apparently the Persians hoped to maintain a bimetallic system.

Of attempts to make profit out of the Persian currency there is no evidence. The *daric* was of a high degree of fineness which was never reduced. Silver was a little less pure than the contemporary Greek coins, but it was well maintained until the closing years of the empire. The debasement which then occurred can, as we have seen above, bear a charitable explanation. Opportunities for profit were probably greatly enlarged during the period of the Persian power. Coins which had hitherto passed by weight only must have begun to be taken by tale. Mint technique, methods of controlling the mint officers, and the public attitude to coins, had all been sufficiently developed for the type on the coin to be taken as a guarantee of weight as well as fineness. In consequence, profit was to be made by deception either as to fineness or weight. The Persians, however, maintained the weight of both gold and silver coin until the fall of the empire. When they established their currency system they adopted as gold unit a piece of about 130 grains or 3 per cent. more than the Lydian unit.[1] At about the same time the silver unit was similarly increased in Athens. Why either unit should have been increased is altogether unknown, unless

[1] The *daric* was a little less pure than the Crœsan unit (Gardner, *op. cit.*, 86). The value of the *daric* was probably not 3 per cent. more than that of the Crœsan unit. But the reduction in fineness probably did not counterbalance the increase in weight.

the forlorn hope was entertained that heavier issues would drive lighter ones out of circulation. Enhancements of units are as uncommon in ancient times as more recently, and no considerations of private profit[1] can be summoned to explain the situation. But one having made the change, the other might follow in order to keep a constant relation between the coins of the two metals.

5. *Macedonian Policy.*

The monetary policy of Macedon possesses an especial interest as obviously the product of a clash of European and Asiatic traditions. Early issues had been made in Macedon since the 6th century by kings and chiefs of tribes, who often advertised their prerogative by placing their names on the coins. Their principal coins were practically always of silver, although bronze was used from early times for subsidiary coins. The weight standards of these early coins were repeatedly reduced. The silver standard based on the "Phœnician" "heavy" unit of 220 grains, which had been in use before the Persian Wars, made way during the last half of the 5th and the first half of the 4th century for a unit of 168 to 173 grains (doubtfully described as the "Babylonian" silver unit), falling early in the 4th century to between 140 and 152 grains. The reason for the change is obscure: possibly a decline in the output of silver or an increase in the supply of gold gave rise to the alteration. If, as has been suggested, the original unit of 220 grains was adopted because the local ratio between the values of silver and gold was such[2] that it was worth exactly one-tenth of the local gold unit, the increase in the gold value of silver may have been followed by a reduction of the silver unit in order that it should remain one-tenth of the gold unit.[3] But if the response to a change in the relative values of the precious metals was to change the silver unit, we may conclude that either gold currency was in use and was regarded as the basis of the currency, or that the policy of the authorities was the maintenance of a gold exchange standard: in either event a unit of value fixed in gold

[1] A desire to benefit lenders at the expense of borrowers is unthinkable. Human psychology being what it is, there is always a stronger desire to attack the lender than the borrower.

[2] 17:1.

[3] At a ratio of 13:1.

was the basis of the system. But our knowledge of the facts is too meagre for any conclusion to be drawn with confidence.

Philip at first showed little interest in the privilege of making coins. When Philippi was established he granted to it the right to coin any metal. But early in the second half of the 4th century his attitude changed, and he commenced to suppress all local issues and those of autonomous allies. He took over local mints and assumed a monopoly of coining. If it is true that in Macedon the export of bullion was prohibited and a seigniorage was charged on coining which exceeded the cost of the operation,[1] it is clear that the preservation of the monopoly was largely an economic consideration. But although in this preservation of the royal prerogative his policy was in the Asiatic tradition, Philip was indebted for the types on the coins to the Greek world. The Greek religious type tempered the monarchical control of coinage.

The influence of the possession of supplies of the precious metals which was evident in Lydia, and partly masked by other influences in Persia, was again a vigorous influence in Macedon. The discovery of the gold mines at Philippi cannot be unconnected with the sudden change in policy which it preceded by a few years. Within a brief period of the commencement of the exploitation of the new mines, the Macedonian policy of silver monometallism was abandoned, and gold took a place as a currency metal: before long it was the principal currency metal. These supplies of gold may also have influenced the weight standards chosen for the gold and silver coins. Philip selected as the units upon which his new system was to rest a *stater* of 133 to 135 grains of gold and a *drachm* of 56 grains of silver. The motives behind this selection are difficult to disentangle. It has been argued[2] that the choice was dictated by purely political considerations. The units he adopted for both gold and silver had already been used by the cities of the Chalcidian League in the first half of the century. In his attempts to raise his barbarous people to the status of a great power, Philip had imported freely of the culture of Asia and of the Greek world, and more particularly of Athens. But he foresaw that Athens would be his most important obstacle in the future. As the Chalcidian League was the bitter commercial rival of Athens,

[1] Lenormant, II, 133. [2] West, *Num. Chron.*, 1923, 200.

particularly for the rapidly increasing and valuable trade of Macedon, he deliberately threw the weight of his favour on their side in the struggle, with the object of undermining the commercial strength of Athens and providing in Chalcidice the markets that would be a vital necessity when the conflict with Athens at last eventuated. By adopting the Chalcidian units he not only facilitated trade by making exchange a little easier, but he also gave visible proof that the interests of the League were his. As early as 356 B.C., by the surrender of Anthemos, he had sought to give expression to his good will. But it is doubtful whether a far-sighted foreign policy is the explanation, or at least the whole explanation, of the standards, although it is attractive because of its simplicity; it is independent of any change in the relative values of the precious metals.

Changes in the relative values of gold and silver, coupled with an interest in foreign trade, and the market for gold, may have been the decisive factors in the reform. The systems which naturally offered a basis for the new currency were those of Persia and Athens. The Persian system was possibly bimetallic, 20 silver *shekels* being worth a *daric*, which means that in coins gold was 13⅓ times as valuable as silver. But in Athens at the end of the 5th century gold had been only twelve times as valuable as silver, and the produce of the new mines at Philippi can only have further reduced its value. A bimetallic system based upon a ratio of 13⅓:1 could no longer survive. Silver did, in fact, disappear from circulation in parts of the Persian Empire. The Athenian system, on the other hand, based upon a ratio of 12:1 between the values of gold and silver, was almost certainly not bimetallic; coins of the two metals were struck upon the same weight unit, and market conditions set up a duodecimal value relation between gold and silver coin of the same weight. Had Philip copied the Athenian system and coined both gold and silver on the unit of 133 grains, a gold unit would have been worth ten silver units.[1] Such a decimal relation between coins of gold and silver would also have been in the Asiatic tradition. But in spite of this, and the fact that Philip was very ready to learn from Athens, he did not accept this system. Possibly its brief

[1] Assuming that gold was then only ten times as valuable as silver.

subsistence in Athens was against the system, or it rendered too obvious the decline in the silver value of gold. The system which he set up rested upon a gold coin which was worth twenty-four silver coins, assuming gold to have been ten times as valuable as silver.[1] Because the value relation between gold and silver coins was the same as it had been in Athens, the change in the value of gold may have been partly concealed. But the silver unit was reduced from 66 to 56¼ grains, and it might be expected that a departure from the weight of the Athenian "owl" would be very obvious. Whether or not such was the case depends whether people notice more changes in the weight of coins or changes in the number of one which is equivalent in value to the other.

It is clear that the motives behind the establishment of this currency are not simple. The difficulty of their identification springs from uncertainty as to the date of the establishment of the new system and the market ratio between the values of gold and silver then prevailing. Bountiful as were the Pangæan mines, some time must have elapsed after their opening in 356 B.C. before the value of gold declined to only ten times the value of silver.[2] Moreover, the gold unit was that used almost everywhere in Asia and Europe for measuring gold,[3] and probably it had for long been used in Macedon for measuring gold by weight and for some early coins,[4] if it did not originate there.[5] The silver unit could be easily fitted into the Persian system.[6] Perhaps a political

[1] $130 \times 10 = 24 \times 56{\cdot}25$.

[2] West, A. B. (*Num. Chron.*, 1923, 169), suggests that this ratio was not reached until 330 B.C. Gold was about ten times as valuable as silver in Athens in 331 B.C. (Gardner, *op. cit.*, 425).

[3] Although Philip's gold unit was approximately equal to the Babylonian gold *shekel*, he did not, in fact, follow the weight (130 grains) of the then universally famous *daric*. He inclined to the European form of the unit as it had been coined at Athens, and his gold *stater* weighed about 133 grains.

[4] It was the basis of the early autonomous gold coinage at Philippi (West, A. B., *Num. Chron.*, 1923, 185).

[5] Ridgeway quotes (125) a statement by Eustathius in evidence of the previous existence in Macedon of a gold *talent* equal to three "Eubœan" *staters*, and suggests that the gold unit was probably of native origin, adding that "unless it already existed, Philip would not have employed it for his gold coinage at a time when he was making changes in his silver, but would have assimilated his gold to his silver standard" (341). But the almost universal use of the unit for gold coins is quite sufficient explanation of its adoption by Philip.

[6] The unit of 56 grains was ⅔ of the Persian *siglos*, and would pass as a Persian *tetrobol*.

rapprochement with Chalcidice was an accessory factor, but it is very doubtful. The system of Philip was the outcome of a desire to establish a currency which would facilitate local trade because it was freely accepted, would encourage trade with Chalcidice and possibly the coast of Asia Minor, would not spoil, if it did not improve, the market for gold, and would further the political plans of Philip. The relative importance of these motives is very doubtful, but the order of their importance is probably the order in which they have been stated.

It is again uncertain whether Philip's coinage was truly bimetallic, whether the gold *stater* was legally rated at the value of twenty-four silver *drachms*.[1] But the subsequent instability of the currency in the face of the continued outflow of gold from the Pangæan mines suggests that a ratio probably was fixed. In this respect, therefore, the system followed what had probably been the Asiatic tradition and rejected the Athenian. The difficulties encountered by the Persians when the silver value of gold fell did not deter Philip, who probably anticipated that if the new market ratio between gold and silver was made also the currency ratio no further trouble need be expected.

The currency reforms of Alexander the Great soon after his accession reorientated Macedonian policy. In the control of coining little change is noticeable, for little is known of the control of the prerogative in his time. But his short reign was so eventful in the political and military spheres, that it is probable that he had no time to impress upon his money lasting signs of the success with which he had met elsewhere. Only in the closing years of his reign, or even later, did a representation of Alexander appear on Macedonian coins. Then the Greek tradition gave way to the Asiatic, and there appeared in Europe a series of coins bearing the effigies of rulers.

His abandonment of his father's silver unit in favour of one of about 65 grains was a much more important aspect of his reform. The new silver unit was already the basis of the gold coins. The currency system was now on the Athenian

[1] Some words of Head (*Hist. Num.*, 225) suggest that no legal ratio was fixed. West (*Num. Chron.*, 1923, 197) also suggests that no legal ratio was established.

pattern, with gold and silver coined on the same standard. As the market ratio between the values of gold and silver was about 10 : 1, twenty silver *drachms* were worth a gold *stater* of two *drachms*. The duodecimal value relation between coins of the two metals established by Philip was abandoned, and Alexander returned to a decimal relation such as had probably prevailed before the time of Philip. But, together with his adoption of the Greek principle of coining both metals upon the same weight standard, he probably accepted the Athenian practice of a parallel currency of both metals not linked together by any legal valuation of coins of one metal in those of the other.[1] The issue of coins on the same weight basis itself suggests more concern for their weight than their values, and that the latter were left to be determined by conditions of supply and demand.[2] But a more convincing reason for believing that the currency was not rigidly bimetallic is to be found in the fact that it continued to be issued by successors of Alexander, without any variation in the weight of the coins of either metal, for over a century after his death, although that century saw frequent and large variations in the relative values of gold and silver. Moreover, Alexander's coins continued to circulate, and were famous throughout the ancient world from India to Gaul until long after Perseus had been defeated by the Romans towards the middle of the 2nd century B.C. A rigid bimetallic system would not have survived changes in the relative values of the metals with such eminent success.

In these changes the influence of Athens is very clear. Immediately, the lines of reform might be traced to the influence of Aristotle, who had only shortly before returned to Athens after acting as tutor to Alexander for eleven years. Aristotle was probably a believer in " hard " money, and he may have acquainted Alexander with the monetary arrangements and traditions of Greece. But the ultimate reasons

[1] *Cp.* Lenormant, *op. cit.*, I, 180.

[2] " The significant fact . . . that Alexander did not seek to maintain his gold coin at an artificially high price by the adoption of a double standard, but issued both gold and silver according to one and the same weight (the Attic), is a proof that gold money was looked on by his financial advisers simply as bullion, and that no attempt whatever was made to fix definitely, as Philip had done, the number of silver *drachms* for which a *stater* should exchange " (Head, *Journal of Institute of Bankers*, I, 183).

for the reform are still to seek. So far as is known, the ratio between the market values of gold and silver did not become any less favourable to gold than it had been when Philip set up his system. But, nevertheless, the bimetallism of Philip was probably the source of the trouble. It is probable that Philip's system had never been stable during the whole period of its life of some twenty years. Silver probably tended to disappear from circulation. After the accession of Alexander the situation cannot have improved. The mines continued to yield a plentiful supply of gold. Alexander coined this supply, to which he added from his father's reserves and, later, the Persian reserves he captured in Susa and Ecbatana. Either there were unrecorded changes in the values of the metals, or the old ratio was maintained by the export of gold. In consequence, it became clear that bimetallism was no policy for a great empire in times of change such as Alexander knew. If bimetallism was to be abandoned, there was no need to maintain the silver unit introduced by Philip. If both metals were to circulate freely, the Athenian system was an obvious model, and the adoption of the "Eubœan" silver unit would assimilate the coinage of the empire to that of Athens and a great portion of the Greek world. Perhaps also there was some political advantage in adopting a unit with all the traditions of empire behind it.[1] It is possible that Alexander was influenced, too, by the currency habits of the Asiatic peoples, although his system was probably established before he had acquired any great Asiatic territory. By reducing the *drachm* from 86 to 65 grains, the gold two-*drachm* piece exchanged for twenty silver *drachms*, a value ratio with which the East had been long acquainted.[2] The motive behind the reform was the economic one of providing a stable and acceptable currency system. In the face of the sudden increase in

[1] West, A. B., *Num. Chron.*, 1923, 197.

[2] The European part of the empire had recently become accustomed to a value relation between gold and silver coins of 24:1, but apparently this part of the empire was less conservative than the East, or perhaps not yet firmly attached to this new system, or even more open to coercion. In any event, it could be persuaded to give up the arrangement to which it was accustomed and accept the 20:1 relation beloved in the East. Further, this part of the empire was required at the same time to suffer the second alteration within a period of twenty-five years in the weight of the silver coin. The *drachm* of silver which twenty-five years before had weighed 86 grains, and had been reduced by Philip to 56·25 grains, was now raised to 65 grains.

the supply of gold this meant the abandonment of bimetallism. The new unit selected was calculated to appeal to the West because it facilitated trade with the Ægean world, which was using the "Eubœan" unit, and to the East because it provided a gold and silver currency in which twenty silver coins were worth a gold unit as they had been since Crœsus set up the first currency of gold and silver.

Throughout this period of change there is no indication that in Macedon any attempt was made to profit out of the currency; no reduction in the fineness of gold or silver money was ever made. Token bronze money was issued, but was severely limited in quantity, and confined to small denominations. The size of the silver was altered, but there is no suggestion that the alterations sprang from any desire to manipulate the currency for profit. Under Alexander, the silver unit was raised—a change unlikely to yield a profit. The policy indicated by currency changes was closely bound up with gold; alterations in the relative values of gold and silver were always met by alterations in the silver unit. It may be, therefore, that from the earliest times the unit of value had been a gold unit, and the discovery of gold in the Pangæum served only to strengthen interest in gold. In any event, it is probable that from the time of Philip, the monetary policy of Macedon, like that of Lydia two centuries earlier, and of South Africa nearly 2,300 years later, was deeply influenced by its possession of supplies of gold. Its policy was simply the maintenance of an unchanging gold standard. Philip's brief success with his bimetallic experiment probably facilitated the introduction of a gold currency, and Alexander's system permitting the free circulation of both metals preserved the silver coins from destruction. The high standard of purity and accuracy in weight always preserved must also have made easy the way of Macedonian gold on foreign markets, where before long it superseded the *daric* and all earlier issues, and became an international coin like the *byzant* in the Middle Ages in Europe. The widespread popularity of the *stater* must have done much to reduce the fall in the value of gold, which never seems to have been worth less than ten times as much as silver.

It is quite impossible to consider the effect of this currency policy upon prices: we do not know whether gold or silver was more stable in purchasing power. It is probable that gold was falling in value, and that the policy of adhering to gold led to rising prices. Alexander, by coining and issuing all the yield of the mines, together with the hoard accumulated by his father, must have temporarily accelerated the rise in prices. But his gold *stater* became famous in other lands. Probably in this form, and because of the fall in its value, gold was much more used, the effect of increased supply being, therefore, somewhat mitigated by an increase in demand. As the gold was spread over an area of increasing size, the local inflation disappeared. In conclusion, it is necessary to keep in mind that the tenuous nature of the evidence as to the relative values of the monetary metals in Macedon is the greatest obstacle to the presentation of clear-cut conclusions as to its monetary policy.

6. *Egyptian Policy.*

The policy of the Egyptians was to avoid the use of coins as long as possible, and rely upon a highly organized commerce based upon payment in metals measured by weight. The Persians did not succeed in establishing any enduring or popular currency. The first coinage was established under the Ptolemies at the end of the 4th century, but subsequent policy is difficult to trace because of the difficulty in assigning dates and denominations to the coins. The Asiatic tradition is evident in the portraits of Emperors on the coins. The monetary material suggests both Asiatic and native influences. Gold and silver were coined, but copper, the metal which had for long been used in Egypt as both a medium of exchange and a unit of account, was important. The Ptolemies issued heavy copper coins, probably circulating at their full weight, from almost the beginning of their era, and from the end of the 3rd century there was a reversion to a copper unit of account. Gold was coined until the middle of the 2nd century, and silver until the Roman occupation. The first coins were issued on the Athenian standards, introduced by Alexander the Great into Macedon. Both coins were coined on the same weight basis, and probably without any legal value relation. But during the succeeding twenty or thirty years, the unit of 133 grains gave place to the " Chian " unit of about

120 grains for silver, and finally to the "Phœnician" unit of about 112 grains for both gold and silver. It is possible that the reduction was effected to secure simple relations with the native units, and particularly with native copper. But the successive reductions suggest devaluation for profit or laxity in the control of the mint. From 80 B.C. until the death of Cleopatra in 30 B.C., the profit motive is very evident in the debasement of the silver coinage that finally brought the whole system to the ground.

Under the Romans Egypt enjoyed a currency almost independent of that of Rome, neither *denarii* nor bronze being imported until the second half of the 3rd century A.D. Roman gold coins of earlier date are, however, found there. In A.D. 19 Tiberius revived the 4-*drachm* piece not struck since the death of Cleopatra, although it was now made of a mixture of silver and copper. This piece was officially tariffed in army pay sheets at 1 *denarius*, although the *denarius* was worth 28 or 29 *obols* against 24 to the *tetradrachm*.[1] These *tetradrachms* were treated in much the same way as the silver currency of the rest of the empire. In Egypt, as in the empire proper,[2] the profit motive dominated. The *tetradrachms* at first contained a fair proportion of silver, but were debased concurrently with the imperial *denarii*. Under Commodus they contained only 10 per cent. of silver, and by the time of Diocletian were only one-half their former weight, and only 2 per cent. of their content was silver. As in the empire, the new pieces drove large copper money out of circulation,[3] and prices rose to extraordinary heights,[4] until finally the currency was no longer acceptable to the government itself, and it demanded the payment of taxes in kind.

7. *Chinese Policy.*

When we turn to the Chinese attitude to coining in ancient times, we find ourselves in a very different environment from that of the Mediterranean. Coins emerged out of implements and utensils in early times, but issues were left to merchants and guilds. The ruling powers intervened to suppress issues in part of China in the later 4th century B.C., but only in the

[1] Head, *Hist. Num.*, 860. [2] *Vide* Chap. XVI.
[3] Head, 860. [4] Petrie, *Social Life in Ancient Egypt*, 155.

last two decades of the 3rd century B.C. was a state coinage issued by the central government. The types on the coins suggest that there was no desire on the part of the issuer to vaunt his own power or encourage any feeling of pride in those who handled the coin. The coins bear nothing more than a sober and businesslike inscription, stating often the name of the issuer or the place of issue, and sometimes the value of the coin. It is true that, in fact, the written word was sacred in ancient China, and perhaps the attitude of mind of the ordinary Chinese to the inscription on the coin was very similar to that of the ordinary Greek to the religious types on his coins. The precious metals were never coined in China in ancient times: until quite recent years all Chinese coins have been of bronze. The weights of the coins are extremely uncertain, largely because of the wide differences between the weights of different specimens owing to the inevitable inaccuracies of cast money. The most obvious reductions in the weight of the standard are to be seen in the shrinkage of the knife money to a mere round coin with a hole through the middle. Presumably the value of the money fell in proportion to its weight, but as the fall was gradual it was probably the result of a long sustained attempt to make small profits out of the coinage. In general, the Chinese coined and used money without enthusiasm. Their coin types and the absence of effort to improve the processes of coining mark this lack of interest. In fact, they never made money the axis about which their economic life revolved. On at least two occasions they abandoned the use of coins altogether for short periods, and endeavoured to return to early mediums of exchange. Down to the present time they have not succeeded in producing a currency which can be regarded by western standards as efficient. For this failure of coined money to strike deep roots in the economic life of China there are two main reasons. In the first place, false coinage has been a serious and constant difficulty for over 2,000 years, no doubt partly owing to the failure to adopt struck coin. Cast coins were so easily imitated that more than 100,000 forgers existed in 48-32 B.C., and a return to barter was considered. Such a return was later actually decreeed, but " it was only opening the door to counterfeiters, who, instead of casting bad metal, put moist grain in the bags, and wove thin and fleecy silk."[1] On another occasion, counterfeit coins were made legal tender.

In the second place, the Chinese attitude to the precious metals is entirely different from that of western peoples. The popularity of coining in the Eastern Mediterranean in early times was often due as much to the desire to find a market for fresh supplies of metals coming from the mines, as to efforts to facilitate the circulation of existing or very slowly increasing stocks of the metals within the community. In Lydia, in Macedonia, and in Athens coining provided a convenient way of making up the metals for export. But in China the attitude of the state to the exploitation of deposits of the metals was fundamentally different. So far as possible, the working of mines was altogether prohibited in normal times. Sometimes private individuals were able to obtain permission to carry on mining operations, but only on payment of very heavy taxes. "The government, in fear, they say, of enriching the wrong people, at the expense of morality and simplicity of life,[2] kept the mines as state property, to be resorted to only in cases of extreme need. The rudeness of mining processes, and the dearth of metal which ensued, caused the metallic currency to suffer."[3] This policy must have tended to increase the value of the metal in China above its value elsewhere where free exploitation of deposits was permitted, importation from abroad being unimportant. But the fact that the philosophers and politicians of the time discouraged any attempt on the part of the state to work the deposits on a large scale meant that the state, never being the vendor of large quantities of metal, was not driven, in early times, to adopt coining as a method of facilitating the marketing of the metals. The introduction of coining depended solely, therefore, on its advantages to trade. The stability of economic life in China, and the organization of trade and exchange on a basis of long-standing custom, probably made even these advantages less significant than in the expanding communities of the Eastern Mediterranean. The currency theorist would like to think that the

[1] Lacouperie, 221.

[2] This Chinese policy bears a strange and partial resemblance to that of Sparta in the beginning of the 6th century B.C. (*vide* p. 352).

[3] Lacouperie, *Catalogue of Chinese Coins*, p. 22.

early Chinese administrators saw that in a static community, if prices were to remain steady, the annual output of the monetary metals must be restricted to an amount just necessary to make good the wear and tear on the coin,[1] and that, convinced of the desirability of an unchanging general level of prices, they took measures to stabilize the value of the monetary metals in this way. It is not difficult to read such explanations into their policy, but there is no evidence of the intentions of the administration. Their policy of dwarfing economic incentives, and placing before all else the stability of society, fits easily into the conventional western conception of the Chinese attitude to life.

8. *Summary.*

The policy of the early empires is notable first and foremost for the complete absence of either debasement or devaluation. The aim of early imperial finance ministers might be to facilitate domestic trade by adopting units already known, to assist foreign trade or those in charge of the imperial finances, or to retain a market for the precious metals, but they never made any attempt to make profits out of currency manipulation.

[1] The above quotation suggests that supplies were not adequate even to cover wear and tear.

CHAPTER XIV

MONETARY POLICY IN THE GREEK WORLD

THE European tradition in monetary matters was cradled in Greece. In the main, it was independent of Asiatic policy, and in many important respects is contrasted with it. In order to discuss within a reasonable compass of words the policy of a number of cities over a period of 500 years, broad generalization is inevitable. This will best take the form of discussions of the more important respects in which Europe and Asia differed, and an attempt to discover the motives behind the action of the Greeks on each occasion. In order that policy may be seen as a whole, it will be necessary to divide the period. The most suitable division is a threefold one—the first period, to the later part of the 6th century, covering the awakening of the Greek peoples; the second, dominated by Athens, covering the 5th century and the first half of the 4th; and the third, the period of the decline, covering subsequent centuries to the loss of Greek independence.

1. *Policy to the End of the 6th Century B.C.*

The first of these periods is full of interest, because it is the time when the foundations of all subsequent monetary arrangements were laid. There was no period of private coining, coins being publicly issued from the first. As soon as we enquire where lay the prerogative of coining, we find the European and the Asiatic worlds following each a separate line. While in the latter monarchical government was the rule and kings controlled the currency, in the former the people were organized in small city-states, and preserved in their own hands the right to issue such money as they thought necessary. The political organization provided channels for the expression of opinion and the control of those entrusted with giving practical effect to the decision of the community. Meetings of all the citizens and Senates discussed what was necessary to be done, and magistrates or special commissioners did it under the supervision of the

Senate. But we may still ask what were the influences that, working through this machinery, produced the policy we are to discuss. In some cities, formally democratic in their constitution, authority was, in fact, in the hands of an oligarchy. The governing families exercised power over the currency as part of their political privilege, and occasionally left their mark upon the coins when they selected the types to be placed on them. The attempt to identify the types on certain supposed 7th-century issues in Athens with the armorial bearings of ruling families has been mentioned. But the types on the early Greek coins suggest that religious influence was more powerful than political. Religious feeling impressed itself upon control of currency in two ways. On the one hand, the temples had in early times been responsible for issuing money. Either they had, in common with other corporations and individuals, marked ingots as they paid them out, and because they paid out frequently and honestly their pieces became common in exchange, or they had been the only available authority to supply currency for use at the fairs which came into being in the vicinity of the temples. When the people came to control coining, the religious symbol had already secured its position on the coin. It is possible that the sacred symbol was sometimes deliberately selected, because in times of illiteracy, but of universal religious feeling, it spoke a language understanded of the multitude. But these purely economic explanations of the importance of religious factors must often have been mingled with political considerations. On the one hand, the presence of sacred symbols might induce greater respect for the coins, and suggest for them an origin less worldly than in fact they had; even this presumes an ultimately economic aim. Religion was, however, a great part of politics. It was intimately associated with the functions of government, and to place emblems of the local divinity upon the coins was as near to a use of the coins for advertisement as was possible when the whole of the people controlled policy and expected to be advertised in their civic capacity. Not all types reflect the political or the religious; some appear to carry a directly economic significance, where they portray what was probably a commodity of great economic importance in the district. Some of these may, however, be brought within the religious sphere, for they may have been sacred symbols, perhaps for the very reason that they were the basis of the economic life of the community. Others, perhaps, were placed upon the coins in a spirit of pride: where some would express their local patriotism in terms of the protecting divinity, others would select emblems reminiscent of local commerce.

The difficulties of inter-state trade, where each small area supplied its own coinage, would appear, at first thought, to be insurmountable. But, in fact, the stamp upon the coin guaranteed nothing more than its quality, and differences in the weight of the coins of different states can be counted as no great difficulty. Furthermore, many cities did not coin until very late in the period. Even then, throughout the whole period of Greek independence in most cities, coining was spasmodic and limited. Except in a few great commercial cities and places commanding deposits of silver, such as Athens, Corinth, Rhodes, Syracuse, and Tarentum, continuous issues were rare. In lesser cities they were unnecessary on account of the smallness of the community: coins were made only on the occasion of the great religious festivals or in time of war. The coins necessary on the occasion of a large festival were often in later times made at the expense of a private citizen, to whom suitable reference was made on the coins.[1] It is quite possible that earlier issues were provided in the same way, and that the bribe of acknowledgment upon the coins was not then necessary as a stimulant to the acknowledgment of civic duty. Issues in time of war were made by coining the stock of bars of metal kept in the temples of many cities against such an eventuality; the military events of Greek history account for the issue of a great part of the Greek coinage that has come down to us. But of the issues made by a great number of the less wealthy cities many are restricted to the smaller denominations. Those cities with foreign trade interests partially solved their difficulty of a confusion of currencies by making their own coins well-known, and a more than local medium of exchange. The coins of Ægina to the east, and Corinth to the west of continental Greece, were so used.

From the earliest times the Greek cities established a distinct policy in the choice of monetary metals. The first

[1] Head, *Hist. Num.*, LXVII, LXXII.

coins of Lydia and Asia Minor had been made of electrum, but in Ægina and Corinth, where coins appeared almost simultaneously with the Lydian pieces, a silver standard was selected. Although bronze and iron had been the original monetary metals, they were not the first to be coined. When gold coins were made early in the 6th century in Asia Minor, the Greek cities adhered to silver, and during this period neither gold nor electrum was ever coined in Greece. This preference for silver is not at all easy to explain. It might be said that Ægina and Corinth coined silver because there were few sources of supply of gold in Europe,[1] whereas silver was produced there. When these two cities had adopted silver, their commercial influence over a considerable area is sufficient to explain the spread of the use of the metal, and the development of a distinct tradition. But, after all, whatever were the supply of and demand for gold, they must have found expression in the local value placed upon gold. In fact, such records as we have of the relative values of the two metals do not suggest that gold was particularly valuable, or so valuable as to be inconvenient for coining. Moreover, gold bullion was used in foreign trade, and could, therefore, have been coined as easily as silver. In fact, few of the cities that coined silver in the early period possessed their own mines. They were compelled, whichever metal was used, to import supplies. Ægina certainly had no metal of its own to sell. It cannot be argued that gold was not coined, because merchants preferred to use gold bullion for the settlement of foreign trade transactions, and to fix in the market a rate of exchange at which it was to be taken.[2] They may have felt that trade was more sheltered from political crises if it was based upon a commodity which could be freely bought and sold, and was immune from the effects of changes of state policy. But, whether coined or not, gold could, and doubtless would, have circulated in foreign trade by weight alone, and currency policy would have had little effect upon its value.[3] There are two pos-

[1] Ridgeway (*op. cit.*, 260) suggests that shortage of supplies of gold, coupled with a large demand for ornament, is the explanation.

[2] Lenormant, *op. cit.*, I, 178.

[3] It is true that if many states had coined gold and used it as an internal circulating medium, the value of gold would have been raised a little when the change was first made.

sible explanations which must be advanced with hesitation. Possibly a preference for silver had grown up in Greece long before coining was introduced, and persisted after its arrival. More probably, there was a broad tendency to use gold for the settlement of large, and silver for small, transactions. The local civic currencies were many of them intended merely to facilitate day-to-day personal expenditure and small local transactions. For these silver was suitable: it was not so valuable that the pieces required for the settlement of these exchanges were inconveniently small. External trade and large bargains were settled in gold. The reason for the failure to coin gold to facilitate these settlements was probably that the gold was still tested for quality and measured by weight, and that to coin it would have been to incur unnecessary expense—unnecessary not only because the minting would not have served any useful purpose, but also because the wide circulation of such coins would have taken them frequently from city to city. Unless each city had been content to allow the coins of many of its rivals to circulate, it would have been involved in continual expense for recoining. The only states likely to be prepared to take up the business were those possessing supplies of gold for which a market had to be found. Lydia had metal of which to dispose and did, in fact, make gold coins during the 6th century. Early silver monometallic currency policy is probably due, therefore, on the one hand, to the number of small communities in Greece, and, on the other, to the fact that trade was still mainly based upon the exchange of metals by weight.

The dominant currency standard in this early period was that established in Ægina. Examination of the many explanations for the selection of a *stater* of about 194 grains by the people of Ægina leads to the conclusion that the only tenable theory is that the new unit in silver represented an old unit of value which had been expressed in bronze or iron. Æginetan policy in this respect was to facilitate commerce and disturb economic relations as little as possible by adopting the more convenient medium of exchange without changing the unit of value. The subdivisions of the unit into *obols*, and later into *chalci*, reveal also the influence of the earlier series of units. But the Corinthians who began to coin only a little (if at all) later than the people of Ægina selected a different unit, one that seems to have entered Greece by way of the Isle of Eubœa. The reasons for the adoption of this unit are even more remote than those for the " Æginetan." Apparently, a weight unit used for gold was now applied to silver. It is clear that the Greeks were not much concerned with the values of silver coins in gold coins of the same weight. They had no gold coins of their own to call for attention, and, apparently as a result of the circulation of gold by weight, and in the interests of simplicity of weighing, one weight unit was used for both metals. In Corinth, however, Asiatic influences are recognizable in the division of the *stater* into three instead of two *drachms*, as in Europe. The new unit proved very successful. Solon made it the basis of the Athenian currency he established at the end of the 7th century, and thenceforward it gained ground at the expense of the "Æginetan" unit. But the coins which have been found do not all fit into a simple system, and a description of the standards of the ancient world in terms of one unit superseded by another contain much that is misleading. Although it is, on the whole, unlikely that Professor Ridgeway is correct in thinking that the types on coins were meant to indicate the value unit they superseded, it is still possible that the departures of local units from the supposed dominant units were in some cities more important than the extent of their approach to foreign units. Many cities may have aimed at the preservation of their ancient unit, as the Æginetans probably did. With this their first concern, difficulties in exchanging local for foreign coins were left to be solved by the money-changer. In subsequent periods, however, these native influences tended to be submerged in a general move towards uniformity.

2. *Policy during the 5th and Early 4th Centuries B.C.*

During our second period the control of policy remained in most cities directly or indirectly with the people. The appearance of the coin suggests a consolidation of religious feeling. But there are other possible explanations for the unmistakable religious motive on the coin types. Until the latter part of the 6th century the engravers had not been ready to attempt the portrayal of human heads. When they were, they found a superstition, political or religious, against such portraiture, and they satisfied their own desires without disturbing public feeling by placing idealized human heads upon the coins and calling them the heads of the gods. This slight and reasonable change from the sacred symbols of the previous period was probably introduced by Peisistratus at Athens in a somewhat delicate political situation, and the subsequent rise of Athens to power gave the new type a great vogue throughout the period. Cities still boasted their civic glory, but their artists pressed a new language upon them.

The disadvantages of a confusion of issues during this period might have been even greater than in preceding years, because coins were beginning to circulate by tale. To the possibility of a confusion of qualities was added that of a confusion of weights. The problem was mainly solved by the vigour of Athens. The Athenian coins bearing the head of Athena and the sacred owl were good to look upon; they were also of a high and unvarying quality, and, most important of all, definite steps were taken to secure uniformity of weight among the coins. Until this time mint regulations probably prescribed the number of coins to be struck from a unit weight of metal (as in England in early times), but the Athenians aimed definitely at fixing the weight of each coin and succeeded to the extent that specimens which have survived suggest that the weight of coins never departed more than 1 per cent. from the average. Having taken all possible economic steps to secure the acceptance of their money, the Athenians brought political pressure to bear upon all the allies in the Delian Confederacy to suppress their issues and forced them to use those of Athens. No doubt the desire to simplify, and, therefore, to encourage, foreign trade was a force in the adoption of this policy, but there were other motives. Athens was working the silver mines at Laurium with great energy; they were the backbone of her finances, and, consequently, she was interested in securing a wide market for the metal which was her staple export. Important, but of less moment, was the necessity for simplifying interstate financial relations arising not out of trade but out of the political supremacy of Athens. The collection of tribute was important enough to influence policy, and there was, in fact, a practice in the later years of the 5th century of encouraging the payment of tribute in Athenian coin. While in 434 B.C. the treasurer's lists at Athens mention separately the silver coins of other cities,[1] after 418 B.C. foreign silver money was quoted merely by its weight in *talents* and fractions,[2] indicating that " owls " were accepted by tale and all other coins by weight. A currency universally acceptable in the Ægean must also have simplified the task of paying the navy. The campaign against Persia, which was the original cause of the Delian federation, prompted Athens to back silver just as Persia had backed gold, and in the same manner. The Persians had as far as possible insisted upon the general acceptance of *darics*. Athens took the same point of view in relation to her own " owls." The mixture of motives of facilitating the disposal of metal, simplifying the public financial arrangements and making political use of the psychological effect of the coins used, is almost exactly similar to that behind the policy followed by Persia at the same time. Rivals were prepared to learn from each other, and in similar circumstances Asiatic and European traditions approach each other very closely.

But policy in the matter of the monetary metal the Greek world still kept apart, and until the closing years of the century silver was practically the only monetary metal in Greece. The silver tradition had doubtless gained the respect due to its age. It is possible also that to commence to coin gold would have been to follow too obviously where the then hated Persians had led. On the other hand, where gold coins were convenient in commerce, there were always adequate supplies of Persian *darics* for use. But the dominant power was that of Athens, and the Athenians adhered strictly to silver monometallism until the end of the century. Their choice of metal and vigorous support of it must have been largely due to their possession of supplies of silver. By the time they secured control of the Pangæan gold towards the middle of the century, the silver policy was so deeply entrenched and so successful that little was to be said in favour of disturbing it. Their rise to power during the century, and their vigorous campaign to extend the use of their coins, only more firmly consolidated the silver monometallic policy.

[1] *E.g.*, the coins of Bœotia, Chalcis, and Phocis.

[2] Gardner, *op. cit.*, 227.

This same campaign and the commercial prestige of Athens resulted in the triumph of the " Eubœan " weight unit, which had been adopted by the Athenians in 600 B.C. With the growth in the number of cities using the " Eubœan " unit for lack of opportunity to select any other, the adoption of the unit held increasing promise for those on whom no pressure could be exerted. The Athenian coins passed by tale over a considerable area, and if local coins were made upon the same basis commerce with that area was simplified.

During the 5th century a fresh era was opened in currency management for which Athens was mainly responsible. The Athenian reforms reveal an originality of mind not surprising in view of the Athenian contributions to art and philosophy during the century. The silver " owls " were of uniform fineness, but also of a greater uniformity of weight than any earlier coins. Uniformity extended also, until early in the 4th century, to the type, which remained unaltered, although great artistic developments had occurred in the 5th century. In consequence, the type on the coins was for the time regarded as a guarantee of weight and the coins were taken by tale. The mint organization was carefully designed to secure the maintenance of the coin. Its economic qualities, together with its enforced currency over the widest possible area, not only made the currency famous, but gave Athenian policy during her period of power an enormous influence over subsequent currencies in the ancient world. The Athenian standard for gold and silver became the prevailing standard. The Athenian gold coins set a fashion for coining gold, while the rejection of bimetallism was followed elsewhere. Representation of divinities upon coins was also imitated. But the rise of Macedon in the 3rd century blew a breath from Asia into Europe and divine types gave way before the new monarchical institutions and the new conception of kingship: silver monometallism was submerged by the flood of gold from Philippi.

3. *Policy from the Middle of the 4th Century B.C.*

In the third period the exercise of the prerogative was still in the hands of the people. Although during the period speculations were made as to the nature of money and the factors influencing its value,[1] they do not appear to have influenced decisions on practical policy.[2] The types remained essentially religious, but there was a feeling after more precise expression of civic patriotism, and some cities portrayed temples, statues, and buildings of which they were proud, made references to contemporary events, or portrayed heroes of the past whose memories they wished to keep fresh. The collapse of Athenian political supremacy meant the collapse of its monetary domination as well. In a reaction from the detested tyranny, cities hastened to reassert their currency privileges, and the Ægean was threatened afresh with a confusion of units. There was now no question of a surrender in the interests of interstate relations, but cities were forced to come to some agreement as to the exercise of their prerogative. Driven together either by military necessity or by the needs of foreign trade, they formed monetary unions to give the necessary uniform coinage and often, incidentally, to reduce the cost of supplying currency by carrying on the business on a larger scale in a centralized mint. The closing years of the 5th century and the 4th century B.C. saw the first breaches in the silver monometallic policy. The introduction of gold as a coinage metal in Athens after the loss of the expedition to Syracuse was plainly a device to relieve the financial pressure under which the city struggled, the severity of which is indicated by their sale of all the temple ornaments.[3] The bullion in the temple treasury and the golden statues in the Parthenon were the national reserve, and they were coined when events called for the use of the reserve. The Athenians had here one advantage over more modern peoples. Their gold reserve was in a sense always in use; any citizen could

[1] See Appendix I.

[2] Possibly Aristotle's preference for "hard money" reinforced general feeling in Athens against the introduction of small change tokens.

[3] Thucydides (II, 13, 3-5; 65, 13) records Pericles as saying previously, at the outbreak of the Peloponnesian War, in 431, that "an average revenue of 600 *talents* of silver was drawn from the revenue of the allies, and there were still 6,000 *talents* of coined silver in the Acropolis. This did not include the uncoined gold and silver in the public and private offerings, the sacred vessels for the processions and games, the Median spoils and similar resources to the amount of 500 *talents*. To this Pericles added the resources of the other temples. . . . Nay, if they were driven to it they might take even the gold ornaments of Athena herself; for the statue held 40 *talents* of pure gold, and it was all removable. This might be used for self-preservation, and must all be restored."

go to the Parthenon and admire the winged statues of victory. But it is not open to any citizen of England, France, Germany, America, or any other modern state, to call at the national bank and see the reserve, and if he could, he would not find it in a form likely to appeal to his æsthetic sense.

For some considerable time issues of gold coins were regarded elsewhere in Greece (and also in Magna Græcia) in the same way as mere devices to be used in time of emergency.[1] But later in the 4th century gold coins were issued by many cities in a spirit of boastfulness, in consequence, probably, of the second issue of gold in Athens which set a fashion. Such issues were presumably examples of conspicuous waste designed by the people or their King to display the civic wealth. They were brought to an end by the bounteous issues of Macedon at the end of the century. But so far as they were made in time of financial stress they constituted the first steps in the evolution of a war-time financial policy —albeit a most righteous step in comparison with subsequent developments. In time of poverty the King or the state, like an individual temporarily pressed for money, sold off less necessary ornaments, and, in order to find as good a market as possible, made them up into lots of convenient and guaranteed weight. It is, in fact, doubtful whether the earliest gold coins served to any very great extent as coins. Those issued in Athens probably did not, owing to their high value. In so far as they did circulate, they would tend, as an addition to the supply of money, to cause a rise in the general level of prices; but if the gold was exportable, and in demand abroad, it would tend to flow out of the country and obviate a rise in prices. The issue of paper, had they thought of it, would have cost them nothing, and would probably not have been exported: it would have remained in the country

[1] " It is a mistake to suppose that the occasional issue of gold coins by Greek cities is indicative of peaceful and prosperous times. The contrary is the case. All the evidence goes to suggest that in Greece proper and the West, silver was long regarded as sufficient for all ordinary commercial purposes in quiet times, and, moreover, that even silver money was chiefly in demand, or that, at any rate, the larger denominations were mostly used on occasions such as the frequently occurring agonistic festivals. Gold money, on the other hand, was only struck exceptionally, and in order to meet the extraordinary cost of maintaining or contributing to the support of an army or fleet in war-time. The sporadic issue of gold coins at Athens may be cited in support of this opinion " (Head, *Hist. Num.*, 60).

and have kept up prices. It is curious that in subsequent times the attitude of silver-using countries to the use of gold has been almost exactly similar to that of Athens. In Rome the first issue of gold was made under pressure of the first Punic War, and was discontinued as soon as the crisis had passed. Ruding, writing[1] of the year A.D. 1257 in England, says that it "is remarkable for the first issue of gold in the kingdom of which any authentic records can be found, and it is extraordinary that it took place in the height of his (Henry III's) distress for want of money."

The 4th century B.C. saw also the invasion of the province of monetary metals by bronze. Silver coins for small denominations were superseded during the century by bronze of a more convenient size. The tradition of silver, and nothing but silver, must have been unusually strong in Athens, for no proper bronze small change was issued until towards the end of the 4th century, and then possibly under Macedonian authority. In all these changes silver remained quite definitely the monetary metal. Gold was always a subsidiary, and there was no attempt to establish a gold and silver bimetallism. By the time gold coins were issued the conditions that had favoured the early bimetallic systems were passing. The silver value of gold was falling, and it may have been that even if they had been prepared to abandon silver so far as to permit the entry of gold as a partner, the proposal lacked support because, on the one hand, bimetallism was an Asiatic notion, and, on the other, it did not appear to be capable of enduring in times of change.

The city of Lacedæmon is a striking exception to almost all that has yet been said about Greek monetary policy. The whole institution of coinage was rejected as well as the use of gold, silver, and even copper by weight. Until the last decade or two of the 4th century B.C., the sole currency consisted of iron bars of nearly one and three-quarter pounds weight. Because the currency was so "heavy and hard to carry,"[2] quite small payments required a pair of oxen and a wagon for their transport.[3] It is doubtless more than a coincidence that Sparta was backward in trade and industry.[4] The ultimate

[1] *Annals of the Coinage*, I, 186.
[2] Plutarch, *Lysander*, 17.
[3] Plutarch, *Lycurgus*, 9.
[4] Ure, *Origin of Tyranny*, 24.

reason for this curious policy[1] lies in the Spartan solution of the over-population problem in the 7th century. Other cities fought the matter out, often under tyrants, and, finally, the less successful party emigrated to some portion of the shores of the Mediterranean, often to Magna Græcia, the whole process resembling nothing so much as the swarming of bees. For the home city this meant frequently the development of a colonial trade which, in its turn, widened the intellectual horizon of those who were left behind. But the Spartans solved the difficulty by conquering and enslaving the neighbouring city of Messenia. Because they had not cast their surplus citizens upon the waters, they gained no commerce, no glimpse of the liberal spirit that was elsewhere overwhelming the old conservatism. A conservative land-owning aristocracy, secure in its wealth, the fruit of the labour of great numbers of slaves, scorned the advantages offered by coinage and commerce. The whole structure of Spartan society was for a brief period threatened at the end of the 7th century by the Messenian revolt,[2] the product of the antagonism between serf and lord, and in consequence the reforms of that somewhat shadowy personage, Lycurgus, were made in about 600 B.C. Having made small democratic concessions, the Spartans established a rigid Constitution to prevent the demand for more. The lives of all citizens were severely regimented, and land was made inalienable. But there was a 7th-century proverb that "money maketh man,"[3] and to prevent the accumulation of wealth in concentrated form, and, therefore, the concentration of power, and to banish covetousness from Sparta,[4] the precious metals and copper,

[1] Ridgeway suggests (57) that in the 8th and 9th centuries iron must have been too valuable to be used as money, although it can never have been so valuable as gold or silver, which were widely used. He suggests (*op. cit.*, 372) that the reason for the later use of iron was "the dearth of precious metals rather than . . . any ordinance of Lycurgus against the employment of the latter." But there is no apparent reason why, in the absence of restrictions, the precious metals should not have been imported until their value in Sparta was much the same as elsewhere. Nevertheless, it is true that the Spartans did not possess mines of the more usual monetary metals, and they had in the mountains of the Malæan Cape and Tærnarium Promontory the chief iron mines in Greece.

[2] *Camb. Anc. Hist.*, III, 539.

[3] *Ibid.*, III, 561.

[4] Plutarch explains (*Lives*, trans. Dryden, I, 115), "Who would rob or cheat another of such a sort of coin? Who would receive as a bribe a thing which a man could not conceal, and the possession of which no man envied him?"

and, almost consequentially, coinage, were banned by law. Change was in this highly socialized community to be resisted with all the power of political organization. " Secure in their immense landed wealth they (the Spartans) kept themselves untouched by commerce, and denied the new coinage any entrance to their state."[1] Never more deliberately did a state refuse the benefits of advances in knowledge.[2] Sparta set the policy for the Peloponnese.

The eclipse of Athens at the end of the 5th century, and the consequent crop of local issues, created afresh the problem of the monetary standard. On its foundation in 408 B.C. the city of Rhodes became almost immediately the centre of Greek commerce in the Mediterranean. It adopted a unit some 8 per cent. lighter than the " Eubœan,"[3] and this became the basis of most civic issues.

4. *Alterations of the Monetary Unit and the Policy Impelling them.*

In the foregoing discussion of Greek policy during each of the three periods somewhat vaguely defined, the reasons for the units of value adopted have been but briefly touched upon. The reason for this was that policy in this matter is not marked off into periods. Much the same variety of motives was behind all policies throughout the period, and can be more conveniently discussed as a whole in this respect. The unit of value depends upon the material and the weight of the standard coin, if it circulates for about the value of its metallic content. So far as possible, and it must be admitted that it is not very far, the objects that impelled those who set up the first currencies in each city have been discussed. But once monetary units had been established, a change in the unit of value implies some fresh influence. Either external circumstances threaten to frustrate the attainment of a preconceived aim, or a fresh aim has suggested itself. A discussion of these changes of unit should, therefore,

[1] *Camb. Anc. Hist.*, 542.

[2] A striking parallel to this policy is to be found in China in the last millennium B.C., when, apparently with the same object as in Sparta, the government prevented the working of the deposits of the precious metals except in times of emergency (*vide supra*, 337).

[3] *I.e.*, the " Chian " or " Phocæan " unit.

illuminate the whole statement of the policy of early currency manipulations.

Dismissing the unlikely possibility that the principal coins were tokens, the standard might be altered by alterations of the fineness, or the weight of the coins, or of both. Where the new standard was already in use elsewhere—as, for instance, where one of the units such as the " Eubœan " or the " Æginetan " was adopted—it has usually been assumed that the motive determining these policies was the encouragement of international trade by simplifying foreign exchange and, possibly, by securing that the local coins should be acceptable in foreign cities: there is no doubt that such aims were important, although they can only have become effective after coins had begun to pass by tale. The policy of Athens in adopting the " Eubœan " unit is typical of the influences operating to induce the adoption of foreign units. Until the end of the 7th century, Athens had used the " Æginetan " unit for silver. But since the first issue of coins there, Corinth had used the " Eubœan " standard. To the east Eubœa used the same unit for weighing metals, although no coins were made. The most important foreign trade of Athens lay with the cities of Eubœa and their numerous and flourishing colonies. In consequence of this trade, the units of weight used by the Eubœans were known, and must gradually have come into use in the Athenian market. Solon, himself a merchant, knew of the concurrent use of two standards, and may have thrown his influence on the side of the " Eubœan " unit as the one most likely to facilitate foreign trade, by assimilating the local currency to that of the Eubœan cities and also to that of Corinth, and, in consequence, with a great part of Magna Græcia. In selecting this unit as the basis for his coins, he did no more than place the seal of public approbation upon the unit selected by the commercial community. But there was probably some political influence at work too. Athens had moved in the orbit of Æginetan trade, and a growing desire to remove all sign of economic inferiority rendered the use of the " Æginetan " unit increasingly distasteful. Solon selected a new unit and Athens issued coins of her own. In his desire for complete independence Solon, although he used a unit similar to that of Corinth, did not, as perhaps Corinth had found advisable in the 7th century when Ægina was still powerful, so divide the *stater* that simple relations were established with the "Æginetan" unit. He cut cleanly off and hoped to supersede, and not to share prosperity with, Ægina. And in course of time the separate coinage and standard of Athens played no mean part in the capture of Æginetan trade. But in some places political pressure was exerted by another city to induce the acceptance of their monetary standard, and its adoption presumably indicates a recognition that it was inadvisable to oppose the foreign pressure. Occasionally agreement between standards denotes neither economic nor political association. When units were falling in different cities, sometimes they reached a common level without any prior agreement. Where units were borrowed, they might be either greater or less than the pre-existing unit: such alterations must have disturbed relations between debtors and creditors where debts were expressed in the silver unit. Although there is no evidence of arrangements for translating old debts into new units at a rate based upon the respective silver content of the coins in order to prevent any disturbance of this kind, such arrangements must sometimes have been made, more especially where the state was a debtor in silver units and the unit was raised. Probably in all places where coin was not taken by weight large alterations in the unit were accompanied by conversion arrangements, while small alterations may have been made gradually and without such provision.

A review of the changes of standard in the Greek world reveals, however, that they were nearly always in a downward direction. But it must not be inferred that profit-making was the reason for the alteration. Lack of proper understanding of the technique of coining, and maintaining a coinage, explains some of the slow but persistent shrinkage that is noticeable. Where, for reasons of economy, old and worn coins were used as blanks and struck again, the standard would decline. The same cause operated slightly differently where the public authority was not prepared to withdraw worn coins from circulation at their face value, and recoin them at their original weight. If it wished to avoid in the process of minting any reduction in the number of coins, the standard of the new issue could be no higher than the actual average weight of the coins withdrawn. In times when coins were not made very uniform in weight and passed by tale, the heavier pieces would tend to be melted or exported, thus reducing the average weight of the new coins at recoinage.[1] In all these ways the standard might fall, not from any intent to profit, but from a desire to avoid loss. The community did not bear directly the cost of maintaining the currency, perhaps from ignorance of the means by which it could be done. In consequence that cost was borne by all those who suffered slight loss owing to the tendency for prices to rise as the unit of value shrank. But the reduction from this cause was small, and must have been easily absorbed into the other influences operating upon prices. Somewhat different from these causes of decline was that due to the adoption of the smaller denominations of foreign units. When, at a later date, cities made larger denominations of proportionate weight, they might be lighter than the corresponding higher denominations in the city from which the unit was borrowed, merely because that city pursued a practice not then uncommon of making small denominations slightly less heavy than the proportion of the large unit which they were intended to represent.

There was, however, one series of alterations of the currency standard in an upward direction. About the middle of the 6th century the *staters* of Corinth and Athens were both raised some 4 per cent. above the standard of 128 grains, until then used in both cities. Not only do early Corinthian and Attic coins substantiate this raising of the unit, but the evidence of Androtion, quoted by Plutarch[2] that the *mina* before Solon's reform was equal to 73 *drachms*, gives a weight for the *drachm* of 130 grains.[3] A number of reasons have been

[1] Hill (*Handbook of Greek and Roman Coins*, p. 31) suggests that when a foreign unit was adopted, it may have been reduced to cover the cost of minting; when it was again borrowed, a further similar deduction was made. It is not clear, however, why it should have been expected that reduced coins would pass for a value equal to that of the *stater*, from which they were derived, if they contained less metal. Deduction for coinage could easily be made by fixing the purchase price of silver at the mint a little below that represented by the coinage, rather than by borrowing the foreign coinage value and using it as the purchase price for metal at the mint.

[2] *Solon*, 15.

[3] *Vide infra*, p. 359, for the discussion of the Solonian reform and its effects. The *mina* was based on the "Æginetan" *drachm* and weighed 9,400 grains $\left(\frac{9{,}400}{73}=130 \text{ grains}\right)$. Aristotle (*Constitution of Athens*, X)

suggested for the raising of the unit, which was probably the work of Peisistratus. The heavier unit was used at Cyrene, to the west of Alexandria, for coins from about the end of the 7th century, but it is difficult to maintain that the unit was borrowed from Cyrene, because it is doubtful whether the earliest coins issued there are any older than the earliest "owls" of Athens which were struck upon the raised unit;[1] moreover, it is not easy to explain why Peisistratus should have borrowed a unit from Cyrene.[2] It is possible that the unit was raised as a result of trade with Egypt. Cyrene, Corinth, and Athens all traded with the Nile delta, especially with Naucratis, during the 6th century B.C., and they may all have adapted their own units in order to facilitate the Egyptian trade. The people of Cyrene were certainly likely to have assimilated their money to that of Naucratis as they wished to do most of their trading there. The traders of Corinth were also interested in the Egyptian trade, as is evidenced by the plentiful remains of Corinthian ware found in the delta.[3] Possibly, desire for trade with Egypt, and rivalry with Corinth, induced Peisistratus to adopt the increased unit. The discovery of many early Athenian coins in the delta at Naucratis, and elsewhere,[4] and of Athenian vases at Naucratis, suggests that Athens was interested in the trade.[5]

The *kedet* varied in different parts of Egypt. The specimens found at Naucratis suggest a weight of 136 to 153 grains,[6] but at Heliopolis it is believed to have weighed only 139

---

said that the *mina* contained about 70 *drachms:* a *drachm* would then have been 134 grains $\left(\frac{9{,}400}{70}\right)$. But on the one hand, Aristotle's round figure suggests approximation, and, on the other, he probably based his calculation on the *staters* of his own day, which, however, were admittedly not introduced until about fifty years after Solon's reform.

[1] The electrum and silver of Samos of early 6th or even 7th century B.C. has also been claimed as evidence of the origin of the unit adopted in Athens. It is, however, heavier than the Athenian unit, and is probably based on the Egyptian *kedet* (Hill, *Camb. Anc. Hist.*, IV, 134), which spread to Samos as well as to Cyrene, Athens, and Corinth.

[2] Cyrene traded with both Greece and Egypt in wool and silphium.

[3] Prinz, *Funde aus Naukratis*, 1908, 73 *sqq.* (*cit.* Seltman, *op. cit.*, 18).

[4] Gardner, *op. cit.*, 157.

[5] It is possible that Peisistratus obtained the unit immediately from Thasos, where he mined silver, and where the *stater* weighed about 140 grains. But that unit may well have been derived from Egypt (Gardner, *op. cit.*, 157).

[6] Petrie, *Naukratis*, 77 *sqq.* Weights supposed to be of Attic *drachm* standard, but uninscribed, vary from 127-148 grains.

grains and, as Heliopolis was one of the cities most accessible to Greece, it might be expected that if any Egyptian unit affected the Greek it would be that of Heliopolis. But, while the unit of Cyrene offers close agreement, that of Greece never rose above 135 grains. There seems to be little advantage in an approach to the foreign unit. Trade might be facilitated if the units could be induced to agree with each other, but no advantage would follow if they nearly agreed.

The reforms of Peisistratus, the adoption of the "owl" type, and the raising of the standard, marked the beginning of Athenian supremacy and of the domination of the Ægean trade by the Athenian *tetradrachms*. It has been argued[1] that the magnificent ideas and the anxiety of Peisistratus to make his city, his temple, his coins, the best in the world were responsible for the rise in the weight of the coins above the normal "Eubœan" unit. Sheer pride may account for his desire to make his coins thus famous, although it is doubtful whether merely by raising their weight 4 per cent. they could be elevated to fame. But if the good repute of the coins was a means to the fame of the city, it is a means of doubtful potency. There is no direct advantage to a country in the use of a standard higher than that of another country. Great Britain is at no advantage in trade compared with the United States because the currency unit of the former is represented by nearly five times as much gold as that of the latter. Similarly, there is no theoretical reason to expect that Athens would benefit by having a currency unit larger than that used by other cities.[2] The increase was so small that its effect on contracts in existence at the time it was made can have been but slight. A more likely explanation might be found in the fact that the supplies of silver had tended to increase. Peisistratus commenced to work the mines of Laurium, although they were not very productive for some considerable time. If silver was tending to become less valuable in Athens, an addition of 4 per cent. to the standard might be made without causing any fall in prices:

[1] Gardner, *op. cit.*, 156.

[2] Adcock (*Camb. Anc. Hist.*, IV, 67) remarks that the coinage of Peisistratus and of his son Hippias "shows a tendency towards a regular fulness or increase of weight, which helped the commercial prestige of Athens," and there is no theoretical reason to believe that "the pure and heavy coins of Athens tended to drive out inferior issues" (Gardner, *op. cit.*, 157).

it might merely neutralize a tendency to a rise. But the merchants of other cities where silver had not fallen in value might find it profitable to exchange their commodities for the Athenian "owls" which would be exported.[1] Where there were fixed tariffs of exchange rates with foreign cities the raising of the Athenian *drachm* would encourage the purchase of Athenian "owls," because for the same price as before more silver would be obtained. Possibly, therefore, the raising of the unit was originally the consequence of a fall in the value of silver, and was aimed at improving the market for the metal without causing a fall in the general level of prices in Athens. In due course Corinth and the cities of Eubœa copied the Athenian increase. Doubtless the Corinthians were not prepared to see their "Pegasi" passing at a discount in Athenian "owls." But it is more difficult to explain why, when the Persians began to coin during the latter half of the 6th century, they raised the *gold* unit, which had been used by the Lydians, by about 3 per cent. to obtain their *daric.* It may be that both Peisistratus and Cyrus, or Cambyses, found expression for their pride in the same manner. If not, one must suppose that the alterations of Greek and Persian units are not unrelated. But if the silver unit was raised after silver had fallen in value there would be no need to alter gold units in order to preserve a simple value relation between the two.[2] If it be suggested[3] that the increase in the Athenian unit was made merely to preserve exchange rates in the face of the raising of the unit by the Persians, it remains to ask why the Persians raised the unit, and no answer appears to be forthcoming. The most satisfactory explanation at the moment is that the increase was initiated in Athens either to facilitate Egyptian trade or, more probably, to encourage the silver market.

[1] Even after the fall of Athens Xenophon wrote that at Athens a merchant could choose what he took in return for his goods. "He can either, in return for his wares, export a variety of goods such as human beings seek after, or if he does not desire to take goods in exchange for goods, he has simply to export silver, and he cannot have a more excellent freight to export, since wherever he likes to sell it he may look to realize a large percentage on his original outlay" (*Ways and Means*, III).

[2] When Crœsus "secured the monopoly of coinage in Asia Minor, 5 Attic *drachms* were exchangeable for 4 *shekels* of Crœsus" (Seltman, *Athens*, 125).

[3] As it is by Seltman, *loc. cit.*

5. *Currency Manipulation for Profit.*

There remains the problem how far the Greeks reduced their monetary standards for motives of profit. Evidence of profit-making is very meagre, the most fruitful source of information being the second book of the pseudo-Aristotelian *Œconomica* of the early 4th century B.C., which is aptly described by the writer himself in his opening lines as "a collection of all the methods that we conceived to be worth mentioning which men of former days have employed or cunningly devised in order to provide themselves with money." The devices described are all of questionable morality, but the writer naïvely explains that the object of the work lay in the belief "that this information also might be useful; for a man will be able to apply some of these instances to such business as he himself takes in hand."[1] The only suggestions of such alterations in Greece proper relate to Athens and the first to the occasion of the change of standards by Solon in the opening years of the 6th century B.C. The evidence is, however, so confused that no interpretation can be advanced with much confidence. It is agreed that Solon was concerned to relieve the burden of debts in the community, and also that he changed the currency standard. It is agreed, too, that the "Æginetan" *drachm* of about 94 grains was the weight unit in Athens until the time of Solon's reform, and that Solon replaced it with a "Eubœan" unit. But the "Eubœan" standard was probably known in Eubœa in both its "heavy" and its "light" forms, the *drachms* in each weighing respectively 129 and 64·5 grains, and it is disputed whether Solon displaced the "Æginetan" unit of 94 grains for a larger one of 129 grains or a smaller one of 64·5 grains. The democratic politician and antiquary, Androtion, thought,[2]

[1] *Œconomica*, II, 27 *sqq.*

[2] Plutarch (who wrote in the second half of the 1st century A.D.) refers to Androtion's view in his Life of Solon (Langhorne translation, 53). He says that "the cancelling of debts . . . was the first of his (Solon's) public acts; that debts should be forgiven, and that no man for the future should take the body of his debtor for security. Though Androtion, and some others, say that it was not by the cancelling of debts, but by moderating the interest, that the poor were relieved, they thought themselves so happy in it, that they gave the name discharge to this act of humanity, as well as to the enlarging of measures, and the value of money, which went along with it. For he

early in the 4th century, that the change of standard and the relief of the burden of debts were related, and that in fact the latter was effected by means of the former. This meant that the new unit was the "light" *drachm* of 64·5 grains. But shortly after Androtion had advanced this view Aristotle stated that the abolition of debts[1] preceded the currency reform. If Aristotle was correct the reason for believing that the "light" standard was introduced is, therefore, demolished. But Aristotle proceeded to explain the alteration of standards. He said[2] of Solon that "During his term of office the measures were made larger than those of Pheidon, and the *mina*, which previously contained about 70 *drachms*, was raised to the full hundred. The standard coin in earlier times was the 2-*drachm* piece. He also appointed as the standard of currency the proportion of 60 *minas* to the *talent*, and the *mina* was also distributed into *staters* and the other values." Sir F. Kenyon adds in a footnote that "the MS. has sixty-three, but this must certainly be a mistake, as there is no evidence that the number of *minas* in a *talent* was ever other than sixty." The passage is, however, ambiguous. Did the *mina* remain unchanged while the *drachm* was reduced from one-seventieth to one-hundredth of it, or did the *drachm* remain unchanged while the *mina* was increased to be equal to 100 *drachms* instead of 70? If we take the first alternative and assume that the *mina* had been one of 70 "Æginetan" *drachms*,[3] the

---

ordered the *mina*, which before went but for 73 *drachms*, to go for 100, so that as they paid the same in value but much less in weight; those that had great sums to pay were relieved, while such as received them were no losers." There seems to be no doubt about Plutarch's interpretation. He thought that the *drachm* was reduced from 94 to 64·5 grains without any adjustment of debts. But he is merely following Androtion in this. Nevertheless, he is by no means clear, for it is difficult to see how such a reduction can be regarded as "enlarging . . . the value of money." Moreover, he does not seem to have understood the effect of the reduction, or he would not have suggested that it relieved debtors without loss to creditors.

[1] He cancelled all debts involving any form of personal servitude, and declared it illegal to accept the person of a debtor as security for a loan.

[2] *Constitution of Athens*, Chap. X.

[3] A *mina* of 70 *drachms* is an unusual unit, but it might be explained by supposing that the "Eubœan" *mina* had been in use before ever the *drachm* was introduced by Solon. Professor Ridgeway (*op. cit.*, 307) claims that this was so, and, in fact, that the "Eubœan" *mina* was the standard for both gold and silver in Athens before ever money was issued. When Athens issued coins of its own, silver pieces on the

resulting new *drachm* was the "Eubœan" "light" unit of about 64 grains,[1] the conclusion to which Androtion came, though by a different path.[2] On the other hand, if the *drachm* remained unchanged and a new *mina* was created equal to 100 *drachms*, the main problem is to find out the weight of the *drachm*, which itself can only a little earlier have been adopted as a silver unit. A *mina* of 70 *drachms* is unlikely to have been deliberately established at any time. The most plausible explanation of its origin is that the units belonged to different series. It is reasonable to suppose that the "Eubœan" *drachm* had been adopted a little previously to the changes to which Aristotle refers, and was then found to be equal to one-seventieth of the old *mina*. Aristotle refers merely to the establishment of a *mina* of one-hundred of the recently adopted *drachms*. It was natural that such a unit should be set up, because the *mina* had always been one hundredfold of the *drachm* in Greece. Proceeding on this assumption, we find that the *drachm* must have weighed about 130 grains, and that the standard adopted was the "heavy" "Eubœan."[3] We must therefore choose between the "light" and "heavy" "Eubœan" units as the basis of the Solonian reform. Reference to the context is none too

---

Æginetan basis being in use, they had to be related to the local unit of weight, and, on the basis of their weight, 70 "Æginetan" *drachms* were rated as worth one native ("Eubœan") *mina*. He holds, therefore, that in coining on the "Eubœan" standard, they were by no means introducing a new standard, but falling back on the one with which they were most familiar.

[1] $70 \times 92{\cdot}1 = 6{,}450 = 100 \times 64{\cdot}5$.

[2] Professor Ridgeway's reading (*op. cit.*, p. 306) brings him to much the same conclusion as Androtion, although he also agrees that the reform of the currency was not part of a scheme of inflation intended to assist debtors. Professor Ridgeway does not follow Sir F. Kenyon in assuming that "63 *minas* to the *talent*" is a mistake for "60 *minas* to the *talent*," although this certainly gives the kind of arrangement we should expect, there being no other instance of a *talent* not sixtyfold the *mina*. He accepts the figure 63, and works back from the Athenian *talent* of later times, which he takes as weighing 405,000 grains, and finds that a *mina* of $\frac{1}{63}$ of this weighed 6,428 grains. Assuming that the *mina* remained unchanged, but that whereas it was before divided into 70 *drachms*, it was thenceforward divided into 100, he obtains a weight for the old *drachm* of 92 grains, and for the new one of 64·28 grains (or, as he expresses it, the *stater* weighed 128·56 grains) (*op. cit.*, 306).

[3] "Æginetan" *mina* = 100 "Æginetan" *drachms* of 92 grains.

"Æginetan" *mina* = 9,200 grains. $\frac{9{,}200}{70} = 131$ grains.

satisfactory, because the sense of the words used is not certain. Aristotle's reference to an " increase in the standards . . . of the currency " could hardly refer to the division of an unchanged *mina* into one hundred instead of seventy parts. The *drachm*, the denomination upon which coins were based, would have been reduced by such an operation.[1] Plutarch's phrase, " the enlarging of the value of money," might more easily be applied to a reform which rated up the *mina* to 100 instead of 70 *drachms* without changing its weight. But, again, it is probable that the *drachm* was referred to, as it, and not the *mina*, was the principal money and the basis of the standard. This suggests the adoption of the " heavy " unit and involves the rejection of Androtion's theory, already weakened by Aristotle's account of the Solonian reform.

Aristotle mentions that " the standard coin in earlier times was the 2-*drachm* piece,"[2] and it is possible that he meant that *didrachms* took the place and were approximately of equal weight to the *tetradrachms* of his own time. Specimens of archaic weights[3] and early coins give some support to this view. Early Athenian silver coins weighing 268 grains bear marks usually indicative of the 2-*drachm* piece.[4] There is a balance of evidence, therefore, in favour of the suggestion that the basis of the Solonian reform was the " heavy " " Eubœan " unit,[5] and that the change of standard took the form of the replacement of a unit of about 94 grains by one of about 130 grains. No profit is likely to have accrued to the city from such an operation. There is no record of any attempt to revalue debts in the new unit, although this is not conclusive evidence that no such arrangement was made. If there was none, it is very difficult to

[1] Seltman (*op. cit.*, 17) considers that " increase of the currency meant increase in the bulk of the coinage, which automatically came from a reduction in the weight of its units." But the *mina* had the same weight as before. And a *drachm* had less bulk than before. The increase was an increase in prices, but it was probably such that the coins necessary to purchase an article had much the same bulk as before.

[2] Reinach regards the phrase as an interpolation, but Ridgeway regards the suggestion as needless (*op. cit.*, 306, n. 2). Seltman (*op. cit.*, 14) contends that the phrase applies to pre-Solonian coins.

[3] Hill, *Camb. Anc. Hist.*, IV, 134.

[4] Head, *Hist. Num.*, 367.

[5] Hill (*Camb. Anc. Hist.*, IV, 134) rejects the light unit. " We may reject the implication that a pre-existing *mina* divisible into 73 'Æginetian' *drachms* was newly divided up into 100 reduced *drachms*, and what follows from it."

persist in the belief that the heavier unit was selected, and for this reason some writers have preferred to accept the lighter unit and to explain the reform as aimed at profit over and above the relief separately given to debtors.[1] If, however, we persist in believing that the "heavy" unit was accepted, and assume that some rating of old debts was made, in the complete absence of any supporting evidence, it remains to explain how the lighter unit came to replace the heavier.

The reduction of the standard by half is ascribed to Hippias towards the end of the 6th century, after his father Peisistratus had slightly raised the *drachm*. It is reported that "Hippias the Athenian put up for sale the parts of the upper rooms which projected into the public streets, and the steps and fences in front of the houses and the doors which opened outwards. The owners of the property, therefore, bought them, and a large sum was thus collected. He also declared the coinage then current at Athens to be base, and, fixing a price for it, ordered it to be brought to him; but when they met to consider the striking of a new type of coin, he gave them back the same money again."[2] From the other actions recorded in the passage, it appears that in an attempt to avert a financial crisis (probably due to the loss of the Thracian mines),[3] a desperate manipulation of the currency was resorted to.[4] The new pieces, which were of the same weight as the old, and were probably the old pieces re-issued, were worth twice as many *drachms* as the old pieces. Thus a piece of 260 to 270 grains, which had formerly circulated

[1] Seltman (*op. cit.*, 16) decides that Solon must have introduced the lighter unit, partly for the same reasons as the Corinthians, and partly because it offered all the advantages (so attractive in emergency) of a devaluation of the coinage. Professor Gardner (*op. cit.*, 148) takes the same view, and thinks that Solon being a moderate man, wishing to destroy neither rich nor poor, is likely to have aimed at reducing the weight of overwhelming debts and mortgages of the poor without abolishing them, and to have managed this by reducing the coinage. Solon is unlikely to have found any reason for raising the coin, and it is unlikely that raising the coin would have made it more popular. Professor Gardner suggests, too (*op. cit.*, 150), that the "enlargement of measures referred to by both Androtion and Aristotle was a further attempt to benefit the people." The success of this policy depends upon the possibility of preventing a proportionate rise in prices. As Pheidonian weights were again used in later times, such increase in size as was made must have been temporary.

[2] *Œconomica*, II, 5.

[3] Owing to the conquest of Thrace by Darius of Persia in 512 B.C.

[4] Ure, *op. cit.*, 64.

as a 2-*drachm* piece, reappeared as a 4-*drachm* piece. The burden of all debts was probably halved, and the state may also have profited out of recoinage.[1] It is possible, therefore, that either Solon or Hippias reduced the currency standard with a view to profit.

Debasement or reduction of the standard by reducing the quality of the coins was extremely rare in Greece,[2] except in a most extreme form the issue of coins of base metal plated to resemble silver. Plated coins are found among Greek issues of the earliest times, but many may be the work of counterfeiters. The best recorded issue is that made in Athens[3] in 407-406 B.C. towards the end of the Peloponnesian War. Athens was reduced to desperate straits: the loss of her fleet was followed by the melting of golden statues in the Parthenon and the issue of gold coins. But this was not enough: plated brass was issued. From the passage already

[1] Seltman, who believes that the lighter unit was introduced by Solon, and cannot in consequence agree that any reduction was made by Hippias, suggests (*op. cit.*, 77) that the coins he demonetized were those that Seltman believes to have been issued in Athens before the time of Solon, bearing heraldic types of the ancient Athenian families. These Hippias attacked, either because of their poor weight, or to satisfy a personal grudge against the families whose coats-of-arms appeared on the coins. The murder of his brother Hipparchus had embittered him against all aristocrats, and Hippias may also have felt it undesirable that the coinage should keep before the eyes of the people the power to which some of those families had attained. He suggests that Hippias made a profit by tariffing the coin below its metallic value, assuming, therefore, that the Athenians would surrender the coin for less than its metallic value.

Professor Gardner, who is in agreement with Seltman, suggests the somewhat lame theory that the passage quoted means that Hippias improved and modernized the types; but that to people expecting something different, it may have appeared to be the same coin over again. He suggests that the coin was called in at a discount and paid out at full value, but it is difficult to see how the Athenians were persuaded voluntarily to give (say) 10 *drachms* for 8 at the Treasury. He thinks that the object of the reform was to exclude from the coinage the barbarous imitations which were then so abundant (*op. cit.*, 158).

[2] It is probable that the ancients had many fairly effective methods of detecting the baseness of metal without an assay. The Chinese possess this skill, and it is probable that the Greeks were equally skilled. Copper, even in small quantities, is revealed by smell when the metal is warmed. Silver was tested by placing it on a red-hot iron shovel; the pure metal retained its whiteness—a not infallible test, however. Silver was also tested by breathing on it. The touchstone may also have been in use.

[3] Although probable, it is not certain that the brass was plated before it was issued (*vide* Chap. XII.)

quoted from Aristophanes,[1] it is evident that both gold and silver were either hoarded or exported, and the brass coins formed the mass of the circulating medium. After the destruction of Athens, in 404 B.C., if not before, the plated coins began to depreciate. Ten years later brass ceased to be legal tender, and Chremes, one of the characters in Aristophanes' *Ecclesiazusæ* (written in the spring of 393 B.C.), complains of them:

> "And a *bad job* for me that coinage proved. I sold my grapes and stuffed
> My cheek with coppers, and then I steered away,
> And went to purchase barley in the market.
> When just as I was holding out my sack
> The herald cried: "No copper coins allowed,
> Nothing but silver must be paid or taken!"[2]

If the brass had been circulating at the same value as the silver it displaced, it would probably not have been demonetized in this way. But, on the other hand, if it had not been passing for more than its metallic value, Chremes would have had no cause to complain, except that he had to go and sell the brass before he could get his barley. But in either event the brass was issued in exchange for silver which was spent in the war, and twelve years later the brass was repudiated. Under the terrible strain of what was then a "world war," even Athens was forced to tamper with her silver standard, and resort to manipulation of the currency for financial support. Plated coins were the nearest approach then known to paper money; they were notes printed on a material more valuable than paper, and when new might deceive recipients.

A different principle was implied in the issue of bronze by Timotheus the Athenian in his campaign against the Olynthians.[3] He met his debts to the troops by issuing a fresh bronze currency to circulate as token money along with the existing silver, and persuaded merchants to accept and circulate the new coins, promising to convert any coin left on their hands. The soldiers he persuaded by promising that "the merchants and retailers would all sell their goods on the same terms as before." Whether this promise was fulfilled so far as prices in the new bronze currency were

[1] *Frogs*, 730.
[2] *Ecclesiazusæ*, 816-22.
[3] *Vide* Chap. XIII, and pseudo-Aristotle, *Œconomica*, II, 2.

concerned, depends on the size of the new issue; perhaps Timotheus realized this when he promised to convert surplus coin. Here the issue of money was clearly used as a means of raising a free loan: it was a common war-time inflation. Temporary token money, in the nature of siege pieces of this kind, was issued by the Greeks from time to time under the burden of political and financial trouble,[1] with promises to redeem in good coin at a later date.

6. *The Policy of the Greek Colonies in Magna Græcia.*

The policy of the Greek colonies in Italy and Sicily is the resultant of the operation of new environmental influences upon a strong tradition brought from the Ægean by the colonists, and nurtured by subsequent commercial contact with the Ægean world. In some respects political conditions were similar to those around the Ægean. Communities were small, but tyranny was probably more common than in Greece. The coin types were usually in the Greek style, consisting of representations of the gods or of divine symbols. Some, however, may well have been heraldic types selected by tyrants. Religious influences found a somewhat unusual form of expression in Sicily, where personifications of rivers and nymphs are particularly common.[2] A greater pride was taken in the artistic qualities of the types than elsewhere, as is demonstrated by the frequent appearance of artists' signatures on the coins, and some of the finest coins of the ancient world were produced in Sicily. Confusion of units in foreign trade was in the main avoided until the end of the 5th century by the general acceptance of Corinthian coins. During the 4th century a monetary union seems to have been established in Sicily in the course of Timoleon's effort to free the island from Carthaginian domination, and in the 3rd century as the power of Rome advanced to the south of Italy, and later to Sicily, Roman coins displaced local issues and uniformity was secured.

The silver monometallic policy of Greece was also the policy of the colonists until the end of the 5th century B.C., when pressure from Athens, as well as Carthage, gave rise, on the one hand, to the issue of gold as a means of realizing civic

[1] Cp. Babelon, *op. cit.*, 415.

[2] Head, *Hist. Num.*, 116.

treasures of gold, and, on the other, to the issue of bronze tokens. As a war-time policy, both these devices were almost immediately adopted in Athens and Carthage, and became part of the war policy of the ancient world. During the 4th century coining of heavy bronze was initiated in Sicily, when Timoleon of Corinth was attempting to liberate the island. The native Sikel peoples rallied to Timoleon and, as they were accustomed to heavy bronze coins, the new issues were probably for their use.

The standard of Magna Græcia was that of Corinth. Much of the trade between the Ægean and Italy and Sicily passed across the Isthmus of Corinth, and for that reason, and because of the considerable commercial influence of Corinth in the Greek colonies, the standard of the former prevailed in the latter. In consequence, the "Eubœan" unit is found with its threefold division into *drachms*.[1] The standard seems to have been selected, therefore, with a view to supporting foreign commerce. But the influence of native conditions, and presumably of a desire to establish commercial relations with the indigenous population, is revealed in the division of the unit of about 129 grains into ten parts, each of which was probably equivalent in value to the bronze *litra* native to the country. In support of this attempt to make the coins attractive to the native population, the coins were also marked to show their value, particularly in *litras* and *unciæ*. Such marks appear on coins of gold, silver, and bronze, and it may be that it was from these cities that the Romans derived the practice which they also followed. It is a practice hardly ever found in Greece. The standard selected for the gold coin of Syracuse in the closing years of the 5th century suggests that the gold coins were intended to represent units of value already represented by silver coins.[2] One specimen of a gold coin, weighing about 90 grains, bears two pellets,[3] and if this signifies, as is probable, that it was equivalent in value to two of the silver 10-*drachm* pieces then current, it is fairly clear that a bimetallic system was established.[4]

[1] Possibly during the 6th century Æginetan influence extended to Magna Græcia, and some of the early pieces of just over 90 grains are "Æginetan" *drachms* and not "Corinthian" *didrachms*.

[2] Head, *Hist. Num.*, 173.

[3] Gardner, *op. cit.*, 413.

[4] On the basis of the ratio of 15:1 between gold and silver (*vide* Gardner, *op. cit.*, 413).

Changes of standard in Magna Græcia followed the general lines of those in Greece in being nearly always in a downward direction. Notably the raising of the Athenian unit by some 4 per cent. in the second half of the 6th century, although it was copied in Corinth, did not affect the South Italian and Sicilian cities. Their units continued to shrink at perhaps a rather greater rate than those of Greece, and doubtless for similar causes. Reduction of the standard with a view to profit is credited to Dionysius or Syracuse. When he captured Rhegium on the Sicilian Straits in 387 B.C., he borrowed money from the citizens. He then ordered all coins to be brought in for counter-stamping. In the course of the stamping the standard was halved : each coin was re-issued at double its nominal value. He was, therefore, left with half the coins in his own hands, and with these he paid off his debt.[1] By this means the burden of the debt was halved, and in its reduced form it was repaid out of profits of re-coinage. Presumably, all the coinage metal was re-issued, so the number of currency units was doubled, and prices must have risen about 100 per cent. Since the discovery of paper money, halving the value of the unit by doubling the supply can be effected directly without any withdrawal of earlier currency.[2] Dionysius is also credited with debasement of the coinage by issuing bronze coins exactly similar to silver *decadrachms* and plated with tin, presumably in order that they might pass as 10-*drachm* pieces.[3] Possibly he issued these base pieces mixed with the good silver, a device which was later to find great favour in the eyes of

[1] "Having borrowed money from the citizens under promise of repayment when they demanded it back, he ordered them to bring whatever money any of them possessed, threatening them with death as the penalty if they failed to do so. When the money had been brought, he issued it again, after stamping it afresh, so that each *drachm* had the value of two *drachms*, and paid back the original debt and the money which they brought him on this occasion" (Pseudo-Aristotle, *Œconomica*, II, 21).

[2] As the coins show no sign of countermarking or restriking, it is possible that the transaction was misunderstood. The *talent* was halved about this time (Julius Pollux, IX, 87), and it is possible that, having borrowed in *talents*, Dionysius halved the *talent* unit of account before he repaid the debt, thus halving the weight of the debt but receiving no recoinage profits (*vide* Gardner, *op. cit.*, 414-15).

[3] Bronze pieces plated with silver were probably issued in Campania during the 5th century (Head, 36).

the Romans. Furthermore, he is said by Aristotle[1] to have forced upon his creditors tin coins worth 1 *drachm* at a value of 4 *drachms*. It is clear from these varying accounts that Dionysius must have manipulated the currency to relieve the state finances. He was a drastic and ingenious financier, as is indicated by the various devices he invented for taxing the people. But his policy may well have been justified by events. The army and the navy, partly maintained out of the proceeds of his manipulations, saved Syracuse from being sacked by the Carthaginians as they sacked Selinus and Agrigentum.

7. *Carthaginian Policy.*

The issues of the city of Carthage are an offshoot of the Sicilian coinage, for not until their invasion of Sicily towards the end of the 5th century did the Carthaginians issue any coins. Their first pieces consisted of gold and silver issued in Sicily, and made from the treasure captured in the island. Coining was a device learned from the native population, and used for disposing of the spoils of war and settling obligations to the mercenary troops. The metals used were dictated, therefore, by the treasure captured. The types[2] and standards were both selected with a view to the easy circulation of the coins in the island, and followed, in the main, the model of the issues of the Sicilian cities.[3] At last, in the latter half of the 4th century, coins were issued in Carthage itself, but during the succeeding century only gold, electrum, and bronze were used. The use of electrum suggests contact with the revived electrum issues of Cyzicus and Phocæa, and the " Phocæan " or " Chian " standard of the cities on the northern half of the coast of Asia Minor was also the basis of the issue. It is possible, however, that the electrum coins resulted from a debasement of gold. The appearance of some of the surviving specimens suggests that attempts were made to remove the silver from the

[1] " When he was in need of money he struck a coinage of tin, and calling an assembly together, he spoke at great length in favour of the money which had been coined, and they even against their will decreed that every one should regard any of it that he accepted as silver, and not as tin " (*Œconomica*, II, 2, and Julius Pollux, IX, 87).

[2] Gardner, *op. cit.*, 347.

[3] Although in addition the " Phocæan " unit was used for gold.

surface of the coins in order that they might be taken for gold. Furthermore, both the so-called electrum and gold were coined on the same weight standard. It is possible, therefore, that debasement for the profit of either the moneyers or the state explains the electrum issues. After the acquisition of the rich deposits of silver in Spain in 242 B.C., interest in the disposal of silver intruded a new influence into monetary policy. Silver coins were issued in great quantity, most of them of very large denomination. They were accompanied, however, by coins of potin, a base alloy[1] confined to smaller denominations, but apparently coined on the same weight basis as electrum and silver. It would seem, therefore, that the smaller denominations were made to appear continuous with the larger, but were, in fact, tokens. By the time coining began in Carthage, bronze was being issued in most of the cities in the Greek world, and the Carthaginians made bronze coins as part of their first issues the pieces representing the electrum *drachms* in size and type. Late in the second half of the last century B.C., larger bronze coins were issued, roughly equivalent to two of the bronze *asses* (of about 840 grains) current in Rome until 217 B.C.[2] Although Carthage was in commercial contact with Egypt, which also issued heavy bronze pieces, there is no simple relation between the two bronze issues. Carthaginian monetary policy was built, therefore, upon foundations imported largely from Sicily, but partly from the Eastern Mediterranean, although in later times it was influenced by interest in the disposal of silver, and possibly also in making a profit from the currency. In this latter direction debasement seems not to have been uncommon, but there is no evidence of any reduction of the standard.

8. *The Policy of the Cities of Asia Minor.*

The cities of Asia Minor were also subject to two influences, the Greek practice on the west, and Asiatic on the east, but the forces were more equal than in Magna Græcia. Political organization along the coast was based upon the small city, but from early times there was a tendency for cities to be

[1] Of tin, copper, lead, and zinc.

[2] Also said to be worth about an "Æginetan" *obol* (*vide* Chap. IX).

dominated by the hinterland power, Lydia and later Persia operating through a local tyrant. The great variety of types on the earliest coins of electrum suggests that for a time the state permitted coining to be carried on by private bankers and merchants. It is possible that the types on the earliest coins were the seals of local merchants who secured political control and with it control of the money. Religious influences reveal their power in the choice of types, but civic types of economic origin are somewhat more frequent than further west. The cities of Asia Minor coined independently until the end of the 6th century. Then, united against Persia in rebellion, a number of cities united also to issue uniform electrum coinage. Early in the 4th century, a second monetary alliance was made to issue the electrum coins, which were famous for over a hundred years. An alliance was also formed to issue silver coins, but the union for the issue of electrum dominated the issues of Asia Minor. It was tolerated by both Athens and Persia during the 5th century, when both were taking their coinage prerogative very seriously. Electrum was probably still necessary for the trade to the Black Sea, and that fact ensured its preservation.

In the selection of the metal to be coined, the Ionian cities were very obviously influenced by their position between the silver standard on the west and gold and electrum standards on the east. The earlier coins of the coast cities were of electrum, silver being unimportant and used mainly for small denominations[1] until the 5th century. It has been noted that the invention of coining is sometimes claimed to have occurred in Asia Minor as a result of the need for electrum of certified composition. If coining did not commence there, punched electrum pieces were being issued[2] very soon after the mint opened at Sardes. Lydia not only coined the metal, but exported considerable quantities. But early in the 6th century coins appeared[3] of an electrum so dark that it was probably intended to pass as gold.[4] This innovation was probably responsible for the abandonment of electrum in

[1] Small silver pieces were issued at Phocæa in the first half of the 6th century (Gardner, 164).

[2] In Ephesus, Miletus, Phocæa, and possibly other cities.

[3] At Phocæa and Cyzicus (Gardner, *op. cit.*, 81).

[4] Gardner, *loc. cit.* They were also coined on a standard usually used for gold (*vide infra*).

Lydia in favour of gold and silver. When Crœsus had effected this reform, electrum fell into disuse in Asia Minor as well. Silver coins were now issued to take the place of electrum. The Ionian revolt at the close of the 6th century brought about a reversion to electrum by the federated cities which rose against Persia, and the suppression of the revolt led only to the temporary lapse of electrum coining; a little later the issues of Cyzicus, Phocæa, and the Mitylene commenced, and lasted almost to the issue of gold by Philip of Macedon in the second half of the 4th century B.C. No important gold issues were made until after the issues in Athens set the fashion. Small denominations appeared within a few years, and, after Athens struck gold *staters* about 394 B.C., similar issues were made in Asia Minor,[1] and continued to appear at intervals.

The principal standard for electrum in early times was the so-called "Phœnician," upon which the Lydians also coined for export to Asia Minor. This unit had, as we have seen, probably been used for many years before coining was commenced for measuring silver. It was convenient to use silver weights for electrum, because the latter was conventionally accepted as ten times as valuable as silver. The dark electrum of Phocæa was, however, coined on the basis of the "Eubœan" unit, an additional reason for believing that it was regarded as gold, for the "Eubœan" silver unit was identical with the gold unit generally used. The 6th century silver coins were based upon the "Æginetan" unit, and there is little doubt that it was adopted because many Æginetan coins found their way to Asia Minor in the commerce of the time, and because Ægina then dominated the Ægean trade. But with the disappearance of electrum, the coining of gold and silver by Crœsus, and the issue of silver in Asia Minor, European influence was thrown off: neither the "Eubœan"[2] nor the "Æginetan" unit was adopted. In the southern portions of Asia Minor (Caria) and in Cyprus, and also on the northern coast, Persian power, and in the former area, the presence of the Persian fleet, resulted in the use of the Persian silver unit. Along the northern half of the west coast the "Phocæan" unit prevailed. In Phocæa

[1] At Lampsacus, Clazomenæ, and Abydos (Gardner, *op. cit.*, 331).
[2] Coins of Attic standard are rare in Asia after 480 B.C.

the unit of 120 grains had been used for dark electrum in very early times, and it is probable that at this period the unit declined from about 130 grains. When silver was issued in the latter half of the 6th century, the Phocæans chose to coin on the standard then used for gold. Along the southern half of the west coast the " Milesian " standard of 102 grains was used, mainly because the commercial greatness of Miletus made easy commercial relations with her the greatest interest of most cities in the neighbourhood. In Miletus the standard probably arose in much the same way as did the " Phocæan " in Phocæa. The unit used for electrum in early times (in Miletus the " Phœnician " unit of 112 grains) tended to shrink. When silver was coined, the shrunken electrum unit was used. It is, however, curious that at this time, when the Lydians, and subsequently the Persians, were probably introducing a bimetallic system, and were almost certainly concentrating their attention on the relative values of the coins, the peoples of the coast were more concerned to coin metals on the same unit of weight regardless of values. Like the Athenians nearly 150 years later, they were more concerned with the weight of the coins than with their relative values. But it is improbable that coins of the two metals were often issued concurrently.[1]

It is particularly true of Asia Minor that the standards in use are difficult to fit into the scale of known units and, in consequence, too much emphasis must not be laid upon the possibility that units were borrowed. Shrinkage of standards was doubtless common in Asia Minor. Two of the prominent silver standards can probably be regarded as the result of the slow devaluation of larger units. Deliberate reduction of standards for profit was not common; the writer of the pseudo-Aristotelian *Œconomica* fails to produce any example. Debasement of the coinage by reducing its quality was, however, more frequent than in Greece. But the whole explanation lies in the fact that Greek cities never attempted to maintain

[1] Gardner (*op. cit.*, 184) says that these silver standards " work in with the *daric* and the gold bars or pellets of 130 grains which preceded the *daric*." The Persian and the " Phœnician " units may have worked in as suggested, but the " Phocæan " unit is about 7 per cent. above the "Phœnician" unit, and the "Milesian" about 7 per cent. below it. In consequence an attempt to establish a gold exchange standard is unlikely.

a coinage of electrum as did the Ionic cities. Electrum proved a temptation to those having control of money from the earliest times, and the abandonment of electrum in both Lydia and Asia Minor as a currency metal was ultimately due to the weakness of states or their moneyers in the face of the temptation. They debased the electrum.[1] Differences in the composition of electrum from place to place and time to time gave rise to difficulties in the use of electrum money. The coins of some cities being known to contain little gold were rated at a discount in the coins of other cities, where the pieces, although of similar weight, were known to contain a greater proportion of gold. Foreign trade was, in consequence, unnecessarily hindered. But the abandonment of electrum suggests also a desire on the part of the civic authorities to make their mark on the coins an unequivocal guarantee of a prescribed quantity of a known metal, a desire probably based more on anxiety for the future of foreign trade than for domestic exchange. Debasement by the issue of plated coins seems to have been exploited by Themistocles when he was tyrant of Magnesia (*c.* 465-450 B.C.), for silver-plated coins have been found.[2]

The most interesting manipulation of the currency recorded in Asia Minor is the substitution of iron for silver coins at Clazomenæ. The writer of the *Œconomica* says of the citizens of Clazomenæ that "when they owed pay to their soldiers to the amount of 20 *talents* and could not provide it . . . paid the generals 4 *talents* a year as interest. But finding that they did not reduce the principal, and that they were continually spending money to no purpose, they struck an iron coinage to represent a sum of 20 *talents* of silver, and then distributing it among the richest citizens in proportion to their wealth they received in exchange an equivalent sum in silver. Thus the individual citizens had money to disburse for their daily needs, and the state was freed from debt. They then paid them interest out of their revenues and continually divided it up and distributed it in proper proportions, and called in the iron coinage."[3] The debt was paid off out of the profit obtained by substituting iron for silver money. If the silver was paid out to the soldiers to whom the city

[1] One specimen of a lead coin plated with electrum is known.
[2] Gardner, *op. cit.*, 257. [3] Pseudo-Aristotle, *Œconomica*, II, 17.

was indebted and, at the same time, the iron money passed into circulation (as apparently it did, for "the individual citizens had money to disburse for their daily needs"), the total supply of money was increased, and its purchasing power must have tended to fall. Unless the iron passed at a discount in silver, we should expect something approaching 20 *talents* of silver to be exported to places where its value had not been reduced by the dilution of the currency with iron. The last sentence in the quotation is anything but clear. It may mean that the interest charge was still included in the budget, but that when the money was raised it was distributed among the citizens in proportion as they had given silver coins for iron, the iron money being redeemed. If so, the currency must have been deflated at the rate of 4 *talents* per annum during a period of five years. When prices tended to fall, silver probably flowed back to take the place of some of the iron demonetized. By inflating the currency with cheap tokens, the government was able to redeem its debt, for token currency carries no interest. This operation recalls the 20th-century device of selling paper tokens, and investing a large part of the proceeds in Government securities, or, in other words, in paying off part of the state debt or diminishing the part that must be raised from the public and carry interest. But the modern practice makes no automatic provision for the subsequent withdrawal of the token notes. On the other hand, the method of issuing the iron tokens in Clazomenæ "among the richest citizens according to their wealth" suggests a forced issue. Demosthenes contended that "the majority of states are quite open in using silver coins diluted with copper and lead: even where our extant coins are not debased, they are in most cases under weight. It is, in fact, an honest coinage which is the exception."[1] And this has led more modern writers to accuse the Greeks of "habitual and shameless" debasement.[2] The wide circulation obtained by the currencies of Ægina, Corinth, Athens, and Cyzicus has been attributed to the honesty with which they were controlled at a time when integrity and efficiency of currency control were unusual.[3] But in the foregoing pages many reasons have been given for the importance of

[1] XXIV, 214.
[2] Zimmern, *Greek Commonwealth*, 304.
[3] Zimmern, *op. cit.*, 307.

these issues. Bounteous issues, owing to the possession of mines, political power, commercial importance (not based only upon a good currency system), technical efficiency in minting, and the control of the mint, were all influences as potent as the honesty of the issuer outstanding from a dishonest world. In fact, the evidence which we possess does not support Demosthenes' vehement and sweeping condemnation. Although these ancient cities did on occasion resort to all the possible methods of inflation, except the issue of paper money, their general policy was one of restraint in the presence of knowledge of the means to profit.[1] Some of the false money that has survived is doubtless the work of counterfeiters and dishonest moneyers. Since the time of Solon, at the close of the 7th century, if not earlier, such practitioners have existed to harass and despoil the user of coin. Most Greek states made the adulteration of money a crime punishable by death,[2] and were perhaps a little too content to regard such severity as exonerating them from effort to remove the causes of debasement.

9. *Conclusion.*

The rectitude of Greek monetary policy might be accounted for by a number of reasons. Communities were small, and required no great quantity of currency for internal trade; in many places the mint worked only at long intervals. The smaller the quantity of currency, the less the profit to be obtained by reducing its weight.[3] While the profits of re-coinage might be small, the device would, however, be as useful as ever as a means of reducing the burden of debts, where the unit of currency was also the unit of account. But the smallness of communities gave rise also to positive arguments against interference. The smaller the society, the greater is the proportion of its trade that is likely to be "foreign," and the more important is it to avoid action likely to hamper such trade.[4] Any state reducing its standard out

[1] "Taken as a whole, Greek money is excellent, the metal is pure, the weight exact, the real value corresponds to the nominal value; nothing better has been produced by the more civilized and more wisely governed peoples of modern times" (Lenormant, *op. cit.*, III, 5).

[2] Demosthenes, *Timocr.*, 212-4.

[3] Ridgeway, *op. cit.*, 224.

[4] Zimmern (*op. cit.*, 305) argues, however, that it was the economic isolation and normal self-sufficiency of the states that made it possible for money to be forced on the people at a value out of proportion to its commodity values.

of harmony with others would feel some reaction upon its relations with neighbouring towns. Coins might be so reduced as to retain a simple relation with the principal foreign units,[1] but such alterations were probably unpopular. The form of political organization, consequent on the smallness of communities, constituted a further important factor, for reductions aimed simply at profit are unlikely to gain acceptance in a democratically governed state. In a small democracy such as that of Athens which gave all citizens a share in the public business, the pressure of those likely to suffer by alterations could be brought more easily and directly to bear upon the authorities to discourage such a policy. The democratic Republic was, therefore, less likely to be afflicted with monetary depreciation. In the Middle Ages Venice and Florence were most fortunate in this. Whether the invention of representative government has brought any relief in this respect to large modern communities is not easy to discover. Other conditions have altered very much. Money has become in modern western communities the pivot about which social and economic mechanism revolves. In consequence, people tend to regard it as fixed and to be much more easily gulled by currency manipulation than ancient peoples who continued to barter (especially for the precious metals by weight) long after money was introduced. The existence of the two systems, side by side, quickly revealed attempts to depreciate money and their consequences. Index numbers of prices as they become more generally understood will probably have the same effect upon modern peoples. But even so, the use of paper money, and the existence of a complex banking system, confuse the question, and the average citizen is not always quite sure that depreciation of the currency is wholly bad; even if he is, he is still not sure of the causes of the rise in prices and of the best method of tackling them. Moreover, the depreciation must be measured against the force of the disaster that causes it: even Athens was forced to debase its coins during the Peloponnesian War. The democratic states which inflated their currencies during and after the War of 1914-18 did so under the stress of war and its consequences, the burden of which was, proportionately to their resources,

[1] The probable halving of the Athenian unit must have permitted as simple foreign exchange quotations in the new unit as in the old.

comparable to the burden which the Peloponnesian War threw on Athens. Their response was much the same as in Athens, with the exception that new monetary devices were employed, but with similar consequences. Depreciation in early times presupposes "sovereign power vested in the hands of a monarch possessed of unlimited authority who has a direct personal interest in the profit to be made from the degradation of the coinage, and who has power sufficient to enable him to force his debased currency on a reluctant people,"[1] or, it should be added, as an alternative, a disaster great enough to secure general acceptance of depreciated money. The rarity of such a concentration of power in Greek cities accounts for the maintenance of standards except in times of disaster; "but in the Greek world one hardly ever meets bad money except among Kings and tyrants,"[2] and they did not always use their powers to depreciate.

There is very little direct evidence of the extent to which, in ancient times, the state attempted to force the acceptance of its currency by making it a legal tender. Specimens of coins give no assistance, and literary records rarely regard it as worthy of mention. Xenophon says[3] that "in most cities (other than Athens) the trader is under the necessity of loading his vessel with some merchandise or other in exchange for his cargo, since the current coin has no circulation beyond the frontier." But whether its circulation within the country is enforced by law is not stated. Bartering for gold was probably a common procedure. Aristophanes, in his reference to the decrying of the bronze coin at Athens, implies that it had previously onjoyed some legal support. Indeed, all issues of plated and debased coins must have been accompanied by legal provisions to secure as free a circulation as possible. It is beyond doubt that legal tender regulations existed in some form or other from the earliest times. No unit of account could come into general use until it was legally defined, and this would involve a statement of the means by which a debt expressed in the unit could be settled.

[1] Ridgeway, *op. cit.*, 224.

[2] Lenormant, III, 13.

[3] *Revenues*, I, 3.

CHAPTER XV

MONETARY POLICY IN THE ROMAN REPUBLIC

During the eight hundred years from the 5th century B.C. to the end of the 3rd century A.D., Roman currency policy developed from that of the small primitive community to an imperial policy built on foundations laid in the Greek democratic city states and the Asiatic empires. Primitive environment gave way to an increasingly complex civilization, and of the change the development of currency and finance was both cause and effect.

1. *The Institution of Coinage.*

There was no era of private coining among the native peoples of Italy. The institution of issues of round coins has, as we have seen, been placed as early as about 340-335 B.C., although more recently there has been a tendency to place the beginning of coining nearly a century later. No at all adequate monetary system existed in Italy outside the Greek cities until the unification of Italy under Rome. In later periods of the Republic, and probably from the time of the issue of the first coins, monetary policy was determined by a vote of all the citizens assembled in tribes. The duty of carrying into practice the decision of the people was in the hands of the chief magistrate, a not altogether satisfactory arrangement, as was realized towards the end of the century. The earliest *as signatum* was marked by the government, although the mark was probably no more than a guarantee of quality, the weight of the coins being determined in the balance.[1] Although the round *as grave* varied very much in weight because they were cast, their type was taken as a guarantee of weight as well as quality. They, and all subsequent coins of whatever metal issued under the Republic, were marked with their value.[2] The state fixed the rate at which coins were to pass, and presumably at this rate they

[1] Mommsen, I, 77.

[2] Mommsen, II, 88.

were legal tender and had to be accepted. They were at no period merely punch-marked ingots to be placed in the balance at the option of the payee. The types of the early *as grave*, and particularly the heads of divinities on one side of the coins, suggest a religious motive borrowed from the Greeks, doubtless partly from the coins of the cities of Magna Græcia which had long been current in Central Italy. But in their limitation of coining to bronze, and their adoption of the *libra* of bronze as the standard, they followed local tradition. Although it has been suggested that coined money possessed a value "independent of its intrinsic value,"[1] it is very unlikely that these early coins ever circulated as tokens above their metallic value. This, the first Roman essay in coining, was aimed simply at facilitating exchange by applying the device of coining to the medium of exchange already in use. The circulation of the coins was encouraged by using the metal and the weight unit already known. The adoption of the *as* as a unit of account and medium of exchange was further encouraged by establishing a special procedure for the enforcement of contracts expressed in *asses*.[2]

2. *The Reduction of the As.*

Soon after its institution the *as* coinage began to fall in weight, although by what stages and at what times are matters upon which there is no decisive evidence. There is a general agreement that by 240 B.C., after the first Punic War, it had fallen to 2 ounces. The supposed reasons for the fall are closely bound up with the dates to which it is ascribed. The crudity of mint technique may account for some reductions. Coins were all cast until 268 B.C., and if coin moulds were

[1] Mommsen, I, 254.

[2] "It was not only to assist in recognition and valuation of pieces that the Romans marked their money. . . . There was a law which gave to money so marked an official value, independent of its intrinsic value . . . these pieces alone were considered as coins, and all other kinds of money were in the eyes of the law but merchandise. All commercial transactions in national money so prescribed gave rise to a special and very severe procedure (*actio pecuniæ certæ*), all others gave the right only to the repayment of equivalent value, and could give rise only to a simple action (*quanti ea res est*). Whoever made a contract by weight doubtless did not lose the right of weighing when it pleased the creditor to pay him in *asses*, but whoever had to receive a fixed sum in *asses* had not the right to ask that they should be weighed, and had to accept them whatever their weight and fineness" (Mommsen, I, 209).

PLATE XII

BRONZE CURRENCY OF CENTRAL ITALY OF THE FIFTH CENTURY B.C.

1

2

Specimens of Bronze *As Signatum* of Central Italy of the Fifth Century B.C. bearing (1) Bull and (2) an Eagle holding a thunderbolt.

[*face p.* 380

obtained by taking castings from other coins each coin would be a little smaller than that from which it was moulded, and a progressive fall in the standard might occur. But the process of casting, even where moulds were uniform, was so inaccurate that it is possible to arrange the coins so as to suggest a gradual fall in their weight. These explanations may well account for small reductions and perhaps the earliest, but they are not adequate for the whole reduction of five-sixths of the original weight of the unit. It is not improbable that moneyers were dishonest as well as incompetent.

If profit was the object of the reduction, such profit must have been derived from the lag of the fall in the value of the coin behind the decline of the value of its metallic content. The idea that the coins were kept up in value, and became tokens at this early period, must be rejected. It is unlikely, however, that the fall from its original weight to 2 ounces in 240 B.C. is all to be explained as due to the profit so obtained from a steady diminution of the coin. It is probable that some definite reductions were made. The *as* had lost at least half, and probably more, of its weight by 268 B.C., although the legal standard may have remained unchanged. Financial relief during, or shortly after, the wars against Pyrrhus (282-272 B.C.) is a possible explanation. The exact nature of the relief is doubtful; there would be little profit on recoinage,[1] or from the lag of prices behind the increase in the number of *asses* in circulation. But as prices rose, the burden of debts payable at par in coined *asses* was lightened,[2] and this result may have been the object of the

[1] The bronze extracted from the coins was not sold on the market, for the coins did not become tokens; they would have done if their weight had been decreased without any increase in their numbers. The bronze was minted, but the recoinage brought profit to the mint only so far as old heavy *asses* could be called in and exchanged at par for light ones. As the rating of the new *as* was half that of the old, few persons can have been prepared to make the exchange. More profit could be made by melting heavy *asses* and selling them as metal than by selling them to the mint, which paid about half their metallic value.

[2] If the *as* persisted as a full-weight coin, prices and wages in coined *asses* must have risen roughly in inverse proportion to the reductions in weight and currency valuation of the *as*. So far as the coined *as* was legal tender in settlement of a debt of 1 *as*, debtors at the time of the reduction would be enriched at the expense of their creditors, unless special arrangements were made for the settlement of existing contracts. The state as debtor for large sums would, if the debt were expressed in coined *asses*, obtain relief from part of its burden of debt.

reduction.[1] The effect of the reduction depends, however, on the unit of account in general use, of which there is very little definite information. There is little doubt that the pound of bronze was the original unit of account. If it was not formally reduced from time to time with the *as* coin, the latter may have been legal tender for payment of debts in *asses*, and profit would then follow upon reduction of the coin. But if coins were taken by weight in payment of debts in libral *asses*, there would be no profit to be obtained from reducing the coins.[2] Against this it may be argued that the democratic constitution of the state rendered it unlikely that it would adopt currency manipulation such as might have commended itself to an irresponsible ruler.[3] But the second Punic War saw both issue of plated coins and the further reduction of standards, although the democratic constitution was still in existence. It is certainly improbable that if the *as* was reduced in 268 B.C., it was to obtain a profit. The issue of the Pyrrhic Wars had been most favourable to Rome, not only in military success, but in treasure, and there is no evident reason why the currency should have been inflated.

On the other hand, the simplificaton of trade relations with silver-using areas may have led to the reduction of the *as* by half, perhaps, in 268 B.C. or ten or twenty years before.[4] Although there is some evidence of such a halving of the unit, it is not at all obvious that it would assist trade. If, as is supposed, it made a *scruple* of silver exchangeable for a bronze *as* instead of half an *as*, that is no great improvement; unless debts in *asses* were adjusted to the new unit, it halved the burden of debts and caused considerable economic upheaval. But the simplification of domestic exchange was as pressing a need as the simplification of foreign exchange. The pound of bronze was not a convenient currency. The

[1] Lenormant, III, 23.

[2] Mommsen (II, 16) suggests that after the supposed reduction to 4 ounces in 268 B.C. the state paid its debts in old *asses* or their equivalent, weight for weight, in new ones, more particularly as for a long time after this the official accounts were kept in old *asses*. Heavy *asses*, he thinks, continued to circulate side by side with new ones, at a value proportional to their respective metallic contents (II, 17).

[3] *Vide* Macdonald, *Evolution of Coins*, 47.

[4] Sydenham, *Num. Chron.*, 1918, 160, who ascribes the halving to 286 B.C.

Roman housewife's journey to the market must have been every bit as fatiguing as her return. In times when trade was unimportant, and public finance of the most elementary, the clumsiness of bronze was not a vital matter, but with the political and economic growth of Rome a more efficient medium of exchange was called for. In consequence, silver coins must have been popular, and the reduction of the *as* may be a sign of its diminishing popularity. It was being confined to ever smaller denominations,[1] although the copper coins remained full-weight pieces. The *denarius* superseded 10 *asses*, weighing at least 20, or possibly 60, ounces of bronze. Nevertheless, it is confusing that instead of allowing the higher and clumsier denominations to lapse together with their names, the whole series of denominations continued to be used, and was shifted downward. The reduction in the denominations, which were represented by bronze coins, must have been the greatest advantage.

It is suggested[2] that the Romans attempted to assimilate their coins to those of other peoples in Central Italy, using a different pound by adjusting the weights of the early subdivisions of the *as*. While the *as* was based upon the pound of 10 ounces, the smaller denominations are thought to have been based upon one of 12 ounces. While such an arrangement would have brought the coins of peoples using the "Oscan" pound into simple weight relation with those of people using the "Neo-Roman" pound, it would have obscured the relation between the denominations. Either the *uncia* passed as one-tenth of the *as*, in which case the lighter pound was in use as the standard, or it passed as one-twelfth of the *as*, in which case the *as* was a token, and, apart from the small

[1] Mommsen (German edition, 293) says: "Also was immer der Zweck jener Abschaffung des Libralfusses sein möchte—wir kommen darauf zurück—so würde dadurch nicht der Werth der Münze verringert, sondern nur der Werthausdruck verändert." This comes to much the same as a much more recent suggestion (Head, 19), that "for convenience' sake the pound of bronze, originally regarded as a single *as*, was gradually split up into a larger and larger number of *asses*." But the convenience may have come from a variety of directions. When (and if) the *as* was halved, the change may have made the *as* equal to 1 instead of 2 scruples of silver. But we cannot thus explain the possible reduction of 60 per cent. in 268. The subsequent reduction in 217 B.C., occurring in time of war, is still harder to explain, for reforms aimed at profit rather than mere convenience are expected in war-time.

[2] Sydenham, *Num. Chron.*, 1918, 164 (following Hæberlin).

profit obtainable, the reduction of its content to 10 ounces was unimportant. But the differences in weight are most probably due to the great variety of weights of the coins of each denomination. Some denominations were coined at one time, and others when the standard had fallen further.

3. *The Institution of Silver Coinage.*

It is difficult to discover the reasons which induced the Romans to issue their first silver coins, because neither the time nor the place of their issue is precisely known. If they were issued at Capua about 335 B.C., their appearance may have been due to the Samnite Wars, or they may have had a purely economic origin in the demand for coins less bulky than *asses* and *unciæ*. On the other hand, these early silver coins are usually found in Samnium, part of Latium, Picenium, and Apulia, and their types suggest Carthaginian as well as Roman influence. Rome was in alliance with Carthage against Pyrrhus from 279 B.C., and it is not improbable that the Carthaginians provided money for the campaign. They were well acquainted with silver coins, and it may have been the fact that they provided treasure in the form of silver bullion that forced the Romans to make silver coins and break with their tradition.[1] The appearance of the coins suggests brief issues from a number of mints, the kind of issue that would be expected during the war. They selected the " Phocæan " or " Campanian " standard, presumably because it was most likely to appeal to the people—a primary consideration if the coining was merely a means of selling the treasure for goods and services more needed by the army. But this silver coinage cannot have lasted for any very long period before it was reduced from about 117 to 105 grains. There are two probable motives for this devaluation. The new unit weighed 6 scruples, and if the scruple was worth either half a pound or a pound of bronze the reduction established an easy relation between the Roman bronze and the extra-Roman silver coins. There is no record of the effect of the alteration; but unless debts were translated into the new units, there must have been a considerable disturbance of economic relations, to the detriment of creditors

[1] Mattingly, *Num. Chron.*, 1924, 186.

SOME COINS OF CENTRAL ITALY PRIOR TO THE COMMENCEMENT OF COINING IN ROME

a b 1 a b 2

a b 3 a b 4

1 Etruscan Gold Coin of about 300 B.C. bearing (a) Male Head and mark of value " XX " and (b) Bull with bird.

2 Roman Bronze *As Grave* of the period before 269 B.C. bearing (a) Head of Janus and (b) Prow of a ship with mark of value " I " above.

3 Six Scruple Silver Piece issued outside Rome probably early in the Third Century B.C. bearing (a) Roma and (b) Victory and inscription " ROMANO."

4 Silver *quadrigatus* Coin issued outside Rome before 269 B.C. bearing (a) Janus and (b) Quadrigatus and inscription " ROMA."

and the benefit of debtors. But the change may have been no peaceful reform made for commercial ends in the last decade of the 4th century.[1] It is possible that the relief of debtors was intended, and that the reduction was a deliberate inflation made during the war with Pyrrhus, and intended to lighten the burden of government obligations for the payment of troops, the purchase of stores, and the financing of the campaign. The *staters* of Tarentum were similarly reduced towards the end of the war, and the Romans may have followed the example set by the enemy. But if the reduction was primarily inspired by military considerations,[2] the fact that the Romans selected the amount of the reduction so as to produce a coin of exactly 6 scruples points to an interest, although perhaps but a subsidiary interest, in the assimilation of Roman bronze and their new silver issues. A new series of 6-scruple pieces (*quadrigati*) was issued outside Rome when the war was over, and possibly contemporaneously with the introduction of the *denarius* in Rome. It was probably struck for a foreign market in Southern Italy or the Adriatic, and is of interest because it was the predecessor of, and was later supplanted by the *victoratus*, issued from Rome, and weighing exactly half as much as the *quadrigatus*. At this period the Romans were prepared to adapt their currency to facilitate foreign trade, either because their own standard was none too well established, or because they were not yet vigorous enough to enforce the general use of their own units. By 268 B.C. the Romans had introduced coinage of both bronze and silver, although the latter was but a provincial issue, and had assimilated the coins of one metal with those of the other. Their bronze unit had sunk below its old pound weight for reasons now impossible to disentangle, although profit from the relief of state debts and the simplification of both home and foreign trade were doubtless important.

4. *The Currency System of* 268 *B.C.*

With the issue in 268 B.C. of *denarii* of 4 scruples, marked to show that they were worth 10 *asses*, we arrive at the first definite landmark in the history of Roman currency. But,

[1] Head (32) suggests 312 B.C.; Sydenham, *Num. Chron.*, 1918, 161.
[2] Mattingly, *Num. Chron.*, 1924, 187.

unfortunately, evidence of the monetary system at that date is still deficient, because the bronze coins of 268 are not identifiable. The principal new elements in the coinage were the introduction of silver coins and the establishment of bimetallism. The issue of silver is not difficult to explain. The Romans had already made silver coins in the provinces during the Pyrrhic Wars, if not earlier, and there is little doubt that they proved popular. The smallness of the value of bronze in proportion to its weight reacted to its disadvantage in that it was difficult to carry any large value in bronze, but also in that it was difficult to make coins of large value except by casting. This process was extremely inaccurate, as well as easy to counterfeit. The desire of the Romans to have coins which would circulate freely by tale, because they varied little in value, may, therefore, account for the adoption of silver and the limitation of bronze to smaller denominations, all of which could be struck.[1] The decline in the weight of the *as* may be the cause or the effect of the growing popularity of silver. The successful conclusion of the Pyrrhic Wars, and the capture of Tarentum, yielded a great booty of gold and silver, and the coining of silver was probably, in part, a means of selling the new-found treasure and settling war obligations. Alexander had coined in this manner before, and the same spirit is noticeable on subsequent occasions in Rome. Coining may be influenced by the desire to dispose of the precious metals, although there is no local source of supply as there was in Lydia, Athens, and Macedon.

The types on the new silver indicate that Greek artistic influence was still strong. The standard of 4 scruples or 72 grains may have been chosen for the silver coin because at the current market rate it was worth just 10 *asses* of bronze. Ten *asses* might be favoured as a multiple, either because of the convenience of a decimal system, or from a long use of decimal multiples going back to the time when the sheep unit was worth 10 *asses*. Although it is suggested that assimilation with the Attic system was desired,[2] it is unlikely that the Romans cared greatly for the encouragement of

[1] After the 2-ounce *as* had been introduced, all *asses* were struck (Sydenham, *Num. Chron.*, 1918, 165).

[2] Mommsen, II, 39.

PLATE XIV

THE ROMAN REPUBLICAN COINS ISSUED IN 269 B.C.

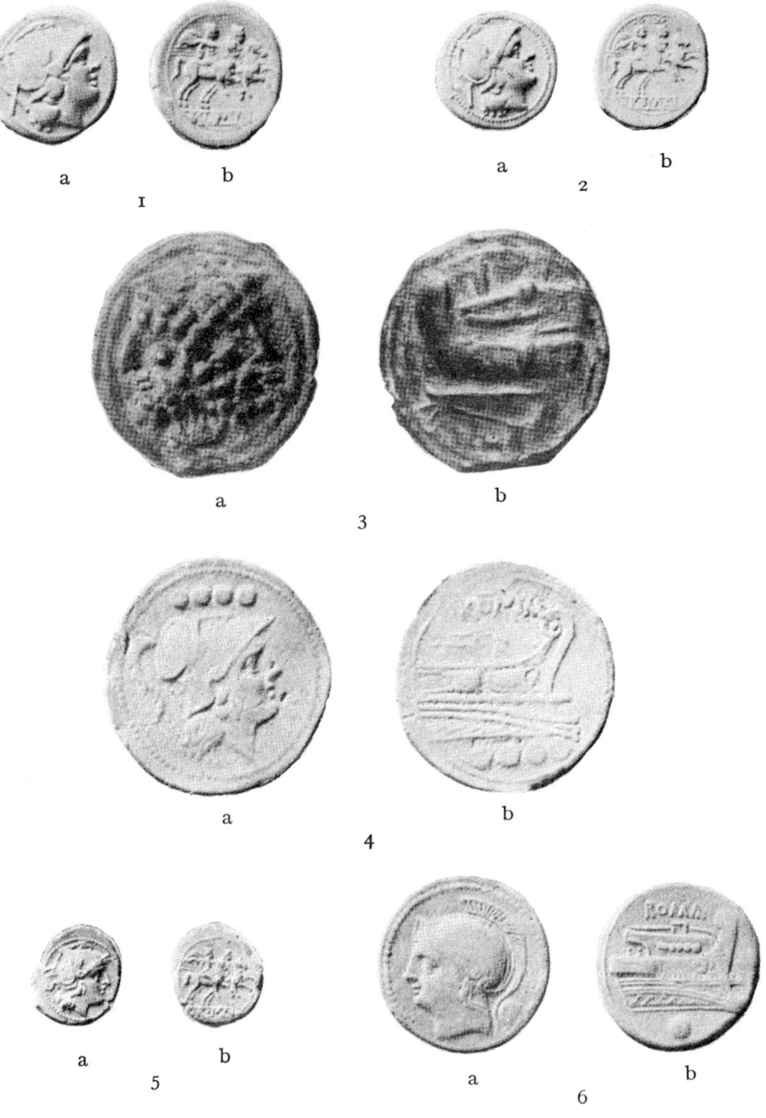

1 Silver *Denarius* bearing (a) Head of Roma with mark of value " X " to the left and (b) the Dioscuri.

2 Silver *Quinarius* bearing (a) Head of Roma with mark of value " V " to the left and (b) the Dioscuri.

3 Bronze *As* with (a) Head of Janus and (b) Prow of ship with mark of value " I " above.

4 Bronze *Triens* with (a) Head of Minerva with mark of value " ● ● ● ● " above and (b) Prow of ship.

5 Silver *Sestertius* bearing (a) Head of Roma with mark of value " IIS " to left and (b) The Dioscuri.

6 Bronze *Uncia* with (a) Roma and (b) Prow of ship with mark of value " ● " underneath.

[*face p.* 386

trade by adopting foreign units,[1] or that if they had they would not have established a unit closer to the Attic *drachm*.[2] They may have preferred a coin of about the size of the *drachm* on grounds of convenience, although it is considerably smaller than most of the famous coins of the ancient world. In fact, both physically as a coin and as a value unit, the *denarius* is unexpectedly small. The marks of value on the silver pieces were doubtless intended to fit the new coins definitely into the bronze system. The establishment of this bimetallic system, based on bronze and silver, was the most important step towards the unification of, on the one hand, the *as grave* coinage which had been the currency of the North and Central Italy during the Pyrrhic Wars, and, on the other, the silver coinage of Campania and Southern Italy. It gave the peoples of Italy their first uniform currency system. The continued use of the marks of value indicates a bimetallic system, although the currency ratio between the values of bronze and silver has, as we have seen, been placed at 1:120, 1:240 and 1:360.[3] It is generally supposed that whatever the ratio, it was also the market ratio, although none but indirect evidence is available, and in fact silver may have been over-valued.[4]

The main driving force behind the currency policy of 268 B.C. was doubtless the desire to consolidate the conquests which had just extended the Roman frontier to the southernmost toe and heel of the peninsula. To that end all the local mints in Italy were prohibited from issuing silver within the next few decades. Roman silver was to dominate Italy before the end of the century. Progress was at first a little slow. The *denarius* was not issued in great quantities, and the *quadrigatus* (worth 1½ *denarii*) continued to be the principal coin in the south.[5]

[1] *Vide infra*. They issued a special *victoratus* for South Italy and Dalmatia, but did not adjust their own system to it.

[2] The *denarius* weighed 70-72 grains, and the Attic *drachm* never more than 67·5 grains.

[3] Mattingly (*Num. Chron.*, 1924, 198) suggests that in practice it was about 1:360, although in law it was still 1:720.

[4] Mattingly, *loc. cit.*

[5] Mattingly, *Num. Chron.*, 1924, 191.

5. *The First Punic War.*

Between 268 and 240 B.C., the period mainly occupied by the first Punic War, changes are observable.[1] If the bronze *as* did not weigh so little as 2 ounces in 268 B.C., it fell to that weight by 240 B.C., and gold coins were issued. Because the fall in the *as* occurred at a time of war, it is plausible to suggest that it was a means of financial relief. If the *as* weighed 4 ounces in 268 B.C., it must have been halved during the first Punic War.[2] But if it weighed a pound in 268, it must have been reduced by five-sixths of its legal weight in 240 B.C.[3] But the reduction in practice was but a fraction of this because the coins were already below the pound in weight. The evidence of the actual effects of the reform gives some suggestions as to the intentions of the government. Festus,[4] although ascribing the reduction to the second instead of the first Punic War, says that the result of the change was that " when payments came to be made, both the Roman people would be freed from debt and private persons to whom a debt had to be paid by the state would not suffer much loss." Pliny[5] says that the reduction of the *as* to 2 ounces was made during the first Punic War at a time " when the resources of the commonwealth were inadequate to meet its expenditure." As to the effects of the alteration, he comments, " so five parts of it (the *as*) were gained, and the public debt was cancelled." Both writers believed that the reduction was from 12 to 2 ounces, while the coins indicate that the reduction was in reality much less. But the effect, rather than the amount of the reduction, is important. There is no warrant for believing that the number of *asses* to the *denarius* was changed during the first Punic War, and if the content of the *as* was reduced it must have become a token unless bronze was rapidly increasing in value—an alternative that may safely be dismissed. If the *as* became a token, its value remaining substantially unaltered, the

[1] Mommsen thought that no legal alteration was made until 217 B.C.

[2] Pliny (*Hist. Nat.*, XXXIII, 13) thought that a reduction was made during the first Punic War, but that it was from 12 to 2 ounces. Festus ascribed a similar reduction to the second Punic War (*De Verb. sig. S. V. Sextantarii*).

[3] Mattingly, *Num. Chron.*, 1924, 194.

[4] *De Verb. sig. S. V. Sextantarii.*

[5] *Hist. Nat.*, XXXIII, 13.

burden of debts in coined *asses*[1] was in no way diminished, but the state profited by being able to sell for the same price as before coins containing much less bronze.[2] But both writers refer to the effect on the public debt. Possibly the profit derived from the replacement of a full weight by a token coinage was applied to the repayment of the debt. But it is doubtful whether this profit would be great enough to bring any large relief, and even whether the coins became tokens at all. Moreover, so far as we know, the *as* was maintained in value during the next twenty-three years, in the face of considerable financial pressure imposed by war. Great restraint is necessary to prevent the over-issue of tokens under such circumstances, and for that reason it is more probable that the *asses* were full-weight coins and not tokens. The alternative is that the reduction in the weight of the *as* directly reduced the burden of the public debt. After 268 B.C. the common unit of account was the *sestertius*, although it is not clear whether the unit was the scruple of silver of which the *sestertius* coin was made or the $2\frac{1}{2}$ bronze *asses* to which it was equivalent.[3] If it was a silver unit[4] contracts expressed in *sestertii* would be unaffected by the reduction of the *as*. But if contracts were expressed in bronze units, originally and still legally libral *asses* or now legally reduced below 1 pound in weight, so long as the coined *as* was legal tender in payment of an *as* debt[5] a fall in the value of the *as* would relieve debtors.

[1] The change must have been comparable in its effects to the reduction of the amount of silver in the British shilling in 1920.

[2] This is presumably what Grueber (*op. cit.*, XXVII) has in mind when he writes that the reduction occurred " when the nation, drained by the demands of the Punic War, sought to recoup itself by lessening the weight of the bronze money. . . . It was a species of state bankruptcy, and its effect was to destroy the old relative value between silver and bronze, and reduce the latter to the condition of a token money."

[3] The official accounts for a considerable period after 268 B.C. were kept indifferently in *as grave* and *sestertii*, and presumably they were regarded as identical (Mommsen, II, 34). Mommsen thinks that the *sestertius* was intended to succeed the old pound of bronze as a *unit*, and that at the time of its establishment it was worth a pound of bronze. Sydenham (*Num. Chron.*, 1918, 168) asserts that in 268 B.C. " bronze was and continued to be the standard by which values were reckoned for the space of five hundred years."

[4] Lenormant, III, 22.

[5] If *as* coins passed by weight in settlement of debts in libral *asses*, no profit was to be made out of reducing the weight of the coin. If coins passed by weight the reduction in the weight of the coins offered no profit. Ridgeway (383) thought that until the first Punic War

If the bronze saved from the coins by the reduction in weight was minted, *asses* must have fallen in value roughly in proportion to the reduction in the value of their metallic content, and a proportionate reduction in the burden of debt was made unless old debts were translated into new *asses* at a rate which was calculated to compensate for the decline of the *as*. But the literary evidence we have examined gives no support to such a suggestion. When the *as* coin had fallen from 12 to 2 ounces the burden of the national debt had been reduced by five-sixths. But Pliny's comment that five parts were gained is justified so far as it applied to debt incurred when both coined *asses* and *asses* of account were of a full pound, which was probably for only a brief period. In 268 B.C. the coin cannot have weighed more than 6 ounces, and was probably no more than 4 ounces, and the relief from debts incurred immediately before or during the first Punic War must have been much less than five-sixths. The more the motive of profit is relied upon as an explanation of earlier reductions, the less is the amount of profit that can have induced those made later. It must be confessed also that this explanation can hardly be brought into sympathy with Festus's remark that "private persons to whom a debt had to be paid by the state would not suffer much loss," while it is rather too mild an explanation of Pliny's assertion that the

the *as* unit of account remained 12 ounces, but during the war the unit of account was reduced to the weight of the coins (*i.e.*, 2 ounces). If previously *as* coins had been accepted by weight in payment of the debt service, the motive of previous reductions is unexplained, for no profit can have been obtained, and the extent of the reduction is too great to be attributed to the badness of mint technique. The effect of the reduction would be concentrated at one point, the burden of the debt suddenly falling to one-sixth. Taxpayers would pay only one-sixth of the number of *asses* formerly necessary to meet the service of the debt, and debt-holders, on the other hand, would receive only one-sixth as many *as* coins as before. Prices would be somewhere about sixfold what they had been. But this would be of no practical importance, because the new prices would be stated in the coins in which they were paid, whereas formerly prices had to be multiplied by six to find the number of *as* coins that were required to pay them. So far as new bargains were concerned, no dislocation would occur; no increased quantity of currency would be called for so long as the size of the population and its methods of doing business remained unchanged. The parties to contracts subsisting at the time of the change would be the persons seriously affected, debtors, both state and private, gaining "five parts" or 80 per cent. of the debts, while lenders lost them. But the explanation in the text seems more reasonable, as it can be applied to earlier reductions as well.

public debt was cancelled. Perhaps he thought that a dividend of 3s. 4d. in the £ approached closely enough to repudiation to justify his term; or the passage may only mean that it became possible to discharge the debt. Probably neither Pliny nor Festus understood quite what happened. Pliny, the older and the principal witness, wrote over three centuries after the event.[1]

Finally, if it is to be argued that the *as* fell both in weight and value between 268 and 240 B.C., it must be explained why its value in *denarii* did not fall, for there is no evidence that the *denarius* was worth more than 10 *asses* in 240. The best explanation is that when the bimetallic system was set up in 268 B.C., silver was over-valued, and subsequent reductions in the bronze coins eliminated the effects of over-valuation and prevented bronze from being melted and exported.[2] During this period from 268 to 240 B.C., if the *as* weighed more than 2 ounces in 268 B.C., it was reduced to 2 ounces during the first Punic War. It is unlikely that the *as* became a token: its value fell roughly in proportion to its weight. The policy of the state was probably aimed at obtaining a profit from the currency both by way of recoinage profit, but more particularly relief in the burden of debts. As silver coins were not important in Rome until the second Punic War, and as also it is possible that in 268 B.C. silver was overvalued, we may glide quickly over the difficulty that, although the *as* is supposed to have fallen in value, it did not fall in terms of *denarii*. But if the *as* had already fallen to 2 ounces by 268, there was no further fall during the first Punic War to discuss. It is probable that this was the true state of affairs, but in view of the vagueness of the evidence as to the dates of the reductions in the value of the *as* it would be foolish to dogmatize upon them. It is quite probable that the war did call forth attempts to manipulate the currency. Perhaps the coins which had previously been taken by weight were now taken by tale in payment of debts in *asses*. Such a measure would reduce by five-sixths the burden of debt service previously paid in 2-ounce *asses* at six to the *as* unit of account and thereafter at par.

The issue of gold coins which was probably made at this

[1] Festus did not write until the 4th century .D.

[2] Mattingly, *Num. Chron.*, 1924, 198.

time has more emphatically the appearance of war-time finance. Although there were precedents for coining gold in Campania, Etruria, and many of the cities of Magna Græcia, it had never been minted in Rome. Moreover, the marks of value on the coins suggest that gold was overvalued in coins.[1] They were clearly a token issue made in an emergency, with a view partly to realizing gold reserves, and partly to getting 30 or 40 per cent. more for them than could be had in the metal market. The Athenians had seen that the striking and issue of gold coins was an excellent means of realizing some of the state treasure in time of financial stress. But the Romans improved upon the Greek policy: by giving gold a monetary status, they not only found an additional source of demand for it, but having a monopoly in the satisfaction of that particular demand for the metal, they also extorted a monopoly profit.

6. *The Second Punic War.*

Between 240 and 217 B.C. the control of policy, the types, and the material of the coinage remained unchanged. Silver *denarii* had neither been very popular nor very plentifully issued, but the *quadrigati* made outside Rome were widely used, and in about 230 B.C. were succeeded by the *victoriatus* of one-half the value of the *quadrigatus*, and issued in Rome. The standard of the coinage as a whole seems to have been imperfectly preserved, both silver[2] and bronze showing a persistent tendency to small reduction. In 217 B.C., when the state was hard-pressed by the war with Hannibal—in fact, when Hannibal had crossed the Apennines and was marching on Rome—the difficulty of financing the war, and particularly of finding funds for the soldiers' pay, led to a financial crisis. Resort was had to remedies more drastic than ever before. The whole of the people voting in *comitia* passed the Lex Flaminia by which the *as* was halved in weight, it being now reduced to about 420 grains, or only one-twelfth of a pound.

[1] Grueber (*op. cit.*, LIV) remarks of the over-tariffing of gold that it "is what would be expected, whether the coinage was instituted after the first Punic War or during the progress of the second one. It was of the nature of fiduciary money, or 'money of necessity,' which the state could at any time redeem at its current value."

[2] Sydenham, *Num. Chron.*, 1918, 169

The *denarius* was reduced by some 14 per cent. to about 60 grains ($3\frac{1}{2}$ scruples), and the legal relation between the value of the *as* and the *denarius* was altered to 16 *asses* to the *denarius*.

In the first place this law established a currency ratio between bronze and silver of 1 : 112. If the ratio in 240 B.C. was 1 : 120, the Lex Flaminia made little change in the currency ratio. If the *as* was previously a full-weight coin it may have now become token, although the margin is so narrow as to make it more probable that it continued a full-weight coin. If the *as* had been reduced to a token in 240 B.C., it was now a little more token than before. But it is surprising that, if the coin was a token, when its weight was reduced its value was correspondingly reduced, especially if on one occasion already its weight had been halved without reducing its value.[1] Mommsen's theory that there was no legal reduction between 269 and 217 B.C., and that the ratio between the market values of bronze and silver was 1 : 240 or 250 merely shifts to 217 B.C. the conversion of bronze coins into tokens ascribed by Grueber to not later than 240 B.C. Although he recognized quite clearly that the Romans were doing no more than the Greeks had done two hundred years before, to the obvious improvement of their coinage system,[2] subsequent writers[3] have wept too copiously and too loudly

[1] This renders somewhat improbable the suggestion that the *as* became token in 240 B.C., and yet twenty-three years later reduction was effected in the same way as in 269 B.C., when it was admittedly not a token. In fact, so far as bronze was concerned, the alteration of 217 B.C., reducing both the silver value and the weight of the *as* in almost equal proportions, is similar to those prior to 240 B.C.

[2] "It is certain that the old Roman idea of considering copper as a precious metal gave way to the Greek idea of considering it as no more than representative of value in silver (Mommsen, II, 73).

[3] Sir John Lubbock (*Journal of Institute of Bankers*, I, 16) says it "recognized a new principle that 'the coin was a sign,'" which "unfortunate error naturally opened the door to further debasement." Lenormant (III, 23) stigmatized it as the only act during the "beaux ages" of the Republic which constituted a real alteration of the money, attempting to give to it an arbitrary and conventional value other than its bullion value. Lenormant regretted it at considerable length, although he was not at all clear about its provisions. He repudiated the idea that the *as* was made a token, and assumed on one occasion that it was the *denarius* that lost its full value status, and yet he was of two minds whether its weight was changed at all by the law. Adopted as a last resort in a time of necessity, when there was no choice of means, this law "remained a fatal precedent on which to base 'la doctrine de la monnaie *signe*,'" the theory that a legislative decision sufficed

over what they arraign as the most deplorable of all Roman currency laws and the beginning of all Roman currency manipulation. They seem to think it is inexpressibly more reprehensible for the state to economize by reducing the weight of the coins while so restricting the supply that the value of the coins shall not fall, than to reduce the weight of the coins and let their value fall in rough proportion. Reductions of the latter type were responsible for the fall of the *as* from 12 to 2 ounces, and were in part merely currency inflation. But it is very probable that the bronze coins remained full-weight coins after 217 B.C. In fact, the changes, so far as they altered the currency ratio between the metals, may have been aimed at the preservation of the bimetallic system then over half a century old.

The silver *denarius* was reduced 14 per cent.[1] in weight, and as the government can have been in no mood to restrict the issue and maintain a token silver coinage, silver prices probably rose, and the value of the *denarius* fell about 14 per cent. The *as* was halved in weight, and we have seen that copper coins were not made tokens, so copper prices must have risen about 100 per cent. There is no record of the translation debts incurred before the change into an increased number of new units, and it must be presumed that they were settled in new reduced coins at par. Again, debtors benefited and creditors were penalized. Those whose debts were payable only in *denarii* gained about 14 per cent. of their debt, while those who were committed to pay in *asses* gained 50 per cent.[2] The importance of these changes depends

---

to give to metallic money a fictitious and arbitrary value. This idea spread to the aristocratic party, which became powerful in the direction of affairs, and the vicious principle that the state had the right to use its power to alter the monetary standard as an ordinary source of revenue became part of their political and financial programme. Not only did they cause serious perturbations in the monetary system of their time, but "they introduced into the world an erroneous principle, the consequences of which are even yet felt after many centuries." Had Lenormant been writing, not in 1878, but forty years or more later, his regrets would doubtless have been keener (*vide* Lenormant, III, 26; Babelon, 408).

[1] And also the *victoriatus*.

[2] If the debts were incurred before 217 B.C., but at a time when the coins had already begun to shrink, the gain was somewhat less than that above stated. Pliny commented on this change that "a profit of one-half was realized by the Republic." This may refer to the gain on

upon the units of account in most common use. So far as contracts were expressed in metal by weight, whether pounds of bronze or libral *asses* used by the state, or scruples of silver used in commerce, the devaluation left the relations between debtor and creditor untouched. Bronze *asses* were, certainly, used as a unit of account. The pay of the troops was expressed in them but, apparently, paid in *denarii*, for the Lex Flaminia provided that, although the *denarius* was in future to be legal tender for 16 *asses*, in paying the troops it was to count only as 10 *asses*.[1] It may have been on this account that the *as* continued[2] to be marked "X." The soldier was saved from the halving of debts in *asses* to which the rest of the population was subjected. Doubtless his satisfaction at this special regulation in his favour diverted his attention from the loss of one-seventh in the weight, no doubt also in the value, of the *denarius*. There was by this time a general tendency to use silver more and bronze less as a unit of account. Familiarity with the use of silver bullion may have induced commercial men to use silver coin, and the fear that former reductions of the *as* would be repeated, probably caused a transference of favour from bronze coins to silver. The latter may even explain why the *denarius* was reduced. But the reduction is also explained by the fact that the Romans were becoming more familiar with silver issues. It was not until the second Punic War that the silver *denarius* was of any great importance as a coin. No very plentiful issues were made until then,[3] although for another thirty or forty years copper remained the most important currency. If there was any such tendency to use silver units of account instead of copper, the Lex Flaminia must have seriously dislocated the commerce of the time. The reduction of the *denarius* was altogether more serious than any of the previous reductions of the *as*, for the latter probably had little effect on the business world.

The state must have benefited out of the inflation by reason of both the lag in prices behind the increased issues of coin,

---

the recoinage of copper pieces, or the gain on state debts expressed in *asses*, if the unit of account was again reduced; he makes no reference to the effects of the simultaneous reduction of silver pieces.

[1] The annual pay of a soldier was at this time 1,200 *asses*, and this continued to be paid in *denarii* at 10 *asses* to the *denarius*, so he continued to get 120 *denarii*.

[2] Until about 140 B.C.

[3] Mattingly, *Num. Chron.*, 1924, 194.

and the reduction of the burden of debts in both metals.[1] In view of the great financial straits in which the government found itself, it is reasonable to infer that these profits made out of the adjustment of the currency were its principal aim.[2] The changes constituted nothing more than a war-time inflation, with perhaps a gesture of affection for the bimetallic system in the alteration of the currency ratio between the values of the two metals to prevent a divergence between the coinage and market ratios from bringing the system to the ground. The new standards adopted were probably based upon the estimates of contemporary politicians as to the amount of inflation that the people would tolerate. The halving of bronze was now hallowed by tradition. The final and most convincing touch to this essentially war-time financial policy was the issue by the state of silver-plated copper coins among the *denarii*. These coins were obviously intended to pass as *denarii*, and they constituted a debasement of the currency

[1] It is possible that some profits were made on the recoinage of *asses*. The effect of the announcement that new small *asses* were to be worth only one-sixteenth of a *denarius* depends on the previous status of these coins. If they were still full-weight pieces, holders of heavy *asses* would be unwilling to exchange them at par for light *asses*. They would sell them as metal, and no profits on recoinage can have been gained. If the old *asses* had become tokens in 240 B.C., as the currency ratio was then halved, they cannot have contained more than one-half of their legal value in silver. They cannot, therefore, have been worth as bullion more than ($\frac{1}{2} \times \frac{1}{10} \times 72$) grains of silver, or 3·60 grains. The new *asses* were to be worth as currency one-sixteenth of 60 grains, or about 3·75 grains. Assuming no change in the market values of the two metals, holders would suffer no loss by handing in old *asses* and taking new ones half their weight in return. The state would thus be able to obtain for one new light *as* enough raw material for two more, and thus secure profits on recoinage.

[2] It has been suggested that there was no sudden reduction in the weight of the *as* in 217 B.C., but that ever since the reform of 268 B.C. the moneyers were gradually reducing the amount of metal in the coin. The state of the coins certainly suggests this. The Flaminian Law was in this event " aimed less at altering the weight of the money than at putting a stop to the successive and arbitrary reductions made by the moneyers " (Mommsen, II, 157). The motive of the reduction then lay in the small but continuous profit derived by the moneyers, mainly from the lag of prices behind the ever-falling metallic value of the *as*. But this would have led in the course of time to different levels in prices in *asses* and *denarii*, in the *as* being valued at less than one-tenth of a *denarius*. Of this nothing is known. The new weight of the *as* may in this event have been fixed at about the level to which the coins had, in fact, sunk. The new weight of the *denarius* may have a similar basis, or it may be that a devaluation of 14 per cent. was the maximum which, in the judgment of the contemporary politicians, the public would stand.

made more effective because of the uncertainty whether any specific coin was good or bad,[1] and by the fact that, as the coin wore all its sterling metal upon its outside, it put up a deceptively good appearance, at least until it was well clear of the mint. There can be no disputing that such coins were issued for profit, and were a means of inflation. The importance of the device lay rather in its potentiality for evil than in any great harm known of it at this time; there are no records of the effect of the issue, or, more particularly, whether the plated coins remained tokens or fell to their commodity value. With the Carthaginian army at the very gates of Rome, the resources of the Republic at their last ebb, and revolt on every hand, the financial administration could not discriminate nicely in their policy between "sound" and "unsound" devices, but within two or three hundred years, under the pressure often of nothing more than incompetence and profligacy, this mean inflation was to bring about the complete collapse of the Roman currency. Although the issue was made as a result of authority given by vote in *comitia*, the decision was doubtless made at a time of panic and in ignorance of the possibility of raising funds by other means. Everything points to an effort to deceive the public at least for a long enough period to enable the mint to get rid of its base productions. This was doubtless due partly to lack of acquaintance on the part of the public in early days with token money, and the fear that it would either reject them or take them at a discount in good coin. To force the people to accept such pieces from the mint was probably less possible in republican days than in the age of tyrants preceding the fall of the Republic or in the empire which succeeded it.

The issue of serrated coins in about 217 B.C. may have been due to the influence of the democratic party which opposed the plating of coins, and the fact that the Gauls preferred the old silver coin and could not be forced to accept the plated pieces. In consequence, the coins were serrated to reveal the presence of any plated pieces,[2] although at least in later years even plated coins were serrated.

[1] It was a blend of the lottery principle with that of coinage debasement, although no prizes were offered. The most that a holder could hope was that he would escape loss.

[2] Mattingly, *Num. Chron.*, 1924, 45.

7. *The Second Century B.C.*

Between 217 B.C. and 91 B.C. policy remained unchanged in the matter of the coinage metals and standards,[1] although in fact after the first one or two decades of the 2nd century silver issues became plentiful. Towards the middle of the century the mint ceased to issue *asses*, and the remaining bronze coins sank below even the much-reduced standard of 217 B.C. According to law, the coinage consisted of full-weight coins, but in fact it was probably a silver monometallic system with bronze tokens for small change. The most notable changes during the period were in the appearance of the coins and in the monetary administration. In the later years of the 3rd century these changes suggest merely a strengthening of central control still exercised according to republican forms. Since 268 B.C. branch mints had been opened and strictly controlled by the Senate, but towards the end of the century all coining was concentrated in Rome. Senatorial control of the mint was at the same time increased by the appointment of Mint Commissioners, independent of the chief magistrate, and responsible direct to the Senate. The Senate saw that the decisions of the people in matters of monetary policy were duly executed. The change was part of a campaign to preserve democratic institutions and prevent

[1] About 140 B.C., a few years after the third Punic War, the *denarius* was marked "XVI" for about fifteen years, and then X̶, which "was not an equivalent of 'XVI' but only 'X' differentiated as a denominational mark" (Mattingly, XLVIII). Grueber (*op. cit.*, XLI) remarks that "it is a remarkable circumstance that the authorities are silent on this important change in the weight of the *denarius*. Silver was substituted for bronze in all commercial regulations, and, in consequence, this new law constituted a fresh depreciation of 37½ per cent." But in his catalogue of coins he does not show any reduction in the weight of the *denarius*. And in fact there is no ground for the suggestion; the *denarius* continued without any change in weight to the end of the Republic. If the same weight of silver became worth 10 instead of 16 *denarii*, and neither was altered in weight, it may be that the purchasing power of silver was falling, or that of copper was rising. In either event the relative value of silver was falling, and the new currency ratio may have been established to bring it into line with the new market ratio. Grueber thinks silver was falling in purchasing power, but there seems to be no evidence of this. A third explanation is possible, that the *as* was becoming a token with a currency value above its bullion value. It is more likely (as Grueber himself assumes elsewhere, 32) that the *as* continued as one-sixteenth of a *denarius*, and that the use of the sign "XVI" on the coins denotes the final disappearance of the reckoning of the *denarius* as 10 *asses* (Mattingly, XLVIII, n.).

unhealthy growth of the powers of the chief magistrate: the machinery of organization was borrowed from Athens. But during the 2nd century the appearance of the coins, and the organization of the mint, clearly reflect a shift of power within the Republic. The constitution still vested the right of decision in monetary matters in the whole body of citizens, but in practice the Mint Commissioners obtained considerable power over the issues. The marks upon the coins at the end of the 3rd century may indicate the emergence of oligarchical government, but more probably they were merely the means by which the Senate fixed responsibility for the issue of each coin. The main types on the coins until this time were directly in the Greek tradition with its taste for the representation of the gods and the rigid exclusion of the effigy of any living person from the coins. But during the 2nd century tradition was steadily undermined. Traditional types were first occasionally replaced by others, apparently harmless, which may well be explained as a revolt from the mechanical repetition of ancient types. But from the middle of the century, and after the last Punic War, reverse patterns changed with each moneyer. The people, in fact, surrendered to the moneyers, or rather the moneyers seized the privilege of selecting types. After a time a personal motive of increasing directness appeared. Down to the end of the Social War, in 88 B.C., mythological types, bearing reference to the more creditable episodes in the history of the moneyers' families, were the fashion. At the same time the moneyers' marks, which had in the 3rd century been but humble crests and monograms, blossomed into full names. It is notable that while the moneyers took advantage of the declining power of the Senate there is no evidence of either depreciation or debasement of the money. They sought no economic gain, but were content with a little swaggering family advertisement. Some twenty years before the Social War the Senate also began to undermine the democratic control of policy; it commenced the practice of making issues of money without the authority of the people or the assistance of the monetary magistrates. During this period such issues were confined to periods of emergency, but they were later to develop into a device of more regular use.

8. *The Social War and the Collapse of the Republic.*

The Lex Papiria, passed under the financial strain of the Social War of 91-89 B.C. and the struggle with Mithridates, was but an episode in this decline of democratic institutions. Nevertheless, it indicated the limitations upon the power of the Mint Commissioners. The new law, which authorized a reduction of the *as* to one-half, and the issue of plated coin, was passed by a general assembly of citizens. As the Act authorized the reduction of the weight of the bronze coins by one-half without any reduction in their value, the coinage ratio of bronze to silver was raised to 56: 1, a ratio admittedly far above any that can have prevailed in the market. For the first time the bronze coinage became legally token, although we have already seen that it was probably token in practice nearly a century earlier. The adoption of the silver standard by law was probably no more than an adjustment of the law to the facts. If this was so, although the change was made during the war, it cannot be explained as a device for yielding a profit to finance the campaign. This it probably was not. The profit to be obtained by reducing the *as* from one to half an ounce cannot have been great. The reason for the coincidence of the reduction with the war lies probably in the fact that considerable supplies of bronze coins were required, more particularly for the war with Mithridates. No *asses* had been issued for sixty years, and the smaller denominations had not been abundantly supplied, and as fresh issues were to be made on a fairly large scale, it was thought desirable to amend the law to authorize the issue of coins on the standard of those that had recently been issued.[1] The profit motive was present

[1] Mommsen (II, 73, n.) and Hill (*Historical Roman Coins*, 90) think that the weight of the *as* was reduced to assimilate it to the local Italian copper issues. The Lex Papiria extended the franchise, with the result that local Italian copper issues were suspended. It is argued that as many cities had already coined half-ounce *asses*, the Lex Papiria reduced the Roman *as* to the same weight in order to facilitate the introduction of Roman coins. But this is, in fact, no explanation. If the local issues were tokens worth one-sixteenth of a Roman *denarius*, the Roman *as* of twice the weight of the local *asses* could quite easily have circulated side by side with them, and at the same value, or could have superseded them.

If the local coins were full weight, they must have been worth only half as much as a Roman *as*, and reducing the weight of the latter without reducing its value in silver would not bring it into line with local issues.

in a most blatant form, however in the clauses of the Act permitting the issue of one silver plated coin with every seven genuine silver coins, an authority of which the magistrates took full advantage.[1] Cicero's remark, that "the value of money was so fluctuating that no one could tell how much he was worth,"[2] suggests that the plated pieces did not pass for the same value as silver *denarii*, and that two price levels existed, one in base and one in good *denarii*.[3]

The period from the close of the Social War to Cæsar's entry into Rome is full of change. The popular power to control monetary policy persisted in law, but was never again exercised. From 89 B.C. the Mint Commissioners openly seized control of monetary types, adding their honours to their full names on the coins, and removing the name of the goddess Roma and the last vestiges of the traditional types. They used both sides of the coins for the effusive expression of personal pride by the representation of contemporary events. The right of family advertisement upon the coins was even let out to private persons after the triumph of Sulla in 81 B.C. The Senate allowed *curule ædiles* to issue money bearing such types as they might select. In return for the privilege the *ædiles* bore the whole cost of the issue, apart from the cost of the metal. During the thirty years between 81 and 50 B.C., some twenty-five such issues were made, many recording the celebration of public games,[4] which were probably the occasion of their issue. Senatorial issues, made without popular authority, became increasingly frequent and large during this period as the popular prerogative sank into the background. The Lex Julia, passed in 90 B.C., granted the right of citizenship to all those states that had remained loyal to Rome in the Social War, and the Lex Plautia Papiria of the next year extended the privilege (with limitations) to all Italy, with the result that all local mints in Italy[5] were closed.

In consequence of the difficulty of financing the army, military commanders were granted, in 91 B.C., power to issue

[1] Lenormant, III, 26. [2] Ciœro, *De Officiis*, III, 20.

[3] It is possible, however, that the plated pieces remained tokens, circulating above their value as metal.

[4] Grueber, LXXII.

[5] Since the latter half of the 3rd century local mints had coined bronze.

coins. No limitation was imposed as to the metal to be used, and from the time of Sulla generals occasionally issued gold coins in the provinces. In appearance these coins followed the style of those of the Roman Mint Commissioners; they bore types that recalled memorable events in the life of the issuer, but never his portrait. This coinage, which was the foundation upon which the whole imperial system was built, embodied two important new elements, the delegation of the power to issue money, and the use of a new monetary material. The first gold pieces were, however, more in the nature of victory medals distributed to the successful troops,[1] and the choice of metals is probably explained by the nature of the booty of the victors. Allied and subject peoples were never allowed to issue gold. As in Persia and Macedon, it was regarded as an imperial monopoly. The original weight standard was probably the 10-scruple unit that was used in early times in Etruria. But it was soon equated to 25 *denarii*, and its weight was reduced to keep it in circulation at that rate. To the end of the republic the Roman moneyers made no attempt to secure any great profit out of their control of the coinage. The weight of the silver coins remained untouched, although the copper sank quickly in weight, *asses* weighing as little as one-eighth of an ounce being issued,[2] and after seven years the issue of copper ceased altogether, never to recommence under the Republic. Attempts to use the control of the currency as a source of profit took the form of debasement by the issue of plated coins, upon the wisdom of which there seems to have been a division of opinion. Sulla and his party made full use of the device, but Marius and the democrats, in their traditional opposition[3] to plated money, favoured serrated coins. When Marius seized Rome

[1] The first three issues can all be identified with the termination of wars. Sulla's issue in Greece and Asia Minor celebrated the successful issue of the war against Mithradates VI of Pontus, those of 72 B.C. (rare) the close of the Sertorian War, and those of Pompey in 61 B.C. the close of the third Mithradatic War (Grueber, LVII).

[2] Mommsen, II, 73. During the sixty-five years between the cessation of copper coinage in 82 B.C., and its resumption under Augustus, the value of the *as* must have fallen considerably. At the earlier date, the copper coins ranged from the *as* to one-sixth of an *as*, while in the opening years of the empire they ranged from the *sestertius* ($2\frac{1}{2}$ *asses*) to the quarter-*as*. But they probably remained token coins (Mattingly, XLVI).

[3] Mattingly (*Num. Chron.*, 1924, 44) suggests that their opposition was as old as the first issue of plated coins (217 B.C.).

in 87 B.C., the currency was in great confusion owing to the Sullan issues, and three years later Gratidianus either redeemed in good coin the Sullan plated issues, or arranged means by which they could be distinguished from the bad.[1] Possibly the serrated coins issued at this time were a Marian issue, the serration being regarded as a guarantee of the homogeneity of the coin.[2] If these coins are identified with the democrats and the round plated pieces with the aristocrats, the discontinuity of each series can be explained. When Sulla drove the Marians from Italy in 82 B.C., plated coins reappeared, and issues continued until the middle of the century. Sulla, although he is said to have used with moderation the power to issue base coins,[3] endeavoured to regularize it in law. The Lex Cornelia provided that the only base money which might be refused was that of counterfeiters; that which issued from the State Mint and bore its official stamp had to be accepted under severe penalties without argument, whatever its weight and fineness.[4] This was, indeed, an attempt to secure recognition of the doctrine that the value of coins should depend on the laws, and not on the content of the coins, and ignored altogether the fundamental factor of the quantity of coins issued. The currency was now the recognized victim of any impecunious tyrant.

The effects of currency manipulation at this time must have fallen mainly upon the private citizen. Wholesale trade, by basing its transactions upon a unit weight of uncoined metal, took shelter from political storms, and freed itself from the uncertainty of government action. Coins were used only for day-to-day transactions and private debts. But in 86 B.C., during the Marian reign of terror, the *sestertius* unit of account was abolished, and debts thus expressed were made payable at par in *asses* of one-sixteenth of a *denarius*.[5] This was yet another way of relieving debtors at the expense of creditors, for where 4 *sestertii* had been lent, only one was to be repaid. Although it relieved much social tension, the law was followed by effects more serious than had been anticipated, and four years later it was repealed by Sulla

[1] Pliny, *Hist. Nat.* XXXIII, 9, 46.

[2] Grueber (I, 159) objects that it can, in fact, have been no such guarantee, because plated coins were serrated.

[3] Lenormant, III, 27.

[4] Lenormant, *loc. cit.*

[5] Mommsen, II, 75.

on his return to Rome.[1] What happened to those whose debts were repaid within this four years is not recorded. The confusion following the repeal may account for the cessation of the issue of bronze.[2] During this period of political intrigue, with the weakening of the republican spirit and the succession of one personal tyrant by another, the monetary policy ceased to be that of the people. The Senate lost control, and the currency became the common prey of the chief magistrates, military commanders, and the Commissioners of the Mint.

Julius Cæsar carried the destruction of the republican system one stage further. When he entered Rome after his triumphs in Gaul, he assumed much of the prerogative of an Emperor in the control of money. He assumed the power to issue money in Rome, although it was never conferred upon him. He seized the Senatorial Mint, but afterwards handed back to the Senate the right to coin silver. He revived, after a lapse of 200 years, the coining of gold in Rome, and established a mint for the production of gold coins, the cost of the maintenance of which was regarded as part of his household expenses. His first issue was, like the provincial gold coinages of the earlier part of the century, at least partly in the nature of a division of the booty from Gaul (and also from the temple of Saturn in Rome) among his successful troops. But the reductions in the weight of the *aureus* suggest either a small measure of deception or an attempt to secure a weight which, at the market ratio between the values of gold and silver, would give the *aureus* a value of 25 *denarii*. Cæsar was making the first attempts to replace the silver monometallic currency with a gold and silver bimetallism.[3] The helplessnes of the Senate in the face of this invasion of its legal prerogative is obvious in the apparent absence of any protest against the

[1] Wells (*Outline of History*, 313) says that Sulla, although he restored the Senate to power and repealed many of the recent laws, was unable to repeal this.

[2] Grueber, XXXII.

[3] Mommsen (III, 19) suggested that Cæsar's intention in coining gold on the basis of an *aureus* of 126·7 grains was to replace the gold *staters* of Philip of Macedon. These pieces weighed originally 133·5 grains, but being now three hundred years old must have been much worn and reduced in weight, although they circulated widely throughout Europe. The weight chosen is, however, but one in a series which was steadily falling, and such agreement as can be found with the Macedonian *stater* is probably a coincidence.

PLATE XV

SOME ROMAN REPUBLICAN COINS OF THE PERIOD FROM THE FIRST PUNIC WAR TO THE END OF THE REPUBLIC

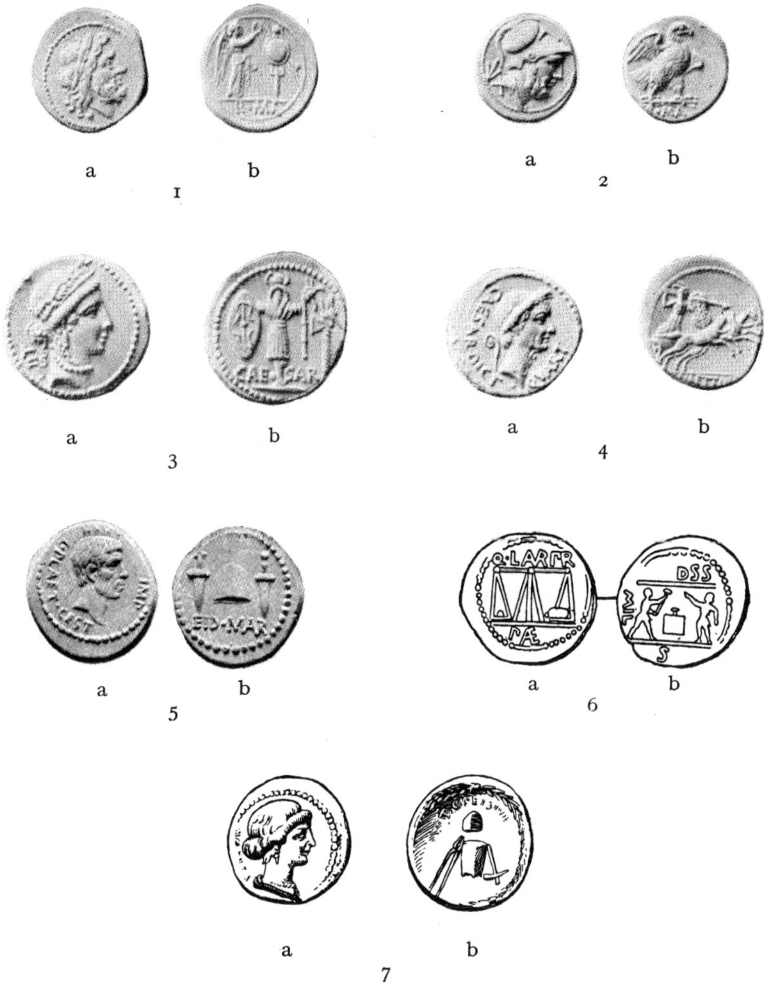

1 Silver *Victoriatus* of 229-217 B.C. bearing (a) Head of Jupiter and (b) figure of Victory with inscription " ROMA " below.

2 Gold Piece of 60 *sestertii* issued during or shortly after the first Punic War bearing (a) Head of Mars with mark of value " ↓X " to left and (b) Eagle with inscription " ROMA " below.

3 *Aureus* of Julius Cæsar bearing (a) Head of Pietas and (b) Trophy of Gallic arms.

4 Silver *denarius* bearing (a) Head of Julius Cæsar and (b) Juno Sospita in a biga.

5 A Silver *denarius* of Brutus bearing (a) Head of Brutus and (b) pointed reference to the assassination of Cæsar in the cap of liberty and inscription " Ides of March " as well as in the dagger.

6 A Bronze Coin of Pæstum, a Roman colony in Lucania illustrating the method of coining in the last Century B.C.

7 Roman Silver *denarius* of about 48 B.C. bearing (a) Head of Juno Moneta and (b) the chief Implements employed in striking Money, the Tongs, the Dies and the Hammer.

issue of gold by Cæsar, and in the subsequent grant to him of authority to place his own effigy upon the coins. This latter was the most obvious departure from Greek and Roman republican tradition. The only portraits of living persons that had hitherto appeared upon coins had, ominously enough, been those of Emperors and Kings in Persia, Macedonia, and the empires into which the Macedonian was partitioned on the death of Alexander the Great. If his reduction of the *aureus* be explained as part of a bimetallic policy, Julius Cæsar was a believer in a stable metallic standard. He did not alter the weight of the silver coins, and he probably indulged in no debasement by issuing plated coins. In fact, he has been credited with redeeming base coins already in circulation.[1] Moreover, he made some effort to produce a more satisfactory series of denominations than those current during the previous thirty years, reviving the bronze *as* and the silver *quinarius* and *sestertius*, as well as instituting the *aureus* and its half. He realized the inadequacy and unsuitability of the Roman system to the conditions of the extending territory of the Republic, and aimed at a much improved system, based, at least in the beginning, on gold and silver bimetallism. Lastly, he abolished the ridiculous anomaly of a *denarius* equal to 16 *asses* in civilian bargains and 10 in military pay. When he increased the pay of the troops, he continued to use the *as* as the unit of account, but it was the *as* of one-sixteenth of a *denarius* current for all other purposes.[2]

The remaining years of the Republic were occupied with internecine conflict, finally giving way to imperial power. From about 37 B.C. the coinage ceased to be republican. The names of the Mint Commissioners disappeared: presumably Octavius took over the control of the mint, and suspended the Commissioners appointed by the now moribund Senate. The coinage was the personal issue of Octavius, for the first ten years as Cæsar, and thereafter as Augustus.

[1] Mommsen, II, 84.

[2] The pay of a soldier was raised from 1,200 to 3,000 *asses*, which meant that the soldier received 188 *denarii* instead of 120.

9. *Summary*

Before passing on to the coinage of the first 300 years of the empire, we may look back over the last 300 years of the Republic. The economic was probably the dominant motive behind the very striking changes in the metallic basis of the medium of exchange and unit of value. The pound of bronze of the 4th century B.C. was superseded at the close of the Republic by a silver coinage, with gold rapidly qualifying to be a monetary medium coequal to, if not supplanting, silver. The need for a portable currency was due to the widening territory of the Republic and the increasing volume of trade and administration. Political changes account for the transfer of the control of the currency from the people to their rulers: for after the attacks upon the prerogative by the Senate, the moneyers, and the military commanders, the control of policy could no longer be said to remain in the hands of the people. It was ready for whomsoever had power to capture it. The Romans, under the Republic, conducted fairly exhaustive experiments in elucidation of the Greek heritage of knowledge of the means to profit out of the coinage by devaluation and debasement. War was the principal cause: the wars of the 3rd century, and those of the early years of the last century B.C., saw the most important experiments. During the last century B.C., the law was adjusted to remove any hindrance to the full exercise of the privilege of debasement, which every tyrant felt to be excused by his need if not justified by right. The stage was set for the monetary follies of the next three centuries.

CHAPTER XVI

MONETARY POLICY IN THE ROMAN EMPIRE

1. *The Policy of Augustus and his Immediate Successors.*

OCTAVIUS secured personal control of the currency in about 37 B.C., when he suspended the Mint Commissioners and issued in his own name. But there was a period of vacillation before he seized the coinage prerogative openly and definitely. In 23 B.C. he restored to the Senate the right to coin bronze.[1] Six years later he also restored the right to issue gold and silver, and for a time it appeared that the control of the currency was reverting to its position under the later Republic. The Mint Commissioners were again in control, and placed their marks upon the coins. But after four years the Senatorial issues of gold and silver were suspended. Even then, however, Augustus was not prepared to make a clean and obvious break with the republican tradition, and he fell back upon the right of military commanders to issue money in the provinces, and opened a mint at Lugdunum (Lyons), from which he issued all his coins. He followed Cæsar's example in placing his effigy upon the coins, and the right of representation upon the money for himself, or, occasionally, for a member of his family, became thenceforward a recognized part of the Emperor's prerogative. Augustus also swept away the surviving distinction between the free allies and subject states of Rome, with the result that local silver issues ceased in all colonies outside Italy. He concentrated in the Emperor the sole right of issuing gold and silver for the whole of the empire. Authority to issue bronze was given as a normal right to local authorities. In Italy the Senate, bereft of the right to make gold and silver coins, became the authority for the issue of small change, although even in that humble capacity it was subject to some control by the Emperor. This division of powers between Senate and

[1] Macdonald, 48.

Emperor in Italy was probably a mere adaptation of the traditional imperial policy of keeping the issue of the principal coins in the hands of the supreme political power, while leaving to local authorities the supply of the small change money necessary for petty local transactions. Nevertheless, it was important that the only portion of the currency which yielded a legitimate profit was in the hands of the Senate and of the local authorities, which were much less likely than the Emperor to increase the bronze issues and bring down their value.[1] They did not feel directly the financial pressure of the empty treasury, and would not themselves profit by manipulating the coinage. Moreover, the results of over-issue would affect them very closely as citizens, and such results could be easily brought home to them as senators or local officials by the populace. In consequence, the bronze money was well-preserved for more than 200 years, and the Emperors, driven by their need for funds to resort to the debasement of the money under their control, concentrated attention for the most part on the silver coins, through which, and not through the bronze tokens,[2] the downfall of the currency was manipulated. As the Senate was strictly confined to small denominations, the possible profit from devaluation was small—perhaps too small to attract the attention of either the Emperor or those who controlled the small change.

The Augustan coinage was definitely based upon a gold and silver bimetallism,[3] although, in fact, silver was the senior partner. The *denarius* continued at the weight of 60 grains, fixed in 217 B.C., and the *aureus* was fixed at 120 grains in weight and in value 25 *denarii*. Gold was rated at a higher silver value than had prevailed since the revival of the coining of gold, but there is no reason to suppose that it had become token. On the contrary, it is probable that the coinage ratio was adjusted to the ratio between the values of gold and silver in the market. In his adoption of bimetallism, Augustus was

[1] Lenormant suggests (II, 404) that the token coinage was allowed to the Senate because it was less likely to debase it, but in view of the political situation at the end of the Republic it is unlikely.

[2] The Senate must have restricted the supply of tokens in some way comparable probably to the limitation upon the issue of bronze and silver applied by the British Mint.

[3] There is no information whether the public had the right to have both metals freely coined: if there was no such legal right it is most probable that in fact both metals were freely coined.

PLATE XVI

THE PRINCIPAL ROMAN IMPERIAL COINS ISSUED BY AUGUSTUS

1 *Aureus* bearing (a) Head of Augustus and inscription " Augustus Divi F " and (b) Bull.
2 *Denarius* bearing (a) Head of Augustus and (b) Gaius and Lucius Cæsar.
3 Brass *Sestertius* (four *as* piece).
4 Copper *as* bearing (a) Head of Augustus and (b) inscription with " S C " in centre.

aiming at the establishment of an imperial currency, with a view to the improvement of both trade and imperial organization. He took steps to have all public accounts and tariffs throughout the empire[1] expressed in Roman *denarii*,[2] and to enforce the use of Roman weights and measures. Imperial gold and silver was made legal tender throughout the empire.[3] His desire to establish an efficient imperial system was again apparent in his attempt to coin a simple but comprehensive series of denominations. The *aureus* and *denarius* were accompanied by coins of half their weight, and the small change system was completely overhauled. No important issue of small coins had been made for sixty-five years, and there was no doubt an inconvenient shortage of bronze coins. Two new bronze denominations, the *sestertius* and *dupondius*, were issued, while the *as* and its quarter were made of copper. These small denominations were doubtless tokens, and the theories based upon the supposition that they were full value coins, because no uniform standard of weight can be discovered as their basis, are without foundation.[4] The use

1 With the exception of Egypt, where *drachms* and *obols* were used until the later years of the 3rd century A.D.

2 Lenormant, II, 148.

3 Hill, *Handbook of Greek and Roman Coins*, 87; Mattingly, XXII.

4 Beanlands (*Num. Chron.*, 1918, 190) suggests that Augustus's desire for centralization extended also to the copper coin, not only for political reasons, but also because of the profit accruing to the mint from the substitution of local issues, and because it would facilitate the adjustment of prices upon a comparable basis. This, he says, could have been effected by the adoption of silver monometallism with bronze as a token currency, but such a policy would have proved unpopular with the bankers and tax-collectors because they would no longer have reaped a profit out of the uncertainties of the exchange, and, in consequence, they would be hostile to such a reform. Moreover, the Roman people, to whom such an ancient bronze standard still meant so much by tradition and association with the past glories of the Republic, would be hardly likely to tolerate a measure which would sweep away one of the last vestiges of their earlier prerogatives. He says (194) that the value of the brass or cadmia was adjusted by state control of the market, so that, in relation to copper, "there was a fixed relation between them (the values of bronze and copper), on the one hand, and again with silver, so as to establish a given ratio, on the other," and then "the copper or bronze coin will be stabilized in its relationship to silver by the intervening medium . . . and a free and fixed interchange between the three coined metals will be maintained." The coinage ratio between copper and silver in *asses* and *denarii* respectively was 48:1 (198), while it is admitted (190) that the market ratio was 250:1. It is quite clear, therefore, that although Augustus is supposed to have rejected the idea of making the *as* a token, it was, in fact, very much a token worth four times as much in *as* coins as in the market. And if so, the stabili-

of the same two metals for small change had been the subject of experiment at the time of the assassination of Cæsar, who in this, and the placing of his effigy upon the coin, the introduction of bimetallism, and the attempted re-introduction of small change, laid down the main line of the reform that Augustus was later to follow. Apart from the fact that it made it possible to provide coins of similar size although different value, the device is not explicable, unless the copper denominations were added, because copper was used for token coins in some provincial areas, and it was desired to establish also a small change money that would circulate widely in the empire.[1] The copper denominations might appeal to many of the Greek-speaking areas, while the bronze appealed to the Romans. Having supplied a full series of denominations in metal of good quality and exact weight, Augustus neither devalued nor debased the coins: he also eschewed the issue of plated coins. During his reign most such coins had been redeemed, and during the first half of the 1st century of the present era the imperial currency was both reliable and suited to the functions it had to perform. Augustus saw clearly the kind of monetary system necessary in an empire as great as the Roman, and he had the vigour and ability necessary to build such a system upon the disorderly ruins of the republican money.

zation of *asses* in *denarii* was as easy as the stabilization of small change tokens in full-weight coins, that had been continuously and successfully managed for four centuries in Magna Græcia and the Greek world. Brass or bronze was coined as if it was one and two-thirds as valuable as copper (199), and was therefore probably also token. If bronze was so little more valuable than copper, it cannot have been much easier to manage the market in the special mixture than the market in copper, and the intrusion of a new metal was but a needless complication. Moreover, the reasons for the supposed rejection of the device of making small change coins tokens are altogether inadequate. Why should Augustus have been so impressed with the need for securing the continuance of the bankers' profits arising out of the instability of the value of money? and if he was convinced of the need to do so, why did he proceed to stabilize the currency? The profit out of issuing small change cannot have been of much importance, for if brass coins were all full weight, the whole profit was to come from the difference between the metallic and face values of the *as*, its half and quarter; and as to the Roman respect for tradition, bronze had lost its full-weight coin status at least seventy-five years before, and lost nothing in the Augustan reform. But the whole theory is based upon a misconception as to the status of the small change money.

[1] Sydenham, *Num. Chron.*, 1918, 182. There is no reason why bronze tokens should not have superseded copper, except the conservatism of the people.

During the first half of the first century A.D. there was a tendency to consolidate the imperial prerogative. About A.D. 38 the mint at Lugdunum was closed, and for the first time Emperors issued gold and silver coins in Rome. The mint was separate from the Senatorial establishment and was supervised by the Emperor's finance minister. The Oriental notion of the divinity of Kings that had infiltrated the declining Republic and finally became patent in the portraiture of Cæsar and his successors on the coins was directed at the beginning of the republic to the idea, also current among the aristocratic party during the previous century, that the value of the currency could be determined by the will of the Emperor expressed in imperial decrees. Their value was even said to spring from the effigy upon the coins. Cæsar and Augustus were strong enough in their belief in the importance of the more prosaic economic influences at work, but their successors fell easy victims to the more flattering theories that attributed to them divine powers which did not stop short at the control of the value of money. Augustus permitted no worship of himself, but after his death coins of gold, silver, and bronze were struck in his divine memory bearing the legend "DIVVS AVGVSTVS."[1] Caligula (A.D. 37 to 41) arrogated to himself the attributes of divinity.[2] In the 'forties of the 1st century plated coins began to appear again. Some authorities state that between A.D. 41 and 54 as many as four-fifths of the *denarii* issued were base. These issues mark the beginning of a series of experiments in debasement, which was to be continued over a perod of 230 years and to disprove tragically but certainly the fallacy that the divine nature of the Emperor would enable him to multiply the number of coins without limit and without effect upon their current value. As an 18th-century writer remarked of this decline: "When money comes to be abased and . . . the mint like the pulse beats too slowly and irregularly, it is an evident symptom of some distemper in the bowels of a state."[3] The seat of the distemper was in the incompetence of Emperors and their belief in their own divinity, two probably not unrelated causes.

[1] Sydenham, *Num. Chron.*, 1917, 259. [2] *Ibid.*, 1917, 277.

[3] Greaves, J., Professor of Astronomy at Oxford: *A Discourse on the Roman Government and Denarius*, London, 1752.

2. *The Policy of Nero.*

The first important changes in the Augustan currency were made by Nero, whose reign falls into two periods, the policies of which are curiously and sharply contrasted. Between A.D. 54 and 63 he displayed an unexpected deference for republican institutions. He seems to have surrendered the prerogative of coining to the Senate, for " Ex. S.C. "[1] appears on all gold and silver issues.[2] He respected the Augustan standards for both gold and silver. The Senate, however, ceased to issue brass, although copper issues continued.[3] But in A.D. 62 after the removal of his advisers, Seneca and Burru, Nero emerged as the tyrant of history books. Towards the end of the following year, after having given the Senate far greater power than it had enjoyed since Octavius became Augustus, Nero reversed his policy and proceeded to crush the Senate. He recovered the privilege of coining gold and silver, and coins ceased to be marked " Ex. S.C." He attacked even the Senatorial privilege of issuing small change, for much of the brass and copper of the period was not marked by the Senate, and the mint was placed under the control of prefects appointed by the Emperor. All reference to the divine Augustus disappeared from the coins, and symbols suggestive of Nero's divinity occur. Boasting on the coin of his divinity was more than Caligula had dared.[4]

The most notable changes, however, were the reduction of the *denarius* by 14 per cent. in weight and 7 per cent. in fineness, and then *aureus* by about 10 per cent. in weight. The *aureus* was still worth 25 *denarii*, and the ratio between the values of gold and silver in coins was altered, therefore, from $12\frac{1}{2}:1$ to about $10{\cdot}6:1$, silver being more highly valued in relation to gold than before. The policy behind this reform is not easy to discover. The rating down of the value of gold suggests that the relative market values of the precious metals had been changing. Either gold had been falling or silver had been rising in value, and having decided that the bimetallic system had to be preserved, Nero adjusted the coins to the new ratio.[5] But the adjustment might have been

[1] " Ex Senatus Consulto." [2] Sydenham, *Num. Chron.*, 1919, 116.
[3] *Ibid.*, 1916, 14. [4] *Ibid.*, 1917, 278.
[5] Mattingly (*op. cit.*, I) states that the reason for the reform was that " the precious metals were clearly of more value as metals than as

effected merely by reducing the weight of the silver coin. The reduction of the weight of both coins and the debasement of silver require more explanation. The encouragement of commerce by the assimilation of the Roman to the Greek coinage system[1] is another possible but partial explanation. Possibly Nero was moved to improve the economic relations between the West and the East, and the currency reform was one of the steps to that end.[2] Nevertheless, the adjustment of Roman to foreign units was repugnant to Roman tradition, and as the theory will explain neither the alteration of the coinage ratio nor the debasement of silver, it has no strong claim to reveal the basis of Nero's conduct. A number of numismatists have explained the reduction of gold and silver coins as the result of a fall in the value of brass of which the smaller coins were made. There is no evidence that these pieces were full-weight coins; in fact, it has been shown that there is every reason to believe that they were not. In consequence, there is no more reason why a fall in the value of brass should have called for a reduction of the gold and silver coins, than that a fall in the market price of silver or copper should involve a reduction of the gold equivalent of the British pound.[3] Moreover, the fall in the value of brass is

---

currency . . . that is to say, that the *aureus* was worth more than 25 *denarii* in metal, and the *denarius* was more in excess of 4 brass *sestertii* or 16 copper *asses* in value than had been contemplated. A loss of metal from currency through foreign trade, and even more through its excessive use for articles of luxury, is probable." If the *aureus* was worth more than 25 *denarii* in metal, it would be necessary to move the currency ratio in favour of gold to maintain both metals as currency. But exactly the reverse was done: the silver coins were reduced by a greater proportion than the gold, and gold was taken at a less value in coins in relation to silver. (The other explanations suggested by Mattingly are dealt with in the text, *infra* 416.)

[1] Soutzo, *Revue Numismatique*, 1898, 659.

[2] Sydenham (*Num. Chron.*, 1916, 20) states that the theory is in keeping with Nero's policy.

[3] In the passage already quoted from Mattingly (50), he suggests as a reason (*inter alia*) for the decline, that "the *denarius* was more in excess of 4 brass *sestertii* or 16 copper *asses* than had been contemplated."

Sydenham (*Num. Chron.*, 1919, 120) thinks that the fall in the value of brass partly explains why no brass coins were issued in the first part of Nero's reign—*i.e.*, the Senate had always made a profit on brass, but ceased coining rather than allow their profit to increase, although it need have had no effect on the value of the coin. He suggests that "in the year A.D. 63 the Senatorial coinage (*i.e.*, bronze and copper only) was entirely readjusted on an orichalcum basis" (120), and that "the reduction in the case of the *aureus* and *denarius* is inseparably associated with the readjustment of the orichalcum and copper coinage"

only inferred from the tendency, evident from about 22 A.D., to make brass coins heavier in weight than they had been under Augustus. As they were tokens the increase in weight proves nothing. It is also remarkable that after the death of Nero the whole elaborate brass and copper system introduced by him disappeared and the brass coins returned to their original Augustan standard.[1] If there had been a fall in the value of brass, either it must have suddenly disappeared, or it was decided that it was not to be permitted to interfere with the currency. There is little denying that the reduction of the fineness of the silver is strong presumptive evidence of a profit motive; it was a common debasement of the currency.[2] Moreover, it suggests that the reduction of the gold and silver

(122). He thinks that copper maintained its value relative to gold and silver, while brass (or bronze or orichalcum) depreciated relatively to copper, and " the Senatorial Mint . . . again confronted with the problem of having to deal with the fluctuating value of orichalcum in relation to the other metals without upsetting the traditional system," hit on the solution of issuing coins of all denominations, from the *sestertius* downwards, in brass, adding to those already in use, the *as*, half-*as*, and quarter-*as*. " It was doubtless the intention of the framers of this policy that the three smaller denominations of orichalcum should supersede the copper coins already in use, although the latter should not immediately be withdrawn from circulation." The brass *asses* were not a success, and copper ones were soon coined again. Thus " the orichalcum coins formed a complete system by themselves, and the copper could pass as money of convenience." Sydenham admits that it would have been both possible and logical to raise the weight of the brass coins (if brass pieces were full value coins) when the value of brass fell, but thinks that the course was rejected mainly for reasons of economy. " The maintenance of a high orichalcum standard, and the slight reduction in that of the gold and silver, brought the three metals into harmony. But since pure copper appears to have retained its original relation to gold and silver, the reduction in the weight of the *aureus* and *denarius* necessitated a slight diminution in the weight of the *as* " (124). This theory means that because brass fell in value (which is not proven) the gold and silver coins were reduced in weight, and an attempt was made to eliminate copper. But both brass and copper were almost certainly tokens; if they were not it is highly improbable that the Romans would have regarded *brass* as the basis of the whole system, to be preserved at any price. If brass had been full-weight, and had to be prevented from becoming token, the obvious course was to raise the weight of brass. The argument that the Roman administrators did not do so for reasons of economy is incomprehensible. They were trying to avoid the brass becoming tokens (according to the theory), and therefore to avoid making a profit on them. If economy was their guiding principle, they would not have objected to their becoming tokens.

[1] Sydenham, *Num. Chron.*, 1919, 126.

[2] It is possible to regard it as part of the attempt to prevent the export of bullion, but as that could have been equally well effected by a reduction in weight, the debasement was probably employed to produce a profit.

coins may have been directed to the same end. The reduction offered some profit out of the lag in the adjustment of prices to the increased quantity of coin, and possibly some recoinage profit. But the rise in prices and incomes caused by the reduction of the unit of value, so far as coined silver and gold were used as units for recording debts, had the usual consequence of relieving debtors at the expense of creditors. The general unit of account down to the last years of the 3rd century was the *sestertius*, which was no longer a bronze unit. "We know for certain that 4 *sestertii* were worth a *denarius* and 25 *denarii* an *aureus*."[1] The *sestertius* was, therefore, either one-quarter of a *denarius* or one-hundredth of an *aureus*; presumably payments within the empire were made in the metal which was the less valuable at the moment, while the more valuable tended to be hoarded or exported. The government, by reducing the weight of both coins, made sure of a reduction in the burden of the public debt, whether it was called upon to pay its interest and capital in gold or silver. The nature of the reduction is in doubt, although its effects are not. Pliny's account[2] suggests that the coins had, prior to the reign of Nero, been gradually reduced in weight. By the time of Nero a series of illegal reductions had accumulated, and Nero merely amended the law to correspond to the actual standard of the coins. If Nero did so amend the law, it was the last occasion upon which the legal weight of the *denarius* was altered until the 3rd century.[3] It is less likely that the reduced weight of the *aureus* was fixed by law, because "several heavier pieces are met with after the time of Nero, and the heavier *aureus* of Nero remained in circulation."[4] Not only does this state of affairs suggest that there was no legal prescription of a new weight for the *aureus*, but also that the *aureus* as a unit was dropping out of use. If both light and heavy coins circulated together, the former would pass at a premium in the latter,[5] and how else should

[1] Mommsen, III, 140.

[2] After the *denarius* of gold had been struck at forty to the pound, "the Emperors gradually curtailed the weight of the *denarius*, until at last, in the reign of Nero, it was coined at the rate of forty-five to the *libra*" (*Hist. Nat.*, XXXIII, 12).

[3] Mommsen, III, 28.

[4] Mommsen, III, 24.

[5] It is unlikely that both passed for the same value, the lighter pieces being, in fact, tokens; sweaters and clippers of coin would, in such circumstances, have reduced all coins to the weight of the lightest acceptable in payment of debts.

the premium be fixed than by a comparison of weights? We approach a system where gold passes by weight. On the other hand, it is probable that so many-sided a reform was deliberate and sudden, and that the reductions of gold and silver resulted in an immediate diminution in the weight of the coins. But it is not important, for if the reduction was gradual losses and profits are the same in kind as if it was sudden, but they are spread much more thinly over time.

But the export of bullion which gave rise to so much complaint towards the middle of the 1st century A.D. also had some bearing on the reform. Gold and silver began to flow abroad very early in the century.[1] Tiberius in the second decade fulminated against "those vanities peculiar to women through which, for the sake of precious stones, our wealth (*pecuniæ*) is transferred to foreign and even hostile nations."[2] Half a century later in A.D. 77 Pliny[3] estimated that at least 550 million *sesterces* (about 5½ million pounds [gold]) were exported annually to India alone to pay for imports. These complaints may have been no more than narrow mercantilist dislike of parting with treasure. The exports of bullion may have been counterbalanced by imports of treasure from other directions. But there are two reasons which render a net export of treasure probable. On the one hand, the gold value of silver had been rising, and as the currency system was bimetallic it is possible that before Nero reformed the currency silver coins were exported and melted because they were undervalued in coins. But Pliny is quite definite in his reference to exports of gold. We have seen that before Nero's time the issue of plated coins had been revived. Nero certainly issued plated coins. These pieces sank in value as their quantity was increased. So far as the law succeeded in preventing them from being taken at a discount in good *denarii*, the tendency would be to raise prices and render both silver and gold less valuable in coins (in which form they had to compete with base coin) than they were abroad or as bullion. The base pieces then drove out the good and caused the export of treasure that gave rise to complaint. Thus the reason for the produce of the West not finding a ready sale in the East whence came the Roman

[1] Mattingly, *loc. cit. supra*.
[2] Tacitus, *Annales*, III, 53.
[3] *Hist. Nat.*, VI, 26.

luxuries[1] was a high price level in Rome which raised the cost price of exports and offered good prices for imports. This high-price level was due to the inflation caused by the issues of base coins and the failure of the exchange to represent the purchasing power parity between Roman and foreign coins. The export of treasure was a natural consequence and would, in time, by diminishing the quantity of currency, have raised the value of money and depressed prices, encouraging exports and discouraging imports. This would have continued until prices had fallen sufficiently to raise the value of the genuine coins at least to the value of their metallic content, or until all the available bullion was exported.[2] The continued issue of base coins would only tend to depress the value of the currency, driving out more bullion before any adjustment was possible. The drain gave rise to so much protest that the reduction of the genuine coins may have been designed to stop it.[3] If the coins were made tokens the outflow could

[1] Bury, *Later Roman Empire*, I, 26.

[2] During and after the war of 1914-18 the immediate effect of inflation was to *increase* the export trade of the area indulging in inflation. This was due to the anticipation of the effects of the policy by foreigners, and the fall in the external value of the inflated currency before the reduction of its internal value. It is doubtful how far the exchange market was organized in Rome, and whether such anticipation of the fall in the value of the currency occurred.

If after 1918 the foreign exchange quotation had not moved in advance of internal prices in countries inflating their currencies, the export trade of such countries would have tended to diminish and their import trade to expand over any period when the foreign exchange quotation did not express a fall in the value of the currency unit as great as that shown by the general level of prices within the country. This was probably the position in Rome. But as in the later period the export of the precious metals was usually prohibited, a fresh equilibrium had to be brought about by means of alterations in the foreign exchange quotation reacting upon the international exchange of goods and services other than the precious metals. In Rome, however, as generally in countries with a metallic standard, metal moved first because of the ease with which it was transported, and the greater rigidity of its price in most markets.

[3] Sydenham (*Num. Chron.*, 1916, 20) remarks that it is not easy "to see how the reduction of the gold and silver currency was likely to affect this drain, although it is not altogether improbable that the reduction may have been partly necessitated by it." In the first place, the reform may have been adopted because it was hoped that it would stop the outflow of treasure, although it may never have been capable of such an effect. Secondly, gold and silver were being exported because they were cheaper than other exportable commodities, but by reducing the metal equivalent of the gold and silver coins the selling price of the two metals was raised and their export was stopped until a further rise in other prices rendered gold and silver again relatively cheap. The latter would happen if inflation was persisted in.

be completely stopped.[1] But in fact they were issued in sufficient quantities to reduce their value to that of their metallic content, and when prices were adjusted to the reduced amount of metal in the coins the export of metal must have recommenced if prices were further depressed by base issues. Pliny's account suggests that this, in fact, happened.

Nero's control of the currency cannot be regarded as the result of any single motive. His desire to maintain a bimetallic system explains the alteration of the coinage ratio between gold and silver. Debasement by reduction of the fineness of the coins may indicate either a purely profit-making motive or an attempt to prevent the export of silver in the face of a rise in its gold value. The issue of plated coins can indicate no motive other than profit-making. The devaluation of gold and silver was probably due to a short-sighted attempt to prevent the export of treasure which, in fact, was the consequence of the adverse movement of the exchanges caused by his issue of plated coins. The devaluation was made more attractive by the small coinage profits and not inconsiderable relief to debtors that accrued from the consequent rise in prices.

3. *From the Death of Nero to the End of the Second Century A.D.*

The Neronian reform marks the beginning of two centuries of inflation. Throughout the period the control of the currency remained constantly in the hands of the Emperor, whose policy was dominated by a determination to make the currency prerogative yield a profit. Although some of the depreciation may have been due to inadequate control of the mint or the technical inefficiency of the moneyers, by far the greater part was the result of sheer profligacy. For the next 200 years the history of policy becomes, therefore, a dissertation upon methods of currency depreciation and their respective consequences. Nero made use impartially of devaluation and debasement by reducing the fineness of

[1] As in Great Britain in 1816 and 1920, when the amount of silver in the coins was reduced.

coins and by issuing plated coins.[1] Although efforts may be made to whitewash Nero's reputation by attributing his depreciatory reform to motives other than those of profit, his determined attack upon the silver coinage resulted in a marked tendency to abandon silver and use gold as the basis of the unit of account, and also as a monetary metal,[2] although the plentiful issues of *denarii* and *sestertii* from the 'seventies of the century suggest that they were both important as exchange mediums.[3] But the *denarius* came to mean one-twenty-fifth of an *aureus* rather than a defined weight of silver. The *sestertius* remained the principal unit of account, but was probably regarded as one-hundredth of an *aureus*.[4] The pay of the army was expressed in gold. By giving up the silver unit of account, the commercial community could escape the effects of the rise in silver prices.

The death of Nero was followed by a period of tranquillity. The additional coins introduced by Nero were abandoned, the brass returned to the Augustan standard, and during the last thirty years of the century coins were minted in considerable quantity and without much change in quality, the most important feature of the period being a definite decline in the importance of plated coins. The self-pressed claims of the Emperor to a divine status were more insistent, and Domitian (A.D. 81-96) described himself as "Dominus et Deus" on his coins.[5] The tranquillity was disturbed towards the close of the century by fresh debasements. Gold was slightly debased. Early in the 2nd century Trajan reduced the fineness of the silver coins by some 11 per cent., and in A.D. 107 organized a great recoinage,[6] but not, as has been suggested, merely to demonetize the coins bearing republican

[1] Pliny, writing within ten years of Nero's death, wished "that gold could have been banished for ever from the earth accursed by universal report, as some of the most celebrated writers have expressed themselves, reviled by the reproaches of the best of men, and looked upon as discovered only for the ruin of mankind. How much more happy the age when things themselves were bartered for one another" (*Hist. Nat.*, XXXIII, 3). But he seems to have been impressed more by the effects of gold upon the development of commerce and upon social organization than by mismanagement of currency.

[2] Mommsen, III, 45; Lenormant, I, 184.

[3] Sydenham, *Num. Chron.*, 1919, 126.

[4] The *aureus* was never adopted as a unit of account for taxes or bargains in the market (Oman, *Num. Chron.*, 1916, 45).

[5] Sydenham, *Num. Chron.*, 1917, 278.

[6] Mommsen, III, 31.

types still in circulation. That these types from long usage had become illegible was merely an excuse for recoining the old money at the reduced fineness and making a profit out of the change. The *denarii* issued by Mark Antony, which had doubtless suffered from wear and tear equally with others, were not recoined, but were left in circulation. Being one-fifth copper, they offered no profits on recoinage.[1] There can be little doubt, therefore, that profit was the main object of the operation. The fineness of silver was similarly reduced by Trajan's successors at intervals throughout the century. By the time of Marcus Aurelius (161-180) silver coins had so far deteriorated in quality that it became profitable to melt down and recoin the base *denarii* of Mark Antony as they were of better quality than the current issues,[2] and by the end of the century the silver currency was only 0·500 fine. During the same period, issues of silver-plated coins became smaller and less common. But in the second and third decades of the century gold plated coins were current, although it is not certain that they were not counterfeits. The troublous later years of Marcus Aurelius, disturbed as they were by earthquake, pestilence, and barbarian invasion, saw the coinage again depreciated. Gold coins ceased to be issued in any quantity: silver was further debased and more plentifully issued than before, perhaps to make up for the deficiency of gold: experiments were again made with the issue of gold-plated coins. Inflation was principally concentrated during the century upon the debasement of the silver coinage, because, on the one hand, the debasement of the small change was not sufficiently remunerative, and, on the other, it was not easy to tamper profitably with gold. Reductions in the weight of the *aureus* and its general irregularity led to its circulation by weight, both in commerce and in payment to the public treasury,[3] by the end of the century. The medium of exchange, as well as the unit of account, was a unit weight of gold. The multiplication of the numbers of *denarii* and their declining quality resulted in the hoarding of gold. The

[1] Mommsen, III, 31. [2] *Ibid.*

[3] " It appears to be beyond doubt that already at this time (early in the 3rd century) gold was received by weight alone in all commercial transactions " (Mommsen, III, 113). Orders on the treasury were expressed in quantities of a stated metal of prescribed fineness.

hoards of the first and 2nd centuries that have been unearthed consist of a large proportion of gold coins, a little silver, and no copper.[1] Nevertheless, there was probably a considerable quantity of gold in circulation until the end of the century.

4. *The Collapse of the Currency in the 3rd Century A.D.*

In the 3rd century inflation entered upon a more desperate phase. In its early years there was a debasement of gold of some 4 per cent. At the same time the weight of the *aureus* was again reduced. This and a series of previous small reductions reduced it from 114 grains (in the time of Nero) to 100 grains. Evidently, for some purposes, gold coins were still used. If gold had always changed hands by weight and private assay, neither of these alterations would have been worth the trouble. It was left to Caracalla in the second decade to lead the final assault on the Augustan system. He debased the silver coinage more rapidly than his predecessors, until the coin was less than half silver, and he multiplied his issues of this poor silver until the public was inundated with them. He introduced a new silver coin, the *argenteus Antoninianus;* this addition to the series of coins seems to have sprung from the necessity to patch up the obvious cracks which appeared in the monetary system as a result of the sapping and mining of the preceding century and a half. The most obvious crack was the difficulty of maintaining the *denarius* as one-twenty-fifth of an *aureus:* the former had been debased and the latter reduced in weight. Gold coins had also become very scarce. The net effect of all these changes is impossible to estimate, but it is likely that the new coin was intended to represent a simple fraction of the *aureus,* either one-twentieth[2] or one-twenty-fifth.[3] Although the *argenteus* was destined to be the means of bringing down the whole system, it was probably not intro-

[1] Mommsen, III, 111.

[2] *Vide* Chap. XI. Sydenham (*Num. Chron.*, 1919, 134) thinks that the debasement of the *as* had caused its value to fall from one-twenty-fifth to one-thirtieth of an *aureus*, and the *argenteus Antoninianus* was one-twentieth of the *aureus*.

[3] Oman (*Num. Chron.*, 1916, 45) suggests that the *aureus* had risen in value above twenty-five *denarii*, in fact, and Caracalla recognized this and made a coin equal in value (at a rate of about 12:1 between the values of gold and silver) to one-twenty-fifth of an *aureus* of about 100 grains. The *aureus* was then worth 37½ *asses*.

duced merely to speed up inflation. The silver coins could easily have been very much further debased if profit had been the only aim. Caracalla has also been credited with further reducing the weight of the *aureus* in about A.D. 214. It is impossible, however, to determine the official standard from coins that present such wide variation in weight from one specimen to another as do those of this period.[1] Gold pieces weighing as little as 100 grains were issued from about A.D. 214, but with them, and bearing the same dates, are others as heavy as 112 grains.[2] The irregularity of the pieces was doubtless due to the fact that they circulated only by weight, which fact also explains why it should not have been worth while to reduce their weight. In fact, there was no official standard, and gold was only coined in very small quantities for the imperial largesses and commemorative purposes. A large proportion of the specimens of the *aurei* of this period that have been found are in so good a condition that they can never have been in circulation. They quickly found their way into hoards.

Elagabalus discovered that a rapid inflation, although it yielded a profit because prices did not rise as quickly as the supply of coins was increased, had the disadvantage that it reacted against the state whenever it was a creditor. He did not, however, stop the depreciation of the silver coins. Although our knowledge of this coinage is in great confusion, it is probable that Elagabalus continued to reduce both the weight and the fineness of silver, and accompanied his shrinking coins with an edict[3] that payment of taxes would be accepted only in gold. As the state was still forcing its creditors to accept base pieces, this act was a sheer repudiation of part of the government debts. It must have caused a severe decline in the value of the debased currency, and have resulted in great hardship. Taxpayers were forced to buy gold with debased coins in order to meet the demands of the tax-collectors.[4] Elagabalus also issued gold pieces lighter than any previously known, and the suspension of the issue of *argentei Antoniniani* that occurred at this time may

[1] Mommsen, III, 61.

[2] Oman, *Num. Chron.*, 1916, 41.

[3] Babelon, 413.

[4] Finlay says that as much as 500 *denarii* was sometimes paid for an *aureus*, and that to an agent of the Imperial Mint (*Greece under the Romans*, App. II).

be due merely to the consequent destruction of the ratio of 25:1 between the value of the *argenteus* and the *aureus*.[1]

Alexander Severus (222-35) further debased the *denarius*, but in about A.D. 227 he showed signs of reform. He improved the appearance of the silver and raised its quality, but did not increase its fineness above 0·5. His plan seems to have been to restore the old relation of 25 *denarii* to the *aureus*,[2] for the improvement of the quality of the *denarius* was accompanied by a reduction in the weight of the *aureus* to 92 grains. But the coinage ratio which he established between gold and silver was much more favourable to silver than the market ratio, and his description of himself on the coins as " Restitutor Mon " (etæ) proved premature.

The successors of Severus, in their dire poverty of ideas, sought to increase the profit from the currency by reducing the cost of production other than the cost of raw materials. Many of the silver coins issued in the provinces, mainly France, Switzerland, and England, but never in Italy, were cast. Whether the change was effected by authority of the law[3] or not is uncertain. Casting was undoubtedly a cheaper, but it was a less accurate and more easily imitated process, and its adoption is but a symptom of the low ebb to which skill in, and perhaps even concern for, the maintenance of the currency had fallen.[4] In A.D. 238 issues of *denarii* shrank to a miserable trickle, and at the same time the *argenteus Antoninianus* was revived and minted in great quantities. The reason for the change lies ultimately in the capacity of the latter to yield a profit. If it was now worth one-twenty-fifth of an *aureus*,[5] it was probably popular as a medium of exchange, which means that it would be slower to fall in value, as its metallic content was reduced and its quantity increased. On the other hand, the cost of manufacturing an *argenteus* was probably much the same as that of making a *denarius*, apart from the cost of raw material.[6] The profit obtainable from an expansion of issue of *argentei* was greater,

[1] Oman, *Num. Chron.*, 1916, 46.

[2] Sydenham, *loc. cit.*

[3] Lenormant, I, 278.

[4] In the succeeding century the evils of economy of this nature seem to have been recognized, for the substitution of any other process for that of hammering money was made illegal (Lenormant, I, 280).

[5] Sydenham, *Num. Chron.*, 1919, 134.

[6] Oman, *Num. Chron.*, 1916, 47.

therefore, than when the issue of *denarii* was inflated, even though the former contained 50 per cent. more metal than the latter. A further reason for preferring the *argenteus* as a means of inflation, which may or may not have been recognized at the time, was that as the *argenteus* was the more valuable more profit would be made before it was reduced to a crude and base memorial to a departed coin. During the next few years the *denarius* and its subdivisions, to all intents and purposes, disappeared from the monetary system, which was dominated for thirty years by the *argenteus*.[1] Even the *aureus* was but occasionally issued for ceremonial purposes. Finally, in the 'sixties, the silver that remained, debased and plated as it was, was as irregular in weight as the gold, although it can hardly have been taken by weight.

By about A.D. 270, the currency consisted almost entirely of *argentei Antoniniani*, containing about 2 per cent. of silver. Third-century hoards contain but a very small proportion of gold pieces.[2] Such gold pieces as are found are often of quite different weights, indicating the irregularity of the currency and possibly that gold was difficult to obtain. Hoards also show that the silver *denarius* of one eighty-fourth of a pound, dating from the period before Nero's reform, had completely disappeared from circulation. They occur quite frequently, however, in hoards across the Danube, whither they had evidently been exported. The *denarii* of one-ninety-sixth of a pound of the period from the middle of the first to the end of the 2nd century were also by this time nearly all driven to Germany, where they formed the principal currency.[3] When they were hoarded in Italy they were set apart as valuable rarities. The *sestertius*, which had remained in circulation until the 'sixties, had to be reduced in order to prevent its continued export.[4] But the *argentei* did not go abroad:[5] their legal tender privilege ceased at the frontier, and there also their circulation ceased. Most of those who hoarded money in Italy were forced, by sheer inability to obtain anything else, to hoard *argentei*.[6] Baked earth moulds, which have been found in great numbers, and were probably

[1] At its value of two-thirds of the *argenteus*, the *denarius* was of little use as a subdivision of the *argenteus*.

[2] Mommsen, III, 111.

[3] Mommsen, III, 121.

[4] Mommsen, III, 148.

[5] Mommsen, III, 121.

[6] Mommsen, III, 148.

the equipment of counterfeiters, suggest that the *argenteus* was not worth counterfeiting. Its cost of production was low, but so also was its value.

The inflation of the period was mainly concentrated upon the silver coins. The occasional reductions in the weight of the *aureus* are signs of a hankering after the depreciation of gold which brought their own remedy. Resort was had to the use of gold by weight as the medium of exchange as well as the basis of the unit of account.[1] This demonetization of gold was a gesture of despair in the utility of money, and a return to the system in vogue in Egypt and Babylon of two or three thousand years earlier. The debasement of gold was never of great importance, although the fineness of the coins was reduced on several occasions. Presumably suspicion of the quality of coins was met by a refusal to accept them, or by a private assay. Gold-plated coins were also important, more particularly during the 3rd century. While these attempts suggest that coins were still occasionally accepted at face value, the general failure to depreciate the gold money must indicate that the government was never able to enforce the acceptance of gold at its face value.[2] In theory there is no reason why the gold should not have been depreciated as much as the silver; in practice it may be that the commercial community resisted any such suggestion. They would not be denied the stable basis for their bargains that they found in the unit weight for gold.

The profit from the silver coins came entirely from debasement. The silver pieces were never reduced in weight after the death of Nero. The Empire inherited from the Republic the device of issuing plated coins and used it to considerable purpose during the 1st century A.D., but one of the most important effects of the progressive reduction in the fineness of silver was the steady decline in the issue of plated money and its entire cessation in the 3rd century. As the value of a " good " *denarius* fell, so did the real sale price of a plated coin. The latter was difficult to make, and there came a

[1] That gold was passing by weight is confirmed by the fact that the gold pieces of the 1st and 2nd centuries were still in circulation in the 3rd century (Mommsen, III, 112). It is unlikely that they would have survived had they been accepted only at their legal value.

[2] Babelon (361) affirms that no one was compelled to take them at their nominal value.

time, early in the 3rd century, when plated pieces were not worth the trouble of manufacture, and debasement was the sole means of depreciation applied to silver. There is considerable difference of opinion as to the plated pieces that were issued by the public authority and those that were counterfeit. But the private coiner was doubtless actuated by the same motives as the state. When the state led the way he also found it easier to profit by issuing coins of lower grade metal instead of plated ones. Inflation by means of the issue of plated coins is a most unsatisfactory method of pursuing an evil course. The plating of the coins was suggestive of cheap deception, which is nowhere more evident than in the device, which seems to be peculiar to Rome, of mixing the plated coins with the good when they were issued from the mint. The profit on any single plated coin was much greater than could have been obtained without a most drastic debasement, although technical difficulties of manufacture were greater, and increased the cost of making plated pieces. While the total profit on an issue could be adjusted by fixing the number of plated pieces issued, it was in practice much more difficult to control than the percentage of alloy in each coin. It was easier for moneyers to deceive the public, and also, in republican times, the Senate, as to the proportion of plated pieces that they had included in an issue. Moreover, when the pieces were issued, they were a great temptation to coiners. Each coin represented a great profit, and so the counterfeiter set to work and added his quota to the output of the public mint.

In their consequences the issues of plated coins were undesirable. If political circumstances were such that it was possible to prevent good and plated coins from circulating at different values, to prevent a double price level, then, if a given amount of profit was to be made by one method or the other, there was little to choose between equal debasement of all coins or the issue of a number of plated coins and the rest good.[1] As soon as the additional coins were issued, prices tended to rise: good coins were then melted or exported until the reduction in the quantity of all coins was sufficient to increase their value as coins to a level high enough to remove any temptation to sell them as bullion. If a uniform debasement was effected, the coins melted would be those in circulation

[1] Except the temptation to counterfeiters.

prior to the issue of debased prices. If plated coins were issued, either old or newly issued good coins could be melted. We have already noted a tendency to export good silver from Rome. The evidence of large hoards of *denarii*, which contain no base coins, indicates that savers very naturally discriminated in favour of good silver and that they buried good *denarii*, leaving the base coins to circulate.[1] In consequence, the currency tended more and more to consist of base pieces.

But there is little doubt that, although refusal to accept plated coins at face value was illegal and punishable by the imposition of very severe penalties, base coins were detected by striking them on the ground or making a hole in the middle to detect any baseness of heart. When the base coins had been identified they passed for a lower value than "good" silver; there were, in fact, two price levels and plated coins fell to a heavy discount in good silver. The unfairness of the reactions of this method of debasement upon the relations between debtors and creditors is obvious. Government creditors were bound to accept a mixture of *denarii* all at their face value. The greater the proportion of base coin which fate or an ill-disposed public official placed in the payment, the greater the loss of the recipient. Private debts incurred before the issue of plated coins had reached any considerable quantity and falling due after, would be unlikely to be paid in good silver. Sheltering behind the law, or the fact that his own debtors had paid him in base coin, the debtor would pay in the same money. To the extent that the base coin had fallen in value below the genuine coin, debtors would gain and creditors lose. There is no doubt that such a mixed issue of good and bad coins is one of the worst methods of manipulating the currency to obtain profit for the treasury. If for any reason the public must be defrauded, instead of taxed, to supply public funds, a method which scatters the incidence of loss by chance can have no defence. The equal debasement of all coins gives a nearer approach to a very rough justice. In the course of time the Romans eliminated the disparity between plated and "good" coins by debasing the latter until their metallic and current value fell to that of the former.

The other important reaction of the debasement of the silver coins was upon the small change money. The reduction

[1] Lenormant, I, 129.

in the value of the *denarius* reduced the purchasing power of the token brass and copper coins which had been issued for three or four hundred years by the Senatorial and local mints, and the value of which was fixed in silver coins. After a time the value of these coins fell to their metallic value, and it no longer paid the Senatorial and municipal mints to continue the issues. Denominations below the *as* ceased to be issued in Rome in about A.D. 180, and *asses* in A.D. 217, after which only small quantities of brass of higher denominations were made. The pieces already in circulation no longer passed at their legal value, but were sought as metal. What had been intended to be purely local issues circulated widely throughout the empire as full value coins preferred to imperial money. The bronze of the east, which was of considerable weight and excellent metal, drifted westward,[1] and circulated with the issues from the Senatorial Mint. Bronze also found its way abroad or into the melting-pot, with the result that bronze money, rare in the time of Commodus (180-193),[2] largely disappeared towards the last quarter of the 3rd century.[3] "It is probable that when Aurelian completely centralized the administration of money to establish his new system there were hardly any old local pieces to demonetize."[4] If the arrangement by which power to issue copper tokens was limited to the Senate and the local authorities had been intended to obviate inflation, it failed: the Emperors found a way of making the Senatorial power to issue tokens quite useless, while at the same time securing for themselves profits from currency manipulation. In consequence of the collapse of local issues, branch mints had to be set up after the middle of the century, particularly in the time of Gallienus.

Lastly it is of interest that, although *denarii* and *argentei* were both debased, the last feverish thirty years of inflation concerned the *argenteus* almost entirely. The *denarius* dropped out of the system before the final collapse, and it

[1] Lenormant, II, 421. "The large number of base pieces and bronze coins of Syria and Egypt which we find on the banks of the Rhine at points where legions were encamped proves that at the end of the 3rd century the provincial and local money of the East was accepted throughout the empire" (Mommsen, III, 353).

[2] Mommsen, III, 48.

[3] Babelon, 412.

[4] Mommsen, III, 355.

was the *argentei* that were so lavishly over-issued that they became the assignats of the period.[1] It is obvious that the purchasing power of the *denarius* and *argenteus Antoninianus* must have fallen very heavily during the 200 years following the death of Nero. But how much they fell we do not know. So little is at present understood of the rates at which the debased coins were rated in the later issues of the reforming Emperors, that it is impossible to estimate the extent of the rise in prices[2] by that method. There must, however, have been a severe disturbance of economic conditions, bringing loss of a fortune to some and the gain of one to others. The social and political unrest of the empire during the 3rd century was in no small degree the outcome of this confusion.[3] It has been argued, however, that an important, if not the main, reason for the debasement of silver during the period lay in the increasing value of silver as a metal. The output of silver was diminishing in the first few centuries of the Christian era, and supplies from Central Asia were cut off by the rise of the Parthian Empire. On the other hand, the demand for silver was increased by the spread of the habit of using silver money with the widening of Roman spheres of administration.[4] It is argued, therefore, that the debasement was the reflex of an increase in the purchasing power of silver: it was part of an attempt to establish a stable unit of value which was from time to time translated into (as it happened) a diminishing weight of silver. It is

[1] Mommsen, III, 147.

[2] If the coins of Aurelian marked "XX" indicate that a new *denarius* was equal to 20 old *denarii*, and the new *denarius* was merely a restoration of the old unit, a rise in prices of 2,000 per cent. is indicated, but this interpretation is very doubtful indeed.

[3] Babelon, 413.

[4] "It would probably be a mistake to regard the selfishness of autocracy as wholly or even mainly responsible for the depreciation. The real explanation is rather to be sought in the fact that a great increase in the demand coincided with a restriction of supply. The Romanization of a larger part of the known world, including considerable tracts that had hitherto been uncivilized, must have added enormously to the number of those by whom coins would be used. On the other hand, the time-honoured sources of silver supply were undoubtedly becoming exhausted. The mines of Laurium, for instance, were virtually worked out by the beginning of the Christian era. At the same time the use of the Parthian Empire had as its direct effect the cutting off of Rome from ready access to the riches of Central Asia. The chances are that if she had been able to 'hold the gorgeous East in fee' her silver scutcheon would not have been so grievously tarnished" (Macdonald, 50).

quite conceivable that the Romans, in the absence of index numbers, endeavoured to maintain a stable gold value for silver: they might have attempted to maintain a bimetallic system with the *denarius* as one-twenty-fifth of an *aureus*. But their resort to alterations in the weight of the *aureus*, and the issue of plated coins, raise a suspicion that is confirmed when the extent of the debasement is considered. Silver cannot have risen in value sufficiently to justify half the debasement that was effected. There is little doubt that the main motive was profit.

5. *The Reforms of Aurelian, Diocletian, and Constantine.*

After the chaos into which the Roman money had been plunged by Gallienus in the 'sixties of the 3rd century, Aurelian (270-5) took the first steps in reform. He centralized the control of currency in his own hands, suppressing the power of the Senate to issue bronze coins and taking over all local mints (with the exception of that at Alexandria). Most of these mints had been driven out of business by the competition of the base imperial silver coins. If he was to issue only good money of silver and gold, denying himself profit by the manipulation of either silver or gold, he claimed control of the only portion of the currency that offered a legitimate profit. According to Zosimus,[1] Aurelian " restored the public credit by delivering out good money in exchange for the bad which people were commanded to bring to the treasury."[2] In all probability his object was the modest one of instituting a uniform plated currency of stable value. The marks of value on the two principal coins " XXI " and " VSV " were doubtless intended to notify the number of old units represented by the new coin, but it has been seen[3] that their interpretation is at present most uncertain. If the new piece is regarded as a new *denarius* which was to pass for the same value as two old *denarii*, debts would be halved when translated into the new units, and it would be expected that some record would have been left of the change. But there is no such record. Nor is there any literary evidence of a change in the weight of the

[1] Writing in the second half of the 5th century A.D.
[2] *Cit.* Webb, *Num. Chron.*, 1919, 237. [3] *Vide* Chap. XI.

coins or of the introduction of a new denomination. It is more probable, therefore, that the two new coins represent merely an attempt to re-establish the *argenteus* and *denarius*.[1] Possibly the "XXI" on the larger coin means that the *argenteus* was stabilized at a value of 20 old *denarii*, or one-twentieth of an *aureus*. Aurelian may have desired to restore the *argenteus* of Caracalla. Having taken it as his model so far as was possible, in type and in the ratio of the coins to gold, and being unable to restore the quality of Caracalla's coin, he issued plated pieces marked to show that they were worth one-twentieth of an *aureus*.[2] He supplemented these plated pieces with revived bronze *sestertius* and *as* coins. The system consisted, therefore, of silver-plated pieces weighing 63-73 grains, which were probably *argentei*, others of 39-46 grains probably *denarii*, bronze *sestertii* of 421 grains, and *asses* of about 126 grains. The metal in the plated *denarius* was thirty-seven times as valuable as that in the bronze *as*. But it is clear that this was not in agreement with the market values of the metals. To maintain the system the plated coins required to be very strictly limited in quantity. If the bronze coins were still token coins, there was a still greater difference between the currency and metallic values of the plated coins. Aurelian aimed at stabilization upon the basis of a silver-plated token coin,[3] looking back to the time of Caracalla for the units of his system. He was unable to issue any silver or gold, although he placed limitations on the melting of gold with a view to its protection. The whole monetary system had been so completely shattered by a century of continuous mismanagement that the deflection of the stream of events from chaos and change towards order and stability was the limit of his achievement. But if, with Gibbon, "we attentively reflect how much swifter is the progress of corruption than its cure, and if we remember that

[1] *Vide* Chap. XI.

[2] If the small "VSV" coin was a new *denarius* which was worth ⅔ of the new *argenteus*, the new *denarius* was worth 13⅔ old *denarii*, a rate which cannot be read into its inscription, although the latter may well not be a mark of value at all (Webb, *Num. Chron.*, 1919, 243).

[3] Sydenham (*Num. Chron.*, 1919, 150) thinks that Aurelian's issue of bronze pieces was "an attempt to force up the plated currency to a fictitious value"—a policy which "was, of course, thoroughly dishonest." But there is nothing essentially dishonest in the issue of token coins. The best governments still do it.

the years abandoned to public disorders exceeded the months allotted to the martial reign of Aurelian, we must confess that a few short intervals of peace were insufficient for the arduous work of reformation."[1] Nevertheless, his achievement in stopping inflation was considerable. It constituted so serious a threat to the profits derived by the moneyers from the issue of base coin, and the sale of gold coins for the payment of taxes, that it produced among them a rebellion[2] which ended in a widespread insurrection, which was suppressed at the cost of the lives of 7,000 soldiers. But under Aurelian's successors, the bronze part of the coinage disappeared,[3] from which it would seem that Aurelian over-issued his money, and that when it fell in value, the bronze money, having a higher "melting-point" than the plated coins, was the first to disappear, leaving the plated money to circulate until after the end of the century.

The reign of Diocletian was one of reforms, and the currency called more urgently for attention than any other department of public administration. Diocletian responded by introducing the most far-reaching reforms that had been made for nearly 150 years.[4] He was faced with a complex problem, for not only were coins irregular in weight and base in quality, they were unpopular, and, in large part, the use of coins by tale was avoided. He recommenced the issue of both gold and silver of excellent quality. In the selection of weight standards for his coins he was governed by a desire to re-establish a gold and silver bimetallism, but he was also impressed with the necessity for taking every possible step to make coins popular. In consequence, he attempted to revive standards of traditional fame. Before 290 he issued gold coins of 4 scruples (about 72 grains);[5] and although later such pieces were introduced with great success by Constantine,

[1] *Decline and Fall of the Roman Empire*, I, 313.

[2] Probably more than this attempt at currency reform went to raise the rebellion (Gibbon, *Decline and Fall of the Roman Empire*, Bury's edition, I, 314).

[3] Sydenham, *Num. Chron.*, 1919, 150.

[4] Tacitus, who succeeded Aurelian, had, as a senator, given powerful support to his reforms. Although he condemned in principle the alteration of the fineness of money and the issue of plated pieces as both disloyal and disastrous in their consequences, he himself probably issued some base pieces.

[5] The original weight of the silver *denarius* of 268 B.C.

at this time they were withdrawn on the occasion of a great currency reform in A.D. 290, embracing coins of gold, silver, and copper. The silver coin was based upon the *denarius* of Nero, and the gold coin was raised to 84 grains presumably so that it might be twenty-five times as valuable as a *denarius* at the current ratio between the market values of the metals. But, having failed in this latter aim, Diocletian reduced the *aureus* to a value of only 20 *denarii*, and finally, in A.D. 301, the *aureus* and *denarius* were both raised, the former to the standard of the Neronian *aureus*, and the latter to a weight such that at a ratio of 12½:1 between the values of gold and silver it was worth one-twentieth of an *aureus*. The very wide variations in the weights of coins of apparently the same denomination leaves much doubt, however, as to the status of the whole coinage of gold and silver. Many of the silver pieces are marked "XCVI." This was presumably a notification that ninety-six of such pieces made a pound of silver—*i.e.*, that they were Neronian *denarii*. But even the pieces so marked vary widely in weight, a number weighing more than one-ninety-sixth of a pound. Perhaps it was necessary to put the good silver in the same position as the gold coins had for long enjoyed, and permit them to pass by weight.[1] By this means the coins were protected from reduction by either the state or by private clippers and sweaters, and would have a reasonable chance of acceptance by the public and of a long circulation. If silver was thus restored to popularity, silver coins might regain public confidence when they became more uniform in weight, and accorded with a known and respected standard. The irregular silver pieces did, in fact, remain in circulation for over 100 years, and unless at least all but the heaviest were tokens, they must have been taken by weight. The gold coins remained as irregular in weight as they had been for the last century or so, and they, too, may have circulated very largely by weight. The variations in the weight of the coins of both metals would suggest that the reign of Diocletian was no more than a period of transition when the attempt to restore silver to monetary status took the form of the institution of the custom of weighing it out in settle-

[1] Mommsen (III, 75) contends "that the silver pieces, like the gold *solidus* of Constantine, were taken by weight."

ment of bargains in the same way as gold. It may have been taken at a fixed ratio in relation to gold.[1] But the supposed irregularity in the weight of the coins is partly due to the confusion between the successive issues made by Diocletian. His reintroduction of marks of value upon the coins for the first time since the beginning of the empire indicates a desire to restore the circulation of silver by tale, and he probably succeeded. He was not so fortunate with gold, in part, no doubt, because of the difficulties inherent in his isolated pursuit of bimetallism, but he probably also encountered administrative difficulties.[2]

The renovation of the Roman currency offered a suitable opportunity for the supersession of local issues of small change and the concentration of the whole of the business of the supply of coin under imperial control. Branch mints were definitely established, often by taking over local establishments that had been closed, and initials were placed upon the coins to denote their place of issue[3]—a device hardly ever previously used under the empire and aimed at the location of responsibility for each coin.[4] Here, too, he seems to have looked back to the Neronian system for inspiration: the principal coin that he introduced was the *follis*, which was based on the copper *as* of the time of Nero.[5] It was probably worth one-twentieth of a *denarius*—a denomination not previously issued. The *liaison* between the new system and that of Aurelian was by way of the coins called the *denarius communis* and the *centenionalis*, which were the respective successors of the coins of Aurelian marked "XXI" and "VSV"

[1] "When Diocletian re-established the coinage of silver on the basis fixed by Nero, he certainly did not try and re-establish the old proportion of twenty-five silver pieces to the *aureus*, nor any other fixed proportion, because it would have been impossible owing to the continual variations in the weight of his *aureus*. He contented himself with fixing legally the proportion between the pound of gold and the pound of silver (1:13·88), and striking new pieces at ninety-six to the pound" (Mommsen, III, 158).

[2] Mommsen (III, 63) blames "audacious frauds, half-measures of reform, simultaneous issues of gold by colleagues, and often by rival rulers on different bases, or the infidelity of officers charged with the control of the money."

[3] Local mints were already issuing gold and silver, but no mint marks had appeared on the coins.

[4] Under Constantine, almost every coin bore a mint mark (Webb, *loc. cit.*).

[5] Sydenham, *Num. Chron.*, 1919, 156.

and passed, the former for two-fifths and the latter for one-fifth of a *follis*. The value marks often, but not always, appear on the coins down to about A.D. 296, after which year they disappear. In order to assimilate these issues to the local coins of various parts of the empire, additional pieces were issued to act as links between imperial and local pieces until the small money fell into a state of complete confusion. The *follis*, the light of this lesser coinage world, fell in weight and apparently in value by some 20 per cent., until the *communis* was worth half a *follis*.[1] There was no renewal of Aurelian's attempt to reintroduce bronze coins. As they had so quickly disappeared from circulation, all Diocletian's issues were plated: they all contain from 4 to 15 per cent. of silver.[2]

He seems to have been troubled, however, by a serious rise in prices. Notwithstanding good harvests, the fall in the value of money caused much distress. Wages tended to rise, and the troops were hard put to to buy the necessary provisions out of their pay. As on so many subsequent occasions, the rise in prices was attributed to speculation, but, in fact, there is no good reason for a fall in the purchasing power of money. Nevertheless, in 301 Diocletian issued an edict prescribing maximum prices for almost every imaginable service and every article that could be brought to market or produced by human industry,[3] "from the price of an onion to the fee of a barrister." The attempt to fix prices by law was a failure; it caused distress and confusion, and largely on that account Diocletian's monetary system was abandoned by Constantine. Diocletian's policy was to establish a currency of gold, silver, and copper for the whole empire, both gold and silver pieces being full-weight coins. His search for a bimetallic basis for his system made all his gold issues unstable: his policy of one small change currency for the whole empire brought that part of the currency into disorder. But his achievement, a stable full-value silver coinage, was of the first importance.

[1] A new denomination resembling the *follis* in type and style appeared some time before 310 A.D., and by 312 the older *follis* had disappeared, the lighter piece taking its place.

[2] Sydenham, *Num. Chron.*, 1919, 170.

[3] Mommsen, III, 158. The *denarius* referred to in the Edict appears to have been the *communis* above referred to, and which was worth about seven-sixteenths of a modern penny (Sydenham, *Num. Chron.*, 1919, 158).

Constantine (A.D. 306-337) introduced the most radical currency reform ever made in the Roman Empire. After a passing lapse into the errors of the previous century,[1] he issued an edict in 312[2] completely reforming the gold and silver money. Both metals were coined on a standard of 4 scruples, or about 71½ grains, the weight of the *denarius* introduced nearly 600 years earlier. The gold coin was the *solidus*,[3] and the silver coin was later called a *miliarense*. The gold coins continued, however, to be as variable in weight as ever. Constantine continued the habit of using marks of value revived by Diocletian, and some of the early gold *solidi* are marked " LXXII " to show that seventy-two of them should weigh a *libra*, but they are so irregular in weight that they can only have been accepted by weight. As gold coin had already passed by weight for some 200 years, it is quite likely that the custom would be continued. In fact, " we know positively that in the reign of Constantine all payments in gold money were by weight, and that ingots of gold regularly controlled were accepted by weight. The government made and deposited in the principal towns standards to facilitate the verification of the gold pieces, and special employees were appointed to carry out the test at the request of individuals."[4] The latter arrangements for the testing of weights of metal probably applied to coins, and may have been the means of restoring their circulation by tale when they became less variable in weight. Although there is no doubt that for many centuries after this date gold coins were weighed, after a time the weighing became more in the nature of a test determining the acceptance or rejection of the coin at its legal value, than a means of calculating its value. Silver was probably more frequently accepted by tale, although it must be admitted that silver coins also display great irregularity in weight, with the result that even their normal weight is not easy to determine.[5] If the coins were tokens the differences in weight could be disregarded, but there is no evidence that they were not full-weight coins. On the other hand, it is

[1] Mommsen, III, 88. [2] Mommsen, III, 65.

[3] Its standard is verifiable by reference to a law of A.D. 325 (Finlay, I, 442).

[4] Mommsen, III, 156.

[5] The *miliarense* and its half are difficult to distinguish from the *denarius* and its half, so great is the irregularity (Mommsen, III, 76).

improbable that silver also passed by weight alone.[1] It is impossible that every transaction was settled, if not in small change money which, we have seen, was in great confusion, in gold or silver weighed in the balance. The only plausible explanation is that the silver intended for small change may have passed for a prescribed value in gold and, although the silver coins were intended to be full-value pieces, they were accepted at their legal value even when their metallic value had fallen. While the heavy pieces were full-value coins, the light ones were not. We have seen that *aurei* were probably taken only by weight. The ratio between the values of silver and gold was not convenient. The silver coin was called a *miliarense*[2] towards the end of the 4th century, because it was worth one-thousandth of a pound of gold. This gives a ratio of 13·88 : 1 between the coinage values of gold and silver.[3] But if both circulated as full-value coins, 13·88 silver *miliarenses* must have been worth a *solidus*. It is not proven that the market ratio was 13·88 : 1 when the system was established. But there is no evidence of any other ratio. It is unlikely, therefore, that the value of the *miliarense* was fixed in *solidi*. However, the name *miliarense* suggests that the pound of gold may have been the larger unit of value, and that it was divided upon a decimal basis, and that its thousandth p .rt was represented by carelessly struck silver coins. The *miliarense* was, therefore, a subdivision of the pound of gold, although not of a *solidus*. If this was so the ratio of 13·88 : 1 must have been accepted as the legal ratio between the values of silver and gold.[4] On the whole, it is

[1] Mommsen, III, 76. Old coins, such as the silver *denarius* of Nero and Diocletian, the base *denarius* of Septimus Severus, and the base *argenteus*, and even some of the coins of the Republic and of Cæsar, still circulated, and must have been accepted at a value dependent on their weight and fineness.

[2] Mommsen, III, 81.

[3] Mommsen (III, 153-4) quotes two other bases for the calculation of the ratio between the values of silver and gold. The *miliarense* was worth $1\frac{3}{4}$ *siliquas* of later times. As the *siliqua* was $\frac{1}{24}$ of a *solidus*, the *miliarense* was $\frac{7}{96}$ of a *solidus*, which gives a ratio of 1:13:17. A *miliarense* was also valued at $\frac{1}{14}$ of a *solidus*, which gives a ratio of 1:14, but he prefers the ratio given above.

[4] Lenormant (I, 186) assumes some legal relation when he says that "a few years after Constantine the value of gold having risen considerably, the silver money which without increase of weight continued to represent the same fraction of a gold unit no longer had a metallic value equal to its nominal value."

probable that there was some legal ratio, because, in addition to the name *miliarense* suggesting a relation to gold, the *siliqua*, the half of the *miliarense*, was called a *siliqua auri*. Furthermore, it is difficult to see how business can have been done, unless the silver coins represented some stable unit. There was no silver unit, because the coins varied so much in weight. The only alternative is to suppose that the units were defined in gold. There was probably, however, no right to have silver coined, and this explains why subsequently silver coins sank to the level of a token currency.[1]

Gold-plated pieces appeared in the period from Diocletian to Constantine, but were few. They were difficult to make, and the gold-plated *solidi* of the reign of Constantine and after can only be false money.[2] The disorganization of the small money in the time of Diocletian continued under Constantine. The Treasury accepted copper only by weight. The mint continued to coin copper, although there was no fixed legal ratio between gold and copper coins, there being a variable price for the former in terms of the latter.[3] During the 4th century, under Constantine and his successors, this money suffered reductions in fineness and weight that reduced its metallic value to an almost negligible quantity. The abundance of the issue in consequence caused great reductions in its exchange value, and the small change money remained in a most unsatisfactory condition.[4]

[1] Mommsen, III, 90. Mommsen (III, 159) attributes to the rating of the silver coin to the pound of gold the fact that "the independence of silver money disappeared completely; this money no longer represented anything but a fraction of the gold money." During the next half-century the pieces became more regular in weight. In about A.D. 360, under Julian, the silver coinage was reformed. The *argenteus* of $\frac{1}{96}$ of a pound, and all the larger denominations, ceased to be issued, and were rare by the middle of the 6th century. The *siliqua* of $\frac{1}{144}$ of a pound became the principal silver coin; it was rated at $\frac{1}{24}$ of an *aureus*, and its status as a subdivision of the gold unit further emphasized. As it weighed exactly one-half as much as a *solidus*, the coinage ratio was 1:12.

[2] "Although that is not to say that several Emperors did not try to make them" (Mommsen, III, 68).

[3] "It is possible that it was sometimes at par . . . it is very doubtful whether the public Treasury was ever ordered to accept copper, even temporarily, like gold and silver. In consequence, it is not surprising that in the time of Constantine, with the immense mass of small money which was issued, the material of which was always changing, continual fluctuations in the value of copper occurred" (Mommsen, III, 170).

[4] Towards the middle of the century difficulties occurred owing to its uneven distribution throughout the empire, and the fact that it

As the *aureus* had not been used as a unit of account, no adjustment was called for when it was replaced by a *solidus* weighing 35 per cent. less than the *aureus*. The commonest units of account under Constantine were still the pound weight of gold and silver. Bronze did not pass by weight, except in transactions with the Treasury. During the reign of Constantine there was added to this a system of purse units. The purse of gold which was used only for payments of the Senatorial tax "most frequently meant nothing more than a pound weight of gold, coined or uncoined."[1] The purse of silver is estimated at 125 *miliarenses* weighing a little under two pounds, and was worth 9 *solidi* or one-eighth of a pound of gold. The purse of copper weighed 312½ pounds, and at a ratio between the values of copper and silver of 1:120 was worth 250 *denarii* of Nero.[2] Another purse of coined bronze was used not only in the time of Constantine, but also for the fixing of fines in a number of laws of the 4th century, A.D.: it is uncertain in size and silver equivalent; but it was possibly worth a little over one-quarter of a pound of silver.[3]

Constantine's policy was directed to building upon the abortive efforts of the previous forty years a money for the whole empire. His success lay in his selection of the pound of gold as the basis of his reform. The pound of gold was the one unit of value and medium of exchange that had persisted through the years of destruction and clumsy rehabilitation. Business men found in the pound of gold, and sometimes also of silver, a haven from the buffetings of imperial finance, and the problem was to induce them to accept a new system not in place of, but rather as auxiliary to, their primitive but reliable medium. Gold, although coined, passed by weight, the stamp being at first only a guarantee of quality. But in time, as it became more reliable as a guarantee of weight as well, it was doubtless accepted as such. Silver was also irregular, but too much can be built upon this irregularity. Roman coins were never as accurate, for some unknown reason, as the better Greek issues had been: during the preceding two

passed at a higher value in some parts than in others. The arbitrage profits offered by this state of affairs resulted in the transport of bronze from places where it was of lesser to those where it was of greater value, and the trade had to be made illegal in 356, except on a very small scale (Mommsen, III, 70).

[1] Mommsen, III, 161. [2] *Ibid.* [3] Mommsen, III, 163.

hundred years coins had been particularly irregular. The silver pieces were probably subdivisions of the gold pound intended to be full-value coins at a prescribed ratio between the values of gold and silver: they were not freely coined, and were regarded rather in the light of somewhat unimportant small change, and apparently not as subdivisions of the *aureus*. The copper coins were plentiful, but bearing no simple or stable relation to the rest of the system. These are most unsatisfactory monetary arrangements, but no better can be devised out of the evidence at present available.

6. *Summary.*

The policy of the empire followed in the main the policies of its Persian and Macedonian predecessors. The control of gold and silver coinage was in the hands of the Emperor, who supervised the issue of bronze coinage which he permitted to be made locally. The Emperor controlled the type on the coins and invariably elected to place his own portrait upon them. The Augustan system was based on gold and silver bimetallism, the standards being those originally taken over from the Republic. From the middle of the 1st century A.D. motives of profit dominated the control of the currency. Nero reduced the standards, issued plated coins and debased silver, and whether or not he was inspired simply by desire for profit, he began the destruction of the Augustan system. Reduction of standards was never again tried, but plated pieces were issued and silver was debased. Slowly the latter was increasingly exploited and the former allowed to lapse, until the silver coins were but washed copper and gold pieces passed only by weight. When the profit motive had been thus thoroughly exploited, reforms were necessarily slow, Aurelian stopped inflation and issued plated coins and copper. Diocletian issued fresh coins of gold, silver, and bronze. Hankering after a bimetallic coinage for the whole empire, supplemented by a uniform small change money, he succeeded only in setting up a silver coinage and a confused mass of small change money. Constantine gave up the idea of simple bimetallism, and issued silver to represent subdivisions of the pound weight of gold, gold coins being allowed still to circulate by weight. During the 5th century confidence in coins slowly returned, and a gold standard with subsidiary silver coins emerged.

CHAPTER XVII

CONCLUSION

1. *Deficiencies in the Evidence.*

We have now examined the available evidence as to early monetary systems, and have inferred therefrom the probable motives behind them. Before we summarize the conclusions to which we have come, it will be well to recall the deficiencies in the evidence to which no positive reference has been made. The most serious deficiency is our lack of knowledge of the legal provisions under which each currency circulated. Throughout the whole period there is no evidence of the legal weight of the coins. Specimens that are found vary greatly, because of the variable amount of wear to which they have been subjected, and also because they were often widely different in weight when issued. The Athenian and Macedonian issues reached a high degree of uniformity, but others, and particularly those of Rome, varied very widely. Standards deduced from coins are, therefore, subject to a wide margin of error. Again, we do not know the circumstances under which coins were legal tender, or even the legal value of some of the coins that have been found, the denominations represented by Roman coins being especially difficult to identify. Again, holders were presumably permitted to melt coins, but were they entitled to have the monetary metals coined in unlimited quantities? If so, what charges were mints entitled to exact for their service? If we may assume that whenever metal was more valuable in coins than as metal the state increased the supply of coins until the margin disappeared, this matter would not be important. But this suggests a second broad deficiency in the evidence. What were the practical conditions in which the law operated and the currency circulated? What was the practice of the government in deciding the quantity of coins to be issued? What was the practice of the commercial world in accepting them? How far was the law effective in preventing variations of the value of different parts of the currency system, especially where base pieces were issued? What were the units in which commercial bargains were made? What was the commercial value of the monetary metals? Many more questions in these two general directions could be asked if there were any chance of answering them. At present there is not, but it is well to bear in mind how much we do not know, while we sum up what we think we know.[1]

2. *The Development of Coining out of Earlier Commercial Organization.*

In the first place, it is now clear that it is useless to seek the inventor of money, the being who by a sublime intellectual effort invented coining. Coining was one stage, far from the beginning, in the organization of commerce. Simple barter as conceived in introductions to the theoretical study of money is no more than a logical device for simplifying exposition. It probably never existed in fact. Units of value must have arisen as soon as any kind of commerce, and depended in each district on the economic environment. The ox was the first unit to be prevalent over a large area, but it was not in general use as a medium of exchange. The metals were probably the first commodities which acted in both capacities over a wide area. Gold and copper attracted man's attention at a very early date, probably because of the ease with which they were worked—gold into ornaments, and copper into tools and weapons. Later silver, and still much later, iron also became common as mediums of exchange. The most primitive method of measuring metals was probably either by large weight units based upon the amount a man could lift, or else by size. They were made up into pots, hoes, or knives of a conventional size, or else into ingots of a shape easily definable by units of length, derived often from the measurement of portions of the human body. These methods were fairly satisfactory for bronze and iron, but gold and silver were so valuable, and small errors so important,

[1] Knapp (*State Theory of Money*, 1 *sqq.*) regards the surviving coins as "but the dead body" of the money, the soul of which is "not in the material of the pieces, but in the legal ordinances which regulate their use." The present study is an attempt to discover from the dead body the manner of life of the living thing to which it formerly belonged.

that ancient people measured them by weight, the weight units being defined in certain well-known seeds found to be uniform in weight. The economic life of the Egyptians, Babylonians, Assyrians, Minoan Cretans, Phœnicians, and Mycenæan Greeks, and perhaps the early Italians, was based upon a unit of value and medium of exchange, consisting of a prescribed weight of metal. Public weigh-masters were appointed in Egypt to verify weights, and the system was brought to such a state of efficiency that the subsequently invented coins were regarded as no improvement, and rejected. In Asia the principal metals circulating in uncoined form were gold and silver. In Egypt, although gold and silver were used, bronze was the basis of the standard. In Europe copper was generally used; in the last millennium B.C. it was superseded by iron in the Peloponnese.

The first contribution towards the idea of coining was the invention of the seal made far back in prehistoric times, and the next the application of the idea to metals. This stage was attained but slowly, partly, no doubt, for want of a suitable material out of which to make punches. After sporadic experiments in various parts of Asia in the 2nd millenium B.C., all of which proved false starts, the first pages of modern currency history were written somewhere round the coasts of the Ægean, probably in Lydia. There, for the first time, monetary ingots were regularly marked, probably by bankers and merchants. Almost immediately the idea spread to the cities on the west coast of Asia Minor, to the Ægean islands the mainland of Greece, and thence on the westward waves of emigration to the cities of Sicily and Southern Italy, and, finally, to Carthage. From Asia Minor it travelled northward to Macedon and the Black Sea. The Persian conquest of Lydia during the 5th century resulted in a Persian coinage, which brought the peoples of Asia into contact with money. In the latter part of the 4th century B.C. great quantities of money issued by Philip and Alexander of Macedon gave a fresh impetus to its propagation, and on this occasion it reached the Gauls and the Britons, by whom it was passed on to Ireland and Scandinavia. Before the beginning of the Christian era the whole of the western and southern European coast lands were using coins. The idea took much longer to penetrate thoroughly into the continental area.

Contemporaneously with the diffusion of the custom of using hall-marked ingots, the coin itself evolved. The placing of the first punch-mark upon ingots of metal in Lydia in the early 7th century B.C. produced merely lumps of metal bearing a small hall-mark on one side. The coin was improved first by placing marks on both sides, then by increasing the size of the types so that they covered the greater part of the face of the coin, and, finally, by making them in relief instead of incuse. Later, coins became thin discs of regular weight and uniform appearance and resembled modern coins. The smallness of the type on the earliest coins and their irregularity in shape rendered the extraction of metal from the coins so easy that, in the absence of legal tender laws, coins must have passed by weight. Moreover, the lack of uniformity in the appearance of primitive coins, resulting from the irregular placing of types and the general crudity of mint technique, made counterfeiting easy, and the presence of counterfeits made it difficult to secure the free currency of the official coins. With improvements in mint technique, in which Athens made the most notable progress, currency by tale became possible. Ancillary to the problem of securing the efficient manufacture of coins which were difficult to counterfeit was that of securing honest coining, and avoiding the enlistment of the official moneyers among the counterfeiters. Greek cities, where democratic institutions were not strong, left such matters to the chief magistrate, but cities democratically organized usually appointed special commissioners to deal with the matter, as in Athens, and required them to place their marks upon the coins. The Roman Republic from the end of the 3rd century controlled its mint in much the same way, but under the Empire the mint was managed by the Emperor, just as in the Lydian, Persian, and Macedonian empires it had been controlled by the King.

3. *The Location of the Prerogative.*

More important than the immediate control of the mint is the ultimate power directing the money. In some districts, probably those east of the Ægean, the power to issue money was at first the uncontrolled right of any citizen, although none but bankers and merchants used it. But with the increasing modification of the practice of sealing metals a new thing—the coin—emerged: coins were increasingly used in commerce, and were not all equally favoured. The seals most frequently met with, and those on which experience taught people to rely, gained special respect, and pieces bearing them became commoner mediums of exchange than pieces with other marks. In some areas, and particularly in Asia Minor and Lydia, it was, in fact, the pieces of the most wealthy and powerful merchant that became best known. Where he elected openly to assume political power the issue of money was vested in the tyrant from the beginning, and by the use of his political power to suppress any small competitors that remained, he secured a monopoly of coining. Further west, the state prerogative developed along different lines. The temples and priestly colleges often possessed more wealth in the form of precious metals than any individual and passed greater amounts through their treasury by reason of the active economic exploitation of their resources. The monopoly of coining tended to drift into the hands of temple authorities, owing to influences similar to those which elsewhere placed it in the hands of local bankers. But religious were identified with civic authorities, and a civic prerogative emerged. Very early in the 6th century B.C. the control of coining was everywhere in the Ægean world vested in the state. In China, however, private issues and issues by guilds of merchants persisted much longer—in the main, no doubt, because coins played a far less important part in Chinese commerce than they did further west. In the Greek cities the prerogative was exercised according to local political forms, the amount of popular control varying widely from city to city. The great Asiatic empires were monarchically constituted, and the coinage was controlled by the monarch. In the Roman Republic the people, in theory at any rate, always made decisions on monetary policy, but with the establishment of the Empire the mint fell under imperial control.

4. *The Exercise of the Prerogative.*

The main problem is to decide the manner in which the prerogative was exercised. In the first place, a state might determine to exercise its prerogative by ceding it or part of it to an ally or to a union of allies. The vesting of the coinage prerogative in the state meant that the area using a common medium of exchange would be also the area of the political state. In the empires of Persia and Macedon this area was so great that foreign exchange difficulties were reduced to very small dimensions. But in the Greek world political units were small and the advantages derived from the use of coining were almost in inverse proportion to the extent to which cities used their freedom to design a separate coinage. A confusion of coins would make commerce with people living outside their own community excessively difficult. In consequence there were practical limitations upon the exercise of the prerogative. During the first two centuries of coining these limitations mainly took the form of voluntary restraint by some cities from the exercise of the right to coin. Certain well-known and reliable coins were used for the settlement of bargains between members of different cities in much the same manner as the coins of some individuals were commonly used within the community in the days when every person could coin. Athenian coins, by reason of their purity, uniformity, and plentifulness would doubtless have dominated the commerce of the 5th century, but in its pride and power Athens reinforced economic with political influences and enforced the use of Athenian coins. The most interesting consequence of this policy was that in the 4th century B.C. the city states were determined to exercise their prerogative to demonstrate the recovery of autonomy, but, realizing that economic conditions demanded some agreement between them, they united to exercise their coinage rights. Monetary unions had been known a century earlier, but now became common. The reason for the desire to issue common currency lay sometimes in the need for military co-operation, sometimes in the recognition of the advantages of free economic intercourse, and to a minor degree in the greater efficiency and economy of minting carried on upon a larger scale than any city except one possessing ample supplies of metal could afford. These motives all disappeared when the Roman Empire developed and introduced into Europe a currency similar to its geographical application in those of the early Asiatic empires.

Turning to those states or unions of states that exercised

their prerogative, we find that in almost all respects there is a contrast in the money and monetary policy in the worlds east and west of the Hellespont. There is no more striking exemplification of this contrast than in the ornaments or types on the coins. In the democratic cities of Greece a strong superstitious objection to the personification of any living individual upon the coins is marked by the absence of any such portrait. The emblems chosen in early times were generally symbols designed to move the citizen to pride in his city. To foreigners the symbol was a claim to respect. In some cities the symbols were religious; they recalled the deity that protected the city, and by implication what was best in the civic life. Others were rooted in the economic life of the city, and secured the same effect by recalling the dominant motive in everyday life, if not the prosperity of the city. Where the staple industry was placed under the protection of the local deity, one symbol touched both religious and secular chords. In later times symbols often gave place to representations of gods—a change which is doubtless as much an expression of artistic changes in the later 6th and the 5th centuries as of any political or economic change. But in Asia, with its large empires and god-Kings, the measure of the imperial power was demonstrated to all by placing on the coins the Emperor's seal. In the early days of the Persian Empire the royal seal bore the King's effigy, and in consequence an imperial tradition of reportraying the Emperor upon the coins grew out of the older practice. The Romans at first accepted the Greek practice, and their republican coins bore the heads of divinities; but the decline of democratic institutions during the hundred years before the Republic finally disappeared is clearly mirrored in the coins. The appearance of Cæsar's effigy upon the money marks the first open avowal of imperialism. The Roman Emperors, like the great Kings of Persia, the Kings of the empires carved out of Alexander's empire, and the majority of subsequent monarchs, down to the 20th century, have maintained this lavish distribution of their portraits. This practice had also a sound psychological basis. It kept before the eyes of the people a boastful assertion of power in which they would do well to acquiesce. The democratic community relied upon loyalty, and used the coins to induce it; the monarchy relied upon servility, and demanded it. Here, then, is a reason for the contrast between Europe and Asia. Broadly speaking, the one was tyrannically governed and the other democratically. Subordinate to these political motives were certain economic influences that affected the types. When later coins travelled far from their place of issue, inscriptions were sometimes added as a better indication of origin than local deistic types. The practice of indicating upon the coins their value was introduced by the Italians, and later continued by the Romans of the Republic, where it was used consistently until the collapse of the Republic. The cities of the Greek world chose other means of indicating the denominations of coins. They adopted in later years a separate type for each denomination, in place of a single type for all the coins of an issuing authority. The need for identifying the coins for which each moneyer was responsible gave rise to moneyers' marks as a subordinate feature on the coins, although during the last century and a half of the Roman Republic these came to overshadow the traditional republican type.

The metals used for coins and for the definition of monetary standards have shown strikingly little variation since the beginning of coining. Electrum, the material of the first coins, was abandoned after but a short period, and since then gold and silver, either jointly or separately, have been the basis of almost all currency systems. In Asia gold and silver provided the basis of the monetary system from the time of the Lydian King Crœsus throughout the life of the Persian and Macedonian Empires. It is impossible to say whether the coinage was bimetallic in the sense that both metals enjoyed an exactly equal status in law, which determined the amount of one metal which was to be accepted in place of a prescribed amount of the other. The uncertainty is less in relation to the Persian Empire and the reign of Philip of Macedon when bimetallism was probably tried. But the outflow of gold from Philippi submerged any hopes of maintaining an isolated bimetallic system, and Alexander permitted the parallel currency of both metals without binding them together by a legal value. In Europe, on the other hand, we find accompanying the city state organization a preference for silver and the almost entire absence of either electrum or gold. Persian gold coins circulated, and it is quite possible that, in fact, the Persian coins performed much the same function in Europe as in the Persian Empire apart from their service in the latter in the collection of tribute. They provided a valuable currency suitable for transport, and one which no small local authority felt prepared to supply. Had there been supplies of gold (and no rival supplies of silver) in Greece to be disposed of, the local state authorities might have copied the Lydian and Persian example. Or perhaps, had the Greeks been restricted to overland instead of marine commerce, the great concentration of value which gold offered might have induced them to import gold and use it much more than they did. The Greeks did occasionally issue gold: the Athenian gold coins of the late 5th century and early 4th century set a fashion for gold coins, more than anything as a means of ostentation, which received some impetus when the gold from Philippi became available. The difference between Greek and Asiatic tradition in the matter of currency materials was not directly a difference between democracy and tyranny. It was a matter of the metal suited for a small area as against that suited for a large one. It was, of course, no coincidence that the larger territory was not governed democratically. Existing methods of political organization were not adapted to the democratic government of large areas, and it may well be argued that the invention of representative government has not solved the problem. The desire for concentration of value in the Asiatic Empire was ultimately due to the necessity for the transport of tribute and commercial payments over long distances where travel was burdensome and none too safe.

Rome passed in turn through all the stages from the barbarous local tribe, the small democracy, to a great empire, and its currency standard changed in accordance with the needs of each period. As a small and primitive community, the Romans were content with a bronze unit to which they adhered in spite of the obvious superiority of the silver coins of neighbouring Greek colonies—a superiority that they recognized by using the silver coins. When the Romans first coined they began with bronze, but they very soon added silver. Although they established a bronze and silver bi-metallism, silver superseded bronze as the real basis of the currency. For a time the Greek traditional silver standard dominated Roman money. But Rome was no city state. Territorial expansion brought her face to face at once with Asiatic currency traditions and with the currency needs of a large empire. The Roman Empire opened with gold and silver bimetallism, in direct line with the Persian and Macedonian traditions. Intentional depreciation of the currency during two centuries from the time of Nero caused the demonetization of gold and the practical abandonment of silver. Gold by weight remained the standard of value, and was the basis upon which early in the 4th century a gold and silver currency was re-established. The subsequent reduction of silver to a token status produced the first gold currency in the ancient world. The long periods during which there was in Rome a bimetallic system were as much the result of the series of changes from one metal to another as of any decision in favour of bimetallism.

The amount of the monetary material selected to represent the principal unit of account and medium of exchange may be chosen for a great variety of reasons, economic and political. Painless transition from the use of uncoined to coined metal was secured by making the first coins equal to the units of weight in use at the time of the introduction of stamping the metals. These units of weight for the precious metals may themselves have been determined by weighing a unit of some commodity previously defined by size perhaps in Babylon or Egypt. Such methods would result in the establishment of a new standard of value. But, in fact, the quality most likely to secure the ready adoption of a weight unit for metals to be used as a medium of exchange would be that the value of the unit of metal fitted easily into the contemporary economic system. It is not improbable, therefore, that the units in which monetary metals were measured were in many places the weight of the metal that corresponded to a known unit of value. Where the ox unit of value was used it would not be surprising to find a unit worth one ox. The ox was very widely used as a unit of value, and the equally wide distribution of the unit of 130 to 150 grains for gold may be explained by supposing that the ox unit of value was translated into gold in a number of places, and the ox and 130 grains of gold were identical value units. It is impossible to prove that this was so, and the uniformity of units can be alternatively explained on the assumption that the unit was invented in some one centre by either of the above methods, and then disseminated throughout the then known world. In fact, units spread from more than one place. So far as similar units were set up in different centres not in contact with each other it is reasonable to assume that similar circumstances gave rise to similar units. This primitive unit of about 130 grains became the standard of the earliest gold coins in Asia. In fact, if we may allow for the tendency of units to shrink, all the important gold coins of the ancient world until gold was demonetized in the Roman inflation of the 2nd century and the 3rd century A.D. can be indirectly traced to this unit. The Persian *daric*, and later Philip's and Alexander's *staters*, the gold coins of the whole of the ancient world, were based upon it. Silver units do not display the same uniformity. A liberal classification may be made to reduce them to five. These units, like the gold unit, may have been derived either from units of weight for other materials or from units of value already in use which were translated into silver. The "Æginetan" unit, which dominated the Ægean trade until the middle of the 6th century B.C., was probably the silver equivalent of a value unit previously represented by iron spits defined by size and number, although it is possible that it was a translation into silver of a fraction of the gold unit. The "Eubœan" unit, with the "Phocæan" unit (probably the result of reducing the "Eubœan" unit), appear to have originated in the use of the gold unit for silver, probably at a time when the market ratios between the values of silver and gold were such as to give a simple value relation between gold and silver units of equal weight. As the ratio in Greece was 12 : 1, a simple duodecimal relation was obtained. The "Eubœan" unit was adopted early in the 7th century at Corinth and at the end of the century at Athens. From Corinth it was carried to Sicily and Magna Græcia, and from Athens it dominated the Greek world from the middle of the 6th century, and particularly in the time of Athenian power during the 5th century. The "Phocæan" (or "Chian") unit, which was common in the northern half of the west coast of Asia Minor, became more widely popular in the Greek world after the decline of Athens and the rise of Rhodes.

The " Babylonian " unit used for silver in the Persian Empire and in parts of Asia Minor, and the " Phœnician " with its dependent " Milesian " used for long in the southern half of the west coast of Asia Minor, are said to have been obtained as a result of the division of the gold unit on a decimal basis and the translation of the result into silver. But the desire for simple value relations between gold and silver units was probably not so great as has been supposed. If it sufficed to give rise to such a system of units, it cannot have survived to maintain it. Adjustment of the units to every change in the ratio between the values of gold and silver would be impracticable. Moreover, in early times when coins were not sufficiently developed to be taken by tale, the advantage of the assimilation of value units in this way can have been but small.

The earliest silver coins of Magna Græcia suggest either the " Æginetan " *drachm* then popular in the Ægean, or the *didrachm* of Corinth then admittedly influential in the Greek colonies in Italy. But during the later 6th century the " Eubœan " unit gained in popularity, presumably because by subdividing it by ten it could be fitted on to the native bronze *litra* unit of value. The " Phocæan " unit was used in Campania during the later 6th century and 5th century, and when the Romans first coined silver late in the 4th or early in the 3rd century they adopted it, and until the last decade or so of the 3rd century B.C. they continued to coin on that basis for the peoples of Central and Southern Italy.

The native Roman standard was, however, the pound of bronze originally perhaps a subdivision of the ox unit or an ancient value unit represented by bars of bronze of a prescribed size. Some time before 268 B.C. the Romans reduced their silver unit to 105 grains or 6 scruples, possibly in an attempt to create a system of interchangeable bronze and silver units, and in 268 B.C. they adopted the silver *denarius* of 4 scruples, or about 72 grains, which became the principal Roman standard. The libral *as*, already rapidly shrinking, faded into a small token coinage. The *denarius* was slightly reduced in 217 B.C., and again under Nero, but it emerged again as the *miliraense* at its original weight after Constantine's reform early in the 4th century A.D. When the gold was again coined in the last century B.C., it was probably based on a standard of 10 scruples, but it was soon rated at

25 *denarii*, and its weight was adjusted during the remaining years of the Republic to that value. Weighing 120 grains at the beginning of the Empire, it was reduced by Nero, and thereafter was practically demonetized and circulating by weight. Constantine finally introduced a fresh gold standard in the *solidus* of 4 scruples, and, although his coins were not taken by tale, later pieces upon the same standard probably were. Europe and Asia followed their own largely separate ways in the choice of weight standards. The gold unit of about 130 grains was limited to Asia by the failure to coin gold in Europe in early times. While the Lydians favoured the " Babylonian " and " Phœnician " silver units, the Greek world rarely used them. The " Æginetan," the " Eubœan," and finally the " Phocæan "[1] were the principal standards in Greece and Italy until the Romans established a new European standard based on the scruple.

Before dealing with the motive behind the selection of these units, two somewhat minor questions call for attention—the origin and basis of the subdivisions of the principal unit, and whether the values of the coins can be judged from their metallic value. Like the principal coins, the divisional money was based upon the scale of weights used for the monetary metal. The origin of these is obscure. On the one hand, it is probable that the considerations of convenience that caused the principal units to be identical with or simply related to previous value units would suggest a similar basis for the smaller units. But, on the other hand, most early systems reveal a mathematical order that seems unlikely to have been accidental. As some degree of order must have been sought before the metals were current by weight, a separate origin for each unit is not precluded, although it remains improbable that all subdivisions are so explainable. It is notable that everywhere the unit of 130 grains of gold or its approximate equivalent was divided decimally. In Asia the silver units are supposed to have represented decimal divisions of the gold unit of value. In Italy the ox was worth ten sheep. This latter ratio may have been widely prevalent and account for this decimal division. But the smaller divisions were on a duodecimal basis. The Greeks probably supplied the sixfold division of the *drachm* into *obols*, which made

[1] Which was also used in Asia Minor, however.

the *obol* a twelfth of a silver *stater*, and the further division of *obol* into 6 *chalci*. The Romans divided the *libra* into 12 *unciæ*, and each of those again into 24 *scripulæ*. Such simplicity of mathematical relation must have been deliberate, and the adoption of both decimal and duodecimal division can only be explained by supposing that some parts of the system were added at a much later period than others when the fashion had changed. Subdivisional coins followed these series, but where only one metal was used the range of denominations that could be represented without using inconveniently large or small coins was limited. The adoption of gold and silver bimetallism in Asia made it easy to represent large values in convenient coins, and the use of bronze made small denominations possible. But the value of bronze was so small in relation to silver that the largest convenient bronze coins were separated by a large gap from the smallest possible silver. The Sicilian introduction of the bronze token solved the problem at the end of the 5th century, and bronze small change was common during the 4th century in the Greek world, and towards the end of the succeeding century bronze became small change even in Rome, where it had not long before been the basis of the standard. The Romans chose a decimal relation between the *denarius* and the *as*, which in 217 B.C. was altered to a sixteen-fold relation, which remained until the *denarius* was swallowed up in the inflation of the 3rd century. The *aureus* was twenty-five times the *denarius* and one hundred times the *sestertius*, and when the currency was restored in the 4th century the silver coins were again related decimally to the gold, the silver piece being one-thousandth of a pound of gold.

Although the device of bronze token small change was introduced before the end of the 5th century, most of the ancient peoples gave most inadequate attention to the supply of a suitable series of small denominations.[1] Many Greek cities supplied little: the Romans under the Republic were careless of it, and when we leave the empire in the 4th century, 350 years from its foundation, when the small money had been adequate and well chosen, we leave it in a chaotic state, with apparently

[1] The British Mint also for long neglected to provide a satisfactory supply of copper pence and halfpence, and tradesmen were permitted to make tokens to perform the functions of small change.

a varying rate of exchange between copper and gold. The need for small money was probably much less in early times than now, but the business of supplying small change was treated too lightly: it was often separated from the coining of the precious metals, the superior authority seizing the latter but scorning the former. In the small Greek communities there was no question of dividing the right of coinage between the superior and inferior authority; both silver and copper were coined by the city. In the early empires, however, in Persia and Macedon, the imperial prerogative was absolute in relation to gold: there was a strong tendency to monopolize silver: the more direct the power of the superior authority in a district, the more likely was the silver coinage to be controlled by the imperial officers. But where copper was coined it was usually left to local authorities. Not improbably there is some connection between this practice and the circumstances of the evolution of the state monopoly. The ingots marked by the wealthy merchant or priestly college and the medium of exchange in which transactions were settled was probably a valuable metal: the problem was not to facilitate personal, day-to-day bargains—then, in any event, much less numerous than now—but rather the larger bargains. When empires emerged the problem most pressing to the Emperor was that of collecting tribute, which it was obviously desirable to receive in material easily portable in quantities representing a considerable value. The weight of and difficulty in transporting bronze made centralized coining impossible. The fact that bronze was the original monetary material in Rome made an allocation on Lydian and Persian lines impossible in early times. When Roman territory was first extended in Italy the coinage of silver was monopolized. Later extensions were not followed by the immediate suppression of local rights of issue, although indirect attempts were often made to render the exercise of the right unremunerative. The coinage of gold was always strictly monopolized. The Emperor established a coinage system that might well have been found in Persia or Macedon. He assumed the monopoly of the right to coin gold and silver for the whole empire, leaving the coinage of copper to the Senate and local authorities. In the reforms after the collapse of the currency in the 3rd century A.D., among other new notions, the Emperors extended their prerogative to include the supply of even small change tokens and recognized the desirability of a uniform system for the whole empire.

There has been a tendency to avoid many difficulties in explaining ancient monetary systems by assuming that coins were tokens. In fact, token coins were a late discovery of which advantage was taken with some reluctance. Tokens were never resorted to as a method of avoiding the disadvantage of heavy standards of bronze and iron, and did not exist at all until they were issued in Sicily under the pressure of the invasions of the last decades of the 5th century B.C. Those issued were doubtless intended to bring relief to the Treasury in time of emergency, but they suggested the use of tokens for small change, and it was to this purpose and this alone that they were applied throughout the Greek world. The Romans used tokens for small change, although bronze was not legally made token until the last century B.C.; they also resorted to their issue in times of emergency. In 240 B.C., during the first Punic War, gold tokens were made and in 217 B.C., during the second Punic War, plated money was issued, and was probably not supplied in sufficient quantity to reduce its value to that of the metal it contained. The device of plating was probably then successful in deceiving people and preventing the circulation of coins at a discount. But when plated coins were issued under pressure of the Social War, they continued to appear spasmodically until the collapse of the Augustan coinage. Because of the liberality of the issues, and the suspicion with which they were regarded, it is doubtful whether they remained tokens. Apart from small change, there was no sustained coinage of tokens. Nothing resembling a note issue with the notes made of metal ever emerged, partly because such systems were not understood, and partly because, if ever there had been wide differences between the metallic and legal value of coins, counterfeiters would have set to work to reduce it. The maintenance of note issues and token coins of any considerable value to-day rests ultimately upon the technical excellence of manufacturing processes, which makes counterfeiting tedious and expensive and the cheaper imitations easy to detect, and the success with which counterfeiters are caught and punished. In both these respects the ancient world lagged behind the modern. The technique of coining was less advanced: the punishment of counterfeiters was more drastic, but detection was less common.

5. *The Motives behind Monetary Policies.*

The motives underlying the policy of the early currency administrators cannot at this distance in time be accurately known. Nevertheless, it is worth while to attempt to elucidate them, because the enquiry offers an opportunity of correlating monetary policy with contemporary economic and political conditions. The reasons for the original seizure of coining as a state monopoly were sometimes economic and sometimes political. The economic interests may have been those of the community as a whole, as, for example, in the democratically constituted Greek cities, and in Rome in the 4th century B.C., which were actuated by a desire to improve the new machine for facilitating commercial intercourse. Or they might be those of the tyrant, as in Lydia, and in some of the cities of Asia Minor, where the benefits of the coinage monopoly, mainly indirect and psychological, were to accrue to the tyrant. It is possible that already at this early stage the tyrant had beheld the gorgeous vision of currency depreciation, for in Lydia private merchants seem to have profited by reducing the percentage of gold in the electrum coins they issued. In the administration of the monetary prerogative, during the next thousand years, there can be detected all the influences which determine modern currency policy.

Behind and overshadowing the Lydian attempt to perfect the new instrument of exchange was the desire to secure a market for supplies of metal. As the metal consisted of a mixture of silver and gold, a means of certifying the quality of the mixture was especially calculated to facilitate its sale. Moreover, the position of Sardes as an entrepôt on the caravan routes from the east to the Mediterranean greatly enhanced the probable benefits from such a practice. This motive is evident in the Lydian selection of weight standards. The Persians had less need to think of the market for the metals: the size of their empire set fresh problems of greater importance. But again in Athens the silver deposits at Laurium, the backbone of civic finance, dominated the coinage. Standards were chosen and coins carefully made with a view to the foreign market, which was then forced to accept them. The coinages of Philip and Alexander of Macedon, in their change from silver monometallism to the use of both gold and silver, were clearly a means of marketing the proceeds of their mining and military enterprises. The Greek, and particularly Athenian, idea that gold was only to be issued in emergency is a further example of the same motive. Coining was used as a means of marketing ornaments and temple treasures. The Romans in early times were influenced by similar considerations. The booty from Tarentum may account for the silver coinage of 268 B.C. In their issue of gold tokens in 240 B.C., the Romans were grafting the Greek principle of coining to realize treasure on to that of issuing tokens. Again, the first issues of gold in Rome by Julius Cæsar were probably a part of a plan for realizing the treasures captured in Gaul. In consequence of this policy, there was a tendency in early times for the powers possessing supplies of metal to supply the principal coinage. The wide circulation of the Persian *darics*, the Macedonian gold *staters* and the Athenian *tetradrachms* of silver all being obvious examples of coinages whose international fame rested upon this basis. The issuing states sold the metal in coins, and others would not incur the expense of recoining with their own types.

A second very early consideration in the shaping of policy was the desire to facilitate the public financial administration, the collection of tribute and taxes and financing the army and navy. This was probably the dominant motive in the Persian administration, where it found expression in the central control of gold and the establishment of one series of weights, where two had existed, in fact, in a general simplification of the system. Again, in Athens during the 5th century, these considerations were important, and there is little doubt that the changes in the Roman system, as her frontiers became wider, were due to the needs of financial administration. Measures, such as the adoption at the beginning of the empire of gold and silver bimetallism, a more complete series of denominations, a greater uniformity among the coins, and the expulsion of plated coins from the system, were all calculated to facilitate government and the collection of taxes which the Romans for the first time made efficient. In the Greek cities generally this motive was absent: financial administration was very simple.

The measures that facilitated the receipt and payment of funds by the state would naturally also simplify commerce. In fact, such measures might be the result of pressure, from either business men or the officials of the Treasury. Firstly, metals suitable for transport were desirable, and in Lydia, Persia, and Macedon we find that gold was coined and carefully protected. The small Greek communities used Persian gold, but did not coin their own, probably for reasons of economy. Secondly, some weight units would be more suitable than others, before coins passed by tale, for weighing the metal, and later as a standard for the coins. The first units adopted in each place were either borrowed from abroad or established locally. If the latter, they were selected because they were identical with an old unit of value or possibly an old unit of weight. But areas which had already established a unit often replaced it by another, either obtained from abroad or locally evolved. We must, therefore, explain, on the one hand, why foreign units were adopted, and the considerations taken into account in their selection, and, on the other, how fresh native units were established.

There were commercial and political arguments for the adoption of foreign units. The use of the same weight standard in two cities for weighing metal or making coin facilitated commercial intercourse by simplifying exchange transactions. The spread of the "Æginetan," the "Eubœan," and later the "Phocæan" standards in the Greek world provides many examples of the adoption of foreign standards for this reason. The Roman issue of coins upon the "Campanian" standard for use in Southern Italy during the second half of the 3rd century B.C. may be similarly explained. But generally the large empires were not concerned with the assimilation of their money to foreign standards. The Roman example quoted above does not constitute an adjustment of the standard, but an issue on a second standard for a special area. In some districts the freer intercourse consequent upon the assimilation of standards was hoped to yield political rather than economic benefits. The spread of units in the Greek world may be also in part so explained. The monetary unions of the 4th century B.C. often rested upon a political basis, and Philip of Macedon's choice of standards has been explained as part of an attempt to court the favour of Chalcidian interests and avoid bringing Macedon within the Athenian orbit by adopting her standards.

Fresh units, including those intended to facilitate intercourse with other areas, were in practice nearly always units smaller than those previously in use. Frequently a shrinking unit can be identified at various stages with some foreign unit, and the reduction may be explained as the adoption for economic or political reasons of a foreign unit. But there is no doubt that other reasons must be sought to account for these reductions. In the first place, it must be noted that they never occurred in Lydia, Persia, or Macedon. In Europe, with its greater variety of units, they were fairly common. They were often due to mere inefficiency in coining or in controlling the moneyers. If coins were irregular in weight, the heavier would tend to disappear; moneyers would seek illicit profit if not supervised; and unless the state was prepared to defray the cost of coining out of taxation or other revenues standards would tend to shrink at each recoinage. Where bimetallic systems were in use, reductions were sometimes due to changes in the market ratio between the value of the metals. The reduction of the fineness of silver towards the end of the Persian Empire, the increase of the weight of the silver coins by Alexander of Macedon, part of the reduction of the Roman silver unit in 217 B.C., and part of Nero's reform in the 1st century A.D., may all be so explained. For the rest, reductions of standard were aimed at yielding recoinage profits and the relief of debtors, the state being usually a debtor on a considerable scale. Reduction in the weight of the coin, without corresponding reduction in its legal value, for the purpose of making it token, could be used as a means of raising a small and steady revenue. But, with the exception of small change, tokens were not often issued. If however, it is a fact that governments made a habit of prohibiting exports of precious metals in uncoined form, and of charging for coining a sum in excess of the cost of the operation,[1] the effect was much the same as if tokens were issued. Devaluation, or reduction of the weight of coins for profit, is rare in pre-Roman

[1] Lenormant (II, 133) says that this was done in Macedon, and in Rome in relation to the produce of the Spanish gold and silver mines.

times: Hippias or Solon may have reduced the Athenian standard, and there are stories of similar reductions in Sicily. The early reductions of the Roman *as* have been ascribed to this, among a number of reasons. The reduction of the silver standard probably during the Pyrrhic Wars, and again under the second Punic War and during the reign of Nero, had probably the same origin. But it must be noted that reductions of the unit supposed to have been made for reasons other than profit were just as remunerative as those where profit was the sole object of the change. Debasement of the coins by reducing their fineness was one of the earliest method of manipulating the coinage for profit; it was almost induced by the use of electrum in early times in Lydia. But it brought its own remedy in the replacement of electrum by coins of silver and gold. These remained of extraordinarily high quality in Lydia and Persia (until nearly the end of the Empire) and the Macedonian Empire. The Greek cities kept the general quality of their silver high, and reveal few examples of debasement, although those of the Ionian cities that returned to electrum in the 5th century B.C. seem to have been unable to prevent its debasement. The Romans under the Republic pursued the same policy of maintaining the quality of silver, but Nero commenced to reduce the *denarius* and started a movement which ceased only when the currency system had been destroyed. The issue of plated coins in imitation of good money was an alternative method of debasement. The early empires never resorted to it, and the Greek cities but rarely. The Athenians issued plated money in the years of stress at the end of the 5th century, and similar issues were made in Sicily. Republican Rome first resorted to the device during the second Punic War, after which it was not again exploited until the last century B.C. In the period of the decline of the Republic and the rise of Empire it was intermittently used until the uniform and drastic debasement of silver rendered plating an unremunerative activity. The contrast in the matter of the exploitation of the coinage is not so much between Europe and Asia as between Rome and the rest of the ancient world. The Asiatic empires seem never to have given way to any temptation to make a profit out of the coinage. The Greek cities experimented in reducing standards, both by debasing and plating, but it was the Romans who turned their knowledge to practical ends. The smallness of the Greek communities, and the form of their political organization, may account for their restraint. Although it is doubtful whether or not the consequences of depreciation were well enough understood for the people to take a strong line and use their political opportunities to thwart any proposal to depreciate the coinage, the quotation of their coins at a discount in foreign coin would disturb them. More probably the volume of the currency was too small to make the temptation to tamper with the money very strong. Perhaps its effect in lightening the state debt was too obvious in its unfairness to receive general approval, and any general tendency to adopt fresh units would have given rise to the most obvious confusion in foreign trade. The Romans turned to good advantage the knowledge of the Greeks: under the Republic they experimented rather as the Greeks had, but as the Republic began to totter they became more frankly mercenary in their currency policy, until under the Empire depreciation of all kinds was exploited almost to the possible limit.

The motives of early currency policy were not, however, merely economic. Where there was any kind of monarchical organization, the tyrant usually seized the currency and used it as a means of advertisement. The Persians and the Roman Emperors placed their portraits upon the coins with this end in view. The Romans of the Republic were equally aware of the psychological significance of the control of the currency. The bimetallic system of 268 B.C. was forced upon all the newly-acquired territory to the southernmost point of Italy. Many of the gold coins issued during the 4th century B.C. had as a basis the purely political motive of display; cities issued gold coins much as individuals might wear gold ornaments. As a means of facilitating the public financial administration, and extending national commerce, a good currency system was of the first importance in peacefully extending the political power of the state, as the Athenians apparently realized. As a means of enabling treasure to be realized, and still more as a means of raising profit, it was of great potency in extending political power in time of war. In consequence, we find that the greatest quantity of currency was issued in time of war, and practically all attempts to depreciate money occurred at the same time. In Rome the association is particularly significant. The first issue of coins was probably made during the Samnite War, the first issues of silver during the Pyrrhic War, a possible reduction of the *as* during the first Punic War, a reduction of both silver and bronze and the issue of silver-plated coins during the second Punic War, and the reduction of the *as* and the reissue of plated coins during the Social War. The provincial issues of gold each commemorated the victorious conclusion of military campaigns, the issue of Julius Cæsar following upon his return from the Gallic War. Periodical festivals and games were the other main cause of coining. Then, instead of a supply of metal calling for disposal, the concentration of a mass of exchanges in a small space and time gave rise to a demand for more money. The most interesting examples of control of monetary policy to political ends are to be found in China and Sparta. In China bronze was the only medium of exchange, the coining of iron in Sparta being prohibited. In China deposits of gold and silver were not normally worked, and in Sparta they were not allowed to be imported—in both areas because a too great inequality of wealth was feared. It was felt that the new commerce was not to be encouraged for fear of the disadvantages it might bring. Sparta became a stagnant backwater of civilization and China a tranquil lagoon. It was doubtless because the Chinese took no real interest in coinage that the state so long postponed taking over the mint; the technique of coining was permitted to continue in a primitive state, and counterfeiters were allowed to batten upon the coinage in great numbers, so that on one occasion the state was prepared to abandon coining altogether.

In the pre-Christian era there were, therefore, two separate currency traditions, the Asiatic and the European, with the coast cities of Asia Minor influenced by both. The former was the policy of absolute monarchs and large territories, and was marked by the open display of power in the personal types and portraits on the coins, a preference for bimetallism, reliance upon the "Babylonian" and "Phœnician" weight standards, and a great stability in both the weight and fineness of coins. The latter was the policy of small territorial units sometimes tyrannically and sometimes democratically organized. No tyrant, however, displayed his portrait on the coin, and the policy of these small units was characterized by types of divine or economic reference, a steady adherence to silver monometallism, the use of standards, such as the "Æginetan," which was probably based upon an ancient iron unit of value, or the "Eubœan," which was possibly adapted from an Asiatic unit. The weight, but not the fineness of coins (except where electrum was coined), was considerably more variable than in Asia. But neither policy gave much emphasis to the profit-yielding capacity of the coinage. As we have seen, that was left to the practically-minded Romans.

6. *Retrospect.*

When we look back now to the first thousand years of coining over an interval of nearly two thousand years from the end of the period, we find that the development of money and monetary policy in early times was not always what we might have expected. Coining was a surprisingly late addition to the human heritage of economic knowledge. But when it came currency problems that have a somewhat modern ring followed with perhaps unexpected rapidity. Bimetallism is almost as old as coining, and the Monetary Union is but little younger. Inflation, both by reducing the monetary standard (devaluation) and by reducing the fineness of the coins (debasement), followed equally quickly. Plated coins were also an early invention; probably at first the work of counterfeiters, they were being used by states at least by the 5th century B.C. They are of interest because they offer the nearest approach in the ancient world to modern paper money: they were a currency of which the metallic value was much less than the legal value, and they offered far greater scope for inflation without resort to recoinage than debasement or devaluation. But, on the other hand, some features of currency policy were unexpectedly slow in appearing. Of these the most interesting is the gold standard, of which there is no example in the first thousand years after the introduction of coining. Less surprising is the fact that token money was not introduced until three hundred years after the first coins.

Modern money was the joint work of many authors. One invented seals, another applied them to metal, the Ionic cities evolved a flat coin with types in relief, the Athenians so far improved the whole business of coining that the coin in the full sense of a piece of metal of agreed weight and fineness was finally achieved. The Romans attended more to the exploitation than the perfection of coining, with the result that their technique was poor, and they gave the world the inestimable curse of practical knowledge of all possible methods of inflation apart from the issue of paper money.

APPENDICES

APPENDIX I

MONETARY THEORY IN EARLY TIMES

SPECULATION as to the nature of money began in Athens in the closing years of the 5th century B.C. References are of the briefest and mostly descriptive of the part played by money in the organization of society. Constructive theory as to who should supply money, what are the best kinds of currency, and how they should be managed with a view to the most effective social organization, is very sparse.

1. *Aristophanes.*

Aristophanes, writing not long before 405 B.C., although no theorist, camc vcry ncar to Gresham's law in the vulgar form when he remarked with reference to the recent issues of emergency money in Athens: " In our Republic bad citizens are preferred to good, just as bad money circulates while good money disappears."[1]

2. *Plato.*

Plato noted, in passing, the need of " money as a symbol for the sake of exchange,"[2] and remarked elsewhere,[3] in elaboration of the same idea, that money " reduces the inequalities and immeasurabilities of goods to equality and measure." He recognized, then, the use of money as both a medium of exchange and a measure of value. In the *Laws*[4] he went further. Money being necessary in the community for the daily buying and selling of the work of the craftsmen and payment of wages, coin must be supplied. But this coin, while of value among the members of the community, is to be " of no worth amongst the rest of mankind." Beyond this and that " no private person be permitted

[1] *Frogs*, 717 *sqq*.

[2] *Republic*, II, pp. 37-38.

[3] *Laws*, XI.

[4] V, 12 (Bohn's edition, p. 179).

to possess gold or silver," he makes no suggestion as to the best material for money. For purposes of war and state services, such as the maintenance of foreign embassies, requiring "the common coin of Greece," it will be essential for the state to possess a supply of such coin. Any private traveller returning from abroad with foreign coin is to be compelled under penalty to sell it to the state in return for domestic currency at the current rate of exchange. Coupled with his earlier reference to money as a symbol, this passage suggests the use of a token money the value of which would considerably exceed the value of its metallic content.[1] The prohibition of the private possession of gold and silver, together with the use of a token currency, would, however, seriously cripple foreign trade. But in the middle of the 4th century B.C. Athens had a silver currency, and Plato's theories had no more effect on the policy of the state than have the efforts of theorists to-day. It is quite possible that his notion of separate currencies for internal and external trade was based on the contemporary use of silver mainly for home and gold mainly for foreign trade.

3. *Aristotle.*

Aristotle followed Plato in his discussion of the functions of money, implying its use as a medium of exchange in his explanation that it arose out of the need for extended exchange of commodities.[2] He elaborated its uses as a measure of value,[3] and pointed to its use as a store of value in that "it is a kind of security to us in respect of exchange at some future time . . . the theory of money being that whenever one brings it one can receive commodities in exchange." The value of money "was at first measured simply by size and weight."[4] He realizes as one of the disadvantages of the use of money as a store of value that "of course this too is liable to depreciation, for its purchasing power is not always the same, but still it is of a more permanent nature than the commodities it represents."[5] The approval with which he

[1] In view of this, the claim that among "all the Greek writers of the autonomous period none bears the least trace of the fatal theory that sees in money only a '*signe conventionnel des échanges*,' subject to the will of the sovereign or the state" (Lenormant, III, 3) is overstated.

[2] *Politics*, 1257a, 38.

[3] *Ethics*, V, 5.

[4] *Politics*, 1257a, 38.

[5] *Ethics*, V, 5.

remarks upon this greater stability of value suggests that he considered such stability a desirable quality in money. The object of coining was, he says, " to save the trouble of weighing " and " marking the value."[1] The last three words are capable of various interpretations. Do they merely refer to the quality of the coin, the fineness of the metal, or does Aristotle mean that the seal on the coin notified the quantity and quality of metal present and, therefore, the value of the coin in terms of the monetary metal? He recognized that the purchasing power of money changed, so he cannot have thought that the state could determine the value of money in terms of commodities. As to the substance of which money should be made he differed from Plato. This substance should be " something which was intrinsically useful and easily applicable to the purposes of life—for example, iron, silver,[2] and the like."[3] This would mark him as the father of the " hard money " theory. But his attitude is not clear, for he writes elsewhere[4] that " money has come to be by general agreement a representative of demand, and the account of its Greek name *νόμιομα* is this, that it is what it is, not naturally, but by custom or law (*νόμος*), and it rests with us to change its value or make it wholly useless."[5] It is true that the monetary commodity is what it is by custom or law. If by a change of law another commodity is adopted in its place, the value of the commodity abandoned is likely to fall, but if it is " something intrinsically useful " it cannot be made wholly useless by such a change of law or custom. It appears that Aristotle is adopting here a view put into the mouths of " others "[6] in the course of a discussion on the art of getting wealth. After stating that riches are thought by many to consist in coin alone he proceeds:[7] " Others maintain that coined money is a mere sham, a thing not natural, but conventional only, because if the users substitute another commodity for it it is worth-

[1] *Politics*, 1257a, 38.
[2] His omission of gold is notable, for, although Athens coined only silver, Aristotle had lived for twelve years in Macedon, where ample gold issues had been made.
[3] *Politics*, 1257a, 38.
[4] *Ethics*, V, 5. [5] *Ibid.*
[6] These " others " were probably some of the Stoics (*vide* Monroe, *Monetary Theory before Adam Smith*, p. 9).
[7] *Politics*, I, 9.

less, and because it is not useful as a means to any of the necessaries of life, and, indeed, he who is rich in coin may often be in want of necessary food. . . . Hence men seek after a better notion of riches and of the art of getting wealth than the mere acquisition of coin, and they are right." This passage suggests that by "valueless" he is thinking of the small utility of money in itself "as a means to any of the necessaries of life" once it ceases to be generally acceptable in exchange owing to an alteration of monetary law. Thus a man may starve though rich in coin. Though the coin may lose its greater usefulness as a medium of exchange when it is demonetized, it retains the utility of the commodity of which it is made. If by demonetization money can be made entirely useless, the material of the money must have been of no value as a commodity, and the coins absolute tokens. In consequence of his conflicting statements, Aristotle has been claimed, on the one hand, as "heading a long line of 'sound money' advocates,"[1] and, on the other, as a supporter of the theory that money is "merely '*le signe représentatif*' of the value of the things exchanged," and "that it is the legislator alone who decrees the value of gold and silver." In fact, he saw the advantages of money which could be converted to other uses by melting, but realized that the possession of such money did not in itself guarantee well-being, which would depend on the facility with which it could be exchanged for other goods and services. This facility would be seriously diminished by the demonetization of the coin, but he went too far in saying that the money would be valueless, for he probably still had in mind a money of some useful commodity. On the whole, therefore, Aristotle believed in "hard" money and presumably had little fault to find with the contemporary silver standard currency of Athens.

4. *The Writer of the Pseudo-Aristotelian "Œconomica."*

The writer of the second book of the pseudo-Aristotelian *Œconomica,* probably some Greek living outside Greece itself, at a period a little later than Aristotle, regarded the management of the coinage, the decision as to "what coin

[1] Monroe, *op. cit.*, 7.

should be struck, and when it should be of a high and when of a low value," as one of the four parts of royal economy which he regarded as the most important of the four kinds of economy.

5. *Xenophon.*

Xenophon, writing in 355 B.C.,[1] turned more particularly to the conditions affecting the value of gold and silver, the reason for his attention being that he had proposed that the city of Athens should remodel the organization for exploiting the silver mines at Laurium; he proposed that the city should follow the example of private capitalists and purchase a slave gang to work in the mines, the consequent profits going to the relief of the Treasury. In defence of his plan he said that the supplies of silver were unlikely to run out, and the silver mining industry differed from all others in that the value of the product did not fall with an increase in the volume of production. The scheme would not result, therefore, in driving any producers out of operation; in fact, "the larger the quantity of ore discovered, and the greater the amount of silver extracted, the greater the number of persons ready to engage in the operation." He attempted to explain this peculiar quality of the metal by saying that, "Of silver no one ever yet possessed so much that he was forced to cry 'enough.' On the contrary, if ever anybody does become possessed of an immoderate amount he finds as much pleasure in digging a hole in the ground and hoarding it as in the actual employment of it. And from a wider point of view when a state is prosperous, there is nothing which people so much desire as silver. The men want money to expend on beautiful armour and fine horses and houses and sumptuous paraphernalia of all sorts. The women betake themselves to expensive apparel and ornaments of gold. Or when states are sick either through barrenness of corn and other fruits or through war the demand for current coin is even more imperative (whilst the ground lies unproductive) to pay for necessaries or military aid.

"And if it be asserted that gold is after all just as useful as silver, without gainsaying the proposition, I may note this fact about gold that with a sudden influx of this metal

[1] *Ways and Means, a Pamphlet on Revenues,* IV.

it is gold itself which is depreciated whilst causing at the same time a rise in the value of silver." The inexhaustibility of the mines at Laurium is no longer in question. But the immunity of silver from changes in value due to the quantity of silver produced calls for explanation. It is quite possible that Xenophon is correct that, although Athens had been on a silver standard, the output from Laurium had caused no rise in silver prices. But wear and tear on the coinage, and the drain of silver for export to parts possessing no mines where the use of silver was extending, are an adequate explanation. The hoarding of silver is a variable factor, because only an excess of the amounts buried over those disinterred would tend to prevent a fall in the value of silver, and a deficiency would have the opposite effect of enhancing the fall in its value. But when he proceeds to a wider view he passes easily to the alternative rise of "silver" and "money" as synonymous. This is not surprising, as the Attic currency was entirely of silver. The presence of more money would not alone make it any easier to purchase luxuries: prices would rise and tend to neutralize the increased size of incomes. But where full value silver coins were in use they could be exported when their domestic purchasing power began to fall, and in this way were the luxuries obtained, and the local value of silver maintained. Similarly in war-time the use of silver lay in its general acceptability abroad. The difference between the effect of increased supplies of gold and silver is not clear. Xenophon does not explain how he determines whether gold or silver changes in value when there is an influx of the former. If gold is valued in silver units, its value would naturally fall. But would the value of the silver unit rise in anything other than gold? Beyond these unsatisfactory suggestions as to the relation between the output of the monetary metal, and the value of money, Xenophon made no contribution to theory.

As was remarked in the text, there is no sign that theory reacted on contemporary policy any more in the 4th century B.C. than two thousand years later.

Roman writers added nothing to the passing comments of the Greek philosophers on the nature of money.

APPENDIX II

THE RELATIVE VALUES OF THE MONETARY METALS

THE age of barter, which passed with the general adoption of the practice of issuing coins, left behind some very troublesome legacies. A study of the monetary standards adopted in early times brings out two salient facts. In the first place, communities adopted as their standard of value the metal which had acted as a medium of exchange and standard of value in the later period of barter; as the metals used for these purposes varied in different communities, early currency standards varied in the same way. In the course of time, bronze and other minor standards were superseded, but two monetary standards—viz., gold and silver—persisted. Where silver monometallic systems were set up, so long as the relative value of gold and silver remained unaltered, no special difficulties arose in transactions with gold-using areas, but changes in the relative values of the two metals at once caused instability of foreign exchange quotations and unsettled trade between them. These difficulties, although vastly less in magnitude, are similar in kind to the difficulties of pure barter. Men, having made great progress in the elimination of the difficulties of barter, failed to attain unanimity in the choice of the material of the standard of value. In consequence, prices in countries using different standards were not directly comparable, and debts expressed in the standard of one country were subject to disturbing variations in their burden in terms of the units of other countries using a different standard. In spite of the disadvantages to foreign trade of the use of two metals as standards, both gold and silver continued in use, as they do still, for China has a silver standard.

In the second place, there emerges from a consideration of monetary standards the fact that as early as the middle of the 6th century B.C. there commenced a long series of attempts to overcome the difficulties consequent on the lack of any universal standard by the use of gold and silver concurrently as monetary metals. Here, again, difficulties did not arise until changes in the relative values of gold and silver occurred. Then, however, when foreign merchants began to give more than before for the coins of one metal, foreign purchases tended to be paid for, as far as possible, in that metal. In such circumstances foreign merchants, finding that purchases in the country can be paid for indifferently at the old rate of exchange in either metal, naturally pay their debts in the country as far as possible in the metal which has not risen in value. Thus one metal tends to flow out of and the other to flow into the country, and, if no reform of the currency is undertaken, one metal disappears from circulation, leaving the country with a monometallic system in practice whatever its currency laws and the intentions of its administrators may be. Moreover, there is a tendency for each of the monetary metals to concentrate in the countries in which they have the greatest value, thus dividing countries into two camps, each with a monometallic currency, but each based on different metals. Then, in all transactions between countries in different camps the foreign exchange difficulties above referred to are encountered.

In the time of the earliest records in Egypt, silver was more valuable than gold, while in about 2000 B.C. in Babylon gold was about six times as valuable as silver. But for some thousand years down to the 5th century B.C. gold was, in the Eastern Mediterranean and throughout Asia and Egypt, about thirteen times as valuable as silver. In Assyria some twenty private contracts of the 9th to the 7th centuries B.C. have been found, in which sums are expressed in silver, but were paid in gold at about this ratio.[1] In Nineveh and Babylon, too, this ratio has been established. At this ratio a mixture of three parts of gold and one part of silver would give an electrum worth ten times as much as silver. The difficulty of assaying early coins has given rise to a suggestion that early electrum coins were accepted at a conventional value of ten times their weight in silver.[2] But the early series of electrum issues petered out in the 6th century, and if ever a conventional value was attached to electrum it had disappeared by the end of the 6th century B.C.

The same ratio of $13\frac{1}{3}:1$ was to be found in Lydia (except in some more remote parts where a ratio of 20 : 1 is believed

[1] Babelon, *Origines de la Monnaie*, 312. [2] Gardner, *op. cit.*, 35.

to have existed) in the latter part of the 6th century, when Crœsus reformed the currency by issuing coins of pure gold and silver in place of the old electrum pieces, and is at the bottom of the decimal relation between the values of the coins of the two metals. The ratio was not disturbed by the Persian conquest, and when the new Persian currency was established it also consisted of both gold and silver coins, rated to each other on the basis of a relation between the values of gold and silver of $13\frac{1}{3}:1$, which ratio persisted throughout the Persian dominions until the 4th century, when gold began to fall in value and the ratio sank to 11 : 1. In consequence, silver coins disappeared from circulation.[1]

In the Greek world also gold was somewhat more valuable than in Asia early in the last millennium B.C. During the 8th and 7th centuries B.C. silver fell in value in Athens and caused some disturbance of the market ratios.[2] If Pheidon when he set up the new silver unit in Ægina attempted to make the silver unit one-tenth of the gold unit (a doubtful possibility), the ratio was then 15 : 1. But the rapid growth of Greek colonization during the 6th century, and the more active commercial relations between the cities of the Ægean and those of Asia Minor, resulted in heavy imports of gold and electrum and a fall in the value of gold until the relative market values of gold and silver approached those current in Asia Minor. By the latter part of the 5th century gold had fallen in value in silver to 14 : 1, the ratio revealed by the accounts for the embellishment of the Parthenon in the time of Phidias and Pericles. Spoils of both gold and silver were sent home to the Treasury after the declaration of peace with Persia in 448 B.C.[3] and may have caused an alteration in the ratio: Herodotus[4] gives a ratio as low as 13 : 1.[5] The Peloponnesian War, which began in 431 B.C., contributed to the fall in the value of gold. It was prodigally distributed to the Greek generals by the Persian King,[6] and the Greek merchants were paid in the same medium. In the last decade of the century, when the output of silver from the Athenian mines

[1] Lenormant, *op. cit.*, I, 17.
[2] Seltman, 116.
[3] Zimmern, *op. cit.*, 402.
[4] III, 95.
[5] Cavaignac, 173-3 (*cit.* Zimmern, 397), says that the general level of prices was rising in Athens in the 5th century (see also Zimmern, *op. cit.*, 414 n.). If the purchasing power of silver was falling, that of gold must have been falling still faster.
[6] Babelon, *op. cit.*, 335.

was suspended, and when also the Athenians coined the gold reserves amassed in the Parthenon by Pericles, it would be expected that the ratio would move against gold and in favour of silver. The gold coins issued in 407 B.C., although not legally rated in silver, probably circulated in practice at about twelve times the value of silver, which continued to be the ratio[1] during the first two or three decades of the succeeding century. In Magna Græcia, however, the ratio seems to have been still as high as 15 : 1.[2] Towards the middle of the century the value of gold began to decline—at first slowly. Gold coins issued in the Cimmerian Bosphorus (Crimea), the market for the metal from the Urals, were apparently based on a ratio of 1 : 11·7. But when the mines were opened at Philippi in 356 B.C., and their plentiful produce appeared on the market, gold fell further in value, and by the end of Philip's reign it was worth only ten times as much as silver.[3] Philip's currency system was probably bimetallic and based upon this ratio. Having reached this level, the value of gold ceased to fall, although Alexander coined not only the produce of the mines, but his father's reserves and, later, the reserves of the Persian Kings from Susa and Persepolis. Moreover, during the later 4th century, the mines at Laurium were beginning to fail. The demand for gold must have increased sufficiently to neutralize the effect of both the increasing supplies of gold and the falling supplies of silver, for the ratio of 10 : 1 probably persisted in Athens down to the Roman invasion. This increased demand came doubtless from fresh areas adopting gold as a principal currency, and often from the substitution of silver currency by gold. This severe fall in the silver value of gold between the Persian Wars and the death of Alexander naturally reacted upon the bimetallic currencies of the time, and was probably accountable for Alexander's abandonment of bimetallism in favour of parallel currencies of gold and silver.

In Egypt, down to the latter part of the 6th century B.C., the relation between gold and silver was about the same as elsewhere in the Eastern Mediterranean, the ratio being 1 : 12

[1] Cp. Pseudo-Platonic dialogue, *Hipparchus*, 231d.
[2] Head, *Coins of Syracuse*, 176.
[3] The Treasurers at Delphi were taking Æginetan *drachms* at one-fifteenth of a *daric* in 331 B.C.—*i.e.*, the ratio was 10 : 1 (Gardner, *op. cit.*, 425).

or 13. The Macedonian conquest, and the hellenization of Egypt under the Ptolemies from the latter part of the 4th century, seems to have left the ratio almost unchanged at about 1 : 12½, the ratio in force under Ptolemy Soter (323-285 B.C.). No Egyptian coins were issued until the 3rd or 2nd century B.C.

In Rome in early times gold and silver circulated as bullion, and nothing is known of their relative values, which, however, were of no importance in relation to the currency. When silver coins were issued at Capua or elsewhere in Campania under Roman control towards the end of the 4th century or early in the 3rd century, the ratio that was important was that between silver and bronze. The new coins circulated with the bronze issues of the Roman Mint. But there is no reliable evidence as to either the currency or the market ratio. Market ratios of 288 : 1,[1] 250 : 1,[2] 180 : 1,[3] 120 : 1[4] have all been suggested. The coinage ratio is generally agreed to have been 120 : 1 in 240 B.C.[5] But from 335 B.C. to 240 B.C. the matter is in dispute. Bronze coins were almost certainly full-weight pieces, but the weight of bronze, which was equivalent to a scruple of silver, depends upon the ratio between the values of gold and silver; the coins do not settle the difficulty, because the Campanian issues are not marked to show their value in bronze, and the difficulty of dating later Roman issues that are so marked renders it impossible to identify the *as* that was worth one-tenth of the *denarius*. In 217 B.C. the currency ratio was altered to 1 : 112 and in 89 B.C. to 1 : 56.

With the disappearance of gold coins during the last century B.C. interest shifts to the relative values of gold and silver. Although the Romans had made no continuous issues, gold coins had been current in Italy since the 5th century, and probably the 6th century. The continuous communication between the Ægean and Italy might be expected to have brought about much the same relations between the values of the precious metals in both places. But at Cumæ in Campania in about 480 B.C. gold coins seem to have been based on a ratio of 15 : 1[6] compared with the 13⅓ : 1 then generally

[1] Babelon, 378.
[2] Grueber, 16.
[3] Ridgeway, 383.
[4] Head, 19.
[5] Mommsen believed that the legal relation remained 240 : 1 until 217 B.C., but the case against his view has been presented in Chap. X.
[6] Head, 36.

current in the East. The same ratio prevailed in Etruria at about the same time, and continued until the end of the 5th century in Sicily, when it was the basis upon which the coins of Syracuse[1] were issued. During the 4th century the flow of gold *staters* from Philippi reduced the ratio to about 12:1.

When gold coins were first issued in Rome in 217 B.C., during the first Punic War, they were marked to show their value in silver *sestertii*, which was based upon a currency ratio between the values of gold and silver of 20 : 1.[2] Gold seems to have been very much over-valued in these coins, for there is no reason to suppose that the silver value of gold had increased generally in the Mediterranean to so high a level. It is difficult to believe that gold was 75 per cent. more valuable in Italy than in the Ægean, for the metal would then have passed westward in quantities sufficient to establish an equal valuation throughout the Mediterranean. In consequence, it must be concluded that the coins were tokens.[3] The silver value of gold declined continuously and steadily until the middle of the last century B.C. The military issues of gold at that time show a wide range of ratios. Those made in the provinces in the first half of the century suggest an under-valuation of gold in the coins. Those of Sulla of about 81 B.C. show a coinage ratio of 1: 9, although the market ratio was about 1 : 11.[4] Those of Pompey in about 60 B.C. were based on a ratio of 1 : 10·7,[5] a closer approach to the probable market ratio. As the coining of gold was a new departure, the coins were perhaps deliberately made a little heavier than the market ratio between gold and silver justified in order to make sure of a good reception. But already in the time of Pompey this consideration was losing force. In the middle of the century the value of gold tended to rise a little, and a ratio of 1:11·9 was reached,[6] but Cæsar brought back great quantities of gold plunder from Gaul, and the market ratio is said to have fallen to 1:8·93.[7] The discovery of the gold mines, in what is now Styria and Carinthia in Eastern

[1] Head, 175.

[2] Grueber, LV. If the gold coins were not issued until 217 B.C., when the *sestertius* of silver had been reduced, the ratio was 1:17·143.

[3] Grueber, LV.

[4] Babelon, 359.

[5] Grueber, LVII, II, 459, II, 464.

[6] Lenormant, I, 166.

[7] Suetonius, *Cæsar*, LIV, says that a pound of gold was worth 3,000 *sestertii*.

Austria, threw a further amount of gold on the market after 60 B.C., but there cannot have been any great or permanent fall in the value of gold from about 12 : 1, for full-weight coins of both gold and silver remained in circulation, and the silver value of gold for coinage was steadily raised by repeated reductions in the weight of the gold coins, without any accompanying alterations either in the weight of the silver *denarius*, or the number of *denarii* to which the gold *aureus* was equated in value. The ratios at which the two metals were coined under the Republic were:

Sulla	1:9
Pompey	1:10·7
Cæsar	1:11·3
Cæsar (46-44 B.C.)	1:12
Triumvirate	1:12
Augustus	1:12·5

During the first half of the first century of the present era the ratio established by Augustus was maintained, but in the time of Nero the weight of the coins of both gold and silver was reduced, and the fineness of the silver coins diminished. The resulting coinage ratio was about 1:10·6, and this had fallen by the end of the century to 1: 9·375.[1] Gold was now clearly falling again in value. No ratio can be traced during the period of the collapse during the 2nd and first three-quarters of the 3rd century A.D. But when Diocletian restored gold and silver it was on a ratio of 1:13 : 88, which was probably also the market ratio. In the coins of the subsequent two or three centuries gold was evèn more highly valued in silver.

[1] Mommsen, III, 43.

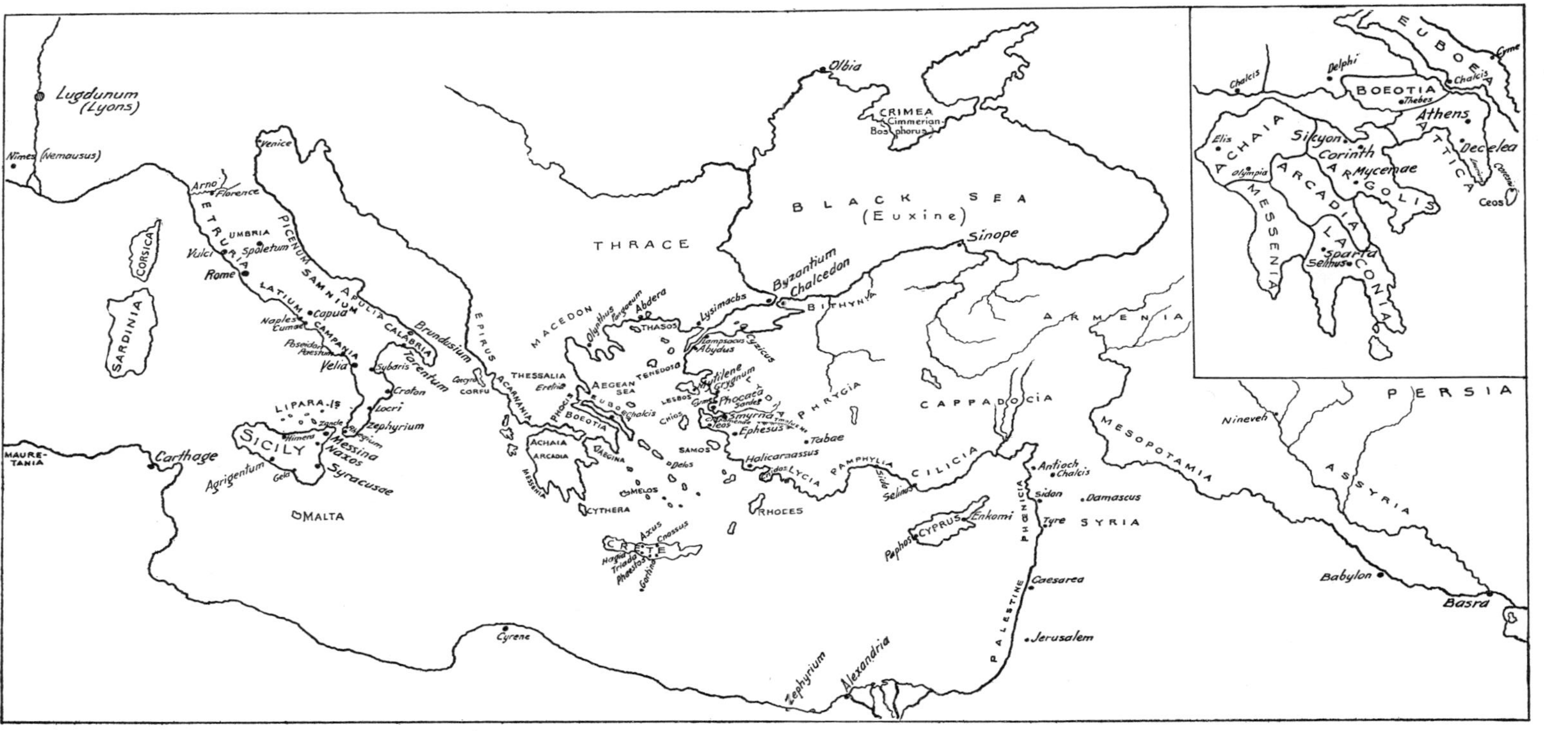

Lugdunum (Lyons)
Nimes (Nemausus)
CORSICA
SARDINIA
MAURE-TANIA
Carthage
Venice
Arno
Florence
ETRURIA
UMBRIA
Spoletum
Vulci
Rome
PICENUM
SAMNIUM
APULIA
LATIUM
Capua
Naples
Cumae
CAMPANIA
Velia
CALABRIA
Brundusium
Tarentum
Sybaris
Croton
Locri
Zephyrium
Messina
Naxos
Syracusae
LIPARA IS
SICILY
Himera
Agrigentum
Gela
MALTA
THRACE
MACEDON
Olynthus
Abdera
THASOS
EPIRUS
CORFU
THESSALIA
ACARNANIA
Eretria
AEGEAN SEA
TENEDOS
PHOCIS
BOEOTIA
Chalcis
ACHAIA
ARCADIA
MESSENIA
AEGINA
Delos
MELOS
CYTHERA
CRETE
Axus
Cnossus
Hagia Triada
Phaestos
Gortina
Olbia
CRIMEA
Cimmerian Bosphorus
BLACK SEA (Euxine)
Sinope
Byzantium
Chalcedon
Lysimachs
BITHYNIA
Lampsacus
Abydus
Cyzicus
Mytilene
Grynium
LESBOS
Phocaea
Sardes
Chios
Smyrna
Teos
Ephesus
PHRYGIA
Tabae
SAMOS
Halicarnassus
Cnidos
LYCIA
PAMPHYLIA
Side
Selinus
RHODES
CAPPADOCIA
CILICIA
ARMENIA
CYPRUS
Paphos
Enkomi
Antioch
Chalcis
Sidon
Tyre
PHOENICIA
Damascus
SYRIA
Caesarea
Jerusalem
PALESTINE
Cyrene
Zephyrium
Alexandria
MESOPOTAMIA
Nineveh
ASSYRIA
PERSIA
Babylon
Basra
EUBOEA
Erme
Chalcis
Delphi
BOEOTIA
Thebes
Athens
ATTICA
Decelea
Ceos
ACHAIA
Elis
Olympia
Sicyon
Corinth
ARGOLIS
Mycenae
ARCADIA
MESSENIA
LACONIA
Sparta
Sellasia

BIBLIOGRAPHICAL NOTE

The following is a list of the more important books, periodicals, and articles consulted in connection with the preparation of this work:

BABELON, E.: La Monnaie de la République romaine. *Paris*, 1886
Les Origines de la Monnaie. *Paris*, 1897
Traité des Monnaies grecques et romaines. *Paris*, 1901, etc.

BEANLANDS, Canon A.: The Origin of the Augustan *sestertius*: an Experiment in Trimetallism. *Num. Chron.* 1918, 187

BRANDIS, J.: Münz- Mass- und Gewichtswesen in Vorder Asien. *Berlin*, 1866

BURGON, T.: An Enquiry into the Motives which affected the Ancients in their Choice of the various Representations which we find stamped on their Money. *London.* 1836

Cambridge Ancient History, edited by J. B. Bury, M.A., F.B.A., S. A. Cook, Litt. D., F. E. Adcock, M.A. *Cambridge*, 1924, etc.

CASPARI, M.: On the Dated Coins of Julius Cæsar and Mark Antony. *Num. Chron.* 1911, 101

DAREMBERG-SIGLIO: Dictionnaire des Antiquités. *Paris*, 1873

DODD, Rev. C. H.: The Cognomen of the Emperor Antoninus Pius. *Num. Chron.* 1911, 6
The Coinage of Commodus during the Reign of Marcus. *Num. Chron.* 1914, 2

Encyclopædia Britannica: Article "Numismatics," by R. S. Poole, H. A. Grueber, and G. F. Hill

EVANS, [Sir] A. J.: Minoan Weights and Mediums of Currency in *Corolla Numismatica*. *London*, 1906

FERENCZI, S.: Contributions to Psycho-Analysis. *London*, 1916

GARDNER, PERCY: A History of Ancient Coinage 700-300 B.C. *Oxford*, 1918

GLOTZ, G.: Ægean Civilization. *London*, 1925

GOODACRE, HUGH: Bronze Coinage of the late Roman Empire. *London* 1922

GRUEBER, H. A.: Roman Coins (in *Coins and Medals*, ed. by R. S. Lane Poole). *London*, 1894
Roman Bronze Coinage from 45-3 B.C. *Num. Chron.* 1904, 185
Coins of the Roman Republic in the British Museum, 3 vols. *London*, 1910
Coinages of the Triumvirs Antony, Lepidus, and Octavian. *Num. Chron.* 1911, 109

HÆBERLIN, E. J.: *Æs Grave*: das Schwergeld Roms und Mittelitaliens. *Frankfurt*, 1910

HALLIDAY, W. R.: Growth of the City State. Liverpool University Press

HANDS, A. W.: Juno Moneta. *Num. Chron.* 1910, 1

HARPER, R. F.: The Code of Hammurabi. *London*, 1904, etc.

HEAD, BARCLAY V.: Catalogue of Greek Coins in the British Museum, *London*, 1873, etc.
The Coinage of Lydia and Persia. *London*, 1877
Greek Coins (in *Coins and Medals*, ed. by R. S. Lane Poole). *London*, 1894
Guide to the Principal Gold and Silver Coins of the Ancients from *circa* 70 B.C. to A.D. 1. *London*, 1895
Catalogue of Greek Coins in the British Museum. *London*, 1901
Corolla Numismatica: Numismatic Essays in Honour of B. V. Head. *Oxford*, 1906
Historia Numorum: a Manual of Greek Numismatics. *Oxford*, 1911

HILL, G. F.: A Handbook of Greek and Roman Coins. *London*, 1899
Historical Greek Coins. *London*, 1906
Historical Roman Coins. *London*, 1909
Catalogue of Greek Coins of Phœnicia. *London*, 1910.
Ancient Methods of Coining. *Num. Chron.* 1922, 1

HOGARTH, D. G.: British Museum Excavations at Ephesus. *London*, 1908

HUNKIN, J. W.: A Note on the Silver Coins of the Jews. *Num. Chron.* 1916, 251

JOHNS, C. H. W.: Ancient Assyria. *Cambridge*, 1912
Ancient Babylon. *Cambridge*, 1910

JONES, ERNEST: Essays in Applied Psycho-Analysis. *London*, 1923
Papers on Psycho-Analysis. *London*, 1913

KEARY, C. F.: in *Coins and Medals* (ed. by R. S. Lane Poole). *London*, 1894

KING, LEONARD: History of Babylon. *London*, 1915

KNAPP, G. F.: The State Theory of Money. *London*, 1924

LACOUPERIE, TERRIEN DE: Catalogue of Chinese Coins in the British Museum. *London*, 1892

LAUM, BERNARD: Heiliges Geld. *Tubingen*, 1924

LENORMANT, F.: La Monnaie dans l'Antiquité. *Paris*, 1878
Monnaies royales de la Lydie. *Paris*, 1876

MACDONALD, G.: Coin Types: their Origin and Development. *Glasgow*, 1905
Evolution of Coinage. *Cambridge*, 1916

MADDEN, F. W.: Coins of the Jews (International Numismata Orientalia). *London*, 1881

MATTINGLY, H.: The Coinage of the Civil Wars 68-9 A.D. *Num. Chron.* 1914, 110
The Last Issues of Gold and Silver from the Senatorial Mint of Rome. *Num. Chron.* 1919, 35
Origins of the Imperial Coinage in Republican Times. *Num. Chron.* 1919, 221
The Restored Coinage of Titus Domitian and Nerva. *Num. Chron.* 1920, 177
The Mints of Vespasian. *Num. Chron.* 1921, 187
Coins of the Roman Empire in the British Museum. *London*, 1923
The Roman "serrati." *Num. Chron.* 1924, 31
The Romano Campanian Coinage and the Pyrrhic War. *Num. Chron.* 1924, 181

McLEAN, J. R.: The Elements of Primeval Finance. *Num. Chron.* 1912, 113
Origin of Weight. *Num. Chron.* 1912, 333

MILNE, J. G.: Roman Coin Moulds from Egypt. *Num. Chron.* 1905
The Leaden Token Coinage of Egypt under the Romans. *Num. Chron.* 1908, 287
Countermarked Coins of Asia Minor. *Num. Chron.* 1913, 389
A Hoard of Persian Sigloi. *Num. Chron.* 1916, 1
The Persian Standard in Ionia. *Num. Chron.* 1924, 1

MOMMSEN-BLACAS: Histoire de la Monnaie romaine. *Paris*, 1865-75

MULLER, F. MAX: India: What can it teach us? *London*, 1892

Numismatic Chronicle: *London*

OMAN, C.: The Decline and Fall of the *Denarius* in the Third Century A.D. *Num. Chron.* 1916, 37

PERRY, W. J.: Origin of Magic and Religion. *London*, 1923
The Children of the Sun. *London*, 1923

PETRIE, Sir W. M. F.: Naukratis. *London*, 1885, etc.
Glass Weights. *Num. Chron.* 1918
Social Life in Ancient Egypt. *London*, 1923

POOLE, R. S. LANE [editor] Coins: and Medals. *London*, 1894

RADET: La Lydie et le Monde grec. *Paris*, 1892

RAWLINSON, G.: Edition of Herodotus (note to Vol. IV). *London*, 1875

RIDGEWAY, Sir W.: The Origin of Metallic Currency and Weight Standards. *Cambridge*, 1892
Companion to Greek Studies, ed. L. Whibley. Article on "Money." *Cambridge*, 1905
Companion to Latin Studies, ed. Sir J. E. Sandys. Article on "Money." *Cambridge*, 1910

Rivista Italiana di Numismatica. *Milan*

ROGERS, Rev. E.: The Type of the Jewish Shekels. *Num. Chron.* 1911, 1

RUDING, R.: Annals of the Coinage of Great Britain, 3 vols. *London*, 1840

SELTMAN, C. T.: Temple Coins of Olympia. *Cambridge*, 1921
Athens: its History and Coinage before the Persian Invasion. *Cambridge*, 1924

SMITH, G. ELLIOT: The Evolution of the Dragon. *London*, 1919

SMITH, SIDNEY: A pre-Greek Coinage in the Near East. *Num. Chron.* 1922, 176

SMITH, W. (and WAYTE, W. and MARINDIN, G. E.): Dictionary of Greek and Roman Antiquities. *London*, 1891

SYDENHAM, E. A.: The Coinage of Nero. *Num. Chron.* 1916, 13
The Mint at Lugdunum. *Num. Chron.* 1917, 53
Divus Augustus. *Num. Chron.* 1917, 258
The Roman Monetary System. *Num. Chron.* 1918, 155; 1919, 114
The Coinages of Augustus. *Num. Chron.* 1920, 17
Coinage of Nero. *London*, 1920

URE, P. N.: The Origin of Tyranny. *Cambridge*, 1922

WEBB, P. H.: The Reform of Aurelian. *Num. Chron.* 1919, 234
Third-Century Roman Mints and Marks. *Num. Chron.* 1921, 226

West, A. B.: The Early Diplomacy of Philip II of Macedon illustrated by his Coins. *Num. Chron.* 1923, 169

Woodward, A. M.: A Note on the First Issue of Gold Coin at Athens. *Num. Chron.* 1911, 351

Zeitschrift für Numismatik. *Berlin*

Zimmern, A. E.: The Greek Commonwealth. *Oxford*, 1911; new edition 1924

INDEX